Reforming the Postal Sector in the Face of Electronic Competition

ADVANCES IN REGULATORY ECONOMICS

Series Editors: Michael A. Crew, *CRRI Professor of Regulatory Economics and Director, Center for Research in Regulated Industries (CRRI), Rutgers, The State University of New Jersey, Newark, USA and* the late Paul R. Kleindorfer, *former Paul Dubrule Professor of Sustainable Development, INSEAD, Fontainebleau, France and Anheuser-Busch Professor Emeritus of Management Science, The Wharton School, University of Pennsylvania, USA*

Edited by Michael A. Crew and Paul R. Kleindorfer, this series aims to advance research in theory, practice and policy in the area of regulatory economics. While regulation is all-pervasive in the modern economy and touches almost every aspect of economic life, this series focuses on micro-economic issues in regulation rather than macro policies. Topics of interest include contributions in the following areas: network industries, environmental, health and safety, risk and insurance, and financial services. Regulatory economics deals with both direct instruments affecting profits and prices in these industries and governance structures in regulated industries, including self-regulation. Contributions may address specific instruments across industries as well as in-depth sector-specific studies.

Titles in the series include:

Liberalization of the Postal and Delivery Sector
Edited by Michael A. Crew and Paul R. Kleindorfer

Competition and Regulation in the Postal and Delivery Sector
Edited by Michael A. Crew and Paul R. Kleindorfer

Handbook of Worldwide Postal Reform
Edited by Michael A. Crew, Paul R. Kleindorfer and James I. Campbell Jr.

Progress in the Competitive Agenda in the Postal and Delivery Sector
Edited by Michael A. Crew and Paul R. Kleindorfer

Heightening Competition in the Postal and Delivery Sector
Edited by Michael A. Crew and Paul R. Kleindorfer

Reinventing the Postal Sector in an Electronic Age
Edited by Michael A. Crew and Paul R. Kleindorfer

Multi-modal Competition and the Future of Mail
Edited by Michael A. Crew and Paul R. Kleindorfer

Reforming the Postal Sector in the Face of Electronic Competition
Edited by Michael A. Crew and Paul R. Kleindorfer

Reforming the Postal Sector in the Face of Electronic Competition

Edited by

Michael A. Crew

Rutgers, The State University of New Jersey, Newark, USA

and

Paul R. Kleindorfer

INSEAD, France and the University of Pennsylvania, USA

ADVANCES IN REGULATORY ECONOMICS

Edward Elgar

Cheltenham, UK • Northampton, MA, USA

Published by
Edward Elgar Publishing Limited
The Lypiatts
15 Lansdown Road
Cheltenham
Glos GL50 2JA
UK

Edward Elgar Publishing, Inc.
William Pratt House
9 Dewey Court
Northampton
Massachusetts 01060
USA

Reprinted 2014

A catalogue record for this book
is available from the British Library

Library of Congress Control Number: 2012946673

This book is available electronically in the ElgarOnline.com
Economics Subject Collection, E-ISBN 978 0 85793 580 9

MIX
Paper from responsible sources
FSC® C013056

ISBN 978 0 85793 579 3

Typeset by Servis Filmsetting Ltd, Stockport, Cheshire
Printed and bound in Great Britain by T.J. International Ltd, Padstow

Contents

Sponsors

Royal Mail
bpost
Deutsche Post DHL
La Poste
R.R. Donnelley & Sons Company
United Parcel Service
Pitney Bowes
Siemens Industry–Mobility
US Postal Regulatory Commission
Consumer Focus
Itella Corporation
IBM Global Business Services
Post Italiane
ANACOM
ARCEP
FedEx Express
FTI
KPMG LLP
NERA Economic Consulting
PostNL
Swiss Post
Oxera
London Economics
SLS Consulting, Inc
Venable LLP
Bird & Bird LLP
Canadian Union of Postal Workers
Commission for Communications Regulation
Copenhagen Economics
Frontier Economics
International Post Corporation
National Association of Letter Carriers
Posten Norge AS
RAND Europe
Accent
An Post
BIEK
Communication Workers Union
Covington & Burling
Diversified Specifics
FratiniVergano–European Lawyers
Jersey Competition Regulatory Authority
K&L Gates LLP
Luis Jimenez Consulting LLC
New Zealand Post Limited
Swiss Economics

Preface and acknowledgements

This book is a result of the Center for Research in Regulated Industries' (CRRI) 20th Conference on Postal and Delivery Economics which was held May 30 to June 2, 2012 at the Grand, Brighton, UK. The 1st Conference was held in 1990 in the UK. Over the twenty plus years after the 1st Conference the industry has seen considerable change. This is reflected particularly in the chapters by Jeff Colvin, Frank Rodriguez, Joëlle Toledano and Tim Walsh, which examine the changes taking place in North America, the UK and Europe during that period. These include the opening of postal markets to competition for most countries in the European Union on January 1, 2011. Even more important is the increasing impact of multi-modal competition, notably, email, social networks, and Internet advertising, which are raising important questions about the future of mail. The conference and this book attempt to address some of the challenges resulting. They follow earlier conferences and workshops. This is the 20th edited volume in CRRI's program on Postal and Delivery Economics.

The conference was made possible by the support of its generous sponsors. We would like to thank sponsors not only for financial support, but also for their intellectual contributions, advice and encouragement, and for service on the organizing committee: José Amado da Silva, John Baldwin, Geoff Bickerton, Larry Buc, Bernhard Bukovc, Peter Burge, Philip Burns, Eduardo Cardadeiro, João Castro, Margaret Cigno, Julien Coulier, John Curran, Robert Curry, Bernard Damiens, Richard Eccles, Colm Farrelly, Charles Fattore, Stephen Ferguson, John Fletcher, Alessandra Fratini, Richard Geddes, Damien Geradin, Ruth Goldway, Stefano Gori, Robert Hammond, Greg Harman, John Hearn, Jan Bart Henry, Paul Hodgson, Stuart Holder, George Houpis, Christian Jaag, Luis Jimenez, Denis Joram, George Kuehnbaum, David M. Levy, Francois Lions, Martin Maegli, Leonardo Mautino, Heikki Nikali, Chris Osborne, Chris Paterson, Ted Pearsall, Wolfgang Pickave, Michael Ravnitzky, Charlene Rohr, Jim Sauber, Michael Scanlon, Gennaro Scarfiglieri, Rob Sheldon, Michael Shinay, Paul C. Smith, Soterios Soteri, Nancy Sparks, Gregory Swinand, Urs Trinkner, Mark van der Horst, Joost Vantomme, Ian Volner, Navin Waghe, Tim Walsh, David Williams, F.W. Worth and Ralf Wojtek.

The host country plays an important role in these conferences, no more so than this year. This year's conference, benefited greatly from the efforts of our host, the Royal Mail Group. Paul Dudley and Marion Frederick were incredibly helpful. Paul provided us with a number of interesting ideas on content and organization. Paul and Marion were also very helpful during the conference, enabling it to operate very smoothly. They and their colleagues provided both advice and assistance on numerous occasions and contributed greatly to the success of the event.

We would like to thank our distinguished dinner speakers, Moya Greene, Chief Executive Officer, Royal Mail Group, Stuart McIntosh, Group Director, Competition Group, Ofcom, and Nick Wells, Chief Executive, TNT Post UK. These speeches addressed current issues of regulation and postal reform against the background of increasing multi-modal competition in the postal sector, maintaining the conference tradition of stimulating presentations by distinguished leaders in the industry.

Finally, we thank all authors and participants of the conference. Absent their contributions, the conference and this book would not have been possible. The usual disclaimers are applicable. In particular, the views expressed reflect the views of the authors and are not necessarily those of the sponsors.

Michael A. Crew and Paul R. Kleindorfer

1. Privatization of postal operators: old arguments and new realities*

Michael A. Crew† and Paul R. Kleindorfer‡

1 BACKGROUND AND MOTIVATION

Privatization of the postal sector has taken on significant momentum with the passage of the Postal Services Act of 2011, which enables the privatization of Royal Mail. Just as in the 1980s when the UK privatization of other network industries and associated regulatory reforms energized these sectors and had an impact well beyond the UK, the current UK proposal promises to have a widespread impact. So, this chapter's re-examination of the topic of privatization of an incumbent postal operator (PO) with the traditional Universal Service Obligation (USO) is particularly timely. The 20th Anniversary Conference on Postal and Delivery Economics is an appropriate place to consider privatization drawing a full circle to the original conference at Coton House in Rugby in 1990, in which the discussion was inspired by the contribution of Roland Hill's innovation of the Penny Post. Hill's reforms coalesced with the other currents of the Industrial Revolution to provide the basis for a model of a postal system for industrial economies in the nineteenth and twentieth centuries. Now is the time for major reform in the postal sector to reflect the 'Communications Revolution', which is taking place at far greater speed than the Industrial Revolution. If the postal sector is to thrive in the Communications Revolution, further significant transformation of the sector, driven by commercialized and privatized POs, will be required to integrate various elements of traditional postal communications with the new communications infrastructure of the Internet and wireless technologies. The form this transformation will take, and the role of private capital in this transformation, requires careful analysis. This will involve weighing the consequences of various forms of restructuring, including privatization, on fulfilling the PO's traditional role, and potential expansion of this role to integrate the activities and resources of the PO with broader communications and logistics markets.

Privatization has been a major topic for several decades. Megginson and Netter (2001) describe both the empirical record of privatization as well as the various forms that privatization has taken internationally, from contracting and outsourcing of major elements of a former public enterprise to the sale of equity. This chapter will consider

† CRRI Professor of Regulatory Economics and Director of CRRI, Rutgers School of Business, Rutgers University.

‡ May 12, 1940–August 24, 2012; former Paul Dubrule Professor of Sustainable Development, INSEAD; and Anheuser-Busch Professor of Management Science Emeritus, the Wharton School of the University of Pennsylvania.

privatization only as the transfer of ownership to private persons, typically through the sale of equity. Nonetheless, it is important, especially in the postal area, to understand privatization against the background of related existing developments to promote commercial operations in the postal sector. The term 'commercialization' will be taken to mean restructuring and management initiatives, short of privatization, that are intended to increase the profit orientation of a postal enterprise. These include changes in pricing, internal accounting systems, marketing innovations to improve revenues and customer loyalty, human resource initiatives designed to improve labor productivity and management incentives, as well as other strategic initiatives that are focused on increasing the profitability of the enterprise. Corporatization has accompanied commercialization, where the governance structure takes on a corporate form, as a private company but still owned by the government. An example is the recent transformation of La Poste in France, and various forms of restructuring to charge the PO explicitly with incentives and licensing agreements to promote profit maximization (for example, through the founding charter for Australia Post). Given the challenges posed by electronic substitution and declining demand, many if not most POs have undertaken significant commercialization initiatives to safeguard their financial viability, but only a few POs have become fully privatized. This suggests that there may be some important reasons for retaining the traditional public enterprise structure of POs. In order to understand the special challenges and opportunities inherent in privatization, this chapter will examine the impact and rationale for moving beyond a commercialized public enterprise to a completely privatized PO.

The topic of privatization is not new to the postal sector. Some aspects of privatization mainly in the context of the United States have been examined in two previous papers, Crew and Kleindorfer (2003, 2008a).The present chapter is intended to go beyond these earlier papers. There have been significant changes recently in postal markets, and these will require significant changes in the approach to privatization. Thus, this chapter aims to provide a fresh look at privatization in the postal sector against the background of the changes that are transforming the postal sector around the world. The primary changes have been increasing competition and volume losses arising not only from the severe worldwide recession but also, and more significantly, from intermodal competition. In addition, interdependencies with electronic media and eRetailing have also been the source of a growing recognition of the difficulties of treating the postal sector as if it were isolated from the broader sectors of communications and logistics. These interdependencies spell increasing complexity for postal regulation, but they also suggest opportunities, which may be better developed if the PO becomes a force for innovation as a privatized entity.

Privatization is not necessarily more efficient than public enterprise or government provision of services. Depending on the extent that there exists an externality or public good, public provision may be more efficient than private provision. National defense is an extreme case for public provision, as are catastrophic losses from terrorism and serious natural disasters, which require some risk bearing on the part of the government. Restaurants and haircuts are examples at the other extreme where the competitive market is recognized as the appropriate means of service provision. In the middle, there is some debate as to what determines the appropriate domain for private, public and mixed provision of services. For example, for infrastructure investments, Helm et al. (2009) argue that private provision may result in inadequate investment. Some roads are most efficiently provided by tolls and some by public provision at least until some improved methods of real-time road pricing are developed. The postal sector, arguably, increasingly resembles the competitive model with minimum externalities. Indeed, the central element in the European Union motivating an analysis of privatization has been the impetus for increased commercialization of the entire sector signaled by full market opening (FMO). However, FMO has also been accompanied by concerns that universal service may be endangered or undermined by a narrow focus on profits, driven by commercialization and competition. The USO will be subject to regulation whether postal service is privately or publicly supplied. Under private ownership the regulator will not be subject to the conflicts of interest and paradoxes that can arise from government ownership. For example, what is the significance of a fine levied on a public enterprise? A fine and surpluses of the enterprise have the same impact on the government's balance sheet. Depending on the incentives provided to management, the fine may affect executive bonuses under public enterprise but it would not have the same direct effect on the enterprise as under private ownership. Under competition, private ownership simplifies issues involving abuse of market power to the extent that there can be no claim that the government is favoring the enterprise that it owns. Under competitive conditions there is little doubt that incentives for efficiency will be increased under private ownership, but these may also lead to resistance to privatization, for example, in respect to anticipated employment reductions and pressures to eliminate wage premiums. These growing tensions provide the backdrop for this chapter.

Section 2 compares private and public governance with special concern for consequences of the lack of a model of public enterprise in economics of similar weight to the theory of the firm for private enterprise. Section 3 examines commercialization of POs as a precursor to privatization. Section 4 examines privatization as a possible solution to the expanded nature of competition arising from the information technology (IT) and communications revolution. The expected impacts of postal privatization are examined for key outcomes of special interest in the postal sector, including efficiency and the USO. Section 5 provides concluding discussion and areas of future research.

2 PUBLIC VERSUS PRIVATE GOVERNANCE AND PERFORMANCE

During the roaring eighties of privatization in the UK there was considerable interest in privatization.[1] The debate *inter alia* concerned the efficiency of private versus public governance structures. This section builds on this literature, as illustrated in Crew and Kleindorfer (1990). Public enterprise (PE) presents a problem for economic theory in that there is no developed and general theory equivalent to the theory of the firm, which provides the basis for analyzing private enterprise. The theory of the firm relies on the notion that firms maximize profit and is employed in market situations from pure monopoly to perfect competition. The first problem with PE is that there is no simple objective. A number of objectives have been attributed to PE, the most common being welfare maximization,[2] which can be stated formally as:

$$W = TR + S - TC, \tag{1.1}$$

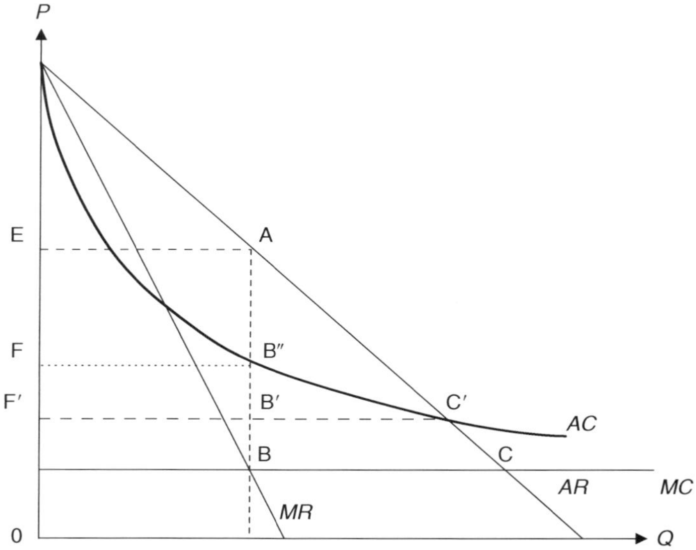

Figure 1.1 *Monopoly rents*

where W = net benefit, S = consumer's surplus, TR = total revenue, and TC = total costs.

This formulation has been used universally and it has appeal in that it results in efficiency, with the identical optimality conditions of perfect competition, namely price = marginal cost. However, the similarity of the conditions is deceptive. The issue is examined initially with the benchmark cases of single-product monopoly and perfect completion. There are a number of problems, however, with the assumption that a PE would act as if welfare maximization were its fundamental objective.

The first problem with welfare maximization is already apparent if the PE is a monopoly with scale economies. Setting $P = MC$ will result in losses. This problem is deceptively easily resolved. The Ramsey or inverse elasticity rule results by assuming that the PE maximizes welfare subject to a break-even constraint. In the single-product case in Figure 1.1 this would be where price equals average cost, $P = AC$. Under the assumption of break-even-constrained welfare maximization, the simplistic implication is that PE is more efficient than unregulated monopoly, where, marginal revenues equals marginal cost, $MR = MC$. However, this simplistic implication has problems in both theory and in practice. First, the comparison should be with a regulated monopoly. Second, and this applies in both cases, it relies on the notion that the monopoly rents as shown in Figure 1.1 will not be contested. In practice, the distribution of rents associated with regulation will be contested. As originally noted by Tullock (1967), rent seekers will expend resources attempting to get a piece of these rents. The rents will be reduced by the deadweight cost incurred in rent seeking. Assuming no rent seeking for the moment, if the PE set $P = AC$ the rents of AB′F′E plus triangle AB′C′ would all go to the consumer in terms of increased consumer surplus. However, if rent seeking is introduced and the only rent seeker is the Treasury, it pockets the rents EAB″F and the consumer loses the net consumer surplus AB′C′. This apparently dominates the unregulated monopoly solution in that all the rents are effectively collected as a tax. However, it implies that the Treasury expends essentially nothing on rent seeking. If rent seekers, for example, labor, other government entities and corporations seek these rents, the activity of rent seeking will create its own costs and so the simple transfer of rents does not occur. Deadweight losses result from rent seeking. Unlike the case of a costless transfer of the rents they are, in fact, dissipated. Price will be increased above 0F′ reducing the triangle AB′C′ and rents will be reduced to less than AB′F′E.

Rents can be dissipated in numerous ways. Labor is a leading contender for rents. Rent seeking by labor can have several effects that result in X-inefficiency.[3] If the rent seeking results solely in a wage premium, then the efficiency loss is the cost of the rent seeking plus the consumer surplus lost as a result of the higher price. If rent seeking results in a rent transfer in the form of excess labor employed, the loss is more complicated since the enterprise is operating off the production frontier resulting in a further loss in the form of X-inefficiency. A third possibility is that the PE pays supra-competitive wages and adjusts its input mix to reflect these. The efficiency loss would be defined as follows if the firm stays on the frontier:

W_{ew} = welfare from supra-competitive input prices, w, + gain to workers from less effort. (1.2)

$W_{ew} < W$ in (1.1) as the loss in total consumer surplus from higher product prices exceed the rents received by workers.

W_{ei} = welfare where PE pays supra-competitive wages and chooses inputs based on these prices. (1.3)

W_{ei} in (1.3) is deceptive in that it appears that the PE is operating on the production frontier and is therefore efficient. The problem is that it would be employing an inefficiently small amount of labor. So, it is difficult to make generalized comparisons between (1.2) and (1.3). What is clear is that they are both inefficient.

A privately owned regulated monopoly would presumably face a regulatory regime that aimed to take it to C′ in Figure 1.1, the same basic idea as in the case of PE. The difference is that its profit motive is attenuated because it is subject to regulation. Its rents have been eliminated by regulation but, like the PE, the incentives for rent seeking remain and so it is also subject to these kinds of rent transfers and inefficiencies. The difference is that the rents would be dissipated differently. Small customers may be the recipients of a greater share of rents in the form of lower prices relative to large customers in both PE and regulated monopoly.[4] The private monopoly would be more likely to respond to the input price signals in (1.3) as it would be more profitable to do so. A regulated private monopoly might be less likely to expand unionized employment but may be not greatly different from PE in expanding management and non-union employment.[5] Similarly, upper management is likely to succeed in obtaining a higher share of the rents than upper management in PE. This brief discussion of static equilibrium implies a priori that there is unlikely to be a major difference in efficiency between PE and regulated monopoly.[6]

The empirical literature comparing the efficiency of privately versus publicly owned enterprises is instructive but somewhat inconclusive. For example, a survey of electric utilities through 1990 found that privately owned enterprises seemed to be slightly more efficient (Crew and Kleindorfer, 1990). Since then these types of comparisons of vertically integrated electric utilities have become less relevant as a result of the restructuring of much of the electric utility industry and the introduction of competition in generation. Megginson and Netter (2001), in their highly extensive survey, provide a discussion of some more recent results where they review studies of the relative efficiency of public versus private in a variety of industries as diverse as telecommunications, banking, and expeditions to the Arctic! In addition, they surveyed the impact of privatization in transition economies, for example, Russia and the Czech Republic. The results showed increased profitability of private enterprise, and private enterprise being mostly more efficient. Similarly, Green et al. (1997) examined privatization of UK electricity generation and transmission and found efficiency advantages for private ownership. Beyond efficiency, there are other impacts of privatization. Following deregulation of generation in parts of the US and privatization of electricity in the UK, there was empirical support for the notion that large customers were likely to benefit and small customers to lose. This is also likely to be a consequence of increased competition in the postal sector where small customers may face increases in the price of a single-piece stamp as competition increases.

So, in terms of static efficiency, the evidence is mixed as to which governance structure performs better under monopoly. However, the situation changes if competitive and dynamic considerations are introduced. There are many reasons why PE is not observed in competitive situations, the main one being the absence of monopoly rents to parcel out. PE frequently involves a web of entanglements with government agencies. Consider US Postal Service (USPS). It is not clear that under its current PE governance structure USPS could come close to maximizing anything! Rather, its behavior is better understood as the result of government agencies and private parties involved in distributing rents through the legislative and regulatory process governing USPS. This type of behavior is only possible because monopoly rents have been historically available. This has radically changed with the emergence of intermodal competition. Competition presents a problem for PE not only because of the absence of rents but because government is vulnerable to claims by competitors of subsidizing its own enterprise. These two features make PE, absent monopoly, problematical for government. The absence of rents means that it cannot pursue policies of rent redistribution. So, instead of a benefit for politicians it becomes a liability. This is the case with USPS. For many years it has performed successfully for a number of pressure groups and the rents have been divided among these. Beneficiaries included especially mailers, who paid low prices for many years, and employees, who had secure well-compensated jobs. The precipitous decline in mail over the last three years or so has pushed USPS into severe losses. For a private business, prolonged losses can ultimately result in bankruptcy. By contrast, a public enterprise cannot go bankrupt as the government is left to pay the bill. This is hardly what government intended. Instead of having rents to disburse, under competition the Treasury faces the prospect of supporting a loss-making PE. PE and competition are somewhat like oil and water in that they do not mix. This matter will now be pursued further in Section 3.

3 DRIVERS OF PRIVATIZATION IN THE POSTAL SECTOR

Competition is arguably the ultimate driver of privatization. While under monopoly regulated private governance of PE may not vary dramatically in terms of efficiency, the same cannot be said under competition. As competition increases, financial viability becomes difficult to achieve unless profit maximization becomes central. This leaves basically two options for PE, either to act more like private firms or to be privatized. Indeed, given the pressures of intermodal competition, many POs have followed one of these two routes, mostly falling short of privatization.

Changing PO behavior in PEs so that they act more like private firms is usually achieved by beginning a process of 'corporatization' and 'commercialization'. In 1990, the postal sector worldwide was in the early stages of the process of commercialization. One of the first to embrace commercialization was a minnow in the postal pond, New Zealand Post. At the time of the first conference in Rugby, NZ Post was in the early stage of what turned out to be a highly successful experiment in commercialization. NZ Post's experiment was observed closely by other POs and in many respects provided a model for commercialization. Toime (1991, p. 275) outlined the origins of, basis for and the early progress in commercialization at NZ Post. He summarized the essence of the New Zealand view of commercialization as follows:

> It was established as a state-owned enterprise on April 1, 1987. In New Zealand, this major economic reform, which transformed a number of former government departments into commercial trading companies, was called 'corporatization' . . . As a state-owned enterprise New Zealand Post is established as a limited liability company, headed by a board of directors. It operates in all respects as a private company, paying all taxes, including the Goods and Services Tax on postage, and returns a dividend to owners.

Significantly,

> New Zealand Post is required by statute to operate as a successful business enterprise, that is to be as profitable as private companies . . . The focus on profitability becomes the driving force for the board of directors and the executive. It explains the progress of New Zealand Post to date; it explains its commitment to customers and service; and it explains its drive for marketing innovation. (Ibid., pp. 275–6)

Toime further explains how NZ Post implemented its new mandate. Its approach involved not only cost savings but the introduction of innovative products and services that the old government department had not delivered and was unlikely to deliver.[7] NZ Post replaced 432 of its post offices by private sector retail outlets and as reported by Toime reduced the labor force by 30 percent. NZ Post was given considerably greater flexibility in its pricing and became increasingly more customer focused and market driven. It increased service quality, reaching 96–7 percent of its delivery targets. In short, corporatization and rapid commercialization provided incentives to innovate and NZ Post took advantage of them as noted by Steele (1991).

Other POs had converted their POs from government departments to corporate entities prior to New Zealand, but none was as radical in its corporatization and commercialization. For example, in the UK the Post Office ceased to be a government department and became a public corporation in 1969. However, it took until the Postal Services Act of 2000 for it to become a public limited company, which gave a similar status to that which NZ Post attained in 1987, both with one shareholder, their respective governments. The United States, in an atmosphere of crisis, abolished the Post Office Department and the United States Postal Service was created in 1970. Canada Post ceased to be a government department in 1981 and became a Crown Corporation, known as Canada Post Corporation (CPC). The big difference between the UK, Canadian and US approaches and that of New Zealand was that the profit objective was fundamental to the NZ corporatization. Contrast this with CPC, which 'was directed to be mindful of "the need to conduct its operations on a self-sustaining financial basis"' (Campbell, 1994, p. 193). The break-even approach for USPS embodied in its 1970 founding legislation was very similar to that envisaged for CPC.

New Zealand may have been the first country to corporatize its PO with the explicit and clear objective that it was to be profitable and judged on its profitability in the same manner as any privately owned company. Other POs were on the same path, notably Sweden and the Netherlands. The Netherlands corporatized in 1989 and commercialized rapidly thereafter. The Dutch Post became increasingly involved with courier services with the acquisition of TNT. It subsequently changed its name to a number of variations involving TNT. It was ultimately fully privatized with all the stock privately held by private individuals or institutions. Privatization was followed by major restructuring, beginning in 2006 with the divestiture of its freight and logistics operations.[8] In 2011, TNT Post underwent a further major reorganization, splitting into two companies, Post NL and TNT Express. The former is a mail company with a USO and the latter is a courier company. Sweden Post corporatized and was the first to open up its market fully to competition in 1993. Like NZ Post it has pursued profitability objectives but has not privatized. Similarly, Finland has corporatized and become increasingly commercialized. Indeed, most European POs have become increasingly commercially oriented including Belgium, Germany, Finland, France and the UK, although only the Netherlands, Germany and Austria have privatized, with the privatization of Royal Mail now legalized by the Postal Services Act. Thus, while only a minority of POs are privatized, almost all are corporatized and increasingly commercialized. Most have not provided plans to privatize but have taken the initial steps of commercialization and corporatization that provide the effective prerequisites of privatization. A notable exception is USPS, which has made little progress in commercialization. As a result, unlike POs in Europe, USPS has not had the opportunity afforded to commercialization POs of gaining experience in how to compete. It never expected to face competition, and never has in letters. When electronic competition came along it was ill prepared to deal with it. Its only strategy was the inwardly focused one of cut, cut, cut.

There are a number of reasons why governments have not privatized their POs. One is that governments have seen them as a source of monopoly rents for distribution among various interest groups. Labor is one of these interest groups and typically PE is preferred by labor in that it seems likely to offer more secure employment and perhaps higher-paying employment. This has been the case with USPS, which has traditionally paid supra-competitive wages. USPS has also retained its reserved area or statutory monopoly protection. The retention of the reserved area, which most POs lost in 2011 or earlier, may in part explain why the US Congress may have believed that there were rents to be distributed and why USPS made minimal progress in commercialization. By contrast POs in Europe, knowing that the reserved area was going to disappear in 2011, embarked on a course of increased commercialization and competitive behavior although few embraced privatization.

In the US there was clearly a mistaken belief. The Postal Accountability and Enhancement Act (PAEA) of 2006[9] is based on the fallacious notion that USPS could continue to deliver monopoly rents for Congress to distribute, which totally ignored the reality of electronic competition. Congress failed to realize that the party was already over. Just because Congress continued the USPS monopoly did not mean that its monopoly rents would continue. Indeed, its rents were already well on the way out when the Act was passed. Congress had failed to see that it had saddled USPS with a governance structure that was not viable with the contraction of the monopoly rents. As a result, USPS has become a millstone round Congress's neck. USPS is something of an outlier among POs. Other countries have made greater advances in commercialization, putting them in better shape to handle the onslaught of electronic competition.

With the noted exceptions of Austria, Germany and the Netherlands, other POs have chosen to commercialize but not to privatize. Traditionally, the public sector has been thought to be a more efficient supplier than the private sector of services that are simple, slow to change and have public good qualities or externalities associated with them. For most of its history, postal service had these attributes. The product was simple and was relatively unchanged for over the 150 years following the Penny Post in 1840. In addition, it had a public good attribute in the form of the USO.[10] Absent the obligation to deliver ubiquitously at a uniform price, the market would not provide this service. Alternatively, competition would mean that competitors would free ride by handing over their remote (high-cost) mail to the universal service provider (USP). The simple and routine nature of the product and the USO were reasons for providing mail as a government service originally. As competition and complexity became more important, POs became more commercially oriented but still remained under public ownership. Partly, this was the result of inertia. However, other considerations were also involved. Governments generally saw their POs as valuable assets. Governments and citizens also considered the USO to be a function of the public sector, and concerns remain as to how effectively the USO would be provided under private ownership. These considerations may explain the continued popularly of PE in the postal sector. The next section examines in more detail the case for public versus private governance of POs.

4 PRIVATIZATION AND POSTAL SERVICE

Major POs have taken the important step of commercialization on the road to privatization but have not become privatized, which raises the question of the role of private governance in the future of postal service. The failure to go beyond commercialization to the next step of privatization could be explained by the superiority of commercialized PE as a governance structure for POs. An alternative explanation is that governments and POs have not understood the competitive situation facing POs today and therefore have not considered the role of privatization. A third possibility is that they foresee some consequences of privatization that they find unacceptable. This includes the notion that the public may trust a publicly owned but commercialized PO to a greater degree than they would a privatized PO. Such concerns are difficult to quantify and analyze but they may be a barrier to privatization. So, the purpose of this section will be to examine the likely consequences of privatization, including potential problems that might hinder its successful implementation. Problems of private governance generally are first examined followed by an examination of several issues likely to be of particular interest in postal privatization.

Critique of Private Governance

Private governance is not without its problems. An extensive literature exists that is highly critical of corporate governance, an early example being Berle and Means (1932). The problem arises primarily from the separation of ownership and control. The firm in economic theory is driven by profits or residual claims.[11] A residual claimant in its most primitive form is the owner operator. He/she pockets all the profits and eats any losses. The owner operator is equivalent to the firm in economic theory. In a private corporation the residual claimants are more diffuse, namely, the stockholders. Although a detailed discussion of the power and nature of the incentives under different forms of ownership is beyond the scope of this chapter, the general idea is summarized here. While the incentives faced by a sole owner (the residual claimant) are clearly high powered in the sense that he/she faces all the consequences of bankruptcy and retains all profits, the same is not true in the case of the corporation. The stock has no value in a bankruptcy but typically stockholders are much more diversified than the sole proprietor. Furthermore, management may not necessarily act to maximize shareholder return. These issues all contribute to the attenuation of incentives for efficiency relative to the unitary actor/residual claimant model of the firm.

Modern finance[12] has examined the issue of attenuation of incentives and has argued that there exist devices to align incentives of executives and stockholders. These involve primarily making executives residual claimants. The basic idea is simple, namely, to make the executive's compensation a fraction of profit. $EC = \pi\alpha$, where EC = executive compensation, π = total profits of the corporation and α = share of profits. The difficulty is to determine how large α should be. Corporate governance places the responsibility upon the board of directors, acting on behalf of the shareholders, to determine the size of α. Critics have argued that boards fail to perform their function effectively, especially in the US. Bebchuk and Fried (2004) argue that boards need to function at arm's length from the CEO and provide numerous instances where this does not happen. In addition, they provide reasons why boards do not function at arm's length including cronyism and identifying with the CEO rather than the stockholders. While Bebchuk and Fried's discussion is mostly normative, they do survey a considerable number of empirical papers. The general thrust of their argument is that the CEO is overcompensated and that the CEO's compensation is not sufficiently closely related to performance. Similar arguments can be made that boards are overcompensated and effectively determine their own compensation. Other criticisms of boards include their being required to spend too much time on compliance with legal and regulatory governance rules rather than in supervising management.[13]

Flaws in corporate governance exist almost everywhere. It would appear that of the major economies, the US system may have greater problems than other countries. One feature of the US that often is problematical is that the CEO often holds the position of chairman of the board, which is not the case in the UK and other countries. Holding both positions gives the CEO considerable power in numerous respects, including controlling the agenda of board meetings. This allows for an abuse of power by executives, which is manifested in the greed that has been at the heart of major corporate scandals. European countries have two boards, a supervisory board and a management board. However, this is not the place for further detail on corporate governance and certainly not the place to propose reforms. What is clear is that private corporate governance suffers from a number of potential imperfections. So also does public governance in the form of a PE, perhaps most importantly the weak incentives for cost efficiency and profitability inherent in the PE structure. The relevant question is whether in the postal context private governance is likely to perform more efficiently than public governance. This is the question which is addressed in the following subsection.

Private versus Public Governance in the Postal Sector

The issues raised in the previous subsection apply generally to private governance. It has recognized flaws manifested in excessive compensation for top management, a practice that has continued following the reforms of a decade ago. In the case of the postal sector, additionally it may provide incentives for curtailing the PO's public missions, in particular the USO, and for using any market power they may have to pursue objectives, for example, in the mergers and acquisitions (M&A) area, that are not in the interest of stockholders or the public. The latter is likely to be less of a problem under competition. However, the alternatives, primarily PE, are also flawed. To evaluate the relative merits of private versus public governance, a comparative assessment is necessary and should be undertaken in light of specific issues that are likely to be critical for the postal sector.

The most important issue currently facing the postal sector is electronic competition, and it has arguably been precisely this issue which has promoted renewed interest in private governance. This phenomenon is outside the realm of anything POs have faced in the past. One of the features of electronic competition is the need to be nimble. The companies in the IT and electronic space have to be exceedingly nimble if they are to survive. Giants, such as Microsoft and Google, have to be constantly innovating to maintain their place in the market. By contrast, PEs have been much slower in responding to changing circumstances. It is true that commercialized postal services have shown an ability to respond to change that is more responsive than under traditional PE. However, at the other extreme is the USPS, which is subject to so many restrictions legislated by the US Congress that it is almost paralyzed in the face of electronic competition. These legal restrictions have given rise to a highly dysfunctional form of micromanagement by the Congress. The combination of strong intermodal competition and congressional micromanagement has left USPS in disastrous shape. One example is that it has operated on a break-even basis over the first thirty plus years following its creation in 1970. This has meant that it has no reserves to call upon now that it is in dire straits.[14] Congress is unlikely to provide it with funding for investment, and innovation is de facto ruled out by the PAEA of 2006. Its only policy has been 'cut, cut, cut'. Cutting is not the way to greatness and is likely only to speed up its decline. The USPS strategy is a polar form of old-line PE, with a sole focus on its traditional declining business rather than on pricing and product innovation. Responding to change through innovation and restructuring is perhaps the strongest suit of private governance relative to PE.

Commercialized POs, by contrast, are in better shape. Indeed, POs such as USPS that are micromanaged by government are increasingly the exception. Accordingly, the comparative assessment that follows will be of commercialized public governance and privatized POs. This assessment will focus on a number of key issues for the postal sector including: innovation, restructuring, USO, market performance, financial viability, human resources, and regulation.

Perhaps the strongest argument in favor of privatization is that it provides more powerful incentives for pricing and product innovation and restructuring.[15] These arise from the incentives provided by privatization relative to commercialization. Under privatization the objectives are much clearer. While a commercialized PO may ostensibly be profit oriented, the incentives and the clarity of the objectives of the organization are likely to be much clearer under privatization. For these and other reasons, the privatized PO is likely to be more successful in both dynamic and static efficiency. In line with these considerations, the two major POs that are privatized have demonstrated both innovation and the ability to restructure their operations in light of changing market conditions and opportunities. Innovations have included significant expansion in logistics, expansion of courier services, and considerable M&A activity to expand their competency in support of B2B (business-to-business) services. Arguably, their ability to identify these new business ventures and the freedom and ability to finance them was enhanced by their status as privatized companies. Innovation is also taking place in commercialized POs but restructuring has been minimal. CPC has a major ($2 billion) investment and modernization program underway. It is known as Postal Transformation. CPC is automating and consolidating its mail-processing operations and modernizing its delivery fleet. In addition, it is entering the electronic space and increasing its efforts in logistics, parcels and small packets. Other POs are taking action. Finland is active in the electronic space, as is Switzerland. The privatized POs have similarly been forward looking and responsive to competition, including the divestiture by the Dutch PO of its TNT courier operation in response to competition.[16] Arguably, the profit orientation of privatized POs allows them freedom and more scope to identify potential profit opportunities for innovation and restructuring activities. The dynamic environment driven by the IT and communications revolution has been the primary engine promoting an interest in privatization. PE works well under stable conditions. In many ways POs have been a great success for most of their history because of stable conditions including steady growth with the economy in general. This is particularly the case for USPS since 1970. It has been successful because of stable conditions. Steadily growing demand allowed it to expand gradually and benefit extensively from scale economies, providing one of the cheapest single-piece stamps of all industrial countries. In addition, USPS continued to make significant efficiency improvements, including a major reduction in career employees down from 760,668 in 1990 to 563,000 in 2011. Unfortunately, USPS's successful record effectively came to an end around the time of the 2006 Act, which envisaged business as usual. Neither USPS management nor Congress saw that they were about to be hit by a massive hurricane with the potential to destroy USPS unless drastic changes were made. However, without residual claimants and the threat of bankruptcy, there was little pressure to change and the only option considered was cutting service and thereby creating a vicious circle of revenue erosion followed by service reductions to save costs, leading to further demand and revenue erosion.

The contrast between a private organization and USPS is stark. A private organization would also be more responsive and likely in better financial condition than a commercialized PE. The private organization would have been in better financial condition initially, would have built up reserves and likely would have taken action to respond to the threat of electronic competition. Because of the incentives facing the residual claimants, the firm would have taken action to avoid bankruptcy and would have been examining ways of innovating and restructuring. Private governance provides the incentives and the vehicle for innovation and restructuring not existing under public governance. In the face of a sea of change, private governance offers much greater potential for responding.

Although privatization is likely to perform better in terms of dynamic efficiency, it does not confer benefits universally. Some benefits of PE are lost. Interestingly, the traditional notion of PE as an organization aimed at maximizing social benefits has already been attenuated by commercialization. However, commercialized POs must still continue to fulfill the USO. Under privatization the USO would be enforced by regulation. However, it may have to be modified if the firm is to compete and remain financially viable. The threat of bankruptcy would clearly act as a discipline to the firm not existing with a commercialized PE. The incentives facing the private firm and the discipline of bankruptcy mean that it is less likely to get into financial distress than the PE. However, bankruptcy of a privatized PO is likely to have serious consequences for the USO that would not occur under a commercialized PO. Even with financial distress that would drive a privatized PO into bankruptcy, the commercialized PE would not be able to go bankrupt. This is likely to mean that adverse effects on the USO arising from financial distress will be attenuated. Even without bankruptcy a commercialized PO might have a more extensive USO than a privatized PO. The higher-powered profit incentives of privatization might work in the direction of a less-expansive USO. *Ceteris paribus* a USO would mean that a company was less profitable. However, as a private corporation required to fulfill a public mission it would have to recognize this constraint and cooperate with the government and its regulator in meeting it. Government would also not be unconstrained. For example, a government with plans for privatization would presumably recognize that the value of its initial public offering (IPO) would be lower if the USO is highly onerous. The regulatory process would clearly be of critical importance with a privatized PO. It would be effectively the sole means of administering and enforcing the USO under privatization. Although regulation would in many ways be more demanding under privatization it would also be more transparent and less subject to any conflicts of interest that arise from government ownership. The design of the regulatory process requires significant attention, which is beyond the scope of this chapter. A seriously flawed regulatory governance structure could be damaging to the PO's public mission and could make a successful IPO almost impossible. Some careful balancing is required in the design of the regulatory process.[17]

Privatization offers the potential for increased static and dynamic efficiency. A privatized PO is likely to respond more rapidly to the impact of competition by increased product and pricing innovation. The benefits will be shared unevenly. Large customers are likely to benefit more than small customers as a result of pricing innovations in that prices may be lower for large customers and higher for small customers. However, since postage is a very small part of consumers' budgets, the impact is likely to be minimal and perhaps will go almost unnoticed. While large customers are also likely to benefit from innovative products the same may also apply, although likely to a lesser extent, for small customers.[18]

The impact of privatization on labor is mixed. A privatized PO is likely to employ less labor and bargain harder on wages and working conditions than a commercialized PO because it faces the higher-powered incentives of bankruptcy and residual claimants. Privatization clearly changes the bargaining process for both sides. Under private ownership, the consequences of failure are likely to be more severe than under commercialized public ownership. This provides the prospect of greater cooperation by both sides since more is at stake. In addition, through its potential for greater innovation, private ownership could lead to greater cooperation between labor and management not possible under public ownership. New compensation arrangements with higher-powered incentives would be possible under private ownership that would not occur under public ownership. There may additionally be innovations in the product mix that are likely to be more significant under privatization. Absent the introduction of new products, workers are going to face a decline in employment, while privatization offers the prospect of retraining, developing new skills. Similarly, pensions will be affected by privatization. Under a commercialized PE that is faced with hard times and cannot cover the pension obligations of its defined benefit plan its owner, the government, will have to intervene. This might include guaranteeing pensions at considerable expense or modifying (reneging on) its promises – something not unknown in government! By contrast, a privatized PO, like other private corporations, will be subject to pension regulation. The privatized PO in these circumstances, may respond as many corporations have by abandoning defined benefit plans for defined contribution plans, where the worker owns the pension account earned from the contributions made by him/her and his/her employer plus any return on the investment. While there are significant differences in the manner in which a commercialized PO addresses human resource issues it is not clear, given the superiority of a privatized PO in responding to competition and the resulting benefits of dynamic efficiency, that workers will necessarily lose under privatization. The issues are complex and the details go far beyond the scope of this chapter. Table 1.1 summarizes the features of public versus private governance for POs.

5 SUMMARY AND CONCLUSIONS

It is widely recognized that with the impact of electronic competition, POs need to become more profit oriented and better able to respond to market conditions and customer needs. This recognition has led worldwide to a transformation of POs. It is not a case of one size fits all. Some POs have restructured their operations to become commercialized PEs, often with a corporate structure. A few have gone beyond commercialization to privatization. As argued in this chapter, the case for private governance becomes more compelling as intermodal competition becomes more intense. Privatization has attributes that make it more effective in addressing product and pricing innovations, as well as necessary changes in financial strategy and accounting systems that are dictated as a result of electronic competition. It provides the opportunity to innovate and

Table 1.1 Comparative assessment of public versus private governance for POs

Performance attribute	Commercialized public enterprise	Privatized enterprise
Financial viability	In the face of volume losses from e-substitution, continuing dependency on public subsidies may be required	Profit orientation provides strong incentives for profitable operations
Static and dynamic efficiency including capital asset productivity	X-inefficiency likely in the form of excess labor and wage premiums. Inaccurate measurement of cost of capital likely leading to inefficient investment strategies	Profit orientation provides strong incentives for static cost efficiency and for investments in long-term productivity gains. Regulation may adversely affect efficiency
Restructuring in response to market conditions and intermodal competition	PE has traditionally been slow to respond to changing market conditions. Tendency to maintain legacy accounting and governance structures in the face of change	Profit orientation provides strong incentives for cost saving restructuring and to respond to new revenue opportunities and to shed losing customers and products
Human resources	Inertia relative to employment levels and contracts. Pension and health obligations often of defined benefit type, with continuing tension/expectation of government funding	In the early stages of privatization, typically strong reduction in excess employment and wage premiums shift to defined contribution type of pension and health benefits
Meeting the needs of small and large customers	PE responsive to public pressure and number of customers, so that households in SMEs tend to receive equal consideration relative to larger customers	As large customers provide the majority of revenues and profits, they receive higher priority in terms of service and product innovation
Pricing and product innovation	PE tends to remain with its traditional product line. Pricing structures tend to be simple and oriented to cost recovery in aggregate rather than value based. Marketing underdeveloped	Profit incentives drive market adaptation, through internal development and external M&A activity. Marketing and customer-driven operations are emphasized
Fulfillment of public missions including the USO	Public missions emphasized by PE. Tendency to maintain USO in its historic form, possibly with government subsidies	Profit orientation provides strong incentives to adapt the USO to shed losing routes and products with the cost of the USO absorbed by the PO

restructure in a more extensive manner than even a commercialized PO. In addition, this competition now means that there are many fewer advantages for governments in owning POs. One of the big advantages of government ownership was the ability to distribute monopoly rents. Now the problem is how to avoid losses. Privatization is arguably the more efficient way of addressing the dramatic effects of electronic competition and the consequent loss of rents. It offers the prospect of making the reduced pie as large as possible. However, privatization will not bring improvements for all stakeholders. There will inevitably be losers as result of the reduction in the pie. Based on results of privatization in other industries, it is likely that the USO and small customers are going to lose relative to the status quo. Large customers are likely to gain from innovative products and their improved bargaining position with respect to a more profit-oriented PO. In addition, the government will gain from shedding PEs that are likely to continue to lose money. It will take time for governments to comprehend this significant change and the longer they delay the more serious the problem will become.

The mechanics of privatization are nontrivial and the process is likely to become more complicated the longer governments wait to address the need of privatizing their POs. Governments will be less and less able to dump their obligations on private owners and they may be required to add some funding for a successful privatization. These problems are not insuperable. The USO will almost certainly remain as an obligation on the PO irrespective of the form of governance. Investments in the network and in new services will be required to reduce profit erosion due to intermodal competition. How much capital to invest is a business decision that should be made in an environment that provides appropriate incentives for valuation of capital. Inherently, private governance is likely to provide better alignment of such incentives than public governance. The decision to privatize also entails important valuation issues. Presumably, if at the margin the expected money raised from the IPO exceeds the (possibly negative) risk-adjusted discounted value of cash flows generated by the PO under continuing public ownership, the government would be interested in privatization. Of course, these pure profit measures of private versus public governance do not capture fully the welfare impacts of a move to private ownership; there may be additional benefits from increased employment and a broader USO under public governance. These issues, and others noted in the previous section, present a more complex decision context than mere profit comparisons, although arguably profitability of the PO will become increasingly important as competition increases. Affecting outcomes on other dimensions, including protecting the welfare of small consumers and assuring fair treatment of employees,[19] will obviously require both legislative and regulatory controls in setting up the privatized PO. This includes specific controls relative to the USO, and these controls must be agreed, at least in principle, with the owners of the privatized PO *ex ante*. Indeed, the governance of the USO will remain a critical element of postal policy, whether or not the PO is privatized. The nature of regulation and the USO under privatization provide fertile ground for future research.

Privatization offers the prospect of providing a more efficient governance structure for POs in the face of competition. Given this, several countries are considering the privatization option, including the UK. The Postal Services Act of 2011, by allowing privatization and reforming its regulatory framework, has opened the door to Royal Mail's potential success as a private corporation in an age of electronic competition. However, more work needs to be done, especially in the area of regulation and the USO.[20] The improved prospects for financial viability under privatization offer benefits not only to the corporation but also to the public. A financially viable and innovative privatized PO will be well positioned to provide products that are responsive to customer needs along with a USO in the fast-changing world of electronic competition. In this spirit, the Act of 2011 could be the kind of milestone in the history of Royal Mail of the same magnitude as was the Penny Post of 1840.

NOTES

* The authors acknowledge the support of Royal Mail Group in the preparation of this chapter. The views expressed are solely those of the authors and do not necessarily reflect those of Royal Mail Group. The authors would like to thank the discussants, Robert Campbell and William Kovacic for their interesting comments. Thanks are also due to Richard Geddes for his helpful comments.

1. Vickers and Yarrow (1988) and Megginson and Netter (2001) are two typical examples and are replete with references on the topic.
2. Alternative behavioral assumptions underlying PE objectives have been examined by a number of authors, including Baumol (1967) and Niskanen (1971), who suggested that sales maximization might be an appropriate assumption for PE. Sappington and Sidak (2003) examined the consequences of sales revenue maximization for pricing and cross-subsidization in a multi-product PE. The consequences of various potential PE objectives are examined in the postal context in Crew and Kleindorfer (2008b).
3. Leibenstein (1966) was the first to use this term, which has now become commonplace to describe inefficient operations of firms. X-inefficiency can take numerous forms as noted in this chapter.
4. The tendency to favor large customers in rent distribution has been observed in a number of regulated industries, for example, in electricity, Green et al. (1997) and Bunn (2006).
5. Williamson (1967) provides an extended analysis of the notion of expense preference, which is the ability of top management to have different preferences among expenses. Staff and management would be preferred to union or shop floor. He further argued that under regulation these preferences were likely to be indulged more fully than absent regulation.
6. Laffont and Tirole (1993, p. 654) reach essentially the same conclusion on the matter of the relative efficiency of public versus private enterprise 'theory alone is thus unlikely to be conclusive in this respect'.
7. With $40 million of losses in its last year of operation, based on its record, the prospects for continuing operation of NZ Post as a government department were not good!
8. The name was changed to TNT Post.
9. The deliberations on PAEA began around a decade earlier and took no account of the changed realities.
10. Interestingly, Toime's discussion of the USO is very brief in the context of a reserved or protected area, where NZ Post had a statutory monopoly. It had the exclusive right to carry items priced below $1.75 or 500g. 'This level of protection carried an obligation (but not a mandatory condition) to provide universal letter service throughout New Zealand at a single price' (Toime, 1991, p. 276).
11. This was understood long ago by Adam Smith, who saw how under competition individuals acting in their own self-interest could increase the wealth of all. In more recent parlance, this is akin to the efficiency of perfect competition.
12. Numerous papers have been written on this topic, an early example being, Jensen and Meckling (1976), who examine *inter alia* the role of debt in aligning incentives of shareholder and management.
13. In the US, Sarbanes–Oxley is one law that adds to board and management responsibility and generates major audit and other costs. It was put together in the panic following the major scandals involving Enron, MCI-WorldCom and others.
14. The issue is far from straightforward. It has arguably considerable assets in real estate if these are marked to market. Similarly, there are other issues in US government accounting that are opaque involving pension and retiree health-care obligations.
15. Bunn (2006) provides an interesting example of how privatized generation in the UK resulted in effectively two firms initially, but evolved into a market with several competitors and changing vertical relationships.
16. It is too soon to determine if this major reorganization will be successful. On the face of it the divestiture appears to be against the accepted wisdom that there are scope economies between mail, parcels and courier.

17. Ofcom (2011) explicitly attempts the kind of balancing act required. While increasing Royal Mail's commercial freedom significantly, it aims to protect the USO and provide safeguards against potential abuse of market power.
18. Given the two-sided nature of the market and the preponderance of B2B and B2C (business-to-consumer) mail, small customers are likely to benefit at least indirectly from innovations aimed at large customers.
19. The treatment of obligations to current and past employees, for example, pensions and health care, has been a fundamental aspect of PE privatizations to date, with the government often assuming part or all of existing obligations as part of the initial valuation of the IPO. See, for example, Maschke (2002) for discussion of these issues in the context of privatization of Deutsche Post.
20. Six-day delivery, for example, should not be something that is written into law. Indeed, such inflexibility might present a problem for successful privatization and reduce the value received by the government for the IPO. Such issues involving the USO are matters for the PO and its regulator.

REFERENCES

Baumol, William J. (1967), *Business Behavior, Value and Growth*, rev. edn, New York: Harcourt, Brace & World.

Bebchuk, Lucien and Jesse Fried (2004), *Pay Without Performance*, Cambridge, MA: Harvard University Press.

Berle, Adolf A. and Gardner C. Means (1932), *The Modern Corporation and Private Property*, New York: Macmillan.

Bunn, Derek W. (2006), 'Institutional intent and strategic evolution in electricity markets', paper presented at The European Electricity Market Conference, Warsaw, May.

Campbell, Robert M. (1994), *The Politics of the Post: Canada's Postal System from Public Service to Privatization*, Peterborough, Ontario: Broadview Press.

Crew, Michael A. and Paul R. Kleindorfer (1990), *Public versus Private: Alternative Ownership Structures for Electric Utilities*, Santa Monica, CA: Reason Foundation.

Crew, Michael A. and Paul R. Kleindorfer (2003), 'Postal privatization: in general and for the United States Postal Service?', in David Parker and David Saal (eds), *Handbook of Privatization*, Cheltenham, UK and Northampton, MA, USA: Edward Elgar.

Crew, Michael A. and Paul R. Kleindorfer (2008a), 'Reform of the United States Postal Service: an unfinished task', in Crew, Kleindorfer and J.I. Campbell (eds), *Handbook of Worldwide Postal Reform*, Cheltenham, UK and Northampton, MA, USA: Edward Elgar.

Crew, Michael A. and Paul R. Kleindorfer (2008b), 'Regulation and the USO under entry', in Crew and Kleindorfer (eds), *Competition and Regulation in the Postal and Delivery Sector*, Cheltenham, UK and Northampton, MA, USA: Edward Elgar.

Green, Richard, David Newberry and Michael Pollitt (1997), 'The restructuring and privatisation of Britain's CEGB – was it worth it?', *Journal of Industrial Economics*, **55** (3), 269–303.

Helm, Dieter, James Wardlaw and Ben Caldecott (2009), *Delivering a 21st Century Infrastructure for Britain*, London: The Policy Exchange.

Jensen, Michael and William Meckling (1976), 'Theory of the firm: managerial behavior, agency costs and ownership structure', *Journal of Financial Economics*, **3** (4), October, 305–60.

Laffont, Jean-Jacques and Jean Tirole (1993), *A Theory of Incentives in Procurement and Regulation*, Cambridge, MA: MIT Press.

Leibenstein, Harvey (1966), 'Allocative efficiency versus X-efficiency', *American Economic Review*, **56**, June, 392–415.

Maschke, Walter (2002), 'Transformation at Deutsche Post World Net: using the example of socially compatible workforce adjustment', in M.A. Crew and P.R. Kleindorfer (eds), *Postal and Delivery Services: Delivering on Competition*, Boston, MA: Kluwer Academic.

Megginson, William L. and Jeffry M. Netter (2001), 'From state to market: a survey of empirical studies on privatization', *Journal of Economic Literature*, **39** (2), June, 321–89.

Niskanen, William A. Jr (1971), *Bureaucracy and Representative Government*, Chicago, IL: Aldine Atherton.

Ofcom (2011), 'Securing the Universal Postal Service: proposals for the future framework of economic regulation', London, October 20.

Sappington, David E.M. and J. Gregory Sidak (2003), 'Incentives for anticompetitive behavior by public enterprises', *Review of Industrial Organization*, **22**, 183–206.

Steele, Ian (1991), 'Comments', in Michael Crew and Paul Kleindorfer (eds), *Competition and Innovation in Postal Service*, Boston, MA: Kluwer Academic.

Toime, Elmar (1991), 'Competitive strategy of New Zealand Post', in Michael Crew and Paul Kleindorfer (eds), *Competition and Innovation in Postal Service*, Boston, MA: Kluwer Academic.

Tullock, Gordon (1967), 'The welfare costs of tariffs, monopolies and theft', *Western Economic Journal*, **5**, June, 224–32.

Vickers, John and George Yarrow (1988), *Privatization: an Economic Analysis*, Cambridge, MA: MIT Press.

Williamson, Oliver E. (1967), *The Economics of Discretionary Behavior*, Chicago, IL: Markham.

2. The UK Postal Services Act 2011

Richard Eccles†

1 INTRODUCTION

The Postal Services Act 2011 came into force on 1 October 2011,[1] setting out the framework for a new UK postal regulatory regime replacing the regulatory provisions of the previous legislation, the Postal Services Act 2000.[2] The 2011 Act makes the safeguarding of the universal service the main regulatory priority. It significantly relaxes the regulatory controls on Royal Mail mainly by reducing the scope of the universal service to exclude bulk mail and by relaxing pricing controls, and by replacing the previous regime on downstream access to Royal Mail's network by a more limited set of controls. The overall result is a considerably more flexible regulatory regime for the incumbent postal operator, Royal Mail. The 2011 Act also provides for a restructuring of Royal Mail Group as a basis for possible privatization, and a framework for the modification and reform of the Royal Mail pension plan.

The specific regulatory controls under the 2011 Act are contained not in the act itself but in the regulatory conditions which have been imposed by the new postal regulator, Ofcom, under the enabling provisions of the act. The regulatory regime introduced by the 2011 Act has a number of important features. First, it makes Ofcom the postal regulator, with the primary duty of securing the provision of the universal postal service on a financially sustainable basis. Second, it introduces a system of general authorization subject to regulatory conditions imposed by Ofcom, in place of the requirement for a license that applied under the 2000 Act. In addition, Ofcom is given competition law powers in the postal services sector under the Competition Act 1998, concurrently with the Office of Fair Trading (OFT), and the power to refer postal services markets to the Competition Commission for a market investigation (under Part 4 of the Enterprise Act 2002).[3]

2 THE CONCLUSIONS OF THE INDEPENDENT REVIEWS OF THE UK POSTAL SERVICES SECTOR

From a regulatory perspective, the 2011 Act introduces into a statutory framework the changes recommended by the UK government's independent review of the UK postal services sector which focused on the policies needed to maintain the universal service in the UK. Two reports were published by the independent review panel chaired by Richard Hooper CBE, 'Modernise or Decline' in 2008 and an update paper in September 2010.

† Partner, Bird & Bird LLP, London.

The 2008 independent review (the Hooper Report) recommended significant changes to the regulatory regime, including the appointment of Ofcom as the postal sector regulator, and the need for new regulatory tools, greater cost transparency of Royal Mail and a review of the regulatory controls on access to Royal Mail's network imposed by the previous regulator Postcomm under the 2000 Act.

The 2008 report took a particularly critical approach to the 'headroom' system of regulating access to Royal Mail's downstream network that had been applied by Postcomm through the license controls on Royal Mail pursuant to the 2000 Act. The 'headroom' access system involved requirements for a specified margin to be maintained between the regulated retail price for a service and the price for the equivalent access service. The Hooper Report pointed out that very few other countries mandate the provision of downstream access in the way required for Royal Mail and, in particular, that no other country operates a comparable system of headroom access. The report observed that while the downstream access regime had kick-started competition, end-to-end competition had declined since the headroom margin system was introduced in 2006, possibly because alternative carriers had been dissuaded by low access prices from developing their own end-to-end networks.[4]

The 2010 Hooper update report went further and stated that the then current regulatory regime was 'not fit for purpose'. It emphasized a need to introduce a new access regime ensuring the right balance between competition and the financial sustainability of the universal service.

3 THE REGULATORY REGIME UNDER THE POSTAL SERVICES ACT 2011

The Hooper recommendations are directly reflected in the regulatory provisions contained in Part 3 of the Postal Services Act 2011. Ofcom is given postal sector regulatory duties requiring it to exercise the functions so as to 'secure the provision of a universal postal service'.[5] This is a primary duty, in that Ofcom's power to impose any other regulatory conditions on postal operators is subject to this requirement. Ofcom is required to have regard to the need for the universal service to be financially sustainable and to be efficient both for a reasonable period and subsequently, which means securing a reasonable commercial rate of return on expenditure incurred in providing the universal service.[6]

The 2011 Act has swept away the requirement for each postal operator to have a license, and instead introduced a system of general authorization to provide postal services.[7] This authorization is subject only to such regulatory conditions as Ofcom may impose. General requirements apply for the imposition of all regulatory conditions by Ofcom,[8] in that they must be objectively justifiable, not unduly discriminate against persons or particular descriptions of persons, be proportionate to their intentions, and be transparent. Likewise, directions can only be given by Ofcom pursuant to regulatory conditions where to do so is objectively justifiable, does not unduly discriminate, and is proportionate and transparent.

There are eight specific types of regulatory conditions, the first three of which relate specifically to the universal service provider (USP).[9] These are: a designated USP condition (requiring the designated operator to provide a universal postal service of a specified description and to specified standards), a USP access condition (requiring access to the universal service provider's network), and a USP accounting condition. The other types of conditions, which can be applied to postal operators generally, are: a notification condition (giving notice to Ofcom of an operator's intention to provide a letters business on a specified scale or to expand such a service), a general universal service condition, an essential condition, a general access condition and a consumer protection condition.

A notification condition is a condition requiring a postal operator to give Ofcom advance notice of the operator's intention to provide a postal service of a specified extent involving the provision of letters or to expand such a letters business of such scale by a specific extent.[10] Ofcom has imposed a notification condition with effect from 1 April 2012[11] requiring any person to give three months' written notice to Ofcom before commencing or expanding a postal services business consisting in the delivery of at least 2.5 million letters in a period of three months in all or any part of the UK. Such written notice must also specify the forecast volume of letters, the geographical areas in which the business will operate and details of when the business will be put into effect.

Essential conditions, which can be imposed on any postal operator, include conditions to safeguard any one or more of the following: confidentiality in connection with the sending, conveyance and delivery of letters, security where dangerous goods are transported, the confidentiality of information conveyed, and also conditions securing the delivery of postal packets to the intended addressees, and guarding against theft or loss of or damage to postal packets.[12] The first three of these types of essential conditions reflect the provisions of EU Directive 2008/6 on postal services (the Postal Services Directive). The last two types of essential conditions are also closely related to the directive's essential requirements. The directive provides in Article 9 that member states may impose conditions on authorizations *inter alia* to ensure compliance with the essential requirements. The Act does not include the further essential conditions allowed under the Postal Services Directive, data protection, environmental protection and regional planning. Ofcom has implemented the act as regards essential conditions by adopting a decision to impose an essential condition on all regulated postal operators, requiring compliance with the Mail Integrity Code with effect from 1 April 2012.[13] The Mail Integrity Code requires the postal operators to adopt recruitment, training and disciplinary procedures to ensure the objectives of minimizing the exposure of postal packets to the risk of loss, theft, damage or interference and maintaining and improving regulated postal operators' performance in respect of such matters. In addition, the Code requires postal operators to maintain procedures in relation to the security of all relevant premises, vehicles and equipment used in the collection, conveyance or delivery of postal items.

Consumer protection conditions which can likewise be imposed on any postal operator, include conditions requiring the operator to establish and maintain procedures, standards and policies with regard to the handling of complaints by users, the resolution of disputes with users, the provision of remedies and redress in respect of the subject matter of complaints and disputes, and information to be made available to users about the service provided. They can also include anything else which appears necessary to Ofcom to protect users.[14]

The Universal Service

While the 2011 Act requires Ofcom to make the provision of a financially sustainable universal postal service its main regulatory priority and contains specific enabling provisions concerning the regulation of the universal service, it is the order made by Ofcom and designated USP conditions imposed by Ofcom under the act, that define the scope of the universal postal service under the new regime. The universal service is now defined in scope by reference to the specific types of products for the first time (rather than individual named Royal Mail services under Royal Mail's license under the old regime). All bulk-mail products are now excluded from the universal postal service, and price controls on the universal postal service as provided by Royal Mail have been considerably relaxed by Ofcom.

Ofcom is specifically required by the 2011 Act to establish, by means of a universal postal service order, a description of the specific services that are to be included within the universal service.[15] These services must in particular include the following minimum requirements: first, daily deliveries of letters six days per week, that is, Monday to Saturday, and daily deliveries of postal packets five days per week, that is, Monday to Friday, in each case to the home or premises of all persons in the UK; second, at least one collection of letters every Monday to Saturday and one collection of postal packets every Monday to Friday; third, the conveyance of postal packets at affordable prices and in accordance with a uniform tariff throughout the UK; fourth, a registered items service at affordable and uniform prices; fifth, an insured items service at affordable prices; sixth, free of charge services (to be specified in the universal postal service order) for blind or partially sighted persons; and seventh, free of charge conveyance services for legislative petitions and addresses.[16]

Ofcom made the Universal Postal Service Order as required by the Act, and it entered into force on 1 April 2012.[17] This specifies the nature of the services that make up the universal service and are to be provided by the USP, in greater detail than in the act. The Order repeats the minimum requirements set out in s.31 of the act that specify the end-to-end services which are to be provided as part of the universal service, all of which are for single-piece services only. The Order sets out more detail concerning the free end-to-end services to be provided (for blind or partially sighted persons and concerning the conveyance of legislative petitions) and further specifies certain addressee services, namely redirection and retention services and *poste restante* services[18] which are to be provided free of charge. All such services are to be provided on fair and reasonable terms. All these services other than those expressed to be free of charge are to be provided at affordable prices in accordance with a uniform public tariff for the whole of the UK. The Order requires both a priority and a standard service for single-piece items based on specified routing times of D+1 for priority services and D+2 for standard services and a registered and insured service for items weighing up to 10kg having a routing time of D+1, where 'D' is the date of collection and 'n' is the number of working days between D and the delivery date (including the delivery date). Single-piece items are stated to be individual postal items (that is, without discount based on quantity, formatting, machine sortation, presortation or the purchase of any other conveyance service). All such postal services must be capable of purchase by postage stamp or by meter and must include a certificate of posting and provision of proof of delivery on application by the sender. The universal service also includes similar services for postal items weighing more than 10kg (which are to be conveyed and delivered within a reasonable period), and the following further services for single-piece items: return to sender services for domestic single-piece items; international services for the EU and for the rest of the world, respectively (with routing times of D+3 for the EU and D+7 or D+72 for the rest of the world countries); and conveyance and delivery services for international items from within the EU (compatible with a routing time for the end-to-end service of D+3) and also from non-EU (rest of the world) countries.

The fact that the Universal Postal Service Order applies only to single-piece postal items means that the UK regime is consistent with the intention specified in the Postal Services Directive with regard to the uniform tariff obligation. A uniform tariff may be imposed by member states (for reasons relating to the public interest) on services provided at a single-piece tariff,[19] although the directive also allows a uniform tariff to be imposed on 'other postal items'. Recital 39 of the directive refers to such other mail items as being, for example, newspapers and books, for the purpose of protecting general public interests such as access to culture, freedom of the press or regional and social cohesion.

The 2011 Act enables Ofcom to impose designated USP conditions on the USP to the extent that it considers it necessary in order to secure the universal service provision in accordance with the description of the universal service in the Universal Postal Service Order. A designated USP condition can require the provision of a universal service throughout the UK to specified standards, to provide access points, to provide specified information to other postal operators and users, and can require the USP to do anything else that Ofcom considers appropriate to ensure the universal service. As regards universal service tariffs, the Act provides that Ofcom may make provision for tariffs but, in exercising such power, Ofcom must seek to ensure that prices are affordable, take account of the costs of providing the universal service and provide incentives for efficient service provision.[20]

Ofcom has designated Royal Mail as the universal service provider by imposing the USP conditions on Royal Mail as set out in the Designated USP Conditions which took effect on 1 April 2012.[21] The Designated USP Conditions set out detailed requirements to fulfill the Universal Postal Service Order. These USP conditions repeat the performance-related requirements of the Universal Postal Service Order[22] and set out detailed performance requirements for each type of universal postal service. These requirements serve to ensure that the specified routing in times of, for example D+1 priority services and D+2 standard services are met. For example, Royal Mail is required to achieve D+1 priority class performance in 91.5 percent of cases for stamped and metered mail and D+2 in prescribed 98.5 percent of cases for standard (second class) mail (items weighing less than 1kg). The Designated USP Conditions also contain obligations on Royal Mail as USP to monitor or procure the monitoring of these performance requirements.

The Designated USP Conditions involve considerable relaxation of price controls under Royal Mail. They do not contain any cost-orientation requirements and contain only a limited price cap, in particular a price cap on the provision of end-to-end services only as regards standard letters sent by second class post, for which the maximum charge is to be 55 pence during the year ending on 31 March 2013, with inflation-based increases, in each subsequent year ending on 31 March up to 2019. The 55 pence cap on second class mail does not appear to constrain Royal Mail's pricing in practice, because

Royal Mail's second class stamp prices have been set at 50 pence following implementation of the new regime. Thus the 55 pence cap can be seen as no more than a safeguard to ensure that second class stamp prices remain within the range of affordability. No price controls are imposed on any of the other universal services.[23]

The fact that the USP conditions do not impose a cost-orientation obligation is also noteworthy. Ofcom stated in its decision document which introduced the regulatory conditions that it would monitor the prices of universal services to ensure that they both remain affordable and take into account the cost of providing the service.[24] It is not clear to what extent the issue of cost orientation has been separately assessed at the outset. Cost orientation of universal service prices is a requirement of the Postal Services Directive (Article 12), but the 2011 Act does not itself directly impose this requirement, leaving it rather to Ofcom as regulator to impose such a requirement when imposing tariff obligations under the designated USP conditions.

The Act allows Ofcom to impose notification conditions and general universal service conditions on any postal operator which is operating 'within the scope' of the universal postal service. A service is 'within the scope of the universal postal service' if it conforms to the description of the service set out in the Universal Postal Service Order, or if it would do so but for the fact that deliveries or collections are not made on a daily basis, or if the service is not provided throughout the UK or if it is not provided at a uniform tariff. In addition, a service can be treated as being 'within the scope' of the universal postal service if, in Ofcom's opinion, the service is of a kind that, from a user's perspective, 'could reasonably be said to be interchangeable' with a service described in the Universal Postal Service Order.[25] The reference to a service being within the scope of the universal service where it fits the relevant description other than the requirements for daily deliveries or collections, national coverage and the uniform tariff, reflects the requirements of Article 9 of the Postal Services Directive. Article 9 allows member states to make the granting of authorizations for postal services subject to requirements concerning the quality, availability and performance of the relevant services,[26] while providing that universal service obligations and obligations set out in Article 3 of the directive (including the requirement for daily collections and deliveries and national coverage) may only be imposed on designated USPs.[27]

The ability of Ofcom to impose general universal service conditions on operators providing services within the scope of the universal postal service, enables Ofcom to ensure that postal services are provided to certain minimum standards, so that non-USPs cannot gain an unfair advantage in relation to the USP and do not thereby undermine the provision of the universal service. However, the act provides that general universal service conditions cannot require an operator to collect or deliver any specific mail and cannot impose any uniform tariff obligations.

Access Conditions

USP Access Conditions can be imposed to require Royal Mail as the USP to give access to its postal network and to maintain accounting separation relating to access matters.[28] USP Access Conditions can be imposed only for the purposes of promoting efficiency and effective competition.

USP Access Conditions have been imposed by Ofcom[29] and their provisions are limited in scope so as to cover only the equivalent access services to Royal Mail's second class *Mailsort* and *Walksort* services. This is a considerable reduction in scope compared with the downstream access price control regime in Royal Mail's license under the previous regime.

Under the USP Access Conditions, Royal Mail is subject, as USP, to a general obligation to provide access services on reasonable request for the purpose of providing D+2 retail services, which are defined as retail services aiming to deliver two working days or later after collection from the sender. Also access services must be provided on fair and reasonable terms, conditions and charges and Royal Mail (as USP) must not unduly discriminate against particular persons or descriptions of persons in relation to such D+2 access services. Royal Mail can be deemed to have shown undue discrimination if it unduly favors to a material extent an activity carried on by it so as to place competitors at a competitive disadvantage.[30] Royal Mail is also required to use all reasonable endeavors to ensure that no information that it receives as a result of giving access to its postal network is disclosed for the benefit of or used by any of its other businesses.

More specially, Ofcom may only impose price controls on Royal Mail's access services if it considers that Royal Mail might otherwise charge excessively high access prices, or impose a price squeeze, with adverse consequences for users.[31] Price controls must take account of such costs incurred in provision of the network as Ofcom consider appropriate. Ofcom may also have regard to the prices at which services are available in comparable markets, and determine what they consider to represent efficiency by using cost-accounting methods.

The provisions in the Act concerning USP Access Conditions guard against excessive pricing, but neither the Act nor the USP Access Conditions actually imposed by Ofcom, require cost orientation (as such) of Royal Mail's prices to its downstream conveyance and delivery costs. Also, the requirement to avoid a price squeeze is to be contrasted with the regime provided for in the Postal Services Directive, which essentially requires nondiscriminatory and transparent pricing by the USP regarding provision of special tariffs for services for business, bulk mailers or consolidators, as between different third parties and as between third parties and the downstream business of the USP supplying equivalent services, taking into account the associated conditions. Recital 39 of the directive further stipulates that for the provision of such services to businesses, bulk mailers and consolidators, USPs should enjoy price flexibility in line with the cost-orientation principle, and the tariffs should take account of the avoided costs (as compared to the standard service covering the complete range of clearance, sorting, transport and distribution features).

The key features to identify a margin squeeze or price squeeze under competition law are the following: (i) two distinct markets must be in existence (an upstream market and a downstream market); (ii) a vertically integrated undertaking must be dominant in the upstream market and active in the downstream market; (iii) operators on the downstream market must have a need for access to an input from the upstream market in order to operate downstream; (iv) the relationship between the dominant company's upstream and downstream prices must be such as to exclude the ability of an 'equally efficient competitor' to compete downstream, by reference to the long-run incremental cost of the dominant operator's downstream operation. The issue is essentially one of whether a competitor having the same cost functions as the downstream arm of the vertically integrated dominant company is able to be profitable in the downstream market having regard to the wholesale and retail prices respectively of the vertically integrated company. Thus the competition law margin squeeze test requires account to be taken of the relevant costs of the vertically integrated operator.

The margin squeeze test requires Royal Mail to take all reasonable steps to ensure that it maintains a minimum margin between the retail prices of relevant retail services (primarily second class Mailsort and second class Walksort services[32]) and access charges for corresponding access services during each 12-month period, so that the relevant upstream revenue is no less than relevant upstream costs. In addition, Royal Mail must ensure that the relevant upstream revenue for each individual contract for any relevant retail services is equal to or more than 50 percent of the relevant upstream cost for that individual contract. Relevant upstream revenue and relevant upstream costs are to be calculated by deducting the relevant downstream revenue and costs from relevant end-to-end revenue and end-to-end costs, respectively.[33] Royal Mail is required to publish its current standard terms and conditions and to keep the publicly available version updated.[34] The actual downstream access conditions imposed by Ofcom on Royal Mail therefore operate in practice as an obligation against cross-subsidy by Royal Mail of its downstream operations to its upstream operations. While the avoidance of cross-subsidy is an important part of avoiding margin squeeze, this obligation against cross-subsidy is not in itself a full margin squeeze avoidance obligation, at least not in the competition law meaning. In the postal services sector, conceptually the physical downstream operations are equivalent to the upstream operations in other sectors in which the incumbent has a virtual monopoly; in the postal services sector, the physical upstream (collection and processing) activities are those that feature the most competition. Therefore the provisions of the USP Access Conditions concerning margin squeeze, in effect require Royal Mail not to cross-subsidize from its downstream delivery operations in which it has a virtual monopoly to its upstream activities which are open to competition.

Ofcom must take into account the following factors in deciding what obligations to impose in a USP access condition: first, the technical and economic viability of installing and using facilities that would make access unnecessary; second, the feasibility of giving the proposed access; third, the investment made by the USP in relation to the relevant facilities; fourth, the need to secure effective competition in the long term; and fifth, any relevant intellectual property rights.[35] These preconditions to the imposition of a USP access condition are derived from the corresponding requirements for the imposition of access requirements in relation to electronic communications networks under the Communications Act 2003. Those requirements are in turn derived directly from the specified preconditions for the imposition of network access obligations on electronic communications operators holding significant market power, as set out in Directive 2002/19 on access to and interconnection with electronic communications networks.

The Act also provides for a power for Ofcom to impose general access conditions on any postal operators, that is, non-USPs. The obligations in a general access condition are essentially the same as those within a USP condition, including provision of access to the relevant postal network and maintaining accounting separation in relation to access matters.[36] However, for purposes of a general access condition, Ofcom does not also have to show that the access condition is necessary for promoting efficiency.[37] Also, any price controls imposed under a general access condition need not be limited to avoiding excessively high prices or a price squeeze.

Significantly, Ofcom is given the power[38] to resolve access disputes between postal operators, regarding the terms and conditions on which network access is to be provided. Ofcom is free to determine the procedure that it considers appropriate, but is required to resolve any such disputes as quickly as possible. Ofcom has various remedial powers, including the making of a declaration as to the parties' rights and obligations, giving directions as to the terms or conditions of relevant transactions and requiring the payment of sums by way of adjustment of an under- or overpayment where Ofcom has determined the proper amount of charges paid by one party to another. These provisions on access disputes reflect the corresponding powers held by Ofcom in relation to the electronic communications sector on network access disputes as set out in the Communications Act 2003. Ofcom has provided guidelines for its resolution of disputes referred to in the postal services sector by publishing a supplement to its existing 2011 guidelines on dispute resolution in the electronic communications sector.[39] Ofcom indicates that it has more discretion in relation to postal services disputes as to whether or not to accept the dispute than it has in relation to disputes arising in the electronic communications sector.

USP Accounting Conditions

Ofcom is given considerable powers under the act to impose accounting conditions on Royal Mail as the USP.[40] Such accounting conditions can require Royal Mail to maintain accounting separation as between different activities specified by Ofcom, for example in relation to different services, facilities or products or in relation to different geographical areas.[41] Ofcom can also require compliance with requirements concerning the identification of costs and cost orientation, and the publication of accounts and other information.[42] Ofcom can impose conditions requiring the application of presumptions in fixing and determining costs and charges for any purpose[43] and rules about the use of cost-accounting systems and requiring annual auditing of compliance with such systems (by a qualified independent auditor).[44]

Ofcom has imposed USP accounting conditions on Royal Mail[45] requiring Royal Mail, *inter alia*, to maintain accounting separation between the activities of four distinct financial reporting entities, namely its end-to-end-only products entity, its downstream services entity, its upstream Universal Service Obligation (USO) products entity and its upstream non-USO products entity. Royal Mail is required to maintain and publish a costing manual setting out a detailed description of its national and zonal costing methodologies, and it must prepare and maintain financial statements for its postal business as a whole and for each of the four distinct financial reporting entities, in accordance with regulatory accounting guidelines to be prescribed by Ofcom. Royal Mail's financial statements must also comply with the *Guiding Principles*, which are the following: *completeness* (that is, that its regulatory accounting methodology takes into account all relevant revenues, costs, assets and liabilities) and *equivalence* (that is, Royal Mail must ensure that transfer prices and/or charges for internal products and services are determined based on similar products and services provided to external parties, reflecting where appropriate any differences in specifications or operational features); and also *causality*, *objectivity*, *accuracy*, *compliance with the statutory accounting standards*, *consistency* and *materiality*. Royal Mail is required to secure an appropriate audit opinion by a qualified independent auditor in respect of its financial statements, and such audit is subject to Ofcom's approval of the appointment and of the terms of the engagement.

Financial Support for the Universal Postal Service

Article 7(3) of the Postal Services Directive allows member states to take action where they calculate that the universal service obligations entail a net cost (calculated taking into account Annex I of the directive) and represent an unfair financial burden on the USP. The member state may then introduce a compensation mechanism (to compensate the USP from public funds) or a cost-sharing mechanism whereby postal services providers share the net cost of the universal service obligation. Article 9(2) of the Directive allows for authorizations to be subject to an obligation to make a financial contribution to such cost sharing. The 2011 Act provides for a cost-sharing mechanism to provide support to the USP where the net cost of the universal service constitutes an unfair financial burden.[46] The general universal service conditions that can be imposed by Ofcom under the act, on postal operators generally, include conditions requiring the making of contributions in accordance with any cost-sharing scheme established under these provisions.[47]

The Act provides that Ofcom may, but is not obliged to, review (from time to time) the extent (if any) of the financial burden for a USP in complying with its obligations. However, no such review can be carried out by Ofcom within the first five years of entry into force of these provisions of the act.[48] In any such review, Ofcom must consider the extent to which the USP is complying with its universal service obligations in a cost-efficient manner.[49] In the absence of any regulations that may be made by Ofcom for assessing the financial burden of the universal service, the financial burden is to be calculated as the net cost of compliance with the universal service obligations after allowing for 'market benefits' accruing to the USP from its designation and the performance of its universal service obligations.[50]

The criteria for assessing the financial burden of the universal service obligations broadly reflect those of Annex I of the Postal Services Directive, in situations where no regulations have been adopted for the review of USP designations and designated USP conditions, but the act is not specific as to the criteria for assessing the financial burden on the USP where such regulations are adopted. In the absence of such regulations, the application of the net cost criteria in the Act is broadly consistent with Annex I of the directive, though the relevant provisions of the act have been simplified in comparison to Annex I of the directive.

Where Ofcom concludes that there is a financial burden on the USP, it must then determine whether it will be unfair for the USP to continue to bear this burden (in whole or in part).[51] Such determination must be made in accordance with regulations made by Ofcom and must be published. Ofcom must submit a report to the secretary of state (the relevant government minister) setting out their recommendations as to how to deal with the unfair financial burden. Such action may include financial contributions by other service providers on a cost-sharing basis, or the making of a procurement determination, that is, a determination by Ofcom as to whether any particular postal operator or operators could provide any of the required postal services in a way which would avoid an unfair financial burden or reduce the unfairness of the burden. Again, Ofcom is required to make any procurement determination in accordance with prior regulations. However, a procurement determination may not be made within the first 10 years of entry into force of these provisions of the act.[52] The secretary of state must determine what action should be taken by Ofcom to deal with the identified financial burden and may direct Ofcom to take such action.[53] Where the secretary of state directs Ofcom to require financial contributions from other service providers, this must be implemented in the form of a scheme to be contained in regulations made by Ofcom.[54]

The Act can be said to set out a fairly thorough implementation of the cost-sharing option under Article 7(3)(b) of the Postal Services Directive, to deal with any unfair financial burden resulting from the net cost of the universal service, though only (at the earliest) after the first five years of the Act.

Enforcement of Regulatory Requirements

The Act provides for a two-stage process for enforcement of regulatory conditions.[55] Ofcom may give a notification where it believes that there are reasonable grounds that a person has contravened a regulatory requirement, specifying the contravention and giving notice, normally of one month, within which the person may make representations, and comply with and remedy the consequences of the notified contravention. However, before deciding to take the statutory steps to enforce the regulatory requirement, Ofcom must decide whether it would be more appropriate to use its competition law powers by proceeding under the Competition Act 1998. Where the operator has failed to comply with and remedy the consequences of infringements of the relevant regulatory requirement, Ofcom can issue an enforcement notification setting out the steps for complying with and for remedying the consequences of infringing the relevant regulatory requirement. The addressee of the enforcement notification has a statutory duty to comply with it which is enforceable in civil proceedings by Ofcom for an injunction or other appropriate remedy or relief. Ofcom can impose financial penalties for contravention of requirements specified in a notification of contravention or a requirement of an enforcement notification. The amount of the penalty must be appropriate and proportionate, but subject to this can be of an amount up to 10 percent of the annual turnover of the operator's postal services business.[56]

Ofcom has the power to give a direction suspending or restricting the scope of postal services that can be provided by an operator that is in repeated contravention of regulatory requirements, where enforcement notifications have failed and the suspension or restriction is considered appropriate and proportionate.[57]

All parties have a duty to comply with regulatory requirements and requirements of enforcement notifications, and breaches causing loss or damage are actionable by persons suffering loss.[58] However, Ofcom's consent is required for the bringing of proceedings concerning breaches of regulatory conditions, as opposed to breaches of enforcement notifications or breaches of a direction suspending or restricting the authorization to provide postal services.[59]

Appeals against Ofcom's Regulatory Decisions

The Act sets out a right of appeal for affected persons against any decision by Ofcom to impose a regulatory condition or a financial penalty or to issue a direction enforcing regulatory conditions. This right of appeal lies to the Competition Appeal Tribunal ('the CAT') and the CAT must apply the same principles as will be applied by a court on an application for judicial review.[60] The CAT has the power to quash the relevant decision and to refer the matter back to Ofcom. Member states are required to give a right of appeal to any user or postal service provider affected by a decision of the national regulatory authority, under Article 22 of the Postal Services Directive.

A person affected can appeal against price-control decisions by giving notice to Ofcom within a period of two months, following which Ofcom must refer the appeal to the Competition Commission. These include decisions on tariff conditions and any decision (other than one reached on a dispute resolution process) on prices for access by an operator to the postal network of another postal services operator. The Competition Commission can allow the appeal or quash the relevant price-control decision if it considers that Ofcom has made a material error. It can then make its own decision on the subject matter or refer the matter back to Ofcom with a direction to reconsider and make a new decision.[61]

4 THE RESTRUCTURING OF ROYAL MAIL GROUP (INCLUDING THE POST OFFICE)

The Act provides for the restructuring of the Royal Mail group so as to enable eventual privatization of all or part of Royal Mail itself while maintaining the Post Office in state ownership. The Act removes certain restrictions on ownership of shares in Royal Mail while providing that Post Office Limited will remain state owned unless the secretary of state makes an order (under Part 1 of the act) that ownership of the Post Office be transferred to a relevant mutual. A relevant mutual is a body whose members have an interest in the use by the public of post office services, including post office employees and other persons engaged in the provision of post offices, and it must have the main purpose of acting for the public benefit by promoting the use of public services provided by a post office. It must also have arrangements in place to prevent disposals of properties or of rights of a post office company that would be inconsistent with these purposes.[62]

5 THE ROYAL MAIL PENSION SCHEME

Part 2 of the Act contains provisions for the reform of the Royal Mail pensions plan. This enables the removal of the burden of the current pension deficit as recommended by the Hooper Report. The Secretary of State can establish a new public scheme for repayment of pension benefits to qualifying members of the current Royal Mail pension plan.[63] The Secretary of State may make an order providing for the transfer of qualifying accrued rights to a new public pension scheme and at the same time discharging liabilities in respect of the transferred accrued rights.[64] The Act further provides that (where such an order has been made) the Secretary of State may also (by order) transfer the assets of the current Royal Mail pension plan to the Secretary of State or the Treasury or to a fund established by the Secretary of State for purposes of holding the assets pending their disposal.[65]

The UK government's use of state funds to relieve Royal Mail of its legacy pension deficit required state aid approval from the European Commission, which approval was announced on 21 March 2012.[66] The Commission's approval decision appears to authorize the payment to Royal Mail Group of approximately £4.5 billion (approximately €5.6 billion) by way of relief of the majority of the Royal Mail pension deficit, and £1.1 billion (approximately €1.3 billion) by way of debt reduction.

6 CONCLUSIONS

There is no doubt that the 2011 Act introduces a total change in the landscape of the regulation of postal services in the UK. It introduces a new regulatory regime enforced by Ofcom to replace the previous regime, which the second Hooper Report (the second report of the government's independent review panel of the UK postal services sector) described as 'not fit for purpose'. The 2011 Act follows directly the recommendations of the two Hooper reports, by making the provision of the universal postal service on a financially sustainable basis the primary regulatory duty. The universal service is now for the first time clearly defined by reference to a description of the services included within the universal service, rather than by reference to specific Royal Mail products as was the case under Royal Mail's license under the previous legislation. Most importantly, the universal service excludes all bulk-mail services and is limited to single-piece items. The uniform tariff is likewise limited accordingly, which is in accordance with the relevant requirements of the Postal Services Directive. This results in a regime which gives considerably more flexibility to Royal Mail than previously.

In relation to price controls, both for universal service prices and for downstream access prices, the key regulatory requirements are to be found not in the act itself, but in the regulatory conditions imposed by Ofcom under the act, because the Act contains enabling provisions which have to be implemented by Ofcom. The regulatory conditions imposed under the Act by Ofcom allow a strong degree of flexibility for Royal Mail. The only price cap so far imposed, of 55 pence on the price for sending a second class standard letter, is considerably above the price level actually set by Royal Mail (5 pence higher) suggesting that Royal Mail is not constrained in practice on such pricing. Moreover, the Designated USP Conditions imposed by Ofcom do not include an obligation of cost orientation on Royal Mail, even though this is a specific requirement of the Postal Services Directive and is referred to in the 2011 Act.

Also, in relation to downstream access pricing, the new downstream access regime imposed by Ofcom under the Act is relatively limited in scope, being specifically for purposes of D+2 retail postal services. While the act enables Ofcom to introduce price controls to avoid a margin squeeze where this would otherwise be likely on the part of Royal Mail, the actual access price controls imposed in the USP Access Conditions do not fully reflect the defined features of a margin squeeze under competition law (that is, ensuring that an equally efficient competitor can compete downstream by reference to the wholesale and retail prices, respectively, of the vertically integrated dominant operator, taking into account the long-run incremental cost of that operator's downstream operations). Rather, the access price controls imposed by Ofcom focus, despite the explanation given for them in Ofcom's decision document introducing the regulatory conditions, on avoiding cross-subsidization of Royal Mail's upstream operations through its charges for downstream access or for the downstream element of its end-to-end service prices. Thus, in the postal services context, this margin squeeze condition is in reality an obligation on Royal Mail not to cross-subsidize from its virtual monopoly downstream delivery operation to its upstream collection and sorting operation which is the main area open to competition. Royal Mail is now given a degree of flexibility in its downstream access pricing as compared to the license regime under the 2000 Act.

Thus there will be some onus on Ofcom to monitor Royal Mail's pricing for the universal service and especially downstream access, by reference to the principles of the Act. Further or revised regulatory conditions, whether on pricing or otherwise, could if necessary be introduced in due course. Competing operators will be able to refer concerns arising to Ofcom, and it remains to be seen whether and to what extent they will do so by means of a complaint-seeking regulatory enforcement, or as regards downstream access issues, by means of a dispute referral in accordance with Ofcom's dispute resolution powers, or by means of a complaint under the Competition Act invoking Ofcom's concurrent competition law jurisdiction with the OFT.

NOTES

1. The Postal Services Act 2011 (Commencement No. 1 and Transitional Provisions Order 2011), SI 2011 No. 2329. Certain amendments in the Act to The Postal Services Act 2000 are, however, not yet brought into force.
2. This chapter covers the position as at 30 April 2012.
3. Schedule 10, Part 2, paragraph 62 of the Postal Services Act 2011, amending s.369(1) of the Communications Act 2003.
4. Paragraphs 198 and 199.
5. s.29(1).
6. s.29(1)–(4).
7. s.28(1).
8. s.53 and schedule 6
9. s.28(2).
10. s.41(2).
11. Statutory Notification: Notification Condition, dated 27 March 2012, Annex 12 to Ofcom's decision document *Securing the Universal Postal Service* dated 27 March 2012.
12. s.49.
13. Statutory Notification: Essential Condition, dated 27 March 2012, included in Annex 13 to Ofcom's decision document *Securing the Universal Postal Service* dated 27 March 2012.
14. s.51.
15. s.30(1).
16. s.s.30(2) and 31.
17. SI 2012 No.936, The Postal Services (Universal Postal Services) Order 2012.
18. *Poste restante* services are services providing for a registered post office to be used as an addressee's postal address for a reasonable period and for postal packets for that addressee to be held at such a post office for a reasonable period for collection by the addressee.
19. Article 12, second indent.
20. s.36, in particular sub-ss. (2)–(5).
21. Statutory Notification: Designated USP Conditions, dated 27 March 2012, contained in Annex 7 to Ofcom's decision document *Securing the Universal Postal Service* dated 27 March 2012. Ofcom may only designate more than one USP where it has made a specific procurement determination (in accordance with s.45 of the Act) or where an administration order has been made in respect of the USP: s.35(2)–(4).
22. However it may be noted that the target routing times for end-to-end international services within the EU are slightly less strict in the USP conditions than in the Order; in the USP conditions only 85 percent of

postal items should be delivered in D+3, while requiring that at least 97 percent of items be delivered in D+5.

23. Ofcom has issued a consultation on a proposal for the introduction of a price cap in relation to second class large letters and packets up to 2kg: *Securing the Universal Postal Service – Safeguard Cap for Large Letters and Packets*, dated 27 April 2012.
24. Ofcom statement *Securing the Universal Postal Service* dated 27 March 2012, section 7 and paragraph 8.65.
25. s.40(1)(c). This criterion of interchangeability is consistent with the statement in the Postal Services Directive on the issue of which services 'fall within the scope of universal service'; recital 27 states that for this purpose member states should assess whether services may from a user's perspective, be regarded as displaying interchangeability with services within the scope of the universal service, taking into account the characteristics of the services, including added value features, such as the intended use and the pricing.
26. Article 9(2), second indent.
27. Article 9(2), first paragraph.
28. s.38(1) and (2).
29. Statutory Notification: USP Access Condition, dated 27 March 2012, Annex 9 to Ofcom's decision document *Securing the Universal Postal Service* dated 27 March 2012. The obligations set out in these Access Conditions are based on the enabling provisions in Schedule 3, Part 1 of the Postal Services Act 2011.
30. USP access conditions 2–5.
31. S.38(4) and (5).
32. The relevant retail services include any substantially similar services offered by Royal Mail, and Ofcom reserves the right to direct Royal Mail to include other services within that group which it reasonably considers fall within the definition.
33. USP access condition 6.
34. USP access condition 7.
35. s.38(8).
36. s.50(1) and (2).
37. s.50(4).
38. Schedule 3, Part 2.
39. Dispute Resolution for postal disputes – Supplement to Ofcom's guidelines for the handling of regulatory disputes (in the telecommunications sector, published on 7 June 2011) (Supplement published in April 2012).
40. s.39.
41. s.39(2)(a) and (3)(a).
42. s.39(4)(b).
43. s.39(3)(b) and 4(a).
44. s.39(2)(c) and (d).
45. Statutory Notification: USP Accounting Condition, dated 27 March 2012, Annex 10 to Ofcom's decision document *Securing the Universal Postal Services* dated 27 March 2012.
46. ss.44–47.
47. s.42(3).
48. s.44(10).
49. s.44(1) and (2).
50. s.44(3) and (4).
51. s.45(1)–(9).
52. s.45(14).
53. s.45(11)–(13).
54. s.46.
55. s.54 and schedule 7.
56. The relevant turnover of a postal operator is defined by statutory instrument as being the turnover from the relevant person's postal services business after the deduction of sales rebates, value added tax and other taxes directly related to turnover: SI 2012 No. 1127, The Postal Services Act 2011 (Penalties) (Rules for Calculation of Turnover) Order 2012.
57. Schedule 7 paragraph 11.
58. Schedule 7 paragraph 16.
59. Schedule 7 paragraph 16(6).
60. s.57(1), (2) and (5).
61. s.59(1)–(3), (6)–(8) and (13).
62. ss.4 and 7.
63. s.17(1).

64. s.17(2) and (3).
65. s.21(1) and (2).
66. European Commission Decision of 21.03.2012 (SA.31479; C(2012)1834 Final); Commission press release: *State Aid: Commission approves pension relief and restructuring aid in favour of the Royal Mail Group*, IP/12/260 dated 21 March 2012.

3. A gravity model of international postal exchanges*

José Ansón† **and Matthias Helble**‡

1 INTRODUCTION

International postal exchanges have been an integral part of global communication for several centuries, first connecting distant locations throughout empires, and then people and businesses from different countries in the world through a single postal territory with the creation of the Universal Postal Union (UPU) in 1874. However, too little is known of the drivers of these exchanges, particularly as regards bilateral flows of letters, parcels and express items between different countries in an era of strong development of e-commerce and greater social and political globalization (KOF, 2012). This chapter proposes an empirical method to identify these drivers and measure their impact on international postal traffic flows so as to gain a better understanding of the functioning of international postal markets.

Almost no empirical research exists on the modeling of bilateral international mail flows with a global coverage of countries and postal operators. International postal traffic has long remained in uncharted waters for economic analysis. However, international trade, migration and foreign direct investment flows have been analyzed empirically over several decades of economic research. The estimation of so-called 'gravity equations' has recently benefited from advances in economic theory (see Anderson and van Wincoop, 2004), is inspired by Newton's law of gravity and was used in most of this research.

This economic research will evaluate whether the above gravity equations methodology can be extended to the analysis of international mail flows, for all classes of mail. Gravity equations rely on the hypothesis that international flows of goods and services between countries depend on the geographic distance between countries and their combined economic weight, as well as number of bilateral variables, representing trade frictions, such as sharing (or not) a common language at origin and destination. Our research will also test whether postal-specific frictions may also matter alongside the traditional trade frictions introduced in empirical models of international trade and migration flows.

The empirical work described in this chapter will rely on the existence of a real-time database covering exchanges of mail between countries' postal operators on a daily basis for the year 2011. High-frequency data is available in this framework, and panel-data econometric methods are applied to estimate for the first-time postal gravity equations,

† Postal Economics Expert, Universal Postal Union, Case Postale, Bern.
‡ Statistics Expert, Universal Postal Union, Case Postale, Bern.

which also corresponds to the first estimation of high-frequency gravity equations in the economic literature.

The econometric estimation results support the validity of applying the gravity equation approach to model flows of international letters, parcels and express EMS (Express Messaging Services) items. It highlights the importance of the geographical distance factor, as well as natural and unnatural trade and postal frictions. The effect of distance on mail flows is lower than for merchandise trade, but still significant. It decreases with higher quality of service and service level. While international postal exchanges are still driven by senders for the international letter post, the model confirms that recipients are almost as influential as senders for international parcel post and express EMS items, and more influential for registered international letter-post items. The estimation of the postal gravity equations also highlights the existence of important postal-specific frictions aside from traditional trade frictions to explain mail flows between countries. Some seasonal effects were also identified.

The rest of the chapter is organized as follows. Section 2 introduces gravity equations and how they could be applied to the analysis of international postal exchanges. Section 3 presents the data and empirical methodology. Section 4 shows the econometric estimation results and Section 5 concludes.

2 GRAVITY EQUATIONS: FROM INTERNATIONAL TRADE TO INTERNATIONAL POSTAL EXCHANGES

This economic research aims to build an empirical model of international postal exchanges using a gravity equations approach for the first time in the postal economic literature. Gravity equations have been used for several decades among trade economists to model bilateral trade flows between countries. Newton's law of gravity in physics inspires them:

$$F_1 = F_2 = G(m_1m_2)/r^2, \tag{3.1}$$

where F_i indicates forces, m_i masses and r distance (G being a parameter). In their simplest form, they postulate that international trade flows between countries are proportional to the combined economic mass of two trading partners and to the inverse of the distance between countries. In other words, the closer two countries are geographically and the more economically developed, the higher the likelihood of greater exchanges between them. While lacking solid microeconomic foundations for several decades, Anderson and van Wincoop (2003) have recently provided a robust theoretical framework to this empirical methodology. Besides international trade flows, the gravity equations have also been extensively used to model international migration or foreign direct investment flows between country pairs.

Gravity equations typically make it possible to distinguish the impacts of natural and unnatural trade frictions, that is, whatever limits the development of international exchanges. Mostly, the latter frictions result from governmental action. In spite of the known link between international postal exchanges and international trade, the use of gravity equations has never been extended to international postal flows in order to estimate the relative influence of natural and unnatural trade and postal frictions.

The extension of the basic gravity equation to international postal exchanges would result in equation (3.2) below, directly expressed in logarithms (ln) after linearization,

$$\ln IPW_{ij,c} = \ln \beta_{0,c} + \beta_{1,c} \ln GDP_i + \beta_{2,c} \ln GDP_j + \beta_{3,c} \ln DIST_{ij} + \ln \varepsilon_{ij,c}, \quad (3.2)$$

where the total weight of dispatches of international postal items (*IPW*) sent from the origination country *i* to the destination country *j*, and for each class of mail *c*, would depend on the gross domestic product *GDP* of the country of origin *i*, the gross domestic product *GDP* of the destination country *j*, and the geographic distance, namely *DIST*, between both countries *i* and *j*. The term $\ln \beta_{0,c}$ represents the constant. While coefficients $\beta_{1,c}$ and $\beta_{2,c}$ are expected to be positive, $\beta_{3,c}$ is expected to be negative. Distance is supposed to provide a measure of trade costs (transportation, and so on), although one could reasonably expect a lower impact of distance for mail communication than for trade flows where the average elasticity of distance is –0.9 according to some meta-analysis of this literature (Disdier and Head, 2008). This means that a 10 percent increase in distance reduces trade flows by 9 percent. The relationship described in (3.2) is multiplicative before linearization, and the error term ε of the econometric equation is assumed to follow a lognormal form. Equation (3.2′) below describes the same relationship but using the total volumes of international postal exchanges, in terms of number of postal items sent from country *i* to country *j*, namely *IPV*, instead of weight:

$$\ln IPV_{ij,c} = \ln \beta_{0,c} + \beta_{1,c} \ln GDP_i + \beta_{2,c} \ln GDP_j + \beta_{3,c} \ln DIST_{ij} + \ln \varepsilon_{ij,c}. \quad (3.2')$$

The chapter tests whether the above-mentioned gravity equations approach can be applied to international postal exchanges or not. If so, it will estimate the relative importance of trade and postal frictions, respectively, whether natural or unnatural. It will also compare how the key gravity equations coefficients, such as the distance coefficient, behave across three classes *c* of international mail: the international letter post, defined as items up to 2 kilograms by the UPU (typically letters, flats or small packets), the international parcel post up to 30 kilograms and the EMS services, an express service for messages and packages provided by a subset of postal operators of the UPU through a cooperative.

3 DATA AND METHODOLOGY

Thanks to the exchange of electronic data interchange (EDI) messages between postal operators, a database comprising more than one billion records was available for developing the first gravity model of international mail flows. The access and management of the data has mobilized great resources and efforts. Millions of records were aggregated to provide daily international mail flows between the designated postal operators participating in the UPUs International Postal System, a platform designed to facilitate the operational management of all classes of international mail exchanges between postal operators. So far, the construction of the database for the gravity equation exercise has been limited to the year 2011 only and covers exchanges between 170 UPU member countries. Typically, each dispatch of mail to and from a country is registered electronically in several centralized databases gathering real-time data. To our knowledge, so far no gravity equation has been estimated on such a high-frequency data basis.

The availability of daily data enables the introduction of daily and monthly dimensions rarely used in gravity equations literature, where the time dimension often corresponds to the year, if any.

Another challenge was that postal operators are still developing the use of these systems for their management of international mail. This entails the possibility of some flow increases being the consequence of starting using exchanges of electronic messages between postal operators rather than reflecting real international postal traffic growth. However, besides the real-time traffic information available through the UPU systems, the level of information exchanged between postal operators can also be controlled for through the number of EDI messages exchanges for each country pair ij.

Therefore, equation (3.3) specifies the international postal gravity equation to be estimated including data for any date t in 2011:

$$\ln IPW_{ijt,c} = \ln \beta_{0,c} + \beta_{1,c} \ln GDP_i + \beta_{2,c} \ln GDP_j + \beta_{3,c} \ln DIST_{ij} + \beta_{4,c} \ln INF_{ijt,c} + \boldsymbol{DAY_t}\beta_{5,c} + \boldsymbol{MONTH_t}\beta_{6,c} + \ln \varepsilon_{ijt,c}, \tag{3.3}$$

where $\boldsymbol{DAY_t}$ and $\boldsymbol{MONTH_t}$ are vectors of dummy variables for each day of the week except one (that is, Sunday) and each month of the year except one (that is, January) in order to avoid perfect co-linearity, and INF is the variable controlling for the number of exchanges of EDI messages for each country pair ij at date t for mail class c. In equation (3.3′), weight (IPW) is replaced by the volumes (IPV) (that is, number of items):

$$\ln IPV_{ijt,c} = \ln \beta_{0,c} + \beta_{1,c} \ln GDP_i + \beta_{2,c} \ln GDP_j + \beta_{3,c} \ln DIST_{ij} + \beta_{4,c} \ln INF_{ijt,c} + \boldsymbol{DAY_t}\beta_{5,c} + \boldsymbol{MONTH_t}\beta_{6,c} + \ln \varepsilon_{ijt,c}. \tag{3.3′}$$

It must be noted that volumes IPV for international letter-post exchanges only cover registered or insured items, unlike IPW which covers all. Equations (3.3) and (3.3′) are typically specified in the manner used previously prior to the seminal paper on gravity equations by Anderson and van Wincoop (2003). One of the most noticeable contributions of this paper to the economic literature on gravity equations was to suggest the use of country of origin and country of destination fixed effects instead of the GDP, so as to take full account of unobservable variations in variables not specified in the traditional models (3.3) and (3.3′). In our case, this could represent the postal network density, or international postal tariffs specific to each country. Therefore, equations (3.4) and (3.4′) incorporate these country-specific fixed effects employing the approach of Anderson and van Wincoop through a vector of country-specific dummies both at origin and destination, that is, $\boldsymbol{SENDER_i}$ and $\boldsymbol{RECEIVER_j}$, respectively, as can be seen below:

$$\ln IPW_{ijt,c} = \ln \beta_{0,c} + \boldsymbol{SENDER}_i \beta_{1,c} + \boldsymbol{RECEIVER}_j \beta_{2,c} + \beta_{3,c} \ln DIST_{ij} + \beta_{4,c} \ln INF_{ijt,c} + \boldsymbol{DAY}_t \beta_{5,c} + \boldsymbol{MONTH}_t \beta_{6,c} + \ln \varepsilon_{ijt,c}, \tag{3.4}$$

$$\ln IPV_{ijt,c} = \ln \beta_{0,c} + \boldsymbol{SENDER}_i \beta_{1,c} + \boldsymbol{RECEIVER}_j \beta_{2,c} + \beta_{3,c} \ln DIST_{ij} + \beta_{4,c} \ln INF_{ijt,c} + \boldsymbol{DAY}_t \beta_{5,c} + \boldsymbol{MONTH}_t \beta_{6,c} + \ln \varepsilon_{ijt,c}. \tag{3.4'}$$

One of the most convenient properties of modern specifications of gravity equations, *post* Anderson and Van Wincoop, is their ability to reduce the gravity equation to variables measuring bilateral influences only. While the set of equations (3.3) and (3.4) were limited to the impact of the geographical distance as a major source of trade costs for international postal exchanges, it is worth examining other bilateral natural and unnatural trade and postal frictions in the context of these exchanges. The first set under consideration represents a number of trade frictions as described in the vector of explanatory variables $\boldsymbol{FRICTIONS}_{ij}$ in equations (3.5) and (3.5′) below:

$$\ln IPW_{ijt,c} = \ln \beta_{0,c} + \boldsymbol{SENDER}_i \beta_{1,c} + \boldsymbol{RECEIVER}_j \beta_{2,c} + \beta_{3,c} \ln DIST_{ij} + \beta_{4,c} \ln INF_{ijt,c} + \boldsymbol{DAY}_t \beta_{5,c} + \boldsymbol{MONTH}_t \beta_{6,c} + \boldsymbol{FRICTIONS}_{ij} \beta_{7,c} + \ln \varepsilon_{ijt,c}, \tag{3.5}$$

$$\ln IPV_{ijt,c} = \ln \beta_{0,c} + \boldsymbol{SENDER}_i \beta_{1,c} + \boldsymbol{RECEIVER}_j \beta_{2,c} + \beta_{3,c} \ln DIST_{ij} + \beta_{4,c} \ln INF_{ijt,c} + \boldsymbol{DAY}_t \beta_{5,c} + \boldsymbol{MONTH}_t \beta_{6,c} + \boldsymbol{FRICTIONS}_{ij} \beta_{7,c} + \ln \varepsilon_{ijt,c}. \tag{3.5'}$$

The set of trade friction variables $\boldsymbol{FRICTIONS}_{ij}$ comprises the participation of a country pair in a common regional trade agreement, in a common currency area, sharing a common legal tradition or sharing a common official language or language roots, or simply being contiguous in terms of geographical borders, among others things, those being the most typically used in the international trade economics literature. They are all expected to exert a positive influence on the levels of trade and postal flows between country pairs *i* and *j*. The CEPII gravity dataset (Head et al., 2010) is used to measure the effects of these influences.

Since the purpose of this exercise was also to measure the weight of international postal frictions relative to other trade frictions, equations (3.6) and (3.6′) include a term (vector) $\boldsymbol{POSTAL}_{ij}$:

$$\ln IPW_{ijt,c} = \ln \beta_{0,c} + \boldsymbol{SENDER}_i \beta_{1,c} + \boldsymbol{RECEIVER}_j \beta_{2,c} + \beta_{3,c} \ln DIST_{ij} + \beta_{4,c} \ln INF_{ijt,c} + \boldsymbol{DAY}_t \beta_{5,c} + \boldsymbol{MONTH}_t \beta_{6,c} + \boldsymbol{FRICTIONS}_{ij} \beta_{7,c} + \boldsymbol{POSTAL}_{ij} \beta_{8,c} + \ln \varepsilon_{ijt,c}, \tag{3.6}$$

$$\ln IPV_{ijt,c} = \ln \beta_{0,c} + \boldsymbol{SENDER}_i \beta_{1,c} + \boldsymbol{RECEIVER}_j \beta_{2,c} + \beta_{3,c} \ln DIST_{ij} + \beta_{4,c} \ln INF_{ijt,c} + \boldsymbol{DAY}_t \beta_{5,c} + \boldsymbol{MONTH}_t \beta_{6,c} + \boldsymbol{FRICTIONS}_{ij} \beta_{7,c} + \boldsymbol{POSTAL}_{ij} \beta_{8,c} + \ln \varepsilon_{ijt,c}. \quad (3.6')$$

At this stage, the postal vector term $\boldsymbol{POSTAL}_{ij}$ will consider the termination charges regime applicable to international letter-post services. One is known as the target terminal dues system and the other is the transition system. These systems are mutually exclusive. In the target terminal dues system, charges for termination of cross-border postal services originated by country *i* and terminated by country *j*'s postal operator are cost related through the application of a termination charge corresponding to a given percentage of the postal domestic tariff, although this is limited by a system of cap and floors for terminal dues rates. Postal operators are also encouraged to separate the three formats defined for international letter-post services, that is, letters, flats and small packets. They are also submitted to quality-of-service incentives where additional remuneration (bonuses) can be obtained or penalties must be paid according to the operators' delivery performance. Finally, terminal dues in the target system are expressed in rates per item and rate per kilogram. Participants in this system are mainly industrialized countries. In the transition system, applied for international postal mail flows originated from and terminated in developing countries, or originated from industrialized countries and terminated in developing countries or the other way around, a single flat access rate is available to all participants. No reference is made to country-specific domestic postal rates. The total access remuneration paid or received depends on the number of kilograms treated at termination, irrespective of the format of the item. In this system, items are rarely separated in trays according to their format, but instead all are mixed in bags. There are no quality-of-service objectives to be met. An unconditional additional charge is paid for flows generated by industrialized countries at destination of developing countries, and feeds a quality-of-service fund to which developing countries can apply for funding of quality of service projects.

In terms of econometric estimation method, a panel-data approach was chosen for estimating equations (3.3) to (3.6) (and (3.3′) to (3.6′)). Except for equations (3.3) and (3.3′), Eicker–White standard errors were computed. All estimates provided correspond to an application of the generalized least squares method with random effects applied to an unbalanced panel. Econometric estimation results are shown in Tables 3.1–4 and discussed in the next section.

4 ECONOMETRIC ESTIMATION: RESULTS

Tables 3.1–4 present the econometric estimation results of the postal gravity equations (3.3) to (3.6) with respect to weight and to number of items (equations (3.3′) to (3.6′)) for the three main classes of international mail, that is, letter-post items (up to 2kg), parcel-post items and express EMS items as managed through the UPU's International Postal System.

Table 3.1 shows the results for the estimation of the historical gravity equations prior to Anderson and van Wincoop (2003), as specified in (3.3) and (3.3′). The GDP variable

Table 3.1 Econometric estimation results for postal gravity equations (3.3) and (3.3′)

Variable	Letters		Parcels		Express EMS	
	ln IPW_{ijt}	ln IPV_{ijt}	ln IPW_{ijt}	ln IPV_{ijt}	ln IPW_{ijt}	ln IPV_{ijt}
ln GDP_i	0.373**	0.273**	0.236**	0.323**	0.256**	0.249**
ln GDP_j	0.245**	0.383**	0.179**	0.251**	0.240**	0.203**
ln $DIST_{ij}$	−0.332**	−0.561**	−0.250**	−0.280**	−0.043**	−0.224**
ln INF_{ijt}	1.220**	0.611**	1.253**	0.442**	1.455**	0.496**
Monday	−0.042**	0.217**	0.094**	0.754**	0.026**	0.835**
Tuesday	0.214**	0.494**	0.155**	0.832**	0.220**	0.935**
Wednesday	0.278**	0.535**	0.188**	0.805**	0.235**	0.928**
Thursday	0.285**	0.556**	0.176**	0.801**	0.228**	0.934**
Friday	0.270**	0.541**	0.141**	0.797**	0.202**	0.931**
Saturday	0.240**	0.428**	0.061**	0.459**	0.159**	0.567**
February	−0.008	0.017	−0.004**	−0.011**	−0.010**	−0.024**
March	−0.023**	0.015**	−0.008**	−0.027**	0.022**	0.006**
April	−0.006	0.013	0.003	−0.045	0.025	0.004
May	−0.056**	−0.015**	−0.020**	−0.093**	−0.013**	−0.064**
June	−0.061**	0.004**	−0.000**	−0.070**	−0.011**	−0.000**
July	−.075**	−0.029**	−0.018**	−0.087**	−0.029**	−0.023**
August	−0.118**	−0.060**	0.034**	−0.054**	0.017**	−0.013**
September	−0.072**	−0.010**	0.045**	−0.071**	0.038**	0.005**
October	−0.020**	−0.031**	0.089**	0.018**	0.085**	0.028**
November	0.059**	0.052**	0.175**	0.114**	0.115**	0.029**
December	0.321	0.121**	0.266**	0.289**	0.222**	0.128**
Constant	−3.074**	−1.722**	−0.541**	−4.023**	−4.131**	−3.451**
R^2	0.59	0.48	0.50	0.50	0.59	0.64
Observations	676,450	517,318	515,200	452,878	447,750	394,363

Note: ** and * denotes statistical significance at the 1% and 5% levels, respectively.

coefficients, $\beta_{1,c}$ and $\beta_{2,c}$, have the expected positive signs and are highly statistically significant. In a balanced communication relationship between senders and receivers of international mail, one would have expected both coefficients for GDP to be almost identical ($\beta_{1,c} = \beta_{2,c}$). This hypothesis can be rejected. Except for international registered letter-post items, it is worth noting that the effect of the GDP of origination of mail is higher than the GDP of destination of mail irrespective of the mail class under consideration ($\beta_{1,c} > \beta_{2,c}$). However, this is true to a much lesser extent for parcels and express EMS. Indeed, the ratio of GDP coefficients for parcels and express EMS suggests that recipients are almost as influential as senders in these segments unlike for international letter post, which clearly seems to be driven by senders in terms of demand.

The estimation of the distance coefficients $\beta_{3,c}$ in equations (3.3) and (3.3′) confirms the validity of the approach of modeling international mail exchanges through the use of gravity equations. As expected, the coefficients are negative and highly statistically significant. Regardless of the class of mail, they are all well below the −0.9 average value found for distance coefficients in the estimation of gravity equations in the international trade literature. This could well be explained by the fact that postal communication is likely to be less sensitive to trade costs related to distance than exchanges of goods, although transportation costs do matter for both activities, that is, postal and merchandise trade. However, postal communication is not fully frictionless since all distance coefficients are statistically different from zero irrespective of the class of mail. The hypothesis that distance does matter for most international mail exchanges is supported by the econometric estimation of $\beta_{3,c}$.

It is also interesting to note that the value of the distance coefficient decreases with the level of postal service offered for the different classes of mail since $\beta_{3,letter\text{-}post} > \beta_{3,parcel\text{-}post} > \beta_{3,express\text{-}EMS}$. Indeed, the postal service has more value added, for instance (but not only) in terms of 'track and trace' and speed of delivery when one moves from international letter post to express EMS services. It thus seems that the impact of distance on international mails flows can be mitigated through higher quality of service and service features as perceived by consumers of these services. The latter seem to be less sensitive to distance when sending international postal items if the service becomes more reliable, can be tracked and traced and/or faster in terms of delivery times. The quality of the logistic postal chain can mitigate the impact of distance as a barrier for communication between countries. The fact that international letter rates tend not to be distance based so quality – time to deliver – is the only postal variable is also consistent with this interpretation of the econometric results. Unlike letter rates, parcels and EMS rates tend to have a distance factor so cost to the shipper becomes a friction.

When using the number of postal items exchanged between country pairs *ij* during one day instead of the weight, the absolute value of the distance coefficient increases. Volumes are more sensitive to distance than weight. This could mean that relatively lighter items within each class of mail are more sensitive to distance than other heavier items. While this explanation could hold for international letter-post items given the exchange of postcards related to tourism (given in turn that tourism flows are themselves sensitive to costs related to distance), the results remain somehow puzzling for international parcel and express services.

The econometric estimation of the postal gravity equations also confirms (see the statistically significant coefficient $\beta_{4,c}$ for ln INF_{ijt}) the need for taking into account the level of electronic information exchanged by postal operators regarding their international mail exchanges, given the variability of their participation in the UPU programs for electronic exchanges of information.

Finally, the modeling of day and month effects through the use of dummy variables proved to be relevant. It enabled the identification of peak international mail traffic in the middle of the week (Tuesday, Wednesday, Thursday) and at the end or beginning of the year (November, December, January) almost irrespective of the class of mail after estimating the vectors of coefficients $\beta_{5,c}$ and $\beta_{6,c}$. All in all, the estimation of the first set of postal gravity equations seems to provide satisfactory results and is encouraging for future empirical research in this area.

Anderson and van Wincoop provided general equilibrium foundations to gravity equations for modeling international trade flows, which in turn modified the econometric specification of gravity equations in subsequent empirical research. The estimation of postal gravity equations reflected this by the introduction of country-specific fixed effects for each sending country on the one hand, and each receiving country on the other. This

Table 3.2 Econometric estimation results for postal gravity equations (3.4) and (3.4′)

Variable	Letters		Parcels		Express EMS	
	$\ln IPW_{ijt}$	$\ln IPV_{ijt}$	$\ln IPW_{ijt}$	$\ln IPV_{ijt}$	$\ln IPW_{ijt}$	$\ln IPV_{ijt}$
$\ln DIST_{ij}$	−0.560**	−0.654**	−0.410**	−0.518**	−0.216**	−0.477**
$\ln INF_{ijt}$	1.226**	0.606**	1.264**	0.460**	1.455**	0.503**
Constant	3.248**	4.220**	3.488**	1.665**	−0.872*	2.034**
R^2	0.67	0.67	0.58	0.63	0.68	0.73
Observations	762,769	575,973	576,180	504,307	516,666	455,628

Note: ** and * denotes statistical significance at the 1% and 5% levels, respectively.

enables all country-specific non-bilateral variables to be taken into account, such as the GDP or the level of literacy. Other possible non-bilateral variables that remain unobservable can thus be taken into consideration. Table 3.2 shows the econometric estimation resulting from this evolution in the empirical development of gravity equations (see equations (3.4) and (3.4′)). The results in Table 3.2 confirm all interpretations provided through the first set of regressions in Table 3.1. Another difference with respect to the estimation in Table 3.1 is the use of Eicker–White standard errors. This increases the values of standard errors without losing the statistical significance for the variables under consideration. Table 3.2 only shows the estimation results for pure bilateral variables in the gravity equation, that is, distance $DIST_{ij}$ and information INF_{ijt}.

Table 3.3 adds additional classic trade frictions, be they natural or unnatural, in the econometric estimation of the gravity equations (3.5) and (3.5′) according to Anderson and van Wincoop's specification. The vector of coefficients $\beta_{7,c}$ is estimated. All new variables are positive and statistically significant without changing the interpretation of the previous econometric estimation results in Tables 3.1 and 3.2. Table 3.3 only shows the econometric estimation results for pure bilateral variables.

The new set of econometric estimation results in Table 3.3 highlights the importance of the geographical contiguity variable for international mail exchanges. *Ceteris paribus*, international letter-post exchanges are increased by 20 to 25 percent for neighboring countries. However, this is not the case for international parcel post and express-EMS exchanges. International mail alliances between some neighboring countries can thus be better explained by this result on the impact of a natural geographical trade friction.

Irrespective of the class of mail, common language features also boost international postal exchanges between countries that share a common official language or within the same ethnology. *Ceteris paribus*, it increases exchanges by 12 to 30 percent illustrating the impact of another natural friction to international postal communication.

Former colonial links between country pairs also increase substantially bilateral mail flows between these countries, with increases varying from more than 30 to almost 80 percent compared to flows between countries without former colonial ties, *ceteris paribus*. Indeed, historical ties seem to matter a lot in international postal communication.

Regional trade agreements (RTAs), as man-made unnatural frictions to trade for non-participants, have a much lower impact though positive, *ceteris paribus*, on international mail flows between countries belonging to a same regional trade arrangement. Effects,

Table 3.3 Econometric estimation results for postal gravity equations (3.5) and (3.5′)

Variable	Letters		Parcels		Express EMS	
	ln IPW_{ijt}	ln IPV_{ijt}	ln IPW_{ijt}	ln IPV_{ijt}	ln IPW_{ijt}	ln IPV_{ijt}
ln $DIST_{ij}$	−0.487**	−0.571**	−0.332**	−0.423**	−0.148**	−0.339**
ln INF_{ijt}	1.226**	0.606**	1.264**	0.460**	1.454**	0.502**
Contiguity	0.195**	0.247**	−0.038	0.091	−0.017	0.096
Common lang.	0.129*	0.269**	0.251**	0.247**	0.226**	0.226**
Ethno. lang.	0.290**	0.328**	0.187**	0.254**	0.074	0.165**
Colony	0.732**	0.678**	0.463**	0.445**	0.386**	0.449**
RTA	0.114**	0.170**	0.062	0.129**	0.107**	0.041
Common leg.	0.100**	0.190**	0.096**	0.114**	0.001	0.080**
Common curr.	0.353**	0.255**	0.238**	0.332**	0.088	0.060
Constant	2.272**	2.992**	2.462**	0.403	−1.589**	0.588
R^2	0.75	0.70	0.60	0.66	0.68	0.75
Observations	762,769	575,973	576,180	504,307	516,666	455,628

Note: ** and * denotes statistical significance at the 1% and 5% levels, respectively.

mostly statistically significant, range from a 6 to 16 percent increase in mail flows in the presence of a regional trade agreement involving both partner countries in the exchange of mail.

A common legal tradition also slightly facilitates international postal exchanges with positive effects on all classes of mail around 10 percent, all other things being equal.

Finally, except for EMS-express international services, the existence of a common currency between countries of both postal partners considerably increases the likelihood of international letter and parcel-post exchanges, with marginal effects ranging from 25 to 35 percent.

Table 3.4 provides the econometric estimation results for the postal gravity equations (3.6) and (3.6′). It confirms that postal frictions also matter along with traditional trade frictions.

The arrangements in the transition system seem to exert a considerable negative influence on the development of international letter-post exchanges between these countries on the one hand, and from or to these countries on the other, with a more than 40 percent negative effect compared to exchanges governed under the so-called 'target terminal dues system'. This is equivalent to a loss of a current full-year international postal traffic for exchanges with and between transition countries' postal operators every two and a half years. While the transition system governs the remuneration of access to the partner postal network at destination for international letter post, an indirect negative impact has also been identified for the development of express-EMS traffic (about 20 percent negative effect). This is probably caused by the lack of incentives, in the transition remuneration system, to develop quality, which in turn undermines postal operators' capacity for developing value-added quality services such as the express-EMS international postal service.

After adjusting and completing the estimation of the basic postal gravity equations

Table 3.4 Econometric estimation results for postal gravity equations (3.6) and (3.6′)

Variable	Letters		Parcels		Express EMS	
	$\ln IPW_{ijt}$	$\ln IPV_{ijt}$	$\ln IPW_{ijt}$	$\ln IPV_{ijt}$	$\ln IPW_{ijt}$	$\ln IPV_{ijt}$
$\ln DIST_{ij}$	−0.467**	−0.566**	−0.340**	−0.409**	−0.143**	−0.328**
$\ln INF_{ijt}$	1.226**	0.606**	1.264**	0.460**	1.454**	0.502**
Contiguity	0.191**	0.246**	−0.036	0.087	−0.017	0.097
Common lang.	0.123*	0.268**	0.253**	0.243**	0.226**	0.225**
Ethno. lang.	0.288**	0.327**	0.187**	0.254**	0.073	0.163**
Colony	0.752**	0.684**	0.456**	0.456**	0.392**	0.466**
RTA	0.110**	0.169**	0.065	0.123**	0.105**	0.037
Common leg.	0.092**	0.188**	0.099**	0.107**	−0.002	0.075**
Common curr.	0.233**	0.224**	0.269**	0.282**	0.050	−0.017
Transition	−0.413**	−0.107	0.098	−0.164**	−0.177*	−0.360**
Constant	2.602**	3.081**	2.396**	0.514	−1.435**	0.902**
R^2	0.75	0.70	0.60	0.66	0.68	0.75
Observations	762,769	575,973	576,180	504,307	516,666	455,628

Note: ** and * denotes statistical significance at the 1% and 5% levels, respectively.

(3.3) and (3.3′), (3.4) and (3.4′), and (3.5) and (3.5′), and (3.6) and (3.6′), one can note that the distance coefficient remains highly statistically significant. A 10 percent increase in distance reduces international letter-post flows by 4.7 percent, the international parcel-post flows by 3.4 percent and the express-EMS exchanges by 1.4 percent in terms of weight, and by 5.71 percent the international letter-post in terms of items, by 4.1 percent the international parcel-post items, and by 3.3 percent the volumes of express-EMS exchanges. This suggests that quality is more important than price where price is variable according to distance in the case of EMS and parcel traffic, but it is less so in terms of letters.

5 CONCLUSION

This chapter has estimated the first postal gravity equations to identify and measure the impacts of the drivers of international mail flows between countries. The econometric estimation results support the validity of applying such an approach to the economic study of international mail flows. While distance matters for international postal exchanges, its impact could be further reduced as implied by the decreasing values of the distance coefficient for postal exchanges associated with higher levels of service and quality. Indeed, there is great scope for improvements and innovation in international postal services that could shrink the postal world in terms of distance, thereby contributing to international postal traffic growth. The application of a two-sided approach so as to better answer customers' needs and preferences, both at origin and destination, could be paramount to achieve this purpose. In this respect, the postal gravity equations have enabled the estimation of the influence of destination relative to origin in driving international postal exchanges. Postal operators should be encouraged to rebalance the development of their services towards the recipients in a number of segments rather than maintaining business models solely oriented towards senders.

Further research must test the panel-data specification of the gravity equations to be estimated (for instance, random versus fixed effects) and the way some dummy variables can be used. It must also test the existence of possible endogeneity problems in some variables, and if so, proceed to an econometric estimation making use of a selection of instruments. The econometric modeling could better take into account the numerous zero values for country pairs in the daily international postal traffic. In this respect, a Poisson process could be added to the modeling. Monte-Carlo simulations could also be run to assess the sensitivity of variable coefficients to the use of high-frequency data.

Finally, more bilateral international postal issues could be tackled besides the impact of the dual remuneration system governing the termination of international letter-post services, particularly those covering the improvement of quality of service or new service features such as returns. The latter could also be further studied on the basis of this gravity equation adjusted for evaluating a range of new services and quality systems and incentives. In the same manner, the model could be reversed to study non-bilateral postal issues that could influence international postal exchanges, such as the accessibility of the postal infrastructure or addressing systems in each country.

NOTE

* The views expressed here are those of the authors and do not necessarily reflect those of the Universal Postal Union.

REFERENCES

Anderson, James E. and Eric van Wincoop (2003), 'Gravity with gravitas', *American Economic Review*, **93** (1), March, 170–92.

Anderson, James E. and Eric van Wincoop (2004), 'Trade costs', *Journal of Economic Literature*, **42**, September, 691–751.

Disdier, Anne-Celia and Keith Head (2008), 'The puzzling persistence of the distance effect on bilateral trade', *Review of Economics and Statistics*, **90** (1), February, 37–48.

Head, Keith, Thierry Mayer and John Ries (2010), 'The erosion of colonial trade linkages after independence', *Journal of International Economics*, **81** (1), 1–14.

KOF (2012), 'KOF Index of Globalization', available at: http://globalization.kof.ethz.ch (accessed March 2012).

4. Price comparisons in the parcel industry: a new approach based on the hedonic price theory*

Claire Borsenberger,[†] Sébastien Bréville[‡] and Aurélie Dehais[§]

1 INTRODUCTION

E-commerce activity is expanding, and the parcel sector is increasingly of interest to the European Commission, who studied in particular the EU cross-border parcels market and will publish a Green Paper on cross-border parcel prices in 2012.

Opened to competition for many years, a part of the parcels sector is subject to the Universal Service Obligation (USO), notably to an affordability constraint. The USO concerns mostly over-the-counter parcels, from private households. In view of the growth of parcels among private households, the affordability issue could become increasingly significant in the future.

Until now, this issue has been dealt essentially through international basic price comparisons based on absolute values, adjusted to take into account differences in purchase power between countries. However, differences in both the costs of parcel delivery processes and the qualitative features of the products offered by European Universal Service Providers (USPs) have not always been taken into account. Often, parcel prices are compared in absolute terms, without any weighing reflecting the quality of the product. This does not prevent national regulators from basing their policy on these comparisons.

To improve international benchmarking, we propose in this chapter to look at USPs' domestic parcel prices in the USO scope as a hedonic function, leaving aside the issue of the costs of the parcel delivery process (explained by the geography and demography of the country, the obligations in terms of delivery frequency, among other factors). In this approach, a good is considered as a vector of characteristics. Therefore, a hedonic equation relates the price of the good to the implicit price of its characteristics. This method has been used for the valuation of public and environmental goods but is also applied in market research for private goods such as houses, cars and food products. Fenster et al. (2006) and Pearsall and Trozzo (2011) applied it to postal services.

Before analyzing the estimation of each relevant characteristic's implicit price given by the hedonic equation, we describe in Section 2 the domestic parcel market for some

† Economist, European and National Regulatory Division, Le Groupe La Poste.
‡ Economist, European and National Regulatory Division, Le Groupe La Poste.
§ Economist, European and National Regulatory Division, Le Groupe La Poste.

European countries and why price comparison is problematical. Section 3 is a first attempt to consider parcel features using international comparisons. In Section 4, we briefly present a survey of economic literature on hedonic theory and its application to different commodities and review econometric techniques to estimate the hedonic function, before presenting our model and the results of our estimation of a hedonic price function for parcels. Section 5 provides a summary and conclusions.

2 THE PARCEL INDUSTRY IN EUROPE

The Scope of the Study

The parcel industry (also called the CEP industry – Courier, Express and Parcel) comprises various types of products, services and operators. This major market is generally segmented according to the speed of delivery (standard or deferred versus express transit time), the weight of the shipment (less than 1kg for documents, less than 2kg for packets, less than 20 or 30kg for postal parcels, over 30kg for truck companies), the destination of the shipment (domestic versus cross-border or international) and the type of senders/recipients (business to business B2B; business to consumer B2C; consumer to consumer C2C; or consumer to business C2B).

According to ITA/WIK (2009), the parcel and express market in the EU27 is estimated at €42.4 billion, accounting for 0.34 percent of the total EU27 GDP. Domestic shipments account for an estimated 70–75 percent share of the total EU27 market value. The intra-European flows add up to approximately 15–20 percent of the market value while intercontinental ones (to/from the EU) account for an estimated 10 percent. Express accounts for slightly more than one-third of the market value while parcel businesses account for slightly less than two-thirds. The largest share of the European parcel and express volumes lies within the B2B area (between 74 and 80 percent in 2008 according to the different studies[1]). According to the ITA/WIK study, the B2C and the C2C segments represented, respectively, a share of 15 and 5 percent in 2008.

In this study, we shall focus on a small part of this market, corresponding to the C2X segments, where the national postal operator, alongside a small number of alternative companies, plays the main role thanks to its nationwide network.

The Problematic Issue of Price Comparison

The European Commission and national regulators often based their parcel price regulation policy on benchmarking analysis. However, comparing parcel prices without taking into account quality through their characteristics seems to be misleading. For example, in a 2009 public report on domestic prices of parcels belonging to universal service scope, the French regulator, ARCEP, argued that 'the domestic parcels prices are higher than those of comparable products offered in other European countries'. This statement was based on a basic comparison between the price of the French La Poste parcel operator's product 'Colissimo' and the price of parcel offers in Germany, Belgium, Spain and Switzerland. As we shall see in the next section, these products do not have the same characteristics in terms of delivery time, insurance, track and trace, weight and so on.

As Campbell noted in a report for the EU Commission (WIK, 2004, p. 152),

> [F]or parcel services, price comparisons are significantly more complex because there is much more variation between parcel products offered by European USPs. Very different tariffs are available for parcels depending on, among other things, weight, size, routing time, destination, and mode of collection. Some of these offerings could be considered express products, reflecting the blurring boundaries between the parcels and express segments. [. . .] Some tariffs include universal delivery while others do not. Routing times for parcels also vary substantially. These differences in service have a significant effect on the cost of parcel delivery that may explain some of the variation in parcel tariffs.

Despite these drawbacks, the method used by ARCEP to compare parcel prices was used in subsequent EC studies.

Swiss Post often publishes reports which compare parcel prices to show that its tariffs are cheaper than those in other European countries. The benchmark method used is based on a Laspeyres index in which all parcel categories are included and weighted. Prices are converted according to exchange rates. Swiss Post chooses this method for the practical validity of the index in spite of several drawbacks such as the dependence on the exchange rate and the ignorance of quality, salary costs or purchasing power.

In the last EC study (2010), Copenhagen Economics simply compares the prices of a 1kg parcel by harmonizing tariffs based on purchasing power parity (PPP), without any deeper analysis of the characteristics of the various products. Postcomm (2009) also uses PPP to weight prices. This method seems to be better than Swiss Post's one since it avoids fluctuations associated with market exchange rates even though it does not take into account quality factors.

Anacom (2009) and WIK Economics (2006) studies compare methods based on exchange rates and PPP. They highlight the fact that these two methods give different results with the same data, which makes it problematic to base price regulation on benchmarking comparisons.

To highlight the significance of such studies, we choose a country, the United Kingdom, and compare its positioning with respect to the European mean, in each benchmark that was described above. Obviously, we have to bear in mind that these studies used data of distinct years and compare different parcel weights (Swiss Post: index of 2010; Anacom: 2kg parcels, 2009 data; WIK Consult: 5kg parcels, 2005 data; Copenhagen Economics: 1kg parcels, 2009 data). In Swiss Post's study, the UK is below the European mean. In the Anacom study, it is also below the EU27 mean but above the EU15 mean by using the method based on the exchange rate, and at the level of EU15 mean by using the method based on PPP. In the WIK study, the UK is largely above the EU25 mean since it is the second most expensive country. Finally, in the Copenhagen Economics study it is just above the mean of the EU27 plus the four members of EFTA (European Free Trade Association). According to these various results, it is hard to draw any conclusions on the relative affordability of the UK's tariffs: are they higher or lower than those charged in other European countries? The answer depends on the study considered. It therefore is necessary to consider the different parcel features to set an international price comparison.

3 A FIRST ATTEMPT TO CONSIDER PARCEL FEATURES

A Common Obligation Translated Nationally

The most evident features we can consider are those imposed by European regulation on universal service. European countries must respect the USO as defined by the Postal Directive.[2] Some obligations concern the parcel activity of USPs. More precisely, the USO includes nationwide collection, sorting, transport and distribution to the home or premises of every natural or legal person, at least five days a week, of domestic postal packages up to 10kg as well as services for insured parcels. Moreover, member states must ensure that postal parcels received from other member states and weighing up to 20kg are delivered within their territory.

European member states can go further than the minimum requirements defined in the directive and extend their parcel services. In particular, they may increase the weight limit of universal service coverage for postal parcels to any weight not exceeding 20kg and may lay down special arrangements for door-to-door delivery of such parcels.

This freedom, related to the subsidiarity principle, results in a variety of situations across the EU, from a minimal implementation of the directive requirements to a more broad interpretation of it. Regarding the main parcel characteristics (weight, home delivery and frequency of delivery per week) we can divide EU countries into three general schemes.

At one extreme, Posti, the Finnish postal operator, includes in the USO only one domestic parcel offer up to 10kg, not delivered to the home: the addressees have to collect their parcels from a postal outlet (during that outlet's opening hours).[3] The shipment is delivered against signature. In Sweden, Posten extends its USO offers to include parcels which weigh less than 20kg.

In the middle range of observed situations, Austrian Post, b-post, Correos, Hellenic Post, An Post, Poste Italiane, P&T Luxembourg, CTT and Swiss Post all deliver parcels, weighing up to 20 or 30kg to the home, five days a week.

Finally, at the other end, Deutsche Post, Post Denmark, La Poste, TNT and Royal Mail provide the more complete USO service by delivering parcels weighing up to 20 or 30kg to the home, six days a week.

Consideration of Non-USO Options

To complete their offer, postal operators provide several extra options which are included in the basic offer. To realize a first benchmark of countries' services which integrate some quality factors, we compare the offer in each country that is the closest to the French Colissimo (within the scope of the USO). In this chapter, these offers are considered as countries' basic offers (see Table 4.1). 'Basic' offers vary across countries with respect to both their characteristics and their price. It is clear that some countries, such as Denmark, Germany, Spain and Luxembourg provide basic offers with a lot of characteristics, whereas others, such as Ireland and Italy, offer a very simple basic offer.

A positive linear relationship between prices and the number of characteristics does not seem to exist: some operators offering sophisticated parcel services price their offer less than other operators offering simple services (for example, Germany and Denmark

Table 4.1 Features of basic parcel offer

Country	Offer	USO options			Extra options								Number of features
		Home delivery	20kg	6-day delivery	D+1/2	Guaranteed delivery time	Insurance	Delivery against signature	Advice of delivery	Track and trace	Second delivery	Return to sender	
Finland	Postal Parcel				X	X	X	X		X		X	5
Sweden	Postpaket				X	X		X		X			3
Switzerland	PostPack Economy	X	X		X		X			X	X		6
Austria	Domestic Parcel	X	X		X		X	X		X			6
Greece	Single Basic Parcel	X	X			X						X	4
Portugal	National Parcel	X	X			X						X	4
Belgium	Bpack LLS	X	X		X	X				X	X	X	7
Luxembourg	Qpack	X	X		X	X	X	X		X		X	8
Ireland	Standard Parcel	X	X		X							X	4
Italy	Pacco Ordinario	X	X								X		3
Spain	Postal Express National	X	X		X	X	X			X	X	X	8
UK	Standard Parcel	X	X	X	X		X				X		6
Netherlands	Pakket	X	X	X	X	X				X	X	X	8
Germany	DHL Paket	X	X	X	X		X	X		X	X	X	9
France	Colissimo	X	X	X	X	X	X			X	X	X	9
Denmark	Postpakke	X	X	X	X	X	X		X	X		X	9

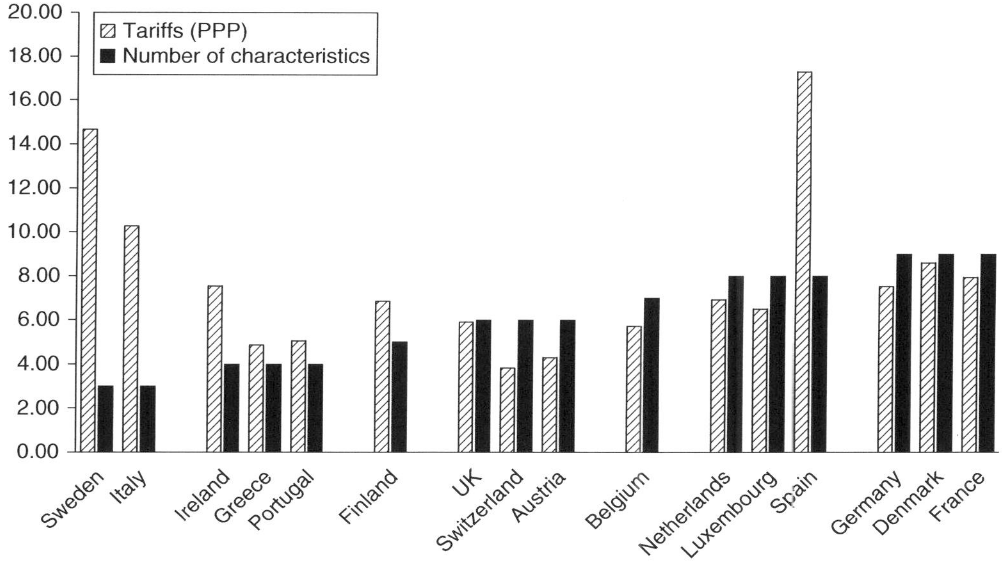

Figure 4.1 Price comparison of basic offer (2kg) in PPP according to number of characteristics

versus Ireland and Italy) (Figure 4.1). As we shall see, this could be explained by the fact that not every feature has the same value in consumers' demand.

To explain different prices among EU countries, we could focus on a fundamental characteristic: the delivery speed, which is, a priori, one of the main cost drivers as well as a feature potentially valued by consumers. All things being equal, one can expect that the shorter the transit time, the higher the cost to transport and deliver parcel (quicker transportation means are often also more expensive) and the higher its price.

This theoretical relationship is not so clear in practice (see Figure 4.2). In some countries, such as Italy, with a long transit time (D+3), the basic parcel price is higher than that in countries with a quicker delivery offer. Consequently, it is likely that other factors drive the price setting, such as combining both dimensions (transit time and number of characteristics). But again no clear conclusion can be drawn.

Besides these basic offers, operators provide alternative offers (at a different price) with additional services such as registration (*Colissimo Recommandé* in France, *Aangetekend* in the Netherlands or *Bpack Secur* in Belgium), or cash on delivery (*Bpack Payback* in Belgium or *Betaalservice* in the Netherlands). Customers can also choose non-free options to personalize their parcel sending. Those options could be added to the existing standard offers proposed by the operator. The most frequent ones are insurance, cash on delivery, and bulky parcels and return to sender options. Our benchmark is summarized in Table 4.2.

With regard to the design of their standard offers, operators' strategies on the panel of non-free options differ. Italy provides a large panel of options, like Finland and Spain, whereas France, Ireland and Portugal limit the number of non-free options that can be added to the standard offers. On average, countries provide three non-free options.

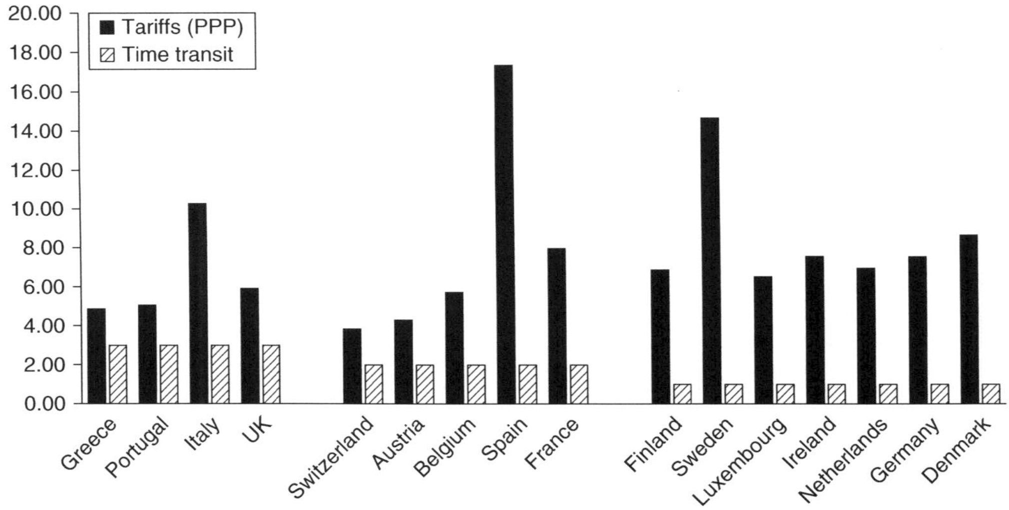

Figure 4.2 *Price comparison of basic parcel offer (2kg) in €PPP according to delivery speed*

Table 4.2 *Non-free options offered*

Option	Countries that provide the option against an additional charge
Registration	Finland, France
Return to sender	Austria, Spain, Finland, Italy, UK
SMS of reception	Belgium, Denmark, Italy
Home collection	Belgium, Italy, Netherlands, Switzerland
Advice of receipt	Spain, France, Italy
Insurance	Germany, Denmark, Spain, Greece, Ireland, Italy, Luxembourg, Sweden
Cash on delivery	Germany, France, Austria, Spain, Finland, Greece, Italy, Luxembourg, Sweden
Handed over against signature	Germany, France, Switzerland
Bulky parcels	Germany, Austria, Denmark, Spain, Finland, Italy, Switzerland, France
Fragile	Austria, Denmark, Finland, Greece

Contrary to expectations, there is no inverse relationship between the sophistication of the basic offer and the number of options that can be added on.

This qualitative comparison of parcel offers proposed by postal operators underlines the differences and the heterogeneity in parcel product within Europe despite common obligations and minimal requirements. As supply responds in general to demand, distinct offers can be the result of different demands. Indeed, operators provide domestic services which satisfy domestic population needs, based on cultural factors among others. For instance, in Finland, the sending of skis is an option that is available for customers.

A possible way to tackle the problem, namely to handle qualitative differences of the features of a same category of goods, is based on the so-called 'hedonic' approach. Its main idea is to identify the quality of a product with a vector of product characteristics. A regression equation is then estimated relating the latter to the price of the product. Once such a relationship between characteristics and price of a product is established, the price of any similar item can be predicted by introducing its characteristics into the estimated hedonic (regression) function. In other words, the hedonic approach allows for quality differences to be controlled over time within the framework of elementary price indices.

4 THE HEDONIC THEORY AND ECONOMETRIC APPLICATION TO PARCELS

Economic Literature Survey and Empirical Applications

Rosen's (1974) article on hedonic prices derives from Lancaster's work related to the consumer theory (1966, 1971) and Griliches's econometric developments (1961, 1971).

Lancaster's new consumer demand theory (1966) asserts that the good *per se* does not give utility to the consumer but it possesses characteristics from which the consumer derives utility. Product characteristics explain why consumers prefer some products to others in the same category. The hedonic model assumes that there is a continuous function relating the price of a good to its attributes (the hedonic price function). In contrast to conventional economic evaluation, where the value of a good is calculated for the whole of the good, the hedonic approach regards a product as a set of attributes and considers the value of a good as a function of each attribute of that good. The value of an attribute is called an 'implicit price' because it cannot be observed in a real market.

Rosen (1974) strengthened the economic foundations of the hedonic method by demonstrating that the functional relationship between the price of a differentiated product and its attribute can be interpreted as an equilibrium outcome from interactions between all the buyers and sellers in a market. Under the assumptions of his model, regressing product prices on their attributes can reveal consumers' willingness to pay for a marginal change in a continuous attribute of a differentiated product.

Even before Rosen's formal model, the hedonic pricing method was already being used empirically. Waugh (1928) studied the variation of prices of vegetables; Court (1939) examined the car market in Detroit; Ridker and Henning (1967) made the first application to the housing market (effects of air pollution on house prices).

Since these early contributions, this method has been applied in various sectors/goods: houses, cars, computers, faxes, and food products (such as rice, cotton, wool, wheat, grapes, wine, pork, tomatoes, asparagus, vegetables and beef) among other commodities and there has been a lot of discussion in the literature on whether one or other regression approach is valid or preferable from an economic point of view for estimating hedonic functions. These discussions are not in the scope of our analysis (for further explanations, see Diewert, 2003; Ekeland et al., 2004; Triplett, 2004).

More recently the hedonic price theory was also applied in the postal sector. Fenster et al. (2006) found that the US postal tariffs over the entire range of US mail services between 1969 and 2006 can be accurately represented by a hedonic price equation (HPE). The HPE relates postal rates to indices of several qualitative properties of the mail, including time to delivery, weight, presorting level, 'machinable' feature of items, distance between collection and delivery points and so on. As explained by the authors, 'the hedonic prices describe the marginal rate customers are charged per piece for varying the amounts of the hedonic properties of their mailings' (p. 370).

In the same vein, Pearsall and Trozzo (2011) developed a hedonic price function for US consumers which related the price of a postal item to variables such as shape, weight, presorting level, and time to delivery, in order to determine the impact of a change in the frequency of mail delivery on volume. The HPE allowed them to determine the impact on prices of a change in the qualitative features of the mail. Then, using a demand model (relating volume to prices), the authors deduced subsequent changes in volume and the impact of revenues and costs of a decrease in delivery frequency (remove the sixth delivery).

Hedonic Price Theory Applied to the Parcel Industry

To estimate a hedonic function of parcel prices, we collected data on the USO parcel offers of 16 USPs[4] at the end of 2011. We chose USO parcels, which are affordable according to EU directives, to diminish the risk that parcels with a highly differentiated margin disturb the regression.

In particular, we collected data on the price paid by customers for sending a domestic parcel (including VAT when relevant) and on 16 attributes assumed price relevant (see Table 4.3). We add in the model a dummy variable representing the country considered, taking France as the reference country. The end result is a cross-section database of 592 observations.

We estimated the three usual functional forms of the hedonic function (linear, semi-log and double log) with all expected relevant variables. Due to the presence of heteroskedasticity, we used the White covariance matrix to correct standard errors and obtain robust estimates. The double-log specification seems to be the most appropriate one since it minimizes the Akaike information criterion and maximizes the coefficient of determination (adjusted R^2).

By a backward stepwise approach, we obtain the following hedonic price equation with, as statistically significant variables, weight, transit time of parcel, return to sender, franking online, cash-on-delivery option, insurance, advice receipt, second presentation and six days a week home delivery through the whole territory. Geographical dummies reflect individual unobservable effects, associated with each country, that are not taken into account by independent variables included in our model. The estimated value of parameters is given in Table 4.4.

$$\begin{aligned}\ln P = {} & C + \beta 1 \ln W + \beta 2 D1 + \beta 3 D2 + \beta 4 Back\_sender + \beta 5 COD + \beta 6 Home\_dev \\ & + \beta 7 Insur + \beta 8 Nat\_cov + \beta 9 Online\_franking + \beta 10 Receipt + \beta 11 Twice\_dev \\ & + \beta 12 Six\_dev + \beta 13 AT + \beta 14 BE + \beta 15 DK + \beta 16 FI + \beta 17 DE + \beta 18 GR + \beta 19 IE \\ & + \beta 20 IT + \beta 21 LU + \beta 22 NL + \beta 23 PT + \beta 24 SP + \beta 25 SW + \beta 26 CH + \beta 27 UK.\end{aligned}$$

Table 4.3 Hypothesized relationships between price and parcel characteristics

Parcel characteristic	Measure/variable used in the regression	Expected/theoretical impact on price
Weight	Middle value of weight class	Positive: the higher the weight, the higher the price
Transit time	Two dummies: • If the parcel is delivered one day after posting, $D1 = 1, D2 = 0$ • If the parcel is delivered two days after posting, $D1 = 0, D2 = 1$ • If the parcel is delivered three (or more) days after posting, $D1 = 0, D2 = 0$	Negative: the longer the transit time, the lower the quality of service
Number of deliveries per week	Dummy: *Six_dev* = 1 if parcels are delivered six days a week; 0 otherwise	Positive: a higher frequency of delivery should improve quality of service and increase the cost for the postal operator
Place of delivery	Dummy: *Home_dev* = 1 if parcels are delivered to the home; 0 otherwise	Positive: home delivery should have a positive value for customers and increase the cost for the postal operator
Insurance	Dummy: *Insur* = 1 if the parcel is insured, 0 otherwise	Positive: insurance should increase the value of the postal service and increase the cost for the postal operator
Signature	Dummy: *Sign* = 1 if the parcel is delivered against signature, 0 otherwise	Positive: signature should increase the value of the postal service and increase the cost for the postal operator
Cash on delivery	Dummy: *COD* = 1 if cash on delivery is proposed, 0 otherwise	Positive: COD should increase the value of the postal service and increase the cost for the postal operator
Advice of receipt	Dummy: *Receipt* = 1 if an advice of receipt is given to the sender, 0 otherwise	Positive: advice of receipt should increase the value of the postal service and increase the cost for the postal operator
Track and trace	Dummy: *Trace* = 1 if the parcel is traced, 0 otherwise	Positive: track and trace should increase the value of the postal service and increase the cost for the postal operator
Online franking	Dummy: *Online_franking* = 1 if the sender can print the stamp online, 0 if he must go to the post office	Ambiguous: online franking should increase the value of the postal service and decrease the cost for the postal operator
Coverage of the territory	Dummy: *Nat_cov* = 1 if the offer is national, 0 if it is local	Positive: national coverage should increase the value of the postal service and increase the cost for the postal operator

Table 4.3 (continued)

Parcel characteristic	Measure/variable used in the regression	Expected/theoretical impact on price
Second presentation at home in case of absence	Dummy: *Twice_dev* = 1 if the parcel is presented twice; 0 otherwise	Positive: a second presentation should increase the value of the postal service and increase the cost for the postal operator
Parcel returned to sender if delivery is not possible	Dummy: *Back_sender* = 1 if the parcel is returned to sender when delivery impossible; 0 otherwise	Positive: the return-to-sender option should increase the value of the postal service and increase the cost for the postal operator
Country	15 dummies: France as the reference	Unknown

As expected, the parameters associated with all independent variables, except the dummy related to the franking of parcels online,[5] have a positive impact on price. In particular, the price charged to consumers increases with the parcel weight (if the weight increases by 10 percent, the price increases by 2.82 percent[6]) and the speed of delivery (if the parcel is delivered in D+1 instead of D+3, the log of the price increases by 0.24; in other words, the price increases by €1.27).

When examining the dummies associated with countries, we could observe that three countries have a negative coefficient: Germany, the Netherlands and Switzerland. However, the coefficient is not statistically different from zero for the two last countries. The coefficients associated with all other countries are positive (note, however, that those associated with Belgium, Denmark and Luxembourg are not statistically significant).

The interpretation of these dummies is the following: a similar offer will be priced at a higher rate in Austria, Finland, Greece, Ireland, Italy, Portugal, Spain, Sweden and the UK than in France. Only Germany will offer a similar product at a lower rate. For Denmark, Belgium, Luxembourg, the Netherlands and Switzerland, differences in tariff are not statistically significant.

These results are illustrated by Figure 4.3, representing the estimated price of a parcel characterized by a weight between 1 and 2 kilograms, delivered two days after posting at home from Monday to Saturday throughout the whole territory, with a second presentation in case of absence, returned to sender and insured.

This model gives preliminary results, which should be improved. Estimated prices seem to approximately reflect reality for some countries but in some cases, the difference between the estimated and the real price is quite high. To illustrate this point, Figure 4.4 compares the estimated and the real price of what we defined as the basic parcel offer in each country. Important differences appear for the UK, Denmark and Italy. The estimated hedonic function for this particular case tends to overestimate the real price, except for Belgium, Luxembourg (underestimation) and Austria, Sweden and Spain (correct estimation). A possible explanation could be that the majority of operators underestimate the real value for consumers of some features of their basic offer or support strong regulatory pricing constraints.

Table 4.4 Estimation results

Variable	Coefficient	Std error	*t*-statistic	Prob.
C	−0.381114	0.179532	−2.122816	0.0342
W	0.292221	0.010131	28.84289	0.0000
*D*1	0.243400	0.077997	3.120620	0.0019
*D*2	0.190606	0.083079	2.294279	0.0221
Back_sender	0.343825	0.076453	4.497207	0.0000
COD	0.215082	0.022446	9.582259	0.0000
Home_dev	0.131941	0.059910	2.202343	0.0280
Insur	0.275153	0.046994	5.855118	0.0000
Nat_cov	0.821604	0.058934	13.94120	0.0000
Online_franking	−0.071719	0.031523	−2.275130	0.0233
Receipt	0.147612	0.025848	5.710708	0.0000
Twice_dev	0.425099	0.083695	5.079140	0.0000
Six_dev	0.464797	0.096714	4.805878	0.0000
AT	0.447447	0.172291	2.597036	0.0096
BE	0.001612	0.120109	0.013421	0.9893
DK	0.056280	0.087612	0.642378	0.5209
FI	1.049901	0.172994	6.069014	0.0000
DE	−0.531049	0.073343	−7.240666	0.0000
GR	0.840619	0.119765	7.018890	0.0000
IE	1.075978	0.116552	9.231774	0.0000
IT	0.566351	0.114413	4.950078	0.0000
LU	0.172922	0.138279	1.250529	0.2116
NL	−0.157369	0.170269	−0.924241	0.3558
PT	1.467787	0.137562	10.67000	0.0000
SP	0.923108	0.102899	8.971014	0.0000
SW	1.877181	0.194402	9.656201	0.0000
CH	−0.013606	0.146596	−0.092811	0.9261
UK	0.703159	0.085300	8.243378	0.0000
Adjusted R^2	0.845196			
F-statistic	120.5081			
Akaike info criterion	−0.219487			

5 CONCLUSION

As the parcels sector is under more scrutiny by regulators and is considered to be an essential factor to promote the development of e-commerce, the robustness and reliability of price comparisons between countries and the affordability character of parcel services become crucial.

Until now, despite some caveats, this issue has essentially been addressed through simple price comparisons based on absolute values, which do not take into account qualitative differences between services offered in different countries. However, as shown in this chapter, the characteristics of parcel offers vary greatly from one country

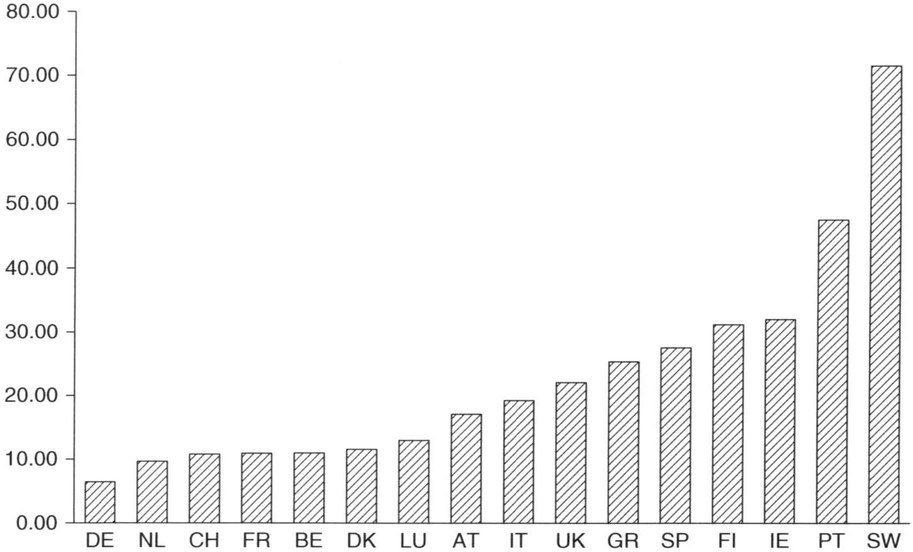

Figure 4.3 *Estimated prices of a same offer in different countries (based on the features of the French Colissimo product) in PPP (€)*

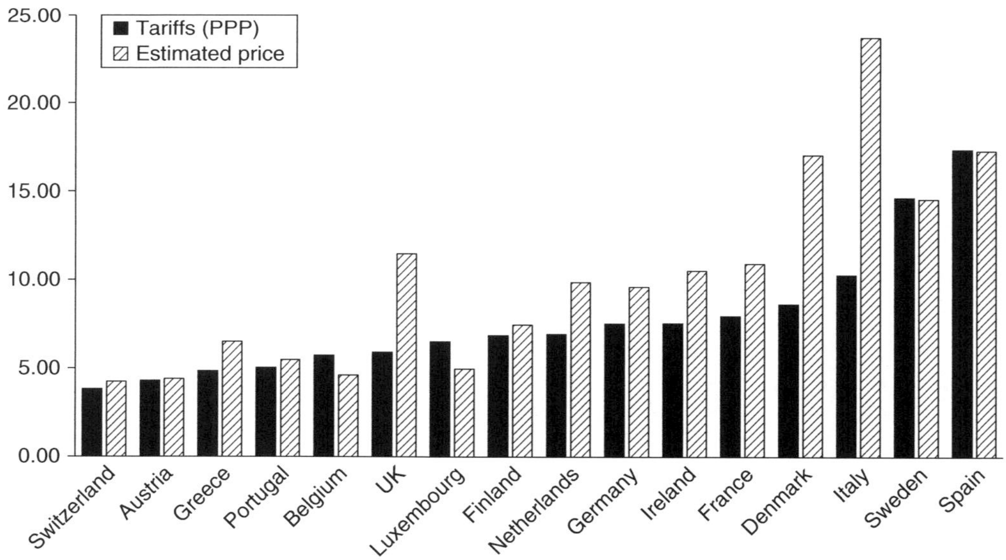

Figure 4.4 *Estimated versus real price of basic offers of 2kg*

to another. The number and the nature of options included in the basic offer differ significantly. So, it could be misleading to take regulatory measures on such comparisons, sometimes irrelevant and non-robust (as we saw in Section 2, the ranking of EU member states according to the price of domestic parcels varies according to the study considered).

To go further and improve the understanding of gaps in price that could exist between offers beyond differences in costs and markups, we estimated a hedonic price function for domestic parcels within the USO scope, in order to take into account the qualitative differences between offers and the implicit valuations of these features by consumers embodied in the tariff.

From this preliminary work, it appears that the most qualitative relevant characteristics of parcels impacting on the price charged to consumers are weight, speed of delivery, six-day-a-week home delivery throughout the territory, second presentation, return to sender, online franking, cash on delivery, insurance and advice of receipt.

The estimation allows new international comparisons to be made which take into account differences in the quality of parcel services offered to individual consumers in Europe. It seems that, *ceteris paribus*, considering parcel features, the most affordable parcel is provided by Deutsche Post, followed by France, Austria and Italy. Delivery costs (from collection) related to geographical and demographical characteristics of the countries, and markups applied by postal operators, determined by the competitive intensity on the parcel market and regulatory constraints, could explain the remaining differences observed in the tariff for some offers.

All these results are preliminary and should be the subject of a more detailed study, for example employing panel data, allowing for changes in prices and changes in parcel feature offerings over several years.

NOTES

* The opinions expressed in this chapter are those of the authors and do not necessarily reflect the positions of Le Groupe La Poste. We would like to acknowledge all persons from postal operators who kindly agreed to answer our questionnaire in order to improve our knowledge of parcel offers.

1. The figures were 74 percent according to IPC (2009); 80 percent according to ITA/WIK (2009).
2. Directive 97/67/EC concerning common rules for the development of the internal market of Community postal services and improving the quality of service.
3. Posti has an alternative scheme ('Parcel to Doorstep') which delivers directly to the addressee, usually by 2pm the working day after posting, but this offer is not part of the USO.
4. Austria, Belgium, Denmark, Finland, France, Germany, Greece, Ireland, Italy, Luxembourg, the Netherlands, Portugal, Spain, Switzerland, Sweden and the UK. Again, we thank all those who kindly answered our questionnaire.
5. As noted by Meloria Meschi, the negative sign reflects the price–cost orientation obligation borne by USPs.
6. If $\log(w)$ increases by 10 percent, $\log(P)$ increases by 2.92 percent. So, P would increase by $[1.1^{0.292} - 1] = 0.0282 = 2.82\%$.

REFERENCES

ANACOM (2009), 'Comparisons of prices of providers of the universal postal service in the European Union in 2009', August.

Copenhagen Economics (2010), 'Main developments in the postal sector (2008–2010), Final Report for the EU DG Market', November.

Court, A.T. (1939), 'Hedonic price indexes with automotive examples', in *The Dynamics of Automotive Demand*, New York: General Motors, pp. 98–119.

Diewert, W.E. (2003), 'Hedonic regressions: a consumer theory approach', in R.C. Feenstra and M.D. Shapiro (eds), *Scanner Data and Price Indexes*, Chicago, IL: University of Chicago Press, pp. 317–48.

Ekeland, I.J., J. Heckman and L. Nesheim (2004), 'Identification and estimation of hedonic models', *Journal of Political Economy*, **112**, 60–109.

Fenster, L., D. Monaco, E.S. Pearsall, C. Robinson and S. Xenakis (2006), 'U.S. Postal Services as composite goods with hedonic properties', in M.A. Crew and P.R. Kleindorfer (eds), *Liberalization of the Postal and Delivery Sector*, Cheltenham, UK and Northampton, MA, USA: Edward Elgar, pp. 369–88.

Griliches, Z. (1961), 'Hedonic prices for automobiles: an econometric analysis of quality change', in *The Price Statistics of the Federal Government*, General Series 73, New York: Columbia University Press for the National Bureau of Economic Research, pp. 137–96.

Griliches, Z. (1971), 'Introduction: hedonic price indexes revisited', in Z. Griliches (ed.), *Price Indexes and Quality Change*, Cambridge, MA: Harvard University Press, pp. 3–15.

IPC (2009), 'Cross-border parcel study', International Post Corporation, Brussels.

ITA Consulting and WIK Consult (2009), 'The evolution of the European postal market since 1997', Report for the European Commission.

Lancaster, K.J. (1966), 'A new approach to consumer theory', *Journal of Political Economy*, **74** (2), 132–57.

Lancaster, K.J. (1971), *Consumer Demand: A New Approach*, New York: Columbia University Press.

Pearsall, E.S. and C.L. Trozzo (2011), 'Evaluating the demand effects of reductions in the frequency of delivery service', in M.A. Crew and P.R. Kleindorfer (eds), *Reinventing the Postal Sector in an Electronic Age*, Cheltenham, UK and Northampton, MA, USA: Edward Elgar, pp. 173–98.

Postcomm (2009), 'European stamp price comparison', available at stakeholders.ofcom.org.uk/binaries/post/952.pdf.

Ridker, R.G. and J.A. Henning (1967), 'The determinants of residential property values with special reference to air pollution', *Review of Economics and Statistics*, **49**, 246–57.

Rosen, S. (1974), 'Hedonic prices and implicit markets: product differentiation in pure competition', *Journal of Political Economy*, **82** (1), 34–55.

Triplett, J.E. (2004), 'Handbook on hedonic indexes and quality adjustments in price indexes: special application to information technology products', Working Paper 2004/9, OECD, Paris.

Waugh, F.V. (1928), 'Quality factors influencing vegetable prices', *Journal of Farm Economics*, **10**, 185–96.

WIK Consult (2004), 'Main developments in the European postal sector', Study for the European Commission.

WIK Economics (2006), 'Main developments in the Postal Sector 2004–2006'.

5. A new governance model for US postal services*

James I. Campbell Jr[†]

1 INTRODUCTION

The United States Postal Service (USPS) is on the brink of collapse. Staggered by debts that it cannot repay, USPS is seeking legislative relief while threatening radical retrenchment. In Congress, prospective decline has evoked sharply contrasting visions of the future of the post. For some members of Congress, six-day, high-quality postal service to every corner of the country remains necessary to 'bind the Nation together' – the lifeline for those on the wrong side of the 'digital divide', the anchor of small and rural communities, the backbone of a vast subsector of the economy. For others, USPS is a bloated federal bureaucracy built for a bygone era – too many offices, too frequent deliveries, an excessive and overpaid workforce, run by a political board incapable of 'right sizing' a business being overtaken by new technologies. Neither vision commands a majority of lawmakers. Current proposals only postpone fundamental reform, while giving postal management detailed, but dubious, instructions on how to run a national postal system.

This chapter proposes a more promising approach. Legislators, it will be argued, should focus less on *what* future postal services should entail and more on *how* such questions should be decided. A wiser strategy for *governing* the postal sector will provide a sounder and more enduring basis for *managing* postal services in the future. Such an approach is well within the mainstream of American postal legislation – in particular, the Postal Reorganization Act of 1970 (PRA) – and consistent with reforms adopted in other national infrastructure industries in the US (for example, aviation, telecommunications) and in the postal systems of other industrialized countries.

This chapter is divided as follows. Following this introduction, Section 2 clarifies the concept of 'governance' by summarizing the current governance model for postal services. Section 3 describes how a new governance model is implied by principles of sound governmental design and key market-based and political imperatives. Section 4 offers a concrete example of how a new governance model could be implemented by outlining the major provisions of one possible example of a Postal Modernization Act (PMA). Section 5 provides a short recapitulation of the argument.

† Attorney in private practice in Washington, DC.

2 THE CURRENT GOVERNANCE MODEL FOR POSTAL SERVICES

The organization and activities of USPS are directed by three distinct sets of rules (Table 5.1). Legislative rules are embodied in statutes enacted by Congress. Regulatory rules are issued by the Postal Regulatory Commission (PRC). Managerial rules and decisions are made by the management of USPS.

Not all rules are created alike. The source of a rule shapes its nature and purpose. Legislative rules embody political compromises because Congress is a political body, designed to mediate between different interest groups, especially those represented in Washington. In the end, the first objective of members of Congress is to satisfy voters. Regulations and decisions of the PRC differ from legislative statutes because regulators are different from legislators. Regulators are less political and more specialized. The first objective of regulators is to satisfy Congress and the courts by applying statutes impartially and expertly. In contrast to legislators and regulators, USPS managers must focus on operational factors, mailers' needs, and market constraints. Each institution has its own pace of decision making, from the usually glacial pace of legislation to the potentially nimble execution of management.

A cardinal principle of good governmental design is that decision-making authority should be allocated among different governmental bodies so that each is assigned responsibility for decisions suited to its nature. An enduring strength of the US Constitution is that it not only divides governmental authority among three branches of government but also organizes each in a manner appropriate to its task. An enduring postal law suited to the needs of society in the early twenty-first century must reflect the same principles.

A review of the current decision-making apparatus clarifies the challenge of postal reform. Under current statutes, Congress makes a major portion of decisions relating to national postal services. Legislation establishes USPS as an independent government

Table 5.1 Decision making by governmental bodies relating to postal services

	Congress	PRC	USPS management
Main question	What do the voters want?	What does the law require?	What do customers want?
Basic nature	Mediation among political interests and values	Application of law and economic principles to specific situations	Organization of costs and products
Major factors	Constituent views; political principles and alliances; interest groups	Statutory requirements; transparent proceedings; economic and legal analyses	Statutory and regulatory requirements; customer and institutional needs
Speed and flexibility	Rules persist over many years; difficult to change	Rules evolve over time but speed and flexibility are limited by due process and precedent	Flexible and anticipatory decision making depends on management

agency directed by nine governors appointed by the President with consent of the Senate. Legislation gives USPS a monopoly over certain services and bars USPS from conveying 'non-mailable' items. Legislation also establishes employment policies and fringe benefits for USPS employees. In the Postal Accountability and Enhancement Act (PAEA) of 2006, Congress divided USPS's products into two categories, market dominant and competitive. For market-dominant products, legislation freezes postage rates in real terms (2006 rates plus inflation), prescribes discounts for preferred types of mail, mandates frequency of delivery and, to a substantial degree, determines the number and distribution of post offices. Legislation further directs USPS to maintain nationally uniform rates for certain products and to provide money-losing freight services to the bush country of Alaska. With respect to competitive products, legislation adopts a more hands-off approach, decreeing only basic rate-making principles.

The PRC is established by Congress as a second independent government agency led by five members also appointed by the President with Senate consent. The PRC's main responsibilities include administration of regulatory accounts, allocation of products between market-dominant and -competitive categories, administration of the statutory price cap for market-dominant products and pricing principles for competitive products, prevention of unfair discrimination, and an annual review of USPS's compliance with the postal laws. The PRC has limited authority over service levels. It defines quality of service measures (but not standards), reviews procedures for closing post offices (but not the decision to close), and reviews major changes in national postal service (but cannot enforce its findings).

The decision making of USPS management is circumscribed by decisions already taken in legislative and regulatory rules. USPS managers establish prices and products for market-dominant products within narrow statutory and regulatory limits. They exercise substantially more discretion in the production and pricing of competitive products. Management negotiates wages with unionized employees and directs USPS personnel but must respect federal hiring preferences and other legislative constraints. In many cases, operational decisions which are not determined by legislation are nonetheless influenced by congressional pressure. USPS also exercises governmental functions. It issues regulations, conducts investigations, and adjudicates accusations to enforce criminal and civil statutes.

The purpose of this chapter is to reconsider this *governance model* for postal services, specifically, the allocation of decision-making authority among Congress, the PRC, and USPS. Can decision making with respect to national postal services be better organized? How and why? This chapter is *not* concerned with the *business model* or commercial strategy of USPS. Many observers have offered detailed explanations why USPS should eschew price increases (or raise rates substantially), focus on last-mile delivery (or diversify into new business areas), sustain high-quality service (or cut back on service levels), and make better use of the network of post offices (or franchise retail operations). While good arguments may be made for different business strategies, the premise of this chapter is that a *lasting* legal framework for an efficient, effective USPS suited to the needs of the nation over the next decade or two requires, first of all, an allocation of decision-making authority that draws upon the strengths and avoids the weaknesses of the several bodies, which determine the business model of USPS.[1]

3 A NEW GOVERNANCE MODEL: IMPERATIVES AND DESIDERATA

A new governance model for postal services must respond not only to the internal decision-making capabilities of government bodies but also to the external environment which is generating the need for decisions in the first place. In the early twenty-first century, there appear to be three fundamental imperatives that must be satisfied by any practicable revision of the governance model for postal services.

First, a new governance model must permit and encourage USPS to develop products at prices that satisfy the needs of commercial customers. Businesses and organizations send 90 percent of all mail. For business mailers, and especially for bulk mailers, use of the mail is increasingly a commercial decision, not an unavoidable cost of doing business. Even catalog mailers, who are closely tied to postal service, post more or fewer catalogs with more or fewer pages depending on considerations of price and service because catalogs and websites have become complementary elements in a modern marketing campaign. The rise of 'commercial mailers' – in the sense of mailers whose use of the mail is motivated by a commercial evaluation of postal services versus alternatives (not merely for ends that are ultimately commercial in nature) – implies a profound break from the past. In the future it will be commercial mailers – rather than first class mailers – who form the financial base of USPS. Unless USPS has the flexibility and motivation to develop efficient, innovative products at prices commercial mailers are willing to pay, there will be no USPS except as a destitute ward of government. A new governance model must recognize not only that USPS requires managerial flexibility to satisfy the demands of commercial mailers but also that USPS's commercial customers can no longer serve as a tax base to pay for public services.

Second, a new governance model must accommodate public expectations for maintenance of public services. However much futurists proclaim the demise of 'snail mail', Congressional complaints and popular protests demonstrate that many citizens and their representatives believe that USPS must continue to perform certain public services. Perhaps post offices should not be closed where the identity of a small town is threatened. Perhaps charitable institutions should continue to receive special discounts. Perhaps in some areas deliveries should remain more frequent than commercially required. Which services should be ensured by the federal government is a question about which reasonable persons may differ, but in a democracy a new governance model must accommodate a political consensus that the USPS should provide *some* public services that do not cover costs.

Third, a new governance model must respond to the fact that the market for postal services is changing rapidly. Mail volume per capita is down 27 percent from its peak in 2000. Worse, first class mail volume, the most profitable portion of the mail, is down 36 percent. While it is commonly observed that this has been the worse decline in mail volume since the Great Depression (when mail volume fell by 31 percent in four years), this observation wholly understates the magnitude of recent market changes. During the Great Depression, the role of mail in society did not change; when the economy eventually recovered so did mail volume. Today volume declines reflect a fundamental change in the function of paper-based communications. In reality, the market for postal services is changing more rapidly and more fundamentally than at any time since the introduction of the railroad in the 1830s.

Table 5.2 Division of USPS revenues by commercial and public service categories

	Commercial products (71%)	Public service products (29%)
Market-dominant products (86%)	Bulk letters Advertisements Periodicals Inbound international letter post and parcels (commercial) (57%)	Universal services for all MD products Single-piece letters Single-piece parcels Bound printed matter Media and library mail In-county newspapers Nonprofit mail Free postage (blind, overseas voting) Inbound international letter post and parcels (social) Alaskan bush services (29%)
Competitive products (14%)	Express mail Priority mail Bulk parcels Bulk outbound international letters (14%)	Universal services for some competitive products (<1%)

What do these three imperatives imply? At the outset a new governance model must introduce a distinction between *commercial products* and *public service products* in much the same way that the PAEA introduced a distinction between market-dominant and competitive products and for much the same reasons: it is not feasible to apply the same regulatory rules to both types of products. There is an increasing tension between services designed to satisfy commercial mailers and maintenance of public services. Commercial mailers may not need, nor be willing to pay for, postal services with all of the attributes of a public service. For example, commercial mailers have little need for retail post offices, and many do not require six-day delivery. On the other hand, there remains an insistent political demand for public services in specific instances, such as maintaining post offices in small towns. A commercial/public service distinction would cut across the market dominant/competitive distinction approximately as shown in Table 5.2.

In addition, the pace of change implies that *allocation of decision making must shift from slower to faster decision-making bodies*. With respect to commercial products, the unsuitability of 'micromanagement' by Congress is apparent. Congress is not organized to gather and evaluate production and marketing information. Nor can Congress function with the speed necessary to keep pace with the evolution of postal markets. Regulators, too, are ill-equipped to address commercial issues in a changing marketplace. For *commercial* products, Congress and the PRC must concentrate on defining and enforcing legal principles that will protect the public interest while establishing operational structures flexible enough to allow USPS to cope with rapidly shifting demand. For *public service* products, the role of Congress must be more direct. To decide how much and what types of public postal services should be federally ensured requires reconciliation of diverse political preferences. This is the sort of decision making that Congress is set up to handle. Even so, social needs are being transformed by new methods of communications. In defining public service products, therefore, Congress should rely as much as possible on broad objectives while allowing the PRC to fill in the blanks.

Beyond these three overriding imperatives, one can imagine additional features desirable in a new governance model. The current governance model, for example, provides remarkably little accountability to the ordinary citizen. Despite soaring rhetoric about the importance of the Universal Service Obligation, it is practically impossible for a citizen to hold the local postmaster to specific standards of service. Then, too, the ultimate aim of any law is to advance the welfare of the United States, not that of USPS and its customers. A new governance model should consider how fruits of the postal system can better serve the national economy.

Taken together, these considerations imply the need for a new governance model that is as different from the 1970 PRA as that act was from prior law. In a new governance model, Congress must become more of a designer of motivated, self-regulating institutions and definer of public interest guidelines and less of a setter of rates, service standards, and employment practices. The PRC must protect public service products and fair competition while adopting a more flexible approach towards commercial products. USPS itself must become more competent, nimble, efficient, self-motivated, and innovative. As a direct consequence, USPS must relinquish governmental authority that might give it an unfair lever against customers or competitors. Elements of the postal system, such as the national system of mailboxes and post office boxes, which can improve the efficiency of the entire national system of delivery services – no longer a system supplied by USPS alone – should be made available to all providers of delivery services in a manner that advances the public interest.

4 FROM NEW GOVERNANCE MODEL TO POSTAL MODERNIZATION ACT

The abstract notion of a new governance model will become clearer with a concrete example. This section sketches out how a hypothetical Postal Modernization Act (PMA) might tackle key legislative issues posed by a new governance model. The PMA described below is illustrative only; one of several possible variations on the theme.

Reorganization of Title 39

An attempt to introduce a new governance model by amending the existing postal law, title 39 of the United States Code, quickly reveals that title 39 is poorly organized for addressing the issues of the twenty-first century. When title 39 was drafted in the late 1960s, postal policy began and ended with USPS. Rules that establish USPS are commingled with others that mandate public services or provide for regulation. A necessary first step in crafting a PMA is reorganization of current law under headings relevant to today.

In the reorganized title 39, provisions of current law could be grouped into five parts as follows: part I, general governmental matters; part II, establishment of USPS as a government corporation; part III, definition of USPS's obligation to provide public products; part IV, general regulatory framework for postal services; and part V, provisions regulating the transportation of mail. The bulk of revisions introduced by the PMA will be concentrated in parts II, III, and IV. Part II will reestablish USPS as a better managed and more efficient government corporation that is equipped to serve commercial mailers and operate in competitive markets. Part III will clarify existing public service obligations and provide a more specific and enforceable Universal Service Obligation. Part III will also include compensation for USPS for the net costs of public services. Part IV will establish a revised regulatory framework that is more focused on protecting public postal services, preventing unfair competition, protecting consumers, and promoting a more efficient national system of delivery services. Parts I and V will deal primarily with the interface between USPS and other departments of government including the Department of Justice (penal postal laws), the Department of State (international postal policies), the Treasury Department (appropriations), and the Department of Transportation (regulation of air transportation of mail).

Reestablishment of the Postal Service

A primary goal of the new governance model is to empower and motivate USPS to produce products at prices that answer the needs of commercial mailers in a rapidly changing market. According to the new governance model, Congress should determine how to establish the USPS so that it can, consistent with government ownership[2] and public service obligations, operate as efficiently and innovatively as possible. Congress should forbear from managing directly the methods of production, products to be offered, and prices to be charged. These decisions must be left to USPS as the body best equipped to address such issues. At the same time, as explained below, the PRC should continue to enforce a regulatory framework appropriate for different categories of postal products.

To implement these goals, the PMA must reestablish USPS so that it becomes a more competent and efficient government corporation. How? One possible precedent is Conrail. In 1976, Conrail was organized as a government corporation established under state corporate law to manage the assets of six bankrupt railroads in the northeastern United States. Conrail had all of the powers of a normal private corporation except where modified by statute. It was managed by a board of 13 directors. Six represented the government while others represented bondholders of railroads and other private interests. The government's directors were not named directly by the President. Instead they were chosen by a second board that included the secretaries of the Treasury and Transportation and nine other presidential appointees. The statutory duty of government directors was to protect the profits of Conrail no less than the private directors.[3] To provide maximum freedom to operate like an ordinary business, the act declared that Conrail 'shall be a for-profit corporation . . . and shall not be an agency or instrumentality of the Federal Government'.[4]

In a similar manner, the PMA could reestablish USPS as a normal corporation organized under state corporate law. So far as possible (there are constitutional limits), it would no longer be an agency of the federal government. The board of directors could be chosen by a committee consisting of the secretaries of relevant departments (for example, Commerce, Labor, Transportation, and Treasury) or, alternatively, by the secretaries acting individually. Directors would be selected based on professional qualifications alone and obliged to protect and advance the ownership interests of government, not the broader interests of the general public. Reestablishing the USPS in this manner would create a more flexible and capable organization, one better equipped to develop commercial products and respond to changing market demands.

The US Constitution, however, raises a red flag over a board of directors appointed in this manner. To preserve accountability, the Founding Fathers set strict limits to how far executive authority may be delegated by the President. In brief, the 'appointments clause' creates only two classes of federal officials: a 'principal officer' appointed by the President and confirmed by the Senate and an 'inferior officer' appointed by the President or by a 'Head of Department' and not confirmed by the Senate.

In a USPS reestablished as described, the board would thus be composed of inferior officers appointed by principal officers. Since a board of inferior officers may *not* appoint another inferior officer, the Postmaster General and other USPS officials would be mere 'employees' of the United States in constitutional terms and unable to exercise sovereign powers of government, such as administering, executing, or authoritatively interpreting the laws.[5] Thus, a USPS board of directors that is less politically accountable and more commercially flexible must, of constitutional necessity, become less governmental. The appointments clause reinforces the conclusion that a more commercial USPS should not exercise governmental authority.

'Degovernmentalization' should work both ways. Under a new governance model, USPS should be insulated from political interference when making specific operational decisions. In the PRA of 1970, Congress prohibited political officials, including members of Congress, from proposing or supporting candidates seeking positions as postmasters. The PMA could extend this protection from political interference to all types of operational decisions. Members of Congress could continue to support public services affecting their constituents in PRC proceedings applying statutory guidelines on public services to specific situations.

The PMA must also address pension and health benefits and the treatment of legacy costs. The critical importance of commercial products to the long-term survival of USPS implies that the PMA should give management and employees the same flexibility to deal with labor costs as a private company. USPS employees should no longer be required to participate in federal benefit programs established for civil servants. Benefits should be decided at the collective bargaining table along with wages. However, in my view, benefits already promised to postal employees must be honored. These are legislative commitments by Congress, not contractual commitments by USPS. Congress has provided funds for these programs by requiring annual contributions from USPS, but funding requirements have been unevenly drawn. It appears that Treasury has collected some $13 billion (as of the end FY 2011) more than required to fund pension programs, but undercollected for retiree health-care programs by about $46 billion.[6] The question is who should get the 'surplus' and who should be stuck for the 'unfunded liabilities', the Treasury or future mailers? It seems unrealistic to expect that large liabilities can be collected from commercial mailers, the primary source of future USPS revenues, without significantly depressing demand. Moreover, it is questionable whether future mailers should bear costs associated with services rendered to other mailers in the past. The fairest and more practicable answer may be simplest. The Treasury should keep the overfunding and cover the underfunding from general revenues, allowing the reestablished USPS to begin with a clean slate.

Universal Service and Other Public Service Products

A second primary goal of the new governance model is to maintain public services that meet the needs of society in a rapidly changing environment. To implement the new governance model, the PMA must address three questions not answered by current law: (i) What universal postal services should be guaranteed to all Americans? (ii) How should such a guarantee be enforced? (iii) How should it be paid for?

The proposed PMA would begin by defining 'essential postal services' to mean adequate and efficient postal services provided at fair and reasonable rates throughout the United States and appropriate for the transmission of *single-piece* letters, documents, and parcels. Bulk mailers would be assured access to essential postal services, so their ability to reach the entire nation at reasonable rates would also be guaranteed. Under this approach, however, the federal government would not guarantee – although it could continue to regulate – special discounted rates suited to bulk mail. The PMA would require that rates for essential postal services must be reasonable, equitable, and affordable for all residents of the United States. The PMA would further require that essential postal services must provide prompt and reliable service in all areas and all communities of the United States. It could require further that services in rural areas, communities, and small towns must be comparable to services in urban areas to the maximum extent practicable.

In short, the idea of a PMA is compatible with a strong universal service obligation. Congress could go further and mandate a minimum number of post offices or days of delivery, but it would be unwise to do so. The market for postal services is changing so rapidly that no one can predict what levels of services will be essential to society in 10 or 15 years. Instead, the PMA should delegate to the PRC the task of translating statutory principles into specific rate and service policies for essential postal services. USPS would be obliged to notify the PRC that it could not profitably provide essential postal services in conformance with rate and service policies set by the PRC. In such cases, the PRC could issue a protective order requiring USPS to maintain such rates, services, and facilities as may be needed to sustain universal service. When operating subject to a protective order, USPS would be entitled to receive compensation for net losses incurred in providing the required service.

In this manner, essential postal services provided under protective order would become one of several public services required by the PMA. Other public services, carried over from current law, would include free and reduced rates for preferred classes of mail, freight services to the Alaskan bush country, franked and penalty mail services, and issuance of semipostals. Not all of these services impose a net cost on USPS, but when there is a net cost, USPS would be entitled to compensation.

Like the original PRA, the PMA proposes that public appropriations should fund the net costs of public services. However, rather than appropriating money directly to USPS, the PMA would direct the money to a special fund in the Treasury under the control of the PRC. USPS have to satisfy the PRC that the public services were satisfactorily provided and net costs correctly calculated before the PRC would disburse the funds. If Congress fails to appropriate sufficient funds, USPS would be permitted to raise rates as necessary without further PRC review (again, as provided in the PRA). As a last resort, USPS could deduct uncompensated losses from any money owed to the Treasury.

Regulation of Postal Rates and Services

Under the new governance model, regulation of postal rates and service would continue – and be extended in some respects – but also simplified and clarified. By concentrating regulatory scrutiny on market-dominant products, the PAEA permitted more flexibility for competitive products. The PMA would again tighten the focus of the PRC's efforts by emphasizing the need to protect public service products while allowing USPS more freedom in the production of commercial products.

The PMA would adopt a more nuanced approach towards rate regulation. As in current law, changes in rates for competitive products, whether public service or commercial, would be required to meet two tests: (i) the rate for each product must cover its attributable costs; and (ii) rates of all competitive products collectively must make a fair contribution to overhead costs. For changes in rates of market-dominant products, review would depend on whether or not the rates pertain to public service products. For essential postal services, USPS could be required to demonstrate that new rates are consistent with PRC policies before implementation. In principle, a priori review could be extended to changes in other public service rates as well; however, most of these rates are either free or tied to changes in the rates of commercial products. For changes in the rates for commercial products, the PRC could be authorized to adopt any form of review it deemed sufficient *except for* a priori review. Criteria for review could be simplified, for example, by requiring only that rates for commercial market-dominant products cover attributable costs, avoid unjust or unreasonable discrimination, and are not excessive or abusive. Rate regulation should no longer be employed to second-guess USPS management as to the flexibility, efficiency, predictability, adequacy, and so on of commercial rates. Similarly, the PMA should relieve USPS of the requirement to seek a PRC opinion before making changes in the nature of services for commercial products. At the same time, the PRC's authority to adopt service standards and issue protective orders would give it more power to protect service levels for essential postal services.

The PMA could also give the PRC new authority to permit access to features of the postal system that can improve the operation of national delivery services. For example, the national system of mailboxes is a secure and inexpensive means of delivery that could reduce the costs of all delivery services. The PMA could authorize the PRC to allow reputable private companies to deliver to private mailboxes provided that public interest criteria are met, such as ensuring the security of the mailbox, the rights of the householder, and the ability of USPS to collect outbound mail. In addition, the PRC could be authorized to open post office boxes to delivery by private companies provided that USPS is compensated for maintenance of the boxes and the preferences of box holders are respected.

General Government Issues

With one prominent exception, the implications of a new governance model are less profound for other parts of the legal framework for postal services. The exception is the set of penal provisions jointly administered by USPS and the Department of Justice. This subsection outlines how a PMA could revise the concept of postal penal provisions and then notes other revisions in current law that could facilitate implementation of a new governance model.

The most significant postal penal provisions are those that establish the postal monopoly. Provisions of title 39 and of title 18, the criminal laws of the United States, prohibit certain delivery services in competition with USPS. Continuation of a postal monopoly is incompatible with the new governance model. The PMA seeks to motivate as well as to empower USPS, while the monopoly creates a shield from competition that undermines commercial incentives. Moreover, a public monopoly cannot be bestowed without public controls, while USPS will need as much flexibility as possible to meet the needs of commercial mailers in the future. Like all major industrialized countries that have adopted comprehensive postal modernization laws (except Australia), the PMA would repeal the postal monopoly after an appropriate transition period.

Repeal of the postal monopoly is, however, only a start in dealing with broader issues posed by postal penal laws. Nonmailability laws prohibit USPS from carrying certain types of items, including items posted for illegal purposes such as perpetration of a fraud, conducting a lottery, or distribution of pornography or alcoholic beverages. Other provisions make it a crime to interfere with USPS in the performance of its duties. To implement such laws, USPS operates its own police force, which is empowered to investigate citizens for violation of regulations adopted by USPS. In some cases, USPS may try persons for such offenses before USPS judges. Violations of postal penal provisions can result in loss of business, fines, and imprisonment.

Such authority is inappropriate for USPS in the twenty-first century. As noted above, under the appointments clause of the Constitution, if USPS is reestablished as more independent and commercially flexible government corporation, it cannot continue to exercise the penal powers of a sovereign. Moreover, postal penal provisions create distortions in the national delivery services market that are neither just nor reasonable. If interstate transmission of an item is lawful, then USPS should be able to offer services in competition with private companies while complying with the same federal and state laws. If unlawful, then the prohibition should apply alike to USPS and private delivery services. Similarly, laws protecting the operations of the postal service should apply in like manner to all providers of similar delivery services. The proposed PMA would, therefore, require a comprehensive review of postal penal provisions and law enforcement activities of USPS by the Attorney General. In the short term, the PMA would transfer to the PRC the authority to adopt regulations and adjudicate guilt with respect to nonmailability laws.

In other areas of general government, more limited revisions in current law could suffice. The PRC should continue as an independent regulatory body of persons appointed by the President and confirmed by the Senate. The Department of State should continue to represent the US in international negotiations relating to trade in postal services, although the PMA should clarify the role of a more commercial USPS in the development of the national policies towards trade in services generally. The Department of Transportation must continue to regulate the air transportation of mail where needed, but the need for such regulation should be reexamined.

5 SUMMARY AND CONCLUSIONS

This chapter has argued that viable and enduring postal reform in the United States requires a new 'governance model' for national postal services. Authority over postal services should be reallocated between Congress, the PRC, and USPS so that each is assigned responsibility for decisions suited to its nature. At the same time, a new governance model must respond to three overriding imperatives of the market and society. First, the financial viability of USPS is dependent on its ability to satisfy the demands of large commercial mailers who can increasingly turn to alternatives to the mail. Second, USPS must continue to provide public services demanded by the American people. Third, the postal market is changing so fundamentally and so rapidly that governmental decision making must stress speed and flexibility.

Taken together, these observations imply the need for a new governance model for postal services that is as different from the current statute as the PRA was from prior law. Congress cannot manage large portions of the business of USPS directly. It must become a designer of self-sustaining institutions and a definer of broad social principles. USPS should be reestablished as a more professional and less political government corporation, perhaps based on the 1976 Act establishing Conrail. The reestablished USPS must be capable of producing efficient and innovative commercial products (about 71 percent of USPS revenues) suited to the rapidly changing needs of commercial mailers. The postal monopoly should be ended, and governmental functions of USPS transferred to other bodies. The role of the PRC should evolve as well. Regulation of rates and services should be maintained, but simplified.

The scope of public services, including 'universal' postal services, to be provided by the Postal Service is a political judgment which Congress must decide. In so doing, Congress needs to specify more clearly the public interest objectives to be accomplished and give the PRC adequate authority to ensure the maintenance and efficient production of public service products. Instead of funding public service products by surreptitiously raising the rates of commercial mailers (who increasingly have alternatives to the mail), Congress should compensate USPS for the net costs of such services by making available public funds to the PRC, which should be responsible for the efficient administration of such funds.

NOTES

* The views expressed in this chapter are those of the author and do not represent the views of any client or other person.

1. Most proposals on USPS reform have eschewed questions of governance in favor of ideas for improving operations. The President's Commission (2003) offered much business advice but proposed only modest regulatory changes and an unworkable revision in the USPS board. Recent reports by USPS (2010) and GAO (2010) are primarily business plans, facilitated by regulatory adjustments and revisions in pension and retiree health-care accounts. Of recent papers, Crew and Kleindorfer (2008) and Panzar (2012) begin to address the core issue of governance. While I agree with much of the commentary in both papers, in my view neither deals adequately with what William Kovacic referred to in his insightful commentary at the 20th Conference on Postal and Delivery Economics (2012) in Brighton as the 'engineering problems' posed by governmental design and legislative drafting. One early discussion of governance deserves special mention. In a paper prepared for USPS, McKinsey & Company (2000) made the case for privatization and a contractual obligation to maintain universal services. This prescient analysis has never been published.

2. Crew and Kleindorfer (2008, pp. 132–34) argue that a privatized USPS would be better empowered and motivated than a commercialized USPS. Panzar (2012, p. 143) maintains that American reliance on USPS as a provider of public services implies that the US is 'best served' if USPS remains a government corporation. I think Panzar is probably right as a practical political matter. In any case, unless and until USPS is successfully commercialized, talk of privatization appears premature.
3. Conrail was reorganized and made operational by the Railroad Revitalization and Regulatory Reform Act of 1976, 90 Stat. 31. Under that act, appointment of governmental directors to the Conrail board was vested in the United States Railway Association whose board, in turn, consisted of the Secretaries of Transportation and Treasury, the Chairman of the Interstate Commerce Commission and eight individuals appointed by the President with the advice and consent of the Senate. The Senate committee said of the governmental directors, 'The responsibilities of these directors are not, of course, different from those of the other ConRail directors – to operate ConRail at a profit for the benefit of its shareholders' (S. Rept. No. 499, 94th Cong., 1st Sess. (1975) at 93).
4. 15 U.S.C. § 741(b) (2010).
5. Department of Justice, Office of Legal Counsel, 'Officers of the United States Within the Meaning of the Appointments Clause' (April 16, 2007), pp. 1, 4.
6. US Postal Service, Form 10-K (2011) at 26, 28.

REFERENCES

Crew, Michael A. and Paul R. Kleindorfer (2008), 'Reform of the United States Postal Service: an unfinished task', in Crew, Kleindorfer, and J. Campbell, Jr (eds), *Handbook of Worldwide Postal Reform*, Cheltenham, UK and Northampton, MA, USA: Edward Elgar, pp 123–42.

McKinsey & Company (2000), 'USPS's preferred regulatory end game and transition path', (unpub.).

Panzar, John C. (2012), 'Towards a 21st century postal service', in M. Crew, and P. Kleindorfer (eds), *Multi-modal Competition and the Future of Mail*, Cheltenham, UK and Northampton, MA, USA: Edward Elgar, pp. 139–49.

United States, Government Accountability Office (GAO) (2010), 'Strategies and Options to Facilitate Progress Toward Financial Viability', Report No. GAO-10455, Washington, DC.

United States, President's Commission on the United States Postal Service (2003), *Embracing the Future: Making the Tough Choices to Preserve Universal Service*, Washington, DC: Government Printing Office.

United States Postal Service (USPS) (2010), 'Ensuring a Viable Postal Service for America: An Action Plan for the Future', Washington, DC: US Postal Service.

6. Estimates of US postal price elasticities of demand derived from a random-coefficients discrete-choice normal model*

Margaret M. Cigno,[†] Elena S. Patel[‡] and Edward S. Pearsall[§]

1 INTRODUCTION

Reliable estimates of demand parameters, particularly own-price and cross-price elasticities, are essential for many applications of economic theory to issues of postal regulation. However, conventional econometric approaches typically fail to produce complete and consistent estimates of these elasticities. The failure occurs because the demand equations for a conventional model typically include each product's own price but exclude the prices of most of the possible postal substitutes. Two recent examples of models fit to US data that truncate the price variables in this way are by Pearsall (2011) and Thress (2012).

In this chapter we present a table of own-price and cross-price elasticities for selected US postal services taken from a complete matrix of consistent estimates of price elasticities for 15 categories of US postal services for the fiscal year (PFY) 2011. They were produced by fitting a model using an econometric method that derives from the random-coefficients discrete-choice logit model and estimation methodology of Berry, Levinsohn and Pakes (BLP, 1995; Nevo, 2000a, 2000b). To our knowledge, the BLP/Nevo approach has not previously been tried in postal economics.[1]

Our model has been fit using two alternative measures of postal prices: average revenue per piece (RPP) and fixed-weight index (FWI) prices. Price and cross-price elasticities have been derived from the parameter estimates for both RPP and FWI prices. The price elasticities with respect to the RPP indices are larger in magnitude than the elasticities with respect to the FWI prices. This confirms and extends an earlier finding that revenues per piece are generally less than unit elastic with respect to the US postal tariff (see Pearsall, 2005).

This chapter will proceed by outlining in Section 2 the basic model underlying the application, including the conceptual indirect utility equation and its distribution assumptions. The specific definitions of postal products, measures of their hedonic characteristics, household demographics variables and other variables used to capture

† Drector of the Office of Accountability and Compliance (OAC) of the US Postal Regulatory Commission (PRC).
‡ Economist and member of the OAC staff.
§ Economist and consultant to the PRC.

changes in postal market conditions are described in Section 3. We then present and discuss our equation fits and the estimates of US postal price elasticities in Sections 4 and 5. Our results demonstrate that we have found a practical method for estimating the complete matrix of price elasticities of US mail products. We provide suggestions for future postal modeling efforts along the line established by our model and estimation method in Section 6. Section 7 concludes.

2 THE MODEL

To represent correctly the effects of substitution possibilities and complementarities among the relevant products in a differentiated product market, the price of each product should appear in every demand equation of a conventional econometric model. The United States Postal Service (USPS), like other posts, offers a wide array of postal products and services, some of which are close substitutes for each other. As a result, the number of cross-price elasticities required to describe demand, except at a highly aggregated level, is necessarily large. Postal prices are geographically uniform and tend to be highly correlated over time. Consequently, the equations used to describe demand must be overly restrictive with respect to the price variables in order to avoid near multicollinearity when fit by standard econometric methods. In conventional postal econometric modeling, each equation is usually specified with its own price but without the entire set of cross-prices. With these restrictions the econometrics yields an incomplete and inconsistent set of estimated parameters including the price elasticities.

A potential solution to the problem exists in the general form of a random-coefficients discrete-choice logit model. The past decade of empirical research in industrial organization has been dominated by the estimation of such models following the method of Berry et al. (BLP, 1995). Their model is founded in individual choice behavior yet can be fit with only market-level price and share data in combination with observable product characteristics, population demographics and, when necessary, an effective set of instrumental variables. Most recent applications of the BLP methodology have followed the 'Practitioners Guide' and have used the routine developed by Nevo (2000a, 2000b).

In this chapter, we harness a model similar to the BLP/Nevo model that we call the 'random-coefficient discrete-choice normal model', to estimate own- and cross-price elasticities of the USPS. Our application is fit using annual USPS volumes, prices, hedonic mail properties, aggregate demographic and economic variables. A series of exponential trends and dummy variables that describe exogenous influences on US postal markets such as the introduction of new services and the entry of competitors is also incorporated. The fitted parameters of the model apply directly to linear functions describing the indirect utility resulting from the purchase of a small additional quantity of each postal service by a single US household.

Following BLP/Nevo, we define the household indirect utility from the purchase and consumption of one additional unit of each of several postal products plus an 'outside good'. The outside good allows for the possibility that the household may not purchase an additional unit of any of the named products.

$$U_{ij} = \xi_j + (Y_i + C_i - P_j)(\alpha + \textstyle\prod_y D_i) + X_j(\beta + \textstyle\prod_x D_i) + Z_j\gamma_t + \varepsilon_{ij} \qquad (6.1)$$

Equation (6.1) describes indirect utility in every time period (or market) $t = 1, \ldots, T$, for every household $i = 1, \ldots, I$, and for every product $j = 1, \ldots, J$, including the outside good, $j = 0$. To simplify notation, the time period index, t, has been dropped. The vector X_j contains the x hedonic properties of product j, with $X_0 = 0$. D_i is a random vector of length d of the demographics characteristics of household i. D_i includes both observable and unobservable characteristics and is mean-centered over the population, allowing us to interpret β as an x-vector of mean responses of the household to changes in the hedonic properties of the products.

Equation (6.1) is a linear indirect utility function with random coefficients and two mean-centered disturbances. In particular, ξ_j is a disturbance to the mean indirect utility from purchasing one unit of product j, and ε_{ij} is a disturbance to the individual household's indirect utility from the purchase. The other terms represent the gains and losses to household i by purchasing and consuming an additional unit of product j.

A gain in utility occurs when a household consumes product j and is captured by the term $X_j(\beta + \prod_x D_i)$. A loss in utility arises because the act of purchasing requires expenditures equal to each product's price. This loss is captured by $(Y_i + C_i - P_j)(\alpha + \prod_y D_i)$. Y_i is household income and C_i is the accumulated consumer surplus derived from the household's current levels of consumption of the J products. The purchase of an additional unit of product j reduces the household's income and consumer surplus by P_j (with $P_0 = 0$ for the outside good). The monetary loss is converted to a utility loss when it is multiplied by the household's marginal utility of income, $(\alpha + \Pi_y D_i)$. $(\alpha + \Pi_y D_i)$ is a scalar random coefficient which combines the mean response to income changes, α, with a component that depends on the d-vector, D_i, of demographic characteristics. $(\beta + \prod_x D_i)$ is a vector of similar random coefficients.

Finally, the term $Z_j\gamma_j$ represents exogenous effects that may either increase or decrease indirect utility in ways that are unrelated to changes in the properties of the products or the demographics characteristics of the households. In particular, Z_j is a vector of exogenous effects in the market for product j (with $Z_0 = 0$ for the outside good), and γ_j is the associated vector of non-random coefficients. In our application, Z_j often contains dummy variables and exponential trends inserted to capture the effects of either structural changes that have occurred in the US postal market or changes in USPS product offerings.

The household indirect utility function together with the mechanics of preference in a discrete-choice framework and a few distributional assumptions implies an associated market share. We solve this model numerically according to the algorithm described in our companion paper (Cigno et al., 2012). Fitting the model ensures that simulated market shares do not differ noticeably from observed aggregate market shares. In addition, analytic demand elasticities are derived from the market-share equations employing information specific to a time period or market. In this sense, all elasticities depend upon the values of the demographic variables, product characteristics, and external effects used to compute them.

3 THE DATA

We fit the model using two different measures of US postal prices. The first fit uses FWI prices taken from worksheets accompanying an econometric demand model submitted by the USPS to the US Postal Regulatory Commission (PRC) (see Thress, 2012). The second fit uses RPP calculated from quarterly revenue, pieces and weights (RPW) reports from USPS. Both FWI prices and RPP were converted to constant 2005 dollars using the implicit deflator for real GDP.

Table 6.1 describes the taxonomy of these models. Listed in the table are the 15 USPS product categories, the variables for price (P) and product properties (X), the demographic characteristics of households (D), and the effective dates and product associations for the exponential trends and other market influences (Z). The models were fit to a 40-year time series of observations corresponding to postal fiscal years from PFY 1972 to PFY 2011.

Most of the product categories we use are US mail classes and subclasses that have existed since 1972. The presort categories for First-Class Letters (2) and Cards (4) did not exist until PFY 1976. Express mail (6) also begins with PFY 1976. Standard Carrier-Route (10) begins with PFY 1979. The shares model representing the early years was solved for only those products that existed. Finally, the shares for the outside good are derived from the shares of the other products.[2]

Market shares, prices and weights per piece were all measured in scaled units. The units were chosen so that a scaled unit of every product except the outside good (0) and penalty, franked and free mail (14) required the same expenditure at average prices over the sample period. The scaled unit for products 0 and 14 is a single average piece. Using scaled units reduces computational error when solving the shares model and allows us to treat the mean disturbance, ξ_j, as homoskedastic but does not alter the estimates of coefficients and elasticities.

The model requires a set of hedonic properties of the mail. To this end, we have included in X_j a subset of the hedonic properties identified in Fenster et al. (2006). Our source for the values of the hedonic properties is the more recent analysis found in Pearsall and Trozzo (2011). We include in X_j the weight per piece, a measure directly reported by USPS in its quarterly RPW reports. Also in X_j is a presortation index representing the number of sort passes on standard USPS sorting equipment left to be done by USPS for a particular class of mail. A high presort index indicates a greater number of sorts that the mail must undergo. A lower presort index indicates mail that has undergone some amount of worksharing before being delivered, or drop shipped, to the Postal Service. A distance index in X_j corresponds to the average distance traveled according to mailing zones and destination entry levels. In addition to the hedonic indices, we have included a set of shape variables (proportions of letters, cards, flats and parcels for each mail category) to measure the effect of mail shape on household utility, and a dummy variable identifying domestic mail auxiliary services.

Except for weight per piece in the RPP model, all of the measurements of hedonic properties are based upon the US mail stream during PFY 2009. The two applications differ slightly with respect to the treatment of weight per piece. For the FWI application weights per piece are standardized for all periods using the most recent (2011) RPW values. For the RPP application weights per piece are variable and are calculated from the RPW reports for each postal fiscal year. Otherwise, the vector X_j does not change over the sample. The seven demographics variables listed in Table 6.1 were all suggested by conventional econometric studies of US postal demand conducted by Pearsall (2005, 2011) and Thress (various years, most recently 2012). Quarterly time series from 1971 to

Table 6.1 Definitions of products and variables

j	Product (Postal Service categories)	Price (P) and properties of mail (X-vector)		
0	Outside Good	P	FWI	Fixed-Weight Index, or
1	First-Class Single-Piece Ltrs, Flats, & Pcls		RPP	Revenue per Piece
2	First-Class Presort Ltrs, Flats, & Pcls			
3	First-Class Single-Piece Cards	X	Std. Wgt/Pc	Weight per Piece in 2011, or
4	First-Class Presort Cards		Wgt/Pc	Weight per Piece
5	Priority Mail			
6	Express Mail		Letters	Proportion of Letters
7	Periodicals In-County		Cards	Proportion of Cards
8	Periodicals Outside County		Flats	Proportion of Flats
9	Standard non-Carrier-Route-Ltrs, Flats & Pcls		Parcels	Proportion of Parcels (large and small)
10	Standard Carrier-Route-Ltrs, Flats & Pcls			
11	Parcel Post and Parcel Select		Presort	Number of USPS Machine Passes to Sort
12	Bound Printed Matter		Distance	Log of Number of Miles to Destination
13	Media and Library Mail			
14	Penalty, Franked and Free Mail		Service	Dummy for Domestic Mail Services
15	Domestic Mail Services ex Evps & Box Rents			

Demographic variables (D-vector)	
hhadults	Adults per Household (22+ years of age)
gdp per hh	Real Gross Domestic Product per Household (Chained 2005 Dollars)
chg gdp per hh	Annual Change in Real GDP per Household (Chained 2005 Dollars)
net worth per hh	Real net Worth per Household (Chained 2005 Dollars)
broadband	Proportion of Households with Broadband and Access
unemployment rate	Unemployment Rate
linear trend	Linear Trend from 1970 to 2012

Service innovations and market conditions (Z-vector)

Effective date	Products	Exponential trend description
07/06/1976	1,3	Start of presort discounts for bulk entry First-Class mail presorted to the 3/5 digit ZIP code level
03/21/1981	1,2,3,4,9	Start of presort discounts for bulk entry First-Class mail presorted by carrier route
02/03/1991	1,2,3,4	Start of discounts for bulk entry First-Class mail with preprinted barcodes

Table 6.1 (continued)

Service innovations and market conditions (Z-vector)		
Effective date	Products	Exponential trend description
07/01/1996	1,2,3,4,7,9,10	Effective date of mail reclassifications and changes for automation resulting from MC95-1
05/24/1997	15	Effective date for MC96-3 reclassification of special (auxilliary) services
04/03/1988	4,10	Start of discounts for bulk mail with extended ZIP code addressing
02/03/1991	11	Introduction of parcel select service and discounts for parcels drop shipped
01/07/2001	5,6,9,11	Effective date of miscellaneous changes resulting from the R-2000 rate case
07/06/1981	7,8,10	Separation of In/Out-county periodicals. Start of Carrier-Route discounts for Standard mail
02/17/1985	12,13	USPS allowed fliers and advertisements to be bundled with catalogues mailed at BPM rates
05/14/2007	1,2,12	Effective date of changes affecting parcels resulting from the R-2006 rate case
01/28/1979	9	Start of presort discounts for bulk entry Standard (Third Class) mail presorted to 3/5 digit level
01/10/1999	9,15	Effective date of miscellaneous changes resulting from the R-97 omnibus rate case
09/13/1975	5	USPS introduces Express mail service
02/03/1991	5	Up to two pound Priority Mail envelope level rate for anywhere in the US
01/01/1995	5	Priority Mail rates are leveled up to 5 lbs
01/01/1979	6	Federal Express enters the express mail delivery market
03/21/1981	6	USPS introduces customer pickup service for Express Mail
04/03/1988	9	5-digit barcode discount introduced for Standard mail
Source/date	Products	Other variable description
USPS	5	UPS Coverage of Lower 48 States
USPS	5	Minimum Weight for Priority Mail
	9,10	Election Year Fraction
USPS	11	UPS Man-Days Lost to Strikes (Normalized)
07/06/1976	12	Bound Printed Matter Definition Expanded
05/29/1978	12	Bound Printed Matter Pound Rates in Effect
01/01/1993	12	Sears Catalog Discontinued
11/21/1993	13	Library Rate Rule Change

2012 are readily available at the national level for all of these variables. The quarterly time series were aggregated and averaged by PFY. 'Real' GDP and net worth per household are measured in thousands of 2005 dollars.[3]

Finally, we have included a set of mostly exponential trend variables to account for exogenous influences on US postal markets. These were selected by scanning the equations fit by Pearsall (2011) and selecting the exponential trends and other variables that appeared in these demand equations with statistically significant coefficients. The exponential trends were recalculated for the PFYs using the rates of adjustment reestimated for the PRC by Pearsall (2011). Exponential trends were first employed to control for the effects of product innovations and other market interventions in Pearsall (2005).

4 RESULTS

Coefficient estimates and *t*-values for the mean responses of indirect utility to changes in the properties of the products using FWI prices are shown in Table 6.2. Each response is *ceteris paribus* and must be considered separate from other responses. The extreme *t*-values for many of the estimated coefficients are primarily a reflection of the exactness of the fit. Price affects indirect utility with a negative sign, implying, as expected, that consumers lose utility with a higher postal tariff.

The remaining coefficient estimates describe the effects of the hedonic properties on mean indirect utility. Regardless of shape, household utility depends positively on the average weight per piece, indicating that households place a higher value on services that permit heavier mailings. The four coefficients for shapes show the relative utility to the mean household of service for differently shaped pieces. Cards and Parcels are the most highly valued, and Flats are the least valued.

The negative coefficient on the presortation index reflects a preference for mail that may be workshared as opposed to single-piece mail which cannot be. Recall that our presort index reflects the amount of sorting left to be done by USPS. Our result may seem counterintuitive when considering household utility. However, 'households' encompasses all mail recipients and senders, including bulk mailers. US bulk mailers are offered discounted rates and other advantages based on the level of presortation before the mail is entered into the USPS mail stream. Presortation allows for an efficient division of mail preparation tasks between USPS and the mailers themselves. Presortation also brings with it many other advantages including bulk entry, simplified weight-based payment, faster service and qualification for a variety of other discounts including many discounts for automated addressing and drop shipping. Therefore, a preference for workshared mail reflects a preference for mail that is eligible, versus mail that is ineligible, for efficient processing, access to better service and a discounted tariff.

Although distance enters positively into the household indirect utility, the relatively low magnitude of the estimate and its *t*-value suggests that the distance that a piece will

Table 6.2 Mean responses of indirect utility, fixed-weight index prices

P, X-vector	FWI	Std Wgt/Pc	Letters	Cards	Flats	Parcels	Presort	Distance	Service
	−Alpha (P)	Beta (x1)	Beta (x2)	Beta (x3)	Beta (x4)	Beta (x5)	Beta (x6)	Beta (x7)	Beta (x8)
Coefficient	−2.5173	1.5007	5.2114	7.9249	3.8575	7.9460	−1.2740	0.0775	2.3103
t-value	−24.5561	13.3440	65.0547	76.6796	34.2338	69.1366	−41.3386	4.5147	32.5296

Table 6.3 (Selected) estimated exogenous effects on the market, FWI

	Coefficient	t-value
Exp. trend from 03/21/1981		
First-Class Single-Piece Letters	1.0209	7.4088
First-Class Single-Piece Cards	0.3706	2.3038
First-Class Workshared Letters	−0.0135	−0.1633
First-Class Workshared Cards	0.3427	3.3216
Express Mail	−0.3399	−2.3300
Standard Non-carrier Route	0.1362	0.8956
Exp. trend from 07/01/1996		
First-Class Single-Piece Letters	0.8090	6.5072
First-Class Single-Piece Cards	−0.2354	−1.9292
First-Class Workshared Letters	−1.0209	−8.2249
First-Class Workshared Cards	−2.0719	−16.9811
Periodicals Within County	−0.1439	−2.2648
Standard Non-carrier Route	−0.2687	−1.9526
Standard Carrier Route	−0.5520	−8.0119

be transported is a hedonic characteristic of low importance to consumers. We have no *a priori* expectation for the sign of the dummy variable identifying domestic mail ancillary and other services.

There are over 25 different exponential trends and other exogenous variables included to account for various structural changes in the US postal market. Table 6.3, based on our fit using FWI prices, highlights only a few statistically significant parameters to illustrate the importance of exogenous effects on US postal markets.

March 21, 1981 marks the start of presort discounts for bulk entry Standard (formerly Third Class) mail presorted to the 3- and 5-digit levels. Our estimates indicate that this change positively affected household utility for First-Class Mail products. On July 6, 1981, the separation of In-County Periodicals from Outside-County Periodicals was implemented, which increased household indirect utility for all Periodicals. July 1, 1996 was the effective date for mail reclassifications and changes that reconfigured automation-based discounts. Modeling this resulted in mean household effects with very high t-values for eight different products.

In general, the estimates and t-values for the coefficients of the variables in the vectors, Z_j, do a remarkably precise job of separating variables that are statistically important from those that are not. The pattern of t-values is unlike the pattern one would get from a conventional econometric fit. Many of the estimated components are statistically significant at extremely high levels. An examination of all estimated exogenous effects reveals that others are quite close to zero, and that there are surprisingly few coefficients with t-values in the middle, with magnitudes in the ambiguous range of one to two. The high t-values confirm previous findings of shifts in utility due to these effects.

5 ESTIMATED PRICE ELASTICITIES

Table 6.4 shows a selection of estimates of own- and cross-price elasticities based on the FWI prices. Own-price elasticities are shown along the diagonal; the off-diagonal elements display the cross-price elasticity of demand for products listed down with respect to the prices of products listed across. The right-hand columns show, respectively, the sum, by product, of the own- and all cross-price elasticities using FWI and, for illustrative purposes, RPP.

Overall, our estimates of price elasticities are larger in magnitude than the estimates that the USPS and the PRC have customarily relied on to recommend and set postal rates. Consider the elasticity of First-Class Single-Piece Letters, Flats, and Parcels with respect to its FWI price. Our estimate is −0.846. While this still reflects an inelastic aggregate demand, it is much higher than previous elasticity estimates. For example, the most recent estimate from USPS of this own-price elasticity is −0.189 (see Thress, 2012).

Nominal postal prices have changed infrequently, but usually in concert, after a period of public consideration and due process dictated by US postal law. Since 2006, postal rates have been tied to CPI-based class-level price caps imposed by the Postal Accountability and Enhancement Act (PAEA). As a result, the movements of all real postal prices are highly correlated over time.

The postal demand models currently in use in the United States mostly include just own prices in the demand equations, and are fit to postal time series. When these equations are fit the own prices become proxies for the movements, not only of each product's own price, but also for movements in the prices of the product's postal substitutes and complements. These movements are nearly proportionate to movements in the own price of the postal products themselves. The conventional econometric own-price elasticity represents (approximately) the sum of the own-price elasticity and all of its postal cross-price elasticities. More formally, if the prices of all other postal products are proportional to the own price of a product then the overall elasticity of a product's demand with respect to movements in the general level of postal prices is equal to the sum of its own-price elasticity and all of the cross-price elasticities. This is the effect that is picked up by the econometrics when a postal demand model is specified without the cross-price terms in order to avoid multicollinearity. Because postal prices all move more or less together, it is impossible to include controls in the demand equations that would allow the econometrics to separate the effects of changes in a product's own price from the effects of the almost-identical movements of its postal substitutes and complements. When fit with just the own price in the equation, the own-price coefficient collects the effects of the simultaneous movements of all the cross-prices as well.

To see this effect one need only examine the sums of own- and cross-price elasticities in the next to the last column of Table 6.4. These sums resemble the estimates of own-price elasticities derived from conventional models and US data. The sum for First-Class Single-Piece Letters, Flats and Parcels, −0.285, is not much different from the USPS estimate of −0.189. The USPS underestimate of the own-price elasticity is approximately equal to the combined cross-price elasticities of First-Class Single-Piece Letters, Flats and Parcels with respect to the prices of all other categories of mail. Our estimates suggest that conventional methods have seriously underestimated virtually all of the own-price elasticities for US postal services.

Table 6.4 Own- and cross-price elasticities using fixed-weight index prices, PFY 2011

Demand for	Own-price or cross-price product (listed across)										
	1	2	3	4	7	8	9	10	11	Sum FWI	Sum RPP
Products (listed down)	FC SP Ltrs	FC Prst Ltrs	FC SP Cards	FC Prst Cards	Period In-Cty	Period. Out-Cty	Std Non CR	Std CR	Parcel		
1 FC SP Ltrs	**−0.846**	0.147	0.005	0.006	0.001	0.018	0.134	0.050	0.045	−0.285	−0.763
2 FC Prst Ltrs	0.137	**−0.878**	0.006	0.007	0.001	0.021	0.152	0.057	0.052	−0.268	−0.492
3 FC SP Cards	0.258	0.326	**−2.288**	0.024	0.005	0.064	0.313	0.137	0.140	−0.557	−1.105
4 FC Prst Cards	0.214	0.263	0.016	**−1.646**	0.003	0.046	0.249	0.106	0.107	−0.292	−0.328
7 Period In-Cty	0.290	0.367	0.030	0.030	**−2.920**	0.080	0.356	0.162	0.171	−0.871	−1.040
8 Period Out-Cty	0.225	0.279	0.017	0.018	0.004	**−1.549**	0.265	0.113	0.114	−0.142	−0.811
9 Std Non CR	0.178	0.212	0.011	0.013	0.002	0.033	**−1.131**	0.083	0.083	−0.251	−0.467
10 Std CR	0.193	0.232	0.013	0.015	0.003	0.039	0.217	**−1.441**	0.094	−0.338	−0.543
11 Parcel	0.199	0.241	0.014	0.016	0.003	0.041	0.226	0.097	**−3.516**	−2.364	0.045

Note: Products 5 (Priority) and 6 (Express) are excluded because they are considered proprietary. For formatting purposes, products 12 (Bound Printed Matter), 13 (Media), 14 (Franked) and 15 (Special Services) are also excluded.

The cross-price elasticity estimates in Table 6.4 reflect plausible substitution patterns among the products. For First-Class Single-Piece Letters, Flats, and Cards, the cross-price elasticity with respect to the price of First-Class Presort Letters, Flats, and Cards is positive and small, 0.147, suggesting that these goods are substitutes. Similarly, the cross-price elasticity with respect to Standard non-Carrier-Route Letters, Flats, and Parcels is 0.134. However, due to content restrictions for Periodicals mail, it would be a near impossibility for a First-Class Single-Piece letter to be sent as an In-Class Periodical, and indeed the associated cross-price elasticity, 0.001, is virtually nonexistent. Likewise, it would be nearly impossible for a piece of In-County Periodical mail to be diverted to the First-Class Single-Piece Cards subclass, and indeed, this estimated cross-price elasticity, 0.030, is negligible. Conversely, the cross-price elasticity for In-County Periodical subclass with respect to First-Class presorts is 0.367 and with respect to Standard non-Carrier-Route mail is 0.356. The cross-price elasticity with respect to First-Class single-piece is 0.290 and with respect to Standard Carrier-Route Letters, Flats, and Parcels is 0.162. For the In-County Periodicals subclass, these cross-price elasticities reflect the most-likely substitute mail subclasses. Due to mail preparation requirements and distribution densities, an In-County Periodical is much more likely to convert to presort First-Class or regular Standard.

Finally, based on the estimates seen in the last two columns of Table 6.4, we make the observation that the elasticities with respect to the FWI are smaller in magnitude than are the elasticities with respect to the RPP. The mathematical relationship between the elasticities that underlies this conclusion is:

$$\frac{\partial \text{Volume}}{\partial \text{RPP}}\frac{\text{RPP}}{\text{Volume}} = \frac{\left[\dfrac{\partial \text{Volume}}{\partial \text{FWI}}\dfrac{\text{FWI}}{\text{Volume}}\right]}{\left[\dfrac{\partial \text{RPP}}{\partial \text{FWI}}\dfrac{\text{FWI}}{\text{RPP}}\right]}$$

When the elasticity of RPP with respect to the FWI price is less than one, the demand elasticity with respect to RPP exceeds the demand elasticity with respect to the FWI price.

This confirms and extends an earlier finding in Pearsall (2005) that revenues per piece are less than unit elastic with respect to the US postal tariff as represented by the FWI prices. USPS tariffs that apply to broadly defined mail categories are actually quite complex. Consequently, when the tariff changes, mailers are able to re-optimize the structure of their mailings, either by reducing content or by otherwise adjusting shapes, weights, and/or worksharing. In the face of increased rates this usually results in an increase in RPP that is smaller than the increase in the FWI price. This less-than-unit-elastic relationship between RPP and FWI helps to explain why both the PRC and USPS tend to overestimate the changes in postal revenues from higher rates.

6 FURTHER RESEARCH

This application to postal services of our random-coefficients discrete-choice normal model and our method of estimation can be further refined. For example, we specified the model using mail class definitions chosen to ease the use of postal data assembled by PFY from 1972 to 2011. Alternatively, the same model could be fit using quarterly data and the post-2006 definitions of mail classes that arose from the PAEA.

Our finding that conventional models underestimate postal price elasticities depends very much on the selection of product categories for our model. Our division of postal traffic into 14 mail and one service categories is not particularly fine. In fact, it was chosen to provide a convenient example for the model and estimation methodology. USPS accounting supports much finer divisions of both mail volumes and postal ancillary services. As the mail stream and service transactions are disaggregated we would expect to find that our own-price elasticities will increase in magnitude. This should happen because disaggregation will tend to introduce products that are ever-closer substitutes. Ideally, our model should be refit using product definitions that reflect the level of aggregation found in postal price decisions. This level is much finer than the 15 products we have used in our initial research.

It may be desirable to include a broader set of demographic variables and/or harness a suitable household-level sample to better estimate the variance–covariance matrix used to calculate the principal components. We have also employed only a subset of the hedonic properties found underlying the US tariff by Fenster et al. (2006). Further explorations may suggest some extensions to the subset that we chose. Also, the low *t*-values of many of the estimates of the coefficients included in the vectors $\gamma_1,\ldots,\gamma_J$ indicate that the model can be fit just about as well using a shorter list of exogenous market effects.

The effect of the regulatory environment on rates and fees is an important aspect of our research that needs further study.[4] To simplify the method of estimation, we omitted the use of instrumental variables and assumed that all postal prices are exogenous. Between 1970 and 2006 the nominal rates were predetermined by a regulatory process; since 2006, they have been linked to the consumer price index under a formula stipulated by Congress. All econometric demand studies of US postal volumes to date have treated postal rates as error free. The generalized method of moments is an estimation method that avoids this probably incorrect assumption. It can be applied to our model, provided that a set of suitable instrumental variables can be identified. Possible data that could be used as effective instruments include unit costs, productivity measurements, and contract labor rates.

Finally, the efficiency of our estimation methodology can be improved by adding a second stage. The first stage would remain the least-squares methodology described in Cigno et al. (2012). The residuals from the first stage would then be used to estimate the variance–covariance matrix of the mean disturbances. The second stage would be to refit the model with the estimation methodology modified to generalized least squares.

7 CONCLUSION

Our estimates of price elasticities are markedly different from those that are produced by conventional econometric methods. The estimates suggest that US postal products are much more sensitive to selective price changes than conventional demand models predict. Our estimates of own-price elasticities using FWI prices range from –0.8 to –3.5, with most in the elastic range. We have also indirectly confirmed an earlier finding that revenues per piece are generally less than unit elastic with respect to the prices in the US postal tariff. The implications for postal pricing and regulation are potentially significant.

Our estimates should be regarded as the early results of an initial exploration. Nevertheless, they stand as a demonstration that a new and effective method has been found to estimate a full set of own- and cross-price elasticities for postal services.

NOTES

* The views expressed in this chapter are those of its authors and do not necessarily represent the opinions of the PRC.

1. This omission may partly be explained by the extreme computational demands of the BLP/Nevo estimation methodology. A thorough survey of modern econometric models of demand behavior may be found in Nevo (2011). This paper also contains an extensive bibliography of the literature regarding the random-coefficients discrete-choice logit model.
2. The largest combined volume of mail pieces and postal service transactions per household in a single PFY, 1933.65, occurred in PFY 2000. Product shares, including the share for the outside good, were calculated for all PFYs using 2000 as the total number of potential pieces and transactions per household per year.
3. The variance–covariance matrix of the demographics variables was estimated from their quarterly series in the absence of a suitable household-level sample. The roots and matrix of characteristic vectors were computed and used with the demographics vectors, D, to calculate the vectors of principal components. All seven principal components were used to fit the models.
4. Virtually everything said here about prices also applies to weights per piece.

REFERENCES

Berry, S., J. Levinsohn and A. Pakes (1995), 'Automobile prices in market equilibrium', *Econometrica*, **63**, 841–90.

Cigno, Margaret M., Elena S. Patel and Edward S. Pearsall (2012), 'A random-coefficients discrete-choice normal model of demand', manuscript available at the PRC webpage www.prc.gov.

Fenster, L., D. Monaco, E.S. Pearsall, C. Robinson and S. Xenakis (2006), 'US postal services as composite goods with hedonic properties', in M A. Crew and P.R. Kleindorfer (eds), *Liberalization of the Postal and Delivery Sector*, Cheltenham, UK and Northampton, MA, USA: Edward Elgar.

Nevo, A. (2000a), 'A practitioner's guide to estimation of random-coefficients logit models of demand', *Journal of Economics and Management Strategy*, **8**, 513–48.

Nevo, A. (2000b), 'Appendix to "A Practitioner's Guide to Estimation of Random-Coefficients Logit Models of Demand" – Estimation: the Nitty-Gritty', manuscript available at: faculty.wcas.northwestern.edu/~ane686/supplements/Ras_guide_appendix.pdf.

Nevo, A. (2011), 'Empirical models of consumer behavior', *Annual Review of Economics* **3**, 51–75.

Pearsall, E.S. (2005), 'The effects of work-sharing and other product innovations on US postal volumes and revenues' in M.A. Crew and P.R. Kleindorfer (eds), *Regulatory and Economic Challenges in the Postal and Delivery Sector*, Boston, MA: Kluwer Academic.

Pearsall, E.S. (2011), 'An Econometric Model of the Demand for U.S. Postal Services with Price Elasticities and Forecasts to GFY 2015', documentation prepared for the US Postal Regulatory Commission, January 11, 2011, estimates and forecasts revised February 2012.

Pearsall, E.S. and C.L. Trozzo (2011), 'Evaluating the demand effects of reductions in the frequency of delivery service', in M.A. Crew and P.R. Kleindorfer (eds), *Reinventing the Postal Sector in an Electronic Age*, Cheltenham, UK and Northampton, MA, USA: Edward Elgar.

Thress, T. (2012), 'Econometric Demand Equations for Market Dominant Products as of January 2012', filed with the PRC January 20.

7. Segmentation and nonlinear pricing in the postal sector*

Claire Borsenberger,† Helmuth Cremer,‡ Philippe De Donder,§ Denis Joram†† and Sébastien Lécou¶

1 INTRODUCTION

Network operators typically use quite sophisticated pricing policies. For instance, nonlinear pricing (second-degree price discrimination) has a long tradition in the telecommunication and energy sectors. Similarly, in these and other sectors, prices are often differentiated according to market segments (third-degree discrimination). Even though it is not the most prominent textbook example to illustrate such pricing policies, the postal sector is in fact no exception. Ramsey pricing is effectively a form of third-degree price discrimination, based on price elasticities. In addition, most postal operators have volume discount programs (a form of nonlinear pricing). While regulators and competition authorities are often reluctant to accept these practices, economists tend to view differentiated pricing policies in a more positive way.[1] For a regulated operator, they are an effective way to cover fixed cost while mitigating distortions that would be associated with linear pricing. When the regulatory policy is well designed and the operator is welfare maximizing, sophisticated pricing policies can only be welfare enhancing. However, when the operator is profit maximizing, this is no longer necessarily true: the scenario where a profit-maximizing operator may engage in pricing policies that are detrimental to welfare can then no longer be ruled out. Nevertheless, the literature has shown that departures from linear pricing are often welfare enhancing (and may be Pareto improving), even when the operator is profit maximizing.[2]

The implications of differentiated pricing policies for the postal sector have received little attention in the literature. A notable exception is Crew and Kleindorfer (2011, 2012) who study the implications of volume discounts. They show that nonlinear pricing can contribute to the financial viability of an operator who faces market opening and intermodal competition (in particular from electronic media).

In this chapter we study pricing policies, which combine market segmentation (third-degree price discrimination) with nonlinear pricing (second-degree price discrimination) – referred to as 'segmented nonlinear pricing' (SNLP). More precisely, we

† Economist, European and National Regulation Division, Le Groupe La Poste.
‡ Professor, Toulouse School of Economics (IDEI, GREMAQ and IuF), Toulouse.
§ Professor, Toulouse School of Economics (IDEI and GREMAQ-CNRS), Toulouse.
†† Chief Economist, European and National Regulation Division, Le Groupe La Poste
¶ Economist, European and National Regulation Division, Le Groupe La Poste.

assume that the operator can group customers into a certain number of categories on the basis of an exogenously observable characteristic at no cost. Under standard third-degree discrimination, the operator charges linear prices that differ across categories. Under SNLP, the operator can use category-specific nonlinear tariffs. This is common practice for telecommunications (particularly mobile phone), in the advertising market and in the airline sector, among others. It is also often referred to as 'tagging', in particular in the public economics literature.[3] In the postal sector, SNLP has a number of potential applications and there already exist some examples where it is used in practice.

One of the advantages of SNLP is that it improves the design of volume discounts by targeting them to the categories of customers who are most likely to switch to electronic substitutes. In a context of decreasing mail volume, such pricing policies could mitigate this decrease and boost volumes. Consequently, this could become a crucial factor in safeguarding universal postal service.[4]

While our analysis provides a methodological contribution that goes beyond the postal sector, we focus our attention on specific postal issues. This is reflected in our illustrative examples, but also in our modeling assumptions. In particular, we include the feature that customers always have the option to use the public stamp rate (reservation utility is determined by a linear tariff and is thus type specific).

The design of nonlinear tariffs is first and foremost an issue of asymmetric information. The operator does not observe the individual customer's willingness to pay. Under full information, the operator would induce an efficient allocation. This is because it can extract the entire surplus and thus chooses a policy to maximize it. Under asymmetric information, there is a tradeoff between rent extraction and efficiency, and quantities are distorted (typically downward) to mitigate informational rents. Under SNLP, the operator observes the customer's category, which provides some information about the distribution of his/her type (willingness to pay). More precisely, it can use the intra-category distribution of types (rather than the overall distribution) to offer segment-specific tariffs.

We characterize the solution under SNLP in a simple four-type, two-category setting and compare it to the standard NLP (nonlinear pricing) solution. We provide a set of sufficient conditions under which SNLP (used by a profit-maximizing operator) is welfare improving. When these conditions are violated, a welfare improvement continues to be possible, but whether it materializes depends on the preference and cost structure. For either case, we use numerical examples to study the impact of the pricing schemes on the various customer groups and on the operator's profit.

We start by presenting some examples of SNLP schemes in various sectors (Section 2). In Sections 3–6 we develop the basic model, wherein the willingness to pay in the two groups does not overlap and where the reservation utility is exogenous and the same for all individuals. This is the simplest setting and yields the most clear-cut results. In Section 7 we study two extensions: the first considers the case of overlapping groups; and in the second, we assume that a simple linear tariff (the stamp price) is available to all customers and determines their reservation utility levels. We examine how this specific feature of the postal sector affects our results. In Section 8 we provide some illustrative numerical examples. Section 9 concludes.

2 SOME EXAMPLES OF SEGMENTED NONLINEAR PRICING SCHEMES

Price discrimination is pervasive in all sectors of the economy. Firms use price discrimination to stimulate demand and increase their profit, but this practice could also be socially beneficial. In particular, in industries with huge fixed costs (and low marginal costs), such as the postal sector, price discrimination allows firms to spread fixed costs over a larger number of units and brings the market equilibrium closer to the social optimum. In sectors where volumes are shrinking, such as in the postal sector which is facing electronic substitution, price discrimination could make sense to maintain the minimum output level permitting to remain financially viable and safeguard the Universal Service Obligation (USO).

In practice, what economists call 'second-degree price discrimination' is particularly widespread: firms set a price per unit which varies with the number of units bought by the customer. This can be achieved through volume discounts or the adoption of a two-part tariff. Through these NLP schemes, the supplier provides incentives for the customers to 'self-select' into categories according to their preferences. Consequently the supplier can charge different prices to the different groups. Volume discounts are particularly well developed in the postal sector as well as in many other sectors producing intermediate goods. In practice, different rates may apply to differences in product quality as well as quantity. For example, airlines often offer multiple classes of seats on flights, such as first class and economy class. Similarly, most postal operators distinguish direct mail from transactional mail, services with different transit time and quality of service. This form of discrimination based on quality is a means to segment mail senders and to charge the transactional mail senders more than direct mailers, because the former have typically a less elastic demand.

When the suppliers are able to differentiate between consumer classes, pricing policy is referred to as 'third-degree discrimination': suppliers charge different prices to different groups of customers depending on their elasticity of demand. Price varies by attributes such as location, time or observed characteristics of the customer. Many movie theaters, leisure parks and tourist attractions have different admission prices according to the market segment; people are segmented into youth, student, adult, and senior groups. Each of these groups typically has a different demand function, based on different levels of disposable income.

These two types of discrimination are not mutually exclusive: a supplier may vary pricing by category of customers and offer volume discounts as well. Such practices are common to many economic sectors. A first example of the combination of second- and third-degree price discrimination can be found in the advertising market. For example, in France, major TV networks offer both rebates based on volume as well as 'sectorial rebates' to advertisers in order to induce them to place more ads on TV programs. For example, *France Télévisions* (French public channels) offer rebates to retailers and distance sellers (4 percent), to telecom providers (7 percent), and to agricultural, gardening or DIY advertisers (7 percent). New advertisers are offered a rebate of 5 percent. Another discrimination criterion is the size of the advertisers: small ones (in terms of revenues) benefit from a discount of 10 percent.

Other examples of policies that combine types of price discrimination can be found in the travel industry. Airline companies typically offer volume discounts to wholesalers, consolidators and tour operators, lower prices for customers who stay over on Saturday nights or buy their tickets in advance, and also roundtrip discounts. Airline price discrimination represents an attempt to charge business travelers more than leisure travelers (because the former have a less elastic demand than the latter), but also to charge more for leisure travel during school holidays and for immediate departure than, respectively, traveling in low seasons and early booking through seasonal pricing and advance discounts.

In the telecommunication sector, prices generally decrease with the quantity of communication time consumed, and vary according to the time of the day (different rates are applied for daytime, evening and weekend calls). In the energy sector, nonlinear tariffs are segmented by time, through peak and off-peak tariffs.

In the postal sector, this double discrimination appears to be less common (at least for the time being). Nevertheless, some examples can be found. In particular, several postal operators offer tariffs that combine second- and third-degree price discrimination for nonprofit organizations. In the US this specific category of mail senders has been benefiting since 1951 from reduced rates compared to other categories of senders. To qualify for these special terms, organizations must prove that they are both organized and operated for a qualifying primary purpose, that they are not organized for profit and that none of the organization's net income is intended to benefit any individual or private shareholder. Eight categories of nonprofit organizations are eligible for this rate: religious, educational, scientific, philanthropic, agricultural, labor, veterans and fraternal. In addition, these nonprofit organizations can benefit from volume discounts. This specific segmented NLP scheme between profit and nonprofit organizations has since then been adopted by several postal operators (bpost, Posten AB, Australian Post, and Poste Italiane among others). Recently, the French operator La Poste has launched an offer: since October 2011, nonprofit organizations, recognized as such by a legal act, are eligible to the offer '*Intégral Utilité Publique*', characterized by a reduced rate. Recently several operators have also experimented with direct mail products that offer discounts when the mailing campaign is targeting new customers. These pricing schemes induce direct mailers to target new customers and to increase their mail demand, the lower return on investment (sending mail to prospective advertising targets is likely to be less profitable than sending mail to already known targets) being partially compensated by lower expenditure on postage. Duncan et al. (2011) present examples which include 'USPS Summer Sale' and 'Royal Mail Sale', where postal operators propose short-term discounts and special offers. These authors also argue that sectorial price discrimination ought to be considered because underlying purposes, costs and revenues of the campaigns vary between sectors.

We now turn to a basic model to study the impact of various pricing schemes, notably the combination of second- and third-degree price discrimination practices (through SNLP schemes), on welfare.

3 BASIC MODEL

The utility of a customer of type i who consumes quantity q_i and pays t_i is given by:

$$\theta_i u(q_i) - t_i,$$

Figure 7.1 *Separate groups*

where u is an increasing and strictly concave function ($u' > 0$ and $u'' < 0$) of the consumption level q_i, while θ_i is a parameter reflecting the valuation of the good. When the consumer does not buy the good he/she has a given utility level u_0 (the same for all types) which we can normalize to zero without loss of generality. There are two categories of customers, a and b, and each category consists of two types of customers, 1 and 2, differing in their willingness to pay, with a higher willingness to pay for customer 2. Overall there are thus four types of individuals characterized by their valuation of the good: $\theta_{1a}, \theta_{2a}, \theta_{1b}, \theta_{2b}$, with $\theta_{1j} < \theta_{2j}$, $j = a,b$. Assume for the moment that $\theta_{2a} < \theta_{1b}$ so that the two groups do not overlap (Figure 7.1). In other words the consumer with the highest valuation in group a has a lower willingness to pay than the consumer with the lowest valuation in group b. The distribution of types is common knowledge and the number of type i individuals is denoted n_i, where $i = 1a, 2a, 1b, 2b$.

There is a single operator whose cost function is given by:

$$C(q_{1a}, q_{2a}, q_{1b}, q_{2b}) = F + \sum_i n_i c_i q_i,$$

where c_i is the constant marginal cost which may or may not be the same for all types.

We consider NLP and SNLP in the worst possible light by assuming that the operator maximizes profit. When the operator is welfare maximizing more sophisticated pricing policies can only lead to a welfare improvement. However, when the operator is profit maximizing, there is a potential conflict between private and social objectives. A more sophisticated pricing policy then necessarily leads to a higher profit, but its impact on welfare is a priori ambiguous.

4 NONLINEAR PRICING WITHOUT TAGGING (NLP)

With the assumption that groups are separate we have $\theta_{1a} < \theta_{2a} < \theta_{1b} < \theta_{2b}$. We assume here and throughout the chapter that incentive constraints are binding according to decreasing (and adjacent) θ.[5] To simplify notation (and without loss of generality) we normalize n_is to 1.

The profit-maximizing problem of the operator can then be written as follows:

$$\max t_{1a} + t_{2a} + t_{1b} + t_{2b} - F - (c_{1a}q_{1a} + c_{2a}q_{2a} + c_{1b}q_{1b} + c_{2b}q_{2b}) \tag{7.1}$$

$$\text{s.t. } \theta_{2b}u(q_{2b}) - t_{2b} = \theta_{2b}u(q_{1b}) - t_{1b}, \tag{7.2}$$

$$\theta_{1b}u(q_{1b}) - t_{1b} = \theta_{1b}u(q_{2a}) - t_{2a}, \tag{7.3}$$

$$\theta_{2a}u(q_{2a}) - t_{2a} = \theta_{2a}u(q_{1a}) - t_{1a}, \tag{7.4}$$

$$\theta_{1a}u(q_{1a}) - t_{1a} = 0. \tag{7.5}$$

The decision variables are (t_i, q_i), $i = 1a, 2a, 1b, 2b$. To set up this problem we have used the standard textbook result that the participation constraint is binding for the low type (equation (7.5)), while the utility level of the other types is determined by a series of binding incentive constraints (equations (7.2)–(7.4)). The easiest way to solve this problem is to substitute the t_is in the objective function from the constraints. Combining the last two constraints we obtain:

$$t_{2a} = \theta_{2a}u(q_{2a}) - (\theta_{2a} - \theta_{1a})u(q_{1a}), \tag{7.6}$$

which together with (7.3) yields:

$$t_{1b} = \theta_{1b}u(q_{1b}) - (\theta_{1b} - \theta_{2a})u(q_{2a}) - (\theta_{2a} - \theta_{1a})u(q_{1a}). \tag{7.7}$$

Combining this equation with (7.2) yields:

$$t_{2b} = \theta_{2b}u(q_{2b}) - (\theta_{2b} - \theta_{1b})u(q_{1b}) - (\theta_{1b} - \theta_{2a})u(q_{2a}) - (\theta_{2a} - \theta_{1a})u(q_{1a}). \tag{7.8}$$

Substituting these expressions into the objective function (7.1) yields the following reformulated problem:

$$\max_{q_{1a},q_{2a},q_{1b},q_{2b}} \theta_{1a}u(q_{1a}) + \theta_{2a}u(q_{2a}) + \theta_{1b}u(q_{1b}) + \theta_{2b}u(q_{2b}) - F - (c_{1a}q_{1a} + c_{2a}q_{2a} + c_{1b}q_{1b} + c_{2b}q_{2b})$$
$$- (\theta_{2b} - \theta_{1b})u(q_{1b}) - 2(\theta_{1b} - \theta_{2a})u(q_{2a}) - 3(\theta_{2a} - \theta_{1a})u(q_{1a}). \tag{7.9}$$

The first line of this expression represents total surplus, while the second line measures the total informational rents that have to be conceded. Under full information (first-degree price discrimination) where no informational rents are conceded, the operator maximizes total surplus, which it can then totally absorb. The objective function then reduces to the first line of (7.9). This would yield a (first-best) optimal solution which is given by:

$$\theta_{2b}u'(q^*_{2b}) = c_{2b}, \tag{7.10}$$

$$\theta_{1b}u'(q^*_{1b}) = c_{1b}, \tag{7.11}$$

$$\theta_{2a}u'(q^*_{2a}) = c_{2a}, \tag{7.12}$$

$$\theta_{1a}u'(q^*_{1a}) = c_{1a}. \tag{7.13}$$

When the customers' willingness to pay is private information the operator cannot extract the full surplus and this introduces a wedge between private and social surplus.

Differentiating (7.9) with respect to the consumption levels of the different types yields the following first-order conditions (FOCs):

$$\theta_{2b}u'(q_{2b}^{nt}) = c_{2b}, \tag{7.14}$$

$$(2\theta_{1b} - \theta_{2b})u'(q_{1b}^{nt}) = c_{1b}, \tag{7.15}$$

$$(3\theta_{2a} - 2\theta_{1b})u'(q_{2a}^{nt}) = c_{2a}, \tag{7.16}$$

$$(4\theta_{1a} - 3\theta_{2a})u'(q_{1a}^{nt}) = c_{1a}, \tag{7.17}$$

where the superscript *nt* is used to refer to the non-tagged (or NLP) solution.[6]

Comparing the NLP solution defined by (7.14)–(7.17) with the first-best allocation given by (7.10)–(7.13) yields:

$$q_{2b}^{nt} = q_{2b}^{*}, \tag{7.18}$$

$$q_{1b}^{nt} < q_{1b}^{*}, \tag{7.19}$$

$$q_{2a}^{nt} < q_{2a}^{*}, \tag{7.20}$$

$$q_{1a}^{nt} < q_{1a}^{*}. \tag{7.21}$$

These expressions show that we have the first-best solution ('no distortion at the top') for the type with the highest willingness to pay, and lower than (socially) optimal consumption levels for all other types. These are all standard properties of NLP models. In particular, the downward distortion on the consumption level of any given group mitigates the informational rents of all types with higher willingness to pay.[7]

5 NONLINEAR PRICING WITH TAGGING (SNLP)

We now assume that the group a or b to which a customer belongs is observable and that the pricing schedule (price-quantity bundle) can be conditioned on $j = a,b$. Note that while categories a and b are observable, the position (1 or 2) of the customer inside the category is *not* observable. For example, if an individual is of type a, the operator knows that his/her willingness to pay parameter is either θ_{1a} or θ_{2a}, but it cannot distinguish between these two types. Observe that since the distribution of types is common knowledge, the operator also knows the distribution of willingness to pay, conditional on the group. Roughly speaking the tagging (or segmentation) thus amounts to using some observable information to get more 'precise' (albeit still incomplete) information on the customers' willingness to pay.

To determine the optimal policy in tag $j = a,b$, we solve:

$$\max_{q_{1j},q_{2j},t_{1j},t_{2j}} t_{1j} + t_{2j} - F - (c_{1j}q_{1j} + c_{2j}q_{2j})$$

$$\text{s.t. } \theta_{2j}u(q_{2j}) - t_{2j} = \theta_{2j}u(q_{1j}) - t_{1j},$$
$$\theta_{1j}u(q_{1j}) - t_{1j} = 0.$$

Within each group the participation constraint of the low type and the incentive constraint of the high type are binding. Observe that we no longer have to worry about incentive constraints 'between groups'. For instance individuals of type $2b$ can take benefit from the pricing scheme designed for type $1b$, but they cannot benefit from any of the pricing schemes designed for group a (because the category to which the individual belongs is observable).

Combining the constraints like in the non-tagged case and substituting into the objective function we obtain in each tag $j = a,b$:

$$\max_{q_{1j},q_{2j}} \theta_{1j}u(q_{1j}) + \theta_{2j}u(q_{2j}) - F - (c_{1j}q_{1j} + c_{2j}q_{2j})$$
$$- (\theta_{2j} - \theta_{1j})u(q_{1j}).$$

Once again, the first line of this expression represents the total surplus (within the group), while the second line represents the informational rent that has to be conceded.

The FOCs are given by:

$$\theta_{2j}u'(q^t_{2j}) = c_{2j} \tag{7.22}$$

$$(2\theta_{1j} - \theta_{2j})u'(q^t_{1j}) = c_{1j}, \tag{7.23}$$

where the superscript t is used to refer to the tagged (that is, SNLP) solution. Comparing this solution with the first-best allocation given by (7.10)–(7.13) yields:

$$q^t_{2j} = q^*_{2j}, \tag{7.24}$$

$$q^t_{1j} < q^*_{1j}. \tag{7.25}$$

These expressions show that we now have the first-best solution for the type with the highest willingness to pay within each group, and lower than (socially) optimal consumption level for the other types.

6 TAGGED VERSUS NON-TAGGED SOLUTION

We are now in a position to compare the two solutions (NLP and SNLP). It is obvious that the solution with tagging yields a higher level of profit for the operator. More precisely, profits cannot be lower because the operator continues to have the option to offer the same pricing scheme as under NLP. This is of course just a fallback option for the operator and in general we can expect the solution to differ, in which case profits will be strictly larger with tagging. The less straightforward question is how welfare is affected by tagging. To deal with this issue, recall that total surplus in our setting (expressed by the first line of (7.9)) depends on only the consumption levels of the various types.

Comparing these consumption levels across solutions by making use of expressions (7.10)–(7.13), (7.14)–(7.17) and (7.22)–(7.23) yields:

$$q_{2b}^{nt} = q_{2b}^{t} = q_{2b}^{*}, \tag{7.26}$$

$$q_{1b}^{nt} = q_{1b}^{t} < q_{1b}^{*}, \tag{7.27}$$

$$q_{2a}^{nt} < q_{2a}^{t} = q_{2a}^{*}, \tag{7.28}$$

$$q_{1a}^{nt} < q_{1a}^{t} < q_{1a}^{*}. \tag{7.29}$$

In words, when tagging is introduced, the solution in the highest group does not change, but we move closer to the optimal solution in the lower tag. More precisely, the high type in the low group now also consumes the efficient level, while the consumption level of the low type increases but remains below the optimal level. These results (along with the property that total surplus, S, is a concave function of any of the consumption levels) immediately imply that welfare (total surplus) is higher with tagging than without.[8] In other words, in our setting the profit-maximizing solution under tagging (SNLP) always yields a higher level of welfare than the profit-maximizing solution without tagging (NLP).

Intuitively, this result can be explained as follows. As shown by equations (7.6)–(7.8) the consumption level of any type, i, affects the informational rents of all the 'higher' types (with a higher willingness to pay) to which type i individuals are 'connected' directly or indirectly via binding incentive constraints. The optimal policy strikes a balance between surplus (which can potentially be extracted) and information rents and to reduce these rents, consumption levels are distorted downwards. From this perspective, we can easily understand that for group b nothing changes when tagging is introduced. Specifically, the q_{1b} equally affects the rents of type $2b$ in both cases (while q_{2b} does not affect any rents). Now in the untagged case q_{2a} and q_{1a} affect the rents of all types in group b and q_{1a} additionally affects the rents of type $2a$. When tagging is introduced, the link between groups is cut; intergroup mimicking is no longer possible. Consequently, q_{2a} no longer affects any rents (and is left undistorted) while q_{1a} solely influences the rents of type $2a$. This argument not only explains the result but it also indicates that it is quite robust and could easily be generalized to more general distributions of the taste parameter. In particular, it immediately follows for the case where the tags constitute a partition of a continuous distribution into two (or more) intervals.

Note that this is exactly similar to age-related discounts in the airline sector. Airlines can give major discounts to young passengers without worrying that this offer would be used by top-level executives with a high willingness to pay simply because there are few such executives in that age group.

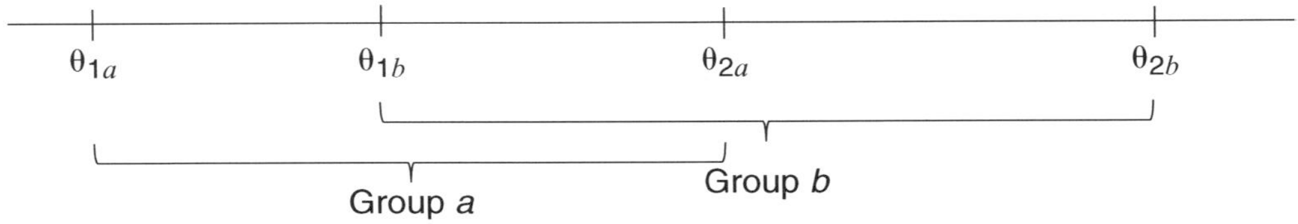

Figure 7.2 Overlapping groups

7 VARIATIONS AND EXTENSIONS

To assess the robustness of this result we now consider two variations and extensions. In the first, we consider the case of overlapping groups. In the second, we assume that a simple linear tariff (the stamp price) is available to all customers and determines their reservation utility levels.

Overlapping Groups

Assume now that $\theta_{1a} < \theta_{1b} < \theta_{2a} < \theta_{2b}$ so that the groups overlap in the sense that (as far as θ is concerned) the high type of the low group is above the low type of the high group (Figure 7.2). It is plain that this has no impact on the rules that determine the tagged solution which continues to be given by expressions (7.22)–(7.23) in Section 5. Note, however, that the actual levels change (θs are different so that the solution will differ). Similarly, the first-best solution is determined by the same expression as above, namely equations (7.10)–(7.13).

However, the untagged solution will change. We show in Appendix 7A that the FOCs defining the solution are now given by:

$$\theta_{2b}u'(q_{2b}^{nto}) = c_{2b}, \tag{7.30}$$

$$(2\theta_{2a} - \theta_{2b})u'(q_{2a}^{nto}) = c_{2a}, \tag{7.31}$$

$$(3\theta_{1b} - 2\theta_{2a})u'(q_{1b}^{nto}) = c_{1b}, \tag{7.32}$$

$$(4\theta_{1a} - 3\theta_{1b})u'(q_{1a}^{nto}) = c_{1a}, \tag{7.33}$$

where the superscript *nto* is used to denote the non-tagged (NLP) solution with overlapping groups. Comparing the different solutions we get:

$$q_{2b}^{nto} = q_{2b}^{t} = q_{2b}^{*}, \tag{7.34}$$

$$q_{2a}^{nto} < q_{2a}^{t} = q_{2a}^{*}, \tag{7.35}$$

$$q_{1b}^{nto} \lesseqgtr q_{1b}^{t} < q_{1b}^{*}, \tag{7.36}$$

$$q_{1a}^{nto} \lesseqgtr q_{1a}^{t} < q_{1a}^{*}. \tag{7.37}$$

These expressions show that the three solutions yield the same level of q_{2b}, while the move to tagging increases q_{2a} and brings it closer to its optimal level. Consequently, the total surplus generated by the high type in each group increases when tagging is introduced. On the other hand, the impact of tagging on the consumption level of low types (and thus on the surplus generated by them) is ambiguous. Depending on the distribution of θs, tagging can thus increase as well as decrease consumption and total surplus of low types. To sum up, with overlapping groups the impact on welfare is ambiguous. We shall revisit this case (and show that a welfare enhancement continues to be possible) in the numerical Section 8.

Linear Pricing as Outside Option

So far we have assumed that the reservation utility was the same for all and normalized to zero. The normalization to zero is not important and has no impact on the results. However, the assumption that the reservation utility is the same for all agents is important. In the postal sector we can think about the reservation utility as being determined by the stamp price; every agent has the option of not accepting the contract and paying the normal stamp price for its mail. The reservation utility of an agent with parameter θ is then given by:

$$v(p,\theta) = \max_q \theta u(q) - pq, \tag{7.38}$$

where p is the stamp price.

To determine the optimal pricing scheme (optimal contract) both without and with tagging, we now have to solve a principal–agent problem with type-dependent participation constraints, which does not necessarily yield nice and simple solutions; see, for example, Laffont and Martimort (2001, Section 3.3). Depending on the profile of binding incentive and participation constraints, many different regimes can occur.[9] Here, the profile of participation constraints is not arbitrary but determined by (7.38) so that we can obtain some results. In particular, we can look for conditions under which the various solutions considered in Sections 4 and 5 remain valid under the reformulated participation constraints. More precisely, we examine when we shall obtain the same quantities for everyone while payments are shifted by a constant.

The participation constraint will be binding for individual θ_{1a} and his/her utility is given by $v(p,\theta_{1a})$ (rather than zero). This positive utility level adds a constant to the (profit-) maximizing problem which has no impact on the FOCs and on the optimal quantities.

With the consumption profile determined in Section 4 the utility of type θ_{2a} is determined by the incentive constraint and now given by:

$$(\theta_{2a} - \theta_{1a})u(q_{1a}^{nt}) + v(p,\theta_{1a}).$$

The solution we derived continues to be valid if:

$$(\theta_{2a} - \theta_{1a})u(q_{1a}^{nt}) + v(p,\theta_{1a}) \geq v(p,\theta_{2a}). \tag{7.39}$$

In words, (7.39) says that the incentive constraint implies a utility level for θ_{2a} that is sufficiently large that the (reformulated) participation constraint is automatically satisfied.

We can derive similar conditions for the other individuals as well as for the tagged solution. Note that even when the optimal quantities are not affected, the sharing of the surplus is affected.

To get a better understanding of these conditions, let us consider an illustration with a simple specification of preferences, namely:

$$u(q) = 2\sqrt{q}. \tag{7.40}$$

The indirect utility is defined by:

$$v(p,\theta) = \max_{q} \; 2\theta\sqrt{q} - pq,$$

which yields:

$$q = \frac{\theta^2}{p^2},$$

and

$$v(p,\theta) = \frac{\theta^2}{p}.$$

Further, we obtain from (7.17) that:

$$q_{1a}^{nt} = \frac{(4\theta_{1a} - 3\theta_{2a})^2}{c_{1a}^2},$$

so that condition (7.39) can be rewritten as:

$$2(\theta_{2a} - \theta_{1a})\frac{(4\theta_{1a} - 3\theta_{2a})}{c_{1a}} + \frac{\theta_{1a}^2}{p} \geq \frac{\theta_{2a}^2}{p}.$$

Rearranging yields:

$$2\frac{(4\theta_{1a} - 3\theta_{2a})}{c_{1a}} \geq \frac{\theta_{1a} + \theta_{2a}}{p}.$$

This condition will certainly be satisfied when p is sufficiently large. Note that p has to be 'much' larger than c, because it includes some markup to cover the fixed cost (or part of it).

To sum up, the solutions derived above, as well as all the welfare comparisons remain valid when the linear tariff becomes available, provided that the stamp price is sufficiently large.

8 NUMERICAL EXAMPLES

We now present some illustrative numerical examples. They are based on the utility function

Table 7.1 *Non-overlapping groups* ($\theta_{1a} = 0.19, \theta_{2a} = 0.24, \theta_{1b} = 0.3, \theta_{2b} = 0.41$)

	First best	NLP (no tag)	SNLP (tag)
q_{1a}	1.965	0.381	1.425
q_{2a}	2.513	1.212	2.513
q_{1b}	3.179	1.965	1.965
q_{2b}	4.416	4.416	4.416
CS_{1a}		0.000	0.000
CS_{2a}		0.953	1.018
CS_{1b}		2.164	0.000
CS_{2b}		4.440	2.276
Sum of *CS*		7.557	3.293
Profit *a*		7.355	7.483
Profit *b*		7.796	12.125
Sum of profit		15.151	19.607
Welfare *a*		8.308	8.500
Welfare *b*		14.400	14.400
Sum of welfare		22.708	22.901

$$u(q) = \frac{q^{\alpha}}{\alpha},$$

with $\alpha = 1/20$. Marginal costs are the same for all types and given by $c_{1a} = c_{2a} = c_{1b} = c_{2b} = 0.1$.

Table 7.1 reports the results obtained when $\theta_{1a} = 0.19 < \theta_{2a} = 0.24 < \theta_{1b} = 0.3 < \theta_{2b} = 0.41$, which corresponds to the separate group case.

The first numerical column of Table 7.1 reports the first-best quantities, while the other two columns contain the results obtained with, respectively, the NLP (no tag) and SNLP (with tag) solutions. The numerical results (of course) confirm the analytical ranking of quantities when nonlinear prices are used; see equations (7.26)–(7.29). Furthermore, we obtain the same ranking for welfare as for profits: tagging is better than no tagging.

We have also studied how the nonlinear optimal solutions resist to the introduction of a linear segment (the stamp price p) as an outside option in the separate group case. Intuitively, the larger the value of p, the lower the reservation utility. Starting with the solution without tagging, we investigate the minimum stamp price p such that the considered solution (NLP or SNLP) gives more utility to the four types of consumers than the linear pricing option which consists of using stamped mail. By definition, the lowest type θ_{1a} receives exactly this reservation utility level in the nonlinear solution with stamps. The minimum value of p is then $p = 0.536$ for θ_{2a}, $p = 0.331$ for θ_{1b} and $p = 0.247$ for θ_{2b}.[10] We then obtain that, even though the reservation utility (with the stamp) increases with θ, the utility (or rent) level at the nonlinear solution increases even faster with θ, so that higher θs resist better to the introduction of the stamp (that is, to smaller values of p) than lower θs.

We have performed the same exercise for the nonlinear tagged solution. Due to the tag, we only have to check two participation constraints, namely those of individual 2 in both groups. We obtain that the minimum value of p satisfying the participation constraint

Table 7.2 Overlapping groups ($\theta_{1a} = 0.19, \theta_{2a} = 0.3, \theta_{1b} = 0.24, \theta_{2b} = 0.41$)

	First best	NLP (no tag)	SNLP (tag)
q_{1a}	1.965	0.381	0.791
q_{2a}	3.179	1.965	3.179
q_{1b}	2.513	1.212	0.687
q_{2b}	4.416	4.416	4.416
CS_{1a}		0.000	0.000
CS_{2a}		2.164	2.174
CS_{1b}		0.953	0.000
CS_{2b}		4.440	3.337
Sum of *CS*		7.557	5.511
Profit *a*		7.428	7.542
Profit *b*		7.723	9.696
Sum of profit		15.151	17.237
Welfare *a*		9.593	9.716
Welfare *b*		13.116	13.033
Sum of welfare		22.708	22.748

with a linear pricing option is $p = 0.153$ for θ_{2a} and $p = 0.186$ for θ_{2b}. Consequently, unlike in the tagging solution, the value of p actually increases with θ. Observe that the value of p is lower, for a given θ_{2j}, with tagging than without tagging. We can see from Table 7.1 that the tagged solution gives more utility than the non-tagged to agent 2 in group a, allowing this solution to better resist the introduction of a linear alternative. In group b, the utility level of θ_{2b} is actually lower with tagging than without, but the participation constraint is also different, since we add the larger $v(p,\theta_{1b})$ to the utility with tagging, compared to $v(p,\theta_{1a})$ without tagging. This latter effect is larger than the former in our setting, resulting in a (slightly) lower minimum value of p with tagging than without.

We now move to the numerical examples with overlapping groups. The easiest way to proceed is to take the same four values of θ, but to swap the values of θ_{2a} and θ_{1b}, to obtain $\theta_{1a} = 0.19 < \theta_{1b} = 0.24 < \theta_{2a} = 0.3 < \theta_{2b} = 0.41$. The results are reported in Table 7.2.

The solutions without tagging are not affected by this change, except for the renaming of θ_{1b} into θ_{2a}, and vice versa. Total consumer surplus, profit and welfare are not affected by this renaming of θs, but of course their distribution among the two categories a and b is affected. In the separate groups' case, we continue to obtain a higher welfare level with tagging than without it.

We have seen in Section 1 that the solution with tagging need not always dominate the one without tagging when groups overlap. Our conjecture is that tagging dominates NLP when the overlap between the groups is 'small enough', but that it may perform less well than NLP when the overlap is 'large enough'. To check this conjecture, we have modified the distribution of θs who now belong to the set $\{0.16, 0.21, 0.3, 0.41\}$. Table 7.3 reports the results with the separate case, where we know from theory that tagging dominates. In the overlapping case, observe that the overlap is larger than in the case studied in Table 7.2, since it now concerns the interval [0.21, 0.3] rather than [0.24, 0.3]

Table 7.3 Non-overlapping groups $(\theta_{1a} = 0.16, \theta_{2a} = 0.21, \theta_{1b} = 0.3, \theta_{2b} = 0.41)$

	First best	NLP (no tag)	SNLP (tag)
q_{1a}	1.640	0.089	1.106
q_{2a}	2.184	0.282	2.184
q_{1b}	3.179	1.965	1.965
q_{2b}	4.416	4.416	4.416
CS_{1a}		0.000	0.000
CS_{2a}		0.886	1.005
CS_{1b}		2.575	0.000
CS_{2b}		4.851	2.276
Sum of *CS*		8.312	3.281
Profit *a*		5.854	6.249
Profit *b*		6.974	12.125
Sum of profit		12.828	18.374
Welfare *a*		6.740	7.254
Welfare *b*		14.400	14.400
Sum of welfare		21.140	21.655

Table 7.4 Overlapping groups $(\theta_{1a} = 0.16, \theta_{2a} = 0.3, \theta_{1b} = 0.21, \theta_{2b} = 0.41)$

	First best	NLP (no tag)	SNLP (tag)
q_{1a}	1.640	0.089	0.184
q_{2a}	3.179	1.965	3.179
q_{1b}	2.184	0.282	0.089
q_{2b}	4.416	4.416	4.416
CS_{1a}		0.000	0.000
CS_{2a}		2.575	2.573
CS_{1b}		0.886	0.000
CS_{2b}		4.851	3.543
Sum of *CS*		8.312	6.116
Profit *a*		6.260	6.388
Profit *b*		6.568	8.559
Sum of profit		12.828	14.947
Welfare *a*		8.836	8.961
Welfare *b*		12.304	12.102
Sum of welfare		21.140	21.063

as previously. Table 7.4 shows that, with overlapping groups, the solution with tagging now performs less well, from a welfare viewpoint, than the solution without tagging. This confirms our conjecture that tagging is better for welfare when the division of types into groups is close to a partition with respect to the willingness to pay. In other words, segmentation (tagging) is more likely to be welfare improving when it conveys 'precise' information about the unobserved distribution (that is, when tags do not overlap or when overlap is not too important).

9 CONCLUSION

We have studied pricing policies which combine market segmentation (tagging) with nonlinear pricing. More precisely, we have assumed that the operator can group customers into a certain number of categories on the basis of an exogenously observable characteristic at no cost. We characterized the solution under SNLP into a four-type, two-category setting and compared it to the standard NLP solution. We have shown that when the groups do not overlap (the highest willingness to pay in the low group is smaller than the lowest willingness to pay in the high group) the profit-maximizing SNLP solution yields a higher welfare (total surplus) than the standard NLP solution. While we restricted our attention to the simplest possible setting, this result could easily be generalized to more general distributions of the taste parameter (and in particular to the case of a continuous distribution). This result shows that the use of nonlinear pricing within categories may eliminate the well-known ambiguity regarding the welfare impact of third-degree price discrimination.

We then considered two extensions. In the first, we analyzed the case of overlapping groups. We have shown that the total surplus generated by the high type in each group increases when tagging is introduced. On the other hand, the impact of tagging on the consumption level of low types (and thus on the surplus generated by them) is ambiguous. We provided an example where the total welfare impact continues to be positive. We have also shown that when the overlap is sufficiently significant, the opposite result can be obtained. Consequently, the welfare impact of tagging in that case is essentially an empirical question which hinges on the distribution of the taste parameter and the capability of the operator to design the tags in a sufficiently informative way. When the observable characteristic is sufficiently revealing to partition the customers into separate groups according to their (unobservable) willingness to pay, segmentation is always welfare improving. In the second extension, we have assumed that a simple linear tariff (the stamp price) is available to all customers and determines their reservation utility levels. We have shown that this specific feature of the postal sector does not affect our results, provided that the stamp price is sufficiently large.

To sum up, this chapter shows that conceding more pricing flexibility to a profit-maximizing operator, who is able to categorize its customers according to their valuation of postal services, can be welfare enhancing. In the current context of declining mail volumes resulting from the competition of electronic means of communication, the positive impact of such discriminatory pricing policy on volume should be taken into account and considered as an instrument to safeguard universal postal service. Hence, identifying relevant customer segments and determining the value of postal services for those customers become relevant issues for postal operators. Regulators have a role to play in facilitating price discrimination when it is welfare enhancing, by assessing pricing policies according to their economic impact rather than by adopting a dogmatic point of view based on some non-discrimination principle.

NOTES

* We thank Michael Crew, Jeanne Golay, Siôn Jones, Paul Kleindorfer and Patrick Legros for their very helpful comments and suggestions.

1. Geradin (2011) and Eccles (2012) give a clear description of the key principles of EU and national competition laws on price discrimination in relation to the Postal Directive.
2. Willig (1978) provided an early discussion. Aguirre et al. (2010) is a comprehensive study of the welfare impact of third-degree price discrimination
3. This paper and a number of others, which are referenced in Cremer et al. (2010) study the design of nonlinear tax schedules that can be conditioned on some observable characteristics (like age or gender). While this appears at first to be a very different question from the one we are considering here, the formal problem is very similar.
4. A similar point is made by Crew and Kleindorfer (2012).
5. With two types this is necessarily the case. With more than two types this involves some assumptions on the distribution of types (similar to the monotone hazard rate assumption in the continuum case). Without such a regularity assumption we could get solutions with 'bunching' (two types receive the same consumption bundles). This would make the analysis more cumbersome without affecting the results.
6. The solution described by these expressions is of course only meaningful when all the *qs* are positive and when the consumption level increases with θ. This is where the assumptions on the distribution of θs we mentioned above are needed. If either of these conditions is violated, the solution involves bunching of two or more types. We would then have to consider a number of different cases. This does not involve any major difficulty but it would complicate the exposition and distract attention away from the main point we want to make.
7. This can be seen from the second line of expression (7.9). This effect is not relevant for the type with the highest willingness to pay which explains that $q_{2b}^{nl} = q_{2b}^{*}$.
8. To see this, differentiate the first line of (7.9) with respect to q_i which yields:

$$\partial S/\partial q_i = \theta_i u'(q_i) - c_i, \partial^2 S/\partial q_i^2 = \theta_i u''(q_i) < 0.$$

9. When the reservation utility is the same for all types, a binding participation constraint for the low type along with the incentive constraints for the other types ensures that no further participation constraints are binding. When the reservation utility level depends on the type, this is no longer necessarily true.
10. To put these numbers in perspective, they are all much smaller than the profit-maximizing linear price, which equals 2.

REFERENCES

Aguirre, I., S. Cowan and J. Vickers (2010), 'Monopoly price discrimination and demand curvature', *American Economic Review*, **100**, 1601–15.

Cremer, H., F. Gahvari and J.M. Lozachmeur (2010), 'Tagging and income taxation: theory and an application', *American Economic Journal: Economic Policy*, **2**, 31–50.

Crew, M.A. and P.R. Kleindorfer (2011), 'Competitive strategies under FMO and intermodal competition', in Crew and Kleindorfer (eds), *Reinventing the Postal Sector in an Electronic Age*, Cheltenham, UK and Northampton, MA, USA: Edward Elgar, pp. 1–19.

Crew, M.A. and P.R. Kleindorfer (2012), 'Non-linear pricing, volume discounts and the USO under entry', in Crew and Kleindorfer (eds), *Multi-modal Competition and the Future of Mail*, Cheltenham, UK and Northampton, MA, USA: Edward Elgar, pp. 1–17.

Duncan, F., D. Longman, L. Mautino and P. Dudley (2011), 'Price discrimination and price differentitation within direct mail', in M.A. Crew and P.R. Kleindorfer (eds), *Reinventing the Postal Sector in an Electronic Age*, Cheltenham, UK and Northampton, MA, USA: Edward Elgar, pp. 243–56.

Eccles, R. (2012), 'Price differentiation: what is acceptable for a universal service provider?', in M.A. Crew and P.R. Kleindorfer (eds), *Multi-modal Competition and the Future of Mail*, Cheltenham, UK and Northampton, MA, USA: Edward Elgar, pp. 18–31.

Geradin, D. (2011), 'Price discrimination in the postal sector and competition law', in M.A. Crew and P.R. Kleindorfer (eds), *Reinventing the Postal Sector in an Electronic Age*, Cheltenham, UK and Northampton, MA, USA: Edward Elgar, pp. 230–42.

Laffont, J.-J. and D. Martimort (2001), *The Theory of Incentives: The Principal–Agent Model*, Princeton, NJ: Princeton University Press.

Willig, R.D. (1978), 'Pareto-superior nonlinear outlay schedules', *Bell Journal of Economics*, **9**, 56–69.

APPENDIX 7A DERIVATION OF THE FOCS FOR THE OVERLAPPING GROUPS CASE

Continuing to assume that incentive constraints are binding according to decreasing θ, we now get a different pattern of binding constraints. Accordingly the profit-maximizing problem of the operator is now given by:

$$\max t_{1a} + t_{2a} + t_{1b} + t_{2b} - F - (c_{1a}q_{1a} + c_{2a}q_{2a} + c_{1b}q_{1b} + c_{2b}q_{2b}) \quad (7A.1)$$

$$\text{s.t.}\ \theta_{2b}u(q_{2b}) - t_{2b} = \theta_{2b}u(q_{2a}) - t_{2a}, \quad (7A.2)$$

$$\theta_{2a}u(q_{2a}) - t_{2a} = \theta_{2a}u(q_{1b}) - t_{1b}, \quad (7A.3)$$

$$\theta_{1b}u(q_{1b}) - t_{1b} = \theta_{1b}u(q_{1a}) - t_{1a}, \quad (7A.4)$$

$$\theta_{1a}u(q_{1a}) - t_{1a} = 0. \quad (7A.5)$$

Proceeding exactly like in Section 4, namely substituting the t_is in the objective function from the constraints and then differentiating with respect to q_is, we obtain conditions (7.30)–(7.33).

8. The proposed reform of EU rules on public procurement: a postal sector perspective

Alessandra Fratini†

1 INTRODUCTION

This chapter aims to review the implications for the postal sector of the ongoing review of the EU rules on public procurement. On 20 December 2011 the European Commission ('the Commission') published its proposals for two new directives on public procurement, one to replace Directive 2004/18/EC[1] (the 'Classic Directive') and one to replace Directive 2004/17/EC[2] (the 'Utilities Directive'), with the stated aims of 'simplification' and 'flexibilisation'. The revision of the public procurement directives is part of an overall program to thoroughly modernize public tendering in the EU, which also includes a directive on concessions.[3]

The proposed public procurement package, which is under examination with the Council and the European Parliament, aims to modernize public procurement rules by increasing the efficiency of public spending and reducing transaction costs for public authorities and private enterprises. This would be done on the one hand by making the public procurement rules more flexible and simple, and on the other by allowing better use of public procurement in support of common societal goals.

It is predictable that amendments and redrafting will take place before the proposals are finalized into new directives and ready for adoption by the member states. Taking into account the draft texts in their progressive stage of development throughout the legislative process, the chapter analyzes the draft new measures from a postal sector's perspective. Section 2 assesses whether the announced simplification and flexibility of public procurement rules is being introduced by the new framework. Section 3 reviews the rationale of the Utilities Directive in the light of the purported aims of the reform to assess its continuing significance for the postal sector.

In the first perspective, the chapter comments on selected provisions of the proposed Utilities Directive that appear to introduce, contrary to the professed aims of the modernization, new and burdensome requirements, which are likely to affect contracting entities in the postal sector.

In the second perspective, the chapter looks at the rationale of the Utilities Directive against the background of accomplished full market opening and fully fledged sector-specific regulation in the postal sector and makes the case for its exclusion from the scope of the directive.

While Section 2 provides an overview of the proposed procurement package, Section 3

† Partner, FratiniVergano – European Lawyers, Brussels.

looks more closely at the proposal that will replace the Utilities Directive, and in particular at the draft provisions that appear to bring in additional requirements compared to the current rules. Section 4 then reviews the rationale for the exclusion of the postal sector from the scope of the directive, and Section 5 concludes.

2 THE PROPOSED MODERNIZATION OF THE EU PUBLIC PROCUREMENT REGIME

EU public procurement rules organize the way public authorities and certain public utility operators purchase supplies, services and public works where the value of those contracts are above specified financial thresholds. The purpose of the rules is to open up public procurement to EU-wide competition and to ensure the free movement of supplies, services and works within the EU.[4] Procurement principles have traditionally been a means of regulating the internal market: by guaranteeing transparent and nondiscriminatory procedures, public procurement regulation primarily aims at ensuring that economic operators from across the Single Market benefit fully from the basic freedoms in competing for public contracts.

Public procurement is a key part of the Europe 2020 strategy for smart, sustainable and inclusive growth,[5] as one of the market-based instruments to be used to achieve its objectives by improving the business environment and conditions for business to innovate. At the same time, the Europe 2020 strategy stresses that public procurement policy must ensure the most efficient use of public funds and that procurement markets must be kept open Union-wide. The Single Market Act[6] identified modernization of the public procurement rules as one of the 12 key priority actions to be adopted before the end of 2012. The revision should 'result in simpler and more flexible procurement procedures for contracting authorities and provide easier access for companies, especially SMEs [small and medium-sized enterprises]'.

Following an evaluation of the impact and effectiveness of EU public procurement legislation and the public consultation on the Green Paper on the modernization of EU public procurement policy[7] in early 2011, the Commission adopted in December 2011 an overall program aiming at an in-depth modernization of public procurement in the EU. This program includes the revision of the Utilities Directive and the Classic Directive,[8] as well as the adoption of a directive on concessions,[9] which were until now only partially regulated at European level.[10] The proposed modernization package announces simplified procedures and reduced administrative burdens, with a view to increasing flexibility for contracting authorities, benefiting economic operators and facilitating the participation of SMEs and cross-border bidders. The improvement of procurement also aims to allow contracting entities to make better use of procurement in support of common societal goals, such as the protection of the environment and the promotion of innovation and social inclusion.

On the other hand, the proposed directive on concession completes the EU public procurement regime by including service concessions, the only concession not yet governed by secondary legislation. The proposed rules aim at ensuring the necessary legal certainty for public authorities when performing their duties and at guaranteeing effective access to the concessions market for businesses, including SMEs, in order to stimulate the development of public–private partnerships, for which concessions constitute a tool of choice. The draft concession directive has been met with strong opposition from the European Parliament.

The proposals on public procurement and concessions are currently under assessment by the Council and the European Parliament in the framework of the legislative process that will lead to their formal adoption. The directives are planned to come into force on 30 June 2014.

The next section will look more closely at the proposal that will replace the Utilities Directive, and in particular at the draft provisions that, far from reducing the complexity of the regime and the burden on participants, bring additional requirements in and limit the discretion of the contracting entities compared to the current rules.

3 THE PROPOSED REVISION OF THE UTILITIES DIRECTIVE: TRUE SIMPLIFICATION AND *FLEXIBILIZATION*?

The current procurement regime[11] treats differently public sector procurement, procurement for defense and sensitive security contracts and procurement in the water, energy, transport and postal services sectors.

The Commission has proclaimed simplification and flexibilization[12] of the existing framework as central pillars of the overall objective of ensuring modernization. The purpose is to make procurement rules, in general, better suited to deal with the evolving political, social and economic context and to support other public sustainable policies (for example, protection of the environment, combating climate change, promoting innovation, employment and social inclusion). As for the Utilities Directive in particular, in view of the nature of the sectors affected, the review of procurement rules should, while safeguarding the application of the principles of the Treaty on the Functioning of the European Union,[13] 'allow maximum flexibility'.[14]

Now, while the proposal indeed provides for some additional flexibility, it has at the same time in many respects brought in more rigidity and heavy requirements for both member states and contracting entities, in particular akin to those already applied in the Classic Directive. Additionally, the codification of the existing EU case law, that has this far shaped the evolution of public procurement law, and other proposed changes are likely to result in a set of rules which is definitely more detailed and complex than the current regime.[15]

In many respects the new rules lead to an increased convergence between the Utilities and Classic directive regimes, which is presumably not desirable in the context of the reform. The Utilities Directive has been justified since 1993 by the specificity and constant evolution of the markets in the sectors concerned, which require a permanent dialogue between contracting entities and economic operators, as well as solutions more flexible than the prescriptive and codified rules of the Classic Directive. The political and economic justification that drove the 'EC' law makers at the time holds even more today and requires the maintenance and reinforcement of the specificity of the Utilities Directive, given the significant progress in the liberalization of most of the utilities sectors. The utilities framework provides for a 'lighter' procurement regime, that is intended to be lifted in relation to the progress of market opening in the relevant sectors: in the absence of sufficient competitive pressure, the discipline provided for by the procedural rules of the Utilities Directive ensures that procurement in these areas is carried out in a transparent and nondiscriminatory manner. Where effective competition has developed in a sector, it should no longer be necessary for the directive to continue to apply. In this context, alignment to the Classic Directive's rules marks a step backwards in terms of flexibilization.

A number of provisions introduced by the proposal hardly fit with the announced simplification and flexibilization of the existing public procurement rules. Some of the changes presented as involving greater flexibility in fact confirm existing options under the directive and actually subject them to greater restrictions (for example, the provision on framework agreements).

This is clearly the case, for the proposal to apply the full rules of the directive to almost all services, by removing the exemption from most rules that applies at present to non-priority services ('Part B services').[16] The current rules distinguish between Part A services, which are subject to the full application of the procurement rules and Part B services,[17] which are subject to limited technical and procedural requirements, because of an assumption of lack of cross-border interest. Compared to the current directive, the Commission proposes the abolition of the distinction between Part A and Part B services (that is, standard rules apply to all services if they are not specifically exempt) and the creation of a new regime for social, health and education services and a limited number of other specified services, listed in Annex XVII. For these specified services, the new regime requires the publication in the *Official Journal of the European Union* (OJEU) of a contract notice and a contract award notice for contracts above a higher threshold of €500,000. While in practice most contracting authorities routinely advertise Part B services in the OJEU, or even follow Part A procedures for Part B contracts in line with a single tendering path, the new burdens in the form of EU-level advertising requirements are certainly unwelcome, given the proven lack of cross-border relevance of these services.

The full application of the directive is instead extended to the other Part B services (such as leisure and legal services), which apparently showed a particularly high percentage of cross-border trade. Yet, it appears that these services retain the same specific characteristics, which made them inappropriate for the application of the regular procedures for the award of public service contracts under the current regime. These services are typically provided within a specific context that varies widely between member states as a result of different administrative, organizational and cultural circumstances and have, by their very nature, only a very limited cross-border dimension.

The above proposal was not well received at the Council level: at the first debate held at the Competiveness Council of 20–21 February 2012, many delegations emphasized that 'the new system should strike the right balance between promoting efficiency through competition in contract awards and delivering on the objective of lighter public procurement rules for certain services'.[18] Subsequently, the Presidency of the Council announced a compromise text to the effect that the proposals may not apply to particular legal services.[19]

Another example is the notion of 'substantial modification' of an already concluded contract.[20] With a view to codifying the case-law indications[21] and defining what will amount to a material change (which will be considered as a 'new award' and will require a new procedure), the proposal states that, where the value of a modification can be expressed in monetary terms, a modification of a contract during its term will be considered substantial when the value of the modification reaches 5 percent of the price of the initial contract. The 5 percent threshold is arguably very low: if it were to remain unchanged, it would prevent any modification of contracts during their term or alternatively impose the use of public procurement procedures to address minor modifications of the contracts.[22]

Similarly, contrary to the intended aims of simplification and increased flexibility appears to be the proposed provision on framework agreements.[23] While under the current directive there is no limitation to the duration of framework agreements concluded in the utilities sectors, the proposal now limits the duration to four years (except in duly justified circumstances) and further provides for mini-competitions for the award of specific contracts based on the agreement. This mirrors the discipline provided for by the Classic Directive and takes away the contracting authorities' flexibility especially as to the duration of the framework agreement, which is inevitably related to the nature of the supply or service purchased and the duration of the investment amortization that can be especially long in the utilities sectors.

A further example is the new definition of 'body governed by public law',[24] which provides that:

> '[A] body governed by public law' means anybody that has all of the following characteristics: (a) It is established for or has the specific purpose of meeting needs in the general interest, not having an industrial or commercial character; for that purpose, a body which operates in normal market conditions, aims to make a profit, and bears the losses resulting from the exercise of its activity does not have the purpose of meeting needs in the general interest, not having an industrial or commercial character.

The definition remains essentially unchanged. The alleged clarification in point (a) has been added in order to reflect better the approach developed by the case law of the Court of Justice.[25] While the proposal makes it clear that minor deviations from the wording or presentation known from the previous directives do not necessarily imply a change of substance, but may be due to simplification of texts, the above definition provides little legal certainty when applied to the case of a postal operator that operates in 'normal market conditions' and has a commercial character, yet receives compensation for net costs of the universal service obligations conferred on to it.

4 THE CASE FOR THE POSTAL SECTOR EXCLUSION

Contracts awarded by contracting entities providing postal services were made subject to the (current) Utilities Directive following the reorganization of the public procurement rules in 2004. This was justified by the need to take into account the further opening up of Community postal services to competition at that time, creating a framework for sound commercial practices and allowing greater flexibility than was offered by the then new Classic Directive.

In the Commission proposal, the postal sector remains within the scope of application of the new Utilities Directive. However, the rationale of both the directive and its Article 30, which enables exemptions to the directive, appears to make the case for the exclusion of the postal sector from the scope of application of the directive, as its rationale might no longer be considered to hold.

The purpose of the Utilities Directive (as well as of the earlier Directive 93/38/EEC),[26] as mentioned, is to ensure the opening up to competition of public procurement contracts awarded by entities operating in the sectors covered. The two traditional reasons given for the introduction of specific rules are the way in which national authorities can influence the behavior of these entities and the closed nature of the markets in which they operate, due to the existence of special or exclusive rights granted by member states concerning the supply to, and provision or operation of networks for providing the services concerned. The aim is to ensure that utility operators, which themselves may not operate in competitive markets, adopt transparent and fair procurement practices to simulate competitive market conditions within the markets in which they procure.[27]

Accordingly, Article 30 of the directive specifically acknowledges that the directive should not apply to an activity if 'in the Member State in which this activity is carried out, it is directly exposed to competition on markets to which access is not limited', the underlying assumption being that if utilities operate in competitive markets, the market conditions create incentives for them to procure on a competitive basis without the need for procurement procedures to be prescribed. In other words, Article 30 establishes the principle that the rationale for the directive can be replaced by the pressure of sufficiently competitive markets, as competition induces incentives to procure efficiently and apply the same kind of fair, transparent practices that the directive requires.

This was specifically recognized in the context of the 2004 review, when the telecommunications sector was taken out of the scope of the new directive because sector-specific regulation had completed the full market opening and introduced effective competition in the sector. Indeed, as then explained by the Commission,[28] the constraints imposed on contracting entities operating in the telecommunications sector were introduced because of the lack of competition resulting from the state's decision to grant a monopoly or a privileged position to an operator (exclusive or special rights). Those constraints were no longer justified following the liberalization, since the sector had been subjected to competitive forces adequate enough to ensure its commercial character operation. Furthermore, the Commission noted that the regulatory process of telecommunications in the EU was centered on the national regulatory authorities, which would provide the necessary interface for implementing EU principles. As a consequence of the above progress, the Commission considered that it was no longer necessary to regulate purchases by entities operating in that sector.

If the absence of competition, with its potential for abuse of market power and inefficient outcomes, is central to the rationale for the directive, it is necessary to consider the full market opening of the liberalized postal sector with a view to assessing whether the constraints the Utilities Directive impose on contracting entities are still justified.[29]

Since 1997, the postal sector has been increasingly subject to competitive pressure. Three milestones in the EU postal *acquis* are relevant in this respect: the first and the second Postal Directives (97/67/EC and 2002/39/EC, respectively),[30] which followed the 1992 Green Paper, set in motion the process of a controlled liberalization and gradually opened the postal markets to competition. The third Postal Directive (2008/06/EC)[31] abolished all exclusive rights in the postal sector and set 31 December 2010 as the deadline for full market opening for the majority of member states (in fact, 95 percent of the EU postal markets in terms of volumes) and 31 December 2012 for the remaining member states. As for the telecommunications sector back in 2004, the existence of a transition period for some member states does not affect the conclusion that full competition in the postal sector is developing across the EU. In any case, by the entry into force of the new public procurement rules, the transition period would be over and full market opening achieved in all the EU postal markets.

Furthermore, as the experience with the application of Article 30 procedure shows, an increasing number of postal services are already excluded from the scope of application of the Utilities Directive. In the seven 'postal' decisions adopted by the Commission until now, it has been acknowledged that the legal and regulatory environment permits access and competition in a variety of postal services (as well as ancillary services) markets, and that postal operators in the markets concerned are subject to competitive pressure. As such, they need not be subject to the Utilities Directive. This was the case for a number of markets in Denmark,[32] Finland,[33] Italy,[34] Sweden,[35] Austria,[36] and Hungary.[37]

It is clear that full market opening does not *per se* correspond to the actuality of competition, which requires that new entrants take up the legal opportunity created by liberalization to compete successfully with incumbents. In that respect, it has been argued that competition is either absent or emerging within the domestic letters sector in every member state.[38]

However, in the assessment of competition (namely of the 'relevant market'), it is submitted that account should be duly taken of the changes that have occurred in the postal sector and of the factors that have emerged in the market. At the crossroads between communications, advertising and transport, the postal sector is evolving substantially. Physical mail is increasingly being supplemented by multi-channel delivery and tailor-made solutions for customers. Postal operators are confronted with a market which is wider than that of the traditional postal operation, where competition (from both the demand and the supply sides) is increasingly coming from electronic messaging services. While this is still to be reflected in the current market definitions, substitution to electronic modes of communication puts a disciplinary force on postal operators' market behavior and can no longer be ignored.

As noted already in the 2008 Commission Report on the application of the Postal Directive,

> At the end of the first decade of the new millennium, postal operators are facing fierce competition from electronic means of communication. . . . Moreover, with the continuous opening of the postal services markets, the incumbent postal operators are also facing increasing competition from new entrants.[39]

Against this background, the radical changes of the competition environment should bring the Commission to reconsider, in the short–medium term, the traditional market definition in a much broader perspective.

In addition, it should be noted that the Utilities Directive not only applies to activities relating to the provision of postal services consisting of the clearance, sorting, routing and delivery of postal items.[40] In addition to the postal services, the Utilities Directive also covers services ancillary to postal services and, in particular, mail service management services (services both preceding and subsequent to dispatch, such as mailroom management services); added-value services linked to and provided entirely by electronic means (including the secure transmission of coded documents by electronic means, address management services and transmission of registered electronic mail); services concerning postal items such as direct mail bearing no address; financial services, including in particular postal money orders and postal giro transfers; philatelic services; and finally, logistics services (services combining physical delivery and/or warehousing with other non-postal functions), on condition that such services are provided by an entity which also provides postal services and that such services are not directly exposed to competition on markets to which access is not restricted.[41] All these services are provided in markets which are *de jure* open to competition and *de facto* very competitive. They fall under the Utilities Directive only insofar as they are provided by a postal operator. This creates a situation in which, in respect of the same service, some operators are subject to public procurement rules and other are not.

It follows from the above that, in the light of the liberalization process, the introduction of fully fledged sector-specific regulation and the evolution of the market since 2004, the rationale of the Utilities Directive is largely less relevant than it was. It is therefore submitted that the postal sector as a whole should be exempted from the directive.

5 CONCLUSIONS

It is not contested that the EU will continue to promote fair, nondiscriminatory and EU-wide competition in order to deliver the best value for money while achieving the best possible procurement outcomes for society. It is hoped that the inevitable amendments and redrafting that will occur in the course of the legislative process will bring the expected adjustments to it and truly minimize burdens for adjudicating entities in the postal sector. The regulatory and market evolutions since 2004 arguably justify the removal of the postal sector from the scope of application of the Utilities Directive.

NOTES

1. Directive 2004/18/EC of 31 March 2004 on the coordination of procedures for the award of public works contracts, public supply contracts and public service contracts, OJ L 134, 30.04.2004, p. 114.
2. Directive 2004/17/EC of 31 March 2004 coordinating the procurement procedures of entities in the water, energy, transport and postal services sectors, OJ L 134, 30.04.2004, p. 1.
3. The new directive on concessions introduces a specific legal framework for the award of concessions within the EU, the current regime originating inefficiencies due to lack of legal certainty.
4. The purpose of EU rules on public procurement is to create cross-border competition in public procurement within the EU, with the aim of ensuring that suppliers from all EU member states have equal access to bidding for public procurement contracts.
5. Commission Communication, *Europe 2020, A Strategy for Smart, Sustainable and Inclusive Growth*, COM (2010) 2020 final.
6. Commission Communication, *Towards a Single Market Act*, COM(2010) 608 final.
7. 'Green Paper on the modernisation of EU public procurement policy: towards a more efficient European Procurement Market', 27.01.2011, COM (2011) 0015 final.
8. Proposal for a Directive of the European Parliament and the Council on procurement by entities operating in the water, energy, transport and postal services sector, COM(2011) 895 final and proposal for a Directive of the European Parliament and the Council on public procurement, COM(2011) 896 final.
9. Proposal for a Directive of the European Parliament and the Council on the award of concession contracts, COM (2011) 897 final. Currently, the award of works concessions is subject to a limited number

of secondary law provisions, while service concessions are only covered by the general principles of the TFEU.

10. The reform brings no changes to the directives on Defence Procurement (2009/81/EC) and on Remedies (89/665/EEC, as amended by 2007/66/EC).
11. The current public procurement directives are the product of a long evolution that started in 1971 with the adoption of Directive 71/305/EEC. In 1993, the procurement directives were extended to apply to public supply contracts, public works contracts and to certain 'excluded sectors' (that is, sectors excluded under the earlier directives), namely water, energy, transport and telecommunications in relation to public bodies or bodies operating under special and exclusive rights. Later, Directive 98/4/EEC amended the earlier Utilities Directive to bring it into line with the World Trade Organization's Agreement on Government Procurement (GPA) and then the 2004 Utilities Directive reorganized the sectors' regime, excluded telecommunications from, and introduced postal services in, its scope of application.
12. See Explanatory Memorandum of the proposal for a new Classic Directive (cited at note 8).
13. In particular, 'the free movement of goods, the freedom of establishment and the freedom to provide services as well as the principles deriving therefrom, such as equal treatment, non-discrimination, mutual recognition, proportionality and transparency'.
14. See recital 2 of the proposal.
15. Sue Arrowsmith, 'Modernising the EU's public procurement regime: a blueprint for real simplicity and flexibility' (forthcoming in (2012) 21 Public Procurement Law Review).
16. Article 84, Annex XVII and recitals 16–17 of the Commission proposal.
17. B-services comprise social services, cultural services, health services, education services, legal services, hotel and restaurant services, security services, and certain transport services. Moreover, services not clearly falling under the A-category are automatically categorized as a B-service.
18. See Press release of the 3147th Council meeting, Competitiveness (Internal Market, Industry, Research and Space), Brussels, 20–21 February 2012.
19. Namely: (i) legal representation of a client in judicial proceedings before the national courts, tribunals or public authorities of a member state by a lawyer within the meaning of Article 1 of Directive 77/249/EEC; (ii) document certification services which must be provided by notaries; (iii) legal services provided by trustees, appointed guardians or other legal services the providers of which are designated by a court or tribunal in the member state concerned; (iv) other legal services which in the member state concerned are connected, even occasionally, with the exercise of official authority.
20. Article 82 of the Commission proposal.
21. Case C-454/06, *Pressetext Nachrichtenagentur*, [2008] ECR I-4401.
22. The European Court of Justice acknowledged that an increase of 10 percent did not require a new procurement procedure (Case C-337/98, *Commission of the European Communities v. French Republic*).
23. Article 45 of the Commission proposal.
24. Article 2(4) of the Commission proposal.
25. *Ex multis*, Case C-44/96, *Mannesmann Anlagenbau Austria AG et al. v. Strohal Rotationsdurck GesmbH*, [1998] ECR I-73; Case C-470/99, *Universale-Bau and Others*, [2002] ECR I-11617; Case C-214/00, *Commission v. Spain*, [2003] ECR I-4667; Case C-18/01, *Korhonen and Others*, [2003] ECR I-5321.
26. Council Directive 93/38/EEC of 14 June 1993 coordinating the procurement procedures of entities operating in the water, energy, transport and telecommunications sectors, OJ L 199, 09.08.1993, p. 84.
27. See *Taking Stock of Utilities Procurement, A Report for DG Internal Market*, Europe-economics, 11 February 2011. The study was commissioned by the public procurement unit and examines all the sectors covered by the current Utility Directive.
28. Commission Communication, *Public Procurement in the European Union*, of 11 March 1998, COM(98) 143.
29. See PostEurop's reply to the Commission's consultation on the 'Green Paper on the modernisation of EU public procurement policy – towards a more efficient European Procurement Market', 10.04.2011.
30. Directive 97/67/EC of 15 December 1997 on common rules for the development of the internal market of Community postal services and the improvement of quality of service, OJ L 15, 21.1.1998, p. 14, and Directive 2002/39/EC of 10 June 2002 amending Directive 97/67/EC with regard to the further opening to competition of Community postal services, OJ L 176, 5.7.2002, p. 21.
31. Directive 2008/6/EC of 20 February 2008 amending Directive 97/67/EC with regard to the full accomplishment of the internal market of Community postal services, OJ L 52, 27.2.2008, p. 3.
32. (BtB) parcel services, domestic and international, light goods/pallet goods services, domestic and international, courier and express services, domestic and international (Commission Decision 2007/169/EC of 16 March 2007).
33. Unaddressed direct mail advertising, standard parcel services (BtB and BtC), national and international, express and courier parcel services, domestic and international, light goods services (also called single

consignments) and freight services, contract logistics, philatelic services (Commission Decision 2007/564/EC of 6 August 2007).

34. Express and courier services, domestic and international (Commission Decision 2008/383/EC of 30 April 2008).
35. Some of non-priority letter services (large sorted non-priority shipments elsewhere in Sweden than in metropolitan areas; including the so-called 'e-brev' (that is, hybrid mail) services, distribution of non-priority newspapers and addressed direct mail), to domestic consumer standard parcel services (BtB, BtC, CtC and CtB), domestic express and courier parcel services, international parcel services (BtB, BtC, CtB, CtC), domestic pallet services, philatelic services, third- and fourth-party logistics (including import, warehousing and distribution as well as direction, control and development of the customer's flows of goods) (Commission Decision 2009/46/EC of 19 December 2008).
36. Standard parcel services, domestic and international (BtB and BtC), domestic express parcel services, combined freight services (that is, freight services relating to consignments consisting of individual parcels and palletized small packages), contract logistics (including the storage of goods and associated stock management, finishing and/or commissioning, marshalling goods ready for dispatch and address management for the sender) (Commission Decision 2010/142/EU of 3 March 2010).
37. Services enabling cash to be placed on a payment account; services enabling cash withdrawals from a payment account; money transfer services; intermediation of current accounts and the related products and services; credit intermediation; intermediation and acceptance of payment cards issued by credit institutions; intermediation of investments and special purpose savings on behalf of others; intermediation of insurance products (Commission Decision 2011/875/EU of 16 December 2011).
38. See *Taking Stock of Utilities Procurement* (above, n. 27). As far as postal services are concerned (§8.35), it concludes that, because of the lack of competition in parts of the sector and the lack of consistent application of sector-specific regulation, the rationale for keeping post 'in' was still relevant (less than it was in 2004, yet still relevant).
39. Report from the Commission to the Council and to the European Parliament on the application of the Postal Directive, COM(2008) 884 final of 22/12/08.
40. Article 6(2)(b) of the Utilities Directive. Pursuant to Article 6(2)(a), a postal item is an item addressed in the final form in which it is to be carried, irrespective of weight. In addition to items of correspondence, such items also include for instance books, catalogues, newspapers, periodicals and postal packages containing merchandise with or without commercial value, irrespective of weight.
41. Article 6(2)(c) of the Utilities Directive.

9. Optimization of the United States postal retail network by applying GIS and econometric tools*

J.P. Klingenberg,† Lyudmila Y. Bzhilyanskaya‡ and Michael J. Ravnitzky§

1 INTRODUCTION

Declining mail volumes worldwide require posts to adapt retail networks to provide postal services more efficiently. This chapter develops an approach to postal retail optimization using both GIS (Geographic Information System) tools and econometric methods.

With over 30,000 retail locations, United States Postal Service (USPS) operates the largest retail network in the United States. However, this retail network is not a direct result of systematic economic decisions by management. Rather, it is a 'legacy' network with most locations established before the 1970 USPS reformation. This legacy retail network may not optimally balance the needs of twenty-first century postal consumers and those of the postal operator for an efficient social result.

Since 2007, consumer transactions at USPS retail outlets have declined 17.9 percent, from 2.5 billion to 2 billion. Similarly, revenue from retail outlets has decreased 21.4 percent over the same period, from $14 billion to $11 billion. As part of its comprehensive five-year business plan, USPS has outlined retail network cost reductions of $2 billion. Optimizing the retail network, maximizing retail revenue[1] while minimizing operating costs, provides USPS the opportunity to achieve the goal outlined in its business plan.

It is a challenge to optimize postal retail networks using rigorous methods that recognize the concerns of all stakeholders and produce useful results. This requires detailed, accurate information as well as thoughtful and tested methodologies. In the US, a practical and methodologically rigorous postal retail optimization process is needed to balance USPS's stated desire to downsize the retail network, reduce costs, and continue to serve the public effectively.

Postal retail network consolidation is also an important international issue, for similar reasons (Berger, 2009). The availability of software and inexpensive computational power facilitates conducting robust optimization analyses. Because optimization of the arrangement and location of postal facilities is a comparatively new task, the principles, methods and tools that can be used are not yet highly developed. Section 2 itemizes major elements

† Economist, US Postal Regulatory Commission.
‡ Senior Econometrician, US Postal Regulatory Commission.
§ Chief Counsel to the Chairman, US Postal Regulatory Commission.

of postal network optimization strategy. Section 3 identifies factors that complicate postal retail network optimization. Section 4 describes applicable econometric analysis, specifically walk-in revenue versus socioeconomic variables. Section 5 reviews optimization of customer access to post offices with supply and demand constraints. Section 6 discusses application of network optimization tools at a national level, and Section 7 concludes.

2 MAJOR ELEMENTS OF POSTAL NETWORK OPTIMIZATION STRATEGY

An essential element of postal retail network optimization strategy is consideration of the interests of both the customer/consumer (mailers and recipients) and the supplier/producer (the postal operator). Classic optimization modeling relies on an optimization function that minimizes or maximizes output, subject to a set of constraints (Intriligator, 1971). Optimization modeling for retail facilities should incorporate the interaction between supply and demand.

It is worthwhile to consider optimization strategy from two sides – the service supplier/producer side and the customer/consumer side (Ruby, 2003). In the postal retail network, USPS supplies services, while mailers (and recipients) represent customers.[2] An appropriate optimization goal of the postal operator as a supplier is the maximization of retail postal revenue and the minimization of related costs.[3] A goal of mailers (in this case – retail customers) is minimization of distances to the nearest post offices where they can satisfy their demand for postal services/products.[4]

Taking into consideration the interests of both suppliers and customers, two main optimization approaches are considered: (i) optimization of postal retail revenue/costs with constraints on the degree of customers' access to postal retail facilities; and (ii) optimization of customers' retail access to postal retail facilities with constraints on postal retail revenue/costs.

To date, studies have adopted either a 'customer-side' approach focusing primarily on optimal access for customers to postal retail facilities (Klingenberg, 2011; Waters, 2011) or else a 'supplier-side' approach focusing primarily on optimization of postal revenue (Yezer, 2010). Applying these methods requires the use of spatial software (that is, GIS tools) and econometric modeling techniques (that is, statistical methods).

Waters (2011) performs his analysis for the state of Kansas. His algorithm allows minimization of total weighted population distance to the post offices in the network (pp. 10–11). However, his analysis lacks supplier-side constraints considering postal revenue/cost levels. His model can propose optimal levels of access to postal facilities, but supply-side limitations may pose practicality concerns.

Yezer (2010) describes optimization of postal facilities focusing on supply-side and maximization of postal revenue. His analysis established a spatial revenue optimization function within a regression model. Revenue is estimated for each postal facility as a dependent variable, using the socioeconomic and geographical characteristics of the market area of each facility as explanatory variables (ibid., pp. 19–20). The spatial revenue function reflects the role of USPS as a service supplier. Yezer compares optimal revenue with actual revenue for each facility. It would be instructive to conduct similar analysis for facility costs. However, the spatial revenue function described in the model contains limitations regarding the description and quantification of customer access.

First, the radius of the market area of each facility is included in the model as part of demand data, and constraints on access are not taken into consideration.

Second, the method used to calculate the radius of a facility's market area is geometrically incomplete. Yezer calculates the radius of a market area as half the distance between adjacent postal facilities (p. 6). Consequently, the Yezer model assumes a circular shape for the market area of a postal facility.[5] The method of radius calculation and the assumption about the shape of the market area creates overlaps in coverage (particularly in urban districts) and leaves certain areas uncovered (particularly in rural areas).

Such limitations suggest a second element of optimization strategy for a postal retail network. The postal network is a transportation network and its optimization should comport with principles of transportation planning. Waters (2011) depicts the postal system as a transportation system. USPS moves 'letters and parcels around a transportation network' and its 'customers travel to . . . post offices' (US PRC, 2011, Vol. 3, p. 1324).

The overall service area of the postal operator should be apportioned into transportation/traffic zones with the retail postal facility as a centroid in each zone.[6] The method of defining the applicable market area for each retail postal facility will thus be different from Yezer's model because the market area of each postal facility will be presented as traffic zone generated as polygon or any other shape derived from transportation planning methods (Lane et al., 1974, pp. 29–34).

Depending upon local topography, there may be significant differences between straight-line distances and driving distances between two points – particularly in rural areas with limited road access; steep, hilly terrain; bodies of water; adjacent forests; or frequent weather-related impediments. For simplicity, both Yezer (2010) and Waters (2011) utilize a straight-line approach to measuring the distance to the nearest retail postal facility. Therefore, another element of postal retail network optimization is that driving distance should be used to measure access to postal facilities because it is more relevant than straight-line distance. Also significant are other less easily quantifiable measures such as availability of parking, average wait time in line, and the quality of retail service assistance. Finally, some retail locations are desirable because they are situated where customers are likely to travel ('anyhow' destinations). In general, this analysis relies on driving distance as a good first-order proxy for purposes of retail optimization of post offices.

Waters measures customers' access to post offices based on population density. This approach may not work well in high-density downtown areas, where a large portion of customers are employees of local businesses who work but do not live in the area. Optimization using residency alone is an oversimplification. A comprehensive analysis of optimal access should take into consideration both residents (population or households) and businesses (employees or establishments), as well as local gathering points such as retail centers. Therefore, modeling customer access to post offices should not be limited to population access.

Yezer in his model establishes a strong statistical relationship between socioeconomic variables and postal revenue. Based on his estimated equation, different socioeconomic variables have different impact on the postal demand in the market area of the post office and, as a result, on the revenue of the post office. The number of households and the number of employees in the market area have the highest positive impact on revenue, while household income has a modest positive impact. Both the size of the market area and the presence of competitive service providers negatively influence postal demand and revenue (ibid., pp. 19–20).

The retail network proposals offered by USPS since 2009 have not included demographic profiles as part of selecting facilities for discontinuance review. USPS has stated that it 'focuses on actual retail transactions of actual customers and local management's knowledge of the retail customer base, based on interactions with those customers' (US PRC, 2011, Vol. 1, p. 63). This approach considers primarily postal revenue and illustrates a supplier-side focus to the analysis. At the same time there is no contradiction between focusing on revenue (actual transactions) and taking into account socioeconomic variables. On the contrary, the Yezer model demonstrates the relationship between revenue and socioeconomic variables. This suggests the following element: economic variables should be considered in the process of optimization of postal retail facilities and their closings. Classical transportation models such as gravity models consider both residents, people who live in the area (households or population), and people who work in the area (employment of the local business) (Travel Demand Forecasting, 2008).

3 FACTORS THAT COMPLICATE POSTAL RETAIL NETWORK OPTIMIZATION

It is important to be aware of the strengths, weaknesses and limitations of the factors and methods used in the optimization process, which can be complicated to varying degrees by a number of factors: (i) geographical/topographical diversity (including water barriers/islands/borders, mountainous terrain or lack or roads); (ii) nonhomogeneous population density or demographic profile; (iii) nonhomogeneous Internet broadband access; (iv) diversity of transportation modes, transit routes or parking regulations; (v) quality of retail counter service/employee helpfulness; (vi) constraints related to the existing retail network since the optimization process does not start from scratch; (vii) change in population and employment over time (demographic trends); (viii) changes in the use of postal services over time (societal trends); (ix) changes in demographic profile over time; (x) changes in transportation networks and transit routes over time; and (xi) accuracy of input data.

Real-world factors can complicate a post office optimization model to varying degrees. In general, geographical features and topographical diversity change the relationship between straight-line distance, driving distance and driving time. Bodies of water, islands or national borders may impose barriers that block passage and require longer or more laborious alternative routes or even alternative forms of transportation. Mountainous terrain is associated with the greatest differential between straight-line distance and driving distance and difficulty, and can cause access issues that may become exacerbated in the wintertime. Some, but not all, of these issues can be addressed by substituting driving routes for straight-line distances.

Population density is non-uniform, varying significantly throughout a service area and even varying throughout a census block or tract. Demographic profiles are similarly non-uniform. As there is a distinct relationship between age cohort and mail usage, areas with a higher average age may make greater use of the mail.

Availability of affordable Internet broadband service can have an impact upon household mail usage, upon the use of packages, and also upon the rate of electronic substitution for letter mail. The existence, alignment and reliability of bus and other transit routes affect post office optimization, as does the availability of parking and the nearby levels of traffic congestion. Customers can be drawn to a post office with more parking available, even if a geographically closer office exists. Similarly, the perceived quality of retail counter service (including wait times on line) and the level of helpfulness of employees is a factor that can draw postal customers toward some locations and away from others. There are locations to which people ordinarily travel for other purposes (anyhow travel). If those places coincide with post office locations, these centers of activity will likely contribute to the postal customer base. Another factor that strongly affects post office optimization is the existence of the current network. The slate is not blank. Locations are not being selected from scratch. Rather, the existing post offices form a base from which changes are to be made. Finally, there are changes that occur over time: population, demographic profiles, and societal trends including the use of postal services, and to a lesser degree, changes in transportation routes. As a result of these factors an exact solution is not possible.

4 ECONOMETRIC ANALYSIS: WALK-IN REVENUE VERSUS SOCIOECONOMIC VARIABLES

Data development, spatial modeling, and further optimization of the mail network are facilitated through the use of software in the areas of GIS, statistical analysis, optimization and database handling. The use of such software makes the application of assessing and including the aforementioned optimization principles practical. This will improve the ability to reconfigure the postal retail network in an optimal and objective manner. This econometric analysis implements some of these principles in optimization of postal retail networks.

First, a relationship is established between walk-in revenue (reflecting transactions between USPS and customers) and socioeconomic variables. The entire US serves as a study area. A transportation zoning system for the US was developed. Each zone is equal to a 5-digit ZIP code area with the post office as a centroid. A base year of 2008 was used.

Original socioeconomic data input into the model included population, number of employees and number of establishments by place of work, adjusted gross income and number of tax returns. The data were collected by 5-digit ZIP code from US Census Bureau and IRS (Internal Revenue Service) online databases. The 2008 data on number of employees and number of establishments was collected from the US Census Bureau (2008). The 2008 data on number of households was estimated based on data on the number of households by 5-digit ZIP code for the years of 2010 and 2000, respectively, from 2010 and 2000 US Census data (2010b). The 2008 data on average adjusted income per tax return was calculated using data on adjusted gross income and number of tax returns from the US Internal Revenue Service (2008). For each 5-digit ZIP code average adjusted income per tax return was calculated as adjusted gross income/number of tax returns.

Walk-in revenue data from individual USPS post offices aggregated by 5-digit ZIP code was set as a dependent variable in a proposed regression model. All socioeconomic and walk-in revenue data were matched together using SQL queries in MS Access. Statistical analysis was performed with SAS Enterprise 4.2 software. After multiple runs, the following three socioeconomic variables were included in a regression model as independent variables: number of employees by place of work, average adjusted income and number of households.[7] The final dataset includes data for 18,629 5-digit ZIP codes in the US. The obtained regression equation exhibits a very strong relationship between walk-in revenue and three socioeconomic variables – households, employment and average adjusted income per tax return. Confidence limits are set at 99 percent and all variables are significant at the 0.01 level. Statistical tests show that all of the coefficients of the independent variables are positive and highly statistically significant and there is no multicollinearity between explanatory variables.[8] The greatest effect on revenue is produced by number of households, followed by the impact from the number of employees. Average income by tax return has a much more moderate positive impact on revenue.

The estimated regression equation is:

$$WIR_{zip5} = -25{,}794 + 73.87HH_{zip5} + 19.48Emp_{zip5} + 2.63AITR_{zip5},$$

where WIR_{zip5} is the walk-in revenue; HH_{zip5} is the number of households in a 5-digit ZIP code area; Emp_{zip5} is the employment by place of work in a 5-digit ZIP code area; and $AITR_{zip5}$ is the average adjusted household income per tax return in a 5-digit ZIP code area.

The estimated regression equation can assist decision making in a number of ways. First, it permits an estimation of optimal revenue as a function of socioeconomic characteristics of the area (on the 5-digit ZIP code level) and making the comparison between the actual and optimal revenues. Second, it provides useful data for making decisions about closing facilities in a particular 5-digit ZIP code area (if the post office is closed, a replacement post office in the same 5-digit ZIP code area is required to assume the functions of the closed one and support customer demand and walk-in revenue). Third, it shows that USPS should take into account socioeconomic characteristics and environment when assessing retail facilities. Fourth, it helps USPS estimate current demand (for example, the negative intercept in the estimated regression equation illustrates that USPS would not achieve positive revenue until households, employment and average income in the area reaches a certain level). Finally, if USPS relies on projected (and not one base year) socioeconomic data, the model can be transformed into a forecasting model and can project walk-in revenue set in a regression equation as a dependent variable from projected explanatory socioeconomic variables.

A similar analysis can be performed for revenue and costs, and net revenue can be estimated. More precise estimates of market area would be useful, using GIS techniques. More precise definition of market areas, especially for urban areas, requires more refined zones based on census tracts, census blocks or traffic analysis zones developed by transportation departments in metropolitan planning organizations (MWCOG, 2010; DRCOG, 2012).

5 OPTIMIZATION OF CUSTOMER ACCESS TO POST OFFICES WITH SUPPLY AND DEMAND CONSTRAINTS

To further illustrate the principles of postal retail network optimization, this chapter establishes an optimization model for the state of Alaska using IBM ILOG LogicNet Plus XE 7.2 software. Alaska was selected as the modeling region for three main reasons. It is an isolated state and can be treated as a relatively independent transportation system and postal network. In addition, it is typically excluded from analysis performed for the US (since it is a non-contiguous state within the US). Finally, it consists primarily of rural areas, and that allows the model to undertake analysis unsuited to urban areas.

IBM LogicNet is a highly capable software package that allows spatial optimization of a network based on various optimization criteria and multiple constraints.[9] There were three primary goals in modeling the postal network using LogicNet. First, this method applies most of the optimization principles described in Section 2. Second, the method analyzes the tradeoffs between customer requirements (that is, access, demand) and supplier interests (that is, revenue, number of post offices). Third, the method analyzes procedural challenges encountered during portions of the LogicNet modeling process (database development, set-up assumptions and network assignments, and multi-criteria optimization itself).

Development of Input Data

LogicNet optimization software allows modeling the spatial interaction between customers and plants with multiple constraints on supply, demand, access, and so on. Each resident of Alaska was modeled as a customer/mailer.[10] Alaska's post offices were represented as plants that provide/ship services/products to customers. Data on population were drawn from each census block based on 2010 US Census data (US Census Bureau, 2010a). To perform spatial network analysis, geographic coordinates for customer and supplier locations were required for the model. Coordinates for the center of population for each census block were obtained from a US Census database (ibid.); coordinates for postal facilities were obtained from USPS facilities database. This is consistent with general transportation network modeling – each census block serves as a transportation zone, and the center of its population serves as a centroid. The LogicNet model also calculates distances as driving distances, and this provides a significant improvement in modeling the approximation of customer access compared to its approximation as straight-line distances applied by Yezer (2010) and by Waters (2011) in their respective analyses.

Modeling Process and Initial Results

We first optimized customer access by minimizing the weighted average distance between customers (located in 534 census blocks) and postal suppliers (203 post offices). Three initial constraints were included in this model: (i) maximum acceptable distance from customers to a post office; (ii) percentage of customer demand satisfied; and (iii) maximum number of post offices that could be kept open.[11] For purposes of this model, it was assumed that each mailer produces equal demand for postal services.[12] The population figure in each census block was adopted by the model as an approximation for customer demand for postal services.

LogicNet permits the user to change optimization criteria or set up additional constraints in an optimization model. For example, the model can calculate optimal results based on optimization criterion and constraints described above with the minimum number of active (open) postal facilities in the network. After several preliminary runs, the maximum distance constraint was set at 50 miles with over 99 percent of customer demand satisfied. The optimal solution obtained in the model showed that in order to serve customers, 126 Alaskan post offices (out of 203 post offices analyzed) could remain open. Weighted average distance between population centers of each census block and the nearest post office is five miles.

One very useful LogicNet modeling feature is an ability to perform so-called multi-objective analysis and generate a graph illustrating the tradeoff between the number of open postal facilities in the network and the weighted average distance from customers to a nearest post office (Figure 9.1).[13]

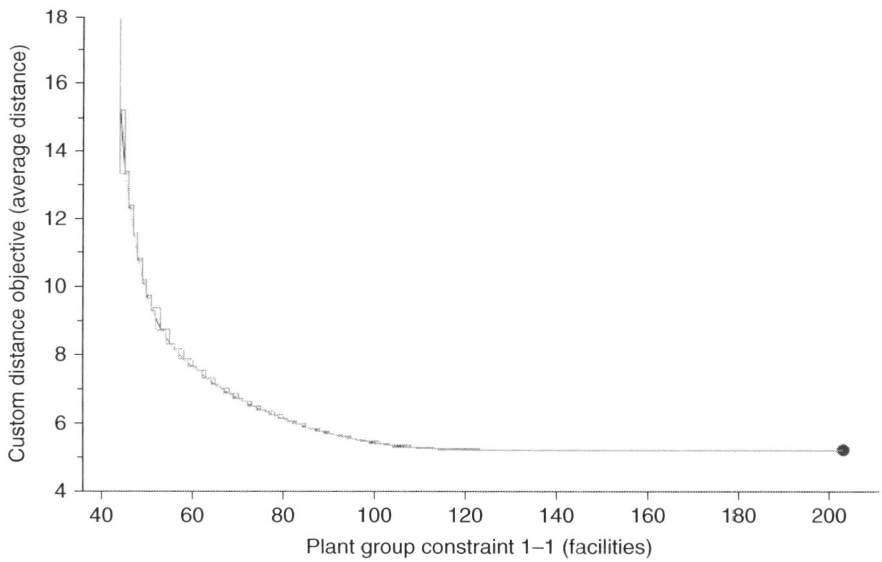

Figure 9.1 Proximity to customers and number of facilities

A review of the plant-to-customer report generated by the LogicNet model (representing the assignment of census block population to post offices) highlighted the need for one additional constraint. In analyzing the LogicNet plant-to-customer report, without a constraint on post office capacity (that is, assuming the unlimited capacity for each post office), the model tends to monopolize (localize) the supply of services in an urban area within one or two post offices. To estimate an upper bound for post office retail capacity, this method analyzed data on the number of retail windows in a post office[14] as well as data that match walk-in revenue and population served by these facilities.[15] Based on these two types of analysis, it was possible to develop a rough estimate for the upper limits of population that can be served by each of five types of postal facilities (related to the number of retail windows in the facility). Upper limits on the maximum number of people that could be served were introduced into the model as a maximum capacity constraint for each post office. Adding capacity constraints into the model while keeping all other parameters unchanged resulted in an increase in the number of post offices that remain open (from 126 to 134). Weighted average distance between population centers of each census block and post offices increased as well – from five to six miles.

A primary modeling goal was to incorporate the interests of both the service supplier and the customers. As it is customer access being optimized, the model incorporated a revenue constraint. Revenue of $10,000 was considered as a minimum floor for each facility.[16] Given the relationship between walk-in revenue of facilities and population served by these facilities, a minimum boundary for post office capacity was assumed in terms of the minimum population that it should serve to generate annual revenue higher than $10,000.[17] However, adding this constraint did not have any notable effect on the results. Therefore, the optimal scenario selected in the previous stage of the modeling process included post offices that would be able to generate walk-in revenue of at least $10,000.

The modeling forms a base for further, more detailed analysis. There are also lessons learned from the modeling. First, it illustrates the broad opportunities for application of modern optimization software to postal needs. Second, similar analysis performed for the State of Alaska could be performed for the US as a whole, or any other country. Third, the main challenge is not the optimization itself, but the development of applicable input data (that is, socioeconomic data by customer and cost-revenue data by post office). Fourth, proper treatment of cost data is required to appropriately consider the postal operator's interests. Fifth, the model can be set up using minimum revenue (net revenue or costs) as optimization criteria with multiple demand and supply constraints. Sixth, additional data on post offices, customers, mail products or transportation can be included in the model to better define a network and/or specify an additional constraint. Accounting for these factors will increase the quality of the retail network optimization model and the value of its potential applications.

6 APPLICATION OF NETWORK OPTIMIZATION TOOLS ON A NATIONAL SCALE

In order to change a retail network, it is important to understand the existing retail network. In the US, this starting point poses significant difficulties. USPS has made important strides in maintaining information on the location and cost of its retail outlets, but this information continues to be fragmented and incomplete for a variety of reasons. At this juncture, a comprehensive optimization analysis using all of these methods is infeasible. That does not mean that informative analysis cannot be developed at this time; analysis using the data currently available highlights where baseline data needs to be improved and where savings opportunities can be realized. The following subsections outline the decisions regarding national-level data which must be made before an optimization solution is developed.

Current Postal Retail Network: Optimization Baseline

USPS has reported operating cost and revenue data for 30,466 post offices in FY 2010 (USPS, 2011). It is important to differentiate between operating revenue and walk-in revenue, which isolates revenue generated by the retail network. USPS has measured the total operating costs for its 30,466 post offices as more than $34 billion in FY 2010, or roughly 50 percent of its total operating costs.[18] The retail network is composed of the post offices, the post office boxes located in post offices, and USPS employees who provide retail counter service at those post offices. However, retail network activities are only a portion of the total activities that occur at post offices. In order to balance the cost of providing retail services at a given location with the demand for that market area, it may be vital to isolate the costs directly attributable to retail activities as input data for an optimization model. For the US, this information is not currently available.

Where data accuracy is an issue, it may be beneficial, from a cost perspective or a time perspective, to model the cost of retail activities as a starting point for a national optimization. If a post chooses to model retail costs at a national level, analyzing the available data at individual locations for deviation from the modeled cost becomes an important task. In order to further a high-level understanding of the cost structure of the US postal retail network, retail costs were modeled. In this model, each retail window costs $80,000 to open (employee wage costs), and the rent and other miscellaneous costs are $45,750 per facility. This leads to a modeled total retail cost of $6.4 billion. Modeling retail costs in this fashion as a starting point for analysis is useful for several reasons. In the US, over 20,000 offices generate retail revenue of less than $150,000 per year, meaning that these offices have a modeled cost greater than actual revenues. Such cost modeling can provide immediate insight into market areas where retail access efficiency can be improved.

Market Areas: Census Data

As discussed in Section 4, both residents and businesses generate retail revenues for USPS. A variety of regional information is available about market areas, including the 5-digit ZIP code employment statistics discussed in Section 4. However, the available geographical information about where people work is currently not as detailed as the census data. For the US, the data provided by the US Census is an accurate informational database that provides the residential location of over 311 million people. Using census block data as a starting point for a national optimization exercise is prudent, although it can be improved upon. The geographical distribution can be used to group residents into market areas, and a distance can be calculated to their nearest postal location.

Each census block is drawn and the centroid is mapped. The distance from the center of each census block (centroid) to the retail facility is measured. This method has limitations, as residents are not captive to the closest post office. This method also assumes that each person is located in the population center of the census block, which is a rough estimate, at best. Since the census block is the smallest unit provided by the Census, this is the most granular data regarding geographic location currently available. Table 9.1 contains the current distance to a postal retail location for the US population using this method.

Much like determining the current cost of operating retail facilities is a key data input for a retail optimization exercise, determining the market area responsibility of each

Table 9.1 Distance between census blocks and post offices

Distance (miles)	Population	Percent of population
More than 20	252,088	0.08
Between 15 and 20	415,466	0.13
Between 10 and 15	1,536,653	0.49
Between 5 and 10	17,098,606	5.49
Between 4 and 5	13,817,934	4.44
Between 3 and 4	26,002,103	8.36
Between 2 and 3	51,288,326	16.48
Between 1 and 2	99,242,719	31.89
Less than 1	101,558,963	32.63
Total population	311,212,858	
Average distance (miles):		2

facility is a key starting point. Perfect market area information is not currently available, but the thorough Census Block data allows for very detailed geographical analysis. If census data of this type are not available to a given post, alternative data can be used to define the problem at that national level, provided that there will be additional detailed analysis to check the accuracy of the broad national assumptions in areas where changes are going to be implemented. One potential starting point for geographical coverage is the distance between current postal locations. This information could be coupled with the number of persons who use each postal facility to develop a market size and area for each facility. If this information is also not available, a postal operator could use the number of retail transactions at each facility to estimate the number of customers served.

By linking each retail facility to a market area, the USPS can determine how each facility fits into the complex geographical coverage web. Understanding this web of coverage will allow posts to determine where retail access can be improved.

7 CONCLUSION

This chapter has outlined potential methods, ideas, and scenarios that can be used for postal retail network optimization. In the current postal market environment, operators are faced with a universal challenge: maximize revenue and minimize costs. Retail access plays a major role in the financial stability of operators. In the US, over 20 percent of revenue is generated through retail channels. In order to ensure that retail revenue is maximized, operators require a clear understanding of their customers and the corresponding market areas. A well-defined market area leads to efficient distribution of postal access. Such a distribution would balance the needs of the customers and the needs of postal operators.

The analytical tools described in this chapter have not yet been applied to the problem of post office optimization. Such optimization should take into account not only supplier and customer perspectives, but also factors such as population density, demographic diversity, local topography and transportation routes. Attempts at optimization without considering interests of both the postal operator/supplier and the postal customers are likely to produce distorted and misleading results.

Moreover, geography, population density and socioeconomic profiles differ among the various nations. Those national differences suggest the value of a flexible analytical approach to optimizing a retail postal network, an approach that can work with a variety of diverse geographies and population profiles. An approach which uses either only GIS tools or only econometric tools lacks the flexibility afforded by utilizing a combination of these methods.

NOTES

* The views represented are solely those of the authors and not necessarily those of the Postal Regulatory Commission.

1. Maximizing retail revenue relates to connecting potential customers with sales locations and reducing geographical and other obstacles to access. It is qualitatively different from profit maximization of the enterprise.
2. Mailers not only receive mail products, but also send them.
3. The supplier (postal operator) must also maintain a service quality level acceptable to customers.
4. These may include the purchase of stamps or money orders, sending of parcels, renting post office boxes, or other services.
5. Professor Yezer recognizes the limitation of such assumption and suggests that it would be useful to consider the precise shape of the market area (Yezer, 2010, p. 20).
6. In transportation and regional models a centroid is a point used to represent the characteristic activity of a zone (University of New Brunswick, Transportation Group, 2008). The centroid may focus on the highest population density and/or transit activity in the zone. In other words, and in accordance with the principles of transportation planning, a zone centroid should be located 'at the centre of gravity of all trips from the zone' (Lane et al., 1974, p. 53). That is why the centroid location in the zone might be very different from the geographical center of the zone.
7. Due to multicollinearity observed between the number of employees and the number of establishments, only one variable remained in a regression model. The choice of the variable left in the model was confirmed by statistical testing.
8. The absolute t-values of estimated regression coefficients are larger than 7, F-value is 11,160 and R-square is 0.64. A variance inflation factor test ensures that there is no multicollinearity between the explanatory/dependent variables.
9. LogicNet Plus XE software could be used for 'supply chain network optimization and . . . decision support solution for ongoing strategic planning' (IBM, 2012).
10. Such simplification would allow modeling the network and performing the desired analysis. However, in the future in modeling the customers, local businesses or their employees should also be represented.
11. Since all post offices included in the model (totaling 203) are pre-existing post offices, it was assumed that they might all be kept open. So, the number of post offices was set to between 1 and 203 in the model.
12. Services provided by postal facilities were considered as one aggregated product. It will be useful in the future to model demand for the most frequently used mail products and services.
13. The distance from the center of population block to a post office is an approximation for customers' access adopted in the model. The more refined the zones (population areas) used in the model, the more precise the results.
14. A nonlinear power regression was established between walk-in revenue and number of retail windows. The analysis was performed for the State of Alaska, which is characterized by substantial isolation from other parts of the country, as well as comparatively low population density. It is possible that similar analysis performed for other states, or at a national level, might produce very different results.
15. Population data were collected by 5-digit ZIP code. All walk-in revenue data by post office were aggregated by 5-digit ZIP code. The population of those 5-digit ZIP codes with no post offices was redistributed by other 5-digit ZIP codes with a post office based on a minimum driving distance criterion. Microsoft MapPoint software was used in this analysis. The relationship between walk-in revenue and population was estimated in a form of a polynomial function.
16. This complies with the recent estimates made by USPS for facilities in the State of Alaska (Boldt, 2011, p. 15).

17. According to the estimates relied upon in this chapter, a post office should serve at least 75 households to be able to generate annual revenue of at least $10,000. It is important to note that the postal revenue will be generated not only by these households, but also by local businesses and their employees. Since the overall analysis was performed for the State of Alaska, these estimates are applicable mostly to low-density areas.
18. The Postal Service total operating cost was $75.6 billion in FY 2010.

REFERENCES

Berger, R. (2009), 'Postal Network Performance. Report on Developments of Central and Eastern Europe's Postal Markets', Issue No. 1, February, available at: http://www.rolandberger.ro/media/pdf/Roland_Berger_CEE_Postal_Snapshot_Issue1_20090303.pdf (accessed 9 May 2012).

Boldt, James. J. (2011), 'Direct Testimony of James J. Boldt on Behalf of United States Postal Service', USPS-T-1, PRC Docket No. N2011-1, July 27, available at: http://www.prc.gov/Docs/74/74143/Testimony.FINAL.pdf (accessed 9 May 2012).

Denver Regional Council of Governments (DRCOG) (2012), 'Transportation Analysis Zones TAZ-2832', available at: http://gis.drcog.org/datacatalog/content/transportation-analysis-zones-taz-2832 (accessed 9 May 2012).

IBM, Inc. (2012), Internet website available at: http://www-01.ibm.com/software/integration/sca/logicnet-plus-xe/ (accessed 9 May 2012).

Intriligator, M.D. (1971), *Mathematical Optimization and Economic Theory*, New York: Prentice-Hall.

Klingenberg, John (2011), 'Direct Testimony of John P. Klingenberg on Behalf of the Public Representative PR-T-2', PRC Docket No. N2011-1, September 26, available at: http://www.prc.gov/Docs/76/76096/PR-T-2.pdf (accessed 9 May 2012).

Lane, R., T.J. Powell and P. Prestwood Smith (1974), *Analytical Transport Planning*, London: Duckworth, available at: http://www.unb.ca/transpo/mynet/mty18.htm (accessed 9 May 2012).

Metropolitan Washington Council of Governments (MWCOG) (2010), 3722 TAZ Reference Maps for Cooperative Forecasts, December 17, Publication Number 20108400, available at: http://www.mwcog.org/store/item.asp?PUBLICATION_ID=400 (accessed 9 May 2012).

Ruby, Douglas A. (2003), 'Digital Economist. The Optimization Principle', available at: http://www.digitaleconomist.org/optimization.html (accessed 9 May 2012).

Travel Demand Forecasting (2008), 'Theory and Concepts. The Gravity Model', available at: http://www.princeton.edu/~alaink/Orf467F08/The%20Gravity%20Model (accessed 9 May 2012).

University of New Brunswick, Transportation Group (2008), 'Transport and Regional Model Centroids, Choosing Centroids', available at: http://www.unb.ca/transpo/mynet/mty18.htm (accessed 9 May 2012).

US Census Bureau (2008), 'County Business Patterns/ZIP Code Business Patterns', available at: http://www.census.gov/econ/cbp/index.html (accessed 9 May 2012).

US Census Bureau (2010a), '2010 Census Centers of Population by Census Block Group', available at: http://www.census.gov/geo/www/2010census/centerpop2010/blkgrp/bgcenters.html (accessed 9 May 2012).

US Census Bureau (2010b), 'American Fact Finder', available at: http://factfinder2.census.gov/faces/nav/jsf/pages/index.xhtml (accessed 9 May 2012).

US Internal Revenue Service (2008), available at: http://www.irs.gov/taxstats/indtaxstats/index.html (accessed 9 May 2012).

US Postal Regulatory Commission (PRC) (2011), Official Transcript of Proceedings before the Postal Regulatory Commission, Docket No. N2011-1, Volume 1, September 8, available at: http://www.prc.gov/Docs/75/75625/110908_PDF.pdf, and Volume 3, October 18, available at: http://www.prc.gov/Docs/76/76832/111017_PRC.pdf (both accessed 9 May 2012).

US Postal Service (USPS) (2011), USPS-LR-N0211-1/5 – Facility Specific Cost and Revenue Data Tracked by USPS Retail Facility Finance Number, available at: http://www.prc.gov/Docs/75/75092/LR.5.pdf, filed on August 24, 2011 (accessed 9 May 2012).

Waters, Nigel (2011), 'Testimony of Nigel Waters PR-T-1', Retail Access Optimization Initiative PRC Docket No. N2011-1, September 26, available at: http://www.prc.gov/Docs/76/76093/PR-T-1.pdf (accessed 9 May 2012).

Yezer, Anthony M. (2010), 'Analyzing the Postal Service's Retail Network Using an Objective Modeling Approach', June 14, available at: http://www.uspsoig.gov/foia_files/RARC-WP-10-004.pdf (accessed 9 May 2012). Conducted for the USPS Office of Inspector General with input from Global Insight.

10. Estimating long-run incremental costs in the postal sector: a UK perspective*

Leonardo Mautino,[†] Paul Dudley,[‡] James Prettyman[§] and Fenella Heagney[¶]

1 INTRODUCTION

In the UK, the presence of both digital and postal competition has led to proposals to reduce the levels of *ex ante* regulation, and move towards *ex post* regulation following the transfer of regulatory duties to Ofcom in 2011. This was accompanied by a greater emphasis on the provision of information by the universal service provider (Ofcom, 2012a). This provision of information includes the estimation of the long-run marginal or incremental costs to assess whether prices are recovering those costs and contributing to fixed costs and profit.

The European Commission guidelines for assessing anti-competitive behavior of a dominant firm in any sector refer to long-run average incremental cost (LRAIC) estimates as one of the relevant cost benchmarks (European Commission, 2009). In general, prices that recover those costs are considered to be reasonable and prices below long-run incremental costs may be reasonable only in more limited circumstances. These cost benchmarks have been applied in several sectors and were used outside of the UK in some EU decisions for the postal sector.

While the approach to estimating LRAICs in other sectors, notably telecoms, provides a useful starting point from which to inform their development for the postal sector, aspects of the postal sector are quite different, and their effects need to be considered carefully. These include the presence of declining volumes,[1] relatively low capital/labor cost ratios, fixed costs attributed to the ubiquity requirement of the Universal Service Obligation (USO) and the incumbent having a potentially high cost base relative to new starters.

In the postal sector there are several studies on cost elasticity estimation for parts of the pipeline (for example, Cazals et al., 2012). There are also some papers exploring marginal costs (for example, Bradley et al., 1993) and the allocation of common costs (for example, Robinson and McMurdie, 2009).

In this chapter we consider the approach and development of LRAICs for the postal sector. In the UK, the pricing structure changed in 2006 to accommodate the item size.

† Managing Consultant, Oxera.
‡ Head of Economics, Royal Mail Group.
§ Business Modeller, Royal Mail Group.
¶ Business Modeller, Royal Mail Group.

The decline in mail volumes commenced around 2004, and has been accompanied more recently by substantial changes to the network operation as well as regulatory change towards greater deregulation, commercial freedom and innovation. Consequently, it is a particularly appropriate time to review LRAICs and to consider how they might be estimated in practice, given the specific characteristics of the postal sector.

We review the alternative methods of LRAIC estimation available in Section 2, consider the alternative cost measures that are related to LRAIC and have been used to inform pricing decisions in telecoms in Section 3 and discuss features of the postal sector that influence the approach to LRAIC estimation in Section 4. In Section 5 we describe the development of LRAIC estimates and we conclude with remarks on guiding principles in Section 6.

2 ALTERNATIVE METHODS TO ESTIMATION

There are two broad approaches to calculating LRAICs. The first, 'top-down' approach starts from the operator's activity costs from the costing system and estimates the expected long-run change in cost arising from a hypothetical reduction or decrement in volume and/or workload. Typically, it assumes that the operator's costs are known and reasonably efficient and therefore representative of the existing network requirements to meet demand. In contrast, the second, 'bottom-up' approach assumes that the operator's network is known and can be represented within a stylized model such that the efficiently incurred costs associated with meeting an increase or increment of demand can be reasonably identified.

In theory these alternative approaches should lead to similar estimates. In practice, the two approaches can yield different estimates where their assumptions are different and not well-aligned. Indeed, a relevant set of assumptions to the different approaches relates to the level of optimization of the network and operational practices. For example, the top-down approach tends to assume the existing network topology (scorched node) as given, while the bottom-up models can also consider additional modifications to the network nodes (modified scorched node) or a greenfield-site (scorched earth) approach.[2] However, this might be an initial position with their alignment improving over time through the review of the costs and network operation, and a common analysis of the future network state. For example, within the first approach, information about the network operation from models that take account of network topology can be used to assess the change in cost arising from a hypothetical reduction or decrement in volume and/or workload and inform the assumptions used.

The choice of models often depends on the purpose, and multiple purposes can lead to multiple approaches. In practice, a number of different models have been applied in regulatory and competition precedents which combine different features of the relevant dimensions that are considered by the alternative methods of estimation.

When assessing the pricing behavior of a firm, there is precedent for commencing with the firm's costs and the top-down approach. As historic costs are audited, updated and known to the firm undertaking the pricing, that party must know when it is pricing in a manner that does not recover costs. However, these are accounting, fully distributed costs, and LRAIC estimates may be formed by applying additional sets of assumptions to those accounting costs. While the LRAICs estimated may not be subject to the same auditing requirements as the accounting costs, the firm must know when it is pricing in a manner that does not recover their LRAICs, and this is a key motivation in the use of top-down estimates in competition law cases.

Even so, the economic costs to inform pricing should be forward looking, as future prices should recover a forward-looking assessment of LRAIC. Under some circumstances, this can lead to the need to amend estimates based on historic costs, particularly where future investments are known to change future activities and costs, and to change the expected cost from a hypothetical decrement/increment in volume and workload.

In many sectors the incumbent firm is often seen to have an advantage over its competitors in that it already has a network with sunk fixed costs, which could enable it to exploit economies of scale. In such circumstances, the incremental cost to the incumbent of an existing network expansion might be expected to be less than that of an entrant who might be expected to incur some additional start-up costs. For example, in the telecoms sector, investigations into the pricing practices have started using the top-down approach, because of the need to look for efficient entry where the incumbent is considered to set an appropriate, efficient benchmark (European Commission, 2007).

However, the advantage of the incumbent over the entrant is significantly more limited in the postal sector. The incumbent's network is less dependent on sunk fixed costs, and more dependent on a labor force with defined, and often less flexible, terms and conditions of employment associated with the provision of the universal service. The potential for the incumbent to have excess capability in a declining market and its need to modernize are calls not only for change in operational costs but also for a forward-looking emphasis for LRAIC estimation. This is all the more necessary if alternative operators can select the customers they wish to offer services, while the incumbent must provide the universal coverage and service. Consequently, there are reasons why LRAIC estimates based on the incumbent's historic costs alone might exceed those formed from a more forward-looking approach to costs or an alternative operator's costs.

There is then a natural progression of thought and development of the LRAIC estimates for the postal sector. It starts with the incumbent's historic costs and network operation, but then moves on to consider the incumbent's expected future costs and network operation, and those of an entrant.

3 ALTERNATIVE COST MEASURES OF ESTIMATION

LRAIC estimates per item and long-run incremental cost (LRIC) in total for all relevant items can be formed for the pipeline activities which are then mapped into products to form LRAIC and LRIC estimates of the products. This mapping can take account of the volume or workload for that product including, for example, the number of times a particular item goes through a specific activity.

The LRIC estimation of pipeline activities can be undertaken at different levels of aggregation, depending on the regulatory and commercial objectives. At the most aggregated level there is the whole business. At a more disaggregated level there are the major pipeline functions including collection, processing, transportation and delivery. At a further layer of disaggregation there are individual activities, with collections

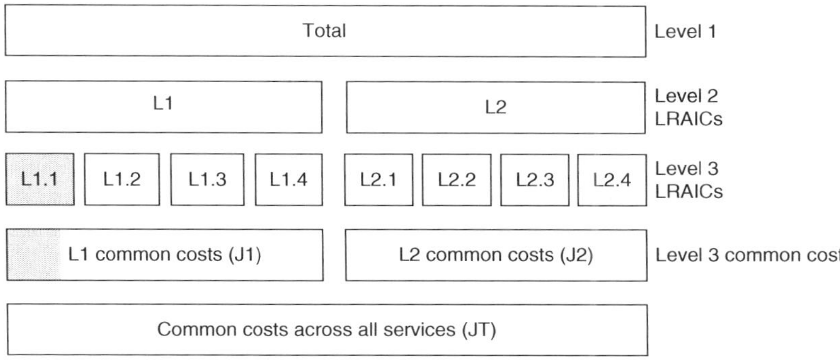

Figure 10.1 Illustration of DLRIC

from postboxes, counters and firms. As the level of aggregation increases, the LRAIC for the defined increment will tend to converge towards the fully allocated cost for that increment.

The Postal Services Directive refers to the need for prices to be cost oriented and this can involve two tests, which become relevant in the presence of common costs. An initial test for cost orientation is that a LRAIC-based price yields revenue between the LRIC and the stand-alone costs (SAC) (IRG, 2000). A price with revenue below the LRIC floor would mean that not all incremental costs would be recovered (with no contribution to common costs); while a price above SAC would mean that an amount in excess of the LRIC plus all of the relevant common costs would be recovered.

Under the first test no individual service would be deemed to be priced excessively if all prices were at SAC, but taken together the services might be priced excessively since revenues would be more than sufficient to recover multiples of all incremental and common costs. A second test might then be necessary whereby the revenues of combinations of services straddling common costs are compared to the LRIC and SAC of these services measured as a single increment. This is sometimes known as the combinatorial test. The second test can become computationally onerous to address all of the possible combinations and has led to some proxies.

In the UK telecoms sector, distributed LRIC (DLRIC) and distributed SAC (DSAC) have been deployed, as guideline cost measures between LRIC and SAC. While they have an accounting and computational definition, they have no specific economic interpretation, which has led some to view them as indicative guideline measures rather than absolute rules. Nevertheless, within the UK telecoms, they have been used in the sense of absolute rules for regulatory determinations on occasions in the past (Ofcom, 2012b).

Figure 10.1 illustrates the DLRIC calculations set out in Appendix 10A. DLRIC is calculated by adding a share of the common costs for a group of services in the incremental cost of an individual service within the service group, such that the sum of DLRICs equals the LRIC for the group of services. The share of common costs is allocated to the individual service by using equi-proportional markup, EPMU (that is, in proportion to the LRIC of the relevant individual services). DLRIC would generally be higher than the pure LRIC of an individual product.

Figure 10.2 illustrates the SAC and DSAC calculations set out in Appendix 10A. The

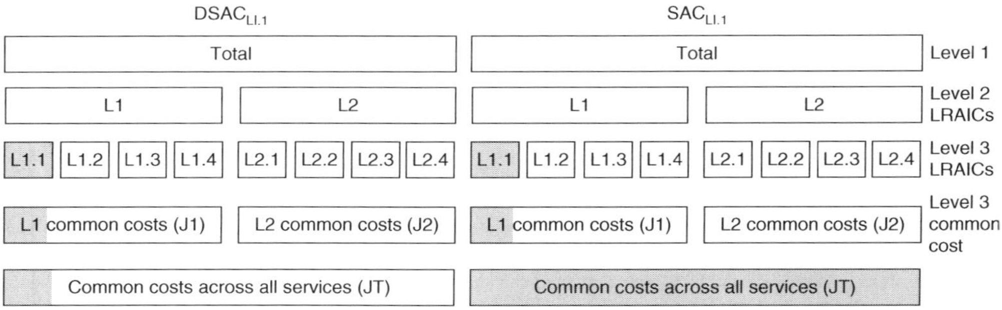

Figure 10.2 Illustration of DSAC

SAC of a service is the cost of providing that particular service on its own, and is equal to the sum of the incremental cost of the service and all the costs that are common between that service and other services. DSAC distributes the stand-alone costs of a broad increment of services pro rata among each of the services within that increment. The DSAC of a service, therefore, includes a proportion of costs that are common across all groups of services. Figure 10.2 shows that the DLRIC of an increment will be higher than LRIC and that the DSAC will be lower than the SAC for the corresponding increment. As such, a cost-orientation rule based on DLRIC and DSAC would result in a narrower range over which prices could be set.

In terms of the level of aggregation, the estimates of LRIC and SAC, DLRIC and DSAC are furthest apart at the greatest levels of disaggregation and gradually converge at higher levels of aggregation. It is also the case that these terms increase in value from LRIC to DLRIC, to DSAC to SAC, and converge towards the fully distributed costs at higher levels of aggregation.

Fully distributed costs, DLRIC and DSAC all apply an EPMU for allocating common costs and are therefore are accounting estimates of what common costs could be borne in different markets. In markets where there is a dominant provider and significant market power, an EPMU may not be unreasonable and may not unduly distort the market, but where there is less market power and competition is present, it may be unreasonable and distortionary (De Donder et al., 2006, 2008). As these measures are proxies, by their nature they are not necessarily appropriate in all market circumstances. While it might be informative to know when revenues are lower than DLRIC, higher than DSAC and lower or higher than fully distributed costs, it would seem important to be wary of using them as universally applicable pricing rules for European or competition law assessments. Rather it would seem more appropriate to view them as benchmarks that enable businesses and authorities to understand when prices might need an enhanced review and justification.

4 FEATURES OF THE POSTAL SECTOR THAT INFLUENCE THE APPROACH

There are several characteristics that are particularly relevant to LRAIC estimation for the postal sector, and while related to the methods applied in other sectors, suggest a different prioritization and emphasis. The mail industry has faced volume decline with the transfer to digital for a sustained period of years; is having to consider more fundamental changes to processes and practices to meet the challenges of falling market demand; has a high labor input with some, but more limited, scope for capital investment and substitution; and undertakes functions where this input is less variable with throughput, and quasi-fixed. The impact of some of these postal sector specificities on the estimation of LRAIC is further explained below.

While other sectors typically have faced stable or growing demand, volume decline and uncertainty are major issues in the postal sector, where electronic substitution or the extent of bypass creates significant uncertainty about future mail volumes. Nevertheless, there are instances where demand has declined over time for specific services in other sectors, such as voice traffic over the legacy PSTN network in telecoms. These have tended to focus on the capacity requirements to meet the highest level of demand in the period (NITA, 2009). In the postal sector this may be less readily defined.

In the presence of declining volume it becomes necessary to consider the degree and cause of demand changes. Declining volumes can cause the LRAIC estimate to increase in the presence of activity with quasi-fixed costs and surplus capacity where existing capacity is not readily divisible. If there is a sustained market decline in volume it would also need to be factored into an entrant's costs. On the other hand, if there is a switch of volume from the incumbent to the entrant such that the entrant volume increases, then surplus capacity would be less relevant to factor into the LRAIC estimation.

It also becomes necessary to consider the quasi-fixed costs and capability necessary for existing and future demand. This is consistent with principles that the dimensioning of the network and its costs should correspond to what an efficient operator facing these demands would do with future changes in demand, as well as possible changes in the volume mix, explicitly taken into account. Furthermore, in the presence of uncertain future demand, it may also be necessary to investigate the extent to which any estimates are sensitive to the demand forecast.

The mail industry needs to consider fundamental changes to processes and practices to meet the challenges of falling market demand. When developing the forward-looking top-down LRAIC model representing the efficient end-state, some recognition of (and emphasis on) the current state of the market in terms of technology and volumes would be important. Several interdependencies may exist, for example, including the organizational development of an integrated network or more distinct networks performing more discrete functions.

A major modernization program indicates transition in operational processes and investment in assets that affect the absolute and relative levels of costs for the main pipeline processes and activities. For example, a reduction in the number of sorting centers (mail centers) may reduce mail center accommodation costs, but potentially increase transportation distances; introducing walk sequencing would increase cost within the mail centers and reduce them in the delivery offices; and a reduction in letter volumes and increase in packets and parcels could lead to a change in delivery methods and associated cost.

A modernization program not only affects the way in which a costing system reports its activity costs, but can also change the very nature of pricing and the categories and LRAIC estimates required to inform pricing. During periods of such substantial change, it becomes less appropriate to focus on historic costs and pricing categories and increasingly necessary to consider forward-looking (future) costs and pricing categories for the formation of LRAIC estimates.

Furthermore, while forward-looking LRAIC estimation needs to take account of these operational changes, it also needs to be based on the assumption that service specification remains constant, so that the comparison of cost with an assumed reduction in volume remains valid. Clearly the approach can then be extended to situations where the service specification is changed at the outset and under the hypothetical volume reduction, but this would require revisions to the historic costs, as well as some additional modeling.

While many sectors also remain heavily dependent on capital and have the scope for greater capital investment for such a program, the mail industry has a high labor input with some, but more limited, scope for capital investment and substitution. In other sectors, much attention to detail is given to the way in which assets are factored into the LRAIC because they represent a substantial component of cost. In contrast, the level of capital is lower for the postal sector and in terms of buildings, machines and vehicles can be leased rather than owned. This opens up the possibility for these costs to enter the LRAIC estimate as market-rate leased costs rather than capital assets.

Where capital assets are relevant, the forward-looking nature of LRAIC has typically applied the lower of the replacement cost or economic value together with a measure of return. In other sectors, the capital costs, whether existing or new, have been valued on the basis of modern equivalent asset (MEA), to reflect the best in class capital investment available, with the following factors considered: the optimization of the asset size, which involves an assessment of the utilization rates; the capital cost or MEA; the productivity/efficiency of the MEA; its maintenance and operating costs; the life of the asset; the depreciation of the asset over time (and the treatment of fully depreciated assets); any terminal value; and the cost of capital. In the postal sector the assets are relatively less significant than the staff costs and the effort in providing robust estimates may then be proportionate to the scale of the relative costs. A less intensive approach may start with current cost accounting values as proxies for the level of depreciation, with a return then added to the cost base.

While many sectors view labor as an input that can vary with throughput, the mail industry undertakes functions where this input is less variable with throughput, and quasi-fixed. An example is the function of outdoor delivery which forms a significant portion of overall costs and is dominated by labor cost. The outdoor delivery cost function has costs increasing with volume but at a decreasing rate. As volume increases the number of delivery points to be reached increases, but increasingly the additional volume is at a delivery point already reached and is consistent with cost elasticities with respect to volume of below unity.

Hence the postal sector has several features that are quite distinct from other sectors, and affect the approach to LRAIC estimation.

5 THE DEVELOPMENT OF LRAIC ESTIMATES

LRAIC estimates reflect the costs incurred in providing a defined increment or decrement of output that might be related to a change to the throughput in part of the network

Table 10.1 Illustrative list of increments

Attribute	Customer type			Format splits						Handling	
Increment	Counter	Firm	Postbox	Letter	Large Letter	Packet size 1	Packet size 2	Packet size 3	Packet other	Machineable	Manual
Attribute	Geography				Speed			Workshare			
Increment	Capital	Non-capital, urban	Non-capital, suburban	Non-capital, rural	Next day	3 day	7 day	Unsorted	Sort to mail centre	Sort to delivery office	Sort to walk

or to the provision of a particular service or product. A core consideration in any LRAIC model is the definition of the increments.

Increments (and decrements) can be defined to take account of network elements, activities and/or pipeline function which, in the postal sector, would mean defining increments on the basis of major pipeline functions: collections, inward sortation, network transportation, outward sortation, local distribution, indoor delivery and outdoor delivery. As mentioned in Section 3, each could be further segmented into activities that reflect a variety of business options for entrants on the supply side. For example, collections could be split between different modes of collection; and transportation could be split between different modes of transport. The greater level of disaggregation provides the scope to examine LRAIC at varying levels of aggregation.

Increments can also take account of product attributes and/or characteristics and in the postal sector, a number of discrete categories of attributes, such as item size, class and machinability could be relevant for the definition of the increments. There are also continuous categories, such as weight, customer mailing size and drop density. The discrete categories are more readily determined and manageable and continuous categories may need to be banded into discrete categories. The LRAIC estimates of specific bespoke products and services offered to customers are a further development of this product approach to increments.

Table 10.1 shows a set of illustrative increments for use in calculating the pipeline LRAICs. Hence, for example, collections include the attributes of customer type and format splits. These are also arranged in order of hierarchy such that the LRAIC can be formed at a higher level of aggregation. For example, in collections the data can be split by customer type and then format splits such that LRAICs can be formed for individual combinations of customer type and format split or at the more aggregated level of customer type and size. The LRAICs by pipeline activity at the most disaggregated level are used to form the product LRAICs.

Having defined the overall approach and set of increments, the cost–volume relationships (CVRs) are key inputs to the top-down LRAIC estimation. The CVR is applied to identify the long-run avoided cost from a reduction in volumes and hence the extent to which certain increments are associated with larger or smaller changes in long-run costs. Figure 10.3 illustrates how the CVR can be used to calculate the cost remaining after removal of an increment. V_t represents the operator's total mail volume, while C_t represents the cost of handling that mail. A volume of mail associated with a given increment

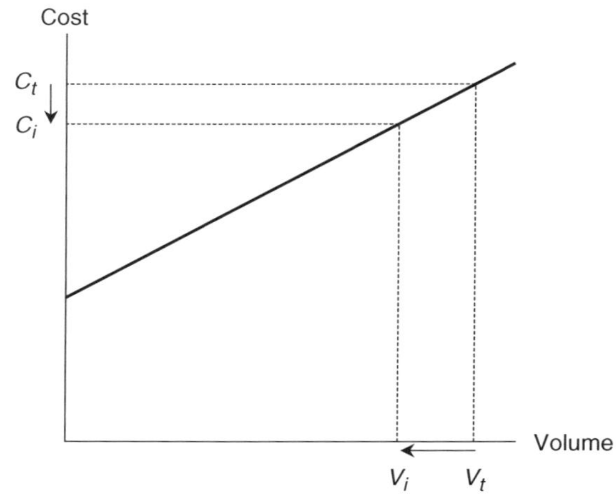

Figure 10.3 Calculating the LRIC for an increment

is deducted from the total volume, leaving a volume V_i costing C_i. The LRAIC for the chosen increment can be calculated as $(C_t - C_i)/(V_t - V_i)$.

CVRs can take many forms and, in essence, aim to capture whether a particular combination of cost category and pipeline function exhibits returns to scale (the slope of the curve) and whether fixed costs would be incurred even if volumes of the respective cost driver were zero (the intercept of the curve). For example, a straight line through the origin would indicate that there are no fixed costs and that there are constant returns to scale; and a curved line with intercept would be consistent with a cost category with quasi-fixed costs and exhibiting economies of scale.

Ideally CVRs should be developed for each homogeneous cost category from a conceptual point of view. In practice, consideration may be given to whether CVRs could be defined for the most significant cost categories only, in line with existing regulatory precedent.[3]

In any event, the definition of these CVRs needs to be based on sound, transparent and, as far as possible, evidence-based parameters. Three main techniques have been identified in precedents, in developing a CVR: (i) industrial engineering simulations are based on operational experience of investment decisions and current best practice; (ii) in some instances, it may be possible to derive a CVR based on statistical analysis or regression to assess the relationship between costs and the identified cost drivers. This is particularly the case where the processes are already considered to be efficient, or where inefficiency can be taken into account in deriving the CVR; and (iii) interviews and fieldwork: when no historical detailed cost information is available, interviews with experts might be used to identify where, within a CVR profile, a structural change in the relationship might take place; this is a more informal variant on using an engineering model. In some instances, there is no direct link between cost and volume, but there may be a series of relationships which, when put together, derive a CVR.

In forming the CVRs, consideration also needs to be given to the treatment of inefficiency (for example, the shape of a CVR might change from that currently observed if

Table 10.2 Illustration of split of collection costs ahead of the application of the CVRs

Category	Description	Cost type			
		Staff	Vehicle	Fuel	Other
1	Set up work	√			
2	Drive to start of route	√		√	
3	Drive on collection route	√	√	√	
4.1	Collect on route from postbox	√	√		
4.2	Collect on route from post office counter	√	√		
4.3	Collect on route from firm	√	√		
5	Drive back from end of route	√	√	√	
6	Consolidation	√			
7	Load feeder vehicle	√			
8	Accommodation				√
9	Network				√
10	Equipment				√

some inefficiencies were removed from the current network) and the approach adopted of scorched node or modified scorched node. For example, if the efficient operation involves fewer mail center nodes this can be incorporated into the LRAIC estimation in a modified scorched node through the CVRs.

We illustrate the approach to cost categorization and CVRs by reference to collections and outdoor delivery. These are two parts of the pipelines where there are known to be some economies of scale and the CVRs are nonlinear. While we illustrate the approach for these two parts of the pipeline, the general approach may be similar for other parts of the pipeline.

The collection activity is divided into cost categories, and then their costs are subdivided by cost type as illustrated by the checkmarks in Table 10.2. For each cost category and cost type with a checkmark there is then not only an allocation of cost, but also the application of a specific cost–volume relationship to form the LRAIC estimate.

The split of the cost categories 1–7 in Table 10.2 illustrates the different stages of the collection activity from the set-up costs prior to going out on the collection through to the loading-up of the collected mail for the onward journey, all of which involve time. Cost category 4 reflects different sources of collection with three main types of firms, counters and postboxes, while greater subdivision could be introduced to take account of different types of counters or firms. Cost categories 8–10 reflect other costs involved in the collection.

The CVRs for cost category 3 can be formed from the relationships of volume to the number of collection points visits and the number of collection visits to cost. The former is nonlinear, with increased volume increasing the number of collection points at a decreasing rate, and the latter is linear if the distance between collection points is assumed to be constant.

The CVRs for cost categories 4.1 and 4.2 in Table 10.2 can be estimated by reference to the ratio of the minimum number of collection visits and the efficient number of collection visits at current volumes, as the proportion of costs that are fixed and an

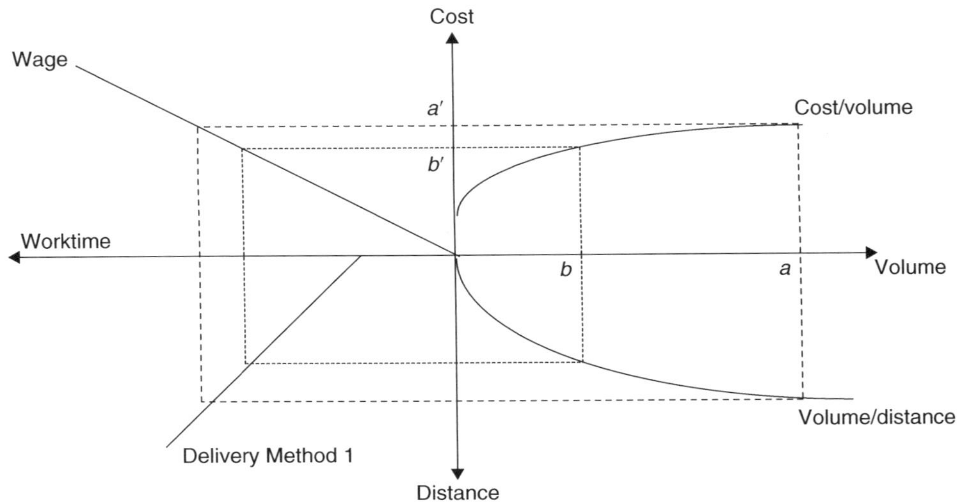

Figure 10.4 Development of CVRs for outdoor delivery

indication of where the CVR meets the y-axis. This reflects the universal service requirement to collect from the access points of postboxes and counters. In contrast, the CVR for cost categories 4.3 for firms depends on whether the number of visits reduces or the average mailing per visit reduces. In practice within the UK we have observed that both occur in the presence of competition upstream, with the volume of large mailers being lost to competitors first. This implies a nonlinear CVR where the rate of cost reduction increases as the volume reduces. In a situation where some volume has been lost to competition, the LRAIC would then be lower for an increment and higher for a decrement of volume.

For outdoor delivery, the CVR is influenced by: the outdoor time where cost increases at a decreasing rate with volume and the number of calls (or delivery points); the presence of attendance and signature costs which require discrete activity and incur additional costs; and the out and return journeys act as fixed costs, irrespective of volume.

For doorstep attendance and signature, the LRAIC may be estimates as the average cost per doorstep call time such that the standard LRAIC calculations for outdoor delivery can be formed by excluding these costs. The outdoor delivery cost by cost type (staff, vehicle and fuel) can then each be split into subcategories by reference to geographical zones (that reflect different unit costs) and delivery methods (that reflect the different modes of transportation for different sized items). This allows separate LRAICs to be estimated by zone and item size.

In Figure 10.4 we illustrate how these factors influence the CVR for a zone and delivery method. In the bottom right quadrant at volume *a* we note that as volume declines the distance declines (effectively as the number of delivery points visited falls) at an increasing rate, specific to the zone. In the bottom left quadrant, we assume a worktime relationship for a specific delivery method, which reflects the speed with which the distance is covered and is a function of delivery method. The function is linear to reflect how worktime changes with distance. We assume an element of fixed worktime to travel to the first delivery point and return from the last delivery point. In the top left quadrant, the function converts worktime into cost and therefore reflects the wage rate. In the top right quadrant, we can put these together to form the CVR where the slope reflects the marginal cost of incremental or decremental volume in outdoor delivery.

We observe the following features of this approach: in the first quadrant (bottom right), the distance per item would be higher for rural than for urban areas; in the second quadrant (bottom left) we might expect the slope to increase the slower the delivery method; and in the third quadrant (top left) the line represents the wage rate inclusive of overtime and so on such that a higher wage rate would cause the CVR in the top right quadrant to move up proportionately.

We also observe that the LRAIC estimate is formed by identifying the reduction in cost associated with the relevant volume decrement and that the size of decrement influences the LRAIC when the CVR is nonlinear. For a volume reduction of a to b the cost reduction is from a' to b', which is equivalent to a straight line CVR through bb' in Figure 10.4. As the volume decrement ($a - b$) increases, then the cost ($a' - b'$) increases. Hence the decrement is an important element in determining the LRAIC estimate. If the increment were applied to the whole of the volume a, the cost would move to zero (in the absence of any fixed costs). A larger volume decrement could then determine a higher LRAIC, but a decrement equal to the full a might be viewed as excessive. The decrement of volume could be applied as a set percentage (x percent) of the total. Given the curved shape of the CVRs, the avoided cost would increase with the value of the x percent. This might lead to counterintuitive results, for example, if the x percent were greater for letters than large letters. It might then be appropriate to set a given value of x percent within an increment. This may need to reflect the likelihood of competition. For example, if there is likely to be n equivalent players in an increment, x = $100/n$ might be appropriate.

Furthermore, if some services are given priority over other services, their LRAICs would differ in the presence of a nonlinear CVR. For example, in Figure 10.4, if the volume b is for universal services and volume '$a - b$' is for non-universal services, then a x percent decrement of 'a to b' would yield a lower avoided cost estimate than an x percent decrement of 'b to 0'.

For a forward-looking LRAIC, account may be taken of changes in both the volume and efficiency. We observe from Figure 10.4 that if there is a decline in delivered volume, the LRAIC would increase *ceteris paribus* because the gradient of the CVR increases with decreasing volume. This would not be a feature of the LRAIC where the CVR is linear, as may be present in some parts of the pipeline other than collection and delivery. Furthermore, for Figure 10.4 we observe that if there is an efficiency improvement in delivery methods through a reduction in the slope of the worktime per distance, this would reduce the gradient of the CVR and reduce the LRAIC. More generally, this would be a feature of the LRAIC where the CVR, whether nonlinear or linear, has an element of fixed cost that is unchanged by efficiency and innovation. In the presence of some fixed cost and efficiency improvement in the variable cost in the pipeline the LRAIC estimate would reduce, but in the presence of quasi-fixed costs and nonlinear CVRs in collection and delivery the LRAIC would increase if volumes decline.

6 CONCLUDING REMARKS

When developing the actual LRAIC estimates, it is useful to consider several guiding principles. These culminate in the provision of estimates that are ultimately fit for the purpose they were intended, to inform pricing and business decisions in the recovery of costs. To achieve this, some principles might be: compliance with the EU Directive and accounting principles, including the principle of causality, so that it remains compatible with the reported accounts; alignment with the allocation of activity costs and mappings of those costs to the historic costing system; future proofing in terms of identifying cost categories that inform future pricing; and consistency with other measures of cost, including, for example, short-run measures and business plans of future costs. Further guidelines might be that the approach is: proportionate with greatest focus towards the largest and most relevant cost categories where there are thought to be some economies of scale; equivalent in measure to the cost categories incurred by would-be competitors; complete in the sense of including all relevant costs;[4] objective with assumptions and inputs informed by robust analysis and consistent logic; practical in recognizing the current limitations in data or analysis to support input assumptions, and the scope for their improvement over time; accurate in terms of updating for developments and changes to the costing system; and transparent in terms of the documentation of assumptions and calculations.

In working to these principles there are several tradeoffs. For example, alignment to the historic costs from the costing system is only the starting point for LRAIC. The process of estimating LRAIC often causes features of the existing costing system to be reviewed in the light of the changes that are anticipated in the future in terms of pricing and operational processes, and therefore how the costing system itself might report those future costs. Alignment to the costing system as the first step then provides the springboard to consider how future developments change assumptions and affect the estimates.

As a further example, and as noted earlier, the level of detail in terms of the level of disaggregation of information can affect the level of LRAIC estimates, and hence there is a tradeoff in terms of the level of detail used in the estimation, which should be informed by the questions that LRAIC is intending to answer. Furthermore, while accuracy in terms of alignment to the detail of the costing system might drive greater detail and disaggregation, this can increase the resource intensiveness of collating, developing and reviewing the inputs and their updates and increase the time for processing and understanding the calculations themselves. Hence there are practical constraints that limit the level of disaggregation and levels of LRAICs that can be attained.

While the development of LRAIC models in other sectors provides a useful basis for developing LRAIC in the postal sector, the specificities of the postal sector are such that a sector-specific approach would need to be developed; and we illustrate what may be involved for collections and outdoor delivery. Nevertheless, the overriding guideline in the assessment of such tradeoffs is that the information should be fit for its intended purpose, taking account of the practical aspects of the provision of the information.

NOTES

* The views in this chapter are those of the authors. The authors also wish to acknowledge the input of Jane McMurdie and Katherine Stoker of Royal Mail.

1. Bradley et al (2012) showed that the short-run marginality is asymmetric, and lower when mail volumes decline. Cazals et al. (2012) showed that the long-run marginality using cross-sectional analysis in delivery is larger than shorter-term marginality.
2. The scorched node approach assumes that the number and location of the network nodes remains unchanged, and aims to optimize operational practices within these nodes. In the postal context the nodes relates to the sorting (mail centers) and delivery offices. The 'modified scorched node' imposes additional optimization requirements, by allowing the closure of some nodes which would not be deemed to be necessary for the provision of an efficient level of service. It should be noted that while the adoption of a 'modified scorched node' approach could be associated with bottom-up models, they could also be applied to top-down models.
3. For example, in the guidelines for the construction of top-down LRAIC in the telecoms sector in Sweden, the recommendation on the number of CVRs was that: 'Unless incremental costs, shared costs and fixed common costs can be correctly identified without the use of cost–volume relationships, the top-down model should estimate cost–volume relationships for the major cost categories (making up at least 75% of the total annual costs in the core and access network respectively), focusing on asset categories where the presence of fixed costs, scale economies and scope economies are likely to be most significant. For the remaining cost categories, the top-down model may assume that the CVR curve is a straight line through the origin' (Post & Telestyrelsen 2002). The European Regulators Group has stated 'NRAs [National Regulatory Authorities] should define the relevant increment that strikes the balance between the disaggregated level needed to demonstrate cost orientation and the disaggregated level that can be practically implemented' (ERG, 2005).
4. Since the LRAIC estimate assumes an efficient end-state operation, it does not need to consider the following factors: the costs incurred in reaching an efficient state, a glide path of efficiency improvements over a time path, redundancy costs, or the historical pension deficit costs.

REFERENCES

Bradley, M.D., J. Colvin and M.K. Perkins (2012), 'Do volume increases and decreases have the same effect on labor hours', in M.A. Crew and P.R Kleindorfer (eds), *Multi-modal Competition and the Future of Mail*, Cheltenham, UK and Northampton, MA, USA: Edward Elgar.

Bradley, M.D., J. Colvin and M.A. Smith (1993), 'Measuring product costs or ratemaking', chapter 8 in M.A. Crew and P.R. Kleindorfer (eds), *Regulation and the Nature of Postal and Delivery Services*, Boston, MA: Kluwer Academic.

Cazals C., P. Dudley, J.-P. Florens and M. Jones (2012), 'Unobserved heterogeneity in panel stochastic frontier: comparison of standard random effect and true random effect methods with simulated data for the postal sector', in M.A. Crew and P.R. Kleindorfer (eds), *Multi-modal Competition and the Future of Mail*, Cheltenham, UK and Northampton, MA, USA: Edward Elgar.

De Donder, P., H. Cremer, P. Dudley and F. Rodriguez (2006), 'A welfare analysis of price controls with end-to-end mail and access services', chapter 4 in M.A. Crew and P.R. Kleindorfer (eds), *Liberalization of the Postal and Delivery Sector*, Cheltenham, UK and Northampton, MA, USA: Edward Elgar.

De Donder, P., H. Cremer, P. Dudley and F. Rodriguez (2008), 'Pricing, welfare and organisational constraints for postal operators', chapter 11 in M.A. Crew and P.R. Kleindorfer (eds), *Competition and Regulation in the Postal and Delivery Sector*, Cheltenham, UK and Northampton, MA, USA: Edward Elgar.

European Commission (2007), 'Commission Decision of 04.07.2007 relating to a proceeding under Article 82 of the EC Treaty (Case COMP/38.784 – *Wanadoo España vs. Telefónica*)'.

European Commission (2009), 'Communication from the Commission: Guidance on the Commission's enforcement priorities in applying Article 82 of the EC Treaty to abusive exclusionary conduct by dominant undertakings (2009/C 45/02)'.

European Regulators Group (ERG) (2005), 'ERG Common Position: Guidelines for implementing the Commission Recommendation C (2005) 3480 on Accounting Separation & Cost Accounting Systems under the regulatory framework for electronic communications', ERG 05(29).

Independent Regulators Group (IRG) (2000), 'Principles of implementation and best practice regarding FL-LRIC cost modelling', 24 November.

NITA (2009), 'Report on the LRAIC Model and User Guide: Revised Hybrid Model', November.

Ofcom (2012a), 'Draft Determinations to resolve disputes between each of Sky, TalkTalk and Virgin Media and BT regarding BT's charges for Ethernet services', February.

Ofcom (2012b), 'Securing the Universal Postal Service: Decision on the new regulatory framework', March.

Post & Telestyrelsen (2002), 'Model reference paper: guidelines for the LRIC bottom-up and top-down models', 13 September.

Robinson, R. and J. McMurdie (2009), 'Postal costing beyond ABC: estimating the economic cost of mails services', chapter 6 in M.A. Crew and P.R. Kleindorfer (eds), *Progress in the Competitive Agenda in the Postal and Delivery Sector*, Cheltenham, UK and Northampton, MA, USA: Edward Elgar.

APPENDIX 10A

In Figure 10.1, the DLRIC of individual service $L1.1$ is represented by the shaded areas, comprising the incremental cost of $L1.1$ and a share of the costs common to $L1.1$, $L1.2$, $L1.3$ and $L1.4$. A simplified illustration of the steps involved in the calculation of DLRIC of individual service $L1.1$ ($DLRIC_{L1.1}$) could be as follows: (a) calculate LRIC of $L1$ ($LRIC_{L1}$); (b) calculate LRIC of $L1.1$, $L1.2$, $L1.3$ and $L1.4$ ($LRIC_{L1.1}$, $LRIC_{L1.2}$, $LRIC_{L1.3}$, $LRIC_{L1.4}$); (c) calculate the joint and common cost ($J1$) of the element $L1$ as follows:

$$J1 = LRIC_{L1} - (LRIC_{L1.1} + LRIC_{L1.2} + LRIC_{L1.3} + LRIC_{L1.4}).$$

$J1$ would then be allocated to $L1.2$, $L1.3$ and $L1.4$ on a cost category-by-cost category basis using EPMU. That is, the DLRIC of service $L1.1$ will be:

$$DLRIC_{L1.1} = LRIC_{L1.1} + J1 * \frac{LRIC_{L1.1}}{LRIC_{L1.1} + LRIC_{L1.2} + LRIC_{L1.3} + LRIC_{L1.4}}$$

As a result of the way DLRIC is calculated and the common costs are allocated, the sum of DLRIC of the individual services within a group is equal to the LRIC of the group of services taken as a single increment. That is, following the previous example:

$$LRIC_{L1} = \sum_{i=1}^{4} DLRIC_{L1.i}.$$

In Figure 10.2, the left-hand side considers the DSAC of individual service $L1.1$, which is illustrated by the shaded area. The top two shaded blocks illustrate the DLRIC of $L1.1$, while the lower shaded block represents the proportion of common costs across all services that are allocated to service $L1.1$. The right-hand figure illustrates the SAC of individual service $L1.1$, and includes the LRIC of individual service $L1.1$, all common costs $J1$, and the common costs across all services, JT. Therefore, reflecting the allocation of only a proportion of the full common costs of the service, the DSAC will be lower than the SAC.

That is, in the example:

$$SAC_{L1.1} = LRIC_{L1.1} + J1 + JT$$

$$DSAC_{L1.1} = LRIC_{L1.1} + \frac{LRIC_{L1.1}}{LRIC_{L1.1} + LRIC_{L1.2} + LRIC_{L1.3} + LRIC_{L1.4}}(J1 + JT).$$

As with DLRIC, the sum of individual service DSACs within a service group is equal to the SAC of the service group taken as a single increment. That is, continuing with the previous example:

$$DSAC_{L1} = \sum_{i=1}^{4} DSAC_{L1.i}.$$

11. Vulnerable users in times of declining demand: the case of basic bank services in Norway and Sweden

Henrik B. Okholm† **and Anna Möller**‡

1 INTRODUCTION

During the past twenty years, communication has become more focused on electronic solutions. Instead of sending letters, people enter social networks and use their mobile phone. Instead of conducting manual bank transactions, people use credit cards and pay bills over the Internet. This development has gone hand in hand with a falling demand for services provided under the postal Universal Service Obligation (USO), resulting in a continuous increase in the unit cost for providing postal universal services.

This chapter examines the need for adapting the postal USO to the digital age and the prospect of ensuring services for vulnerable users by other means than a universal service obligation. It relates to earlier publications by, among others, Cremer et al. (1997), Ambrosini et al. (2006), Econ Pöyry (2010) and RAND Europe (2011), analyzing the cost of and demand for USO services and the impact of reducing the USO scope. The chapter contributes to the earlier findings in at least four ways.

First, it deals exclusively with banking services within the postal USO. This has not been the focus of earlier research. Second, it evaluates the need for public intervention based on actual behavior by analyzing transaction data and establishing a net cost of the USO *per critical transaction*. This approach is advantageous compared with other approaches in estimating the need for public intervention based on consumers' stated preferences. Third, it shows that policy makers can use alternatives to a USO as instruments to solve the problems for vulnerable users. Until now, there has been somewhat minimal discussion on alternative instruments targeting these users. Fourth, while most existing literature provides *ex ante* assessments of expected effects, this chapter also offers an *ex post* analysis of experiences from reduced USO and public tendering of universal services.

This chapter examines the provision of bank services in Sweden and Norway, two small countries with a highly educated population and among the highest GDP per capita in the world. Nevertheless, the lessons learned here can also be applied to the broader USO and in other country contexts. For example, the analysis of transaction data and calcula-

† Partner, Copenhagen Economics A/S.
‡ Senior Economist, Copenhagen Economics A/S.

tions on net costs of the USO per critical transaction instead of basing the analysis on stated preferences can also be applied when analyzing the need for post offices or the need for five or six deliveries per week. Moreover, the impact of electronic substitution on the cost of providing universal services will increase further in the coming years. This development will increase the relevance of the topics addressed in this chapter, not least in countries which today experience relatively modest e-substitution.

Section 2 sets out the broader key questions to which the chapter relates. Section 3 investigates the situation in Sweden where basic payment services have been provided both through a postal USO and through public tendering, and where the national regulatory authority (NRA) has recently suggested new initiatives to improve access for vulnerable users. We shall analyze how demand, and the cost for providing payment services, has developed over time and with different solutions. Section 4 investigates the situation in Norway with focus on the possibility for excluding bank services from the postal USO and introducing alternative solutions to help vulnerable users. The possibility for excluding bank services from the USO is assessed based on individuals' access to alternative service points (for example, bank offices and banks in shops) and alternative products (for example, Internet banking or giro payments). Section 5 summarizes the main findings.

2 THE KEY QUESTIONS

The chapter relates to three fundamental questions:

1. How is the cost of providing universal services affected by increased e-substitution and reductions in the USO scope?
2. What is the need for the services provided under the postal USO?
3. Are there alternative (non-USO) ways of helping vulnerable users?

These issues have been discussed in earlier publications, but to our knowledge never with the same focus as here.

The first question, about how increased e-substitution and reductions in the USO scope respectively affect the cost of providing universal services, is on the agenda of all universal service providers seeking to increase their profitability. For this reason, drivers of USO costs have been subject to considerable attention. A central contribution comes from Ambrosini et al. (2006) who examined what drives the cost of the USO and found population density and traffic (that is, mail volumes) per capita to be the most important cost drivers. As a consequence, changes in mail volumes due to e-substitution will have a significant effect on the cost of providing universal services.

By reducing the scope of the USO, fixed costs (for instance, related to a costly post office network) can be reduced. This could to some extent reduce the negative effect of falling volumes. However, as long as there is a political goal to provide the current service level under the USO, or as long as consumers are willing to pay for the current service level, the USO scope will most likely not be reduced.

The second question, about the need for the services provided under the postal USO, is tightly linked to the previous one since it determines the prospects for reducing the USO scope. The need for universal services is often evaluated through a cost–benefit analysis where the cost of providing the services is compared with consumers' willingness to pay for them. Two recent analyses of this kind have been conducted by Econ Pöyry (2010) and RAND Europe (2011).

In 2010, Econ Pöyry analyzed the demand for universal services in Norway. The motivation was the continuously falling use of the services offered within the postal USO. Based on a stated preference methodology the authors concluded that vulnerable users' willingness to pay for the services, in relation to the cost of providing them, was high enough *not* to justify a reduction in the USO scope. The study focused on delivery time and frequency. It did not explicitly analyze the need for including bank services in the USO.

The need to measure consumer preferences for the USO in markets with falling volumes has also been highlighted by the European Commission, which in 2011 commissioned a study on the appropriate methodologies to measure consumer preferences for postal services. The subsequent report, written by RAND Europe (2011), applies stated preference discrete choice experiments to quantify consumers' preferences for specific aspects of postal services. It shows that businesses and residential consumers are willing to pay for having postal services near their work or home. The authors also found a high willingness to pay for service locations with longer opening hours, but a lower willingness to pay for access to a wider range of postal services or financial services. This indicates that consumers value the access to core postal services, but have a low demand for bank or payment services in the postal network.

However, the inherent problem of stated preference analysis to reveal the demand for universal services is the risk of overestimating consumers' willingness to pay. This might happen, for example, if respondents find it difficult to imagine the value of alternative solutions or if the cost reductions they face as a result of a narrower USO scope are low. To overcome this problem, this chapter focuses on consumers' *actual access to alternative solutions* of sufficient quality and the *actual number of transactions* conducted in the postal network to determine the true need for the services provided under the postal USO.

The third question, examining the possibility of helping vulnerable users through alternative (non-USO) solutions, has not previously been the focus of much attention. However, some earlier contributions have examined the relative efficiency of the entire USO compared to a system with cash transfers, often with the conclusion that the USO is the superior solution. For instance, Cremer et al. (1997) applied this test to the French postal service and found a positive welfare impact of the universal service in the range of 1 billion francs (corresponding to approximately €0.15 billion). These findings do not contradict the fact that it might be more efficient to provide some elements of universal services in alternative ways.

3 SWEDEN

The Swedish Post and Telecom Agency (PTS) is responsible for ensuring the provision of basic bank services at reasonable prices in Sweden when the market fails to do so. This section investigates how access to basic payment services has been ensured in Sweden over time and how the cost of providing the services has changed along with a steady decline of payment volumes in the postal network.

Until 2009: Postal USO on Basic Payment Services

Basic payment services have historically been included in the Swedish postal USO. As the number of post offices was reduced in the late 1990s and early 2000s, the universal service provider, Posten AB, set up a separate entity responsible for the provision of payment services. In most cases this entity, *Svensk Kassaservice* (Swedish Cashier Service), remained on smaller premises where the post office had previously been.

Due to continuously falling volumes of manual bank transactions, Kassaservice turned out to be an expensive venture. Yearly losses of €45 million were covered by government funding, and its position as a competitor to the regular banking system attracted the attention of the Commission, which accused the Swedish government of providing unlawful state aid. The discussions ended with Kassaservice being gradually closed down. There was no discussion as to whether parts of the office network could have been retained in remote areas.

Although Kassaservice had closed, there was still a clear political goal that basic payment services should be available to all citizens in Sweden, at a reasonable cost. It was the duty of the PTS to define which services to include in practice and to analyze the demand for them.

By analyzing living and traveling patterns, the PTS found that 0.5 percent of the population (approximately 40,000 individuals) lacked access to basic payment services in 2007.[1] According to the PTS (2010a), this involved mainly elderly and disabled individuals living in remote locations, defined as more than 30km from a service point providing basic bank services. The remaining population either lived closer to a service point or had traveling patterns such that access was not a problem.

2009–2012: Publicly Procured Services

Since the USO type of solution had failed, another route was tried. It seemed that the only alternative considered was a publicly procured solution. The idea was that the government, through the PTS, would procure the provision of basic payment services in areas where they were not commercially available. Consequently, the provision of basic payment services for 2009–12 in 15 small villages and 73 geographical areas was put up for public tender. The government had prescribed that the bidders had to have 'bank'[2] status, in order to be stable and transparent. This greatly restricted the number of available bidders. There was only one bidder, a joint venture between ICA (Sweden's largest food retailer) and Kuponginlösen AB (a company handling the coupon-clearing business for most of the Swedish retail sector), for the contract. Due to the fact that the budget for the reform was publicly available, the PTS had a bad bargaining position. In the end, a price of €21 million was agreed for the four-year period.

Until 31 August 2012, ICA/Kuponginlösen provides basic payment services for 15 villages through so-called '*Betalservice*' (payment service) at their grocery stores, and for 73 geographical areas through an agreement with Posten AB, providing so-called '*Brevgiro*' (letter giro) services via the rural mailmen/women (Table 11.1). The services provided by rural mailmen/women are only available upon request. Households where all individuals are older than 80 years, or disabled, are automatically allowed to use the service. The services provided at supermarkets are open to everyone. However, the services are not

Table 11.1 Basic payment services procured, 2009–2012

Service type	Functioning	Geography	Services
Brevgiro	Rural mailman/woman visits household and handles transaction	73 remote areas	Payments Payouts
Betalservice	In-store handling of basic payment services at local ICA grocery store	15 small villages with no banking facilities	Payments Payouts Cash withdrawal

Source: PTS (2010b).

Table 11.2 Use of procured payment services, Sweden 2009

Service	Transactions 2009
Paying bills	16,600
Cash payout	4,400
Cash withdrawal	37,100
Total number of transactions	58,100

Source: Copenhagen Economics, based on PTS (2010b).

provided for free. According to Kuponginlösen (2012), there is a fee of €4 to pay a bill and a fee of €3 to withdraw cash within the system.

Despite the fact that the publicly procured solution was a major financial improvement on the earlier USO solution, the use of the system remained very expensive. During 2009, there were only 3,000 active users of the services provided by the rural mailmen/women and only 58,000 transactions were made in total (Table 11.2). The use has decreased further during 2010 and 2011.

Adding up the transactions over the four-year period[3] indicates that it is unlikely that more than 230,000 transactions were made during 2009–12. Splitting the cost of €21 million thus yields a cost per transaction of more than €90.

In 2010–11, the PTS examined the different possibilities for a post-August 2012 solution. Due to the low usage, the PTS did not want to repeat the nationally procured solution, which was, in their opinion, far too expensive (although an improvement on the USO solution). If the government still preferred a second round of public tendering, the PTS argued that the requirement for bidders to be 'banks' should be scrapped, in order to increase the number of possible bidders.

From 2012: Market-based Solutions

On 31 March 2011, the PTS (2011) presented an action plan for 2012–16 to the responsible ministry. The plan recommended that the USO for basic payment services, which had been handled through a tendering procedure, should be abandoned. Instead PTS proposed a plan focused on three market-based solutions: regional support and development, market stimuli and technological development (Figure 11.1). The reason for this

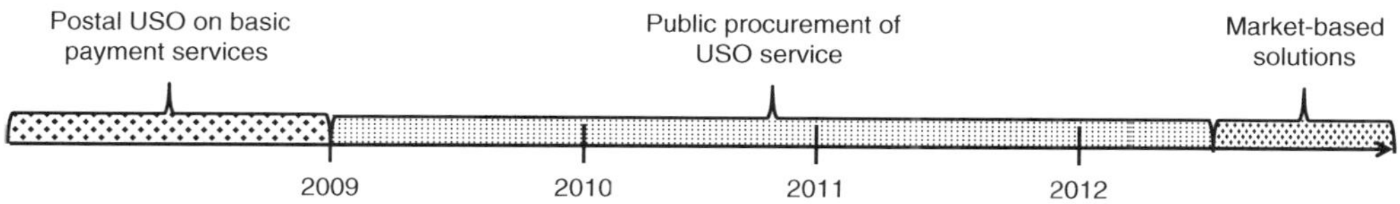

Source: Copenhagen Economics (2010).

Figure 11.1 Provision of basic payment services in Sweden

shift in approach was not that the share of vulnerable users had declined substantially, but that the PTS considered there to be more cost-efficient ways in which the vulnerable users' needs could be met.

The survey conducted by the PTS in 2007 showed that access to basic bank services is most problematic for immobile individuals (mainly elderly or disabled) in sparsely populated areas of Sweden. Since the nature of the problem varies between regions, the PTS has decided to focus on regional solutions. The action plan foresees that the regional counties get more responsibility for identifying and/or designing solutions adapted to each county's specific needs in the coming five-year period. Based on input from the counties, the PTS has suggested four *regional* solutions:

- *Solution 1* Financial support for ATMs, cash deposit boxes and credit/debit card terminals in areas where they are not commercially viable.
- *Solution 2* Mobile ATMs, suitable to deal with cash supply in areas with a large tourist or summer resident influx and where commercial operators do not want to place an ATM all year round.
- *Solution 3* Local circulation of cash where local companies deposit their daily cash into an ATM which in turn uses the deposited cash for withdrawals by private individuals.
- *Solution 4* Combining bank services with other assisted living services for the elderly. Today, elderly people living on their own can get assistance from the municipalities and the state to do grocery shopping. An option could be to combine these visits with visits to a bank or other service points.

The second action in the plan is *market stimuli*, that is, stimulating commercial operators to make their products as accessible as possible for as many as possible. This includes, among other things, discussions with banks on how to improve access to their online bank service or telephone service for elderly or disabled people. As part of this initiative, an 'accessibility survey' evaluating how easy it is for elderly or disabled persons to use different banks' Internet portals has been conducted. The results were highlighted in the media, and promoted changes. The PTS has suggested that the dialogue with banks continues and that more accessibility surveys, possibly with other focuses, could be done.

The third action that will be carried through by the PTS is *technological development* to improve existing technology and to promote innovation. This action is considered to be the main tool for making it easier for elderly and disabled people to use electronic alternatives.

A general problem with access to bank services in sparsely populated areas is Internet access, for example, debit and credit card terminals need Internet access to work, and Internet banking solutions are only available to households with an Internet connection. Developing the broadband network is thus considered important to improve access to basic bank services.

4 NORWAY

This section analyzes the question of whether Norway Post should continue to be obliged by law to provide bank services throughout its entire network.

The bank service obligation required Norway Post to provide five basic services (cash deposit, cash withdrawal, payments, payouts, and opening of bank accounts) at 1,435 post offices and post-in-shops as well as on 1,726 rural delivery routes across Norway. In addition to this obligation, Norway Post was also required to maintain a certain network structure (that is, a minimum number of post offices).

Due to a steady fall in manual bank transactions in the postal network, the two obligations together imposed a net cost on Norway Post. In 2010, the compensation for the net cost of these two obligations amounted to more than €17 million. Estimations for 2012 foresee a net cost of nearly €22 million. The net cost is expected to increase further with continuing volume declines.

National Trends in the Use of Bank Services

Over the past couple of years (2009–2011), basic bank transactions in the Norwegian postal network have experienced yearly declines by 5–10 percent. All else equal, this development suggests a declining need for including bank services in the USO.

In 2010, approximately 10.5 million basic bank transactions were conducted in the postal network. Seventy percent of these were deposits and withdrawals (40 percent made by credit or debit card, 30 percent made without a credit or debit card). Thirty percent were payments and payouts (Table 11.3). The types of bank transactions conducted play

Table 11.3 Bank transactions in the network Norway Post, 2010

Type of transaction	No. of transactions (million)*	Share of all transactions (%)
Payments	2.8	26
Payouts	0.4	4
Cash deposit with card	1.0	10
Cash withdrawal with card	3.2	30
Cash deposit without card	0.9	9
Cash withdrawal without card	2.2	21
Total	10.5	100

Note: * In addition to the transactions in the table, approximately 29,000 openings of bank accounts were made in the postal network in 2010.

Source: Copenhagen Economics, based on Norway Post (2011).

a central role in the analysis. This is because they indicate the availability of alternative solutions, such as Internet banking or letter giro, and thereby determine the level of user vulnerability.

Finding the True Need for the Bank Service Obligation

In the following analysis, vulnerable users dependent on the bank obligation are defined as users without access to comparable and sufficiently good alternatives provided by the market. The analysis is based on four central assumptions about individuals' possibilities to substitute bank transactions in the postal network with alternative solutions:

- *First assumption* There are two possibilities for substitution. On the one hand, transactions can be replaced by *alternative service points* (over-the-counter transactions conducted, for example, at a bank office or bank-in-shop). On the other hand, transactions can be replaced by *alternative products* (non-over-the-counter services such as letter giro, Internet banking, or direct debit).
- *Second assumption* All households located within a distance of 4km from a fixed bank service point (that is, a bank office or a bank-in-shop) can move all their bank transactions to this service point without experiencing worsened access.[4]
- *Third assumption* All households, irrespective of location, can replace all transactions made with a credit or debit card (non-cash-based transactions) by alternative products without experiencing worsened access.[5]
- *Fourth assumption* All households that are *not* dependent on home-care services or other assisted living services for managing daily errands, such as grocery shopping, in addition to the above-mentioned, can move withdrawals made by credit or debit card to ATMs or cash-back[6] in connection to daily errands, such as work or grocery shopping. According to Statistics Norway (2010) and Gabrielsen and Otnes (2011), 2 percent of the Norwegian population had an average to extensive need for home-care assistance in 2009, meaning that they receive on average 10–45 hours of home-care assistance per week. Based on this, 2 percent of the population is defined as *not* being able to replace withdrawals made by credit or debit card by ATMs or cash-back.

The assumptions imply that the only individuals that might be dependent on the bank obligation are those without sufficient access to an alternative (fixed) service point *and* who cannot replace manual services by other types of (self-service) solutions (Figure 11.2).

An investigation of substitution possibilities shows that *all* services in the bank obligation can be fulfilled by banks and bank-in-shops in combination with letter mail (Table 11.4). Hence, individuals with a bank account and sufficient access to a bank or bank-in-shop *cannot* be classified as vulnerable users dependent on the bank obligation.

The investigation also shows that people in sparsely populated areas without access to a fixed service point[7] might have insufficient access to *cash-based transactions* (deposits and withdrawals). The magnitude of this problem, however, depends on when and where cash is needed. For instance, a person who needs cash to spend in the city center is unlikely to perceive this as a major problem since there is usually good availability of ATMs or shops with cash-back in more densely populated areas. However, for a person

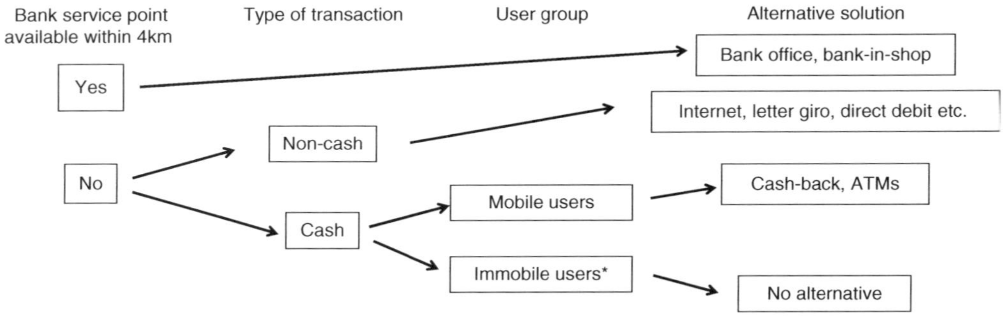

Note: * By immobile users we understand households which are dependent on home-care services or other assisted living services for managing daily errands, such as grocery shopping.

Source: Copenhagen Economics (2010).

Figure 11.2 Defining the true need for a bank service obligation

who needs to withdraw cash to pay the neighbor for doing the weekly grocery shopping, there might be a problem if the rural postman/woman does not provide bank services.

Quantifying the Need for a Bank Obligation

The estimation of the number of vulnerable users builds on a geographical analysis conducted by Bring Dialog (2011), complemented with statistics from Norway Post (2011) on the number of bank transactions[8] within the postal USO in 2010.

Table 11.4 Alternatives to the bank services provided by Norway Post

	Opening of account	Cash withdrawal	Cash deposit	Payouts	Payments
Bank office	✓	(✓)	(✓)	✓	✓
Bank-in-shop	✗	✓	✓	✓	✓
Letter giro	✓[1]	✗	✗	✓[2]	✓[1]
COOP[3]	✓	✓	✓	✗	✗
ATM	✗	✓	(✓)[4]	✗	✗
Cash-back in shops	✗	✓	✗	✗	✗
Internet bank	✓	✗	✗	✗	✓[1]
Telephone bank	✓[5]	✗	✗	✗	✓[1]
Mobile bank	✗	✗	✗	✗	✓[1]

Notes:
1. Requires copy of ID.
2. Requires bank account.
3. Available only to COOP members.
4. Some ATMs allow cash deposit.
5. Requires copy of ID.

Source: Copenhagen Economics (2010).

Underlying assumptions

The analysis relies on two assumptions regarding the geographical distribution of bank transactions and the number of transactions per household and year:

- *First assumption* Bank transactions within a municipality are evenly distributed among individuals.[9] In other words, an individual living close to a service point makes just as many bank transactions per year in the postal network as an individual living far from a service point.
- *Second assumption* An average vulnerable user conducts approximately 12 cash-based transactions per year. This estimate is based on experience from Sweden.[10]

Estimating the number of vulnerable users

The number of users dependent on the bank obligation in rural delivery and at fixed service points, respectively, is estimated by means of a three-step approach:

- *Step 1* Geographical analysis of households, postal and bank service points.
- *Step 2* Analysis of bank transactions that can/cannot be replaced by alternatives.
- *Step 3* Translation of irreplaceable transactions into vulnerable users.

In step 1, the geographical distribution of households in relation to postal and bank service points in a specific area is analyzed. This is central because of the assumption that people living less than 4km from a bank service point can move all transactions conducted in the postal network to the alternative service point.

In step 2, the geographical distribution of transactions within a specific area is assessed.[11] First, an estimation of the number of transactions that lack an alternative service point within a reasonable distance is developed. Thereafter, an estimation of how many of these transactions that *cannot* be moved to alternative products, such as Internet banking or letter giro, is developed. In this way the analysis results in a number of 'irreplaceable' transactions that *might* be dependent on the bank obligation since they lack both an alternative service point and an alternative product.

It is important to keep in mind that the number of transactions derived in this step is most likely an overestimation of the actual number. This is due to the fact that many individuals living far away from an alternative service point have access to alternative service points in relation to work or other daily errands, such as grocery shopping. This is *not* captured by the analysis.

In step 3, the number of 'irreplaceable' transactions in step 2 is translated into vulnerable users by dividing the number of transactions by the assumed average number of transactions per vulnerable user and year.

Results: need for a bank obligation in rural delivery

- *Step 1* More than 19 percent of Norwegian households are located further than 4km from a postal service point with access to basic bank services via the rural mailmen/women. Some of these households are located less than 4km from an alternative service point and are thus, per definition, *not* dependent on bank services within the postal USO. Due to lack of data, all households located along rural delivery routes are assumed to lack an alternative service point within a reasonable distance. This makes the estimate of the number of vulnerable users in rural delivery very conservative.

- *Step 2* In 2009, approximately 450,000 transactions were made on rural delivery routes. Due to lack of updated data, this number is (conservatively) assumed to remain unchanged in 2010.[12] Assuming that the transaction pattern on rural delivery routes mirrors that at post offices,[13] approximately 35 percent of transactions are found to lack an alternative product solution. Thus, at most 155,000 transactions in rural delivery are dependent on the bank obligation.
- *Step 3* Assuming that an average vulnerable user conducts approximately 12 transactions per year, it is found that no more than 12,100 individuals may depend on the rural delivery service for conducting bank transactions. This is an interesting observation since 12,100 individuals correspond to less than 2 percent of the households with access to bank services via the rural mailmen/women. However, it confirms earlier findings by Copenhagen Economics (2010), showing that rural mailmen/women visit approximately 2 percent of households to conduct bank transactions on a regular basis.

The observation reveals that most rural households seem to manage their bank transactions in alternative ways (for example, via alternative products, or via alternative service points located more than 4km from home).

Results: need for a bank obligation at fixed postal service points

- *Step 1* Some 81 percent of Norwegian households are located less than 4km from a post office or post-in-shop, without access to rural delivery. In a situation without bank services in the postal USO, some of these households would suddenly have a larger distance, maybe more than 4km, to the nearest service point.

  However, data reveal that the far largest share (92 percent) of households located less than 4km from a postal service point *also* are located less than 4km from a bank service point. This means that at most 8 percent, or 132,000 households, could be dependent on the bank services provided under the postal USO since they are more than 4km from the nearest bank service point.

  Again, it should be stressed that these individuals *might* have access to alternative service points, for instance in close relation to work or in connection to the running of daily errands such as grocery shopping.
- *Step 2* To estimate the number of 'irreplaceable' bank transactions, the total number of bank transactions in the postal network is used as a starting point, split by the location of the individuals conducting them. The analysis reveals that approximately 2 million transactions are conducted by individuals living more than 4km from a fixed postal service point. Earlier results have shown that 450,000 transactions are conducted via the rural mailmen/women. In other words, approximately 1.6 million transactions are made at fixed service points by individuals with access to rural delivery. As individuals with access to rural delivery are granted access to basic bank transactions through the rural mailman/woman they are not defined as dependent on the obligation at fixed postal service points.[14]

The analysis also reveals that approximately 700,000 transactions are conducted by individuals living less than 4km from a postal service point but more than 4km from a bank service point. Based on the transaction pattern, approximately one-third of these transactions lack not only an alternative service point but also an alternative product solution. Consequently, at most 210,000 transactions conducted at fixed service points cannot be replaced by existing alternatives.

- *Step 3* By dividing the number of transactions in step 2 by the average number of transactions per vulnerable user, the analysis reveals that approximately 16,400 individuals are dependent on the bank services currently provided at the fixed service points of Norway Post.

  The estimations, based on conservative assumptions, thus show that at most 28,500 individuals in Norway might get worse access to bank services if the bank obligation were abandoned. With a net cost of €22 million for providing the bank services in 2012, this corresponds to a cost of more than €750 per user or more than €60 per transaction. Whether this cost of protecting vulnerable users through a USO is justified or not depends on the availability of alternative solutions and the cost of these.

Alternative Solutions and the Savings from Reducing the Postal USO

This subsection contains an evaluation of measures that possibly could ensure the provision of basic bank services to vulnerable users in Norway at a lower cost than a postal USO. There are five possible solutions. Several of these have lately been proposed by the regulator in Sweden as a means of ensuring the provision of basic payment services to vulnerable users in a cost-efficient way (see above). The solutions investigated are (i) increased provision of bank services at alternative service points, (ii) provision of transport service to vulnerable users, (iii) provision of bank services by bank bus or bank car in remote areas, (iv) provision of bank services through a courier, and (v) increased access to self-service solutions.

Increased provision of bank services at alternative service points

If bank services are no longer provided in the postal network, the incentive for other entities to offer bank services at alternative service points would increase. This development could be further incentivised by offering supermarkets, petrol stations, cafés, and similar outlets lump-sum investment support or a direct per-transaction compensation if they provide bank services at their premises.

Provision of transport service to vulnerable users

Another solution could be to increase the mobility of citizens by offering elderly or disabled people a transport service to the nearest bank outlet, for instance twice a month. In the context of Norway, it is foreseen that the current provision of transport services offered to disabled people who cannot use public transport could be extended to also include bank service errands.

Provision of bank services by bank bus or bank car in remote areas
A solution that already exists in some sparsely populated areas in Norway is the provision of basic bank services through a mobile 'bank bus'[15] *or* 'bank car'[16] which visits a selection of rural communities twice a month. These solutions are administered by the local banks and are provided on a commercial basis with the purpose of making services accessible to people living far away from a fixed service point. The bank bus or bank car stops at predefined places according to a schedule. Some stops are only made if the service has been requested in advance. A possible solution could be to incentivize the provision of more mobile bank buses or cars through targeted financial support in problematic regions.

Provision of bank services through a courier
An alternative to the bank bus or bank car is the provision of basic bank services through a courier service. This type of solution is already in place in rural areas where the rural mailmen/women provide basic bank services on behalf of DnB NOR.

The courier solution foreseen in this context is limited to targeted groups of individuals living in areas with more than a predefined distance to the nearest bank service point. The provision of basic bank services would be conducted by a courier, acting on the behalf of a bank or other financial institution, and the individuals using the service would pay a price similar to what they pay for the bank services offered by Norway Post today.

Those experiencing difficulties with access to basic banking services are often elderly or disabled people who cannot use the electronic solutions available and are insufficiently mobile to visit a fixed bank service point. For this reason, a solution is imagined whereby services are offered based on some eligibility criteria, such as age or mobility (instead of distance to the nearest service point).

Increased access to self-service solutions
Good access to self-service solutions decreases the dependence on fixed service points. Consequently, if these alternatives were to be made more accessible to elderly and disabled people, the need for other alternatives would decrease.

5 MAIN FINDINGS

This chapter has investigated the costs of not adapting the scope of the USO to changes in demand. It has assessed the possibilities for excluding basic bank services from the postal USO in Norway and evaluated alternative solutions for providing the services to vulnerable users.

The analysis reveals that at most 28,500 individuals (mainly elderly or disabled individuals or people in sparsely populated areas) are dependent on the bank services provided in the postal network in Norway. However, it also shows that these users can be helped through other alternative solutions, such as transport services, improved self-service solutions, or bank services provided by a courier to targeted households. These solutions seem to be good alternatives in the Norwegian context, as they would target user groups with specific difficulties and also have the potential to improve access to bank services for elderly and disabled individuals in more densely populated areas without access to rural delivery.

By excluding bank services from the postal USO, and loosening the requirements on the network structure, the Norwegian government could save approximately €22 million in 2012. By reducing the bank obligation to cover only rural delivery routes, €15–18 million could be saved. This money could then (at least partly) be used to solve the needs of vulnerable users in more cost-efficient ways.

The findings are supported by evidence from Sweden, where the provision of basic payment services has gone from being included in the USO, to being procured through public tendering, to now being solved by alternative solutions such as targeted regional support, market stimuli, and technological development.

Although the publicly procured solution was a large financial improvement on the earlier USO solution, reducing the yearly cost from €45 million to approximately €5 million, due to decreasing demand, the cost per transaction was still over €90 in 2010. This has encouraged the NRA to suggest new solutions, such as dialogues with banks and continuous follow-up on their accessibility, projects for technological development, and regional support, to ensure future access to payment services.

The research shows that the existence of a group of vulnerable users should not *per se* motivate a broad USO as this could be a very expensive solution. Instead, the research suggests that there are often alternative solutions available to solve the needs of the vulnerable users in more cost-efficient ways.

Based on the results of our research, the Norwegian government has recently decided to exclude the provision of basic bank services at fixed service points from the postal USO.

NOTES

1. It was not clear, however, whether this part of the population had access at an earlier point, either with the old post office network or with the full Kassaservice network. But the political intention was clear: from now on, everyone will have access to basic payment services.
2. To be a 'bank' and provide accounts and administer payments one needs governmental permission, and the company is under the supervision of the Swedish Financial Supervisory Authority.
3. The actual number of transactions is known only for 2009.
4. This is due to the fact that households located within a distance of 4km from a fixed postal service point are considered to have sufficient access to the bank services provided by Norway Post.
5. This assumption is based on earlier findings by Copenhagen Economics (2010), showing that everyone with a bank account can use letter giro or Internet banking for payments, payouts, and deposits made by credit or debit card.
6. Cash-back is currently offered at most shops in Norway.
7. A fixed service point is a post office, post-in-shop, bank office or bank-in-shop where basic bank services are provided.
8. By basic bank transactions we refer to four types of bank services that Norway Post, according to the bank obligation, was required to provide in its network of fixed service points (post offices and post-in-shops) and at rural delivery routes: cash deposit (with and without credit/debit card), cash withdrawal (with and without credit/debit card), payments (for example, bill payments), and payouts (for example, pension payouts).
9. The assumption is necessary since the dataset only allows for a disaggregation of data to the municipality level.
10. Experience from Sweden suggests that this estimate is reasonable. According to the Swedish PTS (2011), 3,000 users of the procured payment service in Sweden conducted slightly more than 37,000 cash withdrawals in 2009 (that is, 12 withdrawals per person per year).
11. We assume that the distribution of transactions mirrors the distribution of households.

12. From 2009 to 2010, bank transactions in the postal network declined by more than 7 percent on average.
13. For instance, if 21 percent of all transactions conducted at post offices are cash withdrawals without a credit or debit card, 21 percent of the transactions conducted on rural delivery routes are also of this type.
14. An analysis of driving distances reveals that households located more than 4km from both a post and a bank service point normally are located closer to the bank service point than to the postal service point. Moreover, in cases where households have a longer driving distance to the bank service point, the weighted average difference in distance is very small, less than 2km. This further supports the decision to disregard the households located along rural delivery routes.
15. For example, Sparebanken Sogn og Fjordane (2011).
16. For example, Tysnes Sparebank (2011).

REFERENCES

Ambrosini, X., F. Boldron and B. Roy (2006), 'Universal service obligations in the postal sector: economic learnings from cross-country comparisons', in M.A. Crew and P.R. Kleindorfer (eds), *Progress toward Liberalization of the Postal and Delivery Sector*, New York: Springer.

Bring Dialog (2011), 'Geografisk avstandsanalyse i forbindelse med en utredning om tilbud av benktjenester i postnettet', Report prepared by Bring Dialog, Oslo, May 2011.

Copenhagen Economics (2010), 'Bank services in the postal network', a study commissioned by the Norwegian Ministry of Transport and Communications.

Cremer, H., M. De Rycke and A. Grimaud (1997), 'Cost and benefits of universal service obligations in the postal sector', in M.A. Crew and P.R. Kleindorfer (eds), *Managing Change in the Postal and Delivery Industries*, Boston, MA: Kluwer Academic.

Econ Pöyry (2010), 'Utredning om behov for leveringspliktige posttjenster', report commissioned by the Norwegian Post and Telecom Authority.

Gabrielsen, B. and B. Otnes (2011), 'Brukerstyrt personlig assistanse (BPA), Statistikk om mottakerne på grunnlag av IPLOS, data for 2009', Report commissioned by the Norwegian Ministry of Health and Care Services, May 2011.

Kuponginlösen (2012), 'Frågor & svar – konsument/företag', available at: http://www.kuponginlosen.se/index.php?option=com_content&view=article&id=103&Itemid=115 (accessed 18 June 2012).

Norway Post (2011), 'Transaksjoner Postbank 2010–2011', Oslo.

RAND Europe (2011), 'Study on appropriate methodologies to better measure consumer preferences for postal services', report commissioned by the European Commission.

Sparebanken Sogn og Fjordane (2011), 'Bankbus – Rute', available at: https://www.ssf.no/wps/portal/3890/!ut/p/c4/04_SB8K8xLLM9MSSzPy8xBz9CP0os3gjIx8nZzcPIwN3C183AyNDV0vPUFMnYwMXQ_3g1Dz9gmxHRQAdLJ2d/?WCM_GLOBAL_CONTEXT=/wps/wcm/connect/3890innhold/ssf+site/about/local+pages/askvoll/bankbuss+-+rute (accessed 18 June 2012).

Statistics Norway (2010), 'Tabell 06972, Brukere av hjemmetjenester (hjemmesykepleie og praktisk bistand) etter alder og bistandsbehov', available at: http://statbank.ssb.no/statistikkbanken/Default_FR.asp?PXSid=0&nvl=true&PLanguage=0&tilside=selectvarval/define.asp&Tabellid=06972 (accessed 18 June 2012).

Swedish Post and Telecom Agency (PTS) (2010a), Interview with Anna-Karin Hellsten, 25 November.

Swedish Post and Telecom Agency (PTS) (2010b), 'Grundläggande betaltjänster, delredovisning av regeringsuppdrag', Stockholm.

Swedish Post and Telecom Agency (PTS) (2011), 'Grundläggande betaltjänster, slutredovisning av regeringsuppdrag', Stockholm.

Tysnes Sparebank (2011), available at: http://www.tysnes-sparebank.no/omoss/kontaktoss/Sider/Kontaktoss.aspx (accessed 18 June 2012).

12. Dynamic letter volume models: how does an economic downturn affect substitution propensities?

Vance L. Martin,[†] **Chris J. Paterson,**[‡] **Heikki Nikali**[§] **and Qiubang Li**[¶]

1 INTRODUCTION

In very recent years discussions about transactional letter volumes worldwide have tended to emphasize the difficulties created by deteriorating economic conditions compounded by substantive movements towards electronic substitutes to the traditional mail item. Structural changes to the postal landscape in the realm of electronic substitution have been well documented throughout the literature (Nikali, 2008, 2011; Paterson, 2008; Martin et al., 2011 Meschi et al., 2011). However, the magnitude of Europe's recent economic instabilities and the global financial crises that immediately predated such events have tended to draw the focus back onto providing a cyclical rationale for letter volume declines as of late. The associated lower levels of domestic demand logically reduce both transactional letter volumes and the level of discretionary spending that drives promotional activities of which letter segments such as Direct Mail are included.

Instead of treating the cyclical and structural change effects as two separate components, a natural generalization is to develop general equilibrium type models linking these, and indeed other, letter volume drivers under a single unifying system. Given that different letter volume segments are exposed to different types of substitution occurring at differing speeds, it is important to recognize the impact that an adverse economic shock might have on accelerating movements towards the electronic alternatives. This is especially the case for letter volume segments that have, until now tended to be characterized by positive growth in the absence of rampant digital substitution. Indeed, contractions in economic growth rates add pressure on senders to change their processes as they seek out alternatives to maintain profit margins. Mail is not immune from these changes. Senders become increasingly likely in such adverse economic conditions to engage in cost containment strategies that might involve substitution, consolidation and rationalization activities. In effect, this widens the net of substitution via accelerated behavioral change that will logically impact negatively on previously well-performing letter volume segments. Of most relevant importance in the current postal environment is the extent to

† Professor of Econometrics, Department of Economics, University of Melbourne, Australia.
‡ Director, Diversified Specifics, Australia.
§ Research Director, Itella Corporation.
¶ Lead Programmer, Diversified Specifics, Australia.

which the presence and magnitude of this added impetus to substitutive alternatives in times of an economic downturn determines how rapidly transactional bill presentment type letter volumes, more commonly thought of as invoices and statements, will decline.

This chapter proceeds as follows. In Section 2 some background to developing a system of econometric models is provided as well as motivating the adoption of Finland as a case study for the development of dynamic models which allow for the interaction of both cyclical and structural change effects in demand. Focusing predominantly on transactional letter segments in Finland, the formal system of equations are specified and estimated in Section 3. This analysis is extended in Section 4 by exploring the linkages between substitution and the level of economic activity in periods of high and low economic growth. Section 5 then draws a set of conclusions in addition to pointing towards future directions given an eventual return to a more stable economic climate.

2 LETTER VOLUMES IN FINLAND

The issue of electronic substitution away from the traditional mail item is symptomatic of not only the Finnish economy but indeed the wider Scandinavian countries in general. Addressed letter volumes in Denmark are now 45 percent lower than the levels prevalent in the year 2000 and also lower in Norway (30 percent), Sweden (20 percent) and Finland (10 percent). These declines are in direct contrast to national economies that have grown by one-quarter in Finland and Sweden over the corresponding period, by one-fifth in Norway and 7 percent in Denmark (Eurostat, 2012). In an era prior to widespread substitutive pressures these natural demand pressures would have generally translated into letter volume increases.

Considering other long-run drivers of letter volumes, price increases have consumed some of the potential demand, although such increases explain only a part of the total decline and are, in some ways inexorably tied to the structural change occurring within the wider postal landscape. Increasing costs, diminishing volumes and expanding delivery points implies, in the absence of fundamental changes to the universal service obligations in delivery, that one of the only levers available to limit revenue declines rests with higher prices. However, the changing environment has led to intertemporal increases in price elasticities across letter volume segments traditionally thought to be very price inelastic only a few years earlier. Therefore, a sound understanding of exactly how letter volumes will respond to price changes in the present climate is required, otherwise such aggressive pricing regimes could be ill conceived and revenue depleting.

The impact of the remaining long-run drivers of letter volumes, population and delivery service performance, has been crowded out by persistent and aggressive surges in substitution over recent times. On average, population growth in the Nordic countries is 0.5 percent annually, which could be expected to increase letter volumes in previous decades (ibid.). However, population growth tends to provide little demand stimulus to letter volumes in the short run. In addition, any gains from delivery service quality on the demand for letter services have also been mitigated by a lack of variability over the medium term.

Unquestionably, recent declines in letter volume demand across each of the Nordic countries can be attributable to some form of substitution. Moreover, its progression at different speeds in different countries across different letter volume segments is reflected in falls of differing magnitudes at all levels. To appreciate fully the true impact on letter volumes it is crucial to understand that there are two different kinds of substitution: direct substitution, whereby a message that was earlier sent as a paper letter, for example an invoice, is transferred to an electronic channel; and indirect substitution, whereby behavioral switches to the electronic channels consumes letter demand potential, for example an energy company may not offer a new customer any other option than to receive invoices in their electronic form (Nikali, 2011).

In reference to mail, transactions necessarily consist of dual activities: bill presentments and bill payments. It is generally accepted that substitution of bill-payment type mail has been occurring for some time since the advent of direct debit payment facilities in addition to the emergence and widespread penetration of Internet and telephone banking. Moreover, the payment of invoices in Finland now exists almost entirely through the Internet (Federation of Finnish Financial Services, 2011).

However, the most significant substitutive factor in very recent times and the most potent threat to future mail volumes has been the realm of bill presentments. That is, the trend towards a fundamental and widespread transfer from paper-based communications to electronic channels of the invoices and statements currently received by consumers.

Indeed, it is the differences in adaptation to this change that explains the considerable variations in very recent letter volume trends within the Nordic countries. When the Danes were asked in 2010 what their main invoice reception channel was, only one-third were still using the paper alternative (Elkelä, 2011a), in contrast to 50 percent of Norwegians, 70 percent of Swedes and 80 percent of Finns. At the same time, letter volumes in Denmark have collapsed, whereas in Finland the fall has, for the time being, been moderate. The significance of consumer invoicing in letter communication in the Nordic countries is overwhelming, since almost every second letter includes an invoice and the majority of these invoices are sent from enterprises to consumers (Nikali and Sandell, 2011). Figures 12.1 and 12.2 suggest that trends in the volume of addressed letters are highly correlated with the importance of a letter in the receipt of an invoice on the part of a consumer. At present, the letter remains the consumers' most important means of receiving invoices in Finland, although in Denmark, for the most part, invoices are already presented electronically.

Letter volume trends in differing sender and receiver segments have been regularly measured in Finland for the last 20 years (ibid.). Itella supplied the Finnish letter volume data utilized in this study, as illustrated in Figure 12.3, and this can be delineated into three main segments which have each tended to behave differently in recent times (Nikali, 2008, 2011). These segments are business-to-business (B2B) paper-based invoice volumes, consumer sent mail and business-to-consumer (B2C) paper-based invoice volumes.

B2B paper-based invoice volumes tend to be bulk bill presentment type correspondence emanating from medium and large enterprises directed at other firms. Substitution of all letters in the B2B sector began as early as the beginning of the 1990s as telefax became common and in pace with EDI (electronic dada interchange) technology. In the last half of the 1990s, email rapidly became a standard feature in enterprises and largely replaced letter communications within this sector. At the same time, telefax was forced to make way for the new technologies. As a result the B2B volume segment has been characterized by a sustained downward trend since 1990, as depicted in Figure 12.3.

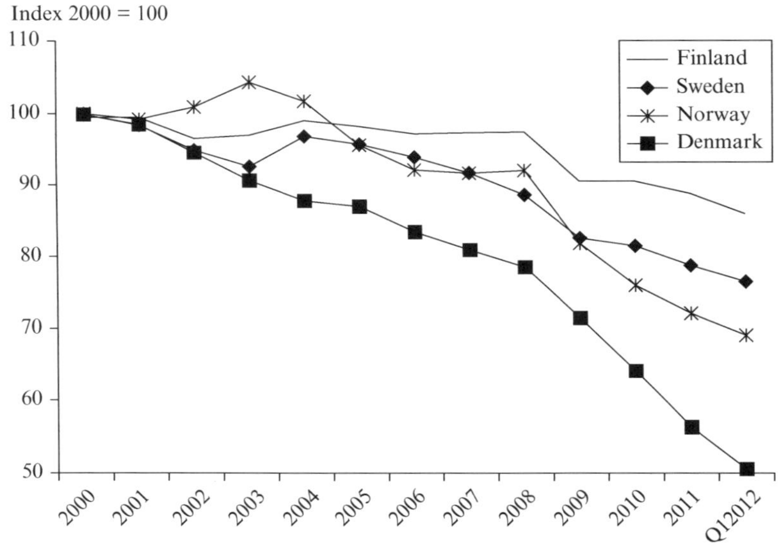

Source: Itella, Quarterly and Annual reports.

Figure 12.1 Addressed letter volumes in the Nordic countries

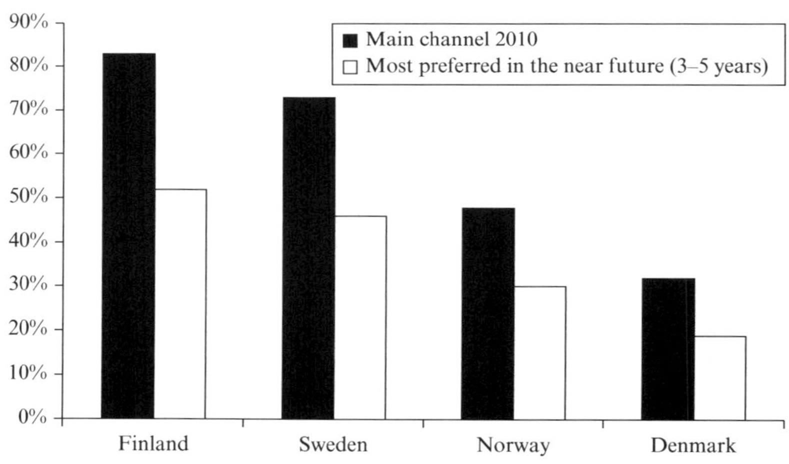

Figure 12.2 Role of letters in consumer invoicing, based on the consumers' own view

Positive growth rates in Finnish consumer-sent letters were evident until 1999, after which volumes in this letter volume segment have exhibited a steady decline. This deterioration can be attributable to the penetration levels of broadband among Finnish households following the turn of the millennium which gave added impetus to the use of email as a substitute to the traditional consumer sent mail item (Nikali, 2008).

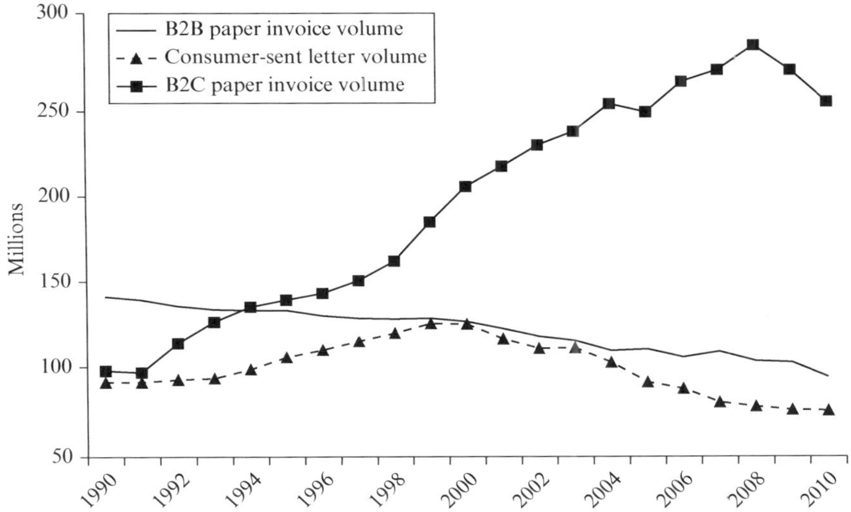

Source: Itella, 2012.

Figure 12.3 B2B paper invoice volume vs consumer-sent volumes vs B2C paper invoice volume (1990–2010)

B2C paper-based invoice volumes may be defined as bulk bill presentment type correspondence emanating from medium and large enterprises sent to households throughout Finland. In contrast to the B2B and consumer-sent mail segments there has been substantial growth in B2C paper-based invoice volumes since the early 1990s (see Figure 12.3). Growth in the B2C segment has largely been a consequence of the explosion in invoices and statements rendered for increases in the number of credit cards, the expansion of mobile phone handsets, increasing penetration rates of the Internet, and so on. Such effects, combined with the absence of a universally accepted alternative platform to the traditional mail item, have delayed the downside impact of substitution in the B2C segment. Similar trends have been observed in other parts of the world such as Australia, for example where PreSort Barcoded small letter volumes experienced comparably high growth rates over the same timeframe (Martin et al., 2011). However, momentum for substitution has been gathering in the last few years. Certainly, the availability and sender–receiver acceptance of electronic substitutes in the B2B segment predated equivalent alternatives in the B2C segment. Since 2008, however, mail recipients have signaled initial movements towards an electronic channel for invoices due to two main 'push' strategies on the part of the sender: a surcharge on the receipt of paper-based invoices; and/or the absence of any paper-based alternatives to the consumer for certain electronic invoices (Elkelä, 2011b). This substitution effect can partially explain why B2C volumes from 2008 have registered a sharp decline. Obviously such effects have coincided with the onset of the global financial crisis providing additional downside pressures on letter volumes in this segment.

The general consensus is that the trend to electronic consumer invoices is now under way in Finland and will progress swiftly over the next few years, in a similar fashion to the trend that has occurred in Denmark during the middle of the last decade (Kiikkilä et al., 2008; Elkelä, 2011a). This chapter attempts to evaluate the extent to which the magnitude and speed of the losses to substitution will be accelerated by a deteriorating global and domestic economic climate.

3 MODELING FRAMEWORK AND ESTIMATED RESULTS

Vector error correction modeling (VECM) techniques have been utilized to analyze letter volumes dynamically by a number of researchers in recent times (Trinkner and Grossman, 2006; Martin et al., 2011). This chapter employs this methodological approach to understanding the impact that economic shocks have on advancing movements towards substitutive alternatives to mail. Such an investigation must focus on a country that has been characterized by a number of quantifiable shocks to provide sufficient evidence of an association. A good example is the Finnish economy, as it has experienced a number of downturns over the same timeframe and therefore represents a sound case study for an application of this econometric methodology. In contrast, Australia represents an economy that does not provide such opportunities, as a sustained resources boom has insulated it against recessionary pressures for the best part of the last two decades (see Martin et al., 2011).

The framework required for this analysis ideally should construct a model that nests the structural and cyclical components of letter volumes. A VECM framework represents an ideal technique to do so as it is based on modeling the interactions of the long- and short-run characteristics of letter volumes. The methodological approach is similar to Martin et al. insofar as the importance of establishing a robust econometric baseline is still relevant as traditional associations continue to hold. However, like Martin et al., it becomes important to delve deeper into different possibilities for augmenting the baseline based upon emerging trends and substantive shocks.

Acknowledging there are m different letter segments, let $VOLUME_{t,m}$ represent the volume of letters at time t and $X_{t,m}$ represent a set of drivers determining letter volumes also at time t for the m letter segment. The relationship between $VOLUME_{t,m}$ and $X_{t,m}$ is given by:

$$VOLUME_{t,m} = \beta_0 + \beta_1 X_{t,m} + u_{t,m}, \qquad (12.1)$$

where β_0 and β_1 are parameters and $u_{t,m}$ is a disturbance term. Under the condition that $VOLUME_{t,m}$ and $X_{t,m}$ are both nonstationary integrated processes with stochastic trends, these variables represent a cointegrated system provided that $u_{t,m}$ is a stationary process. Within this framework $\beta_0 + \beta_1 X_{t,m}$ represents the level of letter volumes in the long run as deviations from this relationship are transitory by definition, as measured by the stationary disturbance term, $u_{t,m}$.

The short-run component of the model is a dynamic multivariate system whereby each variable in (12.1) generally adjusts towards the long-run equilibrium. For simplicity assume that $X_{t,m}$ is a scalar, then the VECM is:

$$\Delta VOLUME_{t,m} = \alpha_{0,v} + \alpha_1 u_{t-1,m} + \phi_{1,1}\Delta VOLUME_{t-1,m} + \phi_{1,2}\Delta X_{t-1,m} + v_{1,t}$$
$$\Delta X_{t,m} = \alpha_{0,X} + \alpha_2 u_{t-1,m} + \phi_{2,1}\Delta VOLUME_{t-1,m} + \phi_{2,2}\Delta X_{t-1,m} + v_{2,t}, \quad (12.2)$$

where $v_{1,t}$ and $v_{2,t}$ are stationary disturbance terms with zero means, constant variances and constant covariances. Although the lag structure is set to one year, longer lags may easily be incorporated. Importantly for the short run, the parameters α_1 and α_2 are the error-correction parameters, which control the speed and direction of the system towards the long run in the next period following a shock to the long run, as given by $u_{t,m}$. The parameters $\phi_{i,j}$ allow for additional short-run characteristics as the process equilibrates towards the long run, such as oscillatory behavior, for example.

Annual letter volume data covering the 1990–2010 timeframe were supplied by Itella with the primary letter segments delineated into three parts: (i) B2B paper-based invoices; (ii) B2C paper-based invoices; and (iii) consumer-sent letters. All VECMs developed contain an intercept in the cointegrating equation and the error-correction component of the model. Indeed, all models are also characterized by a single lag. Finally, contained within the short-run component of the model for each of the three letter segment VECMs is a dichotomous variable denoting the global financial crisis (*DUM_GFC*) and a short-run demand pressure variable given by population growth in Finland (*DLOGPOP*). The initial selection of the prospective structural components of the model was guided by previous studies such as Martin et al. (2011), given that a number of statistical regularities in the model drivers across Finland and Australia were clearly evident.

Model A B2B Paper-based Invoice Model

Given the initial investigation of the drivers, the key variables included in the VECM for B2B letter volumes in natural logarithms consists of:

1. *GDPPC* : Finnish GDP per capita, natural logarithms;
2. *PRICE* : Real company price of letters relative to the consumer price index (CPI), natural logarithms; and
3. *ELECB2BPC* : B2B electronic invoices per capita.

To identify the presence of any long-run relationships among B2B letter volumes and the three key drivers listed above, Table 12.1 provides the results of the cointegration tests among these four variables. The results suggest the presence of two cointegrating relationships among the four variables. Some additional empirical investigations implied that letter volumes and real GDP per capita are cointegrated, a result which is achieved by performing the cointegrating test on a bivariate model consisting of these two variables. The second cointegrating equation is represented by a linear combination of all four variables. To gain insight into the effects of having two error-correction terms compared to having only one error-correction term in the VECM, both systems of equations are estimated. The results show that both models generated similar dynamic structures in the form of similar impulse response patterns. However, due to the loss of degrees of freedom arising from specifying the more general VECM containing two cointegrating

Table 12.1 Mackinnon–Haug–Micheklis cointegration test of the B2B paper-based invoice model

Hypothesized no. of cointegrating equations	*P*-value
None	0.0000
At most 1	0.0000
At most 2	0.1375
At most 3	0.2623

vectors, the impulse responses are presented for the tighter of the two specifications, containing just the one error-correction term.

The estimated long-run cointegrating equation with standard errors in parentheses is:

$$B2BVOL_t = 0.486 + \underset{(0.136)}{1.452}\,GDPPC_t - \underset{(0.454)}{0.911}\,PRICE_t - \underset{(0.003)}{0.047}\,ELECB2BPC_t + \hat{u}_{t,m}, \tag{12.3}$$

where $\hat{u}_{t,m}$ is the residual. All three drivers of B2B volumes in the long run are statistically significant. The long run is characterized by a positive relationship between B2B volumes and GDP per capita with an elasticity of 1.452. There are also inverse relationships between B2B volumes and real price whereby a 1 percent increase in real price results in a fall of 0.911 percent in B2B volumes, and between B2B volumes and B2B electronic invoices per capita with a parameter estimate of –0.047. This translates into increasing (absolute) substitution elasticities of –0.806 in 2007 and –1.001 for 2010, where the elasticities are calculated by multiplying the long-run semi-elasticity estimate of –0.047 for the substitution variable by the values of *ELECB2BPC* in 2007 and 2010, respectively.

The short-run estimated model consisting of four equations corresponding to the four variables in the long-run equation, with standard errors in parentheses, is:

$$\begin{aligned}\Delta B2BVOL_t = &- \underset{(0.039)}{0.059} - \underset{(0.141)}{0.205}\hat{u}_{t-1,m} + \underset{(0.291)}{0.439}\Delta B2BVOL_{t-1}\\ &- \underset{(0.166)}{0.032}\Delta GDPPC_{t-1} + \underset{(0.383)}{0.106}\Delta PRICE_{t-1} - \underset{(0.016)}{0.036}\Delta ELECB2BPC_{t-1}\\ &- \underset{(0.016)}{0.030}DUM_{GFC} + \underset{(7.278)}{0.237}DLOGPOP + \hat{v}_{1,t}\end{aligned} \tag{12.4}$$

$$\begin{aligned}\Delta GDPPC_t = &- \underset{(0.041)}{0.080} + \underset{(0.147)}{0.476}\hat{u}_{t-1,m} + \underset{(0.304)}{0.145}\Delta B2BVOL_{t-1}\\ &- \underset{(0.174)}{0.293}\Delta GDPPC_{t-1} - \underset{(0.399)}{0.348}\Delta PRICE_{t-1} + \underset{(0.017)}{0.012}\Delta ELECB2BPC_{t-1}\\ &- \underset{(0.017)}{0.009}DUM\_GFC + \underset{(7.596)}{20.459}DLOGPOP + \hat{v}_{2,t}\end{aligned} \tag{12.5}$$

$$\begin{aligned}\Delta PRICE_t = &\ \underset{(0.022)}{0.019} - \underset{(0.080)}{0.253}\hat{u}_{t-1,m} - \underset{(0.166)}{0.019}\Delta B2BVOL_{t-1}\\ &+ \underset{(0.095)}{0.037}\Delta GDPPC_{t-1} + \underset{(0.218)}{0.116}\Delta PRICE_{t-1} - \underset{(0.009)}{0.022}\Delta ELECB2BPC_{t-1}\end{aligned}$$

$$+ \underset{(0.009)}{0.000}DUM\_GFC - \underset{(4.139)}{7.698}PDLOGPOP + \hat{v}_{3,t} \tag{12.6}$$

$$\Delta ELECB2BPC_t = -\underset{(0.846)}{0.113} + \underset{(3.060)}{4.241}\hat{u}_{t-1,m} + \underset{(6.314)}{0.843}\Delta B2BVOL_{t-1}$$

$$+ \underset{(3.606)}{5.462}\Delta GDPPC_{t-1} + \underset{(8.289)}{3.468}\Delta PRICE_{t-1} - \underset{(0.349)}{0.353}\Delta ELECB2BPC_{t-1}$$

$$+ \underset{(0.353)}{0.546}DUM\_GFC + \underset{(157.659)}{168.479}DLOGPOP + \hat{v}_{4,t}, \tag{12.7}$$

where $\hat{v}_{1,t} \ldots \hat{v}_{4,t}$ are the residuals from the VECM. With the exception of the last equation all of the error-correction parameters are statistically significant. The other explanatory variables in the VECM are statistically significant in some but not all equations. For example, the population variable is statistically significant in two of the four equations. Following the VECM methodology the strategy is to include all variables in all equations. To examine the substitution effects arising from changes in economic activity, Figure 12.4 gives the impulse response of the substitution variable *ELECB2BPC* with respect to a negative shock in GDP per capita equal to one standard deviation. This corresponds to a –0.0187 percentage change in GDP per capita. The results of the impulse response functions highlight an inverse relationship between income (*GDPPC*) and substitution (*ELECB2BPC*). The substitution dynamics suggest that it takes about four years for the full effects of a shock in GDP per capita to be transmitted through to the evolution of additional substitutive effects. As the impulse responses are expressed in terms of the change in substitution per capita with respect to a percentage change in per capita GDP the values reported in Figure 12.4 represent semi-elasticities. To convert these values to elasticities based on the level of substitution per capita in 2010 these impulses are divided by 21.226, the per capita substitution level in 2010. Performing this calculation for the long-run impulse response value of 0.402 from Figure 12.4 yields an elasticity of 0.019.

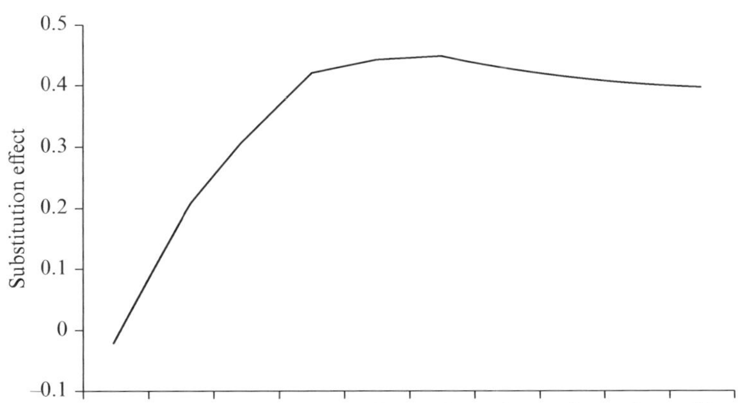

Figure 12.4 How B2B substitution responds to a GDP per capita shock

Alternatively, this suggests that a 1 percent fall in GDP per capita approximately translates into just under a 1 percent increase in substitution per capita approximately after four years. The results are consistent with letter volume trends in Finland after the deep depression in 2009 when GDP fell 8.4 percent. In that case, 2009 letter volumes did not react especially strongly to the economic drop in that same year. The effects of substitution only began to be observable in 2011 and in early 2012 when it manifested itself in a year-on-year fall of approximately 6 percent.

Model B Consumer-sent Letter Model

Given the initial investigation of the drivers the key variables included in the VECM for consumer-sent volumes in natural logarithms consists of:

1. *GDPPC* : Finnish GDP per capita, natural logarithms;
2. *PRICE* : real consumer price of letters relative to CPI, natural logarithms; and
3. *INTHOMEPC* : Internet penetration at home per capita.

As with the B2B letter volume model, a preliminary test of cointegration also suggests two cointegrating relationships among all four variables. The value of the statistic to test at most two cointegrating vectors is 13.588 which yields a p-value of 0.0637 in which case the null hypothesis is not rejected at the 5 percent level. Following the strategy of the B2B model, the VECM is based on the most general cointegrating relationship which includes all four variables.

The estimated long-run cointegrating equation with standard errors in parentheses is:

$$\begin{aligned} CONSVOL_t = & - 4.867 + \underset{(0.256)}{3.045} GDPPC_t - \underset{(0.131)}{0.145} PRICE_t \\ & - \underset{0.007}{0.097} INTHOMEPC_t + \hat{u}_{t,m}, \end{aligned} \tag{12.8}$$

where $\hat{u}_{t,m}$ is the residual. Two of the three drivers of consumer-sent volumes in the long run are statistically significant, namely *GDPPC* and *INTHOMEPC*. Holding all else constant, the long run is characterized by a positive relationship between consumer-sent volumes and GDP per capita with an elasticity of 3.045 which is approximately twice the magnitude of the equivalent income elasticity for the B2B letter volume segment. There is also a non-significant inverse relationship between consumer-sent volumes and price suggesting a highly inelastic response to a 1 percent increase in price that equates to a fall of 0.145 percent in consumer-sent volumes. The remaining association is between consumer-sent volumes and Internet penetration at home which is characterized by a parameter estimate of –0.097. This translates into increasing (absolute) substitution elasticities of –1.184 in 2007 and –1.296 for 2010, where the elasticities are calculated by multiplying the long-run semi-elasticity estimate of –0.097 for the substitution variable by the values of *INTHOMEPC* in 2007 and 2010, respectively.

The short-run estimated model consisting of four equations corresponding to the four variables in the long-run equation, with standard errors in parentheses, is:

$$\Delta CONSVOL_t = \underset{(0.099)}{-0.005} + \underset{(0.162)}{0.057}\hat{u}_{t-1,m} - \underset{(0.371)}{0.799}\Delta CONSVOL_{t-1}$$
$$+ \underset{(0.337)}{0.022}\Delta GDPPC_{t-1} + \underset{(0.304)}{0.263}\Delta PRICE_{t-1} + \underset{(0.033)}{0.022}\Delta INTHOMEPC_{t-1}$$
$$+ \underset{(0.048)}{0.033}DUM\_GFC + \underset{(17.670)}{3.998}DLOGPOP + \hat{v}_{1,t} \quad (12.9)$$

$$\Delta GDPPC_t = \underset{(0.027)}{-0.176} + \underset{(0.045)}{0.375}\hat{u}_{t-1,m} - \underset{(0.103)}{0.308}\Delta CONSVOL_{t-1}$$
$$- \underset{(0.094)}{0.142}\Delta GDPPC_{t-1} + \underset{(0.085)}{0.048}\Delta PRICE_{t-1} + \underset{(0.009)}{0.016}\Delta INTHOMEPC_{t-1}$$
$$+ \underset{(0.013)}{0.055}DUM\_GFC + \underset{(4.920)}{34.740}DLOGPOP + \hat{v}_{2,t} \quad (12.10)$$

$$\Delta PRICE_t = \underset{(0.113)}{0.094} - \underset{(0.186)}{0.051}\hat{u}_{t-1,m} - \underset{(0.423)}{0.201}\Delta CONSVOL_{t-1}$$
$$- \underset{(0.384)}{0.592}\Delta GDPPC_{t-1} + \underset{(0.347)}{0.089}\Delta PRICE_{t-1} + \underset{(0.037)}{0.026}\Delta INTHOMEPC_{t-1}$$
$$- \underset{(0.055)}{0.022}DUM_{GFC} - \underset{(20.158)}{10.781}DLOGPOP + \hat{v}_{3,t} \quad (12.11)$$

$$\Delta INTHOMEPC_t = \underset{(0.733)}{-0.127} + \underset{(1.207)}{0.136}\hat{u}_{t-1,m} - \underset{(2.754)}{3.487}\Delta CONSVOL_{t-1}$$
$$- \underset{(2.502)}{5.217}\Delta GDPPC_{t-1} + \underset{(2.256)}{3.076}\Delta PRICE_{t-1} - \underset{(0.242)}{0.566}\Delta INTHOMEPC_{t-1}$$
$$+ \underset{(0.359)}{0.018}DUM\_GFC + \underset{(131.157)}{93.025}DLOGPOP + \hat{v}_{4,t}, \quad (12.12)$$

where $\hat{v}_{1,t} \ldots \hat{v}_{4,t}$ are the residuals from the VECM. To examine the substitution effects on consumer-sent mail from a shock to economic activity, Figure 12.5 gives the impulse response of the substitution variable with respect to a negative shock in GDP per capita. As with the B2B impulse response results in Figure 12.4 there is an inverse relationship between a negative shock in GDP per capita and the substitution variable. Inspection of the impulse response suggests that the full effects of the GDP per capita shock take about four to five years to be transmitted fully through the system. As the impulse responses given in Figure 12.5 are expressed in terms of the change in substitution per capita with respect to a percentage change in per capita GDP, the values reported in the figure represent semi-elasticities. To convert these values to elasticities based on the level of substitution per capita in 2010, these impulses are divided by 13.406, the value of *INTHOMEPC* in 2010. Performing this calculation for the long-run impulse response value of 0.370 from Figure 12.5 yields an elasticity of 0.028. Alternatively, this suggests that a 1 percent fall in GDP per capita approximately translates into a 2.5 percent increase in substitution per capita after 10 years.

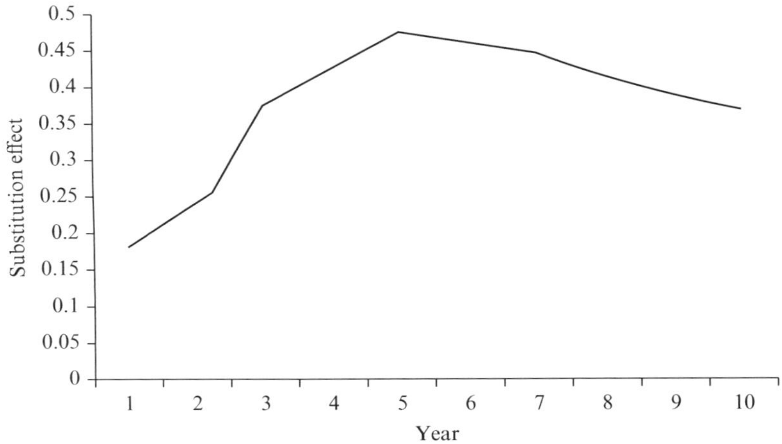

Figure 12.5 How consumer-sent mail substitution responds to a GDP per capita shock

Model C B2C Paper-based Invoice Model

Given the initial investigation of the drivers the key variables included in the VECM for B2C volumes in natural logarithms consists of:

1. *GDPPC* : Finnish GDP per capita, natural logarithms;
2. *PRICE* : real company price of letters relative to CPI, natural logarithms; and
3. *ELECB2CPC* : B2C electronic invoices per capita.

An important feature of the two previous letter volume segments is that substitution effects have been evident over the entire timeframe. In contrast, substitution effects for B2C letter volumes are a fairly recent phenomenon. As already noted in Section 2, there is a large decline in B2C letter volumes in the last three years of the timeframe (see Figure 12.3). To take account of these features the cointegration tests and the VECM model are initially conducted with the sampled period truncated to 2007 prior to the commencement of the global financial crisis. The value of the test statistic to test the null hypothesis of two cointegrating vectors is 11.095 which yields a p-value of 0.2057, showing that the null hypothesis is not rejected at the 5 percent level. Following the strategy of the other two letter segments the analysis is conducted with one cointegrating vector which contains all four variables in the system.

The estimated long-run cointegrating equation with standard errors in parentheses is:

$$B2CVOL_t = 0.549 + \underset{(0.063)}{1.751}GDPPC_t - \underset{(0.461)}{0.921}PRICE_t - \underset{(0.020)}{0.175}ELECB2CPC_t + \hat{u}_{t,m}, \quad (12.13)$$

where $\hat{u}_{t,m}$ is the residual. At conventional levels, all three drivers of B2C volumes in the long run are statistically significant. The long run is characterized by a positive relationship between B2C volumes and GDP per capita with an elasticity of 1.751 which, although marginally higher, bears more of a resemblance to the B2B letter volume income elasticity than it does to that of consumer-sent mail. There is also an inverse relationship between B2C volumes and real price whereby a 1 percent increase in the real price results in a fall on average of 0.921 percent in B2C volumes. The estimated semi-elasticity between B2C volumes and B2C electronic invoices per capita is –0.175. As with the previous letter volume segments, the substitution elasticity is computed as –0.594 in 2007, which more than quadruples (in absolute terms) to an equivalent figure of –2.730 in 2010.

The short-run estimated model consists of four equations corresponding to the four variables in the long-run equation, with standard errors in parentheses:

$$\begin{aligned}\Delta B2CVOL_t = {} & \underset{(0.059)}{0.099} - \underset{(0.086)}{0.495}\hat{u}_{t-1,m} - \underset{(0.163)}{0.114}\Delta B2CVOL_{t-1} \\ & - \underset{(0.245)}{0.041}\Delta GDPPC_{t-1} + \underset{(0.508)}{0.531}\Delta PRICE_{t-1} - \underset{(0.064)}{0.260}\Delta ELECB2CPC_{t-1} \\ & - \underset{(11.109)}{14.340}DLOGPOP + \hat{v}_{1,t} \end{aligned} \tag{12.14}$$

$$\begin{aligned}\Delta GDPPC_t = {} & \underset{(0.004)}{0.005} + \underset{(0.065)}{0.057}\hat{u}_{t-1,\mathrm{m}} + \underset{(0.123)}{0.001}\Delta B2CVOL_{t-1} \\ & - \underset{(0.184)}{0.514}\Delta GDPPC_{t-1} + \underset{(0.383)}{0.018}\Delta PRICE_{t-1} + \underset{(0.049)}{0.020}\Delta ELECB2PC_{t-1} \\ & + \underset{(8.373)}{2.517}DLOGPOP + \hat{v}_{2,\mathrm{t}} \end{aligned} \tag{12.15}$$

$$\begin{aligned}\Delta PRICE_t = {} & \underset{(0.025)}{0.056} + \underset{(0.036)}{0.075}\hat{u}_{t-1,m} + \underset{(0.069)}{0.169}\Delta B2CVOL_{t-1} \\ & + \underset{(0.103)}{0.227}\Delta GDPPC_{t-1} + \underset{(0.213)}{0.375}\Delta PRICE_{t-1} - \underset{(0.027)}{0.012}\Delta ELECB2CPC_{t-1} \\ & - \underset{(4.654)}{8.571}DLOGPOP + \hat{v}_{3,\mathrm{t}} \end{aligned} \tag{12.16}$$

$$\begin{aligned}\Delta ELECB2C_t = {} & - \underset{(0.343)}{0.436} + \underset{(0.496)}{1.141}\hat{u}_{t-1,m} + \underset{(0.945)}{0.505}\Delta B2CVOL_{t-1} \\ & + \underset{(1.415)}{1.044}\Delta GDPPC_{t-1} - \underset{(2.936)}{0.022}\Delta PRICE_{t-1} + \underset{(0.374)}{0.017}\Delta ELECB2CPC_{t-1} \\ & + \underset{(64.245)}{125.957}DLOGPOP + \hat{v}_{4,t}, \end{aligned} \tag{12.17}$$

where $\hat{v}_{1,t} \ldots \hat{v}_{4,t}$ are the residuals from the VECM. An important feature of this model is that it generates similar characteristics as the estimated models for B2B letter volumes and consumer-sent letter volumes. To investigate the very recent changes that have occurred with respect to B2C letter volumes, the following section allows for a more general VECM specification where substitution effects are allowed to differ over the business cycle.

4 INCOME-SUBSTITUTION EFFECTS DURING DOWNTURNS

The previous section established a statistically significant linkage between the level of economic activity and the tendency to substitute away from a traditional mail item to an electronic alternative across the three major letter volume segments in Finland, B2B, consumer-sent mail and B2C. A question that has increasing relevance though given recent periods of economic instability is the degree to which substitutive pressures gather momentum in times of low growth relative to periods characterized by a well-performing domestic economy. An increased impetus for change in a downturn has some sound intuitive basis. When revenues are squeezed senders are increasingly likely to focus on different avenues to maintain their profit margins. In the realm of mail there are a number of channels through which this might be achieved. Substitution is an obvious shift where the alternative represents an ongoing cost saving to the sender. Less obvious though are other forms of cost-containment strategies including consolidating multiple mail pieces into a single mailing. Indeed, rationalization strategies that aim at reducing the frequency of the billing cycle is another means by which firms might attempt to reduce their cost base. Each of these effects exposes downside pressures on letter volumes. While this chapter isolates the impact of slower economic growth on substitutive movements, similar principles apply to consolidation and rationalization strategies. Incorporating these effects into the existing VECM structure involves augmenting the four variate VECM of Section 3 with an additional variable defined as the product of the pertinent substitution variable and a dichotomous variable that revolves around a distinction between periods where the level of economic activity is above and below the long-run trend.

The effects of the global financial crisis on substitution elasticities for all three letter volume segments are given in Table 12.2. When the level of GDP per capita is below the long-run trend there tends to be an additional propensity to substitute across each of the major letter volume segments in Finland. In the case of the B2B letter volume segment the elasticity has changed from –0.684 to –0.786, and for consumer-sent mail the change is from –0.641 to –1.106. In both of these cases the change in elasticities is statistically significant. In the case of B2C there is an extremely large change in the elasticity from –2.729 to –26.477, although in contrast to the other two volume segment elasticity results, this change is statistically insignificant. This result is not too surprising though, as it reflects that the period of substitution for B2C letter volume substitution is rather short, making it difficult to derive a precise estimate to the change in the elasticity during the global economic crisis.

More broadly, there are implications for forecasting letter volumes. It is usually implied that substitution is facilitated by the effectiveness of a prevailing platform and the degree to which an appetite for that platform may be cultivated. Necessarily, this implies some form of behavioral change on the part of the sender to embrace the new platform, and the receiver to make the shift towards accepting that platform as a valid alternative to the traditional mail item. However, the results of this chapter suggest that these motivations and incentives gather momentum in times of low, stagnant or declining economic

Table 12.2 Long-run substitution elasticities evaluated at 2010 values

	Model A: B2B	Model B: Consumer-sent mail	Model C: B2C
Above trend	−0.684	−0.641	−2.729
Below trend (downturns)	−0.786	−1.106	−26.477

growth. That is, there tends to be a greater propensity to substitute away from the traditional mail item in a relatively adverse economic climate.

It is also important to note the magnitude of the results given in Table 12.2. The parameter estimates on the dichotomous business cycle variable are increasingly conclusive for the letter volume segments that have been subjected to protracted periods of sustained substitutive pressures. On the other hand, B2C substitution of bill-presentment type mail (invoices) is generally expected to be on the cusp of the next major wave of electronic substitution and the evidence suggests that, on the back of protracted economic difficulties there quite possibly could be a more rapid rate of substitution for this mail segment as the expected availability, acceptance and usage of electronic platforms are coinciding with some of the most severe economic conditions witnessed in recent decades. The inference is that the atmosphere for substitution has never been greater.

5 CONCLUSIONS

In varying degrees of magnitude and duration, as illustrated in Figure 12.2, recent declines have emerged across all letter volume segments in Finland and there is a need to disentangle the cyclical effects from the effects that represent changes in the underlying structure of letter volumes. Some of the most recent declines in letter volumes have occurred due to the cyclical effects associated with lower rates of economic growth. Diminished demand within the domestic economy reduces the number of transactions and in turn results in declining letter volumes on both sides of a transaction – bill presentments and bill payments. Fewer invoices are mailed, therefore fewer can be settled relative to periods of stronger growth.

As distinguished from the cyclical effects, emerging changes in structural trends represent another threat to letter volumes and can arise in areas such as a consolidation of multiple forms of communication into one letter; a rationalization of billing cycles; and new forms of electronic substitution as an alternative to mail. Trends in these areas threaten to impact greatly on B2C paper-based invoice volumes in the future as profit-maximizing firms seek to reduce their cost base. Up until the onset of the global financial crisis it was this letter segment that had traditionally experienced significant growth for the past two decades. Such growth was largely a consequence of the explosion in bill-presentment type mail as invoices and statements were rendered for increases in the number of credit cards, the expansion of mobile phone handsets, increasing penetration rates of Pay TV, the Internet, and so on.

Complicating measurement difficulties attributable to these affects, the cyclical and structural change effects are not mutually exclusive. Indeed in times of lower rates of economic activity there is a greater propensity for senders to investigate alternatives and enforce change. The results of the estimated models show a strong and inverse relationship between GDP per capita and substitutive effects away from the traditional mail item. Indeed, the results also demonstrate that the severity of the global financial crisis has created an atmosphere that facilitates substitutive pressures and encourages push-and-pull strategies by the senders to enforce a movement away from the traditional mail item for all letter volume segments. Given that substitution has occurred for B2B and consumer-sent mail for some time now, the results would appear to indicate that it is the B2C letter volume segment that will be most prone to downside pressure, and the environment could enforce a more rapid movement away from the traditional mail channel than otherwise observed for the remaining letter volume segments. With a return to more stable economic conditions, it will be of interest to utilize such a system in identifying whether an economic downturn either results in a one-off downward shift in the level of demand or has acted as a catalyst for further substitution resulting in an accelerated downward trend in mail over time.

REFERENCES

Elkelä, K. (2011a), 'Invoicing in 16 European countries', in M.A. Crew and P.R. Kleindorfer (eds), *Reinventing the Postal Sector in an Electronic Age*, Cheltenham, UK and Northampton, MA, USA: Edward Elgar, pp. 20–35.

Elkelä, K. (2011b), 'Sähköinen kuluttajalaskutus Suomessa 2011', Helsinki: Itella Corp., Research Series 46/2011.

Eurostat (2012), Database.

Federation of Finnish Financial Services (2011), 'Säästäminen, luotonkäyttö ja maksaminen', Helsinki: Research Publication, May.

Kiikkilä, L., M. Paakkari and H. Nikali (2008), 'Receiving invoices among Nordic and German consumers', Helsinki: Itella Corp., Research Series 13/2008.

Martin V.L., C.J. Paterson and X. Wang (2011), 'Forecasting letter volumes: augmenting econometric baseline projections', in M.A. Crew and P.R. Kleindorfer (eds), *Multi-modal Competition and the Future of Mail*, Cheltenham, UK and Northampton, MA, USA: Edward Elgar.

Meschi, M., M. Cherry, C. Pace and M. Petrova (2011), 'Understanding the impact of e-substitution on letter mail volumes: a multi-country panel study', in M.A. Crew and P.R. Kleindorfer (eds), *Reinventing the Postal Sector in an Electronic Age*, Cheltenham, UK and Northampton, MA, USA: Edward Elgar.

Nikali, H. (2008), 'Substitution of letter mail for different sender–receiver segments', in M.A. Crew and P.R. Kleindorfer (eds), *Competition and Regulation in the Postal and Delivery Sector*, Cheltenham, UK and Northampton, MA, USA: Edward Elgar.

Nikali, H. (2011), 'Does the level of price elasticity change with the progression of substitution?', in M.A. Crew and P.R. Kleindorfer (eds), *Reinventing the Postal Sector in an Electronic Age*, Cheltenham, UK and Northampton, MA, USA: Edward Elgar.

Nikali, H. and S. Sandell (2011), 'Content Survey for Letter Communication 2010', Helsinki: Itella Corp., Research Series 1/2011.

Paterson, C.J. (2008), 'Postal reform in Australia', in M.A. Crew, P.R. Kleindorfer and J.I Campbell (eds), *Handbook of Worldwide Postal Reform*, Cheltenham, UK and Northampton, MA, USA: Edward Elgar.

Trinkner, U. and M. Grossman (2006), 'Forecasting Swiss mail demand' in M.A. Crew and P.R. Kleindorfer (eds), *Progress Toward Liberalization of the Postal and Delivery Sector*, New York: Springer.

13. Electronic substitution and USO scope definition*

Marcello Cuomo,[†] Tommaso Nardone,[‡] Alberto Rovero[§] and Gennaro Scarfiglieri[¶]

1 INTRODUCTION

Postal markets worldwide are experiencing a long-term trend of decreasing mail volumes as a consequence of e-substitution. Such a trend is likely to be exacerbated over the coming years by a prolonged situation of economic crises. Mail volume reduction, in turn, causes a continuous uptrend in the unit costs of mail, since fixed costs of production are spread over fewer volumes. The increase in unit costs is greater for universal service providers (USPs), since such an obligation makes their cost structure more rigid. USPs cannot balance the increase in unit cost with price increases: such an increase, in fact, would accelerate e-substitution and might result also in the loss of volumes to competitors. Increasing prices may not be the answer as the reduced volume resulting would lead to a further increase in unit costs, potentially triggering a graveyard spiral. Under the condition that the firm providing the service is free to adapt its service level and its base cost to worsening conditions, it is still possible to work out ways to render the firm financially viable. However, the requirement to provide a universal service (national geographical delivery coverage, six days a week service, J+1 service) imposes a number of rigidities on the cost structure of the USP that seriously threaten its financial viability. A USP may well find itself with a shrinking gap between its unit cost and unit revenue that cannot be dealt with, unless universal service requirements are changed.

Studies by Cohen and McBride (2008), Borsenberger et al. (2010), Cohen et al. (2010) and Pearsall and Trozzo (2011) have all addressed reduction in the USO as a means of improving USP finances. Cohen and McBride (2008) and Cohen et al. (2010) estimate the impact on costs deriving from a reduction in delivery frequency and demand level. Borsenberger et al. (2010) divide the territory into homogeneous areas, and for each area identify the delivery frequency that maximizes the profit of the postal operator under three different 'demand scenarios' (low, medium and high). Pearsall and Trozzo (2011) use a hedonic function to estimate the impacts on demand deriving from a reduction of delivery frequency, as well as quantify the impact on cost through an econometric model.

This chapter assesses the impact of USO constraints on the USP cost structure, as

† Strategic Planning, Poste Italiane.
‡ Strategic Planning, Poste Italiane.
§ Strategic Planning, Poste Italiane.
¶ Strategic Planning, Poste Italiane.

well as their combined effect, in a market environment characterized by the shrinking of volumes due to e-substitution. In particular, the chapter will evaluate the single and the joint effect of easing the constraints by eliminating the obligation to provide a J+1 product, by allowing the USP to reduce the frequency of delivery and by reducing the obligation to deliver nationwide. The end result is a grid presenting the simulation results in terms of both number of years in which a simulated USP will keep on presenting a positive profit and loss (P&L) balance and total earnings cumulatively gained by the USP during the years of positive P&L, depending on the extent to which the USP has been allowed to ease USO constraints.

The results are obtained with reference to a specific USP, Poste Italiane in 2009, so further research is needed in order to evaluate the extent to which conclusions are still valid in a more general framework.

The chapter is arranged as follows: Section 2 illustrates the simulation model and data used; Sections 3 and 4 detail the demand and cost function, which are the base for the simulation results that follow (Section 5). Conclusions are in Section 6.

2 MODEL AND DATA

The Universal Service Obligation (USO) involves imposing a variety of constraints on the commercial and operational behavior of the USP. Typically these constraints relate to: uniform price – irrespective of the origin and destination of the postal item – guaranteeing a nationwide coverage in terms of collection and delivery of mail, speed of delivery of the items, and delivery for a certain number of days in a week. This chapter focuses on the three most relevant of these constraints, that is, the provision of quality services, which is defined as the obligation to provide a J+1 product, the provision of a daily delivery service and the provision of a nationwide delivery coverage. In order to assess the impact of each of these constraints on the USP cost structure, in a market environment characterized by the shrinking of volumes from e-substitution, we shall evaluate the effect of easing each constraint by eliminating the obligation to provide a J+1 product, by allowing the USP to reduce the frequency of delivery and by reducing the obligation to deliver nationwide, that is, discontinuing delivery service in the least appealing parts of the national territory.[1]

The approach used in this chapter consists in:

1. simulating the P&L account of universal service provision by Poste Italiane in 2009 and projecting it over the coming years, by holding constant USO scope definition, in order to assess the impact that e-substitution will play on the P&L over the years, with special reference to the moment in time in which the P&L balance will turn into a loss;
2. simulating the impact of easing the three main constraints deriving from USO on the revenue and cost of the P&L over the coming years;
3. presenting the results of the simulation in terms of both number of years starting from 2009 in which the USP will keep on presenting a positive P&L and total earnings cumulatively gained by the USP during the years of positive P&L. In particular, the cumulated USP positive earnings can be interpreted as a mean through which the USP can finance its 'survival' once P&L becomes negative.

The case of Poste Italiane as USP may be especially interesting in that Italy is one of the largest economies in Europe and yet it is one of the least-developed countries in terms of postal items per capita. Therefore, it is particularly interesting to explore the relationship between e-substitution and USO scope definition in relation to Italy, since over the coming years the Italian USP will be facing one of the greatest threats, among its European peers, from e-substitution.

The base year for our simulation model is 2009, since that was the last year of the six days a week delivery. In fact, starting from 2010, in Italy delivery frequency has gradually been reduced to five days a week; since the present work relies on some actual data referring to the current Italian USP, for example, data on yearly postal items and revenues, the year 2009 was chosen as 2010 data were influenced by the ongoing process of reduction in the frequency of delivery.

In order to simulate the universal service P&L of Poste Italiane in 2009, holding the USO scope definition constant (J+1 service, 6 days a week service, 100 percent rural delivery coverage), publicly available data on universal revenues and volumes were used. With regard to cost, a reasonable estimate of each stage of the postal value chain in 2009 was obtained through an application of the Cohen et al. (2006) model.

In order to simulate the impact of different USO scope definitions on demand, the model mainly relies on results by Pearsall and Trozzo (2011). As for cost, in order to highlight the way in which each of the components of USO scope definition affects the cost level of each stage of the postal value chain, the model adapts the PwC (2006) cost model so as to pinpoint the cost variables directly linked with changes in the USO scope definition. As a consequence, it was possible to calculate revenues and costs associated with different definitions of USO scope.

Since the model evaluates universal service P&L under different USO scope definitions in relation to the ongoing process of e-substitution, all simulated P&L accounts refer to future years. Therefore, future volumes are estimated by projecting current volumes on the basis of the previous year's trends and GDP forecasts. In particular, the expected yearly reduction in volume due to e-substitution is set at 3 percent, in line with prevailing estimates for France, Germany, Spain, the United Kingdom and the United States. As for monetary projections, the USP cost base and unit revenue are inflated by a compound annual rate of 1.5 percent – the expected inflation rate in Italy over the coming years.

The USP offering, demand and cost model will be detailed in the following sections.

3 USP OFFERING AND DEMAND FUNCTION

It is assumed that the USP may provide a maximum of two postal products: one product with delivery time in J+1 and another product with delivery time in J+3. The price of the product with delivery in J+1 is higher than that of the product with delivery in J+3. The USO may force the USP to provide either both products or only the J+3 product. The maximum price the USP may charge on any of the two products is set by the regulator.

The model focuses on two further characteristics of USO: weekly frequency of delivery and rural areas delivery coverage. Weekly frequency of delivery varies from one to six days per week and it will be indicated with F^D. Rural areas delivery coverage (C^R) represents the percentage of rural postal routes that will be served by the USP. By ordering rural delivery routes in terms of delivered volumes, it is assumed that USO scope definition in terms of rural areas delivery coverage can be reduced by the regulator from 100 to 90, 80, 70, 60 or 50 percent. It is further assumed that the regulator will never reduce delivery frequency in urban areas.

The J+3 product will be delivered on the third day following the day in which the item has been handed to the USP for delivery, provided that the third day is a day in which delivery actually takes place, depending on the chosen weekly frequency of delivery. If the possible day for delivery is not the third day that follows the handing over of the item to the USP, but the fourth or the fifth day, delivery will actually take place on the fourth or the fifth day. For the sake of simplicity it is assumed that all J+3 items will be delivered with certainty the third or the first possible day thereafter, that is, the quality target and the quality result for the J+3 product are both set at 100 percent.

The demand for each of the two products provided by the USP is represented by a specific function. The demand for the product with delivery in J+1 (D_{J1}) is a function of its own price (P_{J1}), of the weekly frequency of delivery (F^D) and of the territorial coverage provided by the USP (C). The demand for the product with delivery in J+3 is a function of its own price (P_{J3}), of the weekly frequency of delivery (F^D), of the territorial coverage provided by the USP (C) and of the availability of a J+1 delivery product.

Market demand equations for universal service products are as follows:

$$D_{US} = D_{J1} + D_{J3},$$

where:

$$D_{J1} = \begin{cases} f(P_{J1}, F^D, C^R) & \text{if USO scope includes a J+1 product offering,} \\ 0 & \text{otherwise} \end{cases}$$

$$D_{J3} = \begin{cases} g(P_{J3}, F^D, C^R) & \text{if USO scope includes a J+1 product offering,} \\ g(P_{J3}, F^D, C^R) + f(P_{J1}, F^D, C^R) & \text{otherwise,} \end{cases}$$

and where: P_{J1} and P_{J3} are the prices, respectively, of the J+1 and of the J+3 product; F^D is the weekly frequency of delivery, ranging from 6 to 1 and C^R is the rural territorial coverage in terms of delivery provided by the USP, which can be equal to 100, 90, 80, 70, 60 or 50 percent.

The two equations above differ from each other since if the USO scope includes a J+1 offering, the supplied quantity of universal service products is determined by the corresponding demand equation illustrated above. However, if the USO does not include a compulsory provision of a J+1 product, then the USP will not be offering it, since it is a loss-making product.[2] In this case the demand for the J+3 product will be increased by the demand of the J+1 product that would have been expressed by customers at the set regulatory price of P_{J1}; this happens notwithstanding the fact that the quality of the J+3 product is lower, since the best alternative product available for customers on the market is the J+5 supplied by competitors.

The demand for each product offered by the USP is affected by its own price. Prices are assumed to be set at their maximum level by the regulator and any price decrease (discount) would increase USP's volumes only to a very limited extent, since competitors offer only a J+5 product, at a price which is significantly lower than the USP's J+3 price. In other words, the elasticity of demand is very low and the USP worsens its profitability by lowering the price of either of its two products. By charging the regulatory set maximum prices, the USP is capable of keeping its volumes, thanks to the better quality and reliability of its products, in respect to those of competitors.

The demand for both products offered by the USP is affected by the weekly frequency of delivery. The functioning of the contractual agreement between the USP and a customer for a J+1 and a J+3 product, for a given frequency of delivery, has been illustrated above. As for the elasticity of demand in respect to changes in the frequency of delivery, the model relies on the results of the work by Pearsall and Trozzo (2011). Using a hedonic price equation which represents the US Postal Service (USPS) tariff, Pearsall and Trozzo provide the values of the elasticities of different mail products to changes in the frequency of delivery (from 6 days a week to 5, 4, 3, 2 and 1), as well as a weighted average of the elasticity for all products. This chapter uses the weighted average percentage of volume reduction deriving from a reduction in frequency on all products offered by the USP, which is equal to –0.75 percent for the transition from 6 to 5 days per week, to –1.31 percent for the transition from 6 to 4 days per week, to –3.50 percent for the transition from 6 to 3 days per week, to –8.96 percent for the transition from 6 to 2 days per week and to –25.88 percent for the transition from 6 days to 1 day per week.

The demand for both products offered by the USP is affected by the extent of the territorial coverage of rural delivery. In particular, it is assumed that once a certain delivery route will not longer be served (as a consequence of a reduction of C^R), the demand will decrease by the amount of volumes delivered on those specific routes only, since there will be no other effect on the volumes demanded by customers. In other words it is assumed that there is a direct effect on demand deriving from the volumes that will no longer be delivered as C^R reduces, while there will be no negative effect on the volumes delivered in areas that are not impacted by the reduction of C^R. This is because volumes to be delivered in areas that are no longer served by the USP cannot migrate towards competitors (so potentially triggering a migration of further volumes towards competitors), since competitors offer delivery services only in urban areas.

4 COST FUNCTION

In order to evaluate the impact of different USO scope definitions on the cost structure of the USP, the cost model is largely based on two previous studies of the postal sector (Cohen et al. (2006) and PwC (2006)), through a two-step procedure.

The first step aimed at obtaining a reasonable estimate of the cost of each stage of the postal value chain for Poste Italiane in 2009. Cohen et al. derived a general cost function, as well as a cost function for each stage of the postal value chain, as a function of the population to be served and of the volumes to be delivered in a country. The model fitted well with data coming from a variety of countries worldwide. However, since Cohen et al.

provided a 1999 estimate of a postal operator costs, the original model cost functions were updated, in order to obtain a 2009 estimate of the cost functions.[3] The updated equations of the Cohen et al. model are:

$$\begin{aligned}
\text{Collection cost} &= 0.791*(0.0106*V + 5.35*P)\\
\text{Sorting cost} &= 0.791*(0.12*V + 2.42*P)\\
\text{Transport cost} &= 0.791*(0.023*V + 1.06*P)\\
\text{Delivery cost} &= 0.791*(0.06*V + 48.75*P),
\end{aligned}$$

where V represents postal volumes and P population.

The cost of each main stage of the value chain was estimated by referring to 2009 postal volumes managed by Poste Italiane and population in Italy. Thus an estimate was obtained, based on international peer comparison, of the expected average monetary value of each stage of the Poste Italiane value chain in 2009. Considering postal volumes of 5,520 million items managed by Poste Italiane in 2009 and an Italian population of 60.3 million, the following estimates were obtained:

Collection cost = €302.1 million
Sorting cost = €636.0 million
Transport cost = €151.5 million
Delivery cost = €2,592.9 million.

The second step aimed at highlighting the way in which each of the components of USO scope definition affects the cost level of each stage of the postal value chain. To this end the model largely relied on the model built by PwC (2006). In 2006, on behalf of the European Commission, PwC conducted a study to assess the economic impact, for each member state, of the full market opening (FMO) of the postal market which at the time, was assumed to take place in 2009. Clearly, USP cost structure plays a key role in assessing the economic impact of FMO. In order to determine the USP cost structure, PwC used a bottom-up cost model, comprising four main equations, each representing a main stage of the postal value chain (collection, sorting, transport and delivery). In the following we shall present the adaptation of the PwC model. All equations provide yearly values of each activity cost.

Collection Cost

Collection cost is modeled as the sum of the cost of three postal volume collection channels: the cost of collecting postal items through postboxes, the cost of accepting postal items at the sorting centers (for business customers) and the cost of accepting postal items at the post office. Therefore:

Collection cost = cost of collecting from postboxes + cost of accepting at the sorting centers + cost of accepting at the post office.

The cost of collecting postal items through postboxes is obtained by adding the cost of vehicles devoted to the collecting activity to the cost of workers in charge of emptying the postboxes. These two cost items are both assumed to be independent of the collection volumes and depend linearly on the numbers of days in which collection takes place. Throughout the chapter the weekly frequency of collection and the collection territorial coverage are assumed to be constant and equal, respectively, to 6 days and 100 percent of the national territory. Therefore:

$$\text{Cost of collecting through postboxes} = \text{cost of vehicle} + \text{cost of workers},$$

where:

$$\text{cost of vehicles devoted to collecting} = F^C \times 52 \times D^C \times UVC^C \text{ and}$$
$$\text{cost of workers devoted to collecting through postboxes} = F^C \times 52 \times D^C/S^C \times HLC,$$

and where:

F^C	=	Weekly frequency of collection, set equal to 6,
D^C	=	Daily total number of kilometers needed every day to collect mail from mailboxes,
UVC^C	=	Cost per traveled kilometer by vehicles involved in collection (including fuel, maintenance, taxes, depreciation, and so on),
HLC	=	Hourly labor cost of postal workers, and
S^C	=	Average speed of vehicles involved in collection.

The cost of accepting mail at the sorting centers comprises two items: the cost for the infrastructure and the cost of the postal workers involved in the activity. Since the centers devoted to accepting mail from business customers are the sorting centers, and since the infrastructure collection cost represents only a very minor percentage of the infrastructure cost of the sorting centers, all infrastructure costs of the sorting centers were attributed to the sorting activity. Therefore, the cost of accepting mail at the sorting centers comprises only the cost of the postal workers involved in this activity, as detailed in the following equations:

$$\text{cost of workers in sorting centers} = SC \times WSC \times F^C \times 52 \times HWD \times HLC,$$

where:

SC	=	Number of sorting centers,
WSC	=	Average number of workers devoted to accepting per sorting center, and
HWD	=	Average daily opening hours of an acceptance center (post office or sorting center).

The cost of accepting mail at the post office comprises two terms: the cost for the infrastructure and the cost of workers devoted to accepting mail at the counter. Therefore the equation is:

$$\text{Cost of accepting at the post office} = \text{cost of offices} + \text{cost of workers},$$

where:

cost of post offices = $PO \times ACPO \times UA$ and
cost of workers in post offices = $PO \times WPO \times F^C \times 52 \times HWD \times HLC \times UA$,

and where:

PO = Number of post offices,
$ACPO$ = Average annual cost of a post office,
UA = Percentage of hours dedicated to universal postal activity at the post office, and
WPO = Average number of workers per post office.

Sorting Cost

The cost of sorting includes the cost of sorting centers, which depends on the territorial coverage implemented by the USP, and two other components that depend linearly on the number of mail items handled, that is, the cost of sorting machines and the cost of sorting workers.

The cost of sorting machines depends on the weekly frequency of delivery (F^D). In particular, the cost depends on the number of sorting machines necessary to sort the mail in the available time (that is, the number of days in a week in which sorting takes place). When the available time decreases (that is, the weekly frequency of delivery decreases and so the number of days in a week in which sorting takes place decreases) then it will be necessary to use more sorting machines to sort the same amount of mail and this will increase the cost of sorting machines.
Therefore the equations are:

Sorting cost = cost of sorting centers + cost of sorting machines + cost of sorting workers,

where:

cost of sorting centers = $SC \times (DO^R \times C^R + DO^U \times C^U) \times ACSC$,
cost of sorting machines = $\{[(V \times AS)/ASC]/(F^D \times 52 \times 24)\} \times AMC$, and
cost of sorting workers = $SH \times HLC$,

with:

$$SH = \frac{V \times AS}{ASC} \times WSM + \frac{V \times MS}{MSC},$$

and:

SC = Number of sorting centers,
DO^R = Percentage of rural delivery offices,
DO^U = Percentage of urban delivery offices,

C^R	=	Percentage of rural areas delivery coverage,
C^U	=	Percentage of urban areas delivery coverage,
$ACSC$	=	Average annual cost of a sorting center (including insurance, energy, maintenance, and so on),
V	=	Mail volume,
AS	=	Percentage of automatically sorted mail,
ASC	=	Automatic sorting capacity, that is, the average number of items hourly sorted by a sorting machine,
SH	=	Sorting hours,
F^D	=	Weekly frequency of delivery,
AMC	=	Average annual cost of a sorting machine,
WSM	=	Average number of workers per sorting machine,
MS	=	Percentage of mail sorted manually, and
MSC	=	Manual sorting capacity, that is, average number of items sorted manually in one hour.

Transport Cost

Transport cost comprises the cost of transporting mail with trucks on the road and the cost of air mail transport. Road transport is used for the J+3 product only while air transport is used for the J+1 product only.

The cost of transporting mail with trucks is obtained by adding the cost of the trucks to the cost of workers devoted to the road transport activity. Therefore:

Cost of transporting with trucks = cost of trucks + cost of workers,

where:

cost of the trucks $= AD \times SC \times (DO^R \times C^R + DO^U \times C^U) \times URVC^T_{F^D} \times F^D \times 52$ and
cost of workers devoted to road transport $= \{[AD \times SC \times (DO^R \times C^R + DO^U \times C^U)]/RS^T\} \times F^D \times 52 \times HLC$,

and where:

AD	=	Average distance between two sorting centers,
$URVC^T_{F^D}$	=	Cost of trucks per traveled kilometer (including fuel, maintenance, depreciation, and so on). The cost per kilometer traveled by trucks increases when weekly delivery frequency decreases, and
RS^T	=	Average truck speed.

The cost of air mail transport is modeled as the sum of the cost of air vehicles and the cost of workers devoted to this activity. Therefore:

Cost of air transport = cost of air vehicles + cost of workers,

where:

cost of air vehicles $= D^A \times UAVC^T_{F^D} \times F^D \times 52$ and
cost of workers devoted to air transport $= (D^A/AS^T) \times F^D \times 52 \times WAT \times HLC$,

and where:

D^A = Total daily distance traveled by air vehicles,
$UAVC^T_{F^D}$ = Cost per traveled kilometer by air vehicles (including fuel, maintenance, depreciation, and so on). The cost per kilometer traveled by air vehicles increases when weekly delivery frequency decreases,
AS^T = Average air vehicles speed, and
WAT = Number of workers involved in air transport.

Delivery Cost

The cost of delivery is divided into two components: the cost of delivery in urban areas and the cost of delivery in rural areas. The urban areas delivery cost function and rural areas delivery cost function have the same shape and parameters, but the values of parameters in the two equations are different from each other. In the equations below, the index z indicates any of the two kinds of areas, that is, $Z = U$ (urban areas) or $Z = R$ (rural areas).

Delivery cost activity is represented by four main stages: (i) sequencing of items for delivery, (ii) route travel, (iii) accessing the delivery point and (iv) delivery into the postbox.

First, the *cost of mail sequencing for delivery* is modeled through a fixed cost component (the cost relating to delivery offices), and a component that depends linearly on mail volumes handled (the cost of all employees in sequencing). The cost relating to delivery offices depends on the coverage implemented, that is, it depends on the number of delivery offices operating in the territory.

These two components of the cost of sequencing are formally shown below:

cost of delivery offices $= TDO \times DO^Z \times C^Z \times ACDO^Z$ and
cost of workers in sequencing $= [(V \times V^Z)/MSC] \times HLC$,

where:

TDO = Total number of delivery offices,
DO^Z = Percentage of delivery offices in area z (urban or rural),
$ACDO^Z$ = Average annual cost of a delivery office in area z (urban or rural), and
V^Z = Percentage of total volumes to be delivered in the z area.

Second, the *cost of route travel* is considered as a fixed cost in respect to volumes and is divided into two components: the cost associated with vehicles and the costs of the delivery operator. The cost of route travel associated with operators depends on the average number of workers per delivery route. This parameter includes the extra workers which are employed to substitute the worker usually in charge of a specific route, should he/she be unable to serve the route for one or more days. The value of the parameter is higher when the USP has to provide a J+1 product. If the USP does not offer a J+1 product it is able to reduce the stock of extra workers associated with a delivery route. Therefore, equations are:

$$\text{Cost of route travel} = \text{cost of vehicle} + \text{cost of workers},$$

where:

$$\text{cost of vehicle} = DD^Z \times UDVC \times F^D \times 52 \text{ and}$$
$$\text{cost of workers} = (DD^Z / VS^Z) \times WDR_{j+} \times F^D \times HLC,$$

in which:

$$DD^Z = \frac{DP^Z}{AI^Z} \times DS^Z \times F^D \times C^Z \times DZ^Z,$$

where:

DD^Z	=	Average daily distance traveled in the delivery area z (urban or rural),
$UDVC$	=	Unit delivery vehicle cost, that is the cost per kilometer traveled of vehicle (including fuel, maintenance, depreciation, and so on),
VS^Z	=	Average vehicle speed in the delivery area z (urban or rural),
WDR_{j+}	=	Average number of workers per delivery route. The parameter increases when USP has to provide a J+1 service,
DP^Z	=	Average number of delivery points per delivery route in the area z (urban or rural),
AI^Z	=	Aggregate index, that is the number of delivery points per stop in the area z (urban or rural),
DS^Z	=	Average distance between two stops in the area z (urban or rural), and
DZ^Z	=	Total number of delivery routes in the delivery area z (urban or rural).

Third, the *cost of access to the delivery point* has been considered as a fixed cost compared to the volume of items managed and it depends on the number of stops per delivery route. This cost has been modeled as follows:

$$\text{cost of access to the delivery point} = \frac{NS^Z \times DDP^Z \times 2}{HS} \times WDR_{j+} \times F^D \times 52 \times HLC,$$

in which:

$$NS^Z = \frac{DP^Z}{AI^Z} \times ES^Z_{F^D} \times C^Z \times DZ^Z,$$

where:

NS^Z	=	Total annual number of stops in the area z (urban or rural),
DDP^Z	=	Average distance to access the delivery point in the area z (urban or rural),
HS	=	Average human speed, and
$ES^Z_{F^D}$	=	Percentage of actual stops in the area z (urban or rural), depending on

the weekly frequency in which delivery takes place. When the frequency is reduced the percentage of effective stops increases.

Fourth, the *cost of delivery to the recipient mailbox* is linearly dependent on the volume of postal items delivered, according to the following formula:

$$\text{cost of delivery to the mailbox} = V \times V^{Z} \times TD \times HLC,$$

where:

TD = Time of delivering one item in the recipient mailbox.

5 RESULTS

In a first step, by using the demand and cost functions described above, we simulated the P&L account of universal service provision by Poste Italiane in 2009 and it was projected over the coming years, by holding constant USO scope definition, in order to assess the impact that e-substitution will have on it through the years, with special reference to the moment when the P&L balance will turn into a loss.

Assuming the starting USO scope definition as J+1 provision, 6 days a week delivery frequency and 100 percent rural areas delivery coverage, the 2009 universal service economic performance of Poste Italiane was estimated as equal to €336 million (universal revenues equal to €4,020 million and universal operating costs equal to €3,684 million). By assuming a yearly reduction in volume due to e-substitution of 3 percent, a yearly increase in unit price and costs of 1.5 percent and a constant USO scope definition, the USP economic performance turns negative from 2012 onwards (see Table 13.1).

In a second step, we evaluated the impact of easing the three main constraints deriving from USO on the revenue and cost of the P&L over the coming years.

The burden associated with the obligation of providing a J+1 service amounts approximately to €88 million in 2009. This burden derives mainly from the use of an air transportation network and from a greater cost of workers during load peaks in the delivery activities. However, since the J+1 service cost depends on delivery frequency and rural areas delivery coverage, and considering the limited burden generated by the J+1 service obligation, in what follows the impacts of various frequency of delivery and geographical coverage configurations will be illustrated under the assumption that the J+1 product will keep on being provided by the USP.

Table 13.1 USP economic performance at constant USO scope definition (€m) (e-substitution 3%; inflation rate 1.5%)

	2009	2010	2011	2012	2013	2014	2015
Revenues	4,020	3,960	3,900	3,842	3,784	3,728	3,672
Total operative costs	3,684	3,739	3,795	3,852	3,910	3,969	4,028
Operating income	336	221	105	−10	−126	−241	−356

Table 13.2 Number of years with a positive profit for different USO scope definitions

Time to survive (years)		Territorial coverage of rural areas (C^R)					
		100%	90%	80%	70%	60%	50%
Weekly frequency of delivery (F^D)	6 days	3	4	5	5	6	6
	5 days	7	7	8	8	9	9
	4 days	10	11	11	12	12	12
	3 days	13	14	14	14	14	14
	2 days	17	17	17	17	17	17
	1 day	18	18	18	17	17	16

Table 13.3 Cumulative profits generated by the USP for different USO scope definitions during the years in which it generates profits

Total earnings (€/mln)		Territorial coverage of rural areas (C^R)					
		100%	90%	80%	70%	60%	50%
Weekly frequency of delivery (F^D)	6 days	662	1,032	1,302	1,469	1,577	1,539
	5 days	2,311	2,842	3,146	3,294	3,302	3,104
	4 days	5,127	5,703	5,936	5,944	5,763	5,351
	3 days	8,396	8,864	8,904	8,668	8,182	7,406
	2 days	11,805	12,043	11,749	11,136	10,230	9,025
	1 day	10,688	10,502	9,801	8,824	7,555	6,069

Further results are shown in Tables 13.2 and 13.3. Table 13.2 shows the number of years in which the USP maintains a positive profit in connection with every combination of weekly frequency of delivery (F^D) and rural areas delivery coverage (C^R). Table 13.3 shows, for every combination of weekly delivery frequency and rural areas delivery coverage, the cumulative profits generated by the USP during the years in which it maintains a positive balance in the P&L.

A first result is that a reduction of the weekly frequency of delivery determines an economic benefit for the USP significantly higher than that deriving from a reduction of rural areas delivery coverage, on a *ceteris paribus* basis. In fact, by comparing two different possible reductions of USO scope which involve a comparable reduction in the number of delivery workers for the USP, for example, a reduction of F^D to 4 (while holding C^R at 100 percent) and a reduction of C^R to 50 percent (while holding F^D to 6), it emerges that in the first case the USP will keep a positive P&L for 10 years (Table 13.2) while in the second the P&L will be positive only for six years. At the same time, from Table 13.3 it emerges that in the first case the USP will earn cumulative profits of about €5.1 billion before that P&L turns negative, while in the second case cumulative profits are in the range of €1.5 billion. This is due to the fact that a reduction in F^D lets the USP cut delivery cost while maintaining most of the revenues, while a reduction in C^R lets the USP cut costs as well as lose revenues.

A second result is that the optimal level of C^R, in terms of cumulative earnings (Table 13.3), varies greatly with the set level of F^D. In fact, when the frequency of delivery is equal to 6 days a week, the optimal C^R is equal to 60 percent (€1,577 million in Table 13.3), while, when the frequency of delivery is reduced to 1 day per week, the territorial coverage that maximizes total earnings is equal to 100 percent (€10,688 million in Table 13.3). For delivery frequencies below 6 and above 1, the optimal C^R is above 60 percent and below 100 percent. This result is explained by the fact that when F^D is equal to 6 a vast number of rural delivery routes are unprofitable, so that by not serving all of the unprofitable delivery routes the P&L balance improves significantly. However, if F^D is set below 6 days, the number of unprofitable rural delivery routes decreases, since daily delivered volumes per route will be increasing. In this case, it is no longer worth reducing the coverage of rural areas to such an extent as in the case in which delivery frequency is 6, since profitable routes are increasing. Eventually, when delivery frequency is set at 1, all rural delivery routes become profitable, so that the optimal C^R is 100 percent.

A third result is that, independently of rural areas delivery coverage, the optimal weekly frequency of delivery, in terms of cumulative earnings (Table 13.3), is always equal to 2. This is explained by the fact that the Italian USP is characterized by a low level of volume per capita, which implies a significant amount of non-profitable routes in the starting position. Such a situation allows the USP to optimize its offer by significantly reducing F^D.

6 CONCLUSION

The ongoing e-substitution process represents a serious threat on the financial viability of USPs over the coming years. In order to identify possible strategies to counterbalance this trend, this chapter has analyzed the impact of easing USO constraints on the USP P&L balance, in a market environment characterized by the shrinking of volumes due to e-substitution.

Results show that the obligation to provide a J+1 has a relatively limited effect, when compared to the other two main obligations, that is, frequency of delivery and rural areas delivery coverage. A second result is that a reduction of the weekly frequency of delivery determines an economic benefit for the USP significantly higher than that deriving from a reduction of rural areas delivery coverage. When comparing the effectiveness of easing each of the constraints, the following two conclusions can be drawn: the optimal level of rural areas delivery coverage varies greatly with the set level of frequency of delivery, while the optimal weekly frequency of delivery is always equal to 2, independently of rural areas delivery coverage. Any extension of the results of the chapter to a more general level is subject to clear limitations, in that results rely on the value of the elasticity of demand in respect to changes in the frequency of delivery, obtained by previous studies on the US experience, and on the specific characteristics of the Italian postal market. In this sense, further research is essential to extend the results of the chapter to a more general framework.

NOTES

* The views expressed in this chapter are those of the authors and do not necessarily reflect the opinion of Poste Italiane.

1. Throughout the chapter, the analysis will refer only to universal service activities, revenues and costs, ignoring any reference to the non-universal activities that a USP may perform.
2. This is because the difference between the set price on the J+1 product and the set price on the J+3 product, which is a profit-making product, is not sufficient to cover the extra cost incurred by the USP in the provision of the J+1 product.
3. In a first step the cost functions coefficients were actualized from 1999 to 2009, taking into account both the yearly inflation rate and the yearly productivity growth that affected postal production. In particular, the original model parameters were adjusted for the inflation rate registered in the US over the 1999–2009 period, as well as for the productivity growth over the same period. With regard to the inflation rate, we used the consumer price index (CPI), developed by the US Bureau of Labor Statistics, and with regard to the productivity growth updating, we used the total factor productivity (TFP) index of the USPS, which represents the ratio between the output produced and the resources used, including capital, personnel and raw materials. In a second step, the purchasing power parity (PPP) index was used as the relevant input cost factor (ICF) of the Cohen model in order to represent the ratio between the input cost in Italy and that in the US.

REFERENCES

Borsenberger, Claire, Joram C. Magre and Bernard Roy (2010), 'Cross-country comparison of optimal mail delivery frequencies', in M.A. Crew and P.R. Kleindorfer (eds), *Heightening Competition in the Postal and Delivery Sector*, Cheltenham, UK and Northampton, MA, USA: Edward Elgar, pp. 235–52.

Cohen, Robert and Charles McBride (2008), 'Estimates of the current cost of the USO in the US', Appendix F, Section 3 of *Study on Universal Postal Service and the Postal Monopoly*, George Mason School of Public Policy, Fairfax, VA, November.

Cohen, Robert H., Charles McBride and John C. Panzar (2010), 'The cost of the USO in the United States', in M.A. Crew and P.R. Kleindorfer (eds), *Heightening Competition in the Postal and Delivery Sector*, Cheltenham, UK and Northampton, MA, USA: Edward Elgar, pp. 253–62.

Cohen, Robert H., Matthew Robinson, Gennaro Scarfiglieri, Renee Sheehy, Vincenzo Visco Comandini, John Waller and Spyros Xenakis (2006), 'The role of scale economies in the cost behaviour of posts', in A. Dieke and A. Niederpum (eds), *Regulating Postal Markets: Harmonised Versus Country-specific Approaches*, Papers presented at the 8th Königswinter Seminar, WIK Proceedings no. 11, Bad Honnef.

Pearsall, Edward S. and Charles L. Trozzo (2011), 'Evaluating the demand effects of reductions in the frequency of delivery service', in M.A. Crew and P.R. Kleindorfer (eds), *Reinventing the Postal Sector in an Electronic Age*, Cheltenham, UK and Northampton, MA, USA: Edward Elgar, pp. 173–98.

PricewaterhouseCoopers (PwC) (2006), 'The Impact on Universal Service of the Full Market Accomplishment of the Postal Internal Market in 2009', Final Report and Annexes, available at: http://ec.europa.eu/internal_market/post/studies_en.htm#sector2006.

14. Letter traffic demand in the UK: some new evidence and review of econometric analysis over the past decade*

Marzena Jarosik,[†] John Nankervis,[‡] Jonathan Pope,[§] Soterios Soteri[¶] and Leticia Veruete-McKay[††]

1 INTRODUCTION

Prospects for letter mail volumes are an important driver of business decisions for national postal operators. In particular, assessments of the demand for letter traffic inform operational investment decisions, influence the structure of regulatory controls and are a key variable in business valuations. Econometric studies of the demand for mail emphasize the importance of three key factors in assessing the prospects for letter traffic demand: economic activity; multi-modal competition in the communications market; and the price of letters.[1]

This chapter provides new insights to assess prospects for UK letter demand by updating and extending the econometric analysis undertaken by Veruete-McKay et al. (2011) by an additional, and eventful, 15 quarters of information. During this period: the UK entered a severe recession from which it has not yet recovered; technological change affecting the mail market continued at a rapid pace; competition in the upstream mail market substantially increased; and prices for some products rose substantially. This new information provides a rich source of data to further our understanding of the drivers of the demand for letters. In particular, our econometric analysis provides updated estimates for economic activity and price elasticities and also quantitative estimates of the extent to which e-communications and competition from other traditional media are reducing the demand for letters. In addition, this chapter extends the approach to modeling UK letter demand in Nankervis et al. (2002) to provide new insights into the extent to which upstream competition is impacting the price elasticities of specific segments of the letters market.

The chapter also provides a comparison of our econometric findings to a decade of previous research into the demand for mail in the UK to help enhance our understanding of a number of important phenomena. These include whether the link between economic growth and mail volumes has changed significantly in the recent past or even, as some

† Economist, Royal Mail Group.
‡ Professor in Finance, Essex Business School, University of Essex.
§ Senior Economist, Royal Mail Group.
¶ Head of Economics Forecasting, Royal Mail Group.
†† Senior Economist, Royal Mail Group.

have claimed, been 'broken'; whether total letter price elasticities have risen appreciably as a result of changes in the wider communications market; and the extent to which multi-modal communication competition has impacted letter volumes and how this may have developed over time.

Section 2 provides an overview of letter traffic trends for total traffic and three broad substreams of traffic covering Royal Mail First Class non-presort traffic, Second Class non-presort traffic and Other (mainly presort plus access) traffic. Section 3 sets out the estimation methodology and reports the results of the modeling of letter traffic for each of the three streams of traffic. Section 4 provides quantitative estimates of the contribution to total letter traffic demand using the models estimated in the previous section. This section also contains a brief review of econometric letter demand models for the UK contained in the CRRI (Rutgers Center for Research on Regulated Industries) conference books and other publications over the past decade. Finally, Section 5 provides a summary and conclusions.

2 UK LETTER TRAFFIC TRENDS

Royal Mail addressed inland mail (AIM) volumes, of which the vast majority is letters (over 95 percent), peaked in 2005–06 at about 80 million items of mail a day. By 2010/11 this volume declined by over 20 percent to 62 million items per day. An analysis of mail volume projections and outcomes in the UK by Fève et al. (2012) suggests that the majority of this decline is likely to have been due to increasing competition from e-communications and the recession of 2008–09. High and fluctuating rates of letter volume decline in recent years are not unique to the UK and many countries with advanced postal networks have experienced similar phenomena.

Historically total AIM volume growth has tended to move in line with the economy and demographic trends, as shown in Figure 14.1a. However, from around 2002 onwards this simple relationship has become more complex. Other factors, in particular the increasing use of technology to substitute paper communications with electronic media has driven a wedge between economic growth and the demand for letters.

The annual rate of growth of total AIM has been in the range of ± 7 percent per annum for the past 30 years. However, subcomponents of letter traffic differentiated by speed of delivery, payment channels, presort discounts, access traffic and other characteristics have fluctuated within a considerably wider range. For example, Figure 14.1b shows that over the past three decades the annual rate of growth of UK First Class non-presort, Second Class non-presort, and Other (mainly presort plus access) traffic volumes have fluctuated in a considerably wider range than total AIM traffic.[2]

The introduction of discounts in the UK and more extensive presort discounts in the 1980s encouraged the migration of First and Second Class non-presort traffic to the Other (mainly presort and access) stream. Proportionately, discounts earned from presorting mail remained broadly unchanged for much of the period reported in Figure 14.1c. Therefore, initially, the migration of non-presort traffic to the Other stream reflected one-off changes in relative prices and increased customer choice. The main beneficiaries would have been very large mailers. However, over time smaller-scale senders have benefited as a result of advances in new technology lowering the cost of sorting

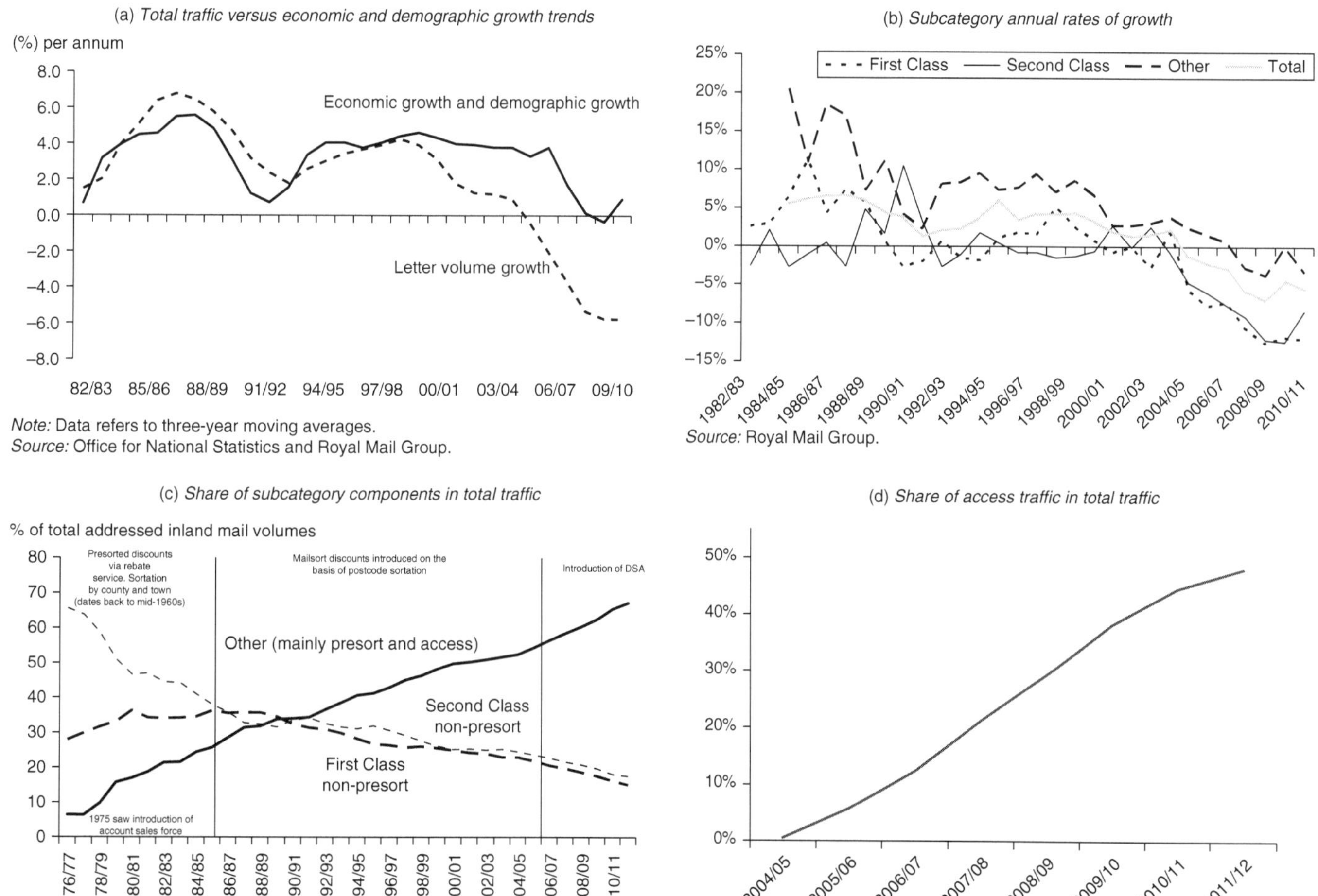

Note: Data refers to three-year moving averages.
Source: Office for National Statistics and Royal Mail Group.

Source: Royal Mail Group.

Source: Royal Mail Group.

Source: Royal Mail Group.

Figure 14.1 UK AIM volume trends for total, First and Second Class non-presort and Other (mainly presort and access) traffic

letters. More recently, the introduction of upstream competition in the UK mail market from 2004 onwards has provided further incentives for mailers sending Royal Mail non-presort mail to switch to consolidators that will collect and sort their mail prior to handing it to Royal Mail to deliver.

The impact of new technology is likely to have had a marked impact on each of the three traffic streams. First Class mail volumes, where customers pay more for speed of delivery, are likely to have a higher exposure to electronic forms of communication than the slower Second Class service, with any negative impact felt from the late 1980s onwards when fax, electronic payment methods and then email and Internet usage developed. Conversely, presort traffic levels should have benefited initially from switching from public tariff services, but over time, this benefit will have dissipated as the relative magnitude of non-presort traffic declined. In addition, advances in technology reduced the cost of acquiring and interrogating marketing databases for direct mail campaigns in the 1980s and initially boosted bulk presort letter volumes. However, more recently, the evolution of technology has created an alternative and relatively lower cost direct marketing medium in the form of Internet 'paid-for-search' advertising[3] that is competing with direct mail letter communications and other media for marketing budgets (see Soteri et al., 2009).

The combined impact of price incentives and falling technology costs is therefore likely to be underpinning the decline in non-presort traffic volumes relative to presort traffic, as shown in Figure 14.1c. In addition, increasing levels of access competition (see Figure 14.1d) have provided senders with an incentive to switch away from Royal Mail non-presort products to Other product offerings (mainly presort and access) traffic.

The following sections provide an econometric analysis of the key drivers of mail for each of the three broad product groups and quantitative estimates of the extent to which they impact AIM volumes and switching between product streams.

3 AN ECONOMETRIC ANALYSIS OF UK LETTER TRAFFIC DEMAND

The demand for the three subcomponents of addressed inland letter traffic (First Class non-presort, Second Class non-presort and Other (mainly presort and access)) are modeled as error-correction models (ECMs) using the following general specification with up to k dynamic terms:

$$\Delta q_{it} = \alpha' D_t + \theta_{i0} q_{i,t-1} + \gamma_i' x_{i,t-1} + \sum_{k=1}^{k=4} \theta_{ik} \Delta q_{i,t-k} + \sum_{k=0}^{k=4} \varphi_{ik}' \Delta x_{i,t-k} + \varepsilon_{it}$$

where lower-case letters for Q_{it} and X_{it} denote variables in logarithms in time period t. The variable Q_i denotes volume per working-day indices for stream i (i = 1, 2, 3); where i = 1 refers to First Class non-presort; i = 2 to Second Class non-presort; i = 3 to Other (mainly presort and access) traffic. The variable X_{it} is a vector of explanatory variables corresponding to each stream i, that includes: the number of households (H); economic activity (Y); real letter price indices for product group i (P_i); the quality of letter service delivery (QoS); the real price of traditional non-mail media advertising media substitutes

(*PA*); and the proportion of Internet advertising expenditure relative to total advertising expenditure (*PIA*). D_t is a vector of deterministic variables, which includes a constant, seasonal dummies and time trends; α, θ, γ and ϕ are unknown parameters; and ε_i are random disturbance terms.

The econometric testing down process for each of the three traffic streams commenced with a general ECM specification containing a similar set of variables to those used by Veruete-McKay et al., 2011 (henceforth referred to as VM) plus the inclusion of time-trend terms starting in 2005 and 2010 and an additional 15 quarters of data (up to and including 2011Q4).[4]

A key difference between the definition of product streams in this study and in the VM paper is the treatment of downstream access volumes. In particular, VM used Royal Mail estimates to quantify the volume of access traffic originating from customers who do not presort their mail and allocated this traffic to the First and Second Class non-presort traffic streams. The econometric analysis in this chapter does not allocate access volumes between the three streams of traffic. Instead, all access traffic is included in the Other category. The broad product categories included in our analysis are therefore determined by the products and services mail customers purchase. This approach has two key advantages over the data methodology adopted by VM. First, it avoids the need to estimate the origin of access traffic and reduces the risk of introducing access allocation errors into our analysis. Second, the clearer mapping of specific products to our broad mail categories allows us to test the extent to which the introduction of access competition has led to switching out of Royal Mail non-presort traffic streams. Ideally, at some future date, when access competition in the UK has fully evolved, this modeling framework can be extended to cover access traffic as a separate and fourth segment of traffic to provide further insights into the drivers of the demand for letters and switching between product groups.

Econometric Models of the Demand for Letters by Broad Product Group

Starting with a general ECM specification for each of the three streams, we used the seemingly unrelated regression estimation (SURE)[5] method to jointly estimate the equations for the First Class, Second Class and Other letter segments of traffic and then tested and imposed the following restrictions on the model: unit long-run elasticities with respect to households; and symmetry between First and Second Class cross-price elasticities. We also allowed for changing levels of switching between Second Class non-presort and Other traffic as the level of access competition increased.[6]

The addressed inland letter traffic model (henceforth referred to as ILTM(2011)) reported in Table 14.1 was estimated by deleting variables from the general specification with low *t*-values subject to the model residuals passing a number of diagnostic tests.[7]

The model reported in Table 14.1 contains estimated elasticities for economic activity and price variables that are consistent with economic theory, all the explanatory variables have reasonably high *t*-statistics and it possesses desirable diagnostic test statistics. This plus Johansen tests which suggest the variables in each equation cointegrate imply that the ILTM(2011) is a statistically sound model.

The sharp decline in Second Class non-presort traffic after 2005/06 is accounted for in the model by evolving and increasing levels of competition with products in the

Table 14.1 Addressed inland letter traffic model by broad product stream (ILTM(2011))

Estimated coefficients and t-values								
	First Class non-presort[1] Dependent variable $\Delta(q_{1t}-h_t)$			Second Class non-presort[1] Dependent variable $\Delta(q_{2t}-h_t)$			Other (mainly presort & access)[1] Dependent variable $\Delta(q_{3t}-h_t)$	
	Coeff.	t-value		Coeff.	t-value		Coeff.	t-value
$q_{1t-1}-h_{t-1}$	−0.48	−6.9	$q_{2t-1}-h_{t-1}$	−0.51	−9.2	$q_{3t-1}-h_{t-1}$	−0.57	−7.0
y_{t-1}	0.67	6.5	y_{t-1}	0.40	3.6	y_{t-1}	0.42	2.3
T87[2]	−0.005	−7.1	T75[2]	−0.007	−7.4	p_{3t-1}	−0.24	−2.5
T02[2]	−0.003	−3.0	T87[2]	0.002	2.3	pa_{t-1}	0.38	4.1
T05[2]	−0.007	−4.3	p_{1t-1}[3]	0.12	3.9	pia_{t-1}	−0.64	−3.5
p_{1t-1}	−0.21	−2.6	p_{2t-1}[3]	−0.12	3.9	T83[2]	0.009	6.4
p_{2t-1}[3]	0.13	3.9	qos_{t-1}	0.40	6.1	T97[2]	−0.007	−5.7
$\Delta(q_{1t-1}-h_{t-1})$	−0.20	−2.7	C06	−0.05	−2.8	C06	−0.02	−2.8
$\Delta(q_{1t-2}-h_{t-2})$	−0.17	−2.9	$(p_{3t-1}-p_{2t-1})$*d07[4]	0.06	0.4	$(p_{2t-1}-p_{3t-1})$*d07[4]	0.02	0.4
			$(p_{3t-1}-p_{2t-1})$*d08[4]	0.26	1.9	$(p_{2t-1}-p_{3t-1})$*d08[4]	0.08	1.9
			$(p_{3t-1}-p_{2t-1})$*d09[4]	0.44	3.0	$(p_{2t-1}-p_{3t-1})$*d09[4]	0.13	3.0
			$(p_{3t-1}-p_{2t-1})$*d10[4]	0.73	4.6	$(p_{2t-1}-p_{3t-1})$*d10[4]	0.22	4.6
			$(p_{3t-1}-p_{2t-1})$*d11[4]	0.70	4.0	$(p_{2t-1}-p_{3t-1})$*d11[4]	0.22	4.0
			Δy_{t-2}	0.65	2.0	$\Delta(q_{3t-1}-h_{t-1})$	−0.25	−3.7
			Δqos_t	0.21	4.9			
			Δqos_{t-1}	−0.11	−2.6			
			$\Delta(q_{2t-1}-h_{t-1})$	−0.18	−3.3			

Table 14.1 (continued)

Diagnostic tests					
First Class non-presort[1] Dependent variable $\Delta(q_{1t}-h_t)$		Second Class non-presort[1] Dependent variable $\Delta(q_{2t}-h_t)$		Other (mainly presort & access)[1] Dependent variable $\Delta(q_{3t}-h_t)$	
R^2 adj.	0.88	R^2 adj.	0.94	R^2 adj.	0.80
Reg. SE	0.03	Reg. SE	0.03	Reg. SE	0.03
Durbin Watson	2.24	Durbin Watson	2.06	Durbin Watson	2.27
Estimation period	1976Q3–2011Q4	Estimation period	1976Q3–2011Q4	Estimation period	1983Q1–2011Q4
Diagnostic Tests[5]	*p* value				
Serial correlation	0.33				
Normality	0.49				

Notes:
1. The estimated equations also included deterministic variables such as constants, seasonal dummies and seasonal dummy break terms which were statistically significant at the 5% level.
2. Refers to a time-trend variable starting in the first calendar quarter of the year referred to after the term T. For example, T87 refers to a time-trend variable equal to: 1 in 1987Q1, 2 in 1987Q2, . . ., and prior to 1987Q1 is equal to zero.
3. The symmetry constraints between First and Second Class were tested using cross-equation restrictions with non-constant volume weights. Wald test statistics indicated that these restrictions were statistically valid and imposed in the model. In addition, the own- and cross-price elasticities in the Second Class equation were tested to be equal and opposite in magnitude. Again this restriction could not be rejected via statistical tests and was imposed in the model.
4. The impact of increasing upstream competition over time was modeled via a series of financial year dummy variable relative price terms and symmetry restrictions were imposed to account for switching between Second Class and Other traffic. For example, D06 is equal to 1 in the UK financial year 2006/07 (that is 2006Q2 to 2007Q1) and equal to zero in all other periods.
5. The serial correlation test is a System Residual Portmanteau test for autocorrelation (lag 4) and the Normality test is the Jarque–Bera test for normality in the residuals.

Other traffic category. In particular, switching from Second Class traffic to the Other traffic stream, resulting from access competition and a divergence in prices between Second Class non-presort traffic and access or Royal Mail presort traffic, are modeled via a constant break term (C06 in Table 14.1) and annual relative price terms from 2007/08 onwards (that is, by the variables $(p_{3t-1} - p_{2t-1})$*d07 to $(p_{3t-1} - p_{2t-1})$*d011 in Table 14.1). The estimated coefficients on these terms suggest that the rate of switching out of Second Class non-presort traffic to the Other traffic stream (which includes access) increased substantially from 2007/08 onwards and may possibly have reached a plateau by 2011.

Long-run Estimated Elasticities and Parameters

The long-run elasticities and parameters corresponding to the ILTM(2011) estimates contained in Table 14.1 are reported in Table 14.2.[8] The long-run elasticities for total addressed inland letter traffic volumes were calculated by weighting each of the product stream long-run parameters by their respective share of total traffic.[9] The magnitude of the estimated long-run elasticities are, in general, broadly consistent with the results of the VM study despite extending the estimation period to include an additional 15 quarters of data.

Similar to VM and previous econometric studies (see, for example, Nankervis et al., 2002 and Fève et al., 2012), the elasticity of UK total traffic letter demand with respect to economic activity is estimated to be close to unity and to vary across streams.[10] In particular, First Class non-presort traffic is estimated to have a relatively high long-run elasticity of demand of around 1.4, while estimates for Other (mainly presort and access) and Second Class non-presort traffic are a little under unity.

The estimated total letter price elasticity (that is, the total net of switching between product groups) of –0.3 (equal to the sum of the three total traffic price elasticity estimates reported in Table 14.2, that is, –0.03–0.00–0.28 ≈ –0.30) is again similar to previous studies, but the estimated cross-price elasticities provide important new insights into switching between traffic streams. In particular, the Second Class non-presort and Other traffic cross-price elasticities suggest that a considerable degree of switching takes place between these two product groups when relative prices change. For example, the ILTM(2011) long-run price elasticities suggest that when the price of the First Class non-presort product group increases relative to the Second Class non-presort stream, by, say 1 percent, then total First Class non-presort volumes would be estimated to decline, on average, by around 0.4 percent, and of this volume 0.3 percent would, on average, switch to Second Class volumes[11] and overall volumes would, on average, be expected to decline by around 0.03 percent.

Similarly, when the price of the Second Class non-presort group increases relative to all other product streams, by say 1 percent, then overall volumes would be expected to remain broadly unchanged, but Second Class volumes would be expected to decline, on average, by around 1.6 percent,[12] of which around 0.2 percent is estimated to switch to the First Class non-presort product group and a further 1.4 percent to the Other stream.[13] An increase in the Other (mainly presort and access) traffic group price of 1 percent relative to First and Second Class traffic, is estimated to lead, on average, to a decrease in Other traffic of around 0.8 percent, of which around 0.4 percent is estimated to switch to

Table 14.2 Addressed inland letter traffic model long-run elasticities and time-trend impacts

	ILTM(2011)				VM estimates
	First Class non-presort[1]	Second Class non-presort	Other traffic (mainly presort and access)	Total traffic[2]	Total traffic
Economic activity (Y)	1.40	0.78	0.74	0.86	1.09
First Class non-presort price (P1)[3]	−0.44	0.24	–	−0.03	−0.07
Second Class non-presort price (P2)[3]	0.27	−0.24	–	0.00	−0.01
Other (mainly presort and access) price (P3)[3]	–	–	−0.42	−0.28	−0.24
Relative price of Second Class and Other (P3–P2)[4]	–	1.36	−0.38	0.00	n.a.
Quality of Service (QoS)[5]	–	0.79	–	0.14	0.13
Proportion of Internet advertising spend (PIA)	–	–	−1.12	−0.73	−0.95
Price of non-mail advertising (PA)	–	–	0.67	0.44	0.24
Net impact of 'unexplained' time trends (% p.a.)[6]	−12.8	−3.9	1.1	−2.0	−2.4

Notes:
n.a. = not applicable
1. Estimated long-run cross-price elasticity for 2010/11.
2 Total traffic estimated elasticities and time-trend effects were calculated by weighting the estimated coefficients in each traffic stream by their respective traffic volume share in 2010/11.
3. Deflated by the all items retail prices index.
4. Long-run estimated coefficients refer to 2011 (that is, $p_{3t-1} - p_{2t-1}$)*d11 in Table 14.1). Variable not tested in VM.
5. Royal Mail First Class quality of service for Stamp and Meter traffic.
6. Estimates refer to the total long-run impact of the time trends. For example, the First Class impact refers to the combined impact of the long-run estimates for T87, T02 and T05.

the Second Class stream[14] and overall total traffic is estimated to decline, on average, by around 0.3 percent.

A key point to note from the results reported in Table 14.2 is that, similar to VM and Nankervis et al. (2002), the estimated long-run own-price elasticities for each of the three traffic streams are relatively low (for example, all are less than –0.5). However, a new result from this chapter is the increase in the Second Class non-presort total cross-price elasticity from 0.2 in 2006 to around 1.6 by 2011 due to increasing competition from Royal Mail presort and access traffic. An important point to note about the estimated price elasticities (which also applies to all other estimated parameters) is that they refer to estimates for each of the three product groups and are not estimates of elasticities for individual products within each stream.

As in previous studies, the impact of QoS was found to be statistically significant only in the Second Class traffic stream. This is consistent with an interpretation of 'trading up'. That is, movements in First and Second Class QoS tend to be highly correlated and hence declines in First Class QoS (and therefore Second Class QoS) reduce Second Class mail volumes as some mailers trade up to First Class services to lower the overall effect on them of declining performance. At the same time, First Class traffic is lost in response to the decline of First Class QoS, so the net impact is that an overall decline in mail volumes is accompanied by First Class volumes remaining more or less unchanged but Second Class volumes falling.

The proportion of Internet advertising expenditure relative to total advertising expenditure (PIA) is estimated to have a significant impact on the demand for Other traffic. The estimated long-run coefficient on PIA suggests that, on average, a 1 percent increase in the share of Internet advertising relative to other media reduces the demand for Other (mainly presort and access) traffic by, on average, around 1.1 percent. This suggests, similar to VM, Soteri et al. (2009) and Cazals et al. (2011) that developments in alternative media communications are exerting substantial downward pressure on letter volumes, and in particular direct mail traffic. However, it is not clear to what extent this variable can be assessed to be impacting solely on direct mail, if, as is the case, the profile of this variable is correlated with that for other technologies that are substituting for letter mail. The magnitude of the ILTM(2011) estimated coefficient for PIA is somewhat lower than that in VM (–1.8).

The model also estimates the price of traditional non-mail media advertising prices[15] (PA) to have significant effects. The long-run elasticity of this variable is estimated to be around 0.7 and is somewhat higher than that estimated in VM (0.4).

Additionally, each of the three submodels contain time-trend variables which perhaps are best considered as primarily reflecting the impacts of technology on the demand for mail. It would have been better to identify directly variables associated with specific technology effects rather than having these reflected by 'unexplained trend' variables. However, in general, models including time trends contained better properties and diagnostic test statistics than those including Internet and broadband penetration rates. This may be because the dynamic impact of technology-related letter substitution is unlikely to be reflected within the properties of a single direct variable. Accordingly, time trends were considered to be a better proxy potentially for numerous and overlapping technology effects, which individually may have an S-shaped impact on mail, but over time cumulate to yield, 'corrugated S-shaped' impacts (see Nikali, 2008) that may be better reflected by time-trend terms.

With regard to First Class non-presort traffic, the estimation of negative time-trend effects from 1987 is consistent with advances in telecommunication technology from the late 1980s onwards. In particular, it coincides with the timing of the widespread adoption of fax machines, the introduction of bill payments by direct debit and the development of electronic communication and business services in the 1990s. The increasing use of the Internet and Internet platform technologies coincides with the much higher negative time-trend estimate from 2002 onwards. The First Class model estimates that the time-trend variable, on average, reduced mail volumes by about 4 percent per annum between 1987 and 2001; by around 7 percent between 2002 and 2005 as broadband subscriptions started to increase; and by approximately 13 percent per annum from 2005 onwards as e-communication technology has evolved and matured.

The net impact of the time-trend variables in the Second Class model has been to reduce traffic volumes in this product stream although the extent of this reduction has slowed down over time. It is likely that the main driving force behind the negative trend in Second Class traffic was initially the offering of worksharing discounts combined with changes in industry structure and advances in technology which reduced letter sorting costs and encouraged switching from Second Class non-presort to Other (mainly presort and access) traffic. The high negative time trend of more than –5 percent per annum prior to 1987 is consistent with this development. The decline in the Second Class time trend to less than –4 percent after 1987 suggests that the pace of such switching has slowed and/or e-substitution effects have been taking place. It is likely that both factors have been at work here but the relative magnitude of each is uncertain.

In contrast to First and Second Class non-presort traffic, the net impact of the time-trend variables on Other (mainly presort and access) traffic is estimated to have been positive throughout the sample period. The two key driving forces underpinning this positive trend are likely to have been the switching from Second Class, as discussed above, and, at least until around the early 2000s, the high rate of growth of direct mail. Prior to 1997 the time-trend impacts account for approximately 6 percent of Other (mainly presort) growth, but from around 1997 this slowed to around 1 percent per annum. The slowdown in the Other time trend is consistent with that in the Second Class model switching into the Other traffic stream plus some potential negative impact from e-substitution

4 USING ECONOMETRIC MODELS TO ASSESS RECENT UK LETTER TRAFFIC TRENDS AND PROSPECTS FOR LETTER DEMAND

The estimates from the ILTM(2011) can be used to quantify the relative importance or contribution of each variable in the model to changes in total inland letter traffic volumes. Table 14.3 contains the results of such an exercise for three time periods: the two years in which the UK was in recession (2008 to 2009); the following two years; and all four years considered together (that is, 2008 to 2011).

Quantitative estimates of the contribution of different variables using the long-run elasticities and parameter estimates reported in Table 14.2 are contained in Table 14.3 (rows 1a to 1d). The sum of the individual contributions (row 2) yields estimates that are reasonably close to the total traffic outcomes (row 4) for the two subperiods, 2008–09 and 2010–11. However, estimates for the full four-year period (2008 to 2011) are much closer, as projection errors in the individual subperiods offset one another (row 5). This suggests that the ILTM(2011) long-run estimated elasticities and parameters may be used to provide reasonable conditional projections for medium- to long-term letter traffic trends, but they are likely to yield less reliable projections over the short term, especially during periods when large changes in the explanatory variables are taking place.

Table 14.3 ILTM (2011) estimates of contribution to total addressed inland letter traffic growth per annum

	Change (%) in total traffic		
	2008 to 2009 (recession years)	2010 to 2011	2008 to 2011
1. Estimated contribution to total traffic growth using long-run elasticities and parameters			
a. Economy and demographic factors	−1.2	2.3	0.5
Economic activity[1]	−2.3	1.2	−0.6
Households[1]	1.1	1.1	1.1
b. Letter prices[1,2]	−1.0	−0.0	−0.5
c. Quality of service[1]	0.3	0.2	0.2
d. Multi-media competition (mainly e-substitution)	−7.0	−5.1	−6.1
Net impact of 'unexplained' time trends[3]	−2.0	−2.0	−2.0
Proportion of Internet advertising expenditure[4]	−2.9	−1.5	−2.2
Price of non-mail advertising[1,2]	−2.0	−1.6	−1.8
2. Estimated change (%) in total letter traffic using long-run elasticities (=1a+1b+1c+1d)	−8.9	−2.6	−5.8
3. Dynamic model estimate for changes in total letter traffic[5]	−6.5	−4.1	−5.3
4. Outcome	−6.1	−4.7	−5.4
5. Outcome minus estimates using long-run elasticities[6] (=4–2)	2.8	−2.1	0.4
6. Outcome minus dynamic model estimates (=4–3)	0.4	−0.6	−0.1

Notes:
1. Estimate relates to average annual growth rate.
2. Deflated by the all items retail prices index.
3. The combined impact of the time-trend coefficients reported in Table 14.2.
4. Refers to the average change in the proportion of Internet advertising expenditure in total advertising expenditure.
5. Obtained from estimates using the model reported in Table 14.1.
6. This difference is due to not taking into account the impact of dynamic estimates on total traffic plus random error.

Estimates using the full dynamic model (row 3) perform considerably better over the two subperiods than those using long-run estimated elasticites (see rows 5 and 6) and suggest that it is important to take dynamic impacts into account when analyzing prospects for letter demand over short- to medium-term time horizons.

The results reported in Table 14.3 suggest that over the period 2008 to 2009 all the key drivers of letter traffic growth, with the exception of QoS and increasing households, were exerting downward pressure on letter demand which declined on average by over 6 percent per annum. In particular, the 2008–09 recession is estimated to have subtracted, on average, around –2½ percent per annum over this two-year period; letter prices about –1 percent per annum; and multi-media competition (that is, mainly e-substitution) approximately –7 percent per annum. In contrast, over the subsequent two years the economic recovery is estimated to have boosted letter traffic by over 1 percent, a turnaround in the contribution from economic activity from –2½ percent to +1.2 percent (that is, an improvement in contribution of around 3½ percent), which helped to reduce the rate of letter volume decline.

An important point to note from the results reported in Table 14.3 is that the decline in total UK letter traffic over the period 2010 to 2011 is estimated to be mainly due to two opposing forces. On one side, economic growth and demographic trends were exerting upward pressure on letter traffic, but pulling in the opposite direction has been the more powerful effect of e-communications and multi-modal competition. This therefore suggests that prospects for UK letter demand over the short to medium term will largely depend on the extent to which gains from improvements in economic activity offset the losses due to e-substitution and other media communications.

Review of Econometric Model Estimates for UK Total Letter Traffic

Table 14.4 contains a summary of econometric time-series estimates for UK addressed inland total letter traffic published over the past decade.

A number of points can be noted from the table. First, the estimated elasticities for economic activity in all models tend to be around unity. This suggests that the link between fluctuations in economic growth and mail volumes is not 'broken' but that these fluctuations are now taking place around a declining trend. Second, the estimated elasticities for factors that are to some extent within postal operators' control, namely letter prices and QoS, are low. Third, multi-modal competition, as modeled via PIA, PA and in particular the net impact of the time-trend variables, is estimated to have increased considerably between 1999 and 2008. Fourth, the estimated price elasticities for total traffic may have increased somewhat over time (possibly from around –0.2 to –0.3). However, the increase in the total estimated price elasticity is mainly due to the increasing proportion of total traffic accounted for by the Other traffic stream which has a higher net of switching estimated price elasticity. For example, reweighting the ILTM(2011) estimated price elasticities with 1999 volume shares would generate a total traffic price elasticity estimate of around –0.25. In the case of economic activity the reweighted estimate would be 0.92, which is very similar to the Nankervis et al. (2002) estimate, and for QoS it would be 0.21, which is somewhat higher.

A decade of econometric research into the demand for letters in the UK therefore suggests that when assessing future letter volume trends, whether using formal econometric models or other methods, postal analysts should focus on three key issues. First, what is the likely profile of economic activity over the time horizon being analyzed. Second, what is the current rate of e-substitution or loss due to multi-media competition? Third, is the impact of e-substitution likely to stabilize, accelerate or decelerate going forward in time?

Table 14.4 A comparison of UK total letter traffic demand estimated long-run elasticities and parameters over the past decade[1]

Publication	Nankervis et al. (2002)	Fève et al. (2012)	VM (2011)	ILTM(2011)
End of estimation period	1999Q1	2003Q2	2008Q1	2011Q4
Economic activity (Y)	1.00	1.02	1.09	0.86
Letter prices (P)[2]	−0.19	−0.19	−0.33	−0.30
Quality of service (QoS)	0.13	0.12	0.13	0.14
Telecom price[2]	0.01	–	–	–
Price of non-mail advertising (PA)[2]	–	0.16	0.24	0.44
Proportion of Internet advertising (PIA)	–	–	−0.95	−0.73
Net impact of 'unexplained' time trends (% p.a.)	1.7	−0.6	−2.4	−2.0

Notes:
1. Total traffic estimated elasticities and time-trend effects were calculated by weighting the estimated coefficients in each of the traffic streams by their respective traffic volumes shares.
2. Deflated by the all items retail prices index.

5 SUMMARY AND CONCLUSIONS

We have applied econometric modeling techniques using time-series data to quantify the impact of key factors driving addressed inland UK letter traffic volumes. The econometric results are broadly similar to the findings of VM, despite including an additional, and eventful, 15 quarters of information. The additional data points covered a period of time in which there was continued downward pressure on letter volumes from increasing levels of multi-media competition aided by advances in technology, and the steepest UK recession in over 70 years.

Our econometric model estimates the total traffic long-run elasticities for economic activity and the number of households to be around unity. These results are consistent with those estimated a decade earlier by Nankervis et al. (2002) and indeed with work undertaken previous to this (see Nankervis et al., 1999). We find the strongest impact from economic activity to be on First Class non-presort traffic (around 1.4) and those for Second Class non-presort and Other (mainly presort and access) traffic to be a little below unity.

These estimated long-run elasticities suggest that the relationship between UK letter traffic and economic activity is not 'broken', as some have claimed. In contrast, our estimates suggest that fluctuations in economic activity continue to have a broadly one-to-one impact on total letter volumes, but these fluctuations are taking place around a downward trend due to increasing competition from other media. Our econometric estimates suggest that in recent years the impact of multi-media competition on letter demand has been around −6 percent per annum, which is consistent with estimates for the structural rate of decline in transactional mail reported in Veruete-McKay et al. (ch. 16, this volume). This implies that, in the absence of letter price increases and quality of service remaining around current levels, the long-run rate of letter traffic growth, assuming that the economy were to grow at around 2 percent and household growth rates by 1 percent per annum, could be around −3 percent per annum if the rate of e-substitution were to remain broadly stable. Unfortunately, as research results contained in CRRI publications over the past decade remind us, the negative impact on letter traffic from multi-modal competition has tended to increase over time. This suggests that assessments of the demand for mail need to explicitly consider the extent to which e-communications and competition from other more traditional media will continue to increase, stabilize, or even potentially slow down over the time horizon under consideration, as recommended in the forecasting methodology proposed by Rodriguez and Soteri (2011) and Fève et al. (2012).

The total traffic letter price elasticity for addressed inland mail is estimated to be low at around −0.3. But, in contrast, cross-price elasticity estimates suggest that there is considerable switching between First and Second Class traffic and also between Second Class non-presort traffic and Other (mainly presort and access) traffic. Furthermore, our results suggest that switching between Second Class and Other traffic has increased as the degree of competition in the upstream letters market has increased.

The extent to which the low estimated total traffic price elasticity is independent of our estimates of relatively high negative impacts of multi-modal competition (mainly driven by e-communications) is a moot point. In future research it may be possible to shed further light on this point by combining econometric time-series data with individual sender and/or receiver information to obtain more robust estimates for price elasticities. Given the importance of price elasticities to inform business decisions, this could be an important avenue for future research.

NOTES

* The analysis contained in this chapter reflects the views of the authors and are not necessarily those of Royal Mail Group. We would like to thank Frank Rodriguez for helpful suggestions and comments.

1. See, for example: Boldron et al. (2010) for an analysis on the demand for mail in France; Meschi et al. (2011) for an EU multi-country study; Nikali (2008) for an analysis in Finland; and Veruete-McKay et al. (2011) for previous analysis in the UK.
2. The First and Second Class non-presort traffic streams have a next working day and within three working days delivery specification, respectively. They include the following addressed inland Royal Mail products: Stamp, Meter, PPI and Cleanmail. The Other stream includes the following products: Mailsort, Walksort, Packetpost, Presstream, Response Services, USO Parcels, Large Mail Order Returns, Tracked, Heavyweight and access traffic.
3. Advertisements triggered by key 'searchwords'.
4. The ECM is a reparameterisation of the general linear autoregressive distributed lag (ADL) model. The research findings of Panopoulou and Pittis (2004) suggest that, in general, the performance of ADL estimators is superior to dynamic ordinary least squares (DOLS) estimators. Therefore, in contrast to Veruete-McKay et al. (2011), we modeled the demand for letters using a single-step ECM.
5. SURE was used to jointly estimate the three equations, which included restrictions between equations, to account for contemporaneous correlation between the errors in each equation.
6. The hypothesis could not be rejected on statistical grounds and was imposed in the model. Symmetry between First and Second Class long-run cross-price elasticities were imposed using the general formula: $e_{ij} = e_{ji} * v_j / v_i$, where: e_{ij} is the price elasticity for traffic stream *i* with respect to changes in the price of traffic stream *j* $(i \neq j)$; v_j and v_i are the volumes for traffic streams *i* and *j*, respectively. In the estimated equations the lagged volumes v_{it-1} and v_{jt-1} were used in order to address endogeneity issues. Changing levels of switching between Second Class non-presort and Other traffic were tested for via the inclusion of a relative price variable multiplied by annual dummy terms for individual financial years 2006/07 to 2011/12 and imposing symmetry restrictions for these terms.
7. Portmanteau tests for autocorrelation and normality tests suggest that the model residuals possess reasonable properties. The model was estimated using the econometric package EViews7.
8. Estimated long-run parameters can be derived from Table 14.1 by dividing the estimated coefficients in each equation by the estimated coefficient for q_{it-1} multiplied by –1.
9. Financial year 2010/11 weights were used.
10. The economic activity variable is UK gross domestic product (GDP). Previous studies of UK letter demand such as VM and Nankervis et al. (2002) used GDP weighted by letter demand. This does not have a material impact on the estimated results.
11. The estimates reported in Table 14.2 suggest that a 1 percent increase in the price of First Class traffic will, on average, increase Second Class traffic by 0.24 percent (the latter is equal, in volume terms, to 0.27 percent of First Class traffic).
12. This is equal to the sum of the estimated Second Class price elasticity terms for Second Class traffic reported in Table 14.2 (column 3), that is –0.24 plus –1.36 (note that the latter is minus the coefficient of the relative price term P3 – P2).
13. The cross-price elasticity estimates between Second Class and Other traffic in Table 14.1 are estimated to be increasing from 2007/08 to 2011/12 (consistent with the observation of increasing access competition over this period) and then flatten out in the final two years of the estimation period. The use of annual dummy variables is a somewhat crude tool to capture the impact of increasing price elasticities over time, but it is highly effective in providing a valuable guide to the potential change in the magnitude of price elasticities in the letters market. The estimated decline in Second Class traffic switching to the Other traffic group of 1.4 percent, referred to in the text, relates to the estimated cross-price elasticity with respect to Other traffic reported in Table 14.2 in 2011 (column 3, estimated coefficient 1.36).
14. The total decline in Other traffic resulting from a 1 percent increase in Other prices is estimated by the sum of the P3 price elasticities reported in Table 14.2 for Other traffic (column 4), that is, –0.42–0.38 = –0.80. The estimated switching to Second Class traffic of 0.4 percent is estimated by the cross-price elasticity term relating to P2, that is –(–0.38).
15. Publishing and TV media rates.

REFERENCES

Boldron, F., C. Cazals, J.P. Florens and S. Lécou (2010), 'Some dynamic models for mail demand: the French case', in M.A. Crew and P.R. Kleindorfer (eds), *Heightening Competition in the Postal and Delivery Sector*, Cheltenham, UK and Northampton, MA, USA: Edward Elgar, pp. 99–115.

Cazals, C., J.-P. Florens, L. Veruete-McKay, F. Rodriguez and S. Soteri (2011), 'UK letter demand: a content-based time-series analysis using overlapping market survey statistical techniques', in M.A. Crew and P.R. Kleindorfer (eds), *Reinventing the Postal Sector in an Electronic Age*, Cheltenham, UK and Northampton, MA, USA, Edward Elgar, pp. 91–108.

Fève, F., J.P. Florens, L. Veruete-McKay, S. Soteri and F. Rodriguez (2012), 'Uncertainty and projections of the demand for mail', in M.A. Crew and P.R. Kleindorfer (eds), *Multi-modal Competition and the Future of Mail*, Cheltenham, UK and Northampton, MA, USA: Edward Elgar, pp. 77–93.

Meschi, M., M. Cherry, C. Pace and M. Petrova (2011), 'Understanding the impact of e-substitution on letter mail volumes: a multi-country panel study', in M.A. Crew and P.R. Kleindorfer (eds), *Reinventing the Postal Sector in an Electronic Age*, Cheltenham, UK and Northampton, MA, USA: Edward Elgar, pp. 47–60.

Nankervis, J., I. Carslake and F. Rodriguez (1999), 'How important have price and quality been to mail volume growth?', in M.A. Crew and P.R. Kleindorfer (eds), *Emerging Competition in Postal and Delivery Services*, Boston, MA: Kluwer Academic.

Nankervis, J., S. Richard, S. Soteri and F. Rodriguez (2002), 'Disaggregated letter traffic demand in the UK', in M.A. Crew and P.R. Kleindorfer (eds), *Postal and Delivery Services*, Boston, MA: Kluwer Academic, pp. 203–18.

Nikali, H. (2008), 'Substitution of letter mail for different sender-receiver segments', in M.A. Crew and P.R. Kleindorfer (eds), *Competition and Regulation in the Postal and Delivery Sector*, Cheltenham, UK and Northampton, MA, USA: Edward Elgar, pp. 89–106.

Panopoulou, E. and N. Pittis (2004), 'A comparison of autoregressive distributed lag and dynamic OLS cointegration estimators in the case of a serially correlated cointegration error', *Econometrics Journal*, **7**, 585–617.

Rodriguez, F. and S. Soteri (2011), 'Uncertainty and long-term projections: a framework for postal sector demand', in Oxera, *Agenda*, August.

Soteri, S., F. Fève, J.P. Florens and F. Rodriguez (2009), 'Internet advertising and direct mail: trends and analysis for the UK', in M.A. Crew and P.R. Kleindorfer (eds), *Progress in the Competitive Agenda in the Postal and Delivery Sector*, Cheltenham, UK and Northampton, MA, USA: Edward Elgar, pp. 209–22.

Veruete-McKay, L., S. Soteri, J. Nankervis and F. Rodriguez (2011), 'Letter traffic demand in the UK: an analysis by product and envelope content type', *Review of Network Economics*, **10**, Article 10.

15. Status of the postal service twenty years after the Green Paper: a Franco–European perspective

Joëlle Toledano†

An idea that is simple but wrong will always carry more weight in the world than an idea that is right but complex.

Alexis de Tocqueville

1 BACKGROUND AND INTRODUCTION

The Green Paper on the Development of the Single Market for Postal Services is now twenty years old. Published on 11 June 1992, it was the outcome of several years of work, consultation and coordination.[1] It stated that 'the absolute policy fundamental is the need to ensure the continuation of the universal service, and thus to ensure that the postal administrations' public service mission is carried out in good economic and financial conditions' (p. 5).

The Green Paper put this principle into practice by advocating Europe-wide accessibility for all national and cross-border services that are affordable and of satisfactory quality. It provided several options for achieving these objectives, ranging from total opening up of the postal market to the status quo, giving preference to a middle-way scenario of gradual market liberalization. At over 350 pages, this report gave a detailed description of the situation on the postal market and of the economic, legal and social issues to be taken into account. It defined the basis for the joint regulatory rules to which postal services and markets in Europe were to be subject, with special rules covering universal service operators, while leaving member states extensive decision-making autonomy. It was welcomed by most stakeholders (governments, major customers, consumer and business associations, public and private postal operators), and the Commission subsequently received more than 200 contributions to the debate.

The purpose of this chapter is to provide an initial attempt to understand the stakes and the economic debates that were current when the Green Paper was written. This approach is necessary in order to take economic stock of the past twenty years before considering the questions which need to be answered now. This strictly economic view of things is obviously very restrictive. In most countries, the postal sector has a centuries-old history and is often a symbol both of political and territorial unity and of solidarity.

Basically, the Green Paper's major achievement was getting economic players with

† Professor of Economics, Supélec.

conflicting interests to almost agree. What pleased some, namely a broad-based universal service and the existence of a reserved area protected by the Community's regulatory framework, was exactly what appealed less to others who were calling for 'strict' regulation of monopoly operators, with a clearly controlled universal service to allow the broadest possible competition to develop. The objective of improving national and European quality of service advocated by the Green Paper met with general approval, primarily from consumers and political staff. Essentially, while the Green Paper opened the door to all possible interpretations, it also had the potential to address all concerns. To understand it, it is necessary to go back briefly to the years preceding its publication.

For postal administrations, the 1980s brought two major institutional innovations. On the one hand, the gradual separation of postal and telecommunications services and on the other, erosion of the postal monopoly, both of which undermined what we would now call the postal business model of the day. In the early 1980s, postal and telecom operations were frequently combined in the same Post and Telecom administration. The British led the way with the separation of Royal Mail and British Telecom from 1981. Then gradually, the twofold separation of administration on the one hand, and between Post and Telecom on the other, established itself everywhere. Independently of all other technical, political and social aspects, the separation of the two operations had the immediate consequence of highlighting the issue of postal service funding, which, in some countries, came partly from telecommunications. In this respect, the Green Paper stated that, in the great majority of the EC's then 12 member states, postal services in the strict sense of the term, that is, without taking account of postal financial services, were operating at a loss in 1988. In those days, only the postal services of the United Kingdom and the Netherlands were making a profit. In four countries (Belgium, Denmark, France and Ireland), the deficit was offset by the surplus generated by financial services (Green Paper, p. 123).

The second shock came with the advent of what were then known as 'integrators' – and now as express couriers – in Europe.[2] As early as 1976, UPS had made an initial acquisition in Germany. Then in the 1980s, integrators (DHL, FedEx and UPS, to name the best known) appeared on the European market offering international mail services based on remailing and/or express services. From the point of view of European postal services (and often of their governments), these American couriers were coming to Europe to do there what they had already managed to do with the American Post, namely to leave low-revenue letter-post business for the Posts and grab the parcels and express markets. In this connection, the 1995 article by E.R. Costich and W.G. Willette perfectly illustrated the fears of European Posts. Indeed the United States Postal Service (USPS) lost the market dominance of the parcel in favor of the integrator UPS with its confining and creaming-off strategy. European Posts did not want this strategy to be repeated at home.

Initially, postal administrations almost everywhere tried to oppose this trend head on. They often came to realize that, because of national regulations which had not changed much over the centuries, the legal monopoly they thought they held did not have a very sound foundation. These monopolies were all the weaker because Community regulations were fairly restrictive in the field of exclusive rights, and postal administrations were not sure of winning any disputes over competition in which they might be confronted.

Thus, member states gradually adopted the Commission's interpretation and accepted that the express service did not legally infringe national, legal monopolies. In 1990, after several legal episodes, two of the European Commission's formal decisions against the Netherlands and Spain confirmed that national and international express services did not come under national postal monopolies. The Court of Justice of the European Communities later confirmed these decisions.

Integrators opened up another legal front – legalizing the opening of the international mail market to competition and calling into question the market practices of traditional monopolies. The Green Paper announced that the Commission would address the complaint brought by the IECC (International Express Carriers Conferences) as to whether the rules enforced by Posts about international mail, and in particular within European Union territory, were permissible under competition law.

The following year, the Corbeau decision once again highlighted the weakness of postal monopolies (European Court of Justice, 1993). Admittedly, the Court of Justice of the European Communities acknowledged that the Treaty of Rome did not prohibit postal monopolies and that they could be justified by the need to finance missions of general interest, such as the public postal service. However, by the same token, the Corbeau decision established that the monopoly was not justified if economic equilibrium was not compromised. The Corbeau decision was in a way the legal counterpart of the more political Green Paper. It had the same effect as the Green Paper and accepted the principle of a monopoly provided it was necessary for providing the public service.

This question of the scope and limits of the monopoly was, in fact, the nub of the integrators' offensive. In a fascinating article, Jim Campbell (1994) recounts how, under the IECC banner, the couriers tried from 1983 on to force a change in European regulations so as to introduce competition on European postal markets.

Because Community law required the postal monopoly to correspond to a mission of general interest, the Green Paper made it possible to reformulate the discussion. For supporters of liberalization, the objective was to show that there was no need to define an overly wide universal service for operators and that the market would often be best able to meet customer needs.

France and other countries took the view that maintaining (or even improving) a public postal service in France justified embracing European ideas about putting in place a single postal market where ambitious goals would be defined for Europe as a whole. To paraphrase *The Leopard* by G.T. de Lampedusa,[3] everything had to be changed for things to stay almost as they were. The 1980s had shown the fragility of the legal and institutional organization of postal services. Radical change was called for, a regulatory framework had to be put in place for the Community, the universal service had to be defined, high-quality targets set for national and intra-European services and then monitored, operator activities separated from those of the postal regulator, and so on. This was the price postal operators would have to pay to preserve the core of the postal service's operational model – a monopoly implementing its internal cross-subsidization policies.

Twenty years thus passed between the Green Paper and liberalization of the postal market in 2011.[4] Compared with the European process of opening up telecommunications or even energy markets, this period may seem very long. Perhaps the Green Paper's very success provides the explanation. It managed to reconcile seemingly incompatible objectives. It took the economic and financial crisis to intensify the slide in traffic which had begun in the early years of the twenty-first century for the contradictions to resolve themselves. In actual fact, the problems have changed, and opening up markets to competition is no longer the central issue.

Consequently, total market liberalization in 2011 has not really had any tangible effect. In practical terms, a look at the countries where liberalization was not yet complete as of 1 January 2011 reveals no new market entrants and no new development plan of any significance in countries which are, in an initial analysis, as different as France, Austria or Belgium. In more general terms, wherever competition has existed since the early years of this century, the question of the impact of loss of market share in recent years is largely relativized in the light of losses as the result of electronic-media substitution.

The chapter now reviews the economic impact of the postal regulatory framework in the 15 member states of Europe, which participated in these changes from the 1990s onward. Countries that joined the Union between 2004 and 2007 are not included in this investigation. Section 2 presents the methodology and summarizes the main trends that developed. Then, Section 3 describes the various forms of competition in Europe, Section 4 proposes various angles to approximate the evolution of jobs and productivity, Section 5 shows the main features of price evolution and Section 6 portrays transformations of incumbent operators. To conclude, Section 7 tries to highlight the main issues that the postal stakeholders will have to answer in the next years.

2 ELEMENTS OF THE REVIEW

In practice, each of these countries conducted its own policy, both as regards liberalization and revised regulation of the market, within the framework of a not very prescriptive directive. Moreover, the initial economic, geographical and regulatory situations differed quite considerably as regards traffic, quality of service, tariffs, population density and the types of services offered, as the Green Paper emphasized. While there was a common regulatory framework, it also left plenty of latitude for national 'subsidiarity' but not much for harmonization. Following on from the numerous studies requested by the European Commission since the Green Paper,[5] two articles in the *Handbook of Worldwide Postal Reform* published in 2008, one on regulatory aspects and the other on socioeconomic aspects, clearly bring out the diversity of situations in Europe (Campbell et al., 2008; Crew et al., 2008). The two studies published in 2009 and 2010 supplement this overview, making it possible to compile the main data needed for a review (ITA consulting and WIK consult, 2009; Copenhagen Economics, 2010).

At a strictly economic level, it would be useful to evaluate the impact of policies by adopting two complementary methods (Winston, 1993). The first, classic method is based on measuring social welfare, the sum of consumer surplus and corporate profits. It is, however, virtually impossible to implement because information about the price and volume indicators for effective measurement of these developments are not available. Sweden is the only country with statistics. For the period under study (1990–2006), increases were on average offset by decreases from which the corporate sector benefited.[6]

The second approach provides less of an overall view but is more qualitative and systematically examines the impact of the new market regulation on competition, jobs, productivity and wages, quality of service, tariffs and any transfers between consumers, traffic volumes, innovation and corporate profits, to mention only the most frequently cited parameters. The studies sponsored by the European Commission provide information about many of these topics but not all of them, because information about certain topics such as jobs, tariffs and volumes is not standardized or does not exist. It is therefore hard to compare it over time (for instance, postal jobs between 1992 and 2011, prices for services paid by the corporate sector, in particular big mailers) and geographically (the definition of total traffic is not necessarily the same in the various countries). Moreover, there are surprising gaps in the information available, as some postal services seem to have a non-transparent information policy which hardly seems compatible with the need for transparency in respect of consumers, which conducting a mission of general interest implies.[7]

In any event, the only economic objective set out in the Green Paper was the continued financing of a good-quality, affordable universal service. On the whole, this objective has been achieved. Despite the economic and financial crisis and, above all, despite lower traffic volumes, the postal operators responsible for providing the universal service were in much better shape at the end of the first decade of the twenty-first century than 20 years before. Furthermore, both national and intra-European quality of service has improved overall, even if there is still room for progress in some countries, and tariffs are affordable.

At the same time, almost all universal service operators have managed to build a profitable economic model based on a more efficient production tool that concentrates and distributes substantial traffic volumes with considerable economies of scale and scope and moderate prices. They have also expanded their non-postal activities by means of diversification strategies on various scales in preparation for the expected slump in postal traffic.

Other review data were much more unexpected and need to be put in perspective. This review will go on to examine four characteristics of the economic model which emerged from the Green Paper: the process of 'gradual' liberalization, led to limited competition, with virtually no innovation (Section 3), there was a marked decrease in postal operation jobs (Section 4), tariff structures have been considerably distorted (Section 5), and universal service operators have used strategies with some characteristics that need to be outlined (Section 6).

All investigations are now focusing on the extent of and the uncertainties affecting the drop in traffic. This chapter will therefore try to see how this slump changes the characteristics of the present economic model. In any event, it destroys economies of scale. If the decrease in traffic is such that tariffs need to be substantially increased or quality of service allowed to deteriorate to ensure funding of the universal service continues, member states and the Commission will have to raise the question of the future of the universal service. As far as universal service operators are concerned, the resilience of their strategy is obviously the fundamental question. This will be dealt with in the conclusion.

3 COMPETITION?

All recent studies have highlighted the weaknesses of competition on European postal markets (Ecorys, 2008; ITA Consulting and WIK Consult, 2009; Copenhagen Economics,

2010). In actual fact, the international mail market is the only niche where competition is overtly present, even though the established operator still dominates this segment. What is more, this market is declining even more than the others. The development of competition upstream of the mail delivery network is structurally linked to regulatory policy. The United Kingdom, where access tariffs allowed competition to develop on the fringe while preventing end-to-end competition, is of course a prime example. On the other hand, despite the repeated affirmations of both companies and regulators, no end-to-end competition has managed to develop by basing itself on customers acquired on the mail preparation market. The British and French examples, where there are sizeable players on markets upstream of mail delivery, testify to the difficulty (and even the impossibility to date) of relying on these operators to develop end-to-end competition.[8]

There are many explanations for the absence of effective end-to-end competition. The strictly economic reasons that are most often cited include the effects of reputation, economies of scale and the learning factor. There are many regulatory entrance barriers, some of which vary from country to country. Examples include the different VAT procedures, problems with accessing letter boxes or the coverage and service quality obligations imposed on new entrants in some countries. Over the past period, there have been no product innovations, as new players have managed to enter the markets on the strength of competition based on price.

In the Netherlands and Germany, they based themselves on labor costs very much lower than those of the incumbent operators. In Sweden, competition is basically confined to one market segment, namely presorted bulk mail delivered to slightly over half of the country's inhabitants living in the most densely populated areas. To date, the product range and operational structure of CityMail dating from the early 1990s, with time-certain delivery and two delivery rounds per week, are the only 'innovations' generated by postal liberalization in Europe. CityMail needed almost 10 years to become profitable (Toledano, 2004). Sweden Post, the incumbent universal service operator, has an 88 percent market share of volume and well over 90 percent of value, after 20 years of a competition that is confined to the cheapest service price category. Service quality and reliability are good.

Very few countries have achieved the same level of competition in the 15 member states of the 'old' Europe. Only in Germany, Spain and the Netherlands is there competition that is anything but marginal.[9] In Spain and Germany, there is a system of local operators networking with a single lead operator covering 70 percent of the territory, such as Unipost the Deutsche Post satellite in Spain and TNT in Germany. SANDD in the Netherlands is partly involved in a branch of CityMail with two rounds a week. However, fast national coverage was made possible by the Netherlands' high population density and by extremely insecure wage and social-insurance conditions. These should in principle improve following the recent postal legislation in the Netherlands. Sweden, Spain, Germany and the Netherlands are all countries where competition was allowed ahead of the Community framework.

The markets liberalized in the wake of the lower price/weight threshold provided for in successive directives were not extensive enough to allow operators to develop financially viable business. No gaining of ground by the competition has been observed in countries where full market liberalization did not come until 2011. The reason is simple. Market development is much too uncertain for new capital investment. Experience has shown that the only way of ensuring the eventual profit of new entrants, where balanced books could reasonably be expected only after several years, was for them to be sold to other countries' incumbent operators as a way of expanding the latter's European coverage. Given the difficulties and uncertainty faced by these operators themselves (above all by Deutsche Post and PostNL), the source of new market entrants has (temporarily?) dried up.

4 JOBS AND PRODUCTIVITY

The Green Paper completely avoided employment issues, with their various aspects: productive efficiency, working conditions, wages and the number of jobs. Based on traffic growth assumptions (6 percent per year) which turned out to be totally invalid, the Green Paper expected 2–3 percent more new jobs overall and job stability for incumbent operators. It did, however, foresee structural problems in respect of skills. Five years later, the PricewaterhouseCoopers (1997) study noted the first signs of employment downturns and predicted that they could continue.

Furthermore, this topic was at the heart of the political debate during the liberalization process, with the issue of new forms of very part-time employment (as little as 15 hours a week or even less in the Netherlands, for instance) with considerably lower wages and very limited social benefits. The postal business is a labor-intensive industry. Opening up the market to competition could not reasonably be expected to create jobs unless, of course, there was strong traffic growth – and this was no longer the case – and/or the players became highly diversified. And even so, existing skills generally did not match those needed for the new jobs.

Increased productivity and roughly 25 percent (that is, 10,000) fewer jobs in the first 10 years of liberalization are the main features of liberalization of the Swedish market. However, as Andersson (2008) clearly shows, these parameters are hard to quantify with any degree of rigor. Changes were made to the business area of the former monopoly, Sweden Post, which has gradually divested itself of its financial services, outsourcing of operations to subcontractors and fluctuating traffic – slightly up during the first 10 years, before falling since 2000 – which greatly complicate any evaluation. Be that as it may, a considerable number of jobs have been shed in Sweden Post's postal business. The number of jobs created by new market entrants lags far behind at less than one-fifth of the jobs cut by the incumbent operator. The results will not always be as simple to analyze in other EU countries, on the one hand because the necessary information is not always available, and on the other because the jobs created are often part-time, making comparison of the resultant magnitudes difficult.

In fact, to fully evaluate changes in employment on the European postal market, the information we would require concerns only staff assigned to mail collection, sorting and delivery for the incumbent operator and for its competitors, but these statistics are not available. Hence the need to fall back on trying to evaluate these changes, country by country, as for Sweden, largely by using the incumbent operator's employment figures. However, many European countries have seen divestments and acquisitions that greatly modified operators' area of activity. The report by ITA Consulting and WIK Consult (2009) estimated that, between 1998 and 2007, jobs with postal operators responsible for the universal service in the 15 member states of Europe under study had risen 17.5 percent, while jobs with these same operators confined to their national territories were down 14.5 percent.

However, the recent structural alterations to the operator in the Netherlands (see below) provide some idea of the magnitude of changes in manpower productivity there. This operator has always been regarded by all players as one of the most efficient. So, this evaluation may be seen as a useful benchmark. The number of jobs at the end of 2011 with the incumbent operator in the Netherlands was around the same level as in 1992 (roughly 65,000 employees). But in terms of full-time equivalents (FTEs), it had fallen 20 percent (34,000 compared with 44,000). Moreover, the current business area covers new postal operations (mainly abroad) accounting for roughly one-third of turnover. Thus, in 20 years, the number of FTE jobs in connection with letter-post and parcel operations in the Netherlands has been halved (though subcontracting has increased). Moreover, industry-restructuring projects aimed at addressing an annual decrease in traffic of 7 percent in the years ahead will result in the shedding of 11,000 more jobs in the years to come.

5 PRICES AND TARIFF STRUCTURES

Sweden is the only country where price changes have been precisely analyzed. The finding that was least expected was probably the very marked change in tariff structure, with an increase in prices paid by private individuals and small mailers that was offset by a proportional decrease in the prices paid by big mailers. Basically, before CityMail, observers lent more towards predicting the development of competition in the B2B (business-to-business) sector. The advent of CityMail revealed underlying cost structures for non-urgent items and slightly heavier items that had previously been overlooked. Hence the price reduction of as much as 65 percent for non-urgent, presorted items weighing 50 grams and price increases of 75 percent (including VAT) for single letters weighing less than 20 grams. Lower prices for corporate mail that are more or less offset by higher prices for single items are found almost everywhere. Obviously, everything depends on the initial situation and the keenness of the competition. In countries where end-to-end competition is virtually non-existent, such as France, Belgium, Denmark or Austria, there is less downward pressure on bulk-item prices.[10] In contrast, lower prices were noted in Germany and the Netherlands.[11] Decreases (admittedly smaller ones) were also registered for franking-machine users.[12] In this case, it is more a question of establishing customer loyalty and responding to competitive pressure from local operators. On the balance sheet, transfers between private individuals and very small enterprises (VSEs), on the one hand, and large and medium-sized mailers, on the other hand, are higher where competition is keener.

So far, price increases for single-piece items have been fairly limited and long-period studies show that in Western Europe, increases over the past 20 years have been lower than increases in the consumer price index in the majority of countries (ITA Consulting and WIK Consult, 2009). However, this basic trend conceals considerable differences in phases. The following are two fairly contrasting examples: Germany is an exception in that Deutsche Post prices have remained stable and have even fallen slightly (€ at current prices), since the year 2000 after being at what was considered a very high level at the end of the 1990s. In contrast, France's La Poste played 'catch-up' in the last decade after a policy of very moderate price increases in the 1990s. Today, German postal tariffs for private customers are among the lowest in the former group of 15 member states of Europe, in terms of nominal value and purchasing power parity. However, new trends seem to be emerging with the traffic downturn.

6 CHANGES IN INCUMBENT OPERATORS

Most incumbent operators have rolled out development strategies, either by acquisition and/or internal expansion, on their national territory and/or at international level, and either upstream of mail delivery or in different market segments, such as express services, unaddressed items, or even banking or logistic operations.[13] The regulatory framework adopted enabled this development into third-party markets which was intended to offset – at least partially – the problems encountered on the mail market. This basically was one of the issues in the debate between integrators and postal operators. How should coexistence between monopoly operations and competitive operations be organized? How could cross-subsidization and state aid be prevented? This option of redeployment towards other activities is not, however, available in the United States where USPS is not authorized to seek new markets beyond its traditional operations. There have been numerous disputes, and they are not over yet. But in any event, Community competition rules did not forbid the introduction of these dynamic strategies.

In 2011, two operators thus had a turnover from mail accounting of less than 30 percent of their total turnover (Poste Italiane and Deutsche Post), and four others a national mail turnover of less than 60 percent (France's La Poste, PostNL, Austrian Post and Finland's Itella). With the exception of Royal Mail, this list covers the biggest postal businesses in Western and Southern Europe. These changes came about very fast, starting from the 1990s in the Netherlands and Germany, and later, in the first decade of the new millennium for the others.

Changes in status and major institutional adjustments took place everywhere, with postal administrations becoming limited companies, mainly with state capital. Three of them (Austrian Post, Deutsche Post DHL and PostNL) are stock-market listed, while Belgium's Bpost has a private shareholder, CVC, that owns half its capital. Almost all these companies have so far ridden out the traffic downturn quite well. Thus, after several years of admittedly more or less sizeable decreases, very few operators are in the red. Finland's Itella made a loss in 2011 for the first time. Moreover, this loss comes at a time when mail was still profitable, though less so than in previous years. The latest figures for the Irish and Greek Posts for 2009 and 2010 are also in the red. One last general comment: in almost all Posts, mail often contributes much more than its weight to generating profit margins. While these margins have fallen in parallel with traffic compared with their previous level, higher tariffs and improved productivity have often helped the Posts to stay profitable.[14] This applies in particular to Germany, Austria, Finland, Sweden and Denmark. The United Kingdom and Italy, where the opposite is the case, seem to be definite exceptions. And Italy is the only country where mail not only represents a very small share of postal business, but also has a negative impact on Group earnings.

The status of the operators has a very significant influence on their strategies. The examples of the Dutch Post and Austrian Post, above, show that financial investors, faced with uncertain demand, show a clear preference for the present and the dividends. Conversely the French La Poste has to deal with different constraints.

From 1996 the Dutch incumbent was making numerous acquisitions, mainly in Europe, but also in Asia and South America. Its turnover rose from €3 billion in 1996 to €12.6 billion in 2004. Very recently the financial markets forced the company to hive off its express operation. PostNL's turnover in 2011 is very close to its 1996 level in constant euro, and staff numbers are the same, though down 20 percent in terms of FTE. So what happened? Why did this international expansion strategy collapse? PostNL is under pressure from two sides. On the one hand, competition makes significant price increases difficult whereas regulation of universal service item prices is restrictive. Since 2007, domestic traffic has fallen by more than 5 percent per year on average. The combination of these two factors, competition and substitution with electronic alternatives, slashed TNT traffic by one-third.

The pressure to divest responds to a very different analysis of its two activities – risky domestic mail faced with regulatory constraints on the one hand, and international express items, whose strategic value is compromised by mail, on the other. From the financial theory angle, two different approaches to investment choices had problems coexisting within the same company. In a stable environment, especially on the basis of revenue generated by future demand, corporate value is maximized by the value of all flows updated to infinity (net present value: NPV), while, in a high-risk environment, the objective tends more towards minimizing the time needed to recover the investment committed. Hence the need to maximize short-term cash flow and dividends; faced with a rocky future for one of these operations, financial operators preferred to trigger the clear separation of two very different assets. One of them, though profitable, was overshadowed by doubts about demand, and this prompted calls for a substantial dividend that was guaranteed in the short term. The other was seen as having greater growth potential that was not reflected in its global value creation.

The example of Österreichische Post (Austria Post) illustrates the same situation, but the other way round. A recent financial analysis by Morgan Stanley (2012) was entitled: 'Cash is king in an uncertain world'. This corporation has been stock-exchange listed since 2006, with the Austria government owning 51 percent. Even though Austria Post has been pursuing regional acquisition since 2006, this strategy has been more restrained and prudent than that of TNT Post and the mail downturn came later (2009) and in a more moderate form (an average of 4 percent over the last three years). Mail accounts for 57 percent of total turnover and for the entire margin. Another major difference from the Netherlands Post is that competition is virtually non-existent. In this way, Austria Post has managed to regularly increase its earnings since 2002, in tandem with an extremely generous dividend policy (a market commitment of at least 75 percent of net earnings and, in practice, closer to 90 percent in 2010 and 2011).

The French incumbent, with state ownership, continues to pursue a strategy of having a business portfolio containing differentiated assets. The La Poste Group has changed radically over the past 20 years. Sticking to the main features, during the 1990s, and above all until 1996, La Poste struggled to keep its accounts balanced. At the beginning of the decade, mail represented two-thirds of turnover and the Group employed more than 300,000 FTE staff (slightly less than 300,000 for the public establishment). By the end of 2011, the Group had been making a profit for many years, managing to keep earnings virtually stable (operating margin of between 3 and 4 percent in the last three years) despite sharply declining traffic (4 percent on average between 2008 and 2011). The mail segment which has expanded slightly, basically upstream of the mail preparation and delivery value chain, now accounts for roughly 50 percent of Group turnover compared with over two-thirds 20 years ago, while the respective contributions of parcels/express items and the Banque Postale to the other 50 percent are roughly the same. The French Post's new economic model builds on three activities with cycles of differing degrees of maturity (letter post, parcels/express mainly in Europe and banking in France). In recent years, its results have been moderate compared with those of several other postal operators (in particular, Belgian, Italian, Portuguese, German and Dutch operators) but always in the black (operating result of between 3.1 and 4.3 percent between 2008 and 2011), with financial services and parcels/express services partly taking over in terms of contribution to the margin.

This kind of strategy now seems difficult to conduct with financial investors, as future privatizations will not take the same form as in previous years. It is hard to imagine, until the great uncertainty over postal markets is resolved, that a form of guarantee on profits and future dividends will not be linked to any privatization process.

7 THE NEW ISSUES

The traffic downturn is radically changing the issues. The future of a universal postal service and of the operators providing it may be at stake. As we have just seen, with the exception of the Italian Post, any significant deterioration in postal business affects the very survival of the incumbent operators. From a certain point on, declining postal business necessarily means higher expenditure for universal service. The competition is so weak that there is no question of relying on them to help fund this service. So when this point in decline is reached, governments will have to choose between changing the universal postal service or financing it, or both.

Postal delivery's high fixed costs mean that the loss of economies of scale *ceteris paribus* inevitably results in smaller margins. To date, operators have tended to demonstrate their ability to make productivity gains that offset the loss of economies of scale. To do so, they used three basic levers – more mechanized sorting, restructuring of the post office network by rolling out franchise networks to replace offices proper and making manpower more flexible, and pushing wages down to cut their wage costs for a set amount of work. In most European postal services, these different methods are used to varying degrees.

However, the reorganization process underway in the Netherlands shows the increasing difficulty of making efficiency gains with the same structure when traffic volumes have been falling by 5 percent per year for several years now, and corporate forecasts are for this trend to accelerate to 7 percent per year by 2015. Perhaps the decreases will be such that productivity gains will no longer be enough? Or perhaps they will be too costly in social terms?

Earnings may also be preserved by two other means, which do not depend solely on the operators and their employees: increasing prices and/or compromising on service quality. Here, the involvement of regulators and even of governments, parliaments and the European Commission could be necessary. Operators would like to be freer to use the quality of service lever to better advantage through changes to universal service obligations. They think that, in the longer term, inflexible universal service obligations in a world where requirements change very fast could become dangerous. Delivery and quality of service obligations are those most often contested. Given the more or less manifest refusal of the authorities to lower service quality targets, some countries have created less urgent services. Where these already exist, higher tariffs go hand in hand with encouragement to promote products with longer transmission times, while ensuring that this does not result in lower turnover. To this end, Austrian Post created a non-priority letter product and France's La Post a 'green letter' in 2011. Higher tariffs in the United Kingdom (with priority letter tariffs rising from 46 to 60 pence, and non-priority letters from 36 to 50 pence) could also encourage the transfer of part of mail flows to non-urgent products. However, the decline in priority traffic together with the items transferred to the non-priority stream will generate net extra cost for priority letters because there will be much less traffic to finance the cost of daily delivery rounds. Consequently, either priority tariffs will have to be increased or more will have to be spent on the universal service, or both.

When it comes to prices, operators are less unanimous. In recent years, some countries have substantially increased their tariffs, apparently not fearing any negative impact on traffic volumes that would wipe out price-increase gains. Royal Mail tariffs for stamped priority letter-post items up to 100 grams rose 30 percent, and non-priority stamped letters nearly 40 percent, at the end of April 2012. The price hikes in the United Kingdom mainly affect small consumers with price increases for companies using franking machines being kept to +10 to +12 percent, depending on transmission speed. Until recently, UK tariffs were among the lowest in Europe. This is no longer the case.

In Belgium, letter-post tariffs have risen sharply from 2008, especially compared with those of PostNL, with single-piece items rocketing nearly 40 percent or 'only' 20 percent if the tariffs for batches of 10 items are included. In a matter of years, and following substantial progress on productivity, the Belgian Post has become the most profitable universal service operator in Europe, with an operating result of 13.8 percent in 2010.[15]

However, this is not the case everywhere, even with marked falls in traffic. In the Netherlands, for instance, PostNL seems reluctant to raise tariffs too much, not just because of the competition and the regulatory framework, but also because of fears of making traffic decrease even further. Apparently for the same reasons, France's La Poste has refrained in recent years from increasing its tariffs to the levels authorized by the price cap, even though there is no competition.

These diverging policies on tariff increases are obviously not directed solely by regulatory constraints but are grounded in considerable uncertainty about demand for postal services. How long will the traffic downturn last and how big will it be? Will it level out? How will future traffic uses, requirements and prices look? And, incidentally and in the shorter term, is price elasticity in the process of changing (Fève et al., 2012)?

How should one regulate in the face of an uncertain future? What checks should be put in place? What tariffs? What quality of service? This could be an important issue for postal economists in the next few years. For postal operators, the answer is clear: with less regulation. This is the right reply if one believes that new technologies obviate the need for a universal postal service. Working on this assumption, one nevertheless wonders whether it would not open the door to new exploitation of monopoly revenue. Indeed, there is little chance for competition to establish itself where it does not already exist. Even when it does exist, it is fairly well contained and likely to remain so in the years to come. Nevertheless, if the sole justification of regulators were competition, an economist might wonder whether competition authorities would not suffice for monitoring a sector where, in any event, uncertainty will make the regulators' task even more difficult. How can one determine what is due to the asymmetry of information which the regulator will have to try to reduce and what is due to lack of information? How can capacities to adapt be given maximum scope?

Another alternative, and currently the most probable one despite declining traffic and the substitution of electronic services for part of the flows, is that the existence of the universal service is not only desirable but what is wanted. In this case, it is *not just* up to operators to assert the general interest. What does society need, and what is the cost of responding to these needs? It would be better for regulators to be able to verify whether financial changes are required. Furthermore, if the universal service is to change, it would be better for regulators to be able to contribute their expertise not just to the political and social but also to the economic debate which will undoubtedly unfold.

NOTES

1. This history has yet to be written. In addition to the facts and economic analyses compiled on this period, the contextual data given in this introduction are mainly taken either from French parliamentary reports and legal or economic articles, or from Jim Campbell (1994 and 1995), that excellent legal historian who nevertheless lobbied for American couriers.
2. Using the word 'integrator' to describe the international transport of letters and goods was an attempt to reflect what actually happened in the mail transport and delivery process. Until then, Posts had set up a structure where items were processed by national postal administrations which interchanged them in accordance with the technical and economic regulations defined within the framework of the Universal Postal Union. For their part, integrators set up end-to-end handling systems, based in particular on efficient information systems. These were high-speed (express) services that were the extension of courier operations.
3. '*Se vogliamo che tutto rimanga come è, bisogna che tutto cambi*', in *The Leopard* by Giuseppe Tomasi de Lampedusa (1958).
4. The 2008 Directive advocated two years' dispensation with total liberalization from 1 January 2013 for the 12 countries which joined the Union after 2002, plus Greece and Luxembourg. Nevertheless, over 95 percent of Europe's total traffic had to be opened to competition from 1 January 2011.
5. See http://ec.europa.eu/internal_market/post/studies_en.htm.
6. Regular studies by Swedish regulator PTS and academic Peter Andersson mean that we now have the most rigorous review possible of Swedish postal policy. The most recent are Andersson (2008) and PTS (2011). There are of course other sources, including Sweden Post, CityMail and government reports. The real difference is that PTS produced homogeneous information about volumes, market shares and prices that is not available elsewhere in Europe.
7. It is therefore astonishing to note that, for about 10 years, the Belgian Post (Bpost) does not appear to have published any exact traffic data. Trends can, however, be identified from the verbatim account of public remarks by its chairman. Indeed, information for stock-market listed companies seems to be the most accessible. However, only the archives of the Netherlands Post can be followed back to the 1990s.
8. For a description of the mailing-firm market in France, see Gallet-Rybak et al. (2008).
9. In Italy too, there seems to be some competition. However, the information available is not very reliable.
10. In this respect, PTS (2011, p. 8) recently expressed the view that rebalancing tariffs had made it possible to limit traffic loss in Sweden, compared with the Danish market.

11. The rebates obtained by large mailers in the United Kingdom have less to do with pressure from competition and more to do, in certain respects, with regulatory pressure on network access tariffs. Royal Mail access tariffs had to comply with rules, and this resulted in a widening of the gap between its own tariffs and those of mail consolidators.
12. In Sweden, the difference is 11 percent, and in the Netherlands 12 percent (April 2012).
13. See ITA Consulting and WIK Consult, 2009, pp. 77ff.
14. All the more since they were high!
15. Whereas the size, geographical density and per capita traffic of Belgium and the Netherlands are comparable, there is a 30–50 percent tariff difference between Bpost and PostNL for letters weighing less than 20 grams. There are of course other cost factors which surely justify this price difference. Part of this difference is definitely in the margin.

REFERENCES

Andersson, Peter (2008), 'Liberalization and market performance: towards higher efficiency in Sweden', in M.A. Crew, P.R. Kleindorfer and J.I. Campbell Jr (eds), *Handbook of Worldwide Postal Reform*, Cheltenham, UK and Northampton, MA, USA: Edward Elgar, pp. 298–315.

Campbell, Jim (1994), 'Couriers and the European postal monopolies: policy challenges of a newly emerging industry', in R.H. Pedlar and M.P.C.M. Van Schendelen (eds), *Lobbying in the European Union*, Aldershot: Dartmouth.

Campbell, James I. (1995), 'A review of efforts to develop a new policy framework for postal services in the European Union', in M.A Crew and P.R. Kleindorfer (eds), *Commercialization of Postal and Delivery Services: National and International Perspectives*, Boston, MA: Kluwer Academic, pp. 1–25.

Campbell, James I., Alex K. Dieke and Antonia Niederprüm (2008), 'National postal policies in Europe on the eve of the Third Directive', in M.A. Crew, P.R. Kleindorfer and J.I. Campbell Jr (eds), *Handbook of Worldwide Postal Reform*, Cheltenham, UK and Northampton, MA, USA: Edward Elgar, pp. 195–215.

Copenhagen Economics (2010), 'Main developments in the Postal Sector (2008–2010)', Study for the European Commission, DG Internal Market and Services.

Costich, E. Rand and W. Gail Willette (1995), 'Regulation of unregulated firms: the postal service and UPS', in M.A. Crew and P.R. Kleindorfer (eds), *Commercialization of Postal and Delivery Services: National and International Perspectives*, Boston, MA: Kluwer Academic, pp. 237–46.

Crew, Michael A., Gonzales d'Alcantara, Paul R. Kleindorfer, Philippe Claeys and Bert Kuypers (2008), 'Economic factors underlying postal reform in the European Union', in M.A. Crew, P.R. Kleindorfer and J.I. Campbell Jr (eds), *Handbook of Worldwide Postal Reform*, Cheltenham, UK and Northampton, MA, USA: Edward Elgar, pp. 216–44.

Ecorys (2008), 'Main developments in the postal sector (2006–2008)', Study for European Commission, DG Internal Market and Services, Rotterdam.

European Court of Justice (1993), Case C-320/91, Paul Corbeau, ECR 1-2563.

Fève, Frédérique, Jean-Pierre Florens, Frank Rodriguez, Soterios Soteri and Leticia Veruete-McKay (2012), 'Evaluating demand for letter price elasticities and technology impacts in an evolving communications market', paper presented at the seventh biannual conference on 'The Economics of the Postal Sector in the Digital World', Toulouse, France, March 22–23.

Gallet-Ryback, Catherine, Cécile Moreno, Daniel Nadal and Joëlle Toledano (2008), 'The French postal market in the wake of the Postal Law of 2005', in M.A. Crew, P.R. Kleindorfer and J.I. Campbell Jr (eds), *Handbook of Worldwide Postal Reform*, Cheltenham, UK and Northampton, MA, USA: Edward Elgar, pp. 316–40.

Green Paper on the Development of the Single Market for Postal Services (1992), COM (91) 476, Commission of the European Communities, Brussels, 11 June.

ITA Consulting and WIK Consult (2009), 'The Evolution of the European postal market since 1997', Study for the European Commission, DG Internal Market and Services.

Morgan Stanley Research Europe (2012), 'Austrian Post: cash is king in an uncertain world', Morgan Stanley, 25 January.

PricewaterhouseCoopers (1997), 'Employment trends in the European postal sector', Study for European Commission, DG Internal Market and Services.

PTS (2011), 'Service and Competition 2011: The postal services market in Sweden', PTS-ER 2011:11.

Toledano, Joëlle (2004), 'La Suède, laboratoire de la régulation postale', in Toledano (ed.), *Économie Postale: Les Fondements*, Paris: Economica.

Winston, Clifford (1993), 'Economic deregulation: days of reckoning for microeconomists', *Journal of Economic Literature*, **31** (3), 1263–89.

16. Electronic substitution and postal price elasticities: a customer market approach*

Leticia Veruete-McKay,[†] Robert Sheldon,[‡] Peter Burge[§] and Alison Lawrence[¶]

1 INTRODUCTION

Advances in technology are blurring the boundary between the delivery of communications via physical and electronic means. There is a consensus among studies that e-substitution has impacted the development of postal markets across the world, reaching various stages in different countries and the impact on mail volumes being dependent upon the type of mail sent and/or business sector.[1] Clearly the use of new technology impacts negatively on postal operators' delivery volumes, with developed countries experiencing sharp falls even before the global recession of 2008–09.

Although this effect is likely to prevail in the future, it is highly uncertain whether it will determine the future path of e-substitution. Postal operators are faced with the challenge to construct medium- and long-term projections in a rapidly evolving market, where e-substitution, due to structural factors, can occur even when prices do not change over a given economic cycle. Because of economies of scale in the sector, as mail volumes decline average costs increase *ceteris paribus*. Rising costs might be compensated by efficiency gains and increasing prices, but the latter can also promote substitution to other ways of communication. Therefore, it is important for postal operators to assess the degree to which future e-substitution could be influenced by structural factors (no price changes) and/or price changes and their impact on mail volumes to inform better their pricing and planning decisions.

Recently, Nikali (2011) noted that the mail market price elasticity has increased over time in Finland and France. Interestingly, this has not been the case for other countries, even though they have included the impact of e-substitution as a driver of demand for mail. This may be explained by the fact that the majority of the econometric studies have estimated the impact of price and technology as being independent drivers of the demand for mail and so might be underestimating the price elasticity. If price and technology were indeed dependent on each other, this might lead to the price elasticity being under or overestimated if ignored. An exception, however, is the recent paper by Fève et al. (2012).

† Senior Economist, Royal Mail Group.
‡ Managing Director, Accent.
§ Associate Director, RAND Europe.
¶ Director, Accent.

Econometric studies rely generally on time-series revealed preference data, where the estimation of mail market price elasticity represents an average figure across senders for a given period. So, these models are not able to capture variations across senders, who might experience different degrees of substitution and price sensitivities (elasticities) as Nikali (2011) found in Finland. Furthermore, these econometric models are backward looking in nature and hence do not allow for the future impact of e-substitution to be captured. Fève et al. (2011) explained the importance of augmenting data-based model forecasts with additional sources of information, such as business opinion polls or customer surveys that aim to take into account the 'non-identified' component of forecasts. The unobserved future impact of e-substitution on mail volumes can be captured in this non-identified component. One way to estimate e-substitution projections is to measure the expected migration away from physical post to electronic channels from business customers. These projections can in turn be added to the data-based model forecasts.

This chapter contributes in three ways to the literature on demand for mail. First, it develops a stated intentions data model, where both structural and price effects are taken together in a scenario analysis to assess the impact on transactional mail in the UK over various time horizons. In particular, the chapter quantifies the impact on prices over the structural decline and estimates price elasticities for different magnitudes of price changes.

Second, in this setting, the degree of heterogeneity among business senders of transactional mail is investigated, and the extent that structural declines and price elasticities vary by type of senders, for example whether senders are banks, utilities, or public organizations and/or what they send (for example, bills, invoices, statements and payments to customers or suppliers). Identifying which sectors and items are at most risk of migrating away from physical post due to structural and/or price factors can enhance information available to postal operators, which in turn can help to develop better their commercial and investment strategies.

Third, it estimates e-substitution projections based on business responses, regarding the expected structural decline in mail volumes, which help to provide better-informed long-term mail market volume projections. This can be seen as an empirical implementation of the Fève et al. (2011) framework.

Section 2 describes the market research methodology used to undertake the quantitative survey. Section 3 summarizes the main results of surveys. Finally, Section 4 provides, a summary and conclusions.

2 QUANTITATIVE STATED INTENTIONS SURVEY: METHODOLOGY

The quantitative stated intentions research was designed to provide robust information on e-substitution from businesses sending (or receiving) transactional mail. Business respondents were asked about sending items either in the post or electronically; 600 business telephone interviews were conducted, with quotas imposed by sector and mail type. All respondents were assigned to a single mail quota although most sent more than one type of mail.

Table 16.1 Sample breakdown

Sector	Transactional mail categories				
	Bills & invoices	Financial (statements & other financial)	Insurance/legal documents/ policy docs/agreements/other	Payments	Total
Financial/Legal[a]	51	56	64	60	231
Government/Utilities[b]	44	32	27	41	144
Other[c]	58	60	57	50	255
Total	153	148	148	151	600

Notes:

a. Includes bank/building society current account, bank/building society mortgage and credit card.
b. Includes government/local authority, water utilities, power utilities (gas and electricity), telephone landlines, telephone mobiles, broadband.
c. Includes insurance (home and car), home shopping (credit), TV providers (satellite or cable), all other sectors.

Sample Size of Business Respondents

Not all quotas were met as a result of different types of sending by the various industry sectors, leading to a lack of available samples in some cells. The numbers achieved in each cell for business interviewing are shown in Table 16.1 with the original target being 50 per cell. Where it proved difficult to achieve this target (for example, senders of financial items in the Government/Utilities sector), the remaining interviews were distributed across the other cells.

The sample was provided from the Royal Mail customer database. This sample included contact details to ensure that the actual respondent was someone within the company who was a high-level decision maker regarding his/her company's future strategy for customer communication. This included people in marketing, finance or procurement roles. In the case of Royal Mail's largest customers, permission was sought by Royal Mail prior to contact and this ensured that the most appropriate person took part in the research. Other companies were sent an email from Royal Mail Group in advance of the research, explaining the nature and scope of the research and the type of respondent within its scope:

> It is important that we target the appropriate individuals in business organizations. In particular, we wish to contact those with responsibility for communication budgets. We appreciate that individuals in marketing, procurement and finance/strategy departments may jointly be responsible for decisions over the form of communications with customers.

Ten percent of business respondents had over 1,000 employees and 10 percent (of those able to say what their annual turnover was) had a turnover of £25 million or more.

A series of questions were developed that asked businesses to report their current sending behavior, before asking them to consider how this may change in the future. Each respondent was asked to consider one element of his/her transactional mail sending; with items relating to bills and invoices, statements or other financial communications, insurance or legal documents, or payments to customers or suppliers.

Business respondents were asked a series of questions about the annual volume they send of these forms of mail by postal services and by electronic alternatives. They were also asked to report the cost of sending paper communications. This was not constrained to be only the price of postage, and other costs (for example, paper, envelopes, and so on) could also be considered by respondents and included in their estimate.

Stated Intentions Survey

One of the key objectives of the survey was to quantify the extent to which customers thought that they would be likely to move some of their existing communication away from postal services over to electronic alternatives in the future. The stated intentions questions used these individual cost and volume estimates as a starting point.

Respondents were then asked to consider how their sending may change in three months' time. Initially they were instructed to assume that the cost of sending paper communications would remain the same as now, and asked what percentage of their communications would continue to be sent by post, what percentage would be sent electronically, and what percentage would not be sent by either means. In considering this scenario they were reminded of the volumes and percentage that they were currently sending, and were provided with information on the cost implications of their choices. They were also asked to indicate how confident they were in their estimate. An example of such a choice is shown in Box 16.1.

Having established the likely allocation in three months, the respondents were then asked to report how this may change in one year, three years and five years. In each case they were shown their responses to previous questions to assist them in making consistent estimates. It was also possible to go back and change the responses to a previous time period if, upon reflection, they decided that they had over or under stated their likely response.

Having completed the series of questions relating to their likely behavior assuming constant prices in real terms, they were then asked to consider how their allocations may change if prices were to vary. Three different price points were considered by each individual corresponding to scenarios where prices may increase by 2, 4 or 8 percent year on year. The price scenarios were presented in turn and for each asking about the impact on allocations in three months, in 12 months, in three years and in five years. In each case respondents were presented with both the annual change in price to be expected and the compound effect of this over their current price over time (for example, an 8 percent annual increase in prices translates to a 26 percent compound increase over three years).

As with the constant price scenario, respondents were asked to consider their allocations in each time period and were reminded of their previous responses to assist them in their reporting. An example of one of the price increase scenarios is shown in Box 16.2.

Theory Underpinning the Stated Intentions Model

Discrete choice models were developed from the stated intention data to explain the patterns of substitution observed, how these develop over time, and the impact of price. In developing these models, various tests were undertaken to identify the extent to which differences in behavior may exist between different groups of respondents.

BOX 16.1 EXAMPLE BUSINESS CHOICE WITH CONSTANT PRICES

For the next few questions, I would like you to think about *bills and invoices* items that you currently send. Think about the *10,000* items you said you send by post at a cost of *46p* and the *5,000* items you send electronically and don't think about any additional volume that you might send in the future if you had more customers, or reduced volume if you had fewer customers.

We will ask you about some different scenarios relating to your use of post and electronic communications over time and then under different pricing scenarios starting with the highest price increase and then looking at lower price scenarios. For each we would like you to estimate what percentage, of the *15,000 bill and invoice* items you send currently, would still be sent by post, what percentage would be sent electronically and what percentage would not be generated in the first place (and so will not be sent by either means).

In *3 months' time*, if the cost of sending paper communications were to *remain the same as now*, how do you expect that the volume will be split between paper and electronic sending? What % of your *bills and invoices* communications would be sent by post, what % would be sent electronically and what % would not be sent by either means?

	Post (Now: 10,000 items – 67%)	Electronic communication (Now: 5,000 items – 33%)	Don't send	Total cost of sending paper communications (Now: £4,600)	How much confidence do you have in your estimate?
3 months' time, same cost	60%	40%	0%	£4,140	A – high B – medium C – low

The discrete choice models developed are based on random utility theory and aim to replicate the stated choices made during the survey, and identify where there are statistically significant differences in these trends between respondent groups, to inform future trends in e-substitution. By pooling the data across the stated intention scenarios, and specifying the utility of the communication alternatives as being composed as both pricing elements and time period constants, it was possible to identify the underlying structural decline in sending, and the impact of different price changes over and above any structural decline.

The models were developed at the level of the decision maker and were based on the principle that each respondent acts to maximize his/her utility. Each choice alternative, i, in a discrete choice model is specified with a utility function for respondent, n, such that:

$$U_{ni} = V_{ni} + \varepsilon_{ni}$$

BOX 16.2 EXAMPLE BUSINESS CHOICE WITH INCREASES IN PRICES

In *3 years' time*, if the costs of sending paper communications were to increase by *8%* per annum above the rate of inflation, (in other words *26% in real terms* after 3 years), how do you expect that the volume will be split between paper and electronic sending?

	Post (Now: 10,000 items – 67%)	Electronic communication (Now: 5,000 items – 33%	Don't send	Total cost of sending paper communications (Now: £4,600)	How much confidence do you have in your estimate?
3 years' time, 26% real cost increase	30%	52%	15%	£2,608	A – high B – medium C – low
12 months' time, 8% real cost increase	45%	45%	10%	£3,353	
3 months' time, 8% cost increase	50%	40%	10%	£3,726	

V_{ni} is the systematic or measurable utility that the individual n receives from adopting choice i. In addition to these observed components, the utility functions contain error terms ε_{ni} that account for the unobserved components of utility.

McFadden (1974) showed that working from the assumption that the individual is a utility maximizer when considering the alternatives, j, available to him/her, that

$$P_{ni} = \text{Prob}\,(V_{ni} + \varepsilon_{ni} > V_{nj} + \varepsilon_{nj}\ \forall j \neq i),$$

and that the error terms ε_{ni} are assumed to be independent and identically distributed with a Gumbel[2] distribution that it is possible to derive a succinct closed form expression for the logit choice probability:

$$P_{ni} = \frac{e^{Vni}}{\sum_j e^{Vnj}}$$

As there is an assumption of independence between observations[3] the likelihood function is given by the product of the model probabilities that each individual chooses the option that he/she is actually observed to select; and the best fit of the model to the data can be established through the maximization of the likelihood function.

The models have been developed by exploring a range of different specifications of the utility equations used to represent the factors influencing the choice of each alternative. The simplest form of these utilities included only the known values of the explanatory variables at each data point; however, these were then further developed by incorporating additional covariates on the price and time variables in the utility functions – allowing us to model how different respondent characteristics may influence the valuations of price and the rate of switching over time – and on the alternative specific constants to describe differences between different groups of respondents in the propensity to switch to a given alternative. These tests were undertaken in a systematic manner: predictions from the model were compared to the stated intention data across each of the characteristics of interest. If a prediction for a subgroup of respondents was found to be inaccurate, this was corrected by including terms in the model to account for the influence of the characteristic in question on the allocation made. For example, it was identified that those respondents that were from government or local authorities were less likely to switch to electronic substitutes than other organizations, and this was captured by including a dummy term in the utility function for the e-substitution alternative.

The coefficients for the final model are shown in Table 16.2.

In interpreting the coefficient values, the following points should be considered:

- *A positive coefficient* means that the attribute level or constant has a positive impact on utility and so reflects a higher probability of assigning items to the alternatives to which it is applied. For example, as base postal volumes increase, the probability of retaining a high proportion of items by post increases.
- *A negative coefficient* means that the attribute level or constant has a negative impact on utility and so reflects a lower probability of choosing the alternative to which it is applied. For example, as the price increases in relation to the base price, the probability of allocating items to the postal alternative decreases.

In interpreting these results it is worth noting that price sensitivity is best represented by modeling the rate of price increases, as opposed to modeling absolute price increases, on different items sent, and considering how the sensitivities may differ according to the items sent.

In particular, it was found that senders of bills and invoices are most sensitive to changes in price. Also senders of statements/other financial communications, and payments to customers or suppliers, are the next most sensitive to changes in price. The least price-sensitive group of senders is the group sending insurance documents, legal documents, contracts or agreements. There are differences in substitution according to the current price of the items being sent. In particular, it was found that business users whose base unit price is less than £0.46 are more likely to shift from post than those sending more expensive items.

This willingness to shift, for those currently purchasing relatively lower-priced items, also increases with time. Also there are time trends on e-substitution. Businesses are likely to increase their substitution over time. Firms which are already sending higher volumes of electronic items, or have been sending their items by these means for longer, are more likely to continue to shift than those sending lower volumes electronically, or doing so for shorter periods. There is a tendency for those sending larger postal volumes to be more likely to retain more of their communication by mail.

Table 16.2 Model results for business respondents

Coefficient	Estimate	*t*-ratio
Utility of post		
Price (as proportion of base) – bills & invoices	−4.8429	−10.4
Price (as proportion of base) – statements & other financial	−4.8137	−11.4
Price (as proportion of base) – insurance, legal, contracts	−4.1049	−8.3
Price (as proportion of base) – payments to customers or suppliers	−4.5690	−11.0
Base postal volume ≤ 200 items/year	0.0000	n/a
Base postal volume 201–1,000 items/year	1.7066	6.5
Base postal volume 1,001–10,000 items/year	3.0010	9.2
Base postal volume 10,001–100,000 items/year	4.2603	10.9
Base postal volume 100,001–500,000 items/year	7.0909	8.7
Base postal volume >500,000 items/year	11.4255	3.2
Base postal volume not known	0.0000	n/a
Base price ≥ 46p – current sending	0.0000	n/a
Base price ≥ 46p – 3 month estimate	0.0000	n/a
Base price ≥ 46p – 12 month estimate	−0.6255	−3.3
Base price ≥ 46p – 3 year estimate	−1.0180	−4.5
Base price ≥ 46p – 5 year estimate	−1.0777	−4.5
Utility of electronic alternatives		
Base electronic volume ≤ 200 items/year	0.0000	n/a
Base electronic volume 201–1,000 items/year	1.6937	6.5
Base electronic volume 1,001–10,000 items/year	3.5817	12.9
Base electronic volume 10,001–100,000 items/year	4.5835	9.2
Base electronic volume 100,001–500,000 items/year	7.0735	7.9
Base electronic volume >500,000 items/year	10.9316	3.1
Base electronic volume not known	0.0000	n/a
Started sending these items electronically within last 2 years	3.0757	7.6
Started sending these items electronically within last 3–5 years	3.3390	6.9
Started sending these items electronically longer than 5 years ago	3.8570	9.3
Government/local authority	−0.5164	−1.8
Telecommunications – primarily mobile or broadband	2.4747	2.3
Health authorities	1.6865	3.4
Constant on e-substitution – current sending	−8.0410	−12.2
Constant on e-substitution – 3 month estimate	−8.1628	−11.6
Constant on e-substitution – 12 month estimate	−7.7200	−11.0
Constant on e-substitution – 3 year estimate	−6.8421	−10.8
Constant on e-substitution – 5 year estimate	−6.4276	−10.6
Utility of don't send		
Constant on Don't Send – 3 month estimate	−22.7975	−9.7
Constant on Don't Send – 12 month estimate	−21.1386	−12.0
Constant on Don't Send – 3 year estimate	−19.6631	−11.1
Constant on Don't Send – 5 year estimate	−18.9489	−11.0
Scale of SI data relative to RP data	0.3611	12.8
Summary statistics		
Observations	17152	
Final log likelihood	−5474.8	
Degrees of freedom	33	
$Rho^2(0)$	0.498	
$Rho^2(c)$	0.222	

The estimated discrete choice models were then used to forecast the levels of substitution under a range of different scenarios, with appropriate weighting of the results by estimates of UK letter content volumes. By comparing the levels of demand for each communication alternative across scenarios it was possible to derive the dynamic price elasticities.

3 QUANTITATIVE SURVEYS OF CUSTOMERS: MAIN RESULTS

This section summarizes main results of quantitative surveys undertaken with over 500 businesses last year, focusing on senders of transactional mail.

Structural Decline, Price Changes and Price Elasticities over Time

As noted earlier, understanding the drivers of e-substitution and its impact on mail volumes is important to postal operators for informing their planning and pricing decisions. More than 80 percent of total mail volumes are sent by businesses in the UK, with a large proportion of total volumes being transactional mail, such as regular bills, invoices, statements, legal documents, other financial transactions and payments to customers or suppliers. However, this type of mail is expected to be the most exposed to e-substitution, as senders adopt new technology to rely less on physical post in comparison to periodicals and direct mail.

Businesses have pursued various strategies to reduce their costs following the global recession. A majority have already been investing in infrastructure to communicate electronically with their clients prior to the recession. Based on the stated intentions analysis, the structural change occurring on postal transactional volumes is estimated to be more than 5 percent per annum over a five-year time horizon. This means that businesses believe they will be sending almost a quarter less volume by post in five years independent of price changes and considering no additional increases to business growth. In addition, price has a further impact on post volumes. When large price increases are also assumed (8 percent pa) the level of structural decline for transactional mail volumes is expected to contract by an additional 13 percent over the same five-year period. The price effect on transactional mail volumes would be different if the price elasticity were to change.

Table 16.3 reports the estimated dynamic market price elasticity of transactional mail based on the stated intention responses. Several points are worth noting. First, the price elasticity of transactional mail is low, ranging from –0.23 to –0.35. These price elasticities are slightly higher than those based on econometric models, for instance, Veruete-McKay et al. (2011) estimated the market price elasticity of transactional mail to be –0.2. Second, the price elasticity increases with the magnitude of the price increases and also evolves with time. As the postal price increases, business senders of physical mail look at alternative communication channels to establish with their customers. In the short term, however, not all business senders will be able to switch their customers to electronic channels, so the substitution is relatively small. However, in the long term, once business senders put in place electronic systems that allow them to move away from letter communications, as the postal price increases the substitution appears to advance faster.

It is also noteworthy that the majority of reallocation was between sending by post and

Table 16.3 Price elasticities of transactional mail, using stated intentions

Time horizon	Low price decline	Moderate price increase	High price increase
1 year	−0.23	−0.23	−0.24
3 years	−0.26	−0.27	−0.29
5 years	−0.29	−0.31	−0.35

Note: The scenario price changes considered a given percentage price change in each year, but it compounded each year and was adjusted for inflation. The impact of price change was estimated over and above the structural decline. The calculations excluded three senders whose levels of sending would have led to them dominating the model forecasts.

Source: Authors' calculations based on Stated Intentions survey.

the substitution to electronic alternatives. Only very small volumes were reallocated to the 'don't send' alternative across the range of scenarios explored.

Figures in Table 16.3, however, mask the heterogeneous behavior of different senders of transactional mail. The quantitative survey found that senders of transactional mail have been communicating electronically with their customers since the early 2000s, and more than a quarter of business respondents have done so over the past two years. It revealed also that the speed for adopting technology has been different among business sectors. On one side of the spectrum were found large senders such as banks and other financial institutions which have put in place electronic systems several years ago. On the other hand, some public organizations have not yet invested in technology, although stated that they have already started to think about this.

Structural Declines and Price Elasticities by Sectors

Figure 16.1 displays the different degrees of e-substitution (structural factors only) among the various business sectors, based on the stated intention analysis. This can be seen as a measure of the expected degree of migration away from post to electronic communications by business senders in the longer term given their current behavior. Large banks and financial institutions expect the largest structural decline in the next five years, almost twice as much as the decline expected by public organizations and utility companies. Companies in the other sector which includes insurance, home shopping (credit) and TV providers (cable or satellite) companies are expected to be more in line with the average of transactional mail.

This is not surprising, as letter communications of large banks and financial institutions with their customers have been switching to electronic channels since the mid-2000s, and it is expected to continue provided that customers have access to the required technology and there is no customer resistance to receiving statements and other financial correspondence via electronic channels. For more detailed information on the different items sent see the next subsection. By contrast, the majority of government correspondence with UK residents is still being sent by post and this sector expects to continue relying on letter correspondence and moving more gradually to use electronic communication as systems of information communications are set in place. Also not all the utilities companies have been sending their correspondence via emails to customers. Although

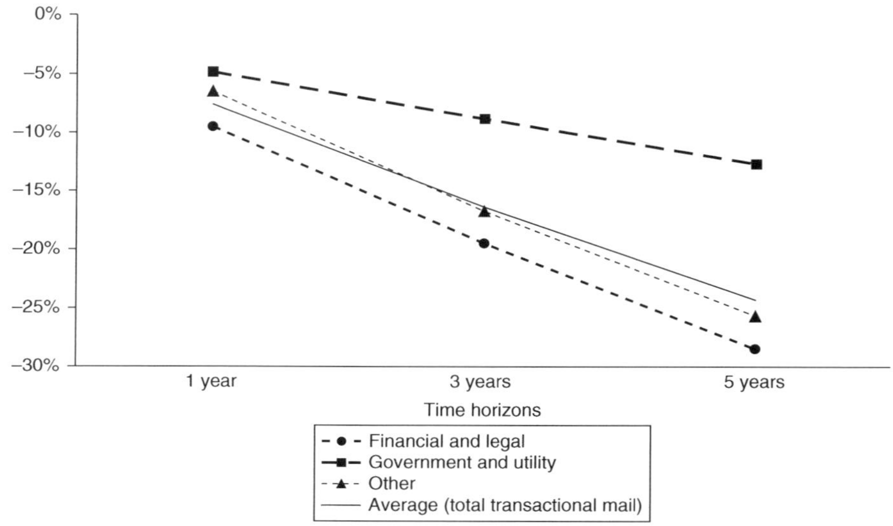

Note: Price increases are adjusted by inflation and responses assume a constant level of business activity over time.

Source: Author calculations based on stated intention responses.

Figure 16.1 Structural decline by sectors

insurance or other home shopping companies might be encouraged to send electronic correspondence to their clients, lack of information on the email addresses can deter them from switching to electronic channels as quickly as they would like.

Furthermore, price elasticities of transactional mail letters are estimated to be different in the various business sectors, indicating different degrees of substitution when considering a high price increase scenario over and above the structural decline stated. The financial and legal sector is less inelastic (–0.34 to –0.47), compared with the more inelastic government and utility sector (–0.18 to –0.25) (Figure 16.2). This suggests that price substitution has advanced more quickly in the financial and legal sector where infrastructure for electronic communications has been put in place with higher emphasis on reducing concern about security than in the government and utility sector, where this has been relatively low. This could reflect also the fact that those businesses sending large volumes (bulk mail) are more concerned with high prices in relation to sending less frequent mail and in smaller volumes.

Structural Decline and Price Elasticities by Item Type Sent

Elkelä (2011) documented that the use of electronic invoices by businesses has been rising sharply in many Scandinavian countries, and this is expected to grow further as the volume of invoices increases between businesses. But the study did not analyze other item types of transactional mail.

Currently, UK business senders of transactional mail, especially those sending bills

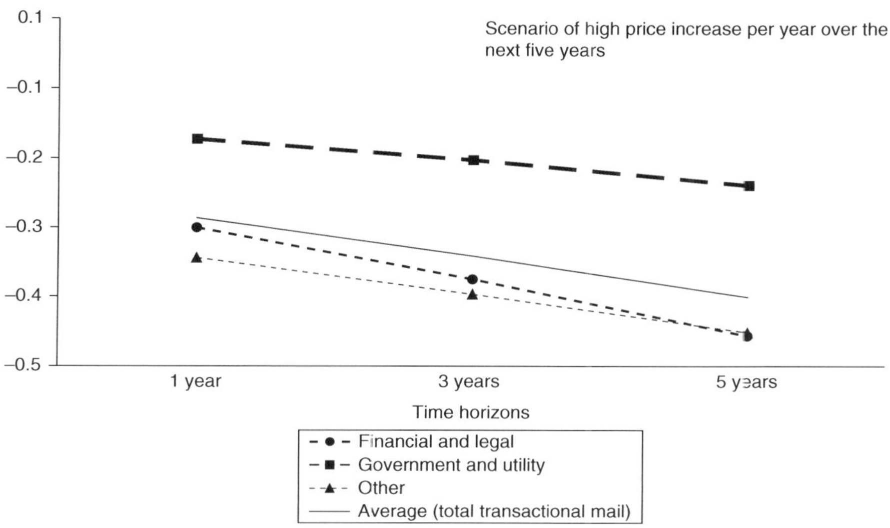

Note: *Price increases are adjusted by inflation and responses assume a constant level of business activity over time.*

Source: Author calculations based on stated intention responses.

Figure 16.2 Price elasticities of transactional mail by sector

and invoices and payments to customers and/or suppliers have already been sending a high proportion via electronic communication channels. But more than half of insurance documents sent by business respondents are done electronically.

From the stated intentions analysis, it was possible to break down transactional mail by types of items and determine the expected structural decline (no price increases) for various time horizons (Figure 16.3).

Independent of price increases and with no additional increases in economic activity, businesses expect to send over a third fewer bills and invoices mail volumes and about a quarter fewer payments to customers and/or suppliers in the next five years. However, those businesses that send insurance and legal documents are expected to send letter correspondence with their customers in such a way that the structural decline will be more gradual (Figure 16.4).

Price sensitivities vary according to item type: payments to customers or suppliers are the most price sensitive, followed by bills/invoices and with insurance/legal/contract documents the least price sensitive.

Business senders when selecting between different communication channels take into consideration not only the price, but other factors that are also relevant. For instance, the speed of communication and benefits to customers/clients are also important factors when communicating using electronic channels. From the survey responses it is known that while saving money is an important reason for sending items electronically, mentioned by eight out of ten, in fact speed is the most frequently mentioned reason, cited by almost nine out of ten.

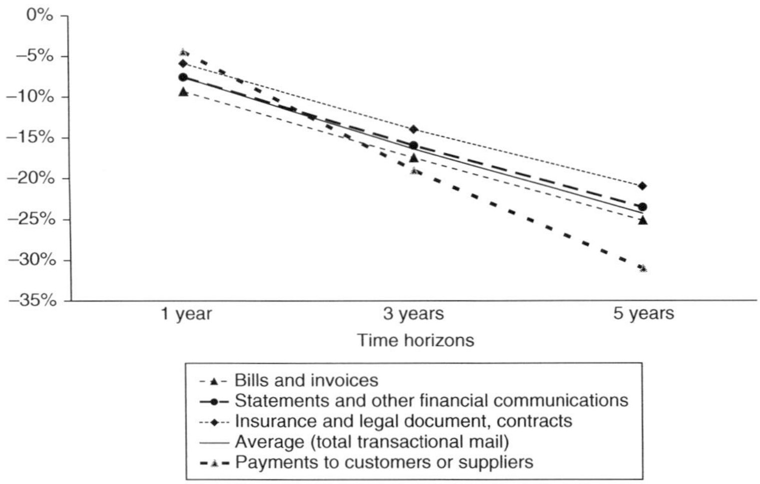

Note: Price increases are adjusted by inflation and responses assume a constant level of business activity over time.

Source: Author calculations based on stated intention responses.

Figure 16.3 Structural decline by items sent

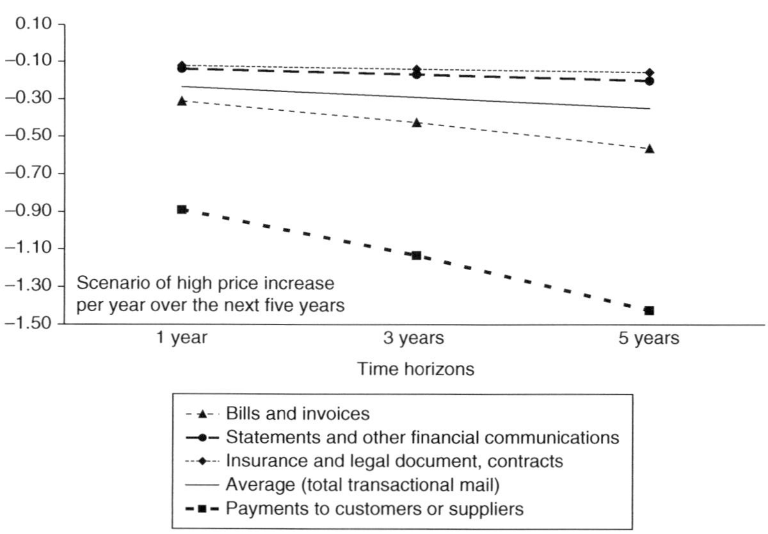

Note: Price increases are adjusted by inflation and responses.

Source: Author calculations based on stated intention responses.

Figure 16.4 Price elasticities by items sent

The reason for choosing electronic communication also varies by the type of item the businesses are sending. For example, saving money is of much less importance comparatively for those sending insurance/legal/contracts/agreements and was mentioned as a reason by only 63 percent. Those sending statements/other financial information are particularly likely to mention customer benefits (84 percent) which are therefore as important as money saving for senders of that mail type. An increase in the cost of sending paper communications was a factor in moving to electronic communication for just over half of businesses, but rose to 66 percent among the senders of statements/other financial items (who tend to be senders of higher volumes on average).

4 CONCLUSIONS

E-substitution remains a major threat to postal markets in various countries, but the scale and future impact is subject to uncertainty. This chapter investigated the extent to which e-substitution is driven by structural and/or price factors in transactional mail in the UK and provided a framework to obtain estimates of e-substitution projections.

It developed a stated intentions data model where the future demand for letters was analyzed from the senders' perspective, based on a wide range of businesses. In this setting, we explored the future evolution of substitution and estimated price elasticities, considering the knowledge of current technology of senders with no changes in economic activity.

The main conclusions from the stated intentions survey and analysis are as follows. First, e-substitution is driven by both structural and price factors and these two effects interact with each other, impacting negatively transactional mail volumes. However, the expected structural decline (no price changes) in transactional mail appeared to dominate over price effects in a five-year horizon; this is partly due to aggressive e-substitution policies implemented by senders since the mid-2000s.

Second, the degree of migration from post to electronic communication is expected to be a gradual process. This is because senders could face customer resistance or receivers might not have in place the required technology or access to the Internet. Furthermore, price did not appear to be the only factor considered by businesses when selecting communication channels. The speed of delivery and convenience were also important determinants in their decision.

Third, the market price elasticity of transactional mail is highly inelastic in the order of −0.2 to −0.4. The lower end of this range is broadly in line with the estimated price elasticity of −0.2 in Veruete-McKay et al. (2011), based on revealed preference data models with data up to 2008. In addition, the price elasticity of transactional mail increases with the magnitude of the price increases, evolving over time.

Fourth, the chapter demonstrated that business senders are heterogeneous, with different degrees of substitution and price sensitivities. Identifying those business sectors and items that are more likely to switch to e-communication therefore is of paramount importance for postal operators to inform their pricing and planning decisions.

Fifth, in an evolving market and with more competition with other communication channels, postal operators are expected to shed more mail volumes due to the continued high e-substitution rates. So firms need to construct medium- and long-term projections of e-substitution rates. The chapter proposed the derivation of these projections following the Fève et al. (2011) approach. That is, this is measured by the expected structural decline rate coming from business responses.

Finally, in order to understand the future development of e-substitution it is not sufficient to understand the demand for mail of senders, it will be important to analyze taking into consideration the sender–receiver relationship. This is important because both parties interact to select the type of communication channel.

NOTES

* The analysis contained in this chapter reflects the views of the authors and may not be necessarily those of Royal Mail Group. We are grateful for the various comments provided by Frank Rodriguez and Soterios Soteri. We would like to thank Marion Frederick for her work on the physical preparation of the chapter.

1. Elkelä (2011) undertook business surveys for different countries, and found that businesses in Nordic and Baltic countries have put in place advanced infrastructure to communicate their invoices with their customers electronically. While in Eastern Europe, Germany and the UK there is still a high preference for sending paper invoices. Nikali (2008) analyzed the evolution of different types of mail letters by type of sectors and found significant e-substitution for business-to-business (B2B) and consumers-to-businesses-or-consumers (C2X), but not for business-to-consumer (B2C) mail.
2. For a fuller discussion of the Gumbel distribution and its use in the derivation of the multinomial logit model, see Ben-Akiva and Lerman (1985).
3. An *ex post* correction for the violation of this assumption is made through bootstrapping the models to correct for any specification error introduced through the consideration of multiple responses from each respondent.

REFERENCES

Ben-Akiva, M. and S.R. Lerman (1985), *Discrete Choice Analysis: Theory and Application to Travel Demand*, Cambridge, MA: MIT Press.

Elkelä, Kari (2011), 'Invoicing in 16 European countries', in M.A. Crew and P.R. Kleindorfer (eds), *Reinventing the Postal Sector in an Electronic Age*, Cheltenham, UK and Northampton, MA, USA: Edward Elgar, pp. 20–35.

Fève, F., J.P. Florens, F. Rodriguez, S. Soteri and L. Veruete-McKay (2012), 'Evaluating demand for letter price elasticities and technology impacts in an evolving communications market', paper presented at the 7th Conference on 'The Economics of Postal Sector in the Digital Age', Toulouse, March 22–23.

Fève, F., J.P. Florens, L. Veruete-McKay, S. Soteri and F. Rodriguez (2011), 'Uncertainty and projections of the demand for mail', in M.A. Crew and P.R. Kleindorfer (eds), *Multi-modal Competition and the Future of Mail*, Cheltenham, UK and Northampton, MA, USA: Edward Elgar, pp. 77–93.

McFadden, D. (1974), 'Conditional logit analysis of qualitative choice behavior', in P. Zarembka (ed.), *Frontiers in Econometrics*, New York: Academic Press, pp. 105–42.

Nikali, Heikki (2008), 'Substitution of letter mail for different sender–receiver segments', in M.A. Crew and P.R. Kleindorfer (eds), *Competition and Regulation in the Postal and Delivery Sector*, Cheltenham, UK and Northampton, MA, USA: Edward Elgar, pp. 89–106.

Nikali, Heikki (2011), 'Does the level of price elasticity change with the progression of substitution?', in M.A. Crew and P.R. Kleindorfer (eds), *Reinventing the Postal Sector in an Electronic Age*, Cheltenham, UK and Northampton, MA, USA: Edward Elgar, pp. 36–46.

Veruete-McKay, L., S. Soteri, J.C. Nankervis and F. Rodriguez (2011), 'Letter traffic demand in the UK: an analysis by product and envelope content type', *Review of Network Economics*, **10** (3), available at: http://ideas.repec.org/a/bpj/rneart/v10y2011i3n10.html.

17. Measuring consumer preferences for postal services

Charlene Rohr,† Urs Trinkner,‡ Alison Lawrence,§ Chong Woo Kim,¶ Dimitris Potoglou†† and Robert Sheldon‡‡

1 INTRODUCTION

Increasing digitalization and the evolution of the Internet have had, and are still having, an impact on the demand for postal services. Letter mail volumes are steadily decreasing in most industrialized countries and there is little doubt that this decline is to be attributed to the substitution of letters by electronic alternatives ('e-substitution'). By contrast, the delivery of physical goods such as small packages and parcels is likely to be increasingly important. These trends can be seen in the growing parcel volumes in most countries.

Increases in e-substitution and e-commerce are likely to have an impact on consumers' needs and preferences for postal services. In the case of regulated postal services, however, such developments in consumer demand are not immediately matched by changes in supply, but must be identified and addressed through policy decisions. Given the significant changes brought about by electronic communication, there is a need for better information on how these developments have affected demand for postal services and on what consumers need from a postal service.

This chapter reports on the implementation of stated preference discrete choice experiments (SPDCEs) to measure business and residential consumers' preferences for specific aspects of postal services in three European member states: Italy, Poland and Sweden. Section 2 sets out the methodology for undertaking the experiments. Section 3 presents the model results; these are discussed in further detail in Section 4.

† Director, RAND Europe, Cambridge, UK.
‡ Managing Partner, Swiss Economics and Lecturer, University of Zürich, Switzerland.
§ Director Accent, London.
¶ Analyst, RAND Europe, Cambridge, UK.
†† Analyst, RAND Europe, Cambridge, UK.
‡‡ Managing Director, Accent, London.

2 METHODOLOGY

In this study, SPDCEs (Hensher et al., 2005) are undertaken with both business and residential postal consumers to quantify consumers' preferences for specific aspects of postal services.

A key aspect of such a study is the specification of the attributes and attribute levels to be tested in the choice experiments. Ideally, the choice experiment would include all meaningful attributes that describe postal services. However, in practice the number of attributes that can be tested is limited by sample sizes and the cognitive abilities of respondents. In this study, limitation on sample sizes meant that it was necessary for all respondents to evaluate all attributes and therefore the maximum number of attributes considered was 15, which is probably an upper limit from a cognitive perspective because of the need to incorporate vulnerable people, including the elderly, in the survey.

In order to be able to compute consumers' willingness to pay (WTP) it is essential that cost is included as one of the attributes. In this study, stamp and parcel prices are used to define the cost vehicle. The price ranges tested in the experiments were specified to test consumers' WTP, and therefore they do not reflect actual costs of providing the services. For realism the prices in the experiments were varied around current prices.

Four sources were used to inform the choice of attributes: (i) a specification of an economic framework for the provision of postal services, and the interaction with consumers, (ii) a review of attributes and levels from other studies, (iii) a review of current minimum levels of the Universal Service Obligation (USO) in the EC, and (iv) views on the importance of specific postal service elements from the relevant stakeholders.

Analysis of the underlying needs of postal services suggested that it was important to take account of three issues: that users are both senders and receivers (the two-sidedness of the postal market); the different exposure of letters and parcels to competition from e-substitutes; and that the services examined in the experiments should reflect the services experienced by users (rather than structure-oriented features of the postal network, such as the number of sorting centers).

It is a challenge to incorporate the two-sidedness of the postal market in the study design. This was done by: (i) ensuring that the preferences of both sides (senders and recipients) were reflected, while avoiding double counting; (ii) computing the WTP considering the needs of both senders and receivers; (iii) framing the choices such that respondents viewed themselves simultaneously both as senders and recipients; and (iv) collecting socioeconomic information regarding respondents' usage of the postal network both as sender and recipient and to distinguish businesses and private consumers.

Second, digital options are also likely to change the underlying needs of consumers. For example, fast letter services might diminish in value as digital alternatives offer effectively instantaneous delivery. While digital competition may result in less WTP for some services, there may be increases in value for other services; for example, the delivery of parcels resulting from online shopping. Consumers' WTP for postal service elements may therefore depend crucially on the availability and usage of digital alternatives. In the study this issue was addressed by: (i) selecting member states with differing levels of digital penetration and e-commerce usage;[1] (ii) distinguishing in choice experiments the delivery of communication (letters, newspapers) and goods (parcels, packages); and (iii) collecting socioeconomic information on respondents' Internet availability and usage, to test for the impact of Internet usage on WTP.

Third, some attributes such as frequency of delivery may be important to operators providing postal services, but may have less direct relevance to users. The experiments therefore focus on service attributes which are directly experienced by users: 'output-oriented' attributes such as speed of delivery rather than 'input-oriented' attributes that relate to the provision of postal services such as the number of sorting and collection facilities or the number of collection and delivery days.

Given the growing importance of parcel services (ITA Consulting and WIK Consult, 2009), separate experiments were undertaken to examine the importance of service attributes for letter and for parcel services. Each quantified the impacts of: speed of delivery, reliability, guaranteed time of latest daily delivery, percentage of lost items, delivery location, and price. The last was based on current stamp prices (for letters and packets) and an average parcel price for parcels. Guaranteed time of delivery was included on the basis that it could be important to customers and could have an important impact on costs for postal providers (sequencing). However, time of collection was not included because it was likely to be less important to consumers. In turn, greater emphasis has been placed on the speed of delivery attribute, which is a direct indication of the time that it takes for an item to reach the recipient.

A Saturday delivery option was also tested in the pilot survey. However, nearly 20 percent of respondents in the pilot survey indicated that they found the experiments too complex, and that they contained too much information and too much text. Therefore, the text was reduced for the main surveys. Furthermore, Saturday delivery attribute was dropped on the basis that this was less interesting to policy makers.

A third experiment was also undertaken to quantify the importance of the following general service attributes: uniform pricing, proportion of the network covered by postal services, accessibility of postal points of contact (measured as distance), available services, opening hours, and price.

For consistency and comparison of findings, the same attributes were tested in the three member states. The costs were based around current price levels in the respective country and were presented in the local currency. Six price levels were tested in the design to ensure that a wide range of costs were tested. Both price reductions (–30 percent) and increases (up to +150 percent) were tested.

The SPDCE was set in the context of choosing between two options describing hypothetical postal services, labeled simply as 'Alternative A' and 'Alternative B', and described by the relevant attributes in each experiment. Respondents were asked to consider each of the choices and to choose the best option for *their own* postal needs, without considering the needs of others (on the basis that the survey would also include elderly and disabled people, who would provide their own views).

The experimental design for the choice experiments was based on an 'efficient' design. In efficient designs, the set of options (or scenarios) that are generated and presented to respondents are constructed on the basis of estimating parameters for a particular model structure, in this case employing a multinomial logit model.

Postal service preferences and priorities may vary by country and customer type. The study design sought to accommodate the range of different customer types within the survey design.

For businesses, quotas were specified for large businesses and small and medium-sized enterprises (SMEs[2]) within each member state.

For residents, the survey design aimed to reflect the demographic profile of the member state. Additionally quotas were specified for vulnerable members of society, notably the elderly, disabled and those on low incomes – those who may be more dependent on postal services and likely to be more heavily impacted by any change to postal service provision.

Four hundred and seventy-five (475) interviews were to be undertaken in each member state: 350 surveys with residential consumers (with a target of 100 vulnerable users[3]) and 125 with business consumers (75 SMEs and 50 large businesses). These were the maximum sample sizes given the project budget. In total 1,438 interviews were undertaken in the three countries: 1,055 among residential consumers and 383 among businesses.

3 ANALYSIS AND RESULTS

Respondents who were judged by the interviewers to be unable to understand the choice exercises or who did not give the questions much consideration (less than 5 percent of the data for business and 5.1 percent for Italian residents, 6.6 percent for Polish residents and 0.6 percent for Swedish residents), were excluded from the analysis.

Discrete choice models were developed from the experimental data. Discrete choice modeling provides an analytical framework to analyze and predict how consumers' choices are influenced by the characteristics of the alternatives and the characteristics of the people making the choices. The basic tenet of discrete choice modeling is utility maximization; that is, given a set of alternatives, people choose the alternative which brings them most utility.

Functions describing the utility of each choice alternative available to a consumer are therefore constructed, incorporating explanatory variables such as price and service quality, multiplied by coefficients (β) that reflect the relative value of the terms, for example for a specific alternative (labeled j):

$$U_j = \beta x_j + \varepsilon_j,$$

where x is a vector of measured variables influencing the SP decision task; β is a vector of unknown parameters (to be estimated); ε is the unmeasured error. In this study, the utility equations reflect the characteristics of the specific hypothetical postal services as presented in the three choice experiments.

All service variables describing the quality of the alternatives were dummy coded. With such coding it is necessary to constrain the coefficient of one of the levels for each attribute to zero to avoid overspecifying the models. As a result, the coefficients that are estimated reflect the value relative to the constrained base level of the variable. For example, the uniform pricing attribute is measured relative to the level of different prices existing for different destinations (which is set to zero). Price was treated as a continuous variable.

Epsilon (ε) is the model error, which is assumed to follow a type I extreme value distribution, with errors distributed identically and independently (iid) for all alternatives and observations. The distributional assumptions of ε permit the derivation of a closed-form expression for the choice probability, the logit model (Train, 2003), that is,

$$P_{ni} = \frac{e^{\beta x_{ni}}}{\sum_j e^{\beta x_{nj}}}.$$

The model coefficients (β) that are estimated in the model estimation procedure assume that each respondent chooses the alternative with the highest utility. The estimation can therefore be conducted within the framework of random utility theory, that is, accounting for the fact that the analyst has only imperfect insight into the utility functions of the responding households and businesses. The standard statistical criterion of maximum likelihood is used. Both the values of the coefficients (in utility terms) and the significance of the coefficients are output (Ben-Akiva and Lerman, 1985).

The business model results are presented below in Table 17.1 (letter and parcel post attributes) and Table 17.4 (general service attributes). The residential model results are presented in Table 17.2 (attributes for letter post), Table 17.3 (attributes for parcel post) and Table 17.4 (general service attributes). Both the model coefficients and their standard errors are presented; both reflect the results after bootstrapping to take account of repeated observations being collected from a single individual.

The ratio of coefficients quantifies the marginal rate of substitution between the attributes – the tradeoff rate between one attribute and another. The ratios of the service coefficients and the cost coefficient provide an estimation of consumers' WTP for service attributes (see Rohr et al., 2011 for values).

Business Consumers' Priorities for Letter and Parcel Service Attributes

In all tables, the coefficients for categorical attributes are measured relative to a base level (labeled, and presented with coefficient value 0.00 and *t*-ratio 'n/a').Shaded areas reflect attribute levels which do not have coefficients in the model. The base level for each service attribute is shown first (and labeled as base). It is assumed to have a value of zero. The value of all other attributes is measured relative to this base value; positive values indicate a positive improvement in service (and increased likelihood of choosing the service alternative), negative values indicate service deterioration. A zero value indicates that the service level is valued the same as the base service level.

First, it is observed that the resulting valuations for businesses have substantial standard errors, even though business responses were pooled across countries. The reason for these relatively large standard errors may be manifold, including: (i) the sample size is too small (it is noteworthy that there is 2.75 times more data for residents than for businesses), (ii) business preferences for SMEs and large businesses may be more heterogeneous in nature than those of consumers; (iii) the cost sensitivity is not well estimated (this may be because stamp costs are a relatively unimportant cost for businesses and therefore larger cost differences could be tested, particularly for big businesses); (iv) the values that businesses place on postal service attributes are relatively small – thus requiring more data to estimate the values significantly, or a combination of all of these aspects; and (v) importance of other attributes, for example, lost items, which may have dominated the choices.

In general, big businesses (BBs) value letter services more than SMEs or residents.

Table 17.1 Business consumers' model results, letter and parcel service attributes (Experiments 1 and 2)

Attribute and levels	Letters				Parcels			
	SME		BB		SME		BB	
	Coef.	*t*-ratio	Coef.	*t*-ratio	Coef.	*t*-ratio	Coef.	*t*-ratio
Number of service classes and speed of service								
One class, delivery by next working day (base)	0.00	n/a	0.00	n/a	0.00	n/a	0.00	n/a
One class, delivery within 2 working days	0.00	n/a	−0.31	−1.9	−0.09	−0.7	−0.29	−2.0
One class, delivery within 3 working days	−0.29	−2.1	−0.50	−2.3	−0.63	−3.7	−0.43	−3.4
One class, local deliveries by next working day, national deliveries within 3 working days	−0.24	−1.6	−0.20	−1.4	−0.35	−2.0	−0.17	−1.4
Two classes, next working day and within 3 working days	0.00	n/a	0.00	n/a	0.00	n/a	0.00	n/a
Delivery location								
Delivered to businesses during work hours only (base)	0.00	n/a	0.00	n/a	0.00	n/a	0.00	n/a
Delivered to secure mail box 100m from business	−0.47	−3.5	−0.35	−4.7	−0.37	−3.5	−0.32	−2.6
Delivered to secure box 1km from business	−0.65	−4.6	−0.38	−2.8	−0.58	−3.2		
Guaranteed time of delivery								
Delivered by 09:00 (base)	0.00	n/a	0.00	n/a	0.00	n/a	0.00	n/a
Delivered by 13:00	−0.17	−1.2	0.00	n/a	0.00	n/a	0.00	n/a
Delivered by 17:00	−0.39	−2.5	−0.22	−1.7				
Delivered by 17:00 (not advertising material)					0.00	n/a	0.00	n/a
Delivered by 17:00 (advertising material)					−0.42	−2.4	−0.32	−2.1
Percentage of items delivered on time								
80% delivered on time (base)	0.00	n/a	0.00	n/a	0.00	n/a	0.00	n/a
90% delivered on time	0.10	1.0	0.36	2.1	0.00	n/a	0.00	n/a
95% delivered on time	0.17	1.5	0.42	2.6	0.21	2.0	0.00	n/a
Percentage of items lost								
No lost items (base)	0.00	n/a	0.00	n/a	0.00	n/a	0.00	n/a
5 out of 100 items lost	−0.53	−4.4	−0.58	−3.7	−0.84	−4.3	−0.72	−3.6
10 out of 100 items lost	−1.34	−5.7					−1.08	−4.4
10 out of 100 items lost (not magazines/newspapers)			−1.41	−5.2				
10 out of 100 items lost (magazines/newspapers)			−0.65	−2.5				
10 out of 100 items lost (visit post office once a year or less)					−1.93	−6.6		

Table 17.1 (continued)

Attribute and levels	Letters				Parcels			
	SME		BB		SME		BB	
	Coef.	*t*-ratio	Coef.	*t*-ratio	Coef.	*t*-ratio	Coef.	*t*-ratio
Percentage of items lost								
10 out of 100 items lost (visit post office several times a year or more)					−1.21	−5.3		
Stamp / parcel prices	−1.58	−6.2	−0.59	−2.3	−0.09	−3.5	−0.08	−2.6
Scale parameter – Sweden (base)	1.00	n/a	1.00	n/a	1.00	n/a	1.00	n/a
Scale parameter – Poland	0.46	4.0	1.21	3.8	0.92	4.1	1.05	3.7
Scale parameter – Italy	0.61	5.0	0.58	3.0	0.81	4.2	1.01	2.7
Model statistics								
Number of observations	1,332		864		1,332		864	
D.O.F	13		14		13		14	
Final log-likelihood	−809.6		−518.0		−778.0		−522.7	
Rho²(c)		0.122		0.131		0.157		0.125

Note:
Coefficients for categorical attributes are measured relative to a base level (labeled, and presented with coefficient value 0.00 and *t*-ratio 'n/a'). Shaded areas reflect attribute levels which do not have coefficients in the model. The base level for each service attribute is shown first (and labeled as base). It is assumed to have a value of zero. The value of all other attributes is measured relative to this base value; positive values indicate a positive improvement in service (and increased likelihood of choosing the service alternative), negative values indicate service deterioration. A zero value indicates that the service level is valued the same as the base service level.

They also are more likely to be senders of large volumes of mail – over 60 percent of businesses in the sample send over 500 pieces of mail per month compared with 14 percent of SMEs. Thus they appear to have a stronger interest in good letter services and are willing to pay for those services. Differences in parcel sending between BBs and SMEs are much less marked, with 15 percent of SMEs and 17 percent of BBs sending over 100 parcels per month, with much more similar valuations of specific service attributes.

For specific service attributes related to letters (see the first columns in Table 17.1), the results indicate the following:

- BBs appear to be more time sensitive, preferring a next-day delivery option, or the two-class alternative, with a next-day option. They also prefer a single next-day service over a non-uniform delivery option. SMEs appear to place less value on speed of delivery, with no observable difference in value between next-day or two-day service delivery options, but they do require compensation for a three-day service. They also prefer a single next-day service over a non-uniform delivery option, where they would require half of the value required by BBs.
- Both BBs and SMEs prefer to have their post delivered to their work location, with increasing dislike for delivery options 100m or 1km from their work – again, SMEs have lower levels of dislike for these options than BBs.

- Both BBs and SMEs prefer to have their post delivered by 9:00 with increasingly lower levels of preferences for deliveries at 13:00 or 17:00 for SMEs and BBs disliking delivery at 17:00, although the relative compensation levels for these service reductions is relatively low.
- BBs are also willing to pay for increased reliability of delivery; SMEs place a much lower value on reliability of delivery.
- Both BBs and SMEs place a high value on reducing loss of letters, with the former being willing to pay substantial amounts to reduce letter loss. Again, these values reflect values for extreme levels of loss. Higher levels of compensation are required for higher levels of loss for items which are not newspapers and magazines. SMEs also view letter loss importantly and are willing to pay to avoid lost letter items.
- For service attributes related to parcels (see the second set of columns in Table 17.1) absolute valuations are much higher than for letters (even larger proportionally when considering the costs of the parcels), as well as more consistent for SMEs and BBs.
- Compared to letter services, there is a stronger preference for next-day delivery options (and two-class services with a next-day delivery option), compared with two or three-day or non-uniform delivery options, by SMEs and BBs.
- There is also a preference for delivery of advertising material by 17:00, but not a need for compensation for delivery by 13:00 compared with 9:00.
- There is no preference for higher levels of delivery reliability, but there is a substantial, very high WTP to avoid parcel loss by SMEs and BBs, particularly for those who rarely visit post offices (with compensation of around nine purchase price standard (PPS) units required for a 5 percent loss of parcels and between 13 and 21 PPS units for a 10 percent loss).

Residential Consumers' Priorities for Letter and Parcel Service Attributes

In Tables 17.2 and 17.3 the valuations for residential consumers are presented. Differently from the business analysis, it was not appropriate to pool together the residential data across member states and therefore separate values are presented for each attribute level for each member state.

Again, there are quite large standard errors for the resulting values, particularly for responses from Italy. In general they are not as large as for businesses. Again, the reasons are manifold, including sample sizes (although the sample sizes for residents were larger for residents than for businesses) and the measure of cost sensitivity, which suggested that larger cost differences could have been tested.[4] These relatively large standard errors may explain why significant differences in valuations across different market segments, for example by age, are not observed.

For letters the following trends from the outputs from the first experiment are observed (see Table 17.2 for the detailed values):

- Resident consumers are not as sensitive to speed of delivery for letter products, although there is some evidence that Polish respondents have higher levels of dissatisfaction with two- and three-day service levels, particularly vulnerable respondents who are dissatisfied with a three-day service, compared with a single-class next-day service. Generally, the non-uniform delivery option is not considered worse than the next-day service. These results are generally consistent with qualitative findings from background questions in the survey. There is less consistency in the results for Italy, where only a small WTP for faster services (or willingness to accept (WTA) compensation for two- or three-day services) is observed compared with the qualitative findings where 37 percent of residents indicated that they would like faster delivery. It may be that the Italian respondents were much more concerned with the lost letters attribute in the experiment, which they valued very highly.

- Home delivery is important to resident consumers, and there is a surprising level of consistency in values across the three member states. In Sweden there is some evidence that delivery location matters to vulnerable people over 44 years of age and non-vulnerable people, although vulnerable people less than 44 years of age did not see this as an important issue.
- The findings indicate that residents in Sweden and Poland prefer later time deliveries – which is opposite from what was found for businesses. Perhaps residential consumers prefer to be at home when their post is delivered. Later time deliveries do not seem to matter to Italian residents.
- Resident consumers in all countries valued improvements in reliability (percentage of mail delivered on time), although the relative valuations are fairly small and with residents in Poland and Italy not differentiating between the 90 and 95 percent levels.
- As with businesses, residential consumers in all countries were willing to pay substantial amounts to reduce the level of lost letters. There is some evidence that non-vulnerable residents may be more sensitive to the level of lost letters (for example, in Sweden and Poland), although this does not seem to be the case in Italy.

There is a similar pattern, but with higher valuations for the parcels market from the outputs of the second experiment (see Table 17.3 for the detailed values).

Again, residential consumers are not so sensitive to speed of delivery for parcel products and there is a preference for delivery for parcels directly to the home. In Sweden, there is some evidence that vulnerable consumers place a higher value on home delivery.

The findings indicate that residential consumers in Poland and Italy prefer later time deliveries for parcels – again opposite to what was found for businesses. Time of delivery of parcels does not seem to be important to Swedish residents.

As with businesses, reliability is not so important for parcels for Swedish and Polish residential consumers, with vulnerable consumers placing a lower value on reliability compared with non-vulnerable consumers. Italian resident consumers do, however, value reliability for parcels.

Again, residential consumers in all countries place a high value on low levels of lost parcels. In Sweden those under the age of 60 seem to place a higher value on lower levels of lost parcels; it can also be seen that vulnerable consumers returning goods place a higher value on lower levels of lost parcels. In Poland, the results indicate higher valuations for non-vulnerable consumers compared with vulnerable consumers.

Table 17.2 Residential consumers' model results, letter service attributes (Experiment 1)

Attribute and levels	Letters					
	Sweden		Poland		Italy	
	Coef.	*t*-ratio	Coef.	*t*-ratio	Coef.	*t*-ratio
Number of service classes and speed of service						
One class, delivery by next working day (base)	0.00	n/a	0.00	n/a	0.00	n/a
One class, delivery within 2 working days	0.00	n/a				
One class, delivery within 2 working days (non-vulnerable)			0.00	n/a		
One class, delivery within 2 working days (vulnerable)			−0.13	−0.7		
One class, delivery within 3 working days	−0.30	−2.8				
One class, delivery within 3 working days (non-vulnerable)			−0.19	−1.8		
One class, delivery within 3 working days (vulnerable)			−0.62	−3.7		
One class, delivery within 2–3 working days					−0.13	−1.1
One class, local deliveries by next working day, national deliveries within 3 working days	0.20	2.1	0.01	0.1	0.03	0.4
Two classes, next working day and within 3 working days	0.00	n/a	0.00	n/a	0.00	n/a
Delivery location						
Delivered to home during work hours only (base)	0.00	n/a	0.00	n/a	0.00	n/a
Delivered to secure mailbox 100m from home			−0.35	−4.8	−0.35	−2.5
Delivered to secure mailbox 100m from home (non-vulnerable)	−0.55	−3.0				
Delivered to secure mailbox 100m from home (vulnerable, age ≤ 44 years)	0.00	n/a				
Delivered to secure mailbox 100m from home (vulnerable, age > 44 years)	−0.63	−4.6				
Delivered to mailbox 1km from home			−0.58	−4.2	−0.35	−2.5
Delivered to secure mailbox 1km from home (non-vulnerable)	−1.24	−4.1				
Delivered to secure mailbox 1km from home (vulnerable, age ≤ 44 years)	0.00	n/a				
Delivered to secure mailbox 1km from home (vulnerable, age > 44 years)	−1.23	−9.0				
Guaranteed time of delivery						
Delivered by 09:00 (base)	0.00	n/a	0.00	n/a	0.00	n/a
Delivered by 13:00	0.17	2.6	0.19	2.2	0.00	n/a

Table 17.2 (continued)

Attribute and levels	Letters					
	Sweden		Poland		Italy	
	Coef.	*t*-ratio	Coef.	*t*-ratio	Coef.	*t*-ratio
Guaranteed time of delivery						
Delivered by 17:00	0.00	n/a	0.31	3.2	0.00	n/a
Percentage of items delivered on time						
80% delivered on time (base)	0.00	n/a	0.00	n/a	0.00	n/a
90% delivered on time	0.22	2.0				
95% delivered on time	0.32	5.2				
> 90% delivered on time			0.37	3.7	0.20	2.0
Percentage of items lost						
No lost items (base)	0.00	n/a	0.00	n/a	0.00	n/a
5 out of 100 items lost (non-vulnerable)	−0.89	−3.7			−0.57	−1.9
5 out of 100 items lost (non-vulnerable, sent letters)			−0.48	−2.4		
5 out of 100 items lost (non-vulnerable, never sent letters)			0.00	n/a		
5 out of 100 items lost (vulnerable)	−0.43	−3.6	−0.24	−1.6	−0.41	−1.9
10 out of 100 items lost (non-vulnerable)	−1.67	−4.2			−0.78	−1.8
10 out of 100 items lost (non-vulnerable, sent letters)			−1.10	−3.1		
10 out of 100 items lost (non-vulnerable, never sent letters)			0.00	n/a		
10 out of 100 items lost (vulnerable)	−0.91	−6.9	−0.32	−2.0	−0.83	−3.7
Stamp / parcel prices	−1.37	−6.1	−0.68	−4.3	−0.50	−1.55
Scale parameter – vulnerable	1.00	n/a	1.00	n/a	1.00	n/a
Scale parameter – non-vulnerable	0.80	4.4	1.11	3.99	1.68	0.71
Model statistics						
Number of observations	2,112		1,968		1,992	
D.O.F	15		15		11	
Final log-likelihood	−1,192.0		−1,186.7		−1,258.4	
$Rho^2(c)$	0.186		0.128		0.088	

Note: See Table 17.1.

Consumers' Priorities for General Service Characteristics

Table 17.4 presents the model results for the third experiment quantifying consumers' priorities for general service characteristics. Generally, there were surprising levels of consistency between the business and residential consumer valuations for general service characteristics.

Both businesses and residential consumers prefer to have post office services located near their home or business location. For residential customers, there was surprising levels of consistency in the estimates for Swedish and Polish consumers. For Italy similar

Table 17.3 Residential consumers' model results, parcel service attributes (Experiment 2)

Attribute and levels	Parcels					
	Sweden		Poland		Italy	
	Coef.	*t*-ratio	Coef.	*t*-ratio	Coef.	*t*-ratio
Number of service classes and speed of service						
One class, delivery by next working day (base)	0.00	n/a	0.00	n/a	0.00	n/a
One class, delivery within 2 working days			−0.17	−1.2	0.00	n/a
One class, delivery within 3 working days			−0.38	−2.4	−0.13	−1.3
One class, delivery within 2–3 working days	−0.19	−1.6				
One class, local deliveries by next working day, national deliveries within 3 working days			0.00	n/a		
One class, local deliveries by next working day, national deliveries within 3 working days (non-vulnerable)	0.22	1.2			0.00	n/a
One class, local deliveries by next working day, national deliveries within 3 working days (vulnerable)	−0.24	−1.4			−0.74	−3.1
Two classes, next working day and within 3 working days			0.17	1.5	0.08	1.1
Two classes, next working day and within 3 working days (non-vulnerable)	0.20	1.3				
Two classes, next working day and within 3 working days (vulnerable)	−0.24	1.8				
Delivery location						
Delivered to home during work hours only (base)	0.00	n/a	0.00	n/a	0.00	n/a
Delivered to secure mailbox 100m from home			−0.15	−1.2		
Delivered to secure mailbox 100m from home (non-vulnerable)	0.00	n/a				
Delivered to secure mailbox 1km from home (non-vulnerable)	−0.27	−1.7				
Delivered to mailbox between 100m and 1km from home					−0.22	−2.2
Delivered to mailbox between 100m and 1km from home (vulnerable)	−0.44	−3.9				
Delivered to secure mailbox 1km from home			−0.51	−4.1		
Guaranteed time of delivery						
Delivered by 09:00 (base)	0.00	n/a	0.00	n/a	0.00	n/a
Delivered by 13:00	0.00	n/a	0.06	0.5	0.10	1.3
Delivered by 17:00	0.00	n/a	0.38	3.4	0.19	2.5

Table 17.3 (continued)

Attribute and levels	Parcels					
	Sweden		Poland		Italy	
	Coef.	*t*-ratio	Coef.	*t*-ratio	Coef.	*t*-ratio
Percentage of items delivered on time						
80% delivered on time (base)	0.00	n/a	0.00	n/a	0.00	n/a
90% delivered on time					0.23	2.5
90% delivered on time (non-vulnerable)			0.00	n/a		
90% delivered on time (vulnerable)			0.00	n/a		
95% delivered on time					0.30	2.9
95% delivered on time (non-vulnerable)			0.34	1.9		
95% delivered on time (vulnerable)			0.00	n/a		
> 90% delivered on time (non-vulnerable)	0.24	2.1				
> 90% delivered on time (vulnerable)	0.10	0.90				
Percentage of items lost						
No lost items (base)	0.00	n/a	0.00	n/a	0.00	n/a
5 out of 100 items lost					−0.59	−5.0
5 out of 100 items lost (non-vulnerable)			−1.44	−5.2		
5 out of 100 items lost (vulnerable)	−0.83	−7.3	−0.46	−2.9		
5 out of 100 items lost (non-vulnerable, age ≥ 60)	−0.49	−1.6				
5 out of 100 items lost (non-vulnerable, age < 60)	−1.25	−3.9				
10 out of 100 items lost					−1.08	−5.5
10 out of 100 items lost (non-vulnerable)			−2.24	−4.7		
10 out of 100 items lost (vulnerable)			−0.70	−5.8		
10 out of 100 items lost (non-vulnerable, age ≥ 60)	−0.57	−1.1				
10 out of 100 items lost (non-vulnerable, age < 60)	−2.32	−4.1				
10 out of 100 items lost (vulnerable, do not use service to return goods)	−0.87	−5.2				
10 out of 100 items lost (vulnerable, use service to return goods)	−1.93	−7.5				
Stamp / parcel prices	−0.24	−6.1	−0.20	−6.8	−0.06	−4.3
Scale parameter – vulnerable	1.00	n/a	1.00	n/a	1.00	n/a
Scale parameter – non-vulnerable	0.85	3.15	0.52	5.76	1.05	3.96
Model statistics						
Number of observations	2,112		1,968		1,992	
D.O.F	18		14		12	
Final log-likelihood	−1,146.8		−1,179.9		−1,180.9	
Rho²(c)	0.217		0.135		0.145	

Note: See Table 17.1.

Table 17.4 Residential and business consumers' model results, general service attributes (Experiment 3)

Attribute and levels	Residents						Businesses			
	Sweden		Poland		Italy		SME		BB	
	Coef.	*t*-ratio	Coef.	*t*-ratio	Coef.	*t*-ratio	Coef.	*t*-ratio	Coef.	*t*-ratio
Accessing postal services										
Distance to travel										
1km from home / business (base)	0.00	n/a	0.00	n/a	0.00	n/a	0.00	n/a	0.00	n/a
3km from home / business	−0.59	−5.8	−0.51	−4.4	−0.23	−1.8	−0.19	−1.7	−0.29	−2.0
5km from home / business	−0.95	−9.1	−0.72	−4.2	−0.55	−2.6	−0.47	−4.1		
10km from home / business	−1.54	−10.6	−1.15	−5.5			−1.15	−7.6	−0.90	−4.1
10km from home / business (non-vulnerable)					−0.79	−2.9				
10km from home / business (vulnerable)					−1.08	−4.7				
Opening hours										
Open 2 hours per day (base)	0.00	n/a	0.00	n/a	0.00	n/a	0.00	n/a	0.00	n/a
Open 4 hours per day	0.60	8.8	0.51	6.4			0.57	5.7	0.63	3.2
Open 4 hours per day (non-vulnerable)					0.56	3.8				
Open 4 hours per day (vulnerable)					0.37	1.9				
Open 8 hours per day	1.31	16.6	0.96	7.9					1.17	5.4
Open 8 hours per day (non-vulnerable)					1.23	3.6				
Open 8 hours per day (vulnerable)					0.85	4.0				

Table 17.4 (continued)

Attribute and levels	Residents						Businesses			
	Sweden		Poland		Italy		SME		BB	
	Coef.	*t*-ratio	Coef.	*t*-ratio	Coef.	*t*-ratio	Coef.	*t*-ratio	Coef.	*t*-ratio
Opening hours										
Open 8 hours per day (no Internet access at home)	0.57						1.42	8.0		
Open 8 hours per day (Internet access at home)							1.05	8.0		
Services										
Basic postal services available (base)	0.00	n/a	0.00	n/a	0.00	n/a	0.00	n/a	0.00	n/a
Full range of postal services available			0.23	3.1	0.12	1.4			0.19	2,9
Full range of postal services available plus financial services	0.30	5.5	0.29	3.6	0.21	2.4	0.30	3.4		
Full range of postal services available plus financial services (visit post office once a fortnight or less)									0.50	3.6
Full range of postal services available plus financial services (visit post office once a week or more)									0.00	n/a

Table 17.4 (continued)

Attribute and levels	Residents						Businesses			
	Sweden		Poland		Italy		SME		BB	
	Coef.	*t*-ratio	Coef.	*t*-ratio	Coef.	*t*-ratio	Coef.	*t*-ratio	Coef.	*t*-ratio
Postal network										
Delivery to 100% of addresses (base)	0.00	0.00	n/a	0.00	n/a	0.00	n/a	n/a	0.00	n/a
Delivery to 99% of addresses	−0.36	−5.0	−0.21	−2.2	−0.34	−3.4	−0.33	−3.7	−0.19	−1.4
Delivery to 95% of addresses	−0.50	−5.0			−0.49	−4.1	−0.69	−4.9	−0.44	−2.8
Delivery to 95% of addresses (non-vulnerable)			−0.64	−4.3						
Delivery to 95% of addresses (vulnerable)			−0.43	−3.0						
Pricing										
Different prices to deliver to different destinations (base)	0.00	0.00	n/a	0.00	n/a	0.00	n/a	n/a	0.00	n/a
Same price to any destination in the country	0.23	3.9			0.09	1.9	2.0	2.6	0.19	1.7
Same price to any destination in the country (non-vulnerable)			−0.19	−2.0						
Same price to any destination in the country (vulnerable)			0.18	1.3						
Stamp prices	−1.05	−10.6	−0.73	−6.3	−0.49	−3.2	−0.82	−4.8	−0.67	−2.7
Scale parameter – vulnerable (base)	1.00	n/a	1.00	n/a	1.00	n/a				
Scale parameter – non-vulnerable	1.06	8.3	0.90	5.9	1.25	2.8				
Scale parameter – Sweden (base)							1.00	n/a	1.00	n/a
Scale parameter – Poland							0.94	5.8	0.77	2.7
Scale parameter – Italy							1.09	5.7	1.23	3.6
Model statistics										
Number of observations	2,112		1,968		1,992		1,332		864	
D.O.F	11		14		15		13		12	
Final log-likelihood	−1,110.9		−1,164.5		−1,128.4		−740.5		−507.0	
$Rho^2(c)$		0.236		0.140		0.182		0.196		0.153

Note: See Table 17.1.

values are observed, but with higher valuations for vulnerable consumers compared with non-vulnerable consumers.

Both businesses and residential customers also prefer longer opening hours – and again, there is a surprising level of consistency in the values for Swedish and Polish residents and evidence of differences between vulnerable and non-vulnerable consumers in Italy (with non-vulnerable consumers valuing longer opening hours more). Interestingly, respondents from SMEs with no Internet access at home place a higher value on longer opening hours than those with Internet access, which may mean that opening hours may be less important in future with higher levels of Internet access.

All consumers place a small but positive value on having both a full range of postal services available as well as financial services (respondents from BBs who visit post offices less frequently place a value on additional financial services).

All consumers value 100 percent coverage of addresses in the postal network and require compensation for reductions in coverage. There is some evidence that non-vulnerable residential consumers place more value on coverage than vulnerable consumers at the 95 percent level of coverage.

SMEs and BBs, residential consumers in Sweden and Poland and vulnerable consumers in Poland all place a small value on having uniform pricing; however, non-vulnerable consumers in Poland do not see value in uniform pricing (and have a small preference for a system with different pricing).

4 DISCUSSION

Generally, the study has found high WTP (and WTA) values for the individual elements of postal services. The values exhibit the expected sign, however with rather large confidence intervals. In important aspects, consumer preferences overlap among customer segments and countries.

On the sender side, it is very important for all customers to be reached within a reasonable distance (not more than three km) and to have a postal contact point with opening hours of at least four or, even better, eight hours. This is despite the fact that most customers agree with the statement that they rarely go to a postal contact point. To a lesser extent, customers care about the scope of services offered in these contact points and prefer having a full range of postal services (as compared to basic services only). Financial services are valued from some BBs as well as from households in Poland and Italy.

On the recipient side, businesses and residential consumers clearly dislike postal services that do not deliver letters or parcels to the doorstep. All customer groups also dislike services that do not deliver to all addresses in the country. Businesses prefer delivery to take place during office hours (before 17:00), whereas households in Italy and Poland favor the latest delivery option, suggesting that households prefer to be at home when delivery takes place (after office hours).

For the service connecting the sender and recipient side, customers value first and foremost a service where no letters or parcels are lost. The attribute can be interpreted as a proxy for the value of the information or goods that are handed over to the postal operators. The very high estimates (up to over 500 percent of base price in Sweden and

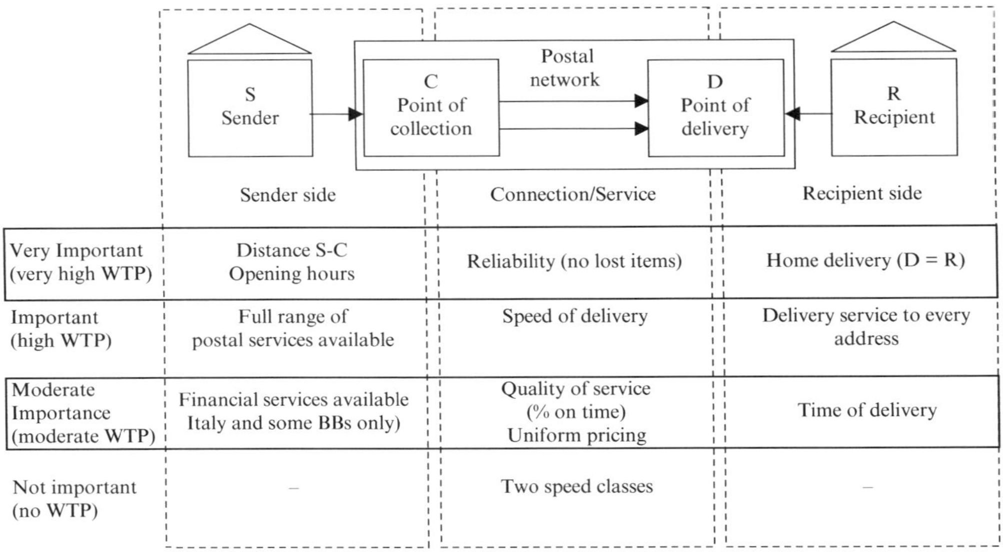

Figure 17.1 Importance of key postal service attributes for consumers

Poland) highlight the importance of postal services and indicate that customers indeed trust postal services in delivering valuable items. Moreover, customers reveal important preferences for services that include a next-day delivery option (same WTP as long as a next-day service is offered). This is in line with the qualitative questions where respondents suggested faster delivery services in countries with slower services (Italy, Poland). The WTP for a next-day service is, in absolute and relative terms, generally higher for parcels than for letters. For the latter, a next-day option seems to be predominantly important for BBs. Businesses, and in particular big businesses, expect uniform delivery standards throughout the country for letters and parcels, whereas households prefer a priority (J+1) treatment of local letters only. SMEs exhibit an important WTP for uniform prices. To a lesser extent, Swedish and Italian households favor uniform prices. BBs care more about reliability (percentage delivered on time) of letters than parcels; small businesses place a higher value on reliability for parcel services. For residents, the WTP for on-time delivery seems to be higher where the actual service levels are lower (Italy, Poland).

Figure 17.1 summarizes the importance of the attributes tested, on the sender and recipient sides of the services, as well as for the service itself. An objective of the study was to examine WTP for senders and receivers of postal services and to take account of the different exposure of letters and parcels to competition from e-substitutes.

The findings from this study suggest that WTP appears to be independent of sending and receiving patterns within consumer groups; net senders have about the same preferences as net recipients. This underpins the view that postal markets are two-sided and that network externalities are very important in this industry. Senders do care about the service provided on the recipient side, and the services offered on the sender side are important to recipients. Otherwise, net senders would set higher priorities for service attributes that are relevant on the sender side and vice versa with net recipients.

To account for the different degree of intermodal competition between letters (against electronic communication, 'e-substitution') and parcels (no alternatives) separate experiments were presented to respondents examining preferences for letter (Experiment 1) and parcel (Experiment 2) services. In absolute terms, the WTP is much higher for parcels than for letters. In relative terms (against the price of the baseline product), there are still significant differences, albeit not that accentuated. As highlighted above, traditional letter service attributes such as speed and on-time delivery remain important for BBs. This may indicate that SMEs and consumers already use different channels compared to big business to satisfy their most important communication needs. It is noteworthy that in the survey sample only 2 percent of business respondents and 6 percent of consumers did not have any Internet access. The highest figures are 19 percent for vulnerable people and 22 percent for ages over 65. Hence, a very large majority of every consumer group in the survey sample had access to electronic substitutes. Against these rather high Internet penetration rates, the result that BBs still exhibit relatively high WTP for letter services is somewhat surprising. If this valuation persists, then this may be interpreted as good news for postal operators, as the substitution potential for sending information to households is limited.[5]

People under 35 from Sweden and living in rural regions are most likely to buy goods online. This is consistent with Internet penetration rates (99 percent under 35, 97 percent in Sweden) and the high opportunity cost of shopping for domestic residents living in rural regions. Italians are least likely to purchase goods online, which may be because of their relatively low WTA for lost items (low trust in domestic parcel services, see above). Based on the results and anticipated generational shifts, further growth in Internet purchases and hence parcel flows is likely.

As noted, standard errors for the WTP estimates are large. The aim of this study was to develop a methodology for quantifying consumers' postal preferences and testing it in three member states. For future studies informing policy interventions in the postal sector, two improvements to the methodology are recommended. First, larger sample sizes should be considered, and the standard errors reported in this study can provide useful information to guide practitioners on this issue. Second, the significance of the measures would be improved with better measures of cost sensitivity and therefore larger cost differentials may be tested.

NOTES

1. As part of the study we selected the three member states for testing the study methodology. We aimed to choose countries that provided a wide range of variation across key background characteristics that might influence postal services and consumers' preferences for postal services, for example, size of country, letter volume, degree of urbanization, market experience, digital penetration, state ownership, and so on. For further information, see Rohr et al. (2011).
2. Small and medium-sized (business) enterprises (less than 250 employees).
3. Vulnerable people were defined as those aged over 65 years, or those with a long-term illness or disability or those from a low-income household.
4. The larger standard errors for Italy are probably explained by the larger confidence intervals on the cost sensitivity attribute, implying that respondents in Italy did not focus on cost levels or that larger cost differences could have been tested in Italy, particularly for the experiments using letter stamp prices (Experiments 1 and 3). More generally, larger cost differences could have been tested in all countries, which could improve

the estimate of cost sensitivity and resulting WTP valuations. Larger sample sizes, more generally, lead to reductions in standard errors, and it is noteworthy that the Accent (2008) study contained around 550 domestic resident interviews and 350 business interviews.

5. A somewhat surprising side result is that e-substitution has not eroded the WTP for next-day letter services. This could have been expected since electronic delivery takes place instantaneously. The results are confirmed by the background questions where faster delivery was suggested as a service improvement in the first place, with respondents under 35 being most likely to suggest faster deliveries. It remains open, however, whether respondents had letters or parcels in mind. An interpretation may still be that people who are used to instantaneous electronic delivery expect the same for physical deliveries.

REFERENCES

Accent (2008), 'Postal universal service obligation: value to the citizen', Report prepared for Postwatch.

Ben-Akiva, M. and S. Lerman (1985), *Discrete Choice Analysis: Theory and Application to Travel Demand*, Cambridge, MA: MIT Press Series in Transportation Studies.

Hensher, D., J. Rose and W. Greene (2005), *Applied Choice Analysis: A Primer*, New York: Cambridge University Press.

ITA Consulting and WIK Consult (2009), 'The Evolution of the European Postal Market Since 1997: A Study for the EC', DG Internal Market and Services.

Rohr, C., U Trinkner, A. Lawrence, P. Hunt, C. Woo Kim, D. Potoglou and R. Sheldon (2011), 'Study on Appropriate Methodologies to Better Measure Consumer Preferences for Postal Services: Final Report', Report for Internal Market and Services DG, available at: http://www.rand.org/pubs/technical_reports/TR1140.html.

Train, K. (2003), *Discrete Choice with Simulations*, Cambridge: Cambridge University Press.

18. Efficiency analysis postal operators: comparison between the United States and Europe*

Maria Rita Pierleoni† and Stefano Gori‡

1 THE BASIC CONCEPT OF EFFICIENCY

This chapter benchmarks efficiency for panel data of five postal operators (La Poste, Deutsche Post, Royal Mail, Poste Italiane and US Postal Service: USPS). The analysis is based on the following parametric and nonparametric techniques: ordinary least squares fixed effects (OLSFE), random effects (RE), stochastic frontier analysis–maximum likelihood (SFA (ML)) and data envelopment analysis (DEA). The analysis of efficiency presented in this chapter is based on an approach proposed by Farrell (1957) and Fried et al. (2008). Two broad paradigms for measuring economic efficiency have emerged from the literature: one based on an econometric/parametric approach where through a regression, a statistically significant relationship between costs and the factors affecting costs is tested to obtain an estimate of theory-based models of cost. With this approach the researcher knows the parameters of the variable of interest in the population. The second is the nonparametric mathematical programming approach whose main method is DEA (Greene, 2008, p. 92). It makes no accommodation for noise and envelops the data (Fried et al., 2008, p. 45).

The above-mentioned methods will be applied to a total cost function and a unit cost function. Furthermore, the effect of the introduction of exogenous variables on the results of the efficiency analysis will be examined. The reason for expanding the analysis to unit cost functions is related to the fact that the operators vary significantly in size, while the inclusion of exogenous factors is linked to the belief that the design of the postal network needs to take into account both geographical and demographic factors.

The chapter is divided as follows. Section 2 introduces the main methods for efficiency analysis; Section 3 discusses the method used and the results obtained, while Section 4 presents the conclusions and lessons learned. Special emphasis will be placed on comparing the results with and without taking exogenous variables into account. More specifically, Section 3 considers the analysis without exogenous variables and then with those variables both for total and unit cost. Furthermore, the efficiency rankings and the tests which can be applied using parametric methods to determine the relative reliability of each method will be presented.

† Research assistant at University of Rome 'Tor Vergata'-Faculty of Economics.

‡ PhD student at Bristol Business School, Head of International Business Strategy at Poste Italiane and Secretary General of Euromed.

2 METHODS FOR EFFICIENCY ANALYSIS

Corrected Ordinary Least Squares

In standard econometric analysis, residuals represent the deviation between observed data and the data predicted and can be interpreted as statistical error, caused by measurement inaccuracies or unobservable heterogeneity (Jacobs et al., 2006, pp. 50–57). Farrell (1957) suggests that residuals can be used to describe the difference between observed and predicted costs and signals the presence of inefficiency or efficiency. Corrected ordinary least squares (COLS) begins with the estimation of a standard cost function (Aigner et al., 1977; Meeusen and van Den Broeck, 1977):

$$\ln C(y_i, w_i) = \alpha_0 + \eta_1 \ln y_i + \beta_1 \ln w_i + \varepsilon_i,$$

where $\varepsilon_i = v_i + u_i$; y_i represents the quantity produced for the ith unit under investigation, w_i represents input prices, v_i is a random error term, and u_i captures nonrandom departures from efficiency.

Modified Ordinary Least Squares

An alternative method known as modified ordinary least squares (MOLS) is based on the argument from Schmidt (1976) that COLS is inadequate if the error term follows a one-sided distribution such as exponential or half-normal (Uğur, 2004). MOLS consists of correcting the intercept with the expected value of the error term (ε_i) and adopting OLS to get a consistent estimate. A problem with the MOLS technique is that the estimates can take on values which have no statistical meaning (Mastromarco, 2008). It does not ensure that all units are bounded from above/below by the estimated production/cost frontier. If a unit has a large positive OLS residual then it is possible that $u_i - \mu_\varepsilon \gtrless 0$; thus the technical efficiency score is greater/less than unity. The most important weakness for both COLS and MOLS is the issue of consistency. The estimators are efficient but not consistent and they are applied mainly in cross-sections.

Ordinary Least Squares with Fixed Effect

If unobservable factors are time invariant, then fixed-effect regression will eliminate omitted variable bias. Including fixed effects in efficiency analysis makes it possible to control for the average differences across operators in any observable or unobservable predictors. The fixed-effect coefficients absorb all the across-group action; what is left over is the within-group action.

The fixed effect offers several advantages: for example, it avoids obtaining distorted estimates of the parameters due to possible correlation between individual effects and the observed regressors (Mundlak, 1978). The disadvantage of using the fixed-effect model is that the regressors, which are invariant to time, are eliminated from the specified model and their effect is captured by the individual dummy variable. This does not allow the introduction in the cost model time-invariant variables. Another disadvantage is that the coefficients of the dummy variables could represent not only the efficiency levels but also the effect of the omitted variables (Dranove, 2010; Vartanian and Buck, 2005).

Generalized Least Squares Random Effect

In the random effects approach, it is assumed that the 'cross-specific effects' and the 'period effect' are modeled like random variables. When these components are independent from the other regressors it is possible to estimate a cost or production model using generalized least squares (GLS). The advantage is that it allows the use of time-invariant regressors in the model. In the random effects (RE) model, the u_i are assumed to be randomly distributed with a constant mean and variance and they are assumed to be independent from both the random errors and the regressors. Given that inefficiency can only take non-negative values, the distribution of u_i is often assumed to be half-normal, truncated normal, gamma or exponential. RE models are used in the analysis of panel data when one assumes no fixed effects. It uses the weighted average of the residuals of the GLS regression with random effects for each country across the years.

Stochastic Frontier Approach

Stochastic frontier models date back to Aigner et al. (1977) and Meeusen and van Den Broek (1997), who independently proposed a stochastic frontier production function with a two-part 'composed' error term. In the production context, where it is often used (Coelli et al., 1999; Knox Lovell and Schmidt, 1993), this error is composed of a standard random error term, representing measurement error and other random factors, and a one-sided random variable representing what Farrell (1957) called 'technical inefficiency'. It reflects the ability of a unit to obtain maximal output from a given set of inputs. When one combines this with allocative efficiency, the ability to use the inputs in optimal proportions, one has a measure of total economic efficiency. The functional forms used more frequently in the literature are Cobb–Douglas and translogarithmic. The first is more easily interpreted while the second is more flexible. A typical stochastic cost frontier would be: $c_i = c(X_i, \beta) + \varepsilon_i$, where (the logarithm of) costs c_i, depends upon a vector of variables, **X**, and parameters, β, and a composite error term $\varepsilon_i = u_i + v_i$ made up of a non-negative random variable, u_i, representing inefficiency, and a random error term, v_i. The stochastic frontier approach implies the application of the maximum likelihood (ML) estimator that considers the residuals to be random variables similar to RE. However, the functional form of the residuals under the ML estimator is also imposed. More specifically, in order to isolate the random component from the inefficiency component, the stochastic frontier method uses a symmetric distribution for the random component while the inefficiency component is modeled according to an asymmetric function, usually a half-normal, because it considers the fact that the inefficiency term cannot be negative and thus needs to be linked to a truncated distribution. The inefficiency and the error terms need to be orthogonal both to the input and output variables and to the other variables used in the specification. An analysis of the probability distribution then needs to be carried out on the inefficiency factor incorporated in the error term to allow for the separation between inefficiency and the random error term. The standard hypothesis which can be found in the literature is a distribution of the error term half-normal with a mean equal to zero. This is a rigid hypothesis, because it assumes de facto that the majority of the entities under scrutiny are close to full efficiency. Greene (1990) stressed that other types of distribution could be more appropriate, for example, gamma distribution of a truncated normal distribution. The ML methodology developed by Battese and Coelli (1995) allows for the estimation of the impact of certain important explanatory variables. With regard to modeling the effects of exogenous factors on costs, these factors, which are beyond the control of the unit under observation, at least in the short run, are often called 'background' or 'environmental' factors. In this sense it is possible to rewrite the cost function as: $c_i = c(X_i,Z_i,\beta) + u_i(E_i,\Delta) + v_i$, where Z_i and E_i represent variables affecting costs directly through the cost frontier and indirectly through inefficiency, and Δ is a vector of parameters to be estimated (Stevens, 2004, p. 4).

Nonparametric Methods: Data Envelopment Analysis

DEA compares each producer with only the 'best' producer (the producer is a decision-making unit: DMU) (Seiford and Thrall, 1990). The production process for each producer is to take a set of inputs and produce a set of outputs. Each producer has a varying level of inputs and gives a varying level of outputs. The objective is to find the 'best' virtual producer and to compare it to the producer under consideration. DEA assigns an efficiency score less than one to (relatively) inefficient units, thus a linear combination of other units from the sample could produce the same vector of outputs using a smaller vector of inputs. To construct the production frontier, there are three assumptions: (i) every observed production plan belongs to the production set; (ii) any unobserved production plan that is weakly dominated by another production plan is also part of the production set; and (iii) the production plan will determine the returns to scale. If they are assumed to be constant (CRS) then the third assumption would read: every unobserved production plan that is a linear combination of production plans is itself part of the output-possibility set. Similarly, if the returns to scale are assumed to be non-increasing (NICRS), then the third assumption states: every unobserved production plan which is a convex combination of production plans, including the origin, also belongs to the output-possibility set. The final variation of the returns to scale assumption is that of variable returns (VRS). DEA can be a powerful tool when used wisely: it can handle multiple input and output models, it does not require an assumption of a functional form relating inputs to outputs, exogenous variables can be taken into account, DMUs are directly compared against peers, and inputs and outputs can have very different units. However, since DEA is an extreme point technique, noise can cause significant problems; it is good at estimating 'relative' efficiency but it converges very slowly to absolute efficiency, and statistical hypothesis tests are difficult; and since a standard formulation of DEA creates a separate linear program for each DMU, it is computationally complex. The list of the methods discussed above is not intended to be exhaustive since within the nonparametric and parametric approaches there are other techniques (Henderson, 2003; Sena, 2003; Greene, 2008). The empirical section below is based on OLSFE, RE, SFA (ML) and DEA techniques following the guidelines in Kumbhakar and Knox Lovell (2000), which presented the main methods that could be applied when using panel data.[1]

3 EFFICIENCY ANALYSIS ON THE TOTAL AND UNIT COST FUNCTIONS

Several studies have investigated the efficiency of a postal operator focusing mainly on the internal efficiency of the postal operator for delivery or processing (Roy, 1999; Horncastle et al., 2006; Fenster et al., 2008) and between postal operators to measure efficiency (Bradley and Baron, 1993; Maruyana and Nakajima, 2002). The efficiency analysis takes into account Deutsche Post (DP), La Poste (LP), Royal Mail (RM), Poste Italiane (PI) and United States Postal Service (USPS) using panel data for the 1998–2008 period.[2] It is based on the main parametric and nonparametric techniques as explained before. Two cost functions will be studied (total and unit) which have labor cost and total volumes as the main determinants. Exogenous variables will also be analyzed. Database sources are: the NERA report (NERA, 2004), Gori et al. (2006) and Visco Comandini et al. (2010), updated using the postal operators' annual reports, the Universal Postal Union (UPU) statistics. For data on population, we used the UPU database and the Economist's *Pocket World in Figures* (Economist, 2003, 2004, 2005, 2007). For the monetary variables we used the euro and for time series concerning the UK and the US we used a fixed exchange rate (£1 = €1.45[3], $1 = €0.86[4]) so that changes in exchange rates would not affect the analysis. The first assumption is that the cost function is Cobb–Douglas:

$$Costs = A^*TV^{\alpha *}(\Pi_{i=1}^{n} Z_i^{\gamma_i}).$$

The empirical analysis implies a log transformation of the CD function:

$$\ln C = \ln(A) + \alpha \ln(TV) + \sum\nolimits_{i=1}^{n} \gamma_i \ln(Z_i) + \mu. \tag{18.1}$$

For the unit cost the log-linear function is:

$$\ln\left(\frac{C}{TV}\right) = \ln(A) + \alpha \ln(VPC) + \sum\nolimits_{i=1}^{n} \gamma_i \ln(Z_i) + \mu, \tag{18.2}$$

where C = total cost, A = constant, TV = total volumes, Z_i = independent variables represented by labor cost and number of employees (mail only), population and urbanization rate, and μ = error term. The coefficients of the log-linear transformation of the CD function measure the elasticity.

Efficiency Analysis without Exogenous Variables

According to the data available, relation (18.1) is defined without the exogenous variables as:

$$\ln(TCM_{it}) = \alpha_o + \alpha_i + \beta_1 \ln(TV_{it}) + \beta_2 \ln(LCM_{it}) + \varepsilon_i, \tag{18.3}$$

where TCM_{it} are the total costs for the mail sector, TV_{it} are the total volumes, LCM_{it} are the labor costs of mail and $\varepsilon_i = u_i + v_i$ is the error term, which in the case of RE and ML estimation methods is decomposed in two parts: u_i is the term of efficiency and v_i

Table 18.1 Efficiency analysis for the total cost function without exogenous variables

	OLS (correc. std. errors)	OLSFE[a]	GLSRE	ML (stoc. frontier model)
Dependent variable: LogTCM_t				
Balanced Panel				
Efficiency model			Time variant	Time variant
Explanatory variables:				
Distrib. effic. terms			Half-normal	Truncated normal
Alfa$_0$	2.173(19.09)***	6.3352.424)**	2.432(3.11)***	2.950(5.82)***
Log LCM_t	0.500(21.59)***	0.579(5.564)***	0.536(5.63)***	0.355(4.75)***
Log TV_t	0.362(19.56)***	0.046(0.238)	0.313(3.49)***	0.443(7.13)***
Alpha_PI		−0.377		
Alpha_DP		0.858		
Alpha_LP		−0.007		
Alpha_RM		−0.164		
Alpha_USPS		0.490		
Observations	55	55	55	55
R-squared overall	0.988	0.981	0.989	
R-squared within		0.524	0.508	
R-squared between		0.986	0.992	
DW		0.632		
Sigma_u			0.112	0.145
Sigma_v			0.055	0.045
Sigma^2_u				0.021
Sigma^2_v				0.002
Sigma^2				0.023
Mean of u				0.128(0.88)
Lambda $\lambda(\sigma_u/\sigma_v)$				3.240
Gamma				0.907
Log likelihood				81.363
Wald chi^2				715.75(0.000)

Note: a. The reported probability for OLSFE is for the t-statistic. For this estimation u_i is assumed to be fixed and it is represented throughout by the cross-fixed effect and is always time invariant.
*** significant 1% level; ** significant 5% level; * significant 10% level.

is the random variable.[5] The results in Table 18.1 shows that the explanatory variables are significant at conventional levels (with the exception for TV with OLSFE) and the signs are as expected. For the OLSFE estimation, the impact of the constant is higher compared to the other estimations. This probably determines the loss of significance of the total volume variable. For the OLS, OLSFE and RE estimations, the goodness of fit (R-squared 'overall') is very high. Moreover for OLSFE and RE, the R-squared 'between' and 'within' are high and similar. For the ML estimation, the lambda and gamma coefficients[6] are 3.2 and 0.9, respectively. Given the values of sigma u (0.14), sigma v (0.04) and the related lambda coefficient, it is possible to affirm that the data have relatively little noise, but the units under consideration are relatively inefficient. Moreover, the value of the gamma coefficient means that if the variance of u_i is a significative component of the total variance of the error term then it is possible to conclude that the technical efficiency effects are present and contain a significant stochastic component. For these estimations a time-variant model is used. Thus the term of efficiency for each cross-section is represented by u_{it}. Moreover, as a distribution of the efficiency terms, for RE it is supposed to be a half-normal and for ML it is a truncated normal distribution. For the ML, the log-likelihood value means that the goodness of fit is high. The Wald chi^2 and the related probability give the information about the validity of the linear relation.

According to relation (18.2), for the unit cost function the following equation is estimated:

$$\ln(UCM_{it}) = \alpha_o + \alpha_i + \delta_1 \ln(VPC_{it}) + \delta_2 \ln(ULC_{it}) + \varepsilon_i, \tag{18.4}$$

where UCM_{it} are the unit costs determined as a ratio between the total costs for the mail sector over the volumes, VPC_{it} are the volumes per capita (a ratio between the total volumes over population), ULC_{it} are the unit labor costs (labor costs over number of employees). $\varepsilon_i = u_i + v_i$ is the error term.

The results in Table 18.2 indicate that the explanatory variables are always significant and the signs are as expected. For the OLS, OLSFE and RE estimations, the goodness of fit is very high. Moreover, for OLSFE and RE, the *R*-squared 'between' and 'within' are high and similar. For the cases of GLS RE and ML estimations, the other parameters estimated are related to the error term which is decomposed in terms of efficiency, u_i, and in the random error term, v_i. More specifically, for the GLS RE, the standard deviations of these terms are presented; while for the ML estimation the variances of u_i and v_i are shown. The lambda and gamma coefficients of the ML estimation are 1.2 and 0.6, respectively. Given the lambda coefficient, the units under investigation are relatively inefficient. Moreover, given the value of the gamma coefficient, it is possible to affirm that the technical efficiency effects are relevant and contain a significant stochastic component. For these estimations a time-variant model is assumed, thus the term of efficiency for each cross-section is represented by u_{it}. Furthermore, as a distribution of the efficiency terms, for RE a half-normal is assumed while for ML a truncated normal distribution is assumed. For the ML, the log-likelihood value means that the goodness of fit is high. The Wald chi^2 and the related probability give the information about the validity of the linear relation.

From the above results, rankings are obtained by the following criteria. For OLSFE the minimum value of cross-sectional fixed effects is obtained and the difference between the value of each cross-section fixed effect (alpha) and the cross-section with the minimum is computed. For the GLSRE estimation, the average of the component errors estimated, u_{it}, which follows a half-normal distribution, is taken for each cross-section.

With ML estimation, taking the measures of technical efficiency calculated with a time-variant model and with a truncated-normal distribution of u_{it}, technical efficiency is determined as a ratio of its mean cost, given the level of inefficiency, to the corresponding mean cost if the inefficiency level were zero. With the DEA technique, the inputs considered are the total costs (unit cost) and the labor costs (unit labor costs) while the output is total volumes (volumes per capita); both the hypotheses of CRS and VRS were taken into consideration. The resulting rankings are shown in Tables 18.3 and 18.4.

The number '1' represents the most efficient and '5' the least efficient. From the tables it emerges that the ranking is different in relation to the method applied. Hence, there is

Table 18.2 Efficiency analysis for the unit cost function without exogenous variables

	OLS (correc. std. errors)	OLSFE[a]	GLSRE	ML (stoc. frontier model)
Dependent variable: LogUCM_t				
Balanced Panel				
Efficiency model			Time variant	Time variant
Explanatory variables:				
Efficiency terms			Half-normal	Truncated normal
Alfa$_0$	1.620(10.83)***	3.253(3.287)***	1.500(7.49)***	1.477(8.12)***
Log ULC_t	0.169(2.41)**	0.304(4.501)***	0.230(3.67)***	0.229(3.27)***
Log VPC_t	−0.532(−24.21)***	−0.902(−4.932)***	−0.550(−18.82)***	−0.553(−18.80)***
Alpha_PI		−0.364		
Alpha_DP		−0.074		
Alpha_LP		0.136		
Alpha_RM		0.010		
Alpha_USPS		0.202		
Observations	55	55	55	55
R-squared overall	0.958	0.958	0.958	
R-squared within		0.405	0.395	
R-squared between		0.992	0.990	
DW		0.696		
Sigma_u			0.027	0.205
Sigma_v			0.056	0.178
Sigma^2_u				0.042
Sigma^2_v				0.032
Sigma^2				0.074
Mean of u				0.034(0.57)
Lambda $\lambda(\sigma_u/\sigma_v)$				1.20
Gamma				0.567
Log likelihood				77.088
Wald chi^2				611.97(0.000)

Note: a. The reported probability for OLSFE is for the t-statistic. For this estimation u_i is assumed to be fixed and it is represented throughout by the cross-fixed effect and is always time invariant.
*** significant 1% level; ** significant 5% level; * significant 10% level.

a need to identify the most reliable approach. The vastly different results obtained lead to different and inconsistent conclusions. To solve this problem for parametric methods, some econometric tests[7] are applied to choose the more reliable method. First the heteroskedasticity test was applied to the OLSFE estimation and the redundancy test; after that the Hausman test was applied to the GLSRE method to check for the presence of correlation between the errors and the regressors and then for testing the presence of misspecification and the dependence between the errors and the regressors.

For the total cost function, the OLSFE estimation displays a Durbin–Watson (DW) statistic of about 0.63, which means that there is some correlation between the residuals; the test of equality of variance between the residuals according to the Levene method leads to rejection of homoskedasticity while the other two methods (Bartlett and Brown-Forsythe) lead to acceptance of the null hypothesis of homoskedasticity between the variance of the residual series. Moreover, the results of the redundant fixed-effect test lead to rejection of the null hypothesis of redundant fixed effects. To summarize for the

Table 18.3 Total cost function

	Parametric			Nonparametric	
	OLSFE	RE	ML	DEA-CRS	DEA-VRS
Poste Italiane	1	2	3	5	2
Deutsche Post	4	5	2	3	5
La Poste	3	3	4	2	3
Royal Mail	2	1	5	4	4
USPS	5	4	1	1	1

Table 18.4 Unit cost function

	Parametric			Nonparametric	
	OLSFE	RE	ML	DEA-CRS	DEA-VRS
Poste Italiane	1	2	4	5	3
Deutsche Post	2	3	3	4	5
La Poste	4	4	2	2	4
Royal Mail	3	5	1	3	2
USPS	5	1	5	1	1

OLSFE estimation, the fixed effects are not redundant and there is only a correlation problem between the residuals. For the GLSRE estimation, the Hausman test leads to acceptance of the null hypothesis of misspecification of RE estimation. According to the parametric methods for the total cost function, it is possible to conclude that the OLSFE estimation gives more reliable results.

For the unit cost function, the OLSFE estimation has a DW statistic of about 0.69, signaling some correlation between residuals; the test of equality of variance between the residuals – according to all the methods (Levene, Bartlett and Brown-Forsythe) – leads to rejection of the null hypothesis of homoskedasticity. Moreover, the results of the redundant fixed-effect test lead to rejection of the null hypothesis of redundant fixed effects. To summarize, fixed effects are not redundant but there are correlation and heteroskedasticity problems.

The Hausman test is used for the GLSRE estimation. If this test leads to rejection of the null hypothesis then the GLSRE is the correct specification. According to parametric methods, for the unit cost function it is possible to conclude that the GLSRE could be the most reliable method. However '[i]f the regressors and the effects can be maintained to be independent, then ML is more efficient than the traditional panel estimators because it exploits distributional information the other estimators do not' (Sena, 2003, p. 15). The ML is a more efficient estimator than the GLSRE because it permits the distribution of the error terms to be defined and the term of technical efficiency to be identified. Generally speaking 'the main advantage is that ML estimation improves (statistical) efficiency in the estimation (as long as the assumption of independence is not a problem) and tighter parametrisation allowing direct individual specific estimates of the inefficiency term in the model' (ibid., p. 13).

The choice between the CRS and VRS techniques cannot be based on the application of statistical tests because DEA is a non-statistical approach that does not easily allow for hypothesis testing. Most of the literature emphasizes that VRS is more appropriate than CRS especially when in the panel the subjects vary in size as in the dataset. CRS could be more reliable if it were possible to restrict the technology capabilities because the main input is labor.

Efficiency Analysis with Exogenous Variables

Relation (18.1) with the exogenous variables (total population and urbanization rate) can be rewritten:

$$\ln(TCM_{it}) = \alpha_o + \alpha_i + \beta_1\ln(TV_{it}) + \beta_2\ln(LCM_{it}) + \beta_3\ln(POP_{it}) + \beta_4 URB_{it} + \varepsilon_i, \tag{18.5}$$

where TCM_{it} are the total cost for the mail sector, TV_{it} are the total volumes, LCM_{it} is the labor cost, POP_{it} is the total population, URB_{it} is the urbanization rate and $\varepsilon_i = u_i + v_i$ is the error term that in RE and ML is decomposed into two parts: u_i is the efficiency term and v_i the random variables.

The estimation results presented in Table 18.5 for OLS, RE and ML show that the explanatory variables have the expected signs and are significant (with the exception of *LCM* with OLS, GLSRE and ML). In this context it is important to note that the variable *URB* impacts the total cost positively; this effect is plausible. It could be understood by the network available for the postal services being completely saturated, with an increase of urban areas leading to an increase in the cost of the structure needed for the new urban areas. The introduction of exogenous variables determines the loss of significance in all the estimations of the variable *LCM*, except in the OLSFE estimation. *LCM* and *URB* are very significant and their impact on the dependent variable is higher than in the other estimations; the other explanatory variables lose significance, with the variable *POP* having a negative coefficient. Moreover, the goodness of fit expressed by the *R*-squared 'overall', 'between' and 'within' is not so high. While for OLS and GLSRE the goodness of fit is very high and the results of the estimations are very similar. For the GLSRE the information of the *R*-squared 'within' and 'between' indicates a strong goodness of fit of the estimation. For the ML estimation the lambda and the gamma coefficients are, respectively, 1.4 and 0.7. Given the lambda coefficient, the units under investigation are relatively inefficient. Moreover, given the value of the gamma coefficient, it is possible to affirm that the technical efficiency effects are relevant and contain a significant stochastic component. For these estimations a time-variant model is assumed, thus the term of efficiency for each cross-section is represented by u_{it}. Furthermore, as a distribution of the efficiency terms, for RE a half-normal is assumed while for ML a truncated normal distribution is assumed. For the ML, the log-likelihood value means that the goodness of fit is high. The Wald chi^2 and the related probability gives information about the validity of the linear relation. For the unit cost function with exogenous variables the equation estimated is:

$$\ln(UCM_{it}) = \alpha_o + \alpha_i + \delta_1\ln(VPC_{it}) + \delta_2\ln(ULC_{it}) + \delta_3\ln(POP_{it}) + \delta_4 URB_{it} + \varepsilon_i, \tag{18.6}$$

Table 18.5 Efficiency analysis of the total cost function with exogenous variables

	OLS (correc. std. error)	OLSFE[a]	GLSRE	ML (stoc. frontier model)
Dependent variable: LogTCM_t				
Balanced Panel				
Efficiency model			Time variant	Time variant
Explanatory variables:				
Distri. Effi. terms u_i			Half-normal	Truncated normal
$Alfa_0$	1.960(16.96)***	7.847(1.227)	1.960(10.15)***	2.077(11.67)***
Log LCM_t	0.102(1.26)	0.353(3.345)***	0.102(1.45)	0.094(1.52)
Log TV_t	0.458(12.48)***	0.201(1.149)	0.458(11.34)***	0.467(12.82)***
Log POP_t	0.414(5.93)***	−0.426(−0.594)	0.414(7.42)***	0.398(8.15)***
URB_t	0.219(3.58)***	5.321(3.356)***	0.219(1.80)*	0.229(2.11)**
Alfa_PI		0.157		
Alfa_DP		−0.417		
Alfa_LP		0.005		
Alfa_RM		−0.848		
Alfa_USPS		1.104		
Observations	55	55	55	55
R-squared overall	0.995	0.400	0.995	
R-squared within		0.666	0.445	
R-squared between		0.398	0.999	
DW		0.848		
Sigma_u			0.001	0.063
Sigma_v			0.047	0.045
$Sigma^2$_u				0.004
$Sigma^2$_v				0.002
$Sigma^2$				0.006
Mean of *u*				0.118(2.95)***
Lambda $\lambda(\sigma_u/\sigma_v)$				1.414
Gamma				0.709
Log likelihood				91.404
Wald chi^2				10,759.99(0.000)

Note: a. The reported probability for OLSFE is for the *t*-statistic. For this estimation u_i is assumed to be fixed and it is represented throughout by the cross-fixed effect and is always time invariant.
*** significant 1% level; ** significant 5% level; * significant 10% level.

where UCM_{it} are the unit costs, VPC_{it} are the volumes per capita, ULC_{it} are the unit labor costs, POP_{it} is the total population and URB_{it} is the urbanization rate; $\varepsilon_i = u_i + v_i$ is the error term.

The results in Table 18.6 show that the explanatory variables are significant (except for *ULC* and *POP* in ML). It is important to note that *URB* also positively impacts the unit cost; this is because the available network is saturated and an increase in urban areas also generates an increase in the unit cost that incorporates the cost. The coefficient estimated for the variable *POP* is negative in all the estimations, while for those of the total cost function this coefficent is positive. The negative impact for the unit cost function is due to the fact that the increase of the population determines an increase of total volumes more than proportional to the increase of total cost.

Table 18.6 Efficiency analysis for the unit cost function with exogenous variables

	OLS (corr. stand. errors)	OLSFE[a]	GLSRE	ML (stoc. frontier model)
Dependent variable: LogUCM_t				
Balanced Panel				
Efficiency model			Time variant	Time variant
Explanatory variables:				
Efficiency terms			Half-normal	Trunc. normal
Alfa$_0$	1.741(10.12)***	14.072(1.762)*	1.741(9.74)***	2.159(10.70)***
Log ULC_t	0.240(3.94)***	0.220(2.459)**	0.240(4.08)***	−0.013(−0.15)
Log VPC_t	−0.529(−22.56)***	−0.678(−3.898)***	−0.529(−25.15)***	−0.485(−21.11)***
Log POP_t	−0.048(−3.03)***	−1.471(−1.875)*	−0.048(−2.65)***	−0.030(−1.53)
URB_t	0.178(2.82)***	6.172(3.789)**	0.177(1.65)*	0.210(1.98)*
Alpha_PI		0.030		
Alpha_DP		−0.594		
Alpha_LP		−0.208		
Alpha_RM		−1.092		
Alpha_USPS		1.865		
Observations	55	55	55	55
R-squared overall	0.967	0.409	0.967	
R-squared within		0.553	0.398	
R-squared between		0.422	0.999	
DW		0.960		
Sigma_u			0.001	0.055
Sigma_v			0.049	0.045
Sigma^2_u				0.003
Sigma^2_v				0.002
Sigma^2				0.005
Mean of u				0.134(2.95)***
Lambda $\lambda(\sigma_u/\sigma_v)$				1.225
Gamma				0.603
Log likelihood				90.29
Wald chi^2				1,525.94(0.000)

Note: a. The reported probability for OLSFE is for the t-statistic. For this estimation u_i is assumed to be fixed and it is represented throughout by the cross-fixed effect and is always time invariant.
*** significant 1% level; ** significant 5% level; * significant 10% level.

For OLSFE, the effects of the constant and *URB* are higher than in the other estimations while the other explanatory variables maintain their significance. Moreover, the goodness of fit is not so high. While for OLS and GLSRE the goodness of fit is very high and the results of the estimations are very similar, for the cases of GLSRE and ML estimations, the other parameters estimated are related to the error term which is decomposed into an efficiency term, u_i, and a random error term, v_i. For the GLSRE the standard deviations of these terms are presented; while for the ML estimation we show the variances of u_i and v_i. For the ML estimation the lambda and the gamma coefficients are, respectively, 1.2 and 0.6. Given the lambda coefficient, the units under investigation are relatively inefficient. Moreover, given the value of gamma coefficient, it is possible to affirm that the technical efficiency effects are relevant and contain a significant stochastic component.

Table 18.7 Total cost function with exogenous variables

	Parametric			Nonparametric	
	OLSFE	RE	ML	DEACRS	DEAVRS
Poste Italiane	4	2	4	5	1
Deutsche Post	2	5	1	4	5
La Poste	3	4	3	2	3
Royal Mail	1	1	5	3	4
USPS	5	3	2	1	2

Table 18.8 Unit cost function with exogenous variables

	Parametric			Nonparametric	
	OLSFE	RE	ML	DEACRS	DEAVRS
Poste Italiane	4	3	4	5	1
Deutsche Post	2	1	1	4	5
La Poste	3	4	3	1	2
Royal Mail	1	5	5	3	3
USPS	5	2	2	2	4

For these estimations a time-variant model is assumed, thus the efficiency term for each cross-section is represented by u_{it}. For the issue of the distribution of the efficiency terms, the log-likelihood value and the Wald chi^2, the same analysis of the total cost function is applied. The resulting rankings are shown in Tables 18.7 and 18.8. The ranking of each postal operator is often different in relation to the method applied; likewise the case without exogenous variables.

Within the parametric methods the heteroskedasticity and the redundant tests were applied for OLSFE, while for GLSRE the Hausman test was used in order to choose the most reliable method. For the total cost function, the OLSFE estimation presents a DW statistic of 0.848, which suggests some correlation between the residuals; the test of equality of variance between the residuals rejects the null hypothesis of homoskedasticity. Moreover, the results of the redundant fixed-effect test lead to rejection of the null hypothesis of redundant fixed effects. For the OLSFE estimation the fixed effects are not redundant, but there are correlation and heteroskedasticity problems. For the GLSRE estimation the Hausman test leads us to reject the null hypothesis (it is the correct specification). According to the parametric methods for the total cost function, it is possible to conclude that the GLSRE method is the correct specification. However, between the GLSRE and ML estimators, the latter is more reliable as explained above.

For the unit cost function, the OLSFE estimation presents a DW of about 0.960, which suggests some correlation between the residuals; the test of equality of variance between the residuals according to the Bartlett and Levene methods rejects the null hypothesis of homoskedasticity. Moreover, the results of the redundant fixed-effect test lead to rejecting the null hypothesis of redundant fixed effects. For the GLSRE estimation, the Hausman test is proposed; if this test leads to rejecting the null hypothesis then the GLSRE is the correct specification. According to the parametric methods for the unit cost function, it is possible to conclude that the GLSRE is the correct specification. However, between the GLSRE and ML estimators, the latter is more reliable. As described above for the nonparametric methods, the choice between the CRS and VRS techniques cannot be based on the application of statistical tests.

4 CONCLUSIONS

From the empirical analysis it emerges that with parametric methods and without exogenous variables, the ranking of operators is not consistent using each cost function in turn. With the exogenous variables, the more appropriate method is the ML using the two cost functions; this results in the same ranking of postal operators and a certain level of reliability is guaranteed. With the nonparametric method both with and without the exogenous variables, the DEACRS leads to consistent results, while the VRS leads to heterogenous results; future research should be carried out on mixed DEA.

The different methods have advantages and disadvantages and it is difficult to identify a priori the best method.[8] For parametric methods there are several tests which can help to identify the most reliable method but unfortunately this is not possible with nonparametric methods. The analysis has produced heterogeneous results which are inconsistent. This is also the case using Spearman's rank correlation coefficients for the two cost functions between pairs of ranks obtained by the methods selected. This could arise first, because when undertaking international benchmarking there is a risk that data may be inconsistent (Oxera, 2009, pp. 5–9). Second, and more relevant for this analysis, the heteregenous results might signal that the operators are similar from an efficiency point of view and that slight changes in the methods impact on the ranking, implying that results need to be interpreted with caution. This suggests that one should not rely on any one technique to infer strong conclusions.

It is also important to take into account the unit cost function signaling the importance of the scale of operations in determining efficiency levels. Furthermore, environmental factors have a relevant impact on the efficiency scores of operators. Future research should expand the set of variables by including other factors, for example, the morphology of territory being served and the amount of mountainous land area. Finally, the evolving competitive and technological environment raises the issue of the tradeoff between efficiency and equity. The effectiveness of operators cannot be based only on efficiency analysis (Bailly and Meidinger, 2011).

NOTES

* Any views or opinions presented in this chapter are solely those of the authors and do not represent those of the affiliated institutions. Detailed results of the tests will be provided on request. Special thanks to an anonymous referee for advice on how to improve the chapter, Alan Horncastle for his comments on DEA and on the impact of the variation on noise on the efficiency levels, Gennaro Scarfiglieri for his advice on Spearman methodology to test rankings, and Mark Fardelli for his comments.

1. COLS and MOLS are not employed because for panel data they are inconsistent.

2. The reason we chose the period 1998–2008 is that 1) before 1998 some operators were still state departments generating possible problems of data inconsistency; and 2) after 2008 the liberalization process and the financial crisis have had an impact on postal volumes. To incorporate the impact of these factors in the research the 'dust needs to settle'.
3. Average exchange rate of the last nine years is applied.
4. The exchange rate used is the average of the 11 years.
5. If time variant, the term of efficiency for each cross-section is represented by u_{it} and the random variables by v_{it}.
6. If $\lambda < 1$ the data are relatively noisy and efficiency estimation is not recommended; if $\lambda = 1$ then the data are measured with relatively little error and the units under investigation are relatively efficient; if $\lambda > 1$ this means that the data have relatively little noise but the units under investigation are relatively inefficient and efficiency estimation is recommended (Badunenko et al., 2011, pp. 10–20). The gamma parameter is the ratio between the variance of u_i and the overall variance of the two error components. This parameter ranges from 0 to 1; a value close to 1 indicates that the technical efficiency is relevant and is stochastic.
7. The approach proposed for the selection of the most reliable method between FE and RE is based on Filippini et al. (2003). In this chapter the DW statistics and the equality of variance test for the heteroskedasticity problem are also considered. However, it is possible to use other specifications of the error component to address the problem (Henderson, 2003).
8. Among these methods it is expected that the best technique would be SFA (ML) since it is important to isolate the term of efficiency by other factors that could be represented by some environmental variables (Filippini et al., 2003). For this reason the OLSFE is not appropriate, also if the consistency of the estimator does not depend on the distribution or independence of the variables (Henderson, 2003). Of the GLSRE and ML, the latter is more efficient (Sena, 2003). Finally, the comparison between ML and DEA when the dataset is a panel data leads to the conclusion that the best estimator is ML (Badukenko et al., 2011).

REFERENCES

Aigner, D.J., C.A.K. Lovell and P. Schmidt (1977), 'Formulation and estimation of stochastic frontier production function models', *Journal of Econometrics*, **6**, 21–37.

Badunenko, O., D.J. Henderson and S.C. Kumbhakar (2011), *When, where and how to perform efficiency estimation*, MPRPA working paper.

Bailly, D. and M. Meidinger (2011), 'The dual trend towards operational efficiencies and social regulation in European postal services', in M.A. Crew and P.R. Kleindorfer (eds), *Reinventing the Postal Sector in an Electronic Age*, Cheltenham, UK and Northampton, MA, USA: Edward Elgar, pp. 336–50.

Battese, G.E. and T.J. Coelli (1995), 'A model for technical inefficiency effects in a stochastic frontier production function for panel data', *Empirical Economics*, **20**, 325–32.

Bradley, M.D. and D.M. Baron (1993), 'Performance in a multiproduct firm: an application to the U.S. Postal Service', *Operations Research*, **41** (3), 450–58.

Coelli, T.J., D.S. Rao and G.E. Battese (1999), *An Introduction to Efficiency and Productivity Analysis*, Boston, MA: Kluwer Academic.

Dranove, D. (2010), 'Fixed Effects Models', Empirical Methods in Strategy Course, Northwestern University, Evanston, IL.

Economist (2003–2007), *Pocket World in Figures*, The Economist.

Farrell, M.J. (1957), 'The measurement of productive efficiency', *Journal of the Royal Statistical Society*, **120**, 253–81.

Fenster, L., D. Monaco, E. Pearsall and S. Xenakis (2008), 'Are there economies of scale in mail processing?', in M.A. Crew and P.R. Kleindorfer (eds), *Competition and Regulation in the Postal and Delivery Sector*, Cheltenham, UK and Northampton, MA, USA: Edward Elgar.

Filippini, M., R. Fazioli and M. Kunzle (2003), 'Valutazione dell'efficienza delle compagnie di bus italiane e svizzere', Bank of Italy, Rome.

Fried, H.O., C.A. Knox Lovell and S.S. Schmidt (2008), 'Efficiency and productivity', in Fried, Knox Lovell and Schmidt (eds), *The Measurement of Productive Efficiency*, Oxford: Oxford University Press.

Gori, S., E. Piccinin, S. Romito and G. Scarfiglieri (2006), 'On the use of cost functions in the assessment of the impact of liberalization on postal universal service burden: restricted versus flexible specifications', in M.A. Crew and P.R. Kleindorfer (eds), *Progress toward Liberalization of the Postal and Delivery Sector*, New York: Springer.
Greene, W. (1990), 'A gamma-distributed stochastic frontier model', *Journal of Econometrics*, **46**, 141–63.
Greene, W. (2008), 'The econometric approach to efficiency analysis', in H.O. Fried, C.A. Knox Lovell and S.S. Schmidt (eds), *The Measurement of Productive Efficiency*, Oxford: Oxford University Press.
Henderson, D.J. (2003), 'The measurement of technical efficiency using panel data', working paper, Department of Economics State University of New York, Binghamton, NY.
Horncastle, A., D. Jevons, P. Dudley and E. Thanassoulis (2006), 'Efficiency analysis of delivery offices in the postal sector using stochastic frontier and data envelopment analysis', in M.A. Crew and P.R. Kleindorfer (eds), *Liberalization of the Postal and Delivery Sector*, Cheltenham, UK and Northampton, MA, USA: Edward Elgar.
Jacobs, R., P.C. Smith and A. Street (2006), *Measuring Efficiency in Health Care: Analytic Techniques and Health Policy*, Cambridge: Cambridge University Press.
Knox Lovell, C.A. and S.S. Schmidt (1993), *The Measurement of Productive Efficiency: Techniques and Applications*, Oxford: Oxford University Press.
Kumbhakar, S.C. and C.A. Knox Lovell (2000), *Stochastic Frontier Analysis*, Cambridge: Cambridge University Press.
Maruyama, S. and T. Nakajima (2002), 'The productivity analysis of postal services: a global comparison of technical efficiency and total factor productivity', in M.A. Crew and P.R. Kleindorfer (eds), *Postal and Delivery Services: Delivering on Competition*, Boston, MA: Kluwer Academic.
Mastromarco, C. (2008), 'Stochastic frontier models', working paper, Department of Economics and Mathematics-Statistics, CIdE, University of Salento, September.
Meeusen, W. and J. van Den Broeck (1977), 'Efficiency estimation from Cobb–Douglas production functions with composed error', *International Economic Review*, **18** (2), 435–44.
Mundlak, Y. (1978), 'On the pooling of time series and cross section data', *Econometrica*, **46** (1), 69–85.
NERA (2004), 'Economics of Postal Services', Final Report to the European Commission, London, July.
Oxera (2009), 'Recommendations on how to model efficiency for future price reviews', prepared for Office of Rail Regulation, London.
Roy, B. (1999), 'Technico-economic analysis of the costs of outside work in postal delivery', in M.A. Crew and P.R. Kleindorfer (eds), *Emerging Competition in Postal and Delivery Services*, Boston, MA: Kluwer Academic.
Schmidt, P. (1976), 'On the statistical estimation of parametric frontier production functions', *Review of Economics and Statistics*, **58** (2), 238–39.
Seiford, L.M. and R.M. Thrall (1990), 'Recent developments in DEA, the mathematical programming approach to frontier analysis', *Journal of Econometrics*, **46** (1–2), 7–38.
Sena, V. (2003), 'The frontier approach to the measurement of productivity and technical efficiency', working paper, University of Leeds, July.
Shepard, R.W. (1953), *Cost and Production Function*, Princeton, NJ: Princeton University Press.
Stevens, P.A. (2004), 'Accounting for background variables in stochastic frontier analysis', working paper, National Institute of Economic and Social Research, London.
Uğur, A. (2004), 'Technical efficiency in Irish manufacturing industry, 1991–1999', Trinity Economic Papers, Trinity College, Dublin.
Vartanian, T.P. and P.W. Buck (2005), 'Childhood and adolescent neighborhood effects on adult income: using siblings to examine differences in OLS and fixed effect models', *Social Service Review*, **79** (1), 60–94.
Visco Comandini V., A. Consiglio, S. Gori, E. Piccinin and M.R. Pierleoni (2010), 'The *Altmark* ruling and approaches to measuring efficiency of postal operators', in M.A. Crew and P.R. Kleindorfer (eds), *Heightening Competition in the Postal and Delivery Sector*, Cheltenham, UK and Northampton, MA, USA: Edward Elgar.

19. Termination charges in the international parcel market*

Andreas Haller,[†] Christian Jaag[‡] and Urs Trinkner[§]

1 THE INTERNATIONAL PARCEL MARKET

The parcel segment is one of the most liberalized segments in the postal industry. A recent market survey commissioned by the EC has revealed that 30 out of 31 European incumbents perceived competition within the parcel segment as 'intense' (Okholm et al., 2010). In the parcels market, incumbents are typically referred to as 'designated operators' (DOs) in that they have been designated by their home country to fulfill the country's international obligations stemming from the Universal Postal Union (UPU). These obligations include the termination of international inbound parcels sent by other DOs according to the UPU's remuneration system referred to as 'inward land rates' (ILRs).

Besides the DOs, the main market players competing in the international parcels market are integrators. Integrators are international companies that provide integrated services between countries, that is, operating in the country of origin and destination under the same brand. Examples include DHL, FedEx, UPS and TNT. Competition for an international parcel takes place in the country of origin between a DO and integrated operators. Generally, DOs do not compete against each other because sending a parcel to country A is not a substitute for sending a parcel to country B and DOs operate in their domestic market exclusively (exemptions are selected integrators that are dominated by a DO, such as DHL or DPD). Hence, the international parcel market consists of separated but interconnected domestic parcel markets.

The international parcel market is a constantly growing market. According to UPU (2010) its growth is mainly driven by international trade and retail prices seem to matter for the allocation of market shares, not for determining overall volumes. From 1998 to 2008, worldwide express and light-weight parcel volumes have grown by 52 percent; revenues by 90 percent.[1] In this growing market DOs have been constantly losing market shares, from 30 to 26 percent in terms of volumes and from 19 to 16 percent in revenues.

Hence, DOs are either losing their competitiveness compared to the other suppliers in the Express and Parcel Services (E&PS) market (for example, in terms of prices or services) or they are not involved enough in the growing segments of the E&PS market. The figures also reveal that revenue shares remain considerably lower than volume shares. This may indicate a weakness of DOs in market segments where quality is of high importance.

† Consultant, Swiss Economics and Research Assistant, University of Zurich.
‡ Managing Partner, Swiss Economics and Lecturer, University of St.Gallen.
§ Managing Partner, Swiss Economics and Lecturer, University of Zurich.

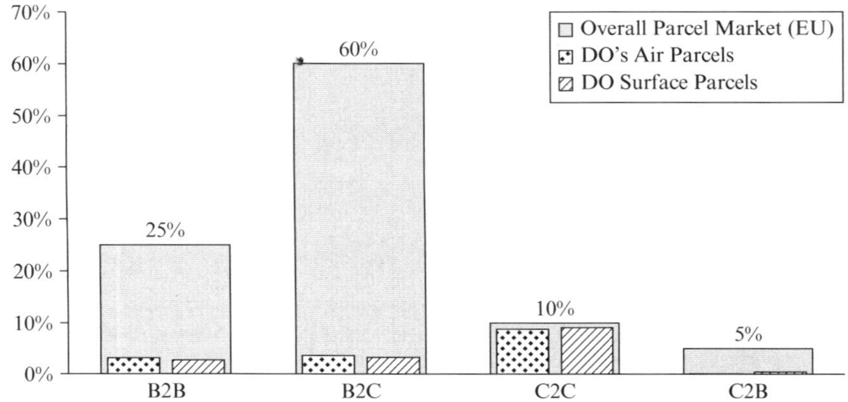

Source: Trinkner et al. (2011).

Figure 19.1 Market share of parcels billed under UPU ILR termination system

The parcels market can be divided into four main sender–receiver segments: business-to-business (B2B), business-to-consumer (B2C), consumer-to-business (C2B), and consumer-to-consumer (C2C). These segments vary by operating costs, barriers to entry, customers' needs, growth rates, and profit margins.

Figure 19.1 shows the segmentation of the European Parcel Market and the approximated market shares of parcels billed under the ILR system in each segment. The figure reveals a rather weak position of the ILR system in the two largest and most dynamic segments, B2B and B2C.

The weak position of the ILR termination system in the international parcel market can be explained by the design of the system itself. Studies find that the ILR rates in some countries are excessive compared to domestic parcel prices: values for the ILR inbound rates of up to 347 percent of domestic parcel prices are reported (see, for example, UPU, 2010). Trinkner et al. (2011) provide additional evidence that the current ILR termination charges seem not to be cost based. They also find that the current ILR termination system is too limited in its accounting for quality. Campbell (2011) finds 'Both types of delivery charges [terminal dues[2] and ILR] are fixed by the UPU by means of elaborate rate agreements that are unrelated to costs. The effect on international trade is distortive, inefficient, and anticompetitive'.

This chapter explains the potentially excessive termination charges and low quality levels with a stylized game-theoretic model of the international parcel market. Within this model it is possible to elaborate the distortions currently in place. The model incorporates quality to account for empirical findings on consumer preferences which indicate that quality of service is a crucial issue in the international parcel market.[3]

Section 2 outlines the current termination charge system of the UPU. Section 3 identifies the main issues that are relevant for the international parcels market: avoidance of double marginalization and provision of adequate incentives for quality and investments. It then discusses these issues based on a game-theoretic model. It is shown that only two-part termination charges will be able to resolve both issues at the same time. Section 4 concludes.

2 INTERNATIONAL TERMINATION CHARGE SYSTEMS

In the cross-border parcel market, non-integrated operators need to purchase final delivery in the country of destination from an operator. There are several systems to price access to such a service/network. This section presents the most important termination charge systems in the parcel market.

The ILR system is a termination charge system led by the UPU. It is decided by its 191 UPU member states in a democratic procedure. All DOs of the member countries can send their international parcels in this pricing regime. It is hence a global, multilateral termination charge system. The ILR pricing system is twofold: the total termination charge is composed of a base rate and a bonus which rewards the supply of defined services with a markup on the base rate.

The base rate is either calculated as 71.4 percent of a country's ILR taken at 2004 levels (plus any inflation-linked adjustment) or set to the 'global minimum base rate' at 2.85 Special Drawing Rights[4] (SDR) per parcel plus 0.28 SDR per kg.

Under this calculation the global minimum base rate applies only if 71.4 percent of a country's ILR in 2004 is smaller than the global minimum base rate. Otherwise the ILR equals 71.4 percent of a country's ILR in 2004 (UPU, 2011). Until 2004, ILRs were set by each DO unilaterally. Hence, the ILR system may be referred to as a 'decentralized market solution' as introduced in Section 4. In addition to the base rate, a DO can qualify for additional bonus payments of between 5 and 40 percent of the base rate when meeting certain quality criteria such as the provision of track and trace, home delivery, fulfilling delivery standards or the usage of the common Internet-based inquiry system. If a country qualifies for the full bonus payment, the current ILR of this country is approximately equal to the ILR in 2004.

In addition to the UPU ILR there are other termination systems such as E-Parcel Group (EPG) and the Kahala Posts Group (KPG). Besides, DOs can buy termination services from integrators. The pricing of these alternatives to the ILR is not disclosed.

3 MODELING INTERNATIONAL PARCEL TERMINATION

As elaborated in Section 1, termination in the international parcel market can be analyzed as two-way access in separated (noncompeting) but interconnected markets.

The two-way access literature has mainly focused on the national telecommunications market. The point of reference for this literature is Laffont et al. (1998). They find that in noncompeting networks, the non-cooperative two-stage game in access charges and retail prices leads to double marginalization, namely, an excessive markup on marginal cost through iterated profit maximization in the upstream and downstream part of the value chain, resulting in suboptimally high prices. Double marginalization occurs when both the upstream and downstream operators have market power and therefore are price setters. Taking the parcels market as an example, when determining the termination charge for final delivery, the downstream operator considers the effect on its own profits only, implying termination charges above marginal costs. This increases input prices for the upstream operator and leads to higher consumer prices and lower volumes compared to a situation with an integrated operator with market power. The externality of the downstream operator on the upstream operator hence results in lower joint profits. Consequently, under double marginalization, consumers as well as operators are strictly worse off compared to a situation with integrated operators. Laffont et al. additionally show that for small substitutability between two networks, the access charge that maximizes joint profits equals marginal cost. This implies that integrators would set their (virtual, internal) access charges equal to marginal cost whereas the non-cooperative determination of access charges between two DOs in the international parcel market cannot be expected to be efficient due to double marginalization.

Laffont et al. do not provide a solution to the problem of double marginalization in noncompeting networks and their results are derived under the assumption of balanced calling patterns, that is, symmetric operators. This assumption of symmetry does not hold in the international parcel market.

Carter and Wright (2003) find that in a model of competing networks allowing for asymmetries, a particularly simple, optimal regulation obtains: if carriers cannot agree on the terms of interconnection, the larger carrier is entitled to select the access price which is then applied reciprocally.

In the following, the quality issues mentioned above are left aside in a first step and it is assessed whether or not the most striking results from the literature on national termination charges apply to the international parcel market. Quality is then introduced later in the section.

Base Model

The ineffectiveness of non-cooperative access prices in noncompeting networks mentioned by Laffont et al. (1998), as well as Laffont and Tirole (2001, p. 184), also applies to the international parcel market as the following game-theoretic model will show. The model in Appendix 19A.1 proves the ineffectiveness of decentralized access charges in the international parcel market in a more general setting.

The international parcel business between two countries A and B is modeled in the simplest way. It is assumed that there are no network externalities.[5] The profit function of a DO $i \in \{A, B\}$ is assumed to be:

$$\pi_i = (p_i - c_i^u - a_j)d_i(p_i,\bar{p}_i) + (a_i - c_i^d)d_j(p_j,\bar{p}_j) - F_i \tag{19.1}$$

where $j \in \{A, B\}$ and $i \neq j$. p_i stands for the retail price of DO i for an outbound parcel and p_j is the retail price of the other DO j for an outbound parcel (which is an inbound parcel for DO i). c_i^u is the constant marginal cost per outbound parcel and c_i^d is the constant marginal cost of an inbound parcel for operator i. a_j stands for the termination charge which has to be paid by operator i to the foreign operator j for the delivery of a parcel. $d_i(p_i, \bar{p}_i)$ represents the domestic demand for international parcels, which depends on the price of the domestic operator p_i as well as on the price $\bar{p}_i$ of an integrated competitor. F_i represents fixed cost.

Hence, the first term of the profit function represents the revenues from outgoing parcels, that is, net revenue per parcel multiplied by the domestic demand $d_i(p_i, \bar{p}_i)$. The second term stands for the revenue of incoming parcels, that is, the termination charge minus marginal costs multiplied by the demand for international parcels in country j.

Following Dietl et al. (2005) and Jaag and Trinkner (2011), a quasi-linear utility function is assumed:

$$U = \alpha_i d_i - \frac{\beta}{2}(d_i)^2 + \bar{\alpha}_i \bar{d}_i - \frac{\beta}{2}(\bar{d}_i)^2 - \varepsilon\beta d_i \bar{d}_i$$

where $\alpha_i, \alpha_j, \beta > 0$ and $\varepsilon \in (0,1)$. A smaller parameter ε indicates a higher degree of differentiation. The parameters α_i and $\bar{\alpha}_i$ determine the market shares of the DO i and the integrated operator, respectively, whereas β determines the slope of the demand function. It is assumed that the parameter constellation is such that the point of local satiation is not reached.

Maximizing the assumed utility function yields the following demand function:

$$d_i = \frac{1}{\beta(1 - \varepsilon^2)}(\alpha_i - \varepsilon\bar{\alpha}_i - p_i + \varepsilon\bar{p}_i)$$

An operator therefore has two strategic instruments to maximize its profit: the price for international parcels and the termination charge. The strategic interaction between the two DOs is treated as a two-stage game. First, they set their termination charges and then given these charges they decide which price to charge. Hence, the game is solved backwards to attain a subgame-perfect Nash equilibrium.

Decentralized market equilibrium

In the decentralized equilibrium, operators can set their access charges without restrictions and profits are defined as in equation (19.1).

In stage two of the game, treating access charges as exogenous, the best-price responses satisfy:

$$\frac{\partial \pi_i}{\partial p_i}: \frac{a_j + c_i^u - 2p_i + \alpha_i + \bar{p}_i\varepsilon - \bar{\alpha}_i\varepsilon}{\beta - \beta\varepsilon^2} = 0$$

Solving for p_i yields the following best responses:

$$p_i = \frac{1}{2}(a_j + c_i^u + \alpha_i + \bar{p}_i\varepsilon - \bar{\alpha}_i\varepsilon) \tag{19.2}$$

Prices are strategic complements and increase with higher termination fees and upstream costs.

Anticipating the best response of the opponent country j in stage two of the game (equation (19.2)) yields in stage one the following profit-maximizing termination charges in a decentralized termination system:

$$a_i^* = \frac{1}{2}(c_i^d - c_j^u + \alpha_j + \bar{p}_j\varepsilon - \bar{\alpha}_j\varepsilon). \tag{19.3}$$

A DO's (inbound) access charge is hence positively related to the integrator's price for the DO's home market $\bar{p}_j$ (strategic complement). The higher the international competitive pressure, the lower will be the termination charge. If own delivery cost c_i^d increase, this will be reflected in a higher access charge. If, however, the partner DO has increasing upstream cost c_j^u, this will be partially offset by lower access charges to increase the competitiveness of the DO stream. These results are in line with intuition.

Industry optimum
If the two countries collude and maximize the joint industry profit:

$$\pi_{IND} = \pi_i + \pi_j,$$

then the following prices are chosen:

$$p_i = \frac{1}{2}(c_j^d + c_i^u + \alpha_i + \bar{p}_i\varepsilon - \bar{\alpha}_i\varepsilon).$$

These prices imply that the optimal termination charge in the industry optimum is equal to the inbound marginal cost, that is,

$$a_i = c_i^d. \tag{19.4}$$

Comparing equations (19.3) and (19.4) it can be shown that operators are strictly worse off with the outcome in the decentralized market compared to the industry optimum for any market constellation, that is,

$$\pi_{IND} > \pi_{iD} + \pi_{jD}.$$

This result can be explained by the issue of double marginalization in the decentralized market equilibrium, which is avoided in the industry optimum (see also Appendix 19A.1).

These results rely on the assumption that the operators strictly maximize profits and that termination charges are not regulated. These are critical assumptions because DOs are often regulated and cannot choose their prices freely. For example, if the retail parcel prices of the originating DO were capped (with a cap independent from termination charges of foreign DOs), then the optimum for the terminating operator in the decentralized market solution would be to set infinitely high termination charges as the retail price of the originating DO, and hence demand, is not affected by the level of the termination charges.

Further, it is assumed here that DOs do not have an alternative to cooperating with foreign DOs to deliver a parcel in foreign countries. In reality, of course, DOs can cooperate with integrated operators. However, abandoning this assumption does not change the previous result of excessively high termination charges in the decentralized market equilibrium; it only results in an upper bound for the level of termination charges.

Social optimum
The optimal termination charge from a welfare point of view depends on the definition of welfare. If one wants to maximize the welfare of a single country, that is, maximize the sum of domestic profits and consumer surplus, a high access charge for incoming parcels

		Operator 2	
		Low Access Charge	High Access Charge
Operator 1	Low Access Charge	Good profit / Good profit	Very Low profit / High profit
	High Access Charge	High profit / Very Low profit	Low profit / Low profit

Figure 19.2 Prisoner's dilemma

and a low (probably below marginal costs) access charge for outgoing parcels are optimal for this specific country. The high access charge on incoming parcels maximizes profits of the domestic operator without inducing any distortions to the domestic market. The distortions from the high access charge take place in the foreign market which the national social planner does not care about. Conversely, the termination rate charged by a foreign DO on outgoing parcels is optimally very low as this access charge can be used as an instrument to intensify competition and therefore maximize consumer surplus. This access charge might optimally be below marginal costs as it might be used to correct upstream market imperfections.

From a global perspective, welfare is the sum of all profits and all consumer surpluses in all countries. Assuming perfect upstream market conditions, the optimal access charge is equal to marginal costs.[6] This coincides with the optimal termination charge from an industry point of view (equation (19.4)).

With balanced parcel streams between two countries, this first-best solution is realizable as operators can cover the fixed costs of the inbound service with the profits from outbound parcels. But with asymmetric streams this first-best result may not be implementable since the net importing operator may not generate enough revenues from outbound parcels to cover the fixed costs of inbound services. Hence, a lump-sum transfer system is needed for asymmetric situations. But such a transfer system between different operators from different countries seems rather unrealistic and the second-best solution therefore is the lowest possible access charge which still covers fixed costs, that is, access charges are set equal to average costs.

Intuitively, unilaterally setting termination charges in noncompeting networks can be interpreted as a prisoner's dilemma (Figure 19.2). The dominant strategy is to set excessively high termination charges (above marginal costs) which leads to a socially undesirable situation of double marginalization, that is, not only are consumers worse off with the decentralized market solution but also operators.

The nature of a prisoner's dilemma implies that DOs will not collaborate in the one-shot game. If the game is played infinitely many times then collusion might be sustained by the reasoning of Friedman (1971). However, even if the game is played ad infinitum, collaboration, that is, low access charges, might not be achieved as an operator can collaborate with an integrator and therefore the 'punishment' for deviating from setting low charges is weakened.

Another solution to this dilemma would be third-party regulation. Optimally, this third party would set the termination charge equal to the marginal cost. But this raises two problems. First, this would require a third party that has the legal power to regulate termination charges in the international parcel market. Such an institution does not exist. Second, marginal cost is private information of the operators and they may not be willing to reveal this information.

In the case of very unbalanced parcel streams, setting termination charges might not be considered a prisoner's dilemma. An operator with large numbers of inbound parcels and only a few outbound parcels (net importer) can always be better off with high access charges independent of the access charge of the other operators. Letting operators set their access charges unilaterally remains a dilemma from both an industry and a welfare point of view, but the solution to this dilemma becomes even trickier. The collusion (setting low charges) by the operators in the case of an infinitely repeated game is no longer an option and one can expect strong opposition to a regulated access charge system with low rates from net importing operators.

The regulation policy in the telecommunication market of reciprocal termination charges might solve this dilemma. Therefore, reciprocal termination charges are analyzed in the following.

Reciprocal termination charges

When DOs are only allowed to set reciprocal termination charges, they face the following profit function:

$$\pi_i = (p_i - c_i^u - a)d_i(p_i,\overline{p}_i) + (a - c_i^d)d_j(p_j,\overline{p}_j).$$

Applying the same procedure as in the derivation of the decentralized market equilibrium to the new profit function yields for operator i the following optimal reciprocal termination charge:

$$a = c_i^d + c_i^u - c_j^u - \alpha_i + \alpha_j + (\overline{\alpha}_i - \overline{p}_i + \overline{p}_j - \overline{\alpha}_j)\varepsilon. \qquad (19.5)$$

If the operators have the same cost structure, that is, $c_i^u = c_j^u$, and their market structures are identical resulting in *balanced parcel streams*, equation (19.5) equals equation (19.4) and hence the chosen reciprocal termination charge is equal to the inbound marginal cost. Hence, for identical markets and operators, reciprocal termination charges provide an efficient solution.

Reducing the choices to either high or low access charges as in the discussion of the prisoner's dilemma above delivers the intuition for this result. Allowing only reciprocal access charges reduces the set of choice in the game described in Figure 19.2 to the choice of setting either low access charges and having good profits or setting high access charges and receiving low profits in the case of balanced parcel streams.

In the case of *unbalanced parcel streams* the game takes on the form illustrated in Figure 19.3, and the net importer would prefer high access charges whereas the net exporter would like to have low access charges. The two operators will not agree on the efficient solution.

Another point of view is that reciprocal termination charges aim to internalize the impact of the chosen termination charge on the profits of the foreign operator to avoid double marginalization. If the termination charge similarly impacts the profits of both operators it is more likely that they will act like an integrator, that is, set

		Operator 2 Net Exporter	
		Low Access Charge	High Access Charge
Operator 1 Net importer	Low Access Charge	Low profit Good profit	
	High Access Charge		Good profit Low profit

Figure 19.3 Reciprocal access charge with asymmetric streams

termination charges equal to marginal costs. The termination charge will impact the profits of two operators in a similar way if they face the same form of competition and have the same market position, which in turn implies that the parcel streams are balanced.

Therefore, the two conditions for efficiency of reciprocal access charges stated above are to understand as conditions on the balance of parcel streams.

In the international parcel market, it is very unlikely that all parcel streams between any two operators are balanced. Carter and Wright (2003) argue that for asymmetric structures the socially efficient termination charges can be attained in the telecommunication market by letting the larger operator choose the termination charge and then applying this charge reciprocally. This does not necessarily apply to the international parcels market.

Assuming $c_i^u < c_j^u$, $\alpha_i > \alpha_j$ and that all other variables are equal for the two operators implies that operator i is larger in terms of outbound parcels than operator j. Then, the approach of Carter and Wright (2003) would suggest that operator i should choose the reciprocal termination charge. The resulting termination charge then might lie below marginal costs. In this case, the smaller operator j will incur negative profits and hence not participate in the international parcel market with operator i. Hence, a pricing system of 'forced' reciprocal termination charges might not have many participants.

Using actual cost data or implementing a mechanism to obtain them indirectly to get cost-based termination charges does not seem to be a viable solution. An alternative would be to use inland tariffs as a proxy for actual costs. However, cost-based termination charges might not solve all issues in the international parcel market. This point will be elaborated in the next subsection.

Accounting for Quality with Linear Termination Charges

As outlined above, quality is an important factor in the parcel market from the consumer point of view and hence from an industry and welfare point of view as well. So far it has been abstracted from quality. This subsection discusses the issues that arise when accounting for quality. Quality is closely linked to investments in network industries. The tradeoff between competition, regulation and incentives for investment is fundamental in economics. This tradeoff becomes particularly important in network industries with access of other operators to the network (Valletti, 2003).

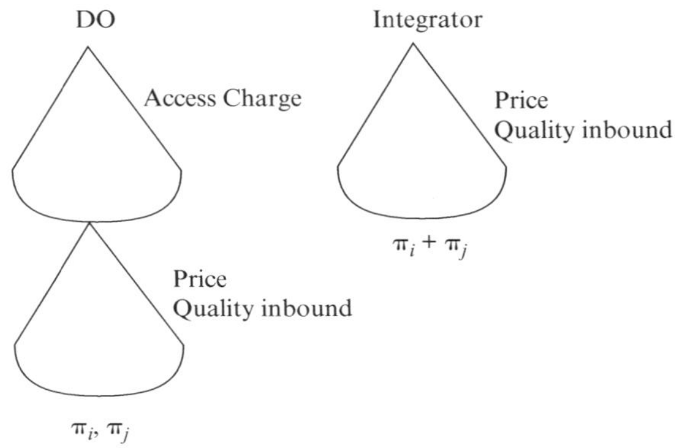

Figure 19.4 Game tree extended model

The literature on termination charges barely deals with the effects of access charges on investment incentives as most of these analyses take place in a static framework and investment only matters in a dynamic context (at least in the telecommunication market) as Gans and Williams (1999) and Valletti (2003) point out. However, investment in the network matters in the international parcel market even in the short run. In the parcel market the network (and especially its quality attributions) is built daily. The decisive quality attributes of the parcel market are the reliability and on-time performance. These parameters can be adjusted in the short run by an operator. Hence investment/quality issues also arise in a static framework. Of course, long-run investments play a crucial role in the parcel market as well, but these issues will be addressed later on.

Accounting for short-run quality considerations makes setting termination charges in the international parcel market a two-stage game which is depicted in Figure 19.4. In the first stage, the operators choose their access charge. In the second stage, given the access charges, the operators determine their prices and inbound quality levels.

It is assumed that only the quality of service by the operator of destination matters for the consumers. The general profit function of a DO is then:

$$\pi_i = (p_i - c_i^u - a_j)d_i(p_i,q_j,\bar{p}_i,\bar{q}_j) + (a_i - c_i^d)d_j(p_j,q_i,\bar{p}_j,\bar{q}_i) - C(q_i) - F, \quad (19.6)$$

and for an integrator (operating in market *i* and *j*):

$$\bar{\pi}_i = (\bar{p}_i - \bar{c}_i^u - \bar{c}_j^d)\bar{d}_i(p_i,q_j,\bar{p}_i,\bar{q}_j) + (\bar{p}_j - \bar{c}_j^u - \bar{c}_i^d)\bar{d}_j(p_j,q_i,\bar{p}_j,\bar{q}_i) - C(\bar{q}_i) - C(\bar{q}_j) - F, \quad (19.7)$$

where $C(q_i)$ are the variable costs arising by short-run quality investments q_i. The rest of the notation is equivalent to that in Section 3 (Base model).

There is no reason to expect the decentralized market equilibrium to be efficient as the issue of double marginalization still occurs when quality is included, as shown in Appendix 19A.1. Intuitively, quality induces an additional free-rider problem. If operator *i* invests in its inbound quality q_i, operator *j* can increase its price without any additional costs given that the access charge does not account for quality investments. Hence, operator i cannot reap all the benefits of its investment into quality and will therefore underinvest if the access charge does not factor in the dimension quality. This is shown analytically in Appendix 19A.2.

The need for regulation of termination charges therefore remains. But what is the optimal termination charge with short-run quality? It is straightforward to show that with quality the optimal termination charge is to be set above marginal costs.

By our assumption of no externalities in the parcel market and our definition of welfare as a global concept the integrator will choose the socially optimal price–quality mix. Hence, the optimal access charge makes DOs act like an integrator, as already argued in the model without quality. Given that the access charge is an exogenous variable determined by some regulator or pricing system, DOs can optimize profits over their price and their inbound quality. Therefore, DOs face the following first-order conditions

$$\frac{\partial \pi_i}{\partial p_i} = d_i(*) + (p_i - c_i^u - a_j)\frac{\partial d_i(*)}{\partial p_i} = 0$$

$$\frac{\partial \pi_i}{\partial q_i} = (a_i - c_i^d)\frac{\partial d_j(*)}{\partial q_i} - C'(q_i) = 0.$$

The integrator's first-order conditions are:

$$\frac{\partial \overline{\pi}}{\partial \overline{p}_i} = \overline{d}_i(*) + (\overline{p}_i - \overline{c}_i^u - \overline{c}_j^d)\frac{\partial \overline{d}_i(*)}{\partial \overline{p}_i} = 0$$

$$\frac{\partial \overline{\pi}}{\partial \overline{q}_i} = (\overline{p}_j - \overline{c}_j^u - \overline{c}_i^d)\frac{\partial \overline{d}_j(*)}{\partial \overline{q}_i} - C'(\overline{q}_i) = 0$$

$$\frac{\partial \overline{\pi}}{\partial \overline{p}_j} = \overline{d}_j(*) + (\overline{p}_j - \overline{c}_j^u - \overline{c}_i^d)\frac{\partial \overline{d}_j(*)}{\partial \overline{p}_j} = 0$$

$$\frac{\partial \overline{\pi}}{\partial \overline{q}_j} = (\overline{p}_i - \overline{c}_i^u - \overline{c}_j^d)\frac{\partial \overline{d}_i(*)}{\partial \overline{q}_j} - C'(\overline{q}_j) = 0.$$

To make DOs act like the corresponding integrator we need:

$$\frac{\partial \pi_i}{\partial p_i} = \frac{\partial \overline{\pi}}{\partial \overline{p}_i} \text{ and } \frac{\partial \pi_i}{\partial q_i} = \frac{\partial \overline{\pi}}{\partial \overline{q}_i}.$$

By corresponding integrator, we mean that the DO and the corresponding integrator have the same demand and costs structure, that is, $\overline{d}_i(*) = d_i(*)$, $\frac{\partial \overline{d}_j(*)}{\partial \overline{p}_j} = \frac{\partial d_i(*)}{\partial p_i}$ and $\frac{\partial \overline{d}_j(*)}{\partial \overline{q}_j} = \frac{\partial d_j(*)}{\partial q_i}$ for $\overline{p}_i = p_i$ and $\overline{q}_i = q_i$, $C'(\overline{q}_i) = C'(q_i)$, $c_i^d = \overline{c}_i^d$ and $c_i^u = \overline{c}_i^u$ for $\overline{p}_i = p_i$ and $\overline{q}_i = q_i$. Then the condition for efficient investment incentives, $\frac{\partial \pi_i}{\partial q_i} = \frac{\partial \overline{\pi}}{\partial \overline{q}_i}$, can be reduced to:

$$a_i^* = p_j - c_j^u.$$

Hence, the optimal access charge a_i^* in terms of investment incentives allocates the total net revenue of a parcel to the operator of destination. As by assumption, only the investment into quality of the operator of destination matters and all costs of the investment are paid by the operator, the DO of destination needs to receive all benefits of the investment. As a consequence, an operator does not earn any profits with its outbound parcels but makes all its profits with its inbound parcels.

From the demand function $d_j(p_j, q_i, \overline{p}_j, \overline{q}_i)$ we know that the price p_j depends on the offered quality q_i, that is, $p_j(q_i)$, and as a consequence the optimal access charge $a^*_i(q_i)$ has to account for quality as well. The exact way the access charge should account for quality depends on how demand interacts with upstream and downstream quality. Upstream quality is of importance as well. As a consequence, some revenue will need to be attributed to the DO of origin. To fully cover this topic, the model would need an extension to reflect upstream quality that is determined by the DO of origin. These issues are beyond the scope of this chapter. The share of revenue allocated to the DO of origin and destination will then depend on the relative importance of price versus upstream and downstream quality. It is expected that such an extended framework will result in optimal termination charges above marginal costs with a markup reflecting downstream quality.

The result that it is necessary to shift the entire margin to the downstream operator to create the efficient investment incentives indicates that it may be a challenge to find conditions under which access prices are able to induce the optimal investment behavior of an integrated firm (ensuring profit-maximizing prices while investing optimally into quality both up- *and* downstream). Related literature on the investment incentives in vertically structured network industries reveals that it is generally difficult to provide optimal up- *or* downstream investment incentives in vertically separated entities relative to integrated operators (see, for example, Buehler et al., 2004, 2006; Buehler and Schmutzler, 2008; Chen and Sappington, 2010). Hence, it will be an even greater challenge to provide adequate incentives up- and downstream at the same time.

Furthermore, an access charge above marginal costs contradicts the 'non-double marginalization' condition, that is, the second condition from above $\frac{\partial \pi_i}{\partial p_i} = \frac{\partial \overline{\pi}}{\partial \overline{p}_i} \leftrightarrow a_j = c_j^d$.

Therefore, the optimal linear access charge does not exist. There is a tradeoff between optimal investment incentives and avoidance of double marginalization when only allowing linear access charges.

Accounting for Quality with Two-part Termination Charges

Two-part access charges can solve this dilemma. If an operator is free to set any arbitrary two-part tariff of the form $T_i(\tilde{a}_i) = A_i + \tilde{a}_i d_j(*)$, it will choose:

$$A_i = \pi_j^{out} = (p_j - c_j^u - \tilde{a}_i) d_i(p_i, q_j, \overline{p}_i, \overline{q}_j)$$

$$\tilde{a}_i = c_i^d.$$

The proposed two-part (affine) access charge follows from profit maximization of the charging operator. The two-part access charge allows the operator of the country of destination to fully extract the rent of an inbound parcel without distorting the behavior of the operator of origin.

By the previous discussion it becomes immediately clear that this two-part access charge is also socially desirable, namely double marginalization is avoided and the optimal level of quality investments is reached. Avoidance of double marginalization is guaranteed by $\tilde{a}_i = c_i^d$.

The optimal quality is supplied as with this access charge the incentive to invest into quality is the same for an integrator and a DO. This can be seen by inserting the two-part access charges into the profit function (19.6) and comparing the result with the integrator's profit function in equation (19.7).

Hence, allowing two-part access charges will lead to a decentralized and (socially) optimal equilibrium. All operators will adapt the optimal two-part access charge irrespective of asymmetric parcel streams.[7]

4 CONCLUSION

Theory predicts that letting operators set their international access prices (termination charges) unilaterally leads to a socially undesirable situation of double marginalization (base model) and underinvestment (quality model).

In the base model of an international parcel market where quality is not accounted for, the first-best access charge is equal to inbound marginal cost. This result fits into the existing access charge literature. The analysis reveals that this first-best solution is difficult to implement in practice as there is no powerful (benevolent) regulator in place, and decentralized solutions such as reciprocal access charges will not always work due to asymmetric parcel flows. The second-best solution in the base model would be to set access charges equal to average cost.

In the quality model it is shown that the access charge is optimally set above marginal costs to align benefits and costs of quality investments. Termination systems that do not appropriately reward for quality will lead to a situation with underinvestment and suboptimal quality. Assuming that only downstream quality is of relevance to consumers, the optimal access charge even implies that an operator does not earn any profits with its outbound parcels but makes all its profits with its inbound parcels. The DO of destination then optimally invests in quality as it fully participates in the additional returns caused by its investment. It can be expected, however, that upstream quality is of importance to consumers as well. As a consequence, optimal termination charges ensure a markup on marginal costs for both operators. But this markup on marginal costs implies again double marginalization. Therefore, the first-best outcome is not achievable through a simple linear access charge. It is shown that two-part access charges can solve this problem and an optimal and decentralized solution is provided.

The identified inefficiencies of the decentralized market equilibrium in the theoretical model closely mirror the observed problems in international parcel markets. The model suggests that the UPU's recent efforts to make termination charges more cost based will offset some of the distortions implied by the current system. However, linear tariffs will not result in an efficient solution in a situation where quality is important. This implies that termination charge systems should move away from item-based linear access charges to two-part pricing.

NOTES

* This chapter is based on Trinkner et al. (2011).
1. Own calculations based on UPU (2010).
2. Terminal dues are the UPU termination charges of international letters.
3. For an overview, see Trinkner et al. (2011). On-time performance, end-to-end speed, reliability, and tracking information are the most important quality dimensions for customers. Generally, quality-of-service attributes appear more important to customers than prices.
4. SDRs are supplementary foreign exchange reserve assets defined and maintained by the IMF (International Monetary Fund).
5. The existence of global externalities in the international parcel market may lead to a markdown on termination charges to encourage senders to demand more parcel services. See, for example, Armstrong (2001) or, for a discussion of the two-sidedness of the postal market, Jaag and Trinkner (2008). It is unlikely that such a markdown would alter the main findings in a significant way.
6. In the absence of perfect upstream market conditions, termination rates below marginal costs may be necessary to achieve optimality. However, in such a situation it would be more straightforward to regulate the competitive distortion where it occurs (in the upstream market) while setting termination rates according to marginal costs.
7. However, a transition from a linear system to two-part tariffs might be opposed by DOs with large net outbound parcel streams as they potentially make lower profits under the new system. At the industry level the net benefits of two-part termination charges are strictly positive.

REFERENCES

Armstrong, Mark (2001), 'The theory of access pricing and interconnection', MPRA Paper 15608, University Library of Munich, Germany.

Buehler, Stefan, Dennis Gärtner and Daniel Halbheer (2006), 'Deregulating network industries: dealing with price–quality tradeoffs', *Journal of Regulatory Economics*, **30**, 99–115.

Buehler, Stefan and Armin Schmutzler (2008), 'Intimidating competitors – endogenous vertical integration and downstream investment in successive oligopoly', *International Journal of Industrial Organization*, **26**, 247–65.

Buehler, Stefan, Armin Schmutzler and Men-Andri Benz (2004), 'Infrastructure quality in deregulated industries: is there an underinvestment problem?', *International Journal of Industrial Organization*, **22**, 253–67.

Campbell, James (2011), 'Towards a United States position at the Doha Congress of the Universal Postal Union', memo, 25 October.

Carter, Michael and Julian Wright (2003), 'Asymmetric network interconnection', *Review of Industrial Organization*, **22**, 27–46.

Chen, Yongmin and David Sappington (2010), 'Innovation in vertically related markets', *Journal of Industrial Economics*, **58** (2), 373–401.

Dietl, Helmut, Urs Trinkner and Reto Bleisch (2005), 'Liberalization and regulation of the Swiss letter market', in M.A. Crew and P.R. Kleindorfer (eds), *Regulatory and Economic Challenges in the Postal and Delivery Sector*, Boston, MA: Kluwer Academic.

Friedman, James (1971), 'A non-cooperative equilibrium for supergames', *Review of Economic Studies*, **38**, 1–12.

Gans, Joshua and Philip Williams (1999), 'Access regulation and the timing of infrastructure investment', *Economic Record*, **75** (2), 127–37.

Jaag, Christian and Urs Trinkner (2008), 'Pricing in competitive two-sided mail markets', in M.A. Crew and P.R. Kleindorfer (eds), *Competition and Regulation in the Postal and Delivery Sector*, Cheltenham, UK and Northampton, MA, USA: Edward Elgar.

Jaag, Christian and Urs Trinkner (2011), 'The interaction between universal service costing and financing in the postal sector: a calibrated approach', *Journal of Regulatory Economics*, **39** (1), 89–110.
Laffont, Jean-Jacques, Patrick Rey and Jean Tirole (1998), 'Network competition: I. Overview and nondiscriminatory pricing', *Rand Journal of Economics*, **29**, 1–37.
Laffont, Jean-Jacques and Jean Tirole (2001), *Competition in Telecommunications*, Cambridge, MA: MIT Press.
Okholm, Henrik, Marcin Winiarczyk and Anna Möller (2010), 'Main Developments in the Postal Sector (2008–2010)', Report prepared for the European Commission.
Trinkner, Urs, Christian Jaag, Helmut Dietl, Andreas Haller, Erwin Verbeek and Oliver Fürst (2011), 'International Parcels – Review of Inward Land Rates', Report prepared by Swiss Economics for the Universal Postal Union.
Universal Postal Union (UPU) (2010), *Market Research on International Letters and Lightweight Parcels and Express Mail Service Items*, Berne: Adrenale Corporation.
Universal Postal Union (UPU) (2011), 'Parcels inward land rates for 2011', available at: http://www.upu.int/en/activities/parcels/inward-land-rates/inward-land-rates-key-documents.html.
Valletti, Tommaso (2003), 'The theory of access pricing and its linkage with investment incentives', *Telecommunications Policy*, **27**, 659–75.

APPENDIX 19A.1 DOUBLE MARGINALIZATION – THE GENERAL CASE

Assume the following general demand function:

$$\pi_i = (p_i - a_j)d_i(p_i, \delta_j, \bar{p}_i, \bar{\delta}_j) + (a_i)d_j(p_j, \delta_i, \bar{p}_j, \bar{\delta}_i) - C(d_i(*)) - C(d_j(*)) - F,$$

where δ captures all parameters which next to the price also might affect the demand, such as, for example, inbound quality. The rest of the notation is equivalent to that in Section 3 (Base model). The usual assumptions on demand and costs are assumed to hold such that the equilibrium exists, is unique and stable. Details of existence, stability and uniqueness of the equilibrium are not examined as they are fairly technical points, which do not deliver any additional insights and a similar model has already been outlined by Laffont et al. (1998) dealing with these technical issues.

As setting termination charges is a two-stage game, as shown in Figure 19.4, the parameter choices of DO j will depend on the access charge a_i of DO i. Hence in the first stage of the game the DO faces the following First Order Condition (FOC):

$$\frac{\partial \pi_i}{\partial a_i} = d_j(*) + (a_i)\frac{\partial d_j}{\partial a_i} - \frac{\partial C_i[d_j(a_i)]}{\partial a_i} = 0.$$

Defining $\varepsilon_j(a_i)$ as the elasticity of demand $d_j(*)$ with respect to the access charge a_i, that is, $\varepsilon(a_i) = \frac{\partial d_j}{\partial a_i}\frac{a_i}{d_j}$, and $C'(*) = \frac{\partial C_i[d_j(a_i)]}{\partial a_i}$ the above FOC can be rearranged to:

$$a_i = \frac{1}{1 - \frac{1}{\varepsilon_j(a_i)}} C'(*).$$

Hence, the access charge is set according to the well-known Lerner markup rule. In the second stage there also is a markup over marginal costs. As access charges are part of the marginal costs of the second stage, double marginalization will always be present in the decentralized international parcel market equilibrium. Analytically, in the second stage DOs face the following FOC:

$$\frac{\partial \pi_j}{\partial p_j} = d_j(*) + (p_j - a_i)\frac{\partial d_j}{\partial p_j} - \frac{\partial C_j}{\partial d_j}\frac{\partial d_j}{\partial p_j} = 0,$$

which can be rearranged to:

$$p_j = \frac{1}{1 - \frac{1}{\varepsilon_j(p_j)}}\left[a_i + \frac{\partial C_j}{\partial d_j}\frac{\partial d_j}{\partial p_j}\right],$$

where $\varepsilon_j(p_j)$ is the price elasticity of demand d_j. Together,

$$p_j = \frac{1}{1 - \frac{1}{\varepsilon_j(p_j)}} \left[\frac{1}{1 - \frac{1}{\varepsilon_j(a_i)}} C'(*) + \frac{\partial C_j}{\partial d_j} \frac{\partial d_j}{\partial p_j} \right],$$

which proves the claim of the general presence of double marginalization in the decentralized equilibrium in the international parcel market.

APPENDIX 19A.2 UNDERINVESTMENT IN QUALITY

Underinvestment in quality takes place if $\frac{\partial \pi_i}{\partial q_i} < \frac{\partial \overline{\pi}}{\partial \overline{q}_i}$ as a necessary condition for existence of the equilibrium implies $\frac{\partial^2 \pi_i}{\partial q_i^2} < 0$ for $i = i, j$. Taking the FOCs of Section 3 (Accounting for quality) and our assumption of the DO and its corresponding integrator having the same demand and costs structure, that is, $\overline{d}_i(*) = d_i(*)$, $\frac{\partial \overline{d}_i}{\partial \overline{p}_i} = \frac{\partial d_i}{\partial p_i}$ and $\frac{\partial \overline{d}_i}{\partial \overline{q}_i} = \frac{\partial d_i}{\partial q_i}$ for $\overline{p}_i = p_i$ and $\overline{q}_i = q_i$ $C'(\overline{q}_i) = C'(q_i)$ and $c_i = \overline{c}_i$ for $\overline{p}_i = p_i$ and $\overline{q}_i = q_i$ the condition $\frac{\partial \pi_i}{\partial q_i} < \frac{\partial \overline{\pi}}{\partial \overline{q}_i}$ can be reduced to:

$$\overline{p}_j > a_i + \overline{c}_j.$$

The first-best access charge which does not account for quality is equal to the marginal costs as derived in Section 3 (Base model). Hence, by the assumption of the symmetry of DO and integrator the underinvestment condition becomes:

$$\overline{p}_j > \overline{c}_i + \overline{c}_j.$$

This will always hold in equilibrium as this is a necessary condition for optimality, that is, $\overline{\pi}_i \geq 0$. Hence, the first-best access charge in static telecommunications market models applied to the international parcel market leads to underinvestment in quality.

20. Competition and the social cost of regulation in the postal sector

Martin Maegli[†] and Christian Jaag[‡]

1 INTRODUCTION

Increased direct and indirect competition in the postal sector represents a great challenge to the traditional business model of postal operators. It is often put forward that regulatory institutions need to evolve in parallel and coherently with developments in the marketplace in order to allow postal operators to cope with these challenges. Crew and Kleindorfer (2008) note that finding an appropriate co-evolution of regulation and market development is one of the primary challenges of postal reform. Jaag and Trinkner (2011) argue that regulatory institutions are intended to remedy market failures and reduce transaction costs. However, they also cause governance costs, including costs resulting from distorted investment and innovation, if these institutions do not respond adequately to changes in consumer preferences and technologies.

Maegli et al. (2009, 2010) develop an analytical framework for the assessment of regulatory governance and its costs in regulated industries. So far, the framework focuses on static effects. In this contribution, the approach is amended by an analysis of the impact of regulatory institutions on investment and innovation; that is, dynamic effects. The main questions of this chapter are:

1. How do regulatory institutions in the postal sector affect incentives for product and process innovation?
2. What is the way forward for these institutions in an age of increasing direct and indirect competition?

Section 2 presents the framework of regulatory governance costs. Section 3 extends it with dynamic governance costs. It then systematically discusses the effect of various institutional aspects on innovation in the postal sector, referring to practical examples, for example, the scope of the Universal Service Obligation (USO), price regulation or access regulation. The section also briefly discusses examples and effects of dynamic costs of regulatory governance in postal markets in Switzerland, Germany and the UK. Section 4 concludes.

† Head of Regulation, Swiss Post.
‡ Managing Partner, Swiss Economics and Lecturer, University of St. Galen.

2 FRAMEWORK OF REGULATORY GOVERNANCE COSTS

In line with Bauer (2005) and his definition of administrative burdens, the governance costs in a regulatory context are defined as the costs related to tasks performed to sustain competitive but fair markets, to set incentives for involved actors to provide a certain level of public service, and to coordinate public authorities involved in regulation. Governance costs are inherently present in any institutional arrangement and as such are influenced by (i) the institutional design and the alignment of competences, (ii) the choice of regulatory instruments as well as (iii) the behavior of the actors within an institutional framework.

The costs are related to tasks and transactions in regulatory regimes concerning bargaining and decision-making processes in policy making and policy enforcement, the control of institutional actors and the industry as well as the search and supply of information.

The choice of adequate or optimal regulatory tools and mechanisms is often related to specific characteristics and the market structure in a particular industry or geographical market. Knieps (2005) argues that many monopolistic bottleneck areas in dynamic sectors gradually disappear owing to rapid technological progress. Arising from the emergence of intermodal competition, it is actually possible for the original need for regulatory intervention to disappear. The regulatory interventions should be reviewed regularly. In this context Knieps (2007) explains two categories of possible regulatory failures: a 'false positive' occurs if regulators intervene in the market while competition is functioning and there is no need for intervention; a 'false negative' occurs if regulatory authorities do not intervene, when the need for regulatory intervention exists from a competition-policy point of view. Other potentially negative impacts of regulation are due to the tendency of the regulatory process to respond slowly to change. If regulated operators link the design of their business model too closely to regulatory rules, their market position may be deadlocked in the long run. Furthermore, the elimination of regulation endangers the companies' means of existence.

Today's regulatory institutions always affect future regulation. Knieps (ibid.) argues that by the time the characteristics of the current market disappear partially (or entirely) – for example, as a result of technological progress – current regulatory intervention may be obsolete. Armstrong and Sappington (2006) state in this context: 'Consequently, although liberalization should ultimately lead to reduced regulatory oversight and control, more pronounced regulatory and antitrust oversight may be required on an interim basis to ensure that regulatory policy is tailored appropriately to the evolving level of competition and that competition is protected' (p. 360). Following Knieps (1997) the process of so-called 'phasing out' of sector-specific regulation may be delayed by a regulator's self-interested behavior and his/her interest in ongoing regulation. It is fairly obvious that regulators are rarely interested in reducing their influence and cutting their own competences. Regulators have some concern for their own survival and may act in their own interests and contrary to the intentions with which they were originally established.[1]

There is a distinction between static and dynamic costs of regulation. Two types of static costs can be identified which are the consequence of the institutional design and the interaction of the actors. While direct costs affect the actors in a rather monetary and resource-based way, indirect costs affect the actors' decisions and, therefore, the outcome in the market. The subcategory of static-direct costs occurs in connection with the institutional design of the regulatory framework and the behavior of actors. In contrast, the category of static-indirect costs arises out of false incentives, resulting in an inefficient supply of goods and services. The category of the dynamic costs is the consequence of direct and indirect costs in relation to distorted innovation and investment incentives.

Direct Costs of Regulation

Regulatory interventions come at a cost. On the one hand, the relevant authorities have to be set up and furthermore given the resources that enable them to monitor markets as well as the involved actors, and consequently to implement the regulatory guidelines. This includes the creation of independent bodies which control the activities of regulatory authorities and coordinate different authorities involved in regulation (for example, competition regulators versus a sector-specific regulator) and compliance requirements. On the other hand, operators in regulated industries also face costs related to regulation. There are three different types of *direct* regulatory governance costs:

- *monitoring costs* arise because of informational asymmetries in their relationships of principals with their agents: regulators have to gather and process information which is costly;
- *compliance costs* are the costs faced by the industry in order to comply with regulatory requirements; and
- *coordination costs* result from multiple institutional actors involved in regulated industries which have to be coordinated.

Table 20.1 summarizes these three aspects of direct regulatory governance costs.

Indirect Costs of Regulation

While the objective of regulatory intervention is to improve market functioning, actions of regulators can have unintended negative outcomes as well. These outcomes may have effects on the nature of the market and the availability of products provided in the market. They may even discourage firms from entering into markets. Hence, *indirect* regulatory governance costs are the costs related to distorted *quantities and prices* as well as *capacity and technology choice*. Table 20.2 summarizes these aspects of indirect regulatory governance costs.

3 DYNAMIC COSTS OF REGULATION

In addition to static effects, regulatory institutions also affect incentives for innovation and investment. In 2005, in a report on the application of the Postal Directive to the Council and European Parliament, the European Commission (2005) stated that the directive intends to 'remove barriers to competition in the postal sector so as to boost innovation and efficiency which in turn should benefit consumers' (p. 2). OECD (1999) published a report on promoting competition in postal services and similarly states that 'introducing competition in postal services . . . has the potential to lead to important

Table 20.1 Summary: categories of static-direct governance costs

Category	Key assumption	Drivers	Components / indicators
Monitoring	Agents/actors do not implicitly share the objectives of their principals and need to be monitored	Agents' behavior Information asymmetries Accountability of agents	Annual budgets of agents Salaries and consultancy fees Staff size Number of active operators in public services
Compliance	Operators face costs when they comply with regulatory directives	Operators' behavior/strategy Relationships (formal/informal) Modalities of information exchange	Labor costs related to compliance activities Administrative overheads Adjustment to regulatory changes Consultancy fees
Coordination	There is more than one single actor involved in regulatory processes and their activities have to be coordinated	Distribution of power Institutional design Alignment of regulators Regulatory processes Interaction of sector-specific regulation	Number of institutional actors involved in regulatory processes Degree of independence of the regulator Accountability of regulators

Table 20.2 Summary: categories of static-indirect governance costs

Category	Key assumption	Drivers	Components / indicators
Quantities and prices	Actions of regulators (or policy makers) can have negative effects on the regulated industries and the consumers	Sector-specific characteristics Degree of liberalization Regulators' knowledge about the industries Regulators' economic knowledge/expertise Price regulation	Degree of competition Regulatory tools to improve competition and sustainability of public services Evolution of product prices
Capacity and technology choice	Regulation may prevent the regulated operators from aligning their supply with the effective demand and consumer needs; it also affects investment activities	Incentives to invest in infrastructure for operators Labor conditions	Market entry barriers Access regimes/bottleneck regulation

improvements in efficiency, productivity and innovation within the postal sector with consequences for overall welfare and growth' (p. 60).

The most important aspect of dynamic costs related to distorted innovation and investment incentives is regulatory risk. There are not only technological and systemic risks, but also risks and uncertainties in relation to regulation and the socio-political goals of the USO. Oxera (2004) defines regulatory risk as 'the risk that arises when the interaction of uncertainty and regulation changes the cost of financing the operations of the firm' (p. 16). Investment activities and thus the development of an efficient market are seriously constrained if these risks are borne by operators (see Jaag et al., 2011).

The important questions regarding the dynamic costs of regulation are whether adequate regulatory models and methods are implemented, if the chosen means are capable of correcting a market failure rather than result in regulatory failure and finally if the chosen means set the right incentives for investment and innovation.

Friederiszick et al. (2008) explain that innovation can generally be interpreted as a form of investment that results in new or better-quality products and services or in more cost-efficient processes. As long as the incentives and protective measures are suboptimal and do not protect investments, there is less innovation and no investment in new technologies or products and services in the sector. This has in turn the effect that the market does not develop to the desired extent.[2]

Therefore, dynamic costs are related to the degree of innovation at the level of products and processes. Concerning *product innovation*, regulation may prevent operators from introducing new products or services because of uncertainty about their investment and pricing. It may also result in a delay of time to market. Furthermore, regulation may result in suboptimal processes and keep operators from optimizing existing processes or introducing *process innovation*. Table 20.3 summarizes these aspects of dynamic regulatory governance costs.

The impact of regulatory institutions on innovation can be explained as follows. In a very simple setting, the marginal benefit of innovation equals marginal cost in the profit-maximizing equilibrium. Marginal benefit is affected by changes in quantity and optimum markup. Increased costs of innovation due to regulatory institutions decrease optimum investments in innovation. Specifically, marginal benefit with respect to product innovation consists of the larger quantity base to which the markup over marginal cost applies. This effect varies directly with the operator's markup.

As to process innovation, marginal benefit emerges from two sources: first, from higher quantity demanded of a lower optimum price. This effect is also the smaller the lower the operator's markup. However, the absolute markup is reduced. This effect is the smaller the lower the operator's quantity. Hence, increased competition which reduces quantity and markup affects innovation incentives at these margins ambiguously.

An increase in marginal production costs, which may be induced by regulation, also has two opposite effects on innovation: the absolute markup increases, which spurs product innovation and reduces process innovation; it also induces a higher optimum price and thereby decreases quantity which reduces the incentives to innovate.

There is interaction between the two dimensions of innovation: higher quantity due to product innovation also strengthens process innovation. Hence, the two kinds of innovation complement each other. Table 20.4 summarizes the effect of institutional dimensions of regulation on direct and indirect costs and subsequently dynamic costs.

Table 20.3 Summary: categories of dynamic governance costs

Category	Key assumption	Drivers	Components / indicators
Product innovation	Regulation may prevent operators from introducing new products/ services	Changing consumer needs and demand Technology change Scope of the USO Production cost structures	Degree of innovation in an industry Time to market for new products Regulatory tools to improve competition and sustainability of public services
Process Innovation	Regulation may result in suboptimal processes and prevent operators from optimizing existing processes or introducing process innovations	Regulatory risk Labor conditions Time needed for institutional change Political willingness for institutional change	Institutional changes in the regulatory frameworks and governance

Table 20.4 Institutional dimensions and regulatory governance costs

Institutional dimensions & cost drivers	Regulatory governance costs			
	Static cost		Dynamic cost	
	Direct cost	Indirect cost	Product innovation	Process innovation
Number of regulatory actors	Unclear responsibilities, necessary coordination	Might result in entry barriers for suppliers	Uncertainty reduces innovation payoff	Uncertainty reduces innovation payoff
Modalities and subject of information exchange	Information exchange and processing	Might result in entry barriers for suppliers	Delayed introduction of innovative services	Delayed introduction of process innovations
Interaction of sector-specific regulation and competition law	Concurrent jurisdiction may lead to ambiguous responsibilities	Might result in entry barriers for suppliers	Uncertainty reduces payoff	Uncertainty reduces payoff
Regulatory processes	Approval process and control leads to costs in information exchange		Approval process delays introduction of innovative services	
Stability of institutions (organizational perspective)	Reduction of direct costs	Certainty about investment payoff and cost	Certainty about innovation payoff and cost	Certainty about innovation payoff and cost
Scope of USO	Rigid requirements need strong control		Existing products cannot be abandoned	Existing processes cannot be replaced
Degree of liberalization	High information requirements and monitoring costs	Uncertainty about investment	More competitors → higher competitive pressure (lower markup) → less volume per firm	More competitors → higher competitive pressure (lower markup) → less volume per firm
Financing of the USO	Implementation and execution of compensation mechanisms	Might result in entry barriers for suppliers	Possibly reduced innovation payoff	Low attractiveness of cost-reduction programs

USO price regulation		Inefficient pricing	New product may not be attractive for firm/consumers	Cost savings from efficient processes have to be passed on to consumers
Access regime	Control and monitoring of access conditions/arbitration process in case of disagreement between operators	Affected market development and end-to-end competition		Reduced economies of scale due to bypass of upstream processes
Stability of institutions (policy perspective)		Certainty about investment payoff and cost, but time to adopt new technologies might be delayed	Certainty about innovation payoff and cost, but time to react on changing consumer needs is very long	Certainty about innovation payoff and cost, but time to react on changing consumer needs is very long
Norms and standardization requirements	Approval process and control mechanisms in order to be compliant	Foster interoperability but might appear as market entry barriers		Increased cost of process innovation due to necessary compliance
Labor conditions	Negotiations with unions and control of labor conditions	Distorted wage rates		Innovation may result in capital replacing labor; innovation is itself capital intensive

In the following, examples of dynamic costs of regulatory governance and its effects on product and process innovation in the postal sector in Switzerland, Germany and the UK are discussed. In general, the costs occur as a consequence of static costs and in combination with unclear regulatory ruling ending in juridical proceedings, with too rigid regulatory regimes that hinder the development of markets or with unforeseen consequences of regulation.

Dynamic Effects on Product Innovation

A first category of dynamic effects on product innovation is related to the USO. Although the stability of institutions has a positive effect on investment security, the influence of the USO on product innovations is rather negative. This is the case if legal stipulations on the USO cannot be adjusted quickly enough per changes in the market. Excessively rigid definitions of the USO prevent the further development of products.

The example of the Swiss postal market shows that the connection of stable institutions can have both positive and negative effects. In effect today is a postal act that was originally enforced in 1997 and later adapted in 2003 and 2009. As early as autumn 2002, the parliament discussed the full opening of the letter market and decided to adopt it stepwise. The emergence of the new Postal Services Act in the UK also took several years. The bases for the adjustments in the regulatory regime were missing, and due to rigid price regulation, together with the access regime and the requirements in the USO, the incumbent got more and more into trouble.

The USO in the postal sector traditionally includes an obligation to deliver nationwide at least five days per week. There have been various attempts at reducing the cost associated with this obligation. Examples include delivery to centralized post office boxes in remote regions instead of doorstep delivery, reduced delivery frequency in remote areas, outsourcing of rural deliveries to partner firms with more flexible labor cost, or differentiated pricing (zonal pricing) to reflect differences in delivery cost across regions.

The most important hindrance for the introduction of such relaxations to the USO is a lack of consumer consent. However, from a technology point of view, in many places, giving away free e-readers would cost considerably less than printing and delivering postal items. Hence, the USO could be adjusted so that convenient alternative forms of delivery means may be chosen as alternatives to physical delivery. The commercial viability of such a service depends on the regulatory possibility of substituting physical delivery processes, which itself depends on the formulation of the USO. Hence, innovative processes and products may only display their full potential in an accordingly formulated or adjusted regulatory regime.

Price control has a decisive influence on product innovation. In some countries, price regulation is part of the USO. In others, there is additional regulation due to presumed market dominance of the incumbent postal operator.[3] Long-lasting approval processes increase the time to market. Moreover, timely reactions to changes in a quickly altering environment, for example, due to intermodal competition and declining volumes, are impossible (see Kleindorfer and Szirmay, 2009). Innovative price models are therefore prevented by extensive price regulation. This used to be the case in the UK. In the former regulatory framework, 80 percent of the turnover of Royal Mail was under price control.

As a consequence, the regulatory authority became rather a product manager – but with limited knowledge regarding cost and market development.

A third category of dynamic effects on product innovation is related to labor conditions. The lengthy debates and the legal disputes concerning the introduction of a minimum wage in the German postal market has hindered the development of competition and therefore had a negative effect on investment incentives there.[4] The legal uncertainty and the introduction of a minimum wage was followed by a wave of bankruptcies. During the first quarter of 2008, the PIN Group let go 7,000 employees. Between 2007 and 2009, a total of approximately 19,000 jobs disappeared, about 17,000 of which were in 2008 alone. It is clear that the economic downturn during this period also played a part in these figures. While TNT did not pay a minimum wage, it had to make provisions for the case that the minimum wage should be fixed after all. During a period of legal uncertainty of more than two years, TNT could invest less in the development of networks and the end-to-end process. As a consequence more effort was expended in the cost reduction in existing processes than in developing new products. The example shows how the length of the procedure leads to high costs for the industry and to regulatory uncertainty.

Dynamic Effects on Process Innovation

The regulatory costs regarding process innovations can be illustrated using the example of the letter market in the UK. Since the market was opened, almost no innovation has taken place. Competition concentrates on prices in the upstream range, and there is no product innovation.

Hence, the de facto regulation of downstream access had various effects. First, it prohibited the development of competing delivery networks. It also created regulatory risk for all involved operators because their business models very much depended on the terms of network access. This translated into investment risk, which deterred investments in innovation and infrastructures. Concerning the development of end-to-end competition in the UK, the Hooper Report (2008) concluded that there was uncertainty about the future development of the market, which made it difficult for operators to assess the likely return on the investment. The consequences of falling volumes, developments in new technologies, and regulation at the end of current price control were difficult to predict. Furthermore, some operators claimed that any investment in an end-to-end delivery network would be threatened by the ability of Royal Mail to hamper competition in the future.

As a consequence, only a small amount of investment was made and innovation incentives were low. In Germany, the access conditions are monitored *ex post*. Consequently, the market development also differed from that of the UK. Both the competitors and the incumbent became innovative at all levels of the postal value chain. Smaller providers have looked for innovative solutions in order to realize a wider area delivery. Hindrances in the development of competition were due not to the definition of access conditions, but to uncertainties in connection with the discussion of minimum wages, as discussed above.

4 CONCLUSION

Various reports provided by the European Commission and the OECD state that one of the original goals of the implementation of the European Postal directives was to remove barriers to competition and to foster innovation in the postal sector. Have the goals been achieved and does current regulation actually support more innovation in the sector?

There is hardly any discussion either in practice or in academia about the impact of regulatory institutions on innovation in the postal sector. In order to fill this gap, this contribution introduced the concept of dynamic costs of regulatory governance, which are a consequence of direct and indirect costs. They result in distorted innovation and investment due to adverse incentives and uncertainty.

The main drivers of the dynamic governance costs are the scope of the universal service, price regulation and approval mechanisms, access regimes and labor conditions, and certainly the stability of institutions itself. In order to allow postal operators to cope with challenges, regulatory institutions need to evolve steadily, concurrently with developments in the marketplace.

NOTES

1. Actors react differently to external threats, constraints and opportunities because they differ in their intrinsic perceptions and preferences but also because these are shaped by the specific institutional setting within which they interact (Scharpf, 1997, p. 37). Crozier (1964) interprets such behavior as 'the active tendency of human agent to take advantage, in any circumstances, of all available means to further his own privileges' (p. 194).
2. Armstrong and Sappington (2006) give a detailed overview on the role of innovation in regulated industries in general, while Dietl et al. (2008) concentrate on innovation incentives for postal operators in particular.
3. The discrepancy of antitrust regulation and competition is increasing in the postal sector where incumbents are often still considered dominant in mail even though they continue to lose market share to alternative means of communication.
4. Dieke and Wojtek (2008) as well as Heitzler and Wey (2010) analyze the impact of the minimum wage discussion in the German postal market in more detail.

REFERENCES

Armstrong, M. and D.E.M. Sappington (2006), 'Regulation, competition and liberalization', *Journal of Economic Literature*, **44** (2): 325–66.

Bauer, M.W. (2005), 'Administrative costs of reforming utilities', in D. Coen and A. Héritier (eds), *Refining Regulatory Regimes: Utilities in Europe*, Cheltenham, UK and Northampton, MA, USA: Edward Elgar.

Crew, M.A. and P.R. Kleindorfer (2008), 'Pricing for postal access and worksharing', in Crew, Kleindorfer and J.I. Campbell (eds), *Handbook of Worldwide Postal Reform*, Cheltenham, UK and Northampton, MA, USA: Edward Elgar, pp. 32–66.

Crozier, M. (1964), *The Bureaucratic Phenomenon*, Chicago, IL: University of Chicago Press.

Dieke, A. and R. Wojtek (2008), 'Competition, wages and politics in the delivery sector: the case of minimum wages in Germany', in M.A. Crew, P.R. Kleindorfer and J.I. Campbell (eds), *Handbook of Worldwide Postal Reform*, Cheltenham, UK and Northampton, MA, USA: Edward Elgar.

Dietl, H., A. Grütter and M. Lutzenberger (2008), 'Deregulation of letter markets and its impact on process and product innovation', *Review of Network Economics*, **7** (2): 231–46.

European Commission (2005), 'Report from the Commission to the Council and the European Parliament on the Application of the Postal Directive', European Commisson, Brussels.

Friederiszick, H., M. Grajek and L.-H. Röller (2008), 'Analyzing the Relationship Between Regulation and Investment in the Telecom Sector', White Paper WP-108-01, ESMT European School of Management and Technology, Berlin.

Heitzler, S. and C. Wey (2010), 'Raising rivals' fixed (labor) costs: the Deutsche Post case', DIW Discussion Paper 1008, DIW, Berlin.

Hooper, R., D.D. Hutton and I.R. Smith (Hooper Report) (2008), *Modernise or Decline: Policies to Maintain the Universal Postal Service in the United Kingdom*, Norwich: TSO.

Jaag, C., B. Stroelin and F. Stahl (2011), 'Commercial and regulatory aspects of reverse hybrid mail', Swiss Economics Working Paper 30, Swiss Economics, Zurich.

Jaag, C. and U. Trinkner (2011), 'A general framework for regulation and liberalization in network industries', in M. Finger and R. Künneke (eds), *International Handbook for the Liberalization of Infrastructures*, Cheltenham, UK and Northampton, MA, USA: Edward Elgar.

Kleindorfer, P.R. and Z. Szirmay (2009), 'Pricing practice in the postal industry: current approaches and challenges under liberalization', Research Paper, INSEAD & Roland Berger.

Knieps, G. (1997), 'Ansätze für eine "schlanke" Regulierungsbehörde für Post und Telekommunikation in Deutschland', *Ordo*, **48**: 253–68.

Knieps, G. (2005), *Wettbewerbsökonomie: Regulierungstheorie, Industrieökonomie, Wettbewerbspolitik*, Berlin: Springer.

Knieps, G. (2007), *Netzökonomie*, Wiesbaden: Gabler.

Maegli, M., C. Jaag and M. Finger (2009), 'Coûts de la régulation des industries de réseaux: enseignements du réseau postal', *Revue d'économie industrielle*, **127** (3): 47–68.

Maegli, M., C. Jaag and M. Finger (2010), 'Regulatory governance costs in network industries: observations in postal regulation', *Competition and Regulation in Network Industries*, **11** (2): 207–37.

OECD (1999), 'Report from the Committee on Competition Law and Policy, Directorate for Financial, Fiscal and Enterprise Affairs', Organization for Economic Cooperation and Development, OECD, Paris.

Oxera (2004), 'Costs and Benefits of Market Regulators', Study for the Dutch Ministry of Economic Affairs, Oxford.

Scharpf, F.W. (1997), *Games Real Actors Play: Actor-Centered Institutionalism in Policy Research*, Boulder, CO: Westview Press.

21. Measuring the environmental benefit of reducing the United States Postal Service's operations*

Norma B. Nieto[†] **and Adam C. Houck**[‡]

1 INTRODUCTION

The United States Postal Service (USPS) has seen mail volumes collapse in recent years, and current forecasts show that the erosion of mail volumes is expected to continue into the future. Mail volumes declined by more than 9 billion pieces in PFY2010, and then further declined by 1.7 percent in PFY2011. Total mail volume in PFY2011 was 168 billion pieces, a figure not seen since 1992 when total mail volume was 166 billion pieces. As a result, USPS has embarked on unprecedented cost-cutting measures, and plans additional cuts to eliminate $20 billion in costs by PFY2015 to return USPS to a positive net income in PFY2013.

To date, much of the public discourse has centered on the financial benefit of reducing the size of USPS's operations. While clear financial benefits exist from consolidating processing operations, retail locations, and the associated transportation, little attention has yet been paid to the environmental benefits realized from reducing the size of USPS operations. So little attention has been paid that in fact, USPS published an advance notice on September 20, 2011 to solicit comments on the Mail Processing Network Rationalization Initiative; at the end of the public comment period on October 21, 2011 not one of the over 4,200 comments received related to the environmental benefit from reducing the size of USPS operations.

This may be somewhat surprising given the negative perception of mail as a major contributor to climate change that is promoted by environmentalists. A recent study by Pitney Bowes (Koljonen, 2008) revealed that mail accounts for 2 percent of total landfill waste, which while not trivial, is perhaps not as significant as the general public may perceive it to be. Comprising paper production, mail creation, collection, transportation, delivery, and disposal, the distribution of letter mail by posts generates, on average, 20 grams of carbon dioxide (CO_2) per letter delivered, compared to an average refrigerator's 127 kg per year, equivalent to receiving 17 years of mail at 300 letters per year.

Despite the potential overestimation of the negative impacts of mail on the environment, there is no doubt that there are opportunities to further reduce mail-related emissions by aligning more efficiently the size and scope of USPS operations to decreased

† Managing Consultant, IBM Global Business Services.
‡ Managing Consultant, IBM Global Business Services.

demand for postal services. The purpose of this chapter is to quantify the environmental benefits associated with reducing the size of USPS operations from their current state to the levels being proposed by USPS. This includes reducing the current complement of USPS processing centers to the numbers currently proposed by both the USPS in its plans submitted to Congress, the Postal Regulatory Commission (PRC) and USPS's Mail Processing Network Rationalization Initiative (Postal Service Office of Sustainability, 2012). Section 2 defines the baseline and the changes included as part of the proposed reductions that will be analyzed in the chapter. Section 3 presents a review of the recent literature and analysis related to the environmental impacts of postal activities. Section 4 introduces the metrics and methodologies used to measure the change in environmental impacts from the proposed reduction in postal operations. Section 5 presents the results of the analysis and conclusions are presented in Section 6.

2 DEFINING THE SCOPE OF THE CHANGES

The analysis will examine the net environmental benefits from reducing the size of USPS operations including mail processing network changes, transportation network changes, retail facility changes, and an examination of moving to five-day delivery. The first step is defining the baseline and future states for all scenarios.

Mail Processing Network Changes

The current complement of mail processing facilities is extremely heterogeneous. For example, processing and distribution centers (P&DCs) sort and distribute both incoming and outgoing mail to the distribution network and local delivery units and post offices. Surface transfer centers (STCs) run a hub-and-spoke operation at strategic geographical locations across the US to increase the utilization of surface transportation, especially for longer haul trips. In all, 487 facilities comprise the existing mail processing network and serves as the baseline for the analysis (Table 21.1).

The net environmental benefit will be examined for the consolidation currently being debated in the public discourse on USPS Network Optimization: the USPS Mail Processing Network Rationalization Initiative. In this scenario, USPS proposed a mail processing center network that would ultimately reduce the number of facilities needed to handle reduced mail volumes. This proposal would decrease or discontinue processing operations at approximately 250 processing facilities, increase and consolidate mail processing operations at approximately 160 processing facilities, and implement revised processing operations at approximately 40 additional processing facilities. The net effect would be a mail processing network of 200 facilities operating in an environment of reduced service standards for First Class Mail (FCM) and Periodicals deliveries within the contiguous United States, and revised business rules for other classes of mail.

Changing the size and composition of the mail processing network has a corresponding impact on the transportation of mail. In its testimony to Congress, USPS presented the results from its analyses to determine the net overall transportation reductions from the optimization effort. By examining large samples of plant-to-plant trips from each

Table 21.1 USPS processing facilities in PFY2011

Processing facilities	Number of facilities
Processing and distribution centers	255
Customer service facilities	137
Network distribution centers	21
Logistics and distribution centers	10
Annexes	46
Surface transfer centers	10
Other	8
Total processing facilities	487

Source: USPS (2012a).

of USPS's eight areas then extrapolating to a nationwide impact, USPS showed an opportunity to reduce annual plant-to-plant transportation by 101,148,250 miles, or 25.4 percent (Martin, 2011). Employing the same approach on processing plant to local post office transportation showed that an estimated 66,183,241 miles or 13.68 percent could be eliminated annually (ibid.). Tempering this overall reduction with the corresponding need to fly more mail to meet service, USPS calculated that an additional 124 million pounds of mail would be diverted from surface to air transportation annually (ibid.). USPS's analysis assumes it will not need to procure any additional flights from its air transportation suppliers, and can meet this increased demand by better cube utilization and procuring additional capacity on existing flights.

Retail Facility Network Changes

The Postal Service manages a network of nearly 36,000 retail facilities across the United States. This legacy network reflects a population distribution more closely mirroring early twentieth-century America than today (Cohen et al., 2006, 2008). The current retail network, excluding the 3,694 contractor-operated retail facilities, comprises 27,077 post offices and 4,794 subordinate stations and branches, and will serve as the baseline.

If USPS were to design a retail network from scratch today it would look very different from the current distribution of facilities and the services they provide. As Adra and Sheehy (2011) articulate, the network's inability to evolve with key demographic changes over the past century has left it with prevalent geographical coverage in sparsely populated rural areas.

The process by which USPS can optimize its retail network has myriad potential approaches. One approach is to align the consumer demand for retail services and the supply of retail facilities across the US by theoretically repositioning its retail locations to maximize postal revenue (Yezer, 2010). Another approach is to optimize the network based on customer access to the postal retail facilities, with population density as a key driver (Klingenberg, 2011; Waters, 2011). Most recently proposed is an approach that optimizes postal revenue against socioeconomic population factors, essentially combining the supplier and customer access optimization approaches (Klingenberg et al., chapter 9 this volume).

While none of these approaches has specified the optimal location and number of facilities required to meet the future demand for retail services, in July 2011 USPS initially proposed that 3,700 retail offices would be studied for potential closure. However, USPS offered a revised plan in May 2012 to reduce operational hours at approximately 13,000 offices instead of closing any post offices completely. In the new proposal, approximately 10 percent of the impacted post offices will have their hours reduced by between 75 and 66 percent, 54 percent will have their hours reduced by 50 percent, 32 percent will have their hours reduced by 25 percent, and less than 1 percent will absorb additional hours. This analysis examines the environmental impact of both approaches.

Five-day Delivery

A key operational change currently being debated involves eliminating Saturday delivery. The five-day delivery scenario involves eliminating the collection of mail on Saturdays and eliminating regular Saturday mail delivery to street addresses. Post offices would remain open six days per week, PO Box delivery would occur six days per week, and Express Mail would continue to be collected from dedicated Express Mail boxes on Saturday and delivered 365 days per year. USPS estimates that these measures will save the organization $3.1 billion per year in operating expenses.

This analysis assumes the current complement of processing facilities and retail locations along with the corresponding current transportation network as the baseline. In the five-day scenario, regular Saturday mail collection and delivery is eliminated, resulting in reduced delivery vehicle trips. On the facility side, it is assumed that there will be reduced delivery operations at post offices, but since the retail component of post offices will remain open on Saturdays, only 50 percent of the operations of a post office on Saturdays can be eliminated.

3 CURRENT USPS SUSTAINABILITY EFFORTS AND ENVIRONMENTAL RESEARCH

USPS has made progress in addressing sustainability, working to instill a 'culture of conservation' (USPS, 2012b). It has set clear goals for success including reducing facility energy usage by 30 percent from PFY2006 to PFY2015, reducing USPS vehicle petroleum fuel use by 20 percent by PFY2015, reducing contract vehicle petroleum fuel use by 20 percent by PFY2020, increasing USPS alternative fuel vehicle use by 10 percent by PFY2015, and reducing greenhouse gas (GHG) emissions by 20 percent by PFY2020, using PFY2008 as the baseline.

Formal research on USPS's environmental impacts is somewhat limited. A 2010 study examined the total environmental footprint of mail, concentrating on characterizing waste, pollutant emissions, and energy consumption 'caused by the four major mail products by conducting a comprehensive life cycle inventory (LCI) analysis of them' (Buc et al., 2010). In total, the analysis accounted for 98.6 percent of total mail volume in PFY2006 and examined the preparation, transportation, handling, delivery, and the major materials that encompass First Class, Standard, Periodicals, and Package Services and allocated shares of emissions and usage by weight, by volume, and by cube. Buc et al. employed published data from government sources and other literature, and utilized Environmental Protection Agency (EPA) methods and data for consistency and repeatability of results over time.

Waste and emissions vary greatly by mail class, due to the significant weight differences among mail products. The significant amount of raw paper materials involved in generating a periodical mail piece causes 'substantially higher unit facility energy consumption, solid waste generation, and hydrocarbon emissions for periodicals than one would otherwise expect, based upon weight and density alone' (Buc et al., 2010, p. 331). The Buc et al. approach is an important step in continuing to ascertain the quantitative impacts of mail piece generation, transportation, delivery, and disposal, and provides a new lens for considering policy implications of product and pricing strategies. The challenge facing any researcher is first defining the boundaries of the overall ecosystem to analyze, as per Buc et al. While not directly used in this analysis, these results present a worthy topic for future exploration; to assess how the environmental impacts from the reduced network estimated in this chapter would change the lifecycle-based results for various classes of mail.

More directly related, USPS published a Programmatic Environmental Assessment (PEA), a nationwide look to examine the options USPS has in making changes to its mail processing network and transportation and associated economic and environmental impacts against a no action alternative. The PEA focuses only on USPS's actions associated with the current Mail Processing Rationalization Initiative; it does not examine the disposition of processing facilities that will be closed as part of the initiative, the resulting impacts of the Retail Rationalization Initiative, or the elimination of Saturday delivery. As articulated in the USPS Mail Processing Network Rationalization Initiative, the PEA focused on the impacts from closing 250 facilities, increasing and consolidating mail processing operations at approximately 160 processing facilities, and implementing revised processing operations at approximately 40 additional processing facilities. USPS anticipates no major modifications to the remaining processing facilities. Minor modifications to 'gaining' facilities will be required, and will mostly involve internal changes such as removing interior structural walls and accommodating new mail processing equipment.[1] The PEA also analyzed the impacts of network transportation changes that result in decreases in surface transportation without significant increases to air transportation (Martin, 2011).

Beyond the impact to USPS operations, the PEA also estimates other impacts to consolidating operations. Reducing the complement of facilities would have an impact on the estimated $11.8 billion in direct labor economic benefit that USPS processing facilities provide nationally. The PEA states that additional economic and environmental benefits would also result from reductions in water treatment and recycling to facility utilities and equipment maintenance. It also concludes that due to facility consolidations, overall USPS-associated privately owned vehicle (POV) usage would decline and result in a net reduction in traffic and potentially a larger share of USPS employees opting for public transportation as many of the 'gaining' facilities would be located in urban areas.

This analysis uses several key inputs from the Mail Processing Rationalization Initiative. First, the proposed list of facility closures to create the first network rationalization scenario; in addition, the analysis uses the results of the network transportation change analysis. This analysis incorporates the results of the PEA estimate of the impact on GHGs of those transportation changes, and applies the same methodology to estimate the impacts of transportation reductions resulting from moving from six-day to five-day delivery for both non-local and local transportation.

4 METHODOLOGY AND ENVIRONMENTAL METRICS EMPLOYED

The principal GHGs which USPS reports and which will be included in the analysis are CO_2, methane, nitrous oxide, and fluorinated gases, which include hydro-fluorocarbons, perfluorocarbons, and sulfur hexafluoride. The non-CO_2 gases are commonly reported as though they were equivalent to a given volume of CO_2. This metric is called the carbon dioxide equivalent (CO_2e) and is the metric used to estimate the impacts of the scenarios in this chapter.

In USPS's Climate Registry 2010 Entity Emissions Detailed Report (CRIS, 2010), the organization published its Direct and Indirect GHG CO_2e emissions at an individual state level. Direct (Scope 1) emissions are GHG emissions from sources that are owned or controlled by USPS, such as fossil fuels burned at a USPS plant, and emissions from USPS-owned vehicles. Indirect (Scope 2) emissions are GHG emissions resulting primarily from the generation of electricity generated offsite but purchased by USPS. The Direct and Indirect emissions data is published for total facility-related emissions and total USPS vehicle-related emissions for each state. This analysis will assess the impacts of changes for both Scope 1 and Scope 2 emissions.

In its Annual Sustainability Report, USPS (2012b) also reports Scope 3 emissions, which it defines as including purchased transportation contract vehicle fuel use, employee travel, contract waste disposal, and transmission and distribution losses from electricity purchases. The PEA assessed the impact of network rationalization on employee-related commuting travel from POVs; however, this analysis considers only the impacts on Scope 3 emissions related to purchased transportation contract vehicle fuel use, which represents approximately 40 percent of USPS's total GHG emissions inventory.

Table 21.2 presents the figures used as USPS's 2010 GHG emissions baseline data.[2]

Table 21.2 USPS 2010 baseline GHG emissions data

USPS 2010 baseline emissions	CO_2e (metric tons)
Scope 1 emissions	1,718,393
Scope 2 emissions	2,989,746
Scope 3 emissions	7,520,000
Total GHG emissions[1]	12,228,139
Scope 3 Purchased transportation related[2]	4,917,948

Notes:

1. Does not include biogenic emissions.
2. Estimated using USPS's 2011 Annual Sustainability Report Total Contract Transportation Fuel Use of 553.2 million Gasoline Gallon Equivalents converted to CO_2e using EPA's GHG equivalencies calculator.

Sources: CRIS (2010); USPS (2012b).

Estimating the Impacts of Facility Consolidation

A facility generates both Direct (Scope 1) and Indirect (Scope 2) emissions from its operations. The main driver of both Scope 1 and Scope 2 emissions for facilities is electrical consumption. For example, one-thousand kilowatt hours of electricity generates 0.69 metric tons of CO_2e. Testimony from Bratta (2011) before the PRC regarding the impacts of network consolidation on facilities states that the main driver of electricity consumption in processing facilities is the heating, ventilation and air conditioning (HVAC) system. He also testifies that mail processing equipment accounts for only a small portion of the total utility consumption within a facility. Thus, the analysis assumes that the two main factors that impact the amount of emissions generated by a postal facility are the hours that the facility is operational, and the square footage of the facility, since the HVAC system needs are likely to increase as facilities get larger. A secondary factor would be the type of facility, since there is likely to be greater electricity consumption in a facility that has mail processing equipment than in one that does not, even if that difference is small. The location of the facility is also a secondary factor impacting GHG emissions, since the local climate will impact the amount of HVAC required.

The proposed USPS Mail Processing Network Rationalization Initiative consists of closing facilities and consolidating their operations into existing facilities. Facilities 'gaining' the operations of the consolidated facilities have sufficient excess capacity to absorb the volume and the transferred mail processing equipment from other facilities without significant facility expansion that would result in additional square feet (Bratta, 2011). USPS concludes that the potential increases in power generated by both running the mail processing equipment for potentially longer periods of time and increasing the amount of mail processing equipment is offset by the elimination of 50 percent of the mail processing equipment and the efficiencies gained from better utilization of the equipment. In addition, since the majority of the emissions are driven by the building itself rather than the equipment, the analysis assumes that all of the Scope 1 and Scope 2 GHG emissions associated with a closing facility are eliminated. This approach does not consider the disposition of the closing facilities. As the analysis is estimating the impact of the network rationalization on USPS's own GHG emissions, it is understood that if the facilities are eventually used for other purposes, some GHG emissions would remain. Thus, the approach to estimating facility closure-related impacts on GHG emissions is to calculate the GHG emissions associated with the facilities proposed to be closed and subtract them from the baseline total GHG emissions.

The process of calculating the GHG emissions for each USPS facility is no easy task, given the lack of publicly available data on emissions. One approach is to simply divide total USPS facility-related GHG emissions by the number of facilities in the United States to calculate the average GHG emissions per facility, and then multiply that by the total number of facilities proposed to be closed to obtain the total GHG emissions for closing facilities. However, this approach does not take into account the heterogeneous nature of the USPS facility network – a 100,000 square foot P&DC in California will have very different GHG emissions from a 1,000 square foot post office in Alaska. Thus, the methodology is to assign GHG emissions to each facility based on the following four factors: facility size (square feet), hours of operation (weekly hours), type (processing facility or not), and location (State).

The first step in assigning GHG emissions to each individual facility was to construct a database containing the four factors above for all 487 processing facilities and approximately 32,000 post offices.[3] When data were not available, the average for that facility type was used. The output of this step was square feet, weekly operating hours, facility type, and location for every USPS facility in the United States. The second step was to calculate a CO_2e factor that could be used to assign relative proportions of CO_2e to facilities within a state. The CO_2e factor reflected the relevant facility characteristics of size, operational hours, and whether the facility had mail processing equipment (MPE). This factor was calculated as follows:

$$CO_2e\ Factor = Facility\ Square\ Feet \times Weekly\ Hours \times MPE\ Adjustment.$$

For non-processing facilities such as post offices, the MPE Adjustment value is equal to 1. For processing facilities such as network distribution centers (NDCs), P&DCs, and vehicle maintenance facilities (VMFs) an MPE adjustment value of 1.15 is assigned, reflecting Bratta's testimony that mail processing equipment contributes only a small portion of the overall electricity consumption of a facility, although he did not specify what that specific portion is. For customer service mail processing centers (CSMPCs), which perform acceptance activities for commercial mailers and represent a significant number of the proposed facility closures, an MPE adjustment factor of 1.05 was used to reflect that the mail processing is less extensive than that which occurs at other processing facilities, but is still higher than what would occur at a post office.

The next step in estimating GHG emissions for each facility is to allocate the state-level USPS-reported CO_2e Scope 1 and Scope 2 emissions across all the facilities in a particular state. The CO_2e factors were summed for all the facilities in the state to get a total, and the percentage for each facility relative to the state total was calculated. This percentage was then applied to the CO_2e emissions for the state to calculate each facility's GHG emissions. The equation is:

$$CO_2e_f = CO_2e\ Factor_f / \Sigma_s CO_2e\ Factor_{fs} \times CO_2e_s,$$

where f = facility and s = state. As an illustration, the reported 2010 Scope 1 CO_2e emissions for the State of Alaska were 3,471 metric tons. Of the 184 facilities in Alaska, the majority are post offices, with the exception of one P&DC, one air mail facility (AMF), one VMF, and three CSMPCs. Based on CO_2e factors, the Anchorage P&DC, which has over 131,000 square feet and is presumed to be operational 24 hours a day, seven days per week, accounts for over 45 percent of USPS's Alaska CO_2e, while each post office, with a range of 4,000 to 15,000 square feet and are only open during normal business hours, primarily account for 0.05–0.24 percent of the Alaska CO_2e factor each.

The final step in estimating the impact of facility closures depends upon the scenario and component estimated. For the USPS Mail Processing Network Rationalization scenario, the estimated GHG emissions of each processing facility identified as approved for consolidation are subtracted from the baseline.

For the retail facility closures scenario, the estimated GHG emissions of the approximately 3,700 facilities that USPS has identified as being under study are subtracted from the baseline estimated for all post offices. For the retail reduction in hours scenario, the

GHG emissions are estimated as proportional with the proposed reduction in operational hours for each of the impacted post offices. For example, if an office reduces its operational hours by 25 percent, it receives a corresponding reduction in GHG emissions of 25 percent. Results of the analysis are presented in Section 5.

Estimating the Impacts of Network and Local Transportation Changes from Network Consolidation

As previously described, USPS estimates that network consolidation will result in a reduction in annual transportation of 167,331,435 miles. The PEA calculated the nationwide decrease in GHG emissions based on USPS's mileage decrease estimates and the emission factor from the EPA's MOBILE 6.2 model for truck trailer vehicle types.

Reducing the number of facilities while maintaining service standards will require an increase in the volume of mail that must travel by air rather than by surface transportation. USPS estimates that 124 million pounds of mail would be diverted from surface to air transportation annually but assumes it will not need to procure any additional flights from its air transportation suppliers, and can meet this increased demand by better cube utilization and procuring additional capacity on existing flights (Martin, 2011). USPS concludes that the air transportation changes are not expected to increase GHG emissions primarily because of the excess capacity available on the current commercial air and cargo carriers (UPS, FedEx) which currently carry USPS's volumes, thus not requiring additional flights. Although the additional weight of mail has the potential to increase GHG emissions for these existing flights, the majority of GHG emissions for air transportation occur during takeoff and landing. Since no new flights are being added, USPS's PEA has concluded that the additional GHG emissions from the increased volume on air are negligible.

While the conclusion that additional flights will not be needed may be an overly optimistic assumption by USPS, re-analyzing the potential for increased flights is outside the scope of this analysis. Thus, this analysis takes USPS's transportation reduction methodologies and outputs and the PEA's estimate of the environmental impacts of those as given.

Estimating the Impacts of Moving to Five-day Delivery

There are two sources of potential environmental impacts from eliminating Saturday delivery – the changes in facility operations from eliminating the need for delivery operations at the local post office and the reduction in the transportation required to deliver mail to individual businesses and households.

In USPS facilities, retail and delivery operations are often co-located. Since post offices will remain open on Saturdays, it is anticipated that the potential impact of not needing to have the delivery portion of the post office open for the lighter-volume Saturday will be relatively minimal on an individual facility-basis from an environmental standpoint. However, given the large number of post offices in the United States, even a marginal decrease in operational hours for each facility has the potential to have a significant effect on the overall GHG emissions of USPS. In order to estimate this impact, the potential decrease in operational hours associated with no delivery on Saturdays is estimated first.

Most post offices are open for only a half-day on Saturdays, so it is assumed that there are four operational hours on that day. The analysis then adjusts that by 50 percent to account for the space that is retail rather than delivery for a possible reduction in operational hours of two hours per week. For the post offices not slated for closure, the operational hour reduction of two hours per week is divided by the total weekly hours the post office is operational (usually 44) to calculate the percentage reduction due to the elimination of Saturday delivery, and apply it to the GHG emissions for that specific post office to calculate the overall impact. The calculation is:

$$\Delta CO_2e_{6\text{-}5} = Reduced\ Hours\ per\ Week_f\ /\ Total\ Hours\ per\ Week_f \times CO_2e_f,$$

where f = facility. Results are presented in Section 5.

The primary impact of eliminating Saturday delivery is the reduction in transportation which includes the elimination of vehicle trips from delivery units to individual businesses and residential delivery points. Grossman (2010) estimates that there will be a 42 percent reduction in Saturday miles for vehicle service driver (VSD) transportation, which is the USPS-operated delivery fleet. This is not eliminated completely because USPS will still deliver to post office boxes and will deliver Express Mail to individual addresses. The elimination of Saturday delivery also reduces transportation across the entire network. Grossman explains that the Postal Service typically uses contracted transportation for overnight and two-day volume between clusters within the same area and between P&DCs within the same cluster. In an environment without outgoing processing for Saturday collection mail, Grossman states that this volume will not require transportation Saturday evening and Sunday morning, and estimates that the Postal Service can reduce Saturday transportation by approximately 30 percent and Sunday transportation by approximately 80 percent. He provides similar estimates for the amount of transportation reduction associated with each type of transportation. Bradley estimates the actual reduction in miles, which is used to estimate the change in GHG emissions due to transportation-related reductions.

The first step is assigning a vehicle type for each type of transportation with mileage reductions. With the exception of intra-CSD (customer service direct) and VSD transportation, which are highly localized delivery to individual addresses, the vehicle type of truck-trailer is assigned to all types of transportation, which is consistent with the assumptions by USPS and in the PEA. For intra-CSD and VSD, which can range from personal vehicles to a small delivery truck, a vehicle type of Light-Duty Gasoline Trucks 1 (LDGT1) is assigned based on average weight for USPS delivery vehicles of 3,000lbs. For non-intra CSD and VSD transportation, the impact on GHG emissions resulting in the reduction of miles is estimated using the same ratios of reduction in miles by transportation to GHG emissions from the USPS Mail Processing Network Rationalization Initiative analysis for the transportation impacts from network consolidation in the PEA. Due to the complexity and requirements for non-publicly available date of the EPA's Mobile 6 model which was used by the PEA to estimate transportation impacts, a publicly available GHG emissions calculator was used to estimate the impacts of the reduction in miles from intra-CSD and VSD transportation which is based on vehicle type, weight, and miles to estimate CO_2e. The results are presented in Section 5.

5 RESULTS

Facility-related Environmental Impacts of Network Consolidation

The reduction in GHG emissions arises from proposed closure of facilities and all associated activities. Table 21.3 summarizes the results. The Scope 1 and Scope 2 CO_2e emissions presented in the table for the baseline facilities row reflect the total for all USPS facility-related GHG emissions regardless of the type. Although nearly 60 percent of processing facilities are proposed to be closed in this scenario, the overall impact on facility-related GHG emissions is much less for several reasons. First, the facilities proposed to be closed are in general much smaller than the facilities proposed to remain open, and second, is that processing facilities do not cause significantly more electricity consumption than non-processing facilities. However, there is still a material impact of a reduction of 15.4 percent on the Postal Service's GHG emissions, for a total reduction of 519,349 tons of CO_2e. This reduction is equivalent to the emissions generated by 92,381 passenger vehicles.

Impacts of Retail Facility Network Changes

The reduction in GHG emissions (CO_2e) associated with the previously proposed potential closure of the 3,700 post offices under study by USPS were estimated and compared with USPS's newly proposed reduction in hours at approximately 13,000 post offices. Table 21.4 summarizes the results. The Scope 1 and Scope 2 CO_2e emissions presented

Table 21.3 Facility-related impacts of mail processing network consolidation

Mail Processing Network Consolidation Initiative scenario	Processing facilities	Scope 1 CO_2e emissions	Scope 2 CO_2e emissions	Total CO_2e
Baseline facilities	487	372,086	2,989,746	3,361,832
Reductions due to network consolidation	287	57,968	461,381	519,349
As a percentage of baseline	58.9	15.6	15.4	15.4

Table 21.4 Impacts of retail facility network changes

Retail Network Reduction scenarios	Impacted facilities	Scope 1 CO_2e emissions	Scope 2 CO_2e emissions	Total CO_2e
Baseline	32,000	372,086	2,989,746	3,361,832
Scenario 1: Reduction due to post office closures	3,700	3,159	26,142	29,302
As a percentage of baseline	11.6	0.8	0.9	0.9
Scenario 2: Reduction due to reducing post office hours	12,983	16,313	134,685	150,998
As a percentage of baseline	40.6	4.4	4.5	4.5

Table 21.5 Transportation reductions from network consolidation

Air emissions (annual)	VOC	NO_x	CO	PM_{10}	$PM_{2.5}$	SO_2	CO_2e
Baseline purchased transportation related							4,917,948
Air transportation change							0
Network transportation reduction*	39	575	143	19.4	13.5	1.4	
Local transportation reduction*	26	376	94	12.7	8.9	0.9	
Total purchased transportation-related reduction*	65	951	237	32.1	22.4	2.3	114,125
As a % of baseline purchased transportation emissions							2.3

Source: *USPS Programmatic Environmental Assessment.

in the table for the baseline reflect the total for all USPS facility-related GHG emissions. Although nearly 12 percent of post offices are proposed to be closed in Scenario 1, the overall impact on facility-related GHG emissions is much less because the offices proposed to be closed are in general much smaller than both the processing facilities in the network and the post offices proposed to remain open. However, the reduction in GHG emissions of almost 1 percent is still equivalent to the emissions generated annually by 5,212 passenger vehicles.

However, the results of Scenario 2 show that reducing hours in a greater number of post offices has over five times the impact in GHG emissions than completely closing some smaller post offices. Scenario 2 results in a 4.5 percent decrease in baseline GHG emissions, the equivalent of the emissions generated annually by 26,859 passenger vehicles.

Impacts of Network and Local Transportation Changes from Mail Processing Network Consolidation

As previously described, network consolidation will reduce the number of trip-miles required across various transportation types including both network and local trips that support the overall USPS network, reducing the overall GHG emissions from USPS transportation. The PEA used the reduction in miles in purchased transportation as calculated by Martin to calculate the following reductions in GHG emissions. While CO_2e factors for some of the emissions type below are not easily calculated, the PEA states that the CO_2e reduction for these emissions is 114,125 metric tons; this result is used to estimate the overall impact to GHG emissions.

Because these estimates all pertain to purchased transportation, the changes presented in Table 21.5 impact only Scope 3 emissions. The reductions represent a 2.3 percent reduction in USPS's purchased transportation-related Scope 3 emissions, and a 1.5 percent reduction in USPS's total Scope 3 emissions. Since some segments of transportation remain unaffected, including air transportation which uses higher amounts of fuel per mile relative to highway transportation, the overall impact on purchased transportation emissions is significantly less than the mileage reductions for impacted segments,

Table 21.6 Facility impacts from moving from six- to five-day delivery

6- to 5-day facility impacts	Impacted facilities	Scope 1 CO_2e emissions	Scope 2 CO_2e emissions	Total CO_2e
Baseline	32,000	372,086	2,989,746	3,361,832
Reductions due to decreased hours		4,550	36,663	41,213
As a percentage of baseline		1.2	1.2	1.2

Table 21.7 Transportation impacts from moving from six-day to five-day delivery

Transportation	Baseline miles	Miles reduction	CO_2e/mile	CO_2e reduction
INTER AREA	353,106,306	50,128,601	0.00068203	34,189
INTER CLUSTER	99,917,696	13,470,000	0.00068203	9,187
INTER P&DC	56,852,485	6,672,655	0.00068203	4,551
INTRA BMC	181,708,106	21,543,947	0.00068203	14,694
INTRA CSD	175,920,575	27,199,912	GHG Calculator	44,000
INTRA P&DC	493,846,941	62,446,970	0.00068203	42,591
VSD	18,808,653	7,899,634	GHG Calculator	13,000
Total	1,380,160,762	189,361,719		162,211

which are estimated as high as 25.4 percent. However, this reduction still has an overall positive and significant environmental impact, as it is the equivalent of eliminating 20,300 passenger vehicles annually.

Impacts Resulting from Five-day Delivery

Next, the environmental impacts from eliminating Saturday delivery are estimated. Using the methodology described in Section 4, the facility-related change in GHG emissions for all post offices not proposed for closure is estimated based on a reduction in delivery operational hours of approximately two hours per week. The results of this analysis are in Table 21.6.

Next, the impacts related to transportation reductions as estimated by Grossman (2010) and Bradley (2010a, 2010b) are presented, which include both network-related transportation and local transportation. The results of this analysis for each transportation type are in Table 21.7.

In the table, all miles reductions are for purchased transportation and impact only Scope 3 emissions, with the exception of VSD, which are Scope 1. The reduction in miles of 42 percent for VSD results in a CO_2e reduction of 13,000 tons, which is approximately 1 percent of the 1,332,701 total CO_2e Scope 1 vehicle-related emissions reported by USPS in 2010. The total reduction in Scope 3 emissions for purchased transportation of 149,211 tons of CO_2e represents a total reduction in Scope 3 purchased transportation-related emissions of 3 percent. The combined reduction in CO_2e for both facility and transportation GHG emissions of 203,424 tons is equivalent to eliminating the burning of 1,108 railcars' worth of coal annually.

Table 21.8 Aggregated CO_2e reductions from all activities

Scenario	Total Scope 1 and Scope 2 CO_2e (metric tons)	% change in Scope 1 and 2 CO_2e from baseline	Total Scope 3 CO_2e (metric tons)	% change in Scope 3 CO_2e from baseline
Baseline USPS-related GHG emissions	4,708,139	N/A	7,520,000	N/A
Network consolidation – facility impacts	−519,349	−11.0%	N/A	N/A
Network consolidation – transportation impacts	N/A	N/A	−114,125	−1.5%
PO hour reductions – facility impacts	−150,998	−3.2%	N/A	N/A
6-day to 5-day – facility impacts	−41,213	−0.9%	N/A	N/A
6-day to 5-day – transportation impacts	−13,000	−0.3%	−149,211	−2.0%
Total change	−724,560		−263,336	
As a percentage of baseline		−15.4		−3.5

Summary of Results for All Activities Related to Operational Reductions

If USPS is allowed to pursue all the reductions in operations that it proposes, the positive impact on USPS-related Scope 1 and Scope 2 GHG emissions would be significant, with smaller, but still measurable, impacts on Scope 3 emissions related to purchased transportation. Table 21.8 presents the summary impacts of all the proposed actions discussed that are under active consideration by USPS, which results in a significant decrease in GHG emissions from the baseline for both facilities and vehicles. For retail network changes, this is the reduction in post office hours scenario rather than the closure of post offices since that is the scenario currently being proposed.

As illustrated in Table 21.8, the biggest reductions in absolute terms on USPS's overall GHG emissions result from the facility and transportation reductions related to network consolidation, and from the reduction in operational hours in post offices. The total reduction in CO_2e for all the proposed actions of 987,896 tons of CO_2e is equivalent to eliminating the CO_2e emissions associated with 175,726 passenger vehicles annually, the electricity generated by 111,746 homes, or the burning of 4,880 railcars' worth of coal.

6 CONCLUSION

Despite the substantial cost savings associated with reducing postal operations that have been quantified to date, the Postal Service still faces significant political opposition from its labor unions, legislators whose constituents are affected by the proposed closures, and the PRC. The recent debate has been focused on the cost and labor impacts, and to our knowledge, has not considered the additional beneficial environmental benefits that could result from USPS's proposals. The results of this analysis demonstrate that USPS's proposed operational changes will produce significant decreases in the agency's CO_2e emissions. The positive environmental benefits of the efforts to reduce the size of postal operations are an important component that should be a part of the current debate as postal operators internationally strive to operate their networks in both an operationally efficient, and thus, environmentally responsible manner, reflecting the new realities of decreased demand for postal services.

NOTES

* The views expressed in this chapter are those of the authors and do not necessarily express those of IBM Global Business Services. The authors are indebted to David Post from IBM for his contributions to this chapter.

1. As defined in the PEA, a 'gaining' facility obtains additional volume, work hours and mail processing equipment with the consolidation of operations associated with the Mail Processing Network Rationalization Initiative; 'Study' facilities contain mail processing equipment that is being considered for possible consolidation or closure under the Mail Processing Network Rationalization Initiative (Postal Service Office of Sustainability, 2012).
2. Although 2011 figures are published in the 2011 Annual Sustainability Report (USPS, 2012b), 2010 data are used as the baseline because detailed 2011 GHG emissions by state and type are not yet published in the Climate Registry.
3. This figure does not include the 3,694 retail locations operated by contractors.

REFERENCES

Adra, Mohammad and Renee Sheehy (2011), 'A Framework for Optimizing and Modernizing the U.S. Postal Service Retail Network', paper presented at the 30th Annual Eastern Conference and Advanced Workshop on Regulatory Economics, Skytop, PA, May 18–20.

Bradley, Michael D. (2010a), 'Direct Testimony of Michael D. Bradley on Behalf of the United States Postal Service', Docket No. N2010-1, USPS-T-6, March 30.

Bradley, Michael D. (2010b), Docket No. N2010-1, Postal Service Library Reference USPS-LR-N2010-1/8 in support of Bradley Testimony, Purchased Transportation Highway Contract Costs by Day of Week. Uploaded to PRC website on March 30, 2010.

Bratta, Dominic L. (2011), 'Direct Testimony of Dominic L. Bratta on Behalf of the United States Postal Service', Docket No. N2012-1, USPS-T-5, December 5.

Buc, Lawrence G, Peter A. Soyka and Sander S. Glick. (2010), 'The environmental impacts of the US mail: initial life cycle inventory model and analysis', in M.A. Crew and P.R. Kleindorfer (eds), *Heightening Competition in the Postal and Delivery Sector*, Cheltenham, UK and Northampton, MA, USA: Edward Elgar, pp. 323–37.

Climate Registry Information System (CRIS) (2010), Entity Emissions Detailed Report for the United States Postal Service.

Cohen, Robert, Luigi Di Paola, Renee Sheehy and Vincenzo Visco Comandini (2008), 'The distribution of post offices in Italy and the United States', *Review of Network Economics*, **7** (2), June, 325–36.

Cohen, Robert, Matthew Robinson, Renee Sheehy, Tom Sharkey, John Waller and Spyros Xenakis (2006), 'The conflict about preserving small rural post offices; difference in the distribution of pharmacies and post offices', paper presented at the Winton M. Blount Symposium on Postal History, National Postal Museum, November 3–4.

Grossman, Luke T. (2010), 'Direct Testimony of Luke T. Grossman on Behalf of the United States Postal Service', Docket No. N2010-1, USPS-T-5, March 30.

Klingenberg, John (2011), 'Direct Testimony of John P. Klingenberg on Behalf of the Public Representative PR-T-2, Retail Access Optimization Initiative', PRC Docket No. N2011-1, September 26.

Koljonen, Denice (2008), 'The Environmental Impact of Mail: A Baseline', Pitney Bowes, June 20.

Martin, Cheryl D. (2011), 'Direct Testimony of Cheryl D. Martin on Behalf of the United States Postal Service', Docket No. N2012-1, USPS-T-6, December 5.

Postal Service Office of Sustainability (2012), 'Programmatic Environmental Assessment United States Postal Service Mail Processing Network Rationalization Initiative', February 6.

United States Postal Service (USPS) (2012a), PFY 2011 Annual Report, March 1.

United States Postal Service (USPS) (2012b), PFY 2011 Annual Sustainability Report, April 30.

Waters, Nigel (2011), 'Testimony of Nigel Waters PR-T-1. Retail Access Optimization Initiative', PRC Docket No. NP2011-1, September 26.

Yezer, Anthony M. (2010), 'Analyzing the Postal Service's Retail Network Using an Objective Modeling Approach', Report Number: RARC-WP-10-004, Postal Service Office of Inspector General (OIG), Risk Analysis Research Center, June 14.

22. Economic regulation and the UK postal sector, 2000–2011*

Tim Walsh[†]

It is, perhaps, the only mercantile project which has been successfully managed by, I believe, every sort of Government. The capital advanced is not very considerable. There is no mystery in the business. The returns are not only certain, but immediate.
Adam Smith, *The Wealth of Nations*, 1776
Book 5, Chapter 2 Part 1

1 INTRODUCTION

In 1990, Royal Mail delivered 58 million letters each day and returned a profit of £30 million on a total letters' turnover of £3.6 billion. By 2010, Royal Mail were delivering 71 million items per day but reported a loss of £333 million on a turnover of £6.6 billion. When the first Rutgers postal economics conference was opened at Rugby in 1990 by its former chairman, Sir Ron Dearing, Royal Mail was recognizably a leader in the postal world. Yet by the mid-2000s, Royal Mail was described by its then chairman as 'a basket case' (Leighton, 2011: 5).

This chapter reviews the experience of independent postal regulation in the UK and evaluates the decisions of the Postal Services Commission (Postcomm) in respect of liberalization, downstream access and price control. It assesses the economic merits of the regulatory disputes that developed between Royal Mail and Postcomm over the 2000s, in the context of business performance and the broader governance design.

Section 2 outlines the principles behind UK postal reform and the institutions created by the Postal Services Act, 2000. Section 3 reviews Postcomm's decisions in respect of liberalization in the context of what Leighton described as 'the last of UK's really big corporate turnarounds' (2007: 29). Section 4 evaluates the economic case for Postcomm's decision to facilitate downstream access including the cost basis for access. Section 5 assesses the nature of price control regulation (PCR) during the period and its contribution to supporting the Universal Service Obligation (USO), protecting users and stimulating efficiency. The chapter concludes with an overview of the wider lessons for economic regulation from the experience in the UK postal sector during the 2000s.

† Vice President Corporate and Regulatory Affairs, Pitney Bowes.

2 GOVERNANCE AND REGULATORY DESIGN, 2000–2011

By the end of the 1990s there was widespread recognition that public sector financial frameworks were not helpful in supporting the transformation of Royal Mail to emerging market and technological realities. There was, however, little political support for privatization and so a policy emerged embracing limited commercial freedoms for Royal Mail as a state-owned plc, combined with commercial disciplines.

The Postal Services Act, 2000 thus created an independent regulator, Postcomm, and established an oversight executive body to mimic the role of capital markets (the Shareholder Executive, SHEX). The act was described at the time by a Treasury adviser as 'a dog's breakfast' (quoted in Macintyre, 2000: 474–8) and, in more measured terms, by Campbell as a 'hybrid or transitional' model, compared to the mercantile, market and national archetypes being developed elsewhere in the postal world (Campbell, 2002: 331).

In particular, the context for the new institutions was rather unique and their relationships somewhat unclear. PCR in the UK had been designed to enable transfer of state-owned businesses to the private sector, as a monopoly, thereby both capturing value for the taxpayer while protecting consumers and overseeing the phased introduction of competition. That PCR was the most efficient regulatory solution rested on private ownership and the incentives resulting from effective residual claimants in the form of shareholders. Yet, Royal Mail was to remain in state hands posing, what Wachter et al. had prefigured, 'unique difficulties in subjecting a government-owned, labor intensive firm to PCR' (1997: 4) and resulting in the absence of residual claimants to drive efficiency so essential for the effective implementation of PCR (Crew and Kleindorfer, 2000).

SHEX was formally charged with the residual claimant function to drive profits as its return. However, SHEX operated from inside the industry ministry and was subject to prevailing political objectives that might have impeded a singular focus on maximizing shareholder value. Moreover, its levers over management, the intensity of its performance monitoring and influence in the wider system were weak. SHEX reviewed the Royal Mail business plan, advised ministers and provided oversight on key financial metrics, but the only transparent objective of expected performance was soon surrendered.[1]

SHEX did not join the Royal Mail board in the way that the German state-owned bank, KfW Bankengruppe, has an influential voice on the board of Deutsche Post. SHEX believed that to fulfill its role it required independence from the Royal Mail, for fear of taking on 'holding company' characteristics. While SHEX's neutrality was thus preserved, this may have been at the expense of any meaningful influence. It could easily be ignored by management and failed in practice to exert that 'capital market' pressure on the business in support of Postcomm's effort to stimulate product market and other incentives.

3 ROYAL MAIL AND LIBERALIZATION

Postcomm's primary statutory duty was to protect the financial viability of the universal service, at an affordable and uniform tariff. A subsidiary duty to promote effective competition was additionally subservient to the goal of furthering user interests. Postcomm viewed the universal service as a competitive advantage, not a burden, and believed that

Source: Royal Mail total inland mail. Department for Communities and Local Government for Household Data.

Figure 22.1 Total delivered items (First and Second Class) per delivery point per delivery day

in the absence of competition there would be inadequate incentives for cost reduction. Despite viewing the challenges facing the business as 'breathtakingly straightforward' (Leighton, 2011: 5), Royal Mail's progress on cost reduction was indeed slow, even during the period up to 2006 when total delivered volumes per delivery point per day grew strongly (Figure 22.1).

The removal of the second daily delivery, targeted at saving £350 million 'added to Royal Mail's costs by £23m' (LECG, 2005: 238–9). Necessary operational modernization was 'insufficient' (Postcomm, 2008a: 4) and Hooper et al. concluded that it was Royal Mail's own inefficiency which had 'the most significant impact on the company's operating profitability' (2008: 53). Royal Mail themselves acknowledged that 'the pace and extent of change in business performance and culture must improve' (Royal Mail, 2008).

The Postal Services Act, 2000 itself imposed no reserved area as would have been permitted under the EC Directive, 97/67[2] (at that time 100 grams and a price of not more than three times the tariff in the first weight step) and Postcomm's decision to liberalize the market in 2006 was not unexpected, nor perhaps unreasonable in terms of promoting economic efficiency.

While Royal Mail supported the Postal Services Act, accepted its license and welcomed market opening, it was evident that institutional design was far from ideal. Having created an independent regulator the secretary of state immediately began to put pressure on Postcomm in respect of particular decisions in support of the state-owned business (Campbell-Smith, 2011: 672). Royal Mail's chairman, Allan Leighton[3] sought to undermine Postcomm publicly, rather than leverage the incentives so provided to achieve what the business required in any event (Leighton, 2011: 175).

Royal Mail resented not so much that Postcomm was liberalizing, but that it was promoting competition as an end in itself. While Postcomm saw the risk of anticompetitive practices by the incumbent as 'well founded' (Postcomm, 2008b: 52), Royal Mail argued that the regulator was overzealous in applying non-discriminatory requirements, based on form rather than the effects-based impacts, and that pro-competitive license conditions (such as the avoidance of undue discrimination) impeded their freedom to innovate. In fact, 99 percent of mail revenue prices were controlled and this was still around 85 percent in 2010. Three months' notice of price or product changes was required, with no allowance to adapt its product portfolio without permission. Thus, Eccles charged that Royal Mail was 'over-regulated . . . in that too many operational decisions require regulatory approval' (2008: 352).

Royal Mail did innovate during the period in terms of strategic pricing changes: channel pricing (approved by Postcomm without challenge); pricing in proportion (proposals resubmitted to Postcomm but approved after significant delays due to costing); wholesale zonal pricing (approved); and retail, bulk mail, non-USO zonal tariffs (rejected in 2007 by Postcomm on grounds of reasonableness and inconsistency with wholesale zonal rates). However, with just five new products launched over the period, controls established by Postcomm were not in themselves the constraint on product or process innovation within Royal Mail. Royal Mail marketing efforts, particularly in its retail letters' business, concentrated more on tactical 'price discounts' rather than product innovation (Postcomm, 2008a: 21).

4 DOWNSTREAM ACCESS

Postcomm required Royal Mail (Condition 9 of Royal Mail's license) to provide third-party access to its domestic downstream operations, and not simply to respect the non-discrimination principle of the postal services directive. For Royal Mail this represented an additional requirement and that it was not 'appropriate' to go further than the directive (Eccles and Kuipers, 2008: 279).[4] However, it was not unreasonable for a UK economic regulator to be attracted to the economic benefits of access. Postal networks have 'an obvious hierarchical structure' (Panzar, 1993: 92) and economies of scale represented a significant barrier to facilities-based competition (Cazals et al., 2005). Access would allow 'process and product innovations to find their way into the marketplace on a piece-meal, component by component basis, rather than requiring the entrenched practices of the dominant firm be replaced all at once' (Panzar, 2002: 113).

Postcomm's view was that a decision to 'share' the incumbent's scale benefits with new entrants was a 'reasoned regulatory decision' (Moriarty and Smith, 2005: 113) based on pragmatic observations that brand awareness of entrants was low;[5] customers did not want to split their mail between operators; and that Royal Mail's VAT exemption represented a 14 percent cost advantage on around half of the total mail. In fact, Leighton supported Postcomm's proposal to facilitate access (Royal Mail, 2003).

Rather, the main point at dispute concerned the terms on which access was made available. Royal Mail supported a retail-minus approach to access costing and argued that subsidy-free access must respect the efficient component pricing rule (Willig, 1979) such that access prices be set on the retail price less the universal service providers' (USPs') avoided long-run marginal cost of upstream activity (De Donder et al., 2002).

They further cited Article 12 of the postal directive which required that where access was provided tariffs must be non-discriminatory and 'take account of the avoided costs, as compared to the standard service'.

However, the same directive required that tariffs shall apply without discrimination 'both as between different third parties and universal service providers supplying equivalent services'. Postcomm interpreted this as requiring, as a minimum, that Royal Mail must recover costs directly attributable to the handling of access, meaning a cost-plus pricing rule allowing for the recovery of the downstream fixed and variable costs plus a proportion of joint costs.

Thus, under the threat of a Postcomm determination, Royal Mail negotiated commercial terms[6] with Business Post Group (UK Mail) in February 2004 for mail center access at uniform prices ranging from 13.75p for 60g letters £3.65 for items up to 2kg, and differentiated-based format and level of presort. Critically, prices were set on the basis that the profile of accessed mail displayed a typical 'fall-to-earth' pattern as mail generally, thereby protecting Royal Mail from the risk of what Panzar called 'wasteful' cherry picking (2002: 114) and consistent with Crew and Kleindorfer's protection for the USO whereby access providers are charged 'not according to the work they have by-passed, but according to the work yet to be performed in delivering the mail they repost with the PO' (2002: 13).[7]

Royal Mail's agreement with UK Mail meant that access competition took place 'on a similar geographic footprint to Royal Mail' (Dudley et al., 2009: 54) and that access prices 'reflect the costs of work yet to be done in each delivery zone' (Hill and Robinson, 2006: 128). Leighton wrote that it could 'earn a commercial return . . . while preventing the sort of cream-skimming which would damage our ability to continue providing the one-price-goes-anywhere universal service' (Royal Mail, 2004: 2).

However, access traffic grew rapidly rising from 100 million items in 2004–05 to 6.5 billion items by March 2010 (though of these about half of the access traffic represented Royal Mail's own wholesale, customer-direct contracts). Postcomm saw such growth 'competition working', and welcoming the 'greater efficiency' and 'closer customer intimacy' of the new entrants that could 'handle addressed mail upstream for less than half of Royal Mail's fully allocated costs' (Postcomm, 2008a: 15). In contrast, from 2006–07, Royal Mail's complaint was that it made a loss (on a fully allocated cost basis) from delivering access mail (Dudley et al., 2009: 61). Postcomm's view was that the access price was not too low and that despite limitations in Royal Mail's costing systems, the evidence suggested that any loss was substantially less than Royal Mail claimed and that, if it existed, it reflected Royal Mail's own 'slower than expected progress in improving their efficiency' (Postcomm, 2008b: 16).[8]

While Postcomm did not directly set or regulate access prices, as part of the 2006 price control it did set a headroom control between Royal Mail's retail price and respective access prices to protect competition from margin squeeze. Postcomm saw 'considerable risks' of non-equivalent price and non-price treatment of access operators (Postcomm, 2008a: 44). The headroom margin was set on the basis of the differential between relevant retail and wholesale services as existed on 31 March 2006 and were estimated at 3.5p.

Royal Mail contended that it was unfair that efficiencies in its upstream business (reflected in downward improvements in prices for its own bulk retail services) had to be automatically passed on to competitors and that headroom regulation guaranteed a margin for access entrants. The 'very presence of access volumes and their growth', Royal Mail argued, 'can be taken as an indication of the absence of "margin squeeze"' (Dudley et al., 2009: 53); besides, access was 'manufactured competition' (Royal Mail, 2008: 4).

In the absence of cost transparency, however, there was an efficiency rationale to protect access operators from the risk of discriminatory behavior. Headroom control provided a margin within which access competitors competed – access operators' profitability was not guaranteed, and such was the level of competition in the access market that margins were much below the level of the headroom control. Postcomm acknowledged that the headroom control was 'lumpy' and 'problematic' applying to each individual price point rather than an alternative approach which might have required maintenance of an average headroom but allow the incumbent to lower price for the more competitive segments (Postcomm, 2008b: 62). The benefit for access operators was that they always knew Royal Mail's retail price they were competing against; whereas Royal Mail could not selectively target particular customers whose volumes were critical to the 'base loading' for efficient new entrant access operations.

While access volumes grew spectacularly, the revenue dilution impact on Royal Mail was limited. Access operators' combined non-postage revenue amounted to no more that £100 million by 2010, a tiny fraction of total Royal Mail revenue, which included some 70 percent of the total revenue (around 13p) for each accessed item delivered. Access did not threaten the USO but rather may have protected and underpinned it by bearing down on business mail tariffs and reinforcing Royal Mail's dominance in the delivery market, particularly after 2006 when volumes had begun to decline.

However, the absence of end-to-end competition (just 1 percent of volumes in the UK compared to 10 percent in Sweden, Germany and the Netherlands) would have failed to provide incentives for efficiency in Royal Mail's delivery business (where some 50 percent of the costs reside) and thus Postcomm's access regime may have deterred facilities-based competition. Proponents of bypass argued that, in the context of generic non-discrimination principles and sector-specific regulation, mandatory downstream access 'was not needed . . . may be counterproductive . . . [and] may bias entry strategies towards a specific entry mode, thereby possibly limiting innovation' (de Bijl et al., 2006: 154).

Overall, the license condition opening up access in the UK was not economically unreasonable; nor was the cost-plus basis of the access price, particularly as Royal Mail protected itself against delivery density cream-skimming through the terms and prices of access contracts. Transparent, *ex ante* margin squeeze protection was economically reasonable at the time of its introduction in 2006 when Royal Mail was still dominant in the upstream market and competition was primarily between access operators and Royal Mail retail (rather than between access operators). However, by 2008 Royal Mail's upstream dominance had been significantly weakened, suggesting that headroom control, certainly its 'lumpy' nature, was no longer suited to the market.

5 PRICE CONTROL

The PCR that Postcomm established for Royal Mail was typical of their type in terms of form, scope, structure and length, including controlling for quality of service. PCR was reviewed periodically (2001–03; 2003–06; 2006–10, rolled over to 2012) to ensure that a balance was struck between allowing time for efficiency gains to be made and rewarded, while recouping the benefits of cost reduction for users. While there was nothing that was fundamentally unreasonable about the principles and nature of the three price controls set by Postcomm, the wider governance environment in which they were set, combined with technical and calibration errors, served to compromise the controls' effectiveness at various times in respect of protecting customers, the USO and driving efficiency.

Price control applied to regulated services, not just those within the USO, thus capturing certain bulk mail, non-USO services. Royal Mail argued that such a broad PCR would 'limit the ability of the USP to amend prices and pricing structures in order to make them more cost-reflective' (Dudley et al., 2005: 122). A tariff basket structure allowed some room to adjust prices, but the freedom to rebalance was limited by subsidiary pure price caps on individual services (albeit limited to products that accounted for little revenue) to ensure that there were no real terms price rises at the product level.

For Royal Mail, a global price control would avoid the need for any detailed review of cost allocation between competitive and noncompetitive markets, and allow it freedom to gear prices to costs in markets which would become 'prospectively competitive' within the period of the price control (ibid.: 123). Postcomm rejected the idea that PCR was hindering Royal Mail's ability to compete. Royal Mail could apply to be removed from the price control where there was evidence that competition had sufficiently developed and Postcomm had deemed four out of the five new products that Royal Mail introduced during PCR 3 as substantially different, and so excluded from PCR.

For PCR to be effective it needs to be 'well-structured and robustly specified' (da Silva et al., 2004: 160) and depends on 'regulatory commitment . . . not just on the part of the regulator . . . but also on the part of the firm' (Crew and Kleindorfer, 2001: 43). Moreover, the incentive is most effective where the control is focused on those elements wholly within the management's control, with an in-built flexibility for other factors, and where once set, the price control is not reopened. Indeed, the 'core concept' of PCR is that 'it is a target that does not get adjusted based on the performance of the regulated company' (Wachter et al., 1997: 19).

Against these principles, the structure of the first substantive price control, 2003–06, was poorly specified in that it failed to embed an automatic volume adjustor. Traffic projections had assumed that bypass competition would take off during the period such that by the end of the control period in 2006 volume outcomes were considerably higher than forecast, allowing Royal Mail to benefit from the scale economies which drove unit cost reduction and profits, but blunting the efficiency incentive on management. PCR 2 posed no risk to the USO but rather favored Royal Mail insofar as the benefits of unit cost reduction arising from volume growth (compared to the price control assumptions) were not shared with customers as a condition of the control.

In contrast, PCR 3, 2006–10, did seek to allow for the uncertainty of volume trends through a growth factor (G), whereby Royal Mail had the ability to raise prices more than RPI-X. A further error-correction method, P (Pension), adjusted the PCR and allowable revenue in line with the needs of funding the pension. In addition, following increased public concern over falling First Class service quality in 2003 and 2004 (and thus perhaps representing a political as much as a regulatory goal) Postcomm increased the relative weight attached to the automatic revenue adjuster pertaining to the quality on non-bulk mail (the C factor) from 0.9 to a maximum of 5 percent. The X factor in PCR 3 was –0.1

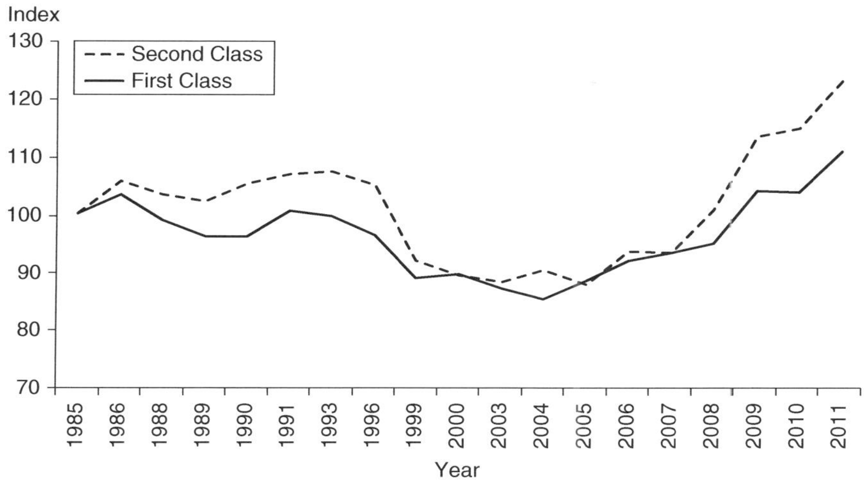

Source: Calculated From Royal Mail and Office of National Statistics data.

Figure 22.2 Real stamp prices, First and Second Class mail, 1985–2011

which allowed Royal Mail £1.2 billion from mail revenues for new investment and an average of £320 million a year to help Royal Mail reduce its pension fund deficit.

Nonetheless, while Royal Mail had welcomed PCR 3 as 'a manageable package of price controls' (Royal Mail, 2006) less than 12 months later the business requested a review to take into account volume erosion, to reduce headroom control to a level which reflects the underlying upstream costs and to rebalance prices more rapidly, despite a growth in average annual real stamp prices of 2.7 percent between 2003 and 2010 (Figure 22.2).

It may have been that with mail volumes falling and the pension deficit ballooning, PCR, however sophisticated, was no longer appropriate. The protection of the USO – Postcomm's primary statutory duty – was becoming the cardinal objective as it became clear from the national strike in 2007 (as well as 2003 and 2010) that Royal Mail management simply could not take out costs quickly enough to provide any assurance on the financial viability of the USO.

Thus, while it is not necessary to agree with Ofcom's precise conclusion that controls on mail revenues 'were too tight in light of what had subsequently happened in terms of the level of demand', it was the case that 'the incentive properties' of PCR that operated well in the case of privatized UK companies were not working in the case of a nationalized Royal Mail (BIS, 2012: para. 16). While PCR 1 and 2 (and liberalization and access) had not been responsible for the cash crisis that was engulfing Royal Mail, PCR was no longer relevant to the problem of falling volumes, growing pension costs and management's inability to become more efficient. On its own estimates, Royal Mail was 20 percent less efficient than its rivals (Postcomm, 2008b: 31).

Postcomm rejected headroom reduction as it was not supported by cost data but conceded additional revenue relief for Royal Mail in support of the USO, even if Postcomm were not convinced in 2007 that the challenge facing Royal Mail was one of inadequate revenue, as opposed to one of excessive cost: 'Royal Mail is using an attack on the regulatory structure as a smokescreen for its own lack of progress in tackling their high labor costs . . . Royal Mail has failed to bring its costs into line as would be expected of an efficient mail operator' (Postcomm, 2007: 1).

Royal Mail were permitted to raise the price of a Second Class stamp to 29p by 2010 (the original price cap was 26p) and to rebalance the subcap controls in the 'captive' and 'non-captive' basket by up to 8.5 percent per year (from 3 percent). Postcomm made further changes from April 2010 allowing Royal Mail to use a zero inflation figure rather than negative inflation when setting its prices. In reopening PCR 3 it became, in the words of Wachter et al., the 'safety valve of last resort', easing not only 'dislocations outside the posts control' (pensions, volume) but also the failure to implement efficiency improvements (Wachter et al., 1997: 19). A fundamental review of PCR 3 at this time would have been desirable but regulatory blight had set in as the whole 2000 governance arrangements came under scrutiny.[9]

6 PERSPECTIVES AND CONCLUSIONS

A significant constraint on the efficacy of the economic regulation during this period was the 'serious limitations' and 'poor transparency' of Royal Mail's costing systems (Postcomm, 2008a: 4). The absence of consistent cost data bedeviled the relationship between Postcomm and Royal Mail; made the basis for regulatory decisions uncertain; and probably delayed a move from *ex ante* to *ex post* regulation. Postcomm argued that Royal Mail were gaming their use of data as a strategic asset, that it withheld its own studies (for example, on efficiency in 2006) and that information provided was often late or subject to substantial revision.

In contrast, Royal Mail argued that Postcomm failed to understand that costs changed as Royal Mail itself was changing, and that Postcomm did not appreciate the heterogeneity of postal costs across networks, processes and products. Royal Mail's ABC product costing was 'a substantial system that deals with over 200 activities (some of which are subdivided) and over 1000 cost objects' (Robinson and McMurdie, 2009: 84). Estimating postal costs is a non-trivial exercise, including a level of complexity below product level (in terms of weight, format, readability, delivery destination); difficulty in measuring and apportioning volume across activities; and the fact that over half of total costs are common costs across many products.

With no agreement on costs and the absence of yardstick data, much of the dialogue between Royal Mail and Postcomm turned on the appropriateness of various analytical or econometric techniques in casting light on particular issues; for example, the debate on the appropriateness of data envelopment analyses to assess costs (Horncastle et al., 2006: 164; Moriarty et al., 2006). Regulatory decisions, however, embrace 'shades of grey', rather than provide unequivocally right or wrong answers, and cannot in themselves resolve disputes without a shared acceptance of the purpose and direction of regulatory intervention.

Consensus as to purpose was lacking and Postcomm's legitimacy in the eyes of the regulated firm had been compromised from the earliest days. Certainly, the idea of price control as a regulatory contract that could support the business in its modernization did not take hold in the company under the chairmanship of Allan Leighton. The failure to work with Postcomm incentives combined with the absence of effective scrutiny of management's performance by SHEX may have meant that regulation became 'more intrusive' than would otherwise have been the case, becoming 'a surrogate for the incentives that would normally come from the workings of the capital markets' (Postcomm, 2008b: 41).

In particular, the period of economic regulation under Postcomm was characterized by the incumbent's consistently poor performance in reducing costs, modernizing its networks and growing new profitable revenue streams.[10] Costs and jobs were reduced over the 2000s but a large part of the gross savings were distributed to employees and managers in the form of real pay increases, bonuses, reduced hours and phantom shares with little or no benefit to industrial relations, service or employee engagement (Walsh, 2012). For example, the grip that Royal Mail had established on comparative earnings during the 1990s was lost, with 'substantial evidence' suggesting that operational pay grades' base pay was between six and 25 percent above market rates (LECG, 2005).

Lack of transparency in the reporting of financial and other results also soured the Postcomm–Royal Mail relationship. In 2002 Leighton 'came up with a figure' for public relations purposes to present Royal Mail as a business that was losing a million pounds a day (Campbell-Smith, 2011: 680). The claimed savings from the three strands of the 2002–05 renewal plan (single daily delivery, transport and mail center review) were 'hard to understand' (Postcomm (2008b: 131, Annex 12), and the targeted reduction in 30,000 jobs appeared to be based on 'a bit of funny accounting' (Peston, 2008: 312; Walsh, 2012). Postcomm also found 'irrefutable evidence' that between July 2006 and February 2010 there was the widespread, deliberate and organized deception to cheat the independent, test letter performance monitoring system (Postcomm, 2010). Even in 2010, Royal Mail letters reported an operating profit of £121 million (before exceptional items, including core costs), whereas the actual result was loss before tax of £333 million (Royal Mail, 2010: 62).

The facts of the business were made subservient to the crafting of a 'corporate turnaround' narrative undermining Postcomm's confidence in Royal Mail's leadership. The 'turnaround' narrative went unchallenged by others in the system until the first Hooper report called time on the post-2000 institutional design and signaled, as the capital market might do in the case of a failing privatized company, that the existing leadership could not deliver corporate renewal without externally provided private sector 'corporate experience' (Hooper et al., 2008: 13).

In conclusion, Postcomm's decision to liberalize and to require access was not unreasonable, particularly in the context of Royal Mail's troubled progress in becoming more efficient. Market opening in the form that Postcomm introduced may have sustained volumes for the benefit of the USO both in terms of lower business mail prices and by constraining bypass entrants. Headroom control was justified to protect access providers though the establishment of that margin based on an earlier, commercially negotiated formula had limitations, and had outlived its economic rationale by 2008 when upstream competition had been firmly established.

The effectiveness of PCR on a publicly owned company was always likely to be challenging, particularly as SHEX did not drive a focus on efficiency necessary for effective PCR. Institutional design flaws were perhaps compounded by misjudgments in the detailed calibration of particular controls. The volume projections on which PCR 2 was based were overpessimistic (and thus overly generous to Royal Mail), thereby blunting the effectiveness of the control. In addition, the quality controls in PCR may have been dialed up too high at a time when Royal Mail was seeking to modernize operations. The efficiency assumptions underpinning PCR were strongly evidenced based but, in the absence of effective oversight of management, gained no traction on performance.

Adam Smith was wrong. Running a postal business is not a straightforward affair, at least not in the UK. Independent postal regulation was not, however, responsible for Royal Mail's failure to modernize networks and reduce costs in line with volume decline. That responsibility rested with the leadership of the regulated firm, and with SHEX. It was not so much that Postcomm did not work but rather that it could not work in the context where the shareholder interest was so inadequately exercised and where the hubris of the leadership undermined any commitment on the part of the business to the regulatory contract. By 2008, it was clear that independent economic regulation had become irrelevant to the task of maintaining the Royal Mail's solvency.

The Postal Services Act, 2000 was replaced by the 2011 Postal Act marking a political consensus that any future for Royal Mail required full commercial freedoms and the discipline that comes from capital markets as a privatized entity. Royal Mail will continue to enjoy significant market power with some 80 percent of the upstream business and 99 percent of the delivered mail business, and so the need for an appropriate level of regulatory oversight will remain, particularly if the return to profitability risks being borne more by customers in terms of higher prices than by underlying efficiency improvements and innovation.

NOTES

* The views expressed here are the author's alone and do not necessarily represent those of Pitney Bowes.

1. While the act provided for a 40 percent dividend of post-tax profits to be returned to government as shareholders this was only paid once, in 2001.
2. Directive 97/67/EC, amended by 2002/39/EC required that member states establish an independent economic regulator for the sector as well as laying out minimum standards with respect to the scope of the USO, quality of service and frequency of delivery. *Official Journal* 2000 L 176/21 10 June 2002.
3. Leighton was not in the normal mode of post office chairmen. Peston writes that 'you think he was a showbiz magnate or a Premier-League football manager . . . And quite a lot of the time he's a hair's breadth from (talking) nonsense' (2008: 304–5). His style was certainly unconventional and perhaps less focused on the detail of business and the complexities of the challenges than would have been ideal. It was a style that failed to foster trust among senior officials (ibid.: 304).
4. The EU Postal Notice had identified delivery as a separate product market. European Commission Notice on the application of the competition rules to the postal sector and on the assessment of certain state measures relating to postal services, *Official Journal* C. 39/2, 6 February 1998.
5. Postcomm was wrong on this point. As de Bijl et al. noted, any lack of awareness of competition in the UK market would be a 'transitory phenomenon' and that 'large customers quickly switch to better offers when these are available' (2006: 162).
6. Postcomm believed that a negotiated access model would ensure that the regulator was not 'dragged into "micro managing" the business' (Moriarty and Smith, 2005: 110–15).
7. Other safeguards for Royal Mail were built into the initial UK Mail contract including a requirement that the operator had to access a minimum 40 mail centers, including 25 named centers every day, with a minimum daily posting of 25,000. In October 2004 variable zonal access rates were made available to regional operators further reducing 'the likelihood of access customers looking for arbitrage opportunities' (Dudley et al., 2009: 57).

8. For example, Postcomm reported that far from making a significant loss, Royal Mail's 'latest costing now suggest it makes a small profit' (2008b: 65). Postcomm reviewed the control in 2007 and decided that there were no grounds to make reductions or to increase it (as requested by access operators), as access costing data 'was not sufficiently robust' (Postcomm, 2008b: 62).
9. The 2008 Hooper review and the failed Postal Services Bill of 2009 created a hiatus in regulation and the loss of one-third of Postcomm staff as it prepared for the anticipated merger with Ofcom in 2009. After the failure of the 2009 Bill in Parliament, Postcomm began to rebuild its team when the new government's postal services bill was presented to Parliament, also proposing a merger of Postcomm into Ofcom.
10. Leighton quotes his CEO, Adam Crozier, in a way that unwittingly demonstrates leadership's lack of focus on mail center productivity. Crozier describes how on a visit to a mail center local management was proud of their improved 'EP' (Royal Mail's measure of mail center's effective performance) score from 77 to 80 over the previous 12 months. Crozier describes how the term was 'complete gobbledygook to them' as EP meant 'earnings price ratio' (quoted in Leighton, 2011: 116–17). Similarly, the lack of grip of pay is illustrated by the fact that up until late 2006 one of Royal Mail's claims for the success of its transformation was that postal workers' pay was 'up almost 25 percent since March 2002' (Crozier, 2006: 3). Yet within months, the 2007 national strike had begun turning on the issue that 'Royal Mail staff were paid 25 percent more than workers in rival post firms and other companies in the business were 40 percent more efficient' (Crozier, *The Times*, 9 October 2007, quoted in Postcomm, 2008b: 57).

REFERENCES

BIS (2012), 'Stamp Prices, Ofcom Evidence', Report 1, Business, Innovation and Skills Select Committee, House of Commons, London: HMSO.

Campbell, R. (2002), *The Politics of Postal Transformation*, Quebec: McGill Queen's University Press.

Campbell-Smith, D. (2011), *The Masters of the Post: The Authorised History of Royal Mail*, London: Allen Lane.

Cazals, C., J.-P. Florens and S. Soteri (2005), 'Delivery costs for postal services in the UK', in M.A. Crew and P.R. Kleindorfer (eds), *Regulatory and Economic Challenges in the Postal and Delivery Sector*, Boston, MA: Kluwer Academic.

Crew, M.A. and P.R. Kleindorfer (2000), 'Privatizing the U.S. Postal Service', in E.L. Hudgins (ed.), *Mail @ the Millennium: Will the Postal Service Go Private*, Washington, DC: CATO Institute.

Crew, M.A. and P.R. Kleindorfer (2001), 'A critque of the theory of incentive regulation', in Crew and Kleindorfer (eds), *Future Directions in Postal Reform*, Boston, MA: Kluwer Academic.

Crew, M.A. and P.R. Kleindorfer (2002), 'Balancing access and the Universal Service Obligation', in Crew and Kleindorfer (eds), *Postal and Delivery Services: Delivering on Competition*, Boston, MA: Kluwer Academic.

Crozier, A. (2006), 'Getting ready to compete', presentation to The UK Mail Show, London, April.

Da Silva, L.C., P. Dudley, L. Mautino and S. Richard (2004), 'RPI-X price control regulation in the postal sector', in M.A. Crew and P.R. Kleindorfer (eds), *Competitive Transformation of the Postal and Delivery Sector*, Boston, MA: Kluwer Academic.

De Bijl, P.W.J., E. Van Damme and P. Larouche (2006), 'Regulating access to stimulate competition in postal markets in the UK', in M.A. Crew and P.R. Kleindorfer (eds), *Progress Toward Liberalization of the Postal and Delivery Sector*, New York: Springer.

De Donder, P., H. Cremer and F. Rodriguez (2002), 'Funding the Universal Service Obligation under liberalization: an analysis of the postal market', in M.A. Crew and P.R. Kleindorfer (eds), *Postal and Delivery Services: Pricing, Productivity, Regulation and Strategy*, Boston, MA: Kluwer Academic.

Dudley, P., S. Agar, L. Mautino and F.F. Duncan (2009), 'Competiton through downstream access in the UK postal sector: the first four years', in M.A. Crew and P.R. Kleindorfer (eds), *Progress in the Competitive Agenda in the Postal and Delivery Sector*, Cheltenham, UK and Northampton, MA, USA: Edward Elgar.

Dudley, P., H. Jenkins, L. Mautino and S. Richard (2005), 'Competition and the coverage of price controls in the postal sector', in M.A. Crew and P.R. Kleindorfer (eds), *Regulatory and Economic Challenges in the Postal and Delivery Sector*, Boston, MA: Kluwer Academic.

Eccles, R. (2008), 'United Kingdom postal service regulation', in M.A. Crew, P.R. Kleindorfer and J.I. Campbell (eds), *Handbook of Worldwide Postal Reform*, Cheltenham, UK and Northampton, MA, USA: Edward Elgar.

Eccles, R. and P. Kuipers (2008), 'The proper scope of the rules on abuse of dominant position in a liberalized postal services market', in M.A. Crew and P.R. Kleindorfer (eds), *Competition and Regulation in the Postal and Delivery Sector*, Cheltenham, UK and Northampton, MA, USA: Edward Elgar.

Hill, R. and R. Robinson (2006), 'Establishing non-uniform access prices in the UK', in M.A. Crew and P.R. Kleindorfer (eds), *Progress toward Liberalization of the Postal and Delivery Sector*, New York: Springer.

Hooper, R., D. Hutton and I.R. Smith (Hooper Report) (2008), *Modernise or Decline: Policies to Maintain the Universal Postal Services in the UK*, Norwich: TSO, 16 December.

Horncastle, A., D. Jevons, P. Dudley and E. Thanassoulis (2006), 'Efficiency analysis of delivery offices in the postal sector using stochastic frontier and data envelopment analyses', in M.A. Crew and P.R. Kleindorfer (eds), *Liberalization of the Postal and Delivery Sector*, Cheltenham, UK and Northampton, MA, USA: Edward Elgar.

LECG (2005), 'Future Efficient Costs of Royal Mail's Regulated Activities', Excised Version, August.

Leighton, A. (2007), *On Leadership*, London: Random House.

Leighton, A. (2011), *Tough Calls: Making the Right Decisions in Challenging Times*, London: Random House Business Books.

Macintyre, D. (2000), *Mandelson and the Making of New Labour*, London: Harper Collins.

Moriarty, R. and P. Smith (2005), 'Barriers to entry in post and regulatory responses', in M.A. Crew and P.R. Kleindorfer (eds), *Regulatory and Economic Challenges in the Postal and Delivery Sector*, New York: Springer.

Moriarty, R., S. Yorke, G. Harman, J. Cubbin, M. Meschi and P. Smith (2006), 'Economic analysis of the efficiency of Royal Mail units and the implications for regulatory policy', in M.A. Crew and P.R. Kleindorfer (eds), *Liberalization of the Postal and Delivery Sector*, Cheltenham, UK and Northampton, MA, USA: Edward Elgar.

Panzar, John (1993), 'Competition, efficiency and the vertical structure of postal services', in M.A. Crew and P.R. Kleindorfer (eds), *Regulation and the Nature of Postal and Delivery Services*, Boston, MA: Kluwer Academic.

Panzar, John (2002), 'Reconciling competition, downstream access and universal service in postal markets', in M.A. Crew and P.R. Kleindorfer (eds), *Postal and Delivery Services: Delivering on Competition*, Boston, MA: Kluwer Academic.

Peston, R. (2008), *Who Runs Britain*, London: Hodder.

Postcomm (2007), 'Postcomm calls for radical action over Royal Mail's costs', Press release, London, 27 February.

Postcomm (2008a), 'First Submission to the Independent Review of the Postal Services Sector', March, as amended May.

Postcomm (2008b), 'Second Submission to the Independent Review of the Postal Services Sector', May.

Postcomm (2010), 'Quality of service decision', Press release, London.

Robinson, R. and J. McMurdie (2009), 'Postal costing beyond ABC: estimating the economic cost of mails services', in M.A. Crew and P.R. Kleindorfer(eds), *Progress in the Competitive Agenda in the Postal and Delivery Sector*, Cheltenham, UK and Northampton, MA, USA: Edward Elgar.

Royal Mail (2003), 'Royal Mail Group Annual Review and Report 2002–03', London.

Royal Mail (2004), 'Royal Mail Group Annual Report 2003–04', London.

Royal Mail (2006), 'Royal Mail Group Annual Report 2005–06', London.

Royal Mail (2008), 'Submission to Phase One of the Independent Review of the Postal Services Sector: Supporting Exhibits to Terms of Reference 1 and 2 (Royal Mail, Renewal Plan Closure Summary, August 2005)'.

Royal Mail (2010), 'Royal Mail Group Annual Report 2009–10', London.
Wachter, M.L., B.T. Hirsch and J.W. Gillula (1997), 'Difficulties of deregulation when wage costs are the major cost', in M.A. Crew and P.R. Kleindorfer (eds), *Future Directions in Postal Reform*, Boston, MA: Kluwer Academic.
Walsh, T.J. (2012), 'Royal Mail, 1986–2010: A Business and Regulatory Review', mimeo, London.
Willig, Robert (1979), 'The theory of network access pricing', in H.M. Trebing (ed.), *Issues in Public Utility Regulation*, East Lansing, MI: Michigan State University Press, Public Utility Papers.

23. What's past is prologue: understanding developments in North American postal markets*

Michael D. Bradley,[†] Jeff Colvin[‡] and Mary K. Perkins[§]

1 INTRODUCTION

Research on postal economics, whether presented in regulatory forums or in the series of Rutgers Center for Research on Regulated Industries Conferences on Postal and Delivery Economics (CRRI conferences), has exercised an important influence on postal policy over the past 22 years. Tracing the debates and their relation to actual developments in North American postal markets since the first of the CRRI conferences in 1990 is the purpose of this chapter.

A proper analysis of the recent history of the postal industry in the US and Canada requires understanding the fundamental nature of postal markets and the basic issues that have arisen. Such issues have been debated at these conferences throughout the relatively peaceful years of the 1990s. Such issues have reappeared in intriguing new forms in the years since.

In this chapter, we focus on four such issues, which have been important in recent postal policy considerations in North America and have been treated at length at the CRRI conferences. The first is governance/regulatory policy, the second is the Universal Service Obligation (USO), the third is the measurement of postal costs and the fourth involves pricing of postal products, including access pricing. Section 2 briefly reviews the recent history of the post in the United States and Canada. Section 3 discusses issues surrounding the appropriate governance of postal services. Section 4 examines the USO, including efforts to measure the cost of the obligation. Section 5 turns to the issue of postal cost measurement. Section 6 discusses issues in pricing. Section 7 offers conclusions and suggestions for future research.

2 TWENTY YEARS OF POSTAL HISTORY: EXTREME REDUX

The first CRRI postal conference took place in 1990 in Rugby, UK. From then until 1995, United States Postal Service (USPS) volume grew steadily. In fact, volume had increased steadily since the early 1970s, First-Class mail growth tracking the growth in

† Professor of Economics, George Washington University, Washington, DC.
‡ Director, USPS Office of Inspector General, Arlington, VA.
§ Associate Professor of Economics, Howard University, Washington, DC.

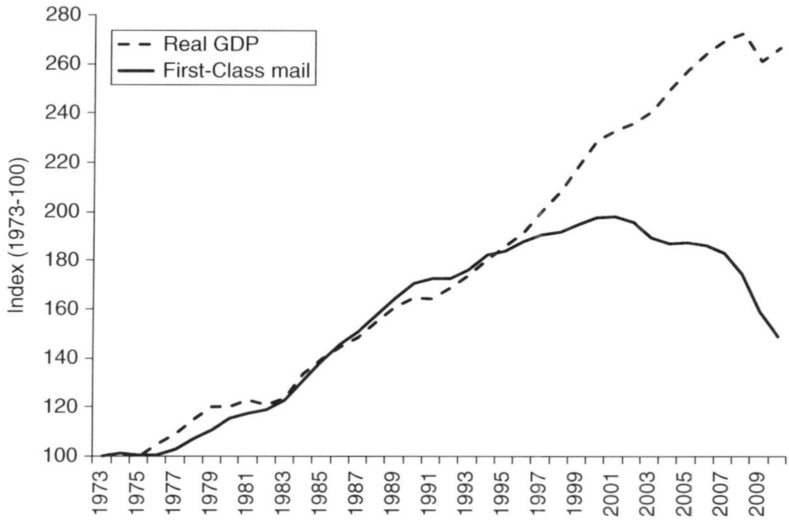

Source: USPSOIG (2012d).

Figure 23.1 GDP and First-Class mail volume

real GDP (Figure 23.1). In the mid-1990s, USPS hit the first of several bumps, the first being the initial growth spurts of the Internet. Broadband connections began to replace slower dial-up services, and free bill pay service appeared on bank websites, ushering in the era of electronic substitution.

USPS ran into further bumps in the road as the relatively mild recessions of 1991 and 2001 took a bite out of First-Class and Standard mail volumes. The effects of these downturns were minor compared to the 2008 recession, in which First-Class mail, already weakened by the migration to email, continued its decline, while Standard mail markets essentially collapsed, volume falling by nearly 17 percent in 2009 alone (Figure 23.2).

These events also brought about a major change in the mix of mail, dramatically increasing the proportion of business mail in the mail stream, a fact of post-Internet postal life that (i) makes USPS finances subject to the uncertainly of the business cycle, and (ii) raises tricky questions about long-held goals of public policy, such as the USO. Standard mail advertising represents 48 percent of volume, 25 percent of revenue and 22 percent of contribution (Table 23.1).

Along with the declines in volume came declines in revenue and contribution. These have led to a serious financial crisis, with real net income (in 2010 dollars) falling from $4.6 billion in 2003 to a loss of $8.5 billion in 2010 (see USPS Annual Reports, 2003 and 2010).

Canada Post Corporation (CPC), like USPS, felt the pressure of electronic substitution. Total volume has fallen sharply since 2008, but not as sharply as that of USPS, and is well below where it was in the mid-1990s (Table 23.2).

Yet at the same time as CPC faces an ongoing volume decline, its network responsibilities, as measured by points of delivery, continue to expand. For example, in the

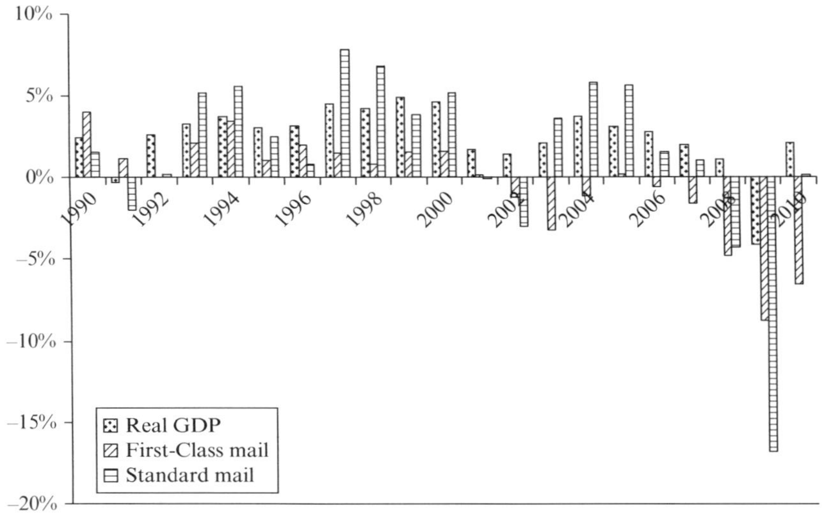

Source: USPSOIG (2012d).

Figure 23.2 Year over year growth in GDP and mail volume

Table 23.1 2010 USPS mail volume by segment

Mail type	Proportion (%)
FCM correspondence	9.00
FCM transactions	21.00
FCM advertising	4.00
STD advertising	48.00
Periodicals	4.00
2 & 3 day packages	1.00
Overnight flats & packages	0.02
Ground packages	1.00
Other	12.00

Source: USPSOIG (2012d).

mid-1990s Canada Post had about 12,000 points of call but by 2011 that had increased to over 15,000. As in the similar case of USPS, network growth increases the difficulty of remaining financially solvent in an era of declining volume.

In the US a reform act was passed in 2006 (the Postal Accountability and Enhancement Act: PAEA). Prior to that date, the most recent postal reform had been the Postal Reorganization Act of 1970 (PRA). This law required USPS to 'bind the Nation together' without, for the most part, taxpayer subsidies. This placed importance upon the rates charged to mailers as the only means to fund USPS operations. The ensuing regime established a form of utility style cost-of-service regulation between 1990 and

Table 23.2 Canada Post volume performance in two decades

Year	Millions of pieces	% change
1992	10,410	
1993	10,910	4.8
1994	11,573	6.1
1995	11,753	1.6
2008	11,754	
2009	10,765	−8.4
2010	10,572	−1.8
2011	10,101	−4.5

Source: Canada Post Annual Reports.

2006. A major drawback of the PRA, one the 2006 law attempted to address, was the lack of incentive for postal management to increase efficiency. Increased costs could be passed on to mailers without examination of the need for increased expenditures. Unlike private utility litigation, with its intense struggles over the return to capital, the proceedings before the Postal Regulatory Commission (PRC) focused on the rate structure. In the 2006 law, USPS got some pricing flexibility but constraints were placed on diversification, the cost of future liabilities were to be recovered from current customers, and restrictions on access pricing were written into the law. PAEA froze prices in real terms by placing a set of CPI-based caps on 'market-dominant' products, leaving USPS free to set 'competitive' prices subject to some constraints on cross-subsidy. Workshare discounts were tied to the costs avoided by the activity. Perhaps most importantly, as discussed in Bradley et al. (2008), the law removed the break-even constraint; USPS was left free to earn profits (or losses) as long as it complied with the regulations, regulations enforced by a strengthened third-party regulator, the PRC.

The transformation of CPC proceeded along somewhat different lines. CPC struggled to become a profitable Crown Corporation with just one shareholder, the Canadian government, while maintaining important social obligations. Canada Post was given substantial pricing freedom, with a price cap on just the basic letter rate, but faced a moratorium on closing small rural post offices. CPC proceeded on its path toward corporatization and by 2007 had become debt free and was poised to begin an ambitious modernization plan.

In 2008, a perfect storm of bad economic news struck and both North American posts found themselves in dramatically worsening environments. The worst recession since the 1930s, which accelerated the diversion of business-related letter mail, the pull-back in advertising, and other factors led both institutions down the path toward substantial losses, leading to the loss of billions of dollars in both countries by 2010. In addition, losses in its pension fund sharply increased CPC's pension liabilities and USPS was hit with a legislative shift requiring it to spend billions of dollars a year prefunding its retiree health-care liabilities. Such theoretical issues as the death spiral, intermodal competition, bypass and price caps, now became components of postal reality. Again, the interplay of ideas and reality demonstrate the importance of ongoing research in postal economics.

Since 2008, USPS has mounted efforts to downsize its network, shedding delivery routes and work hours, and putting forward plans to reduce the USO by lowering the frequency of delivery and changing delivery standards. In Fiscal Year 2010, USPS proposed eliminating Saturday delivery in order to save both delivery and transportation costs. In Fiscal Year 2012, USPS proposed lowering the delivery standard for First-Class mail, essentially eliminating overnight delivery for the product and replacing it with two-day delivery. Such a change would allow it to restructure its mail processing network and expand the operating windows for sorting mail. In both instances, USPS predicted multi-billion dollar savings.

Canada Post suffered both a strike and a lockout in 2011, with postal services suspended for nearly three weeks. It now contemplates reducing delivery frequency to three days from five days. Meanwhile, debates rage over the fundamental changes confronting postal markets in the digital age, the cost savings available from changes in the USO, how to combine competition and cooperation, and over the best strategy in the face of recession, all amidst new calls for reform of the business model.

3 GOVERNANCE AND REGULATION

A foundational issue in the debate on the postal industry concerns the type of governance under which the post operates. In Europe, changes in governance have been dramatic since 1990, as most posts have been transformed from agencies under direct control of parliament to corporatized state-owned enterprises (SOEs), as part of the broad liberalization movement accompanying European integration. On the other hand, the basic governance platform of USPS has remained largely unchanged since 1970; even after the passage of PAEA, USPS remains an 'independent establishment', supported by rates but obliged to perform certain loss-making activities to fulfill its USO, managed by a nine-member board of governors and regulated, via one mechanism or another, by a presidentially appointed commission. Bradley et al. (2008) and Crew and Kleindorfer (2008b) offer discussions of the new law.

Crew and Kleindorfer (ibid.) emphasize the failure of the reform to go further in the direction of privatization, expressing doubt that what steps toward commercialization the law takes are likely to fail, due to Congress's long-established penchant for managing postal affairs. The Congress exercises considerable power over the management of postal activities, blocking post office closures, facility consolidations, service changes, and even restricting the use of contractors. Moreover, PAEA mandated large annual payments to the Retiree Health Benefits Fund (RHBF) through 2016; it seems likely that were USPS management free to do so, it might well accrue the future costs at a slower pace, under current circumstances. The challenges presented by congressional control over items that would, in a private business, be within the power of management, are among the factors leading Crew and Kleindorfer to strongly favor privatization.[1] They also cite the improved efficiency incentives associated with the threat of bankruptcy, the discipline of capital markets and pressure from residual claimants (shareholders) as reasons favoring a governance structure similar to that of regulated investor-owned utilities in other sectors. Holder and Smith (2012) make similar arguments.

Privatization has not, at least so far, been given serious attention as an alternative in the United States. Both Holder and Smith (2012) and Panzar (2012) suggest, while noting the superior efficiency properties of private firms, there is nevertheless a large and important gap between good and bad management of an SOE. Such thinking has led some to favor a commercialization approach to governance, one focused on creating the conditions under which SOE management will be more profit oriented, on the possible reform of labor relations, and reducing the degree of congressional influence over management.

As Panzar (ibid.) notes, factors tipping the balance toward commercialization, that is, toward the maintenance of USPS as a regulated SOE, are the continued requirement that USPS assume an obligation of universal service, and the natural monopoly characteristics of USPS's most vital function, delivery (see Panzar, 1991). While it is not difficult to imagine a private postal service fulfilling such obligations, Panzar (2012) finds that such practices have proven unwieldy in other sectors, such as railroads and telecommunications. Adherents of privatization often assert the benefits of the threat of bankruptcy and yet find no difficulty in the idea that a USO might be required of a private entity. One wonders to what extent the USO would be fulfilled by today's postal service, were it allowed to file for bankruptcy protection. Fundamentally, the requirement to make losses on certain activities seems to run counter to the motives underlying private sector behavior.

The need for regulation, on the other hand, stems from the likelihood that a single firm will dominate the postal industry, whether it enjoys a *statutory* monopoly or not, owing to the powerful advantages it gets from strong economies in delivery. It may be that such advantages are sufficient to preserve the postal monopoly, at least as against traditional letter mail competition, or it may be that secure financing requires protection. Either way, the case remains strong for some form of price regulation to mitigate monopoly exploitation.

Twenty years of history and debate both point to a continued role for government in the postal industry, at least in the United States, and at least in the near term. Those same twenty years, however, provide ample examples of the difficulty of operating a business-like entity under conditions of close government involvement. In short, USPS appears destined to remain a regulated SOE, but to provide a secure financial foundation for the infrastructural role it is expected to play, its management will need the flexibility and incentives to operate effectively.

The regulation of Canada Post has evolved along the lines of a commercialization approach. Since its transformation from a government department to a public enterprise in 1980, Canada Post has operated in a far more autonomous environment than USPS, with more focus on being financially self-sufficient. Unlike USPS, which operated under a break-even mandate until 2006, as a Crown Corporation, CPC is expected to earn a positive profit for its sole shareholder – the government of Canada. In this respect, it has been more successful than the USPS. Although CPC did make a loss in 2011, it has reported profits in the previous 16 years.

Canada Post does not have an external regulator analogous to the PRC. Rather, government regulation comes in several forms. First, there is a minister responsible for Canada Post who receives and reviews CPC's annual reports and corporate plans. The government has the authority to reject Canada Post's corporate plan, as it did in 1985, and to replace Canada Post's chief executive officer. In addition, Canada Post has an independent board of directors, all of which are appointed by the Government of Canada. Finally, the government periodically undertakes thorough external reviews of Canada Post's operations, financial performance, commercial behavior, and strategic plans such as the 1996 Mandate Review and the 2008 Strategic Review.

Nevertheless, Canada Post has considerably more operating flexibility than the USPS. It has substantial pricing freedom in its competitive markets and has the ability to engage in commercial activities outside its core mail delivery function. Whether such differences in operational and pricing flexibility, diversification, and labor relations are sufficient to explain CPC's superior financial performance is an excellent topic for further research.

4 UNIVERSAL SERVICE OBLIGATIONS

When USPS and CPC were transformed from government departments to public enterprises, each inherited a universal service mandate. However, the precise obligations embodied in the mandate were not specified in detail. This should not be surprising because universal service was inherent in the mission of a government (postal) department and the cost of carrying such a burden was not an issue.

In the years immediately following the establishment of the posts as public enterprises, little attention was focused on the USO. The nature of the obligation was historically determined and, moreover, the economic burden of the obligation was relatively easy to bear in an era of rising volume and revenue. However, in more recent years, the USO has become the subject of focused research. As governments began discussion of moving their public posts down the road toward corporatization and/or privatization, the necessity of specifying, and quantifying the obligations a self-sustaining post would need to sustain became an important public policy issue. As the subsequent decline in the economic environment raised the issue of the financial sustainability of posts, consideration of ways to reduce the scope of the USO came to the fore of policy discussion.

PAEA included a stipulation that the PRC and USPS undertake a study of the nature and costs of USPS's USO.[2] Similarly, the 2008 Strategic Review initiated by the minister responsible for Canada Post included the CPC's universal service obligation as one of its primary topics.

As research on the USO increased, quantitative methods to measure its financing cost were developed (Rodriguez et al., 1999; Bradley and Colvin, 2000; Cremer et al., 2000). In addition to considering the cost of the USO, the recent difficult economic environment has also brought attention to ways of restricting the size of the obligation. For example, CPC has been successful at replacing postal-run retail facilities with franchise operations and has reduced the cost of fulfilling its retail obligation. USPS has recently focused on closing small retail facilities and/or reducing their hours of operation.

Another margin at which the USO can be trimmed is through changing the mode of delivery. Centralized delivery in which delivery points are concentrated in mail rooms or community mailboxes (CBUs) reduce the cost of delivery but make it more inconvenient for customers to retrieve their mail. Both postal operators have attempted to move delivery from 'door' or 'curb' to 'central', and, as Table 23.3 shows, Canada Post has been more successful in this effort.

Table 23.3 A comparison of delivery points by type

	CPC		USPS	
	Number of delivery points	Percentage	Number of delivery points	Percentage
Door	5,321,000	36.9	57,807,861	38.3
Central	3,167,000	22.0	19,012,701	12.6
Community mailbox	3,329,000	23.1	11,280,391	7.5
Rural mailbox	828,000	5.7	42,771,358	28.3
PO box	1,770,000	12.3	20,095,372	13.3
Total	14,415,000	100.0	150,967,683	100.0

Sources: Canada Post Corporation (2008); USPSOIG (2010).

Despite the profusion of methods purporting to quantify the financing costs of the USO, there is some agreement that the cost is pretty large once one considers the added losses from bypass in a liberalized environment. Hence, the question of financing the USO remains an important part of the policy debate, as do means of reducing the scope of the USO and the social costs they entail. Both North American posts have engaged in the attempt to reduce the size of the USO, with CPC apparently achieving greater success to this point than USPS.

5 MEASURING POSTAL COSTS

Postal product cost measurement has been of special importance in the United States because of the traditional relation between costs and prices. PAEA broke this link to some extent, though the avoided cost of workshare products still plays an important role in setting access prices.

In the pre-PAEA years, rates were chosen by the PRC which would enable USPS to break even in a future test year. Numerous economists emphasized the opportunity to price postal products efficiently by estimating marginal costs and demand elasticities (Baumol, 1984; Panzar, 1990; Bradley et al., 1993). That left unanswered the question of fairness and this prompted USPS to provide estimates of incremental cost as a test of cross-subsidy (Bradley et al., 1997, 1999). Debate over the accuracy of cost measurement was plentiful before the PRC, and at the CRRI conferences. USPS provided cost estimates of delivery, transportation and mail processing costs; all estimates were challenged and debated before the PRC (Bradley and Colvin, 1995, 1999; Bradley et al., 2007; Bozzo, 2009). At the same time, estimates of costs avoided by mailers performing worksharing activities played a growing role, especially during the years in which the mailing industry grew at a rapid rate.

Since PAEA, cost measurement has focused more on cross-subsidy detection than on providing inputs to efficient pricing exercises. However, the use of incremental cost as a test for cross-subsidy has been challenged by Sappington and Sidak (2003) on the grounds that an SOE is motivated to make investments in assets whose costs are impossible to allocate to specific products, thus confounding the incremental cost test. Bradley et al. (2004) note that USPS prices are set (or were at the time set) by a regulator and show that using a maximand more typical of a regulator than an incumbent leads to an *over*statement of competitive prices. They conclude that the issue calls for careful monitoring of incremental cost measures for competitive products. Panzar (2008, 2012) views the danger of cross-subsidy to be sufficiently strong to recommend prohibition of USPS entry into adjacent markets. Perkins (2001) and USPSOIG (2012a, 2012b), on the other hand, find that horizontal integration, especially in the digital area, is the key to long-term success for USPS, and possibly to resolution of the set of issues referred to as the 'digital divide'.

Because CPC operates in a very different regulatory environment from USPS, it takes a different approach to cost calculation. Except for the price cap on its stamped letter product, CPC has flexibility in setting its prices. It also has the ability to tailor prices to meet the needs of individual customers. This flexibility translates into less reliance upon product costs in setting prices than USPS and more reliance upon market signals. As a result, CPC's product costing system, the Annual Cost Study (ACS) is designed to measure long-run incremental costs rather than marginal costs. CPC thus uses its ACS to check the profitability of its products and product lines.

In addition, CPC uses the ACS to satisfy its regulatory requirements. CPC is prohibited from cross-subsidizing its competitive products with revenues earned on its exclusive privilege (monopoly) products. It uses the long-run incremental costs for these groups of products, as calculated in the ACS, to demonstrate annually that it is not cross-subsidizing its competitive products.[3]

Cost measurement has shifted, as North American posts have moved in the direction of commercialization, from an emphasis on major product costs to providing the information needed for more differentiated pricing (see USPSOIG, 2012c for discussion of this issue). The debate on the use of SOE cost information in cross-subsidy tests is not settled, at the theoretical level, though both North American posts use cost estimates in this way.

6 PRICES

PAEA placed USPS under a price-cap regime applied to several baskets within which the average product price was constrained to increase at or below the consumer price index for all urban consumers (CPI-U).[4] No 'X factor' was applied to the mechanism, probably reflecting limitations in USPS's ability to increase productivity.

Analysts promptly raised issues with the new legislation. Bradley et al. (2008) noted that the impact of the legislation depended somewhat upon the maximand pursued by USPS management and emphasized the importance of cost control for success of the reform. Crew and Kleindorfer (2008b) offer a broad array of criticisms of PAEA, but note that the incentives the price cap offers are profoundly weakened for want of residual claimants.

Theoretical predictions aside, two real-world issues surfaced almost immediately upon implementation of the reform. First, the caps were set without a final rate case to bring revenues up to expenditures. As a result, USPS began in a financial hole. Second, demand collapsed quite suddenly, with 2006 being the year the price cap was implemented as well as the historic peak of USPS mail volume (213 billion pieces). As mentioned above, successful price-cap implementation depends upon productivity growth, which, in the absence of fundamental technological change, depends in turn upon pushing a lot of volume through the network. As Bradley et al. (2012), and many others, have noted, the benefit of scale economies as volume grows becomes a disadvantage during the downturn. Given these two problems, it is questionable whether the price cap, as it is now constructed, is financially sustainable.

As noted by Laffont and Tirole (1993), incentive regulation involves a tradeoff between a strong efficiency incentive, which will likely afford the incumbent the ability to appropriate rents, and a weaker incentive at the cost of greater inefficiency. In the case of PAEA and USPS, the dynamic is similar except that the rents 'earned' are negative ones. Clearly, a procedure which perpetually revised the cap (allowing price changes greater than the CPI-U) to compensate for USPS losses would constitute a very weak incentive, but one which might allow for a more secure financing of the USO.

Within the orbit of continued price-cap regulation at least three alternatives present themselves.

The first has to do with modification of the price-cap standard itself. Under the PAEA, price increases are limited by reference to the CPI-U. Such an index has the advantage of providing strong efficiency incentives to postal management, but it could be weakened by tailoring the cap to the conditions in the industry. In its most extreme form, the cap could be based on an index of postal input prices, but that would seem to take most of the 'incentive' out of 'incentive regulation'. More moderately, adjustments might be made to the cap, either by adding 'factors' to the price restraint for differences between postal productivity and that of the industry as a whole (see Christensen et al., 2003). Or an adjustment to the mechanism could be made to account explicitly for the fall in volume. This would be similar to 'revenue per customer' adjustments sometimes made in the electricity and telecommunications industry (see FCC, 1990 and Ontario Energy Board, 2008). Further research is needed before choosing a specific modification as the impact on managerial incentives is still unknown, and that was the perceived problem that the postal price cap was designed to solve.

Two other modifications to the cap mechanism might be noted. Some have argued for a replacement of the current cap with a global cap, which would allow USPS to trade off higher prices for customers with more inelastic demand for lower increases in more price-elastic markets. As discussed by Borsenberger et al. (2012), global price caps offer better efficiency properties than the current multiple basket approach. However, the suggestion raises the interesting question of what is the structure of demand under multi-modal competition. Crew and Kleindorfer (2011) note the likely increase in the price elasticity of postal products as electronic substitution grows, whereas Nikali (2011) suggests that price increases have little if any impact on the decision to move to the Internet. In any case, further research on demand would benefit policy decisions regarding the appropriate cap mechanism.

Finally, some posts have implemented a less encompassing price-cap mechanism. CPC pricing is constrained by a cap on the basic letter rate; the remaining products are priced flexibly. USPS appears to contemplate a gradual transferring of products onto the competitive (uncapped) side of the menu, consistent with this approach.

Access pricing has provided a frequent theme of the CRRI conferences, and has been a powerful source of growth for USPS. A straightforward attempt to introduce competition and increase efficiency begun in 1976, the basic structure of 'worksharing', as it is termed in the US, has been described many times (Panzar, 1993; Crew and Kleindorfer, 2002, 2004, 2008a). The practice benefited immensely from the growth of computing power throughout the 1980s, as it proved to be markedly easier to sort addresses than letters.

Practitioners were quick to borrow the efficient component pricing rule (ECPR) from other regulated network industries and apply it to this problem. ECPR, which sets the discount off of the E2E (end-to-end) prices at the cost avoided by the worksharing activities, has two powerful advantages: (i) it ensures that the most efficient producer performs the activity and (ii) it provides the incumbent with the same contribution whether the entrant accepts the offered discount or not. Such an arrangement may have appeal during a period of 'peace' in which growing volumes provide benefits for all parties involved, and may lose some of that appeal as competitors struggle over the remains of a shrinking pie.

In any case, the issue becomes more complicated as elements of reality are brought into the picture. For instance, as shown by Billette de Villemeur et al. (2003), surplus maximizing discounts set for an operator with fixed network costs serving customers with heterogeneous demand will not in general be equal to ECPR discounts.[5] Further, Crew and Kleindorfer (2002, 2004) noted that access prices that take into account differential delivery costs could dominate ECPR uniform discounts from the point of view of efficiency. Along these lines Bradley et al. (2010) used 2007 USPS data to show that even keeping total revenue constant, adjusting prices to delivery costs, would increase contribution by $800 million by shifting volume from high- to low-cost delivery areas.

The price-cap regime initiated by postal reform added a further complication. As Panzar (2008, 2012) has emphasized, the introduction of a price cap that is 'global' in the sense of including both retail and workshared products within the same weighted-average price constraint, provides a profit-maximizing incumbent with a motivation to set discounts below avoided cost, thus 'excluding' efficient entrants and inviting antitrust concerns.[6] Crew and Kleindorfer (2008b) note, however, that to the extent that cost-avoided *measures* include higher labor compensation than that offered by entrants, ECPR discounts equal to avoided cost will encourage inefficient entry. It may be that the ground of access pricing, though pretty well trodden, could benefit from further analytical survey, the mail obstacle perhaps being the difficulty in keeping up with rapidly changing practices.

7 CONCLUSIONS AND FUTURE RESEARCH

In this chapter, we have examined several key areas of research and their relation to postal policy over the past two decades. We have argued that the events of the past twenty years suggest that the way forward is to steer a path between privatization, which seems on the face of it to miss something of the close relation between postal services and the communication infrastructure of the country, and full agency status, which is very likely to inhibit the potential efficiency gains available to the post. Future research suggestions include a more thorough analysis of the impact of price on postal demand in the digital world, further understanding of incentive regulation (or alternatives to it) under conditions of falling volume, as well as the potential long-term impact of postal entry into the adjacent digital market place, possibly as a supplier of government services (see Ravnitsky, 2011; Ravnitsky and Klingenberg, 2012).

Is past prologue? Is the pattern of the recent past to be repeated? It does not seem unfair to characterize postal/government relations, over the past two decades in the US, as torn between a strong desire to create a free-standing 'economic' institution capable of sustaining a powerful USO, and an equally pressing, if often conflicting, need to address a variety of short-tem fiscal or political problems. Improvement in this fundamental relationship would require a break with the recent past, so it is to be hoped that past is indeed *not* prologue in this sense.

NOTES

* The views expressed in this chapter are those of the authors and do not necessarily reflect those of George Washington University, the Office of Inspector General or Howard University. The authors are indebted to Luis Jimenez and Stephen Littlechild for their comments on an earlier draft.

1. In this context, it is worth noting the rather large list of government agencies, apart from Congress, that have oversight responsibilities with regard to USPS, or otherwise has a strong influence on its activities. The list would include the Postal Regulatory Commission, the Office of Inspector General, the General Accountability Office, the Office of Management and Budget, the Office of Personnel Management, the Federal Trade Commission, the Department of Justice, the Department of State, the Department of Homeland Security and the Treasury.
2. That study was completed in 2008 (see USPRC, 2008).
3. ACS cost calculations are also used to defend CPC against charges of anticompetitive behavior in regulatory proceedings such as the 1996 Mandate Review and the NAFTA challenge brought by United Parcel Service (UPS). In that case, UPS charged that Canada Post was cross-subsidizing its packet and parcel lines of business.
4. 39 U.S.C. 3622(d)(1)(A). There was some consideration, in the years leading up to the reform, given to other inflation indices, such as the GDP deflator and the Employment Cost Index (ECI), but the CPI-U won out as it was not under the control of the regulated entity and it was used in so many industries around the world.
5. Crew and Kleindorfer (2008a) provide an extended discussion of the theoretical issues at the heart of the controversy over optimal access pricing.
6. Interestingly, PAEA requires USPS to explain discounts greater than avoided cost, it seems to permit discounts to be less than avoided cost.

REFERENCES

Baumol, W. (1984), 'Testimony before the United States Postal Rate Commission', Docket No. R84-1.

Billette, de Villemeur, E., H. Cremer, B. Roy and J. Toledano (2003), 'Optimal pricing and price-cap regulation in the postal sector', *Journal of Regulatory Economics*, **24** (1), 40–62.

Borsenberger, C, and S. Bréville, H. Cremer, P. De Donder, and D. Joram (2012), 'Price cap regulation in the postal sector: single versus multiple baskets', in M.A. Crew and P.R. Kleindorfer (eds), *Multi-modal Competition and the Future of Mail*, Cheltenham, UK and Northampton, MA, USA: Edward Elgar.

Bozzo, T. (2009), 'Using operating data to measure labor input variability and density economies in the USPS mail processing operations', in M.A. Crew and P.R. Kleindorfer (eds), *Progress in the Competitive Agenda in the Postal and Delivery Sector*, Cheltenham, UK and Northampton, MA, USA: Edward Elgar.

Bradley, M. and J. Colvin (1995), 'An econometric model of postal delivery', in M.A. Crew and P.R. Kleindorfer (eds), *Commercialization of Postal and Delivery Services: National and International Perspectives*, Boston, MA: Kluwer Academic.

Bradley, M. and J. Colvin (1999), 'Productivity and technical change in a public service enterprise', in M.A. Crew and P.R. Kleindorfer (eds), *Emerging Competition in Postal and Delivery Service*, Boston, MA: Kluwer Academic.

Bradley, M. and J. Colvin (2000), 'Measuring the cost of universal service for posts', in M.A. Crew and P.R. Kleindorfer (eds), *Current Directions in Postal Reform*, Boston, MA: Kluwer Academic.

Bradley, M., J. Colvin, N. Nieto and G. Tobias (2010), 'Estimating the impact of a uniform price rule in a liberalized postal environment: the case of the USPS', in M.A. Crew and P.R. Kleindorfer (eds), *Heightening Competition in the Postal and Delivery Sector*, Cheltenham, UK and Northampton, MA, USA: Edward Elgar.

Bradley, M., J. Colvin and J. Panzar (1997), 'Issues in measuring incremental cost in a multi-function enterprise', in M.A. Crew and P.R. Kleindorfer (eds), *Managing Change in the Postal and Delivery Industries*, Boston, MA: Kluwer Academic.

Bradley, M., J. Colvin and J. Panzar (1999), 'On setting prices and testing cross-subsidy with accounting data', *Journal of Regulatory Economics*, **16**: 83–100.

Bradley, M., J. Colvin and M. Perkins (2004), 'Testing for anti-competitive behavior in public enterprises', in M.A. Crew and P.R. Kleindorfer (eds), *Competitive Transformation of the Postal and Delivery Sector*, Boston, MA: Kluwer Academic.

Bradley, M., J. Colvin and M. Perkins (2007), 'Measuring scale and scope economies with a structural model', in M.A. Crew and P.R. Kleindorfer (eds), *Liberalization of the Postal and Delivery Sector*, Cheltenham, UK and Northampton, MA, USA: Edward Elgar.

Bradley, M., J. Colvin and M. Perkins (2008), 'An economic model of the regulatory structure created by the PAEA of 2006', in M.A. Crew, P.R. Kleindorfer and J.I. Campbell (eds), *Handbook of Worldwide Postal Reform*, Cheltenham, UK and Northampton, MA, USA: Edward Elgar.

Bradley, M., J. Colvin and M. Perkins (2012), 'Do volume increase and decreases have the same effect on labor hours?', in M.A. Crew and P.R. Kleindorfer (eds), *Multi-modal Competition and the Future of Mail*, Cheltenham, UK and Northampton, MA, USA: Edward Elgar.

Bradley, M., J. Colvin and M. Smith (1993), 'Measuring product costs for ratemaking: the United States Postal Service', in M.A. Crew and P.R. Kleindorfer (eds), *Regulation and the Nature of Postal and Delivery Services*, Boston, MA: Kluwer Academic.

Canada Post Corporation (2008), 'Strategic Review of Canada Post'.

Christensen, L., P. Schoech and M. Meitzen (2003), 'Telecommunications Productivity', in Gary Madden (ed.), *Traditional Telecommunications Networks*, Cheltenham, UK and Northampton, MA, USA: Edward Elgar.

Cremer, H., A. Grimaud and J.J. Laffont (2000), 'The cost of universal service in the postal sector', in M.A. Crew and P.R. Kleindorfer (eds), *Current Directions in Postal Reform*, Boston, MA: Kluwer Academic.

Crew, M.A. and P.R. Kleindorfer (2002), 'Balancing access and the USO', in Crew and Kleindorfer (eds), *Postal and Delivery Services: Delivering on Competition*, Boston, MA: Kluwer Academic.

Crew, M.A. and P.R. Kleindorfer (2004), 'Access and USO for letters and parcels', in Crew and Kleindorfer (eds), *Competitive Transformation of the Postal and Delivery Sector*, Boston, MA: Kluwer Academic.

Crew, M.A. and P.R. Kleindorfer (2008a), 'Pricing for postal access and worksharing', in Crew, Kleindorfer and J.I. Campbell (eds), *Handbook of Worldwide Postal Reform*, Cheltenham, UK and Northampton, MA, USA: Edward Elgar.

Crew, M.A. and P.R. Kleindorfer (2008b), 'Reform of the United States Postal Service: an unfinished task', in Crew, Kleindorfer and J.I. Campbell (eds), *Handbook of Worldwide Postal Reform*, Cheltenham, UK and Northampton, MA, USA: Edward Elgar.

Crew, M.A. and P.R. Kleindorfer (2011), 'Competitive strategies under FMO and intermodal competition', in Crew and Kleindorfer (eds), *Reinventing the Postal Sector in an Electronic Age*, Cheltenham, UK and Northampton, MA, USA: Edward Elgar.

Federal Communications Commission (FCC) (1990), CC Docket No. 87 – 313, Second Report and Order, Washington, DC.

Holder, S. and H. Smith (2012), 'Privatization: could the benefits seen in other network industries be realized in postal industries?', in M.A. Crew and P.R. Kleindorfer (eds), *Multi-modal Competition and the Future of Mail*, Cheltenham, UK and Northampton, MA, USA: Edward Elgar.

Laffont, J and J. Tirole (1993), *The Theory of Incentives in Procurement and Regulation*, Cambridge, MA: MIT Press.

Nikali, H. (2011), 'Does the level of price elasticity change with the progression of substitution?', in M.A. Crew and P.R. Kleindorfer (eds), *Reinventing the Postal Sector in an Electronic Age*, Cheltenham, UK and Northampton, MA, USA: Edward Elgar.

Ontario Energy Board (2008), EB-2007-0606, Decision.

Panzar, J. (1990), 'Testimony before the United States Postal Rate Commission', Docket No. R90-1.

Panzar, J. (1991), 'Is postal service a natural monopoly?', in M.A. Crew and P.R. Kleindorfer (eds), *Competition and Innovation in Postal Services*, Boston, MA: Kluwer Academic.

Panzar, J. (1993), 'Competition, efficiency, and the vertical structure of postal services', in M.A. Crew and P.R. Kleindorfer (eds), *Regulation and the Nature of Postal and Delivery Services*, Boston, MA: Kluwer Academic.

Panzar, J. (2008), 'Interactions between regulator and antitrust policies in a liberalized postal sector', in M.A. Crew, P.R. Kleindorfer and J.I. Campbell (eds), *Handbook of Worldwide Postal Reform*, Cheltenham, UK and Northampton, MA, USA: Edward Elgar.

Panzar, J. (2012), 'Towards a 21st century postal service', in M.A. Crew and P.R. Kleindorfer (eds), *Multi-modal Competition and the Future of Mail*, Cheltenham, UK and Northampton, MA, USA: Edward Elgar.

Perkins, M. (2001), 'Text services and universal service obligations', *Netnomics*, **3**, 173–89.

Ravnitzky, M.J. (2011), 'Offering sensor network services using the postal delivery vehicle fleet', in M.A. Crew and P.R. Kleindorfer (eds), *Reinventing the Postal Sector in an Electronic Age*, Cheltenham, UK and Northampton, MA, USA: Edward Elgar.

Ravnitsky, M. and J.P. Klingenberg (2012), 'Government use of the postal system: an ignored USO component', in M.A. Crew and P.R. Kleindorfer (eds), *Multi-modal Competition and the Future of Mail*, Cheltenham, UK and Northampton, MA, USA: Edward Elgar.

Rodriguez, F., S. Smith and D. Storer (1999), 'Estimating the cost of the Universal Service Obligation in postal service', in M.A. Crew and P.R. Kleindorfer (eds), *Emerging Competition in Postal and Delivery Services*, Boston, MA: Kluwer Academic.

Sappington, D. and J. Sidak (2003), 'Incentives for anticompetitive behavior by public enterprises', *Review of Industrial Organization*, **22**, 183–206.

United States Postal Regulatory Commission (USPRC) (2008), 'Report on Universal Postal Service and the Postal Monopoly'.

United States Postal Service (USPS) (2003, 2010, 2011), 'Annual Report'.

United States Postal Service Office of Inspector General (USPSOIG) (2010), 'Audit Report – Modes of Delivery'.

United States Postal Service Office of Inspector General (USPSOIG) (2012a), 'Digital Currency: Opportunities for the Postal Service', Risk Analysis Research Center, Report Number RARC-WP-12-001.

United States Postal Service Office of Inspector General (USPSOIG) (2012b), 'USPS Global Card: A Conceptual Analysis of a Smart Card Platform', Risk Analysis Research Center, Report Number RARC-WP-12-06.

United States Postal Service Office of Inspector General (USPSOIG) (2012c), 'Primer on Postal Costs', Risk Analysis Research Center, Report Number RARC-WP-12-09.

United States Postal Service Office of Inspector General (USPSOIG) (2012d), 'State of the Mail', Risk Analysis Research Center, Report Number RARC-WP-12-010.

24. Human capital and diversification choices for postal operators

Dominique Bailly[†] and Margaux Meidinger[‡]

1 INTRODUCTION

Faced with a decline in their traditional core business, diversification seems to be recognized today as the best way forward for incumbent operators to find new sources of revenue to guarantee their sustainable economic development. Within such a labor-intensive sector, these diversification choices are intrinsically linked to both economic and social considerations in two ways. First, the transformation of activities and the need for increased flexibility has significant social consequences in terms of employment and work organization. Second, within an increasingly customer-driven economy, diversification strategies are influenced by the operators' potential in terms of human resources but also by other intangible changes assets.

This chapter analyzes, therefore, the relationship between diversification choices and postal operators' social capital. To give the key elements of context, Section 2 presents the reality of the social impact of current developments in the sector and the diversity of social developments between the different European operators.[1] Section 3 analyzes the extent to which the postal companies' diversification can have protective social effects and lead to more well-balanced social adaptations. Section 4 explains why the emerging trend towards customer-driven diversification of companies, combined with the rise of a digital society calls for increased use of intangible assets, in particular human capital, as levers of economic development. Section 5 concludes that a successful customer-driven diversification and the development of the employees' employability can be mutually reinforcing.

2 SOCIAL IMPACT OF THE CURRENT CHANGES

The prospect of full market opening alongside increased e-substitution due to the development of new technologies has given rise to many concerns regarding social developments in the postal sector. National postal operators (NPOs) as a whole are facing similar technological, economic and regulatory challenges and must step up the pace and intensity of adaptation. This situation of unavoidable continuous change is acknowledged by the sector's European social partners in the Joint Declaration signed on 18 April

† Adviser to the General Delegate, Director of HR Development and Innovation, Le Groupe La Poste.
‡ Head of European Social Affairs Coordination, Le Groupe La Poste.

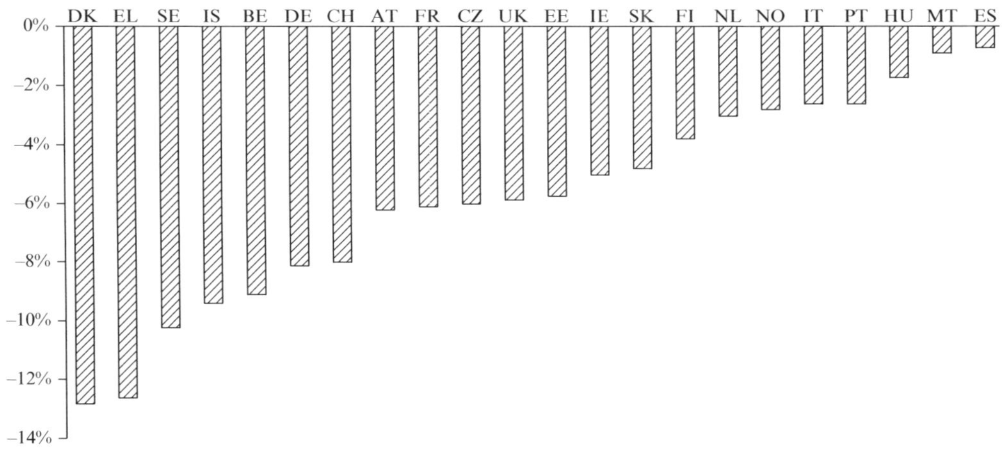

Source: Copenhagen Economics (2010).

Figure 24.1 General decline in staffing levels in all EU NPOs

2012[2] which also recognizes that various adaptation approaches are possible. The Social Observatory project indeed highlights a very diverse situation among EU members in terms of size of operations, social dialogue and the regulatory framework. These national differences are important in gaining a better understanding of the strategic choices made by operators. The objective of this section is therefore to assess the reality of social impacts of the current changes in the sector and examine whether or not there is uniformity in these developments.

Overall Decline in Staffing Levels Generally Managed by Natural Attrition

The first major social impact of the current changes within incumbent operators is the decline in staffing levels. In an industry where labor costs represent a large proportion of operating costs, staffing levels are key optimization levers. This decline can be seen in almost all European NPOs, as shown by Figure 24.1; sector studies report an average drop of 6 percent in staffing levels between 2007 and 2009 in the European Union. However, statistics point to significant variations in situations between operators, with a decrease ranging from more than 12 percent to less than 1 percent. This reduction is mainly managed by natural attrition, through the non-replacement of retired workers, and is actively encouraged with the development of early retirement programs in many NPOs, with financial incentives for employees wishing to follow these schemes. Despite the economic constraints, it seems that there are currently a limited number of redundancies, with nine companies from this project having reported using social plans.

External mobility, through voluntary departures, is also a method of decreasing the company workforce. Companies can thus guarantee former employees an equivalent job position outside the company and decrease their workforce in a responsible manner. Even if organized external mobility still remains limited, some programs have been put

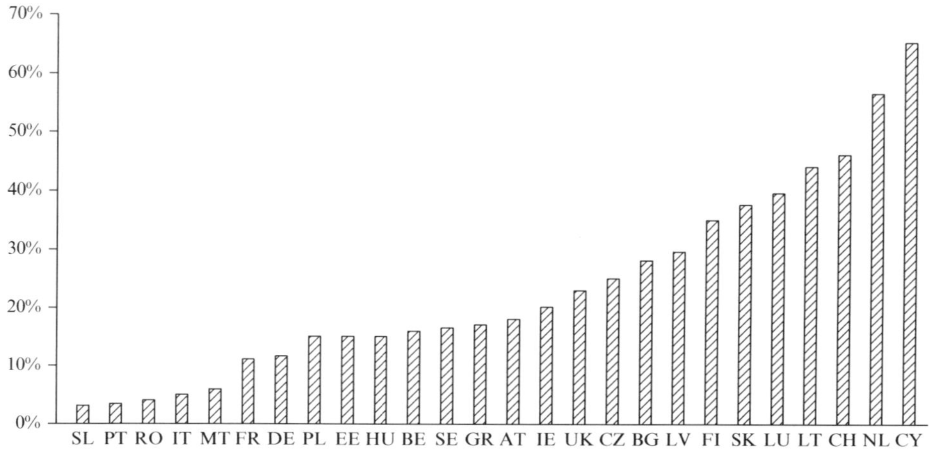

Source: Copenhagen Economics (2010).

Figure 24.2 Rates of part-time employment in 2008

in place within postal operators in order to favor mobility to other companies, to public administration or police as well as for the creation of companies. Some operators such as PostNL with PostNL Mobility and Posten AB with the Futurum program have put in place large-scale initiatives enabling thousands of employees to leave the company and find new job positions elsewhere.

Changes in Job Type and Status within the NPOs

The New Joint Declaration on Postal Sector Evolution also sets out as a key principle to accompany change, the need 'to improve the adaptability of the work organization in order to better cope with new customer requirements and to increase productivity' (European Social Dialogue Committee for the Postal Sector, 2012). This flexibility to work variations can be based either on adapting the production tool by introducing more flexible working hours while maintaining a stable workforce or, alternatively, on adapting employment by making greater use of flexible types of employment. In the study, half of the companies report an increased use of part-time workers but their level varies largely between companies. Figure 24.2 shows a general increased tendency of NPOs to rely on part-time employment. The study shows that traditional activities such as sorting and delivery, which are becoming increasingly automated, have been the most affected by these social developments, in addition to the direct impact of the drop in mail volumes.

The increased use of short-time contracts is also a means of increasing the flexibility of work organization, depending on the intensity of the activities. As shown in Figure 24.3, some operators have extensively developed this type of employment while others have chosen to have limited recourse to it.

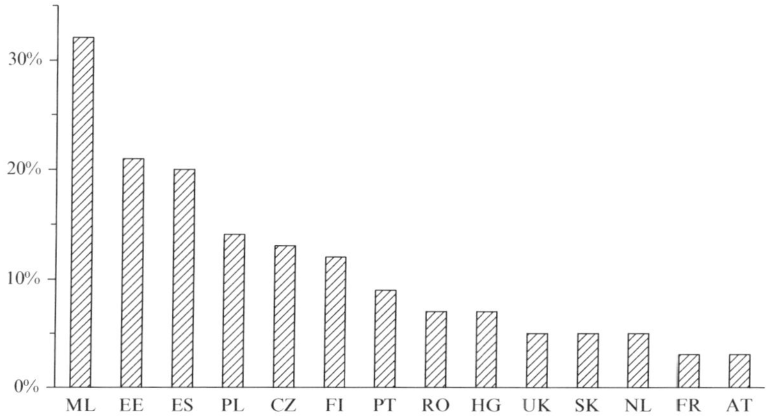

Source: SDC Questionnaire, in European Social Dialogue Committee for the Postal Sector (2011).

Figure 24.3 Rates of short-time contracts in 2010

3 PROTECTIVE SOCIAL EFFECT OF DIVERSIFICATION

By underlining some common trends and revealing the diversity in the degree of social optimization across the different countries, the Social Observatory project has confirmed that NPOs have opted for different adaptation strategies. This chapter aims, therefore, at gaining a better understanding of the link between diversification and the adaptation of the social model. It appears that lack of diversification puts increased pressure on operators to reduce costs, in particular labor costs, and therefore leads to both quantitative consequences, with increased pressure on staffing levels, and qualitative consequences, with radical social adaptations. On the other hand, diversification generates alternative ways of increasing flexibility and fostering a more balanced social adaptation.

Diversification as Protection against Restructuring

Even though it may take several forms, today diversification appears to be the only way forward for operators in order to find new sources of revenue. Several studies, like the one from Accenture (2010), claim that performance and diversification of operators are directly linked. This study shows that less-diversified NPOs are mainly low performers while the ones that have diversified the most show high performance. Indeed, non-mail activities are proving to be the most dynamic and represent a large majority of growth at a time when mail revenues are shrinking. In view of these findings, it appears that operators which diversified the least are the most exposed to significant social restructuring. Indeed companies which focus on their core business do not have any other choice but to follow a cost-reduction strategy. There is greater pressure on decreasing operating costs, with the social leverage in such labor-intensive companies being one of the main tools to achieve it. A non-diversified company also has a more restricted internal employment market: there are fewer opportunities for developing internal mobility between the different activities in order to manage the excess employment and external regulation therefore becomes the main way of cutting costs.

As explained before, the decline in staffing levels by natural attrition has been commonly used by almost all NPOs. Therefore, operators faced with the need to cut operating costs further have no choice but to reinforce the reduction of employees by resorting to redundancies. United States Postal Service (USPS), which is classified by Accenture as a traditionalist with diversification of less than 13 percent, still relies mainly on one core activity and is therefore one of the operators that are most exposed to the drop in mail volumes. At the same time, in the absence of new sources of revenue, there is heightened pressure to cut labor costs which are still very high in USPS. In March 2011, the sector's trade unions and the company reached an agreement which guaranteed no layoffs, and yet, in August 2011, the American postal operator officially begged Congress to eliminate the layoff protections in the company's collective bargaining agreements in order to allow it to resort to layoffs. In their Workforce Optimization White Paper, they estimated that natural attrition, which would enable them to decrease their staffing levels by around 100,000, would not be sufficient because, in total, 220,000 job positions needed to disappear by 2015 (USPS, 2011).

Increased Employee Differentiation, in particular within Delivery Activities

Besides curbing staffing levels, increased flexibility in the type of employment is also a lever for cutting operating costs. In some NPOs, therefore, increased employee differentiation can be observed. This differentiation relies first of all on wages, with different levels for employees with more seniority and new recruits, whose wages are lower. Operators now tend to implement wages according to market trends rather than internal equity. This differentiated wage policy raises fundamental questions in terms of internal organization as it creates differentiation within the internal social structure and is also an obstacle to internal mobility. By creating a more fragmented activity this wage differentiation has a direct impact on the social but also economic organization of the postal industry.

The increased differentiation of the job type and status of delivery workers is also a means of social optimization, with the development of several kinds of workers. This can be clearly seen in the differentiation between traditional postmen/women and mail deliverers. As an example, PostNL is currently undergoing a complete restructuring process of its delivery activities, moving from a company relying on full-time employees who are mainly traditional postmen/women to one employing part-time employees who are supposed to have very few contacts with the customers. PostNL which aims, in the future, to have mail delivered only by part-time workers, seems to be engaged in a real paradigm shift of its business and social model. Figures show that the composition of its delivery activities' payroll has changed very quickly in a few years. In 2005 there were 20,000 traditional delivery workers compared to 16,000 in 2010. By contrast, the number of part-time delivery workers rose from 6,000 in 2005 to 13,000 in 2010. Ultimately, the aim is to have a fully part-time structure in delivery activities. As shown by Figure 24.4, the increased use of independent and part-time workers in the delivery activity relies on a cost-based strategy as this workforce is indeed more flexible and less costly for the employer. Not only is the status of these employees different but also their work is different, with a simplification of their competences. Customer contact no longer represents a core activity

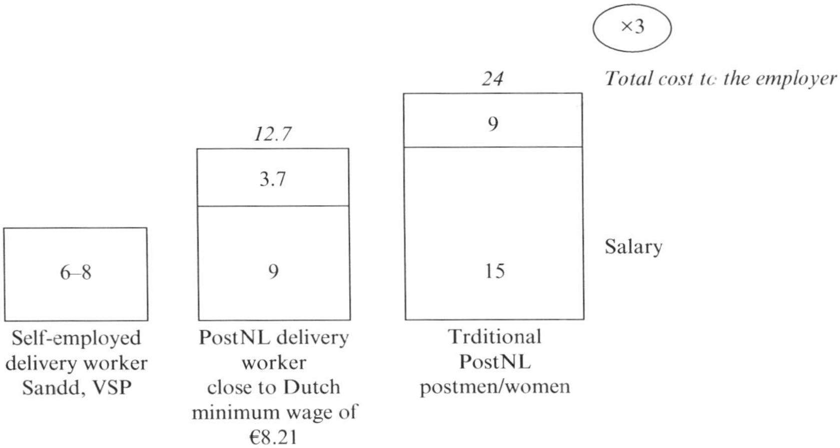

Figure 24.4 The case of the Netherlands: differentiation in wages and types of employment within the delivery activity

for deliverers who generally no longer have their own delivery route. It appears, therefore, that as part of a trend towards industrial mail, the quality of customer relations is not relevant, implying that there is no need to maintain the regularity of contact between employers and consumers.

Differentiation in terms of type of employment and wages within the delivery activity leads to an evolution of the nature of this activity. In companies opting for a move towards industrial mail, the nature of the delivery worker's role but also, ultimately, the nature of the postal operator's role itself is totally different. This tendency is reinforced at sector level with the business models put in place by most new entrants, which rely on the use of delivery personnel, who are mainly independent workers with lower wages and a very different activity.

Balanced Diversification Helps in Finding Internal Levers for Social Optimization

While diversification makes it possible to avoid radical social adaptation in historic postal companies, the need to optimize labor costs and increase flexibility remains a major challenge for all incumbents. Choosing balanced diversification of activities, however, seems to offer greater internal levers for managing social costs. It gives companies the opportunity to have an extensive internal employment market for managing mobility between their different activities. Moreover, a diversified portfolio of activities offers some protection from business cyclical effects, thus fostering economic solidarity between activities as revenues from the most dynamic areas can compensate for those with falling revenues. Social solidarity also exists between activities as businesses with a surplus of activity can integrate the excess number of employees coming from less dynamic activities, thus helping to compensate for the blow to staffing levels triggered by the drop in mail volumes. Several companies have therefore set up programs for internal mobility which can be either functional, in particular from back to front office, or geographical.

Interesting initiatives such as financial incentives, mobility departments and personalized career advisers have been put in place by some incumbents to promote internal mobility. This system of inner regulation should be further improved, in particular by focusing on relevant training and organized internal mobility.

Companies that are better protected against social impacts can opt for weaker social optimization policies and lower their staff costs by increasing the adaptability of work organization while maintaining a primarily full-time employment model. As an example, La Poste promotes internal 'flexicurity' in order to combine the company's commitment to quality employment and the employees' commitment to the adapting to new market circumstances and customer services (Bailly and Meidinger, 2011). Within the delivery sector, the '*Facteurs d'avenir*' program, which aims at reconciling the flexibility required by a variable activity with a stable quality job, is a good illustration of this double commitment. More concretely, postmen/women are organized in teams of 12 to 15 individuals with a manager and are responsible for a specific area. The organization of the team enables mutual substitution between postmen/women and the adaptation of their working time to the variations of the activity while guaranteeing them a full-time position. This program contributes to a more flexible organization of work as well as promoting mobility and enhancing skills by giving employees the opportunity to become more versatile, flexible and responsible.

4 DIVERSIFICATION INTO SERVICES DRIVEN BY HUMAN CAPITAL

Diversification does indeed appear to be beneficial, but, as confirmed by the Social Observatory, a one-size-fits-all strategy cannot apply to all operators. The choices of diversification depend on several factors, assets and constraints, which are both internal and external and can be specific to a country or operator or, indeed, common to all. In such a labor-intensive industry, human capital is a key lever and this section aims to analyze the extent to which, if it is well combined with other assets which are specific to postal operators, it can be considered as being a strategic advantage for a customer-oriented diversification.

Diversification Should Be Based on Existing Assets

While it appears to be the main way forward, diversification is a risky strategy because, in developing new activities, operators enter markets in which they are small competitors or even newcomers. Indeed, the study from Accenture underlines that the synergies between logistics or financial services and the mail activity are low and shows that operators such as the Italian, Japanese, Hungarian and French posts, which have achieved a strong position in the banking sector, are the ones that historically already had some business in this market. In order to develop the necessary capabilities, incumbents should therefore take into consideration their existing assets and the extent to which they can be transferred into new markets; these assets could become key competitive advantages, in particular, if they cannot be imitated or substituted.

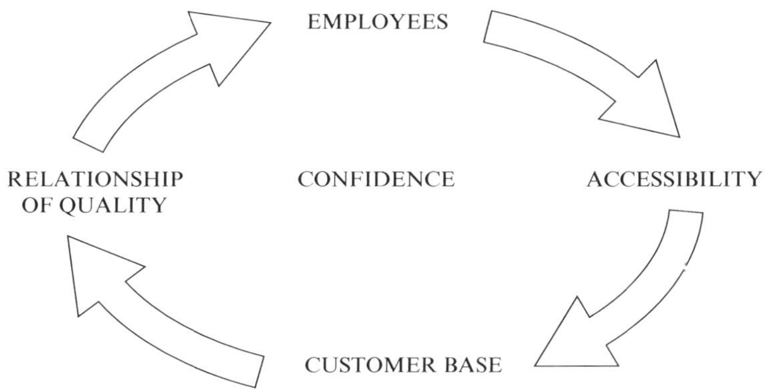

Figure 24.5 NPOs' intangible assets are a competitive advantage

Postal Operators Have Several Specific Intangible Assets to Diversify into Services

Within this diversification process, postal operators benefit from several resources which give them a competitive advantage in comparison with their main competitors. In such a labor industry, human capital, that is to say the knowledge, skills, expertise and experience of employees but also other less measurable elements such as their commitment and adaptability, is one of the operators' major assets. A sound analysis of this human capital is necessary to determine the strategic directions to be taken and its development is a focal point of investment for ensuring the company's long-term sustainability. Qualified and well-trained employees, who are committed to their companies, are assets, which are largely non-substitutable. The human resources of postal operators should of course be considered in their own right, but they are even more valuable if they are adequately combined in a supportive relationship with other intangible assets that are specific to incumbent operators as shown by Figure 24.5.

Postal operators are strongly rooted in society and have developed a trust-based relationship with citizens; this trust is a key intangible asset which is highly valuable as it cannot be duplicated. It is important to maintain this relationship built through stable, quality jobs with employees committed to their companies and upholding a deep-seated culture of quality service. At the same time, postal operators are the companies with the highest number of customers, and therefore customer base, which, in theory, can be all of society. This unique knowledge of customers is an important lever of development in working towards services which need to be increasingly personalized.

The incumbents' widespread network is a competitive advantage which is highly valuable as it represents an important fixed cost that competitor firms are unable to build. Operators successfully diversifying into services are those that have taken their network's advantages and used them efficiently to find alternative sources of revenue. When developing into services such as banking and insurance but also mobile phones, the accessibility of operators that are present all over the country and serving all citizens is an important lever for gaining market shares, in particular among specific segments of the population. The employees working in the network are key promoters of this accessibility. These assets taken as a whole can guide the diversification choices of operators and in particular the effective diversification into services.

Customer Needs at the Center of a Diversification Strategy into Services

The idea that companies' diversification choices should be driven by customers is gaining traction (Gori, 2010). Thanks to their large customer base but also their historical knowledge of consumers, incumbents are particularly well-equipped to answer but also to shape customers' needs. Better understanding evolving consumers' needs is key to innovating and developing new and personalized products, services but also experiences that are more adapted to these needs. New priorities have arisen for postal market consumers. In particular, the issue of shipment reliability is today a main concern and seems more important to consumers than speed. Increasing environmental concerns within society also have to be taken into consideration in order to develop appropriate green solutions. As an example, the green stamp introduced by La Poste considers many of these evolving needs as it guarantees delivery within D+2, is less expensive and ensures that the letters have been carried by road transport, which has a lower environmental impact.

These changes strongly support a diversification into services which focus on customers' needs. Indeed, what appears to be important for customers is not only the actual quality of the products themselves but also the services that are related to these products; their choices largely depend on intangible criteria such as perception. Postal operators have major assets to shape this perception positively and in this sense the quality of service and customer relations are important. Poste Italiane is one of the postal operators that have diversified most, and its strategy to become a service provider seems to have met with success. The Italian operator has made the choice to develop a wide range of services better matching customers' needs. In 2010 the share of mail revenues in total revenues was only 23 percent, while financial and insurance services accounted for almost 74 percent of the revenues. Coupled with its growing diversification, the revenue of the company has shown steady growth from €8,150 billion in 2002 to €21,837 billion in 2010.

Postal Operators Have Key Assets to Diversify into Digital Services

The rise of the digital society and the development of new technologies will have a major impact on the postal industry. New activities, especially in terms of data storage and processing, are being developed at a time when there is a need for a more personalized customer approach. Even if at first glance NPOs' traditional activities seem very different from and even endangered by new technologies, postal companies have key assets for playing a major role in digital society where customers will be the focal point. Quality customer relations, extensive access to customers in quantitative but also qualitative terms with in-depth knowledge of their needs and behavior, represent key elements of differentiation and of leadership in this economy. The role of the postal employees, who will be constantly interacting with the customers, is essential to maintain the quality of the relationship but even more importantly, to identify and understand consumers' needs. Trust is also a key asset in an Internet-driven society where customers need to control their virtual identity and to have enough guarantees that the data they are communicating is securely handled. The NPOs' position as a trustworthy company is a key asset in several digital services. The management of data by being a provider of solutions, such as Cloud computing or digital safes, in particular, can be sound areas of development for operators. In an increasingly virtual society, the notions of accessibility and proximity may also gain a new valuable dimension. Developing a multi-channel approach with complementary but also easily and quickly accessible services will be crucial for postal operators. Diversification into e-services seems to offer numerous new opportunities and appears necessary for a solid diversification combining quality physical and virtual services, based on a relationship of trust between the company, its employees and the consumers.

5 CONCLUSIONS

One of the major issues at stake for postal operators is developing new business areas while keeping the same workforce. The trend towards digital services, in particular, will represent a major challenge in terms of human resources (HR) management. The postal operators rely on a labor-intensive structure largely composed of a low-skilled and aging workforce that is not well-acquainted with new technologies. At the same time, the development of new technologies places significant pressure on staffing levels, with employees being increasingly substituted by machines and reduced requirement of physical contact with customers.

Employability, adaptability and mobility are therefore major issues at stake for NPOs in modernizing and diversifying successfully into new services. As underlined in the new Joint Declaration on Postal Sector Evolution signed in 2012, key principles to accompany change are 'to develop the employees' employability . . . as a shared responsibility of the social partners and of each employee' (European Social Dialogue Committee for the Postal Sector, 2012). Enhancing employees' employability through adequate training, re-skilling and lifelong learning programs enables them to gain new skills, increased responsibilities and to have more opportunities for mobility and promotion. Changes in ways of thinking will also be essential. Indeed, in keeping with new customer needs, greater consideration should be given to the changing expectations of employees. They are willing to embrace personalized HR policies which cater more specifically to their individual needs and offer them development opportunities. A solid, tailored HR strategy will be essential to support this diversification.

Successful and appropriately managed diversification into services, and in particular digital services, could provide an opportunity to reinforce the role of the employees, who are at the center of the relationship, whether physical or virtual, with the customers. The development of new services in post offices and in the delivery sector has already led to the expansion of workers' responsibilities in terms of welcoming clients, advising and selling; they can be further strengthened by the development of virtual services. As a unique point of contact between the company and the customer, they will be able to better identify, collect and analyze customer needs and submit this feedback to the company in order to consolidate its knowledge of the customers. They will become proactive players in service innovation. It appears then that the diversification choice into services, in particular digital ones, could represent an opportunity for change and development of the human capital of NPOs. Developing a culture of quality services but also a digital culture among employees is therefore crucial to the long-term economic development of incumbents.

Postal companies opting for diversification into services largely rely on the positive link between job quality and the quality of customer relations, which brings added value to their products and services. They have decided that their development depends on the relationship connecting the interests of all stakeholders – the employees, the company and the customers – and that developing HR and the company strategies can be mutually beneficial. Such strategies are based on a balance between the economic and social aspects of the diversification process and offer the prospect of enhancing the long-term sustainable development of incumbents.

NOTES

1. This chapter is based on the results of the 'Social partners preparing for change' project conducted by the European Social Dialogue Committee for the postal sector (SDC) in 2010–11 within the framework of the Social Observatory. The Observatory established a solid overview of the main social developments in most EU member states. The project's final report can be downloaded from the European Social Dialogue Committee's website at: http://www.postsocialdialog.org/.
2. Following the Social Observatory initiative, a new Joint Declaration on Postal Sector Evolution was signed by the social partners of the SDC to establish a common assessment of the situation and define four key principles to accompany change. This Declaration builds on the 2007 Joint Statement on Postal Sector Evolution and the main findings of the two successful projects under the Social Observatory conducted from 2008 to 2011.

REFERENCES

Accenture (2010), 'Is Diversification the Answer to Mail Woes? The Experience of International Posts', study commissioned by US Postal Service.

Bailly, Dominique and Margaux Meidinger (2011), 'The dual trend towards operational efficiencies and social regulation in European postal services', in Michael A. Crew and Paul R. Kleindorfer (eds), *Reinventing the Postal Sector in an Electronic Age*, Cheltenham, UK and Northampton, MA, USA: Edward Elgar.

Copenhagen Economics (2010), 'Main Developments in the Postal Sector 2008–2010', study commissioned by DG Internal Market, November.

European Social Dialogue Committee for the Postal Sector (2011), 'Final Report of the project social partners preparing for change', European Social Dialogue Committee for the Postal Sector.

European Social Dialogue Committee for the Postal Sector (2012), 'New Joint Declaration on Postal Sector Evolution', European Social Dialogue Committee for the Postal Sector.

Gori, Stefano (2010), 'Postal operators at a crossroads: what are the strategic options?', Ch. 4 in Derek Osborn and Kristian J. Sund (eds), *The Future is in the Post: Perspectives on Strategy in the Postal Industry*, Faringdon, Oxon: Libri.

USPS (2011), 'Workforce optimization', national press release, United States Postal Service.

25. Welfare and pricing with single-piece and bulk mail access competition in the postal sector*

Philippe De Donder,[†] **Helmuth Cremer,**[‡] **Paul Dudley**[§] **and Frank Rodriguez**[¶]

1 INTRODUCTION

Following the full opening of the postal market to competition, the third European Directive makes a distinction between single-piece (SP) mail and bulk mail (BM) to include the SP mail in the universal service and exclude BM from the universal service. SP mail comprises social and business mail, and there is the option for the BM market to include access to the incumbent operator's network.

This opens up to competition the upstream market in collection, outward sortation and transportation not only for BM, but also for all upstream mail if entrants can consolidate SP and BM upstream. While the fixed upstream costs for the social mail network may be prohibitively high for entry with respect to collection from postboxes, it may be less so for business mail where collection of larger mailings is made from businesses directly or from dedicated collection hubs. This form of market opening appears to leave the universal service provider (USP) exposed in its recovery of fixed upstream costs for business mail.

Furthermore, when direct *ex ante* regulation is withdrawn and replaced by *ex post* regulation as may be appropriate in a declining market, it can be accompanied by greater regulatory information requirements including accounting separation and transfer pricing. Transfer prices are implicit or explicit internal charges levied by one part of a vertically integrated business to another part of its business. This information can then be used by the business to inform pricing decisions, and by the regulatory authorities to inform assessments of whether behavior by a firm amounts to an abuse of dominance.

If the USP offers an access price for BM business mail, there is neither an explicit access price for SP business mail nor explicit internal transfer prices for SP or BM business mail. In general the transfer prices might be expected to have similar characteristics to the access prices offered to third parties, where those access prices exist, and to reflect what market access prices might be if they were to be offered to third parties but are not in fact offered. Indeed, within the postal sector if the incumbent operator is unable to

† Professor of Economics, Toulouse School of Economics (IDEI & GREMAQ-CNRS).
‡ Professor of Economics, Toulouse School of Economics (IDEI & GREMAQ-CNRS).
§ Head of Economics, Royal Mail Group.
¶ Associate, Oxera.

distinguish between SP and BM from entrants for access pricing purposes, then the effective access price for these two markets may be the same.

This chapter explores the impact of upstream competition on the USP, under different assumptions, through a model framework that is an extension of that developed by De Donder et al. (2008). That paper explored cases where the incumbent postal operator (PO) or USP comprises a mail network operator (MNO) with a single good for the SP market and an access good (for both urban and rural zones) in the BM market, and retail business (RB) selling a BM good (for both urban and rural zones) with a competitive fringe in BM. De Donder et al. assumed welfare maximization subject to break-even for the USP and looked at the effect on welfare and pricing of different break-even constraints and pricing rules on the PO, MNO and RB, including the effect on urban and rural access prices in the BM market.

In this chapter, the MNO and RB introduce a market distinction between SP social and SP business mail in addition to BM business mail, with access and transfer prices in both business mail markets. Hence the MNO has one end-to-end service for SP social mail and two access services for SP business and BM, and the RB has two end-to-end business services. Imperfect competition in the upstream SP business and BM business mail markets is assumed. Geographical zones are excluded to focus on the impact of competition upstream on prices, welfare and finances of the USP. The model is calibrated to gain numerical results and provide further insight, including the effects of different levels of intensity of competition, switching to entrants and access pricing rules.

Section 2 sets out the details of the model and scenarios considered. The inputs to the model are calibrated in Section 3 with numerical examples then applied in Section 4. Section 5 concludes.

2 THE MODEL

There are three postal operators: an RB, an MNO and entrants. The MNO sells one final good to customers: SP social mail, while the RB sells two: SP business mail and BM business mail. For simplicity, we assume that the three types of goods have independent demands. The entrants sell SP and BM business mail, while there is no competition for SP social mail. The two goods sold by entrants are imperfect substitutes of the corresponding two goods offered by the RB, but the demands for entrants' SP business mail and BM business mail are independent from each other.

Let x denote (generic) SP and y = BM, with a subscript S for social (SP) and B for business (SP), and with a superscript I for the RB (incumbent) and E for the entrants. There is one representative sender of SP social mail, whose utility is:

$$u(x_S) - qx_S + I_1,$$

where x_S denotes the quantity of SP social mail sold by the RB, q its final price and I_1 the sender's exogenous income. The demand function $x_s(q)$ is obtained by maximizing $u(x_s)$ with respect to x_S.

The quantity of SP business mail sold by the RB is denoted by x_B^I, and its price by q_B^I.

Similarly, x_B^E denotes the quantity of SP business mail sold by the entrants, and q_B^E its price. There is one representative sender of SP business mail, whose utility is:

$$v(x_B^I, x_B^E) - q_B^I x_B^I - q_B^E x_B^E + I_2,$$

where I_2 is the sender's exogenous income. The demand functions $x_B^I(q_B^I, q_B^E)$ and $x_B^E(q_B^I, q_B^E)$ are obtained by maximizing this utility with respect to quantities (x_B^I and x_B^E).

Similarly, for BM: y^I (resp., y^E) denotes the quantity of BM sold by the RB (resp., entrants), and p^I (resp., p^E) its price. There is one representative sender of BM, whose utility is:

$$w(y^I, y^E) - p^I y^I - p^E y^E + I_3,$$

where I_3 is the sender's exogenous income. The demand functions $y^I(p^I, p^E)$ and $y^E(p^I, p^E)$ are obtained by maximizing this utility with respect to quantities (y^I and y^E).

There are two types of activities in the postal sector: upstream (collection, sorting and transportation) and downstream (delivery). The MNO performs the downstream (delivery) activities for all five goods (x_S, x_B^I, x_B^E, y^I and y^E), and also the upstream activities for SP social mail (x_S). The RB takes care of the upstream activities for BM (y^I) and SP business (x_B^I). The RB then has to buy access to the MNO's delivery network and to pay the MNO an access charge for both x_B^I and y^I. For each unit of mail delivered requiring access to the MNO delivery network, the RB pays an access charge of a_B^I for SP business mail and of a_y^I for BM.

The entrants sell SP business mail and BM business mail, but they only perform the upstream activities and buy access to the MNO delivery network, for which they pay a unit access charge of a_B^E for SP business mail and a_y^E for BM. Bypass is not allowed.

The cost structure of the industry is as follows. The MNO faces one large fixed cost for all its downstream activities, denoted by F_D (subscript D stands for downstream). Downstream marginal costs are assumed to be the same for all five goods (SP social mail, SP business mail by RB and by E, and BM by I and E) and denoted by c_D. The MNO also faces an upstream fixed cost for SP social mail, denoted by F_{US}. The upstream marginal cost for SP social mail is denoted by c_{US}.

The RB faces fixed costs in its upstream activities for both SP business mail (denoted by F_B^I) and for BM (denoted by F_y^I). The (constant) upstream marginal cost of the RB is denoted by c_B^I for SP business mail and by c_y^I for BM.

The (constant) upstream marginal costs of the entrants are the same across entrants and are denoted by c_B^E for SP business mail and by c_y^E for BM. For simplicity the entrants are assumed to face no fixed costs.

The RB's profit function is given by:

$$\Pi^I = (q_B^I - a_B^I - c_B^I)x_B^I(q_B^I, q_B^E) - F_B^I + (p^I - a_y^I - c_y^I)y^I(p^I, p^E) - F_y^I,$$

where the RB controls the two final prices q_B^I and p^I.

The MNO's profit function is given by:

$$\Pi^N = (q - c_{US} - c_D)x_S(q) - F_{US}$$

$$+(a_B^I - c_D)x_B^I(q_B^I, q_B^E) + (a_B^E - c_D)x_B^E(q_B^I, q_B^E)$$
$$+(a_y^I - c_D)y^I(p^I, p^E) + (a_y^E - c_D)y^E(p^I, p^E) - F_D,$$

where the MNO controls the final price q and four downstream access charges (a_B^I, a_B^E, a_y^I and a_y^E).

The entrants' profits are given by:

$$\Pi^E = (q_B^E - a_B^E - c_B^E)x_B^E(q_B^I, q_B^E) + (p^E - a_y^E - c_y^E)y^E(p^I, p^E),$$

where the entrants control two final goods' prices: q_B^E and p^E.

Finally, social welfare is given by:

$$\begin{aligned} W &= u(x_S) - qx_S + I_1 + v(x_B^I, x_B^E) - q_B^I x_B^I - q_B^E x_B^E + I_2 \\ &+ w(y^I, y^E) - p^I y^I - p^E y^E + I_3 + \Pi^I + \Pi^E + \Pi^N \\ &= u(x_S) + v(x_B^I, x_B^E) + w(y^I, y^E) \\ &- (c_{US} + c_D)x_S(q) \\ &- (c_B^I + c_D)x_B^I(q_B^I, q_B^E) - (c_B^E + c_D)x_B^E(q_B^I, q_B^E) \\ &- (c_y^I + c_D)y^I(p^I, p^E) - (c_y^E + c_D)y^E(p^I, p^E) \\ &+ I_1 + I_2 + I_3 - F_{US} - F_D - F_B^I - F_y^I. \end{aligned}$$

The pricing behavior of the postal operators is studied assuming that the MNO and the RB maximize welfare subject to a profit constraint and concentrate on Ramsey prices to consider several sets of constraints, in addition to the profit constraint. The objective is to focus on numerical examples, in order to shed light on the impact of these different sets of constraints on prices, volumes, contribution to profits, consumer surplus and welfare. Numerical simulations also make it possible to check whether there exists a vector of prices that satisfies all the constraints. The various optimization problems solved for are described briefly before moving to the sections devoted to the calibration and numerical results.

Initially a hypothetical monopoly situation is examined. Appendix 25A derives demand functions $x_B^{IM}(q_B^I)$ and $y^{IM}(p^I)$ and profit functions Π^{IM} and Π^{NM}. Initially also the profit constraint is assumed to be global,

$$\Pi^{IM} + \Pi^{NM} \geq 0,$$

which would be the case for instance if both the RB and the MNO were part of the same postal operator.

The Ramsey problem with one global profit constraint is then:

$$\begin{aligned} \max_{q, q_B^I, p^I} W^M &= u(x_S) + v(x_B^I, 0) + w(y^I, 0) \\ &- (c_{US} + c_D)x_S(q) - (c_B^I + c_D)x_B^{IM}(q) - (c_y^I + c_D)y^{IM}(p^I) \end{aligned}$$

$$+ I_1 + I_2 + I_3 - F_{US} - F_D - F_B^I - F_y^I,$$

subject to $\Pi^{IM} + \Pi^{NM} \geq 0$

$$\Leftrightarrow (q - c_{US} - c_D)x_S(q) + (q_B^I - c_B^I - c_D)x_B^{IM}(q_B^I) + (p^I - c_y^I - c_D)y^{IM}(p^I)$$

$$\geq F_{US} + F_D + F_B^I + F_y^I.$$

The following Ramsey prices are obtained:

$$\frac{q - c_{US} - c_D}{q} = \frac{\lambda}{1 + \lambda} \frac{1}{|\varepsilon_S(q)|},$$

$$\frac{q_B^I - c_B^I - c_D}{q_B^I} = \frac{\lambda}{1 + \lambda} \frac{1}{|\varepsilon_B^{IM}(q_B^I)|},$$

$$\frac{p^I - c_y^I - c_D}{p^I} = \frac{\lambda}{1 + \lambda} \frac{1}{|\varepsilon_y^{IM}(p^I)|},$$

where λ is the Lagrange multiplier of the budget constraint $\Pi^{IM} + \Pi^{NM} \geq 0$ and where $\varepsilon_S(q)$, $\varepsilon_B^{IM}(q_B^I)$ and $\varepsilon_y^{IM}(p^I)$ represent, respectively, the direct price elasticity of the demand for SP business mail, SP business mail and BM in a monopoly situation.

It is easy to show analytically that the same retail prices would obtain if one were to look at the same problem with two separate profit constraints: $\Pi^{IM} \geq 0$ and $\Pi^{NM} \geq 0$. The intuition is that the two access prices a_B^I and a_y^I are used so that both the RB and the MNO break even. This result was already underlined in De Donder et al. (2008).

Entrants are then introduced into the model. Imperfect competition is assumed between entrants and the RB and, further, to simplify matters, entrants are assumed to post an exogenous markup over marginal costs for the two goods they sell. The markup for SP business mail is denoted by m_B^E, and the markup for BM by m_y^E. Then:

$$q_B^E = (1 + m_B^E)(a_B^E + c_B^E),$$

$$p^E = (1 + m_y^E)(a_y^E + c_y^E),$$

and the MNO and RB's Ramsey prices are solved, given these entrants' prices. The two markups m_B^E and m_y^E can be considered to reflect the intensity of the competition between entrants, so that the numerical section reports how Ramsey prices are affected when the entrants' markups are exogenously changed. In addition, this formulation encompasses the case of a competitive fringe, where the entrants' markups are both zero. Note that whether the profit constraint imposed is global or imposed separately on the MNO and the RB is immaterial, because the planner can use the access charges a_y^I and a_B^I to transfer income from one operator to the other so that both break even.

Finally, the case is considered where access charges follow the equi-proportional markup (EPMU) rule and are set according to:

$$a_B^E = a_B^I = a_y^E = a_y^I = (1 + m)c_D.$$

Observe that, since the downstream marginal costs are by assumption the same for the four goods, the EPMU rule results in the same access charge level being set for the four goods. Section 4 provides numerical illustrations of final prices and reports how the EPMU setting of the access charges impacts Ramsey prices when separate profit constraints for the RB and the MNO are imposed.

3 CALIBRATION

The calibration assumptions are based on De Donder et al. (2008) modified to take account of the fact that SP mail is split between social and business. The assumptions are not estimates from a particular postal operator, but they are intended to reflect the general nature of postal markets and cost structures given published empirical studies.

The initial situation is a hypothetical one where the RB faces no competition. The USP sets a price of 0.50 for SP social mail and a price of 0.40 for SP business mail and for BM. Total quantities sold at those prices are 2bn, 3bn and 5bn items, respectively. The direct price elasticities are –0.2 for SP social mail, –0.25 for SP business mail and –0.5 for BM. Linear demands are calibrated based on these quantities, prices and elasticities.

Further information is required to calibrate the (linear) demand functions for SP business mail and for BM in the presence of competition by entrants. With regard to the extent of entry, it is assumed for both SP business mail and for BM that the entrants' total market share is 10 percent if their price is the same as the RB's and 50 percent if they are 20 percent cheaper.[1] On substitution, the displacement ratio of both SP business mail and BM offered by the entrants is assumed to be 0.9.[2]

The MNO's marginal downstream cost c_D is set at 0.12. The marginal upstream cost of SP social mail c_{US} is set at 0.18 so that the total marginal cost of social SP is 0.3. The marginal upstream cost of SP business mail is 0.15 for both the RB and the entrant ($c_B^E = c_B^I$, so that its total marginal cost is 0.27 for both operators), while the marginal upstream cost of BM is 0.102 for both the RB and the entrants ($c_y^E = c_y^I$, for a total marginal cost of 0.222). The USP faces a total fixed cost of 1.680 billion which is assumed to include the normal remuneration of capital. There is no need for the analysis or calibrations to segment this, though in Section 4 the contribution to total upstream fixed cost of the RB ($F_B^I + F_y^I$) is examined on the assumption that this could be separately imposed in the budget constraint. The reader can check that, with these demand and cost calibrations, the sum of the profits of the RB and of the MNO is zero (that is, revenues exactly cover the sum of variable and fixed costs).

4 NUMERICAL ILLUSTRATIONS

For ease of reference the results of the monopoly case are reported under the same assumptions as De Donder et al. (2008) in the first column of Table 25.1. The comparative welfare-maximizing results subject to the USP (MNO + RB) breaking even are shown, where there are two access services and two entrants' services and the MNO can distinguish SP business mail from BM. The results are for two scenarios where the entrants first have ($m_B^E = m_y^E$) 20 percent markups on their marginal costs (in the second column of figures) and second have greater competition intensity and a competitive fringe with no percent markup on their marginal costs (in the third column of figures). The consequences of the MNO being unable to distinguish the access prices are then reported, with the same EPMU markup on downstream marginal costs, for the two scenarios (in the fourth and fifth columns, respectively).

In each case all prices are above marginal costs, including the access prices charged to the entrant. The implicit transfer prices paid by the RB to the MNO play no role in the formulation of results shown in Table 25.1 because of the combined RB + MNO break-even constraint, but observe that in each case both prices of the RB exceed their corresponding access price plus upstream marginal cost. For the scenarios shown, when the MNO can set distinct access prices the RB's prices exceed those of the entrants, but when the MNO cannot the relative prices of the RB and entrants depend on the level of markup applied and competitive intensity of the entrants. Observe also that the end-to-end price for SP business mail is higher than that for BM business mail, and this is the case even when the access prices are set to be the same.

With distinct access prices and a low competitive intensity (in the second column) the MNO sets a higher access price for SP business than for BM to reflect the more inelastic demand for the SP business market and the same marginal downstream cost. The overall level of the access prices are set sufficiently low to avoid the SP business and BM prices from rising sharply compared to those under the monopoly case. The contributions toward the recovery of fixed costs of business (SP and bulk) mail for the MNO and the RB are reported based on the assumption that internal prices are equal to access charges paid by the entrant. Compared to the monopoly situation,[3] the MNO loses some contribution from the introduction of upstream competition and the USP raises all its end-to-end prices as it becomes more difficult for it to break even.

In contrast, when the competitive intensity increases upstream (in the third column of figures) so that entrants' profit is zero, the USP has the opportunity to raise its access prices more without introducing higher end-to-end prices. In fact, the RB lowers its end-to-end prices (compared to the second column), which further reduces the differences between its prices and the access prices. The end-to-end prices are remarkably similar to the monopoly case.

The higher access prices enhance the contribution to the fixed network costs from the business mail, and the contribution from RB upstream reduces from €0.484 billion to €0.068 billion, but this is more than offset by the increase in contribution from the MNO prices which increases from €1.196 billion to €1.612 billion (as the entrants' profit reduces to zero). The lower markup by the entrants both grows the market (marginally) and their market share (from 12 to 16 percent), which has the effect of making it easier for the USP

Table 25.1 Illustrative results for the USP (MNO and RB)

		With distinct access prices			With same access prices	
		Monopoly	Low competitive intensity with entrant markup of 20%	High competitive intensity with entrant markup of 0%	Low competitive intensity with entrant markup of 20%	High competitive intensity with entrant markup of 0%
Prices (€):						
SP social – MNO	p^x	0.592	0.606	0.591	0.618	0.604
SP business – RB	q_B^I	0.457	0.463	0.456	0.420	0.410
SP business – Entrant	q_B^E	–	0.456	0.441	0.410	0.393
BM business – RB	p^I	0.328	0.331	0.327	0.350	0.349
BM business – Entrant	p^E	–	0.330	0.321	0.352	0.345
Access SP business – MNO	a_B^E	–	0.230	0.291	0.192	0.243
Access BM business – MNO	a_y^E	–	0.173	0.219	0.192	0.243
Quantities (bn):						
SP social – MNO	x^S	1.926	1.915	1.927	1.905	1.916
SP business – RB	x_B^I	2.893	2.593	2.484	2.572	2.470
SP business – Entrant, MNO	x_B^E	–	0.322	0.455	0.434	0.567
BM business – RB	y_I	5.452	4.789	4.668	4.781	4.642
BM business – Entrant, MNO	y_E	–	0.715	0.873	0.587	0.753
Total		10.271	10.333	10.408	10.279	10.348
Contribution to fixed cost – USP (€bn):						
SP social – MNO		0.562	0.586	0.561	0.606	0.582
SP business – MNO		0.541	0.319	0.503	0.215	0.374
BM business – MNO		0.576	0.291	0.548	0.385	0.664
Subtotal – MNO		1.680	1.196	1.612	1.206	1.620
SP business – RB			0.216	0.038	0.202	0.042
BM business – RB			0.268	0.031	0.272	0.019
Subtotal (upstream) – RB			0.484	0.068	0.474	0.061
Profit subtotal – MNO+RB		0.000	0.000	0.000	0.000	0.000
Profit subtotal – Entrant		–	0.064	0.000	0.064	0.000
Consumer surplus (€bn)						
SP social		2.320	2.293	2.321	2.269	2.295
SP business		2.218	2.218	2.240	2.346	2.380
BM business		2.371	2.371	2.394	2.262	2.275
Total		6.929	6.882	6.956	6.877	6.950
Welfare (€bn)		6.929	6.945	6.956	6.941	6.950
Lagrange multiplier		0.138	0.146	0.137	0.154	0.146

to break even (as reflected by the lower Lagrange multiplier) and marginally increasing consumer surplus in all three markets as well as welfare.

With the access prices set the same by applying an EPMU rule to the same marginal costs for the two business segments (in the fourth and fifth columns of figures), the access prices increase for BM business mail and reduce for SP business mail. There are corresponding price movements for RB's prices and an increase in the contribution from the BM business market. However, this reduces overall market volumes and welfare, and it becomes more difficult for the USP to break even. It would then be in the interests of the USP to have distinct access prices between the two markets of business mail if they could be applied.

Overall, the effects of changing assumptions are all rather small for the calibrations used in the numerical illustrations. The difference in welfare between having distinct access prices and the same access prices for the two business segments is just €4–6 million and the difference in welfare between having low and high competitive intensity is just €8–9 million. Indeed, the potential welfare enhancement of high competitive intensity within these illustrations is based on a market growth of less than 1 percent from greater entrants' market share, which may be overshadowed, in practice, by other movements in the market from digital competition. Hence, perhaps the most significant result here is that the BM access price would be higher and therefore the contribution from BM greater, if the MNO cannot distinguish SP business and BM items for pricing.

The relatively small effects of changing assumptions may be due in part to the low propensity to switch to entrants' services assumed and so the case is considered where the USP can set distinct access prices for SP business mail and BM but faces a greater propensity to switch to the entrants. More specifically, for both the SP business and BM markets, it is assumed that the entrants would obtain 50 percent of the market for equal prices and 90 percent if they were 25 percent cheaper than the USP.

Table 25.2 considers the case where the entrants' services are more attractive and the entrants have a greater market share of the business mail. This is done for the two scenarios of Ramsey pricing with 20 and 0 percent markups on their marginal costs by the entrants (in the first and third columns of figures, respectively), with the difference relative to the corresponding case from Table 25.1 (from the second and fourth columns of figures, respectively) also shown. As this change has the effect of reducing the RB's upstream contribution to just €7 million for the high competitive intensity case, the directional change to the results is also shown when a higher contribution is imposed on the RB in Table 25.2 (final column).

The RB's share of business mail reduces to 46–51 percent under the two scenarios presented and the higher entrants' shares leads to an increase in the access prices. When the entrants apply a high (20 percent) markup in Table 25.2 (in the first column of figures), the entrants and USP both raise their end-to-end prices, but the USP increases them to a lesser degree, and sets a BM price below the entrant price (as compared to equivalent case in Table 25.1 where the RB sets its prices above those of the entrant). The RB's prices remain above the sum of the access price and marginal upstream cost. The lower market share for the USP reduces its contribution from business mail as well as its contribution from RB while the MNO's contribution increases (including from the SP social market). Total volume, consumer surplus and welfare all increase. The SP social price increase

Table 25.2 Illustrative results for the USP (MNO and RB) with lower market share conditions

		Distinct access prices				
		Low competitive intensity with entrant markup of 20%	Change relative to lower entrant share from 2nd column of Table 25.1	High competitive intensity with entrant markup of 0%	Change relative to lower entrant share from 3rd column of Table 25.1	Direction of change when RB required to increase contribution relative to 3rd column of this table
Prices (€):						
SP social – MNO	p^x	0.643	+0.037	0.582	−0.009	+
SP business – RB	q_B^I	0.476	+0.013	0.451	−0.005	+
SP business – Entrant	q_B^E	0.477	+0.021	0.444	+0.003	–
BM business – RB	p^I	0.338	+0.007	0.324	−0.003	+
BM business – Entrant	p^E	0.346	+0.016	0.325	+0.004	–
Access SP business – MNO	a_B^E	0.247	+0.017	0.294	+0.003	–
Access BM business – MNO	a_y^E	0.186	+0.013	0.223	+0.004	–
Quantities (bn):						
SP social – MNO	x^S	1.885	−0.030	1.934	+0.007	–
SP business – RB	x_B^I	1.571	−1.022	1.450	−1.034	–
SP business – Entrant, MNO	x_B^E	1.430	+1.108	1.616	+1.161	+
BM business – RB	y_I	3.054	−1.735	2.938	−1.730	–
BM business – Entrant, MNO	y_E	2.589	+1.874	2.818	+1.945	+
Total		10.530	+0.197	10.756	+0.348	+
Contribution to fixed cost – USP (€bn):						
SP social – MNO		0.647	+0.061	0.546	−0.015	+
SP business – MNO		0.382	+0.063	0.532	+0.029	–
BM business – MNO		0.375	+0.084	0.595	+0.047	–
Subtotal – MNO		1.404	+0.208	1.673	+0.061	–
SP business – RB		0.123	−0.093	0.010	−0.028	+
BM business – RB		0.153	−0.115	−0.003	−0.034	+
Subtotal (upstream) – RB		0.276	−0.208	0.007	−0.061	+
Profit subtotal – MNO+RB		0.000	0.000	0.000	0.000	0
Profit subtotal – Entrant		0.263	+0.199	0.000	0.000	0
Consumer surplus (€bn)						
SP social		2.221	−0.072	2.338	+0.017	–

Table 25.2 (continued)

	Distinct access prices				
	Low competitive intensity with entrant markup of 20%	Change relative to lower entrant share from 2nd column of Table 25.1	High competitive intensity with entrant markup of 0%	Change relative to lower entrant share from 3rd column of Table 25.1	Direction of change when RB required to increase contribution relative to 3rd column of this table
Consumer surplus (€bn)					
SP business	2.238	+0.020	2.325	−0.085	–
BM business	2.435	+0.064	2.534	−0.140	+
Total	6.894	+0.012	7.198	−0.243	–
Welfare (€bn)	7.157	+0.212	7.198	+0.243	–
Lagrange multiplier	0.171	+0.025	0.132	−0.005	+

lowers its consumer surplus but this is more than offset by the increase in consumer surplus for business mail.

When there is a high competitive intensity and a competitive fringe (with entrants' markups of zero), the levels of RB contribution were already low when the entrants' market share was low in Table 25.1 (in the second column of figures), and is even lower with a greater propensity to switch to the entrants in Table 25.2 (in the third column of figures). Something different happens when the USP has a lower market share and sets higher access prices. The entrants increase their prices, but the USP lowers all of its end-to-end prices to the point where the RB price is above the entrants' prices in SP business and below the entrants' prices in BM business, such that RB's contribution from BM is negative. This is illustrated where the RB prices below access price plus marginal cost and enhances welfare, with the entrants retaining a high market share. The RB makes a negative contribution to fixed network costs in the BM market and a low overall contribution from business mail of just €7 million. The welfare gain from raising the access price is greater than that from raising the SP social price, because of the greater entrants' market share and the consumer surplus increases in each of the three customer segments to raise welfare.

With the RB's upstream contribution only just positive for the higher propensity to switch and high competitive intensity case, the effect of imposing the constraint of a higher contribution on the RB is explored. This might be internally or externally imposed as a requirement for RB to make a greater contribution to its fixed network upstream costs.

The directional changes arising from the introduction of this additional constraint are shown in Table 25.2 (in the final column). While welfare maximizing subject to the revised budget constraint and overall break-even, the USP increases its end-to-end prices (RB prices and MNO's SP social price) and reduces its access prices. The contribution from SP social and business increases and welfare reduces. It becomes more difficult for the USP to break even as reflected in the increase in the Lagrange multiplier of the USP's profit constraint. For the calibrations assumed, the RB is limited in the contribution it can make. Consequently imposing additional constraints upon the RB is beneficial neither to the USP, nor to overall welfare and is unnecessary for competition to have a high market share.

5 CONCLUSIONS

This chapter has explored the development of upstream competition and its impact on prices, the financing of the USP and welfare where the USP maximizes welfare. The numerical illustrations indicate the relative scale and direction of movement arising from changes in market assumptions, which for the USP as a whole are often relatively small but for the RB and MNO are more material.

Transfer prices were confirmed to play no direct role in the analysis and do not affect the behavior of the USP, as was shown in De Donder et al. (2008). They are therefore not necessarily informative for pricing decisions by the USP or its regulatory authorities.

The chapter has shown that the access prices charged by the MNO to entrants rise as competition intensifies (and the markup on entrants' marginal costs falls). As the contribution to fixed network costs made by the RB reduces, the USP also relies more heavily on recovering its fixed costs from both SP and BM business markets. Greater market share loss upstream by the RB further reduces its contribution to the recovery of fixed costs and further increases the access prices and the MNO's contribution.

When the USP charges the same access price for both SP and BM business markets or the BM market alone, the RB's end-to-end price was shown to not always be above that of the entrants, but can be below (depending on the level of competitive intensity). Furthermore, when there is a greater propensity to switch to the entrants, it can lead to the RB reducing its business prices and a situation where its prices are below the access price plus upstream marginal cost and entrants' prices, with the entrants still holding a high share of the market. Hence the RB prices that maximize welfare may be above or below the entrants' prices or access prices plus marginal upstream costs, with competition still having a high market share.

The chapter has also demonstrated that if higher contributions to the fixed upstream costs are imposed on the RB (either internally or externally), the USP finds it more difficult to break even and further there is a limit to the contribution that the RB can make. The imposition of additional constraints upon the RB is beneficial neither to the USP nor to overall welfare and is also unnecessary for competition to have a high market share.

If the MNO can apply distinct access prices to business mail with different market elasticities (in this case SP and BM business mail), this can improve the USP's financial position (by making it relatively easier to break even). This reduces the burden on the business market with the higher price elasticity (in BM). Furthermore, the RB distinguishes between the two business markets even when the downstream access charges are the same. Hence, more distinct pricing by USP can improve its financial position and increase welfare in the presence of upstream competition.

The analysis did not include bypass competition, competition from digital media, and the potential relationships between upstream and bypass competition, so as to focus on the impact of upstream competition alone. The development of upstream competition not only reduces the contribution to fixed network costs and raises access prices as has been shown, but also increases drop density of the mail volume held upstream by entrants, which would both increase the likelihood of bypass competition. Hence the development of competition in the postal sector as a whole may be informed by the development of upstream competition and remain a subject for further research under full market opening and alongside competition from digital media.

NOTES

* This chapter reflects the views of the authors and may not necessarily be those of Royal Mail Group.

1. The sensitivity of the results to this assumption is checked by also looking at results obtained when the entrants' market share of both SP business mail and BM is 50 percent for equal prices and 90 percent if the entrants are 20 percent cheaper than the RB.
2. With linear demands, this means that for any 10 items sold by the entrants, nine are displaced from the RB and one is net volume creation. A higher displacement ratio would have the effect of reducing the market growth arising from the transfer of mail to the entrants, and therefore reduce the welfare benefit of entry. The figure of 0.9 is used for illustrative purposes. The growth in that market from the switching of mail to entrants is not easily discerned and may be even lower in a declining market.
3. For the monopoly case, in the absence of access charges and thus of a benchmark for internal prices, it is assumed that all contributions accrue to the MNO.

REFERENCE

De Donder Philippe, Helmuth Cremer, Paul Dudley and Frank Rodriguez (2008), 'Pricing, welfare and organizational constraints for postal operators', in M.A. Crew and P.R. Kleindorfer (eds), *Competition and Regulation in the Postal and Delivery Sector*, Cheltenham, UK and Northampton, MA, USA: Edward Elgar

APPENDIX 25A

The demand functions for SP business mail and BM in the case when the RB has a monopoly over these two goods can be obtained easily:

$$x_B^{IM}(q_B^I) \text{ is obtained from } \max_{x_B^I} v(x_B^I, 0) - q_B^I x_B^I + I_2,$$

$$y^{IM}(p^I) \text{ is obtained from } \max_{y^I} w(y^I, 0) - p^I y^I + I_3.$$

The profit functions of the operators are also easy to adapt to the monopoly situation:

$$\Pi^{IM} = (q_B^I - a_B^I - c_B^I)\, x_B^{IM}(q_B^I) - F_B^I + (p^I - a_y^I - c_y^I)\, y^{IM}(p^I) - F_y^I,$$

$$\Pi^{NM} = (q - c_{US} - c_D)\, x_S(q) - F_{US} + (a_B^I - c_D)\, x_B^{IM}(q_B^I) + (a_y^I - c_D)\, y^{IM}(p^I) - F_D.$$

26. The postal economy in the UK and Rutgers CRRI conferences since 1990: a review of developments and economic themes*

Frank Rodriguez[†]

1 INTRODUCTION

The first Rutgers CRRI[1] conference on Postal and Delivery Economics was held in Rugby in the UK in 1990. That conference and succeeding ones have contributed much to the analysis and understanding of developments in the sector and, throughout, the enduring theme of the conferences has been the analysis of postal markets and policy and the factors affecting these in a period of major change. In 1990, the postal sector in the UK was dominated by the Post Office Group, a public corporation.[2] The Group consisted of three main businesses: Royal Mail (all mail including international and unaddressed); Parcelforce (parcels); and the Post Office (counters). Of these, Royal Mail was by far the largest and had a monopoly in the addressed mail market for items under £1, except for exempted areas such as document exchanges. Following a period of growth during the preceding decade, total addressed mail volumes were about 16 billion items, of which only about 600 million were international and the remainder inland, while the Group employed about 210,000 employees, of which about 170,000 were in Royal Mail.[3] Unaddressed mail was outside the monopoly, as were parcels, and there were a large number of private operators in these sectors. The Post Office network contained both directly operated (Crown) and franchise offices.

By 2010–11 Royal Mail's volume of addressed delivered mail was similar to that in 1990 but, after continued steady growth to the mid-2000s, volume peaked in 2005–06 before beginning to decline. The Postal Services Act (2000) had defined the Universal Service Obligation (USO) in legislation for the first time and had set up an independent economic regulator, Postcomm, which opened the postal market to licensed entrants in two stages, with full market opening (FMO) in January 2006. Competitors entered the UK letter market from 2003, mainly through downstream access after the negotiation and signing of the first access agreement in February 2004, so that, in 2010–11, nearly a half of Royal Mail's delivered addressed mail was access traffic. In 2010–11 employment in Royal Mail Holdings plc (the successor company) was around three-quarters of its level in 1990 and, although the company had diversified into profitable parcels, logistics and express markets, overall its finances were under pressure as they had been for a number of years.

† Associate, Oxera.

The Hooper review (2008) was commissioned by the government in the light of concerns regarding the decline in the postal market and the financial position of Royal Mail. It made recommendations on the governance of the sector. These included the introduction of private capital into Royal Mail; the assets and liabilities of the employee pension fund up to a cut-off date to be retained by government as part of a wider financial restructuring; and regulation to pass to Ofcom. Postcomm was abolished in 2011 and its functions as the independent regulator taken up by Ofcom under the Postal Services Act (2011). A new regulatory regime came into effect in April 2012. This included a substantially increased degree of pricing flexibility and commercial freedom for Royal Mail, and a move towards economic regulation of the company by *ex post* competition rules subject to certain safeguards. After satisfying EU state aid rules, clearance was given for the financial restructuring of Royal Mail Group. The UK government intends to proceed with the privatization of Royal Mail.

There were a number of key questions then that were of major relevance to UK stakeholders in the sector over this period. The remaining sections of the chapter consider the contribution of the conferences to the understanding of some of these.[4] These include, first, on the demand for mail (Section 2): what were the prospects for the growth or decline of the mail market, and hence what factors underpin the demand for mail? How would these be affected by electronic (e-) substitution? Second, on costs and efficiency (Section 3): what were the best ways for the company to continue to improve its efficiency? To what extent would stronger or weaker volume growth impact on costs? Third, on universal service and competition (Sections 4 and 5): to what extent would market opening affect the ability of Royal Mail to meet its obligations on the provision of universal service? What factors determined the nature, pattern and extent of entry? More generally, how compatible are competition and universal service with the financial viability of universal service providers (USPs), particularly in the context of a declining market for mail? Fourth, on economic regulation and pricing (Section 6): what would be the effects of moving from control by government department to control by independent regulator? How should the regulatory design for the postal sector respond to the changing market environment of declining volumes and increasing competition? Finally, Section 7 concludes.

2 DEMAND FOR MAIL

In the UK, as in most developed economies, addressed mail volumes for the total market grew robustly during the 1980s and 1990s but began to fall after the mid-2000s. Understanding past trends and trying to forecast future volumes are of critical importance and the conferences have provided the main forum internationally for the analysis of mail demand.

Estimation of Demand Elasticities

The most common approach to the estimation of demand elasticities has been the use of time-series macro models of demand where the dependent variable is total mail volume in a particular country or total mail there divided into no more than three segmentations. Total volume in these studies has usually been that of the USP, and mail volume is typically a function of economic activity, own mail price, competitor prices, and a trend or e-substitution proxy variable. Some studies include additional variables, such as demography or quality of service. Generally, the broad similarities in the estimated elasticities across many of these studies are more striking than the differences. The results usually contain GDP or another economic activity indicator with an elasticity typically around or a little below unity for total traffic, and differences by individual streams of traffic.[5] Own-price elasticities for total mail at the market level are low, typically in the range of around –0.2 to –0.5. At a more disaggregated level of traffic, price elasticities vary across streams and also by whether a time-series macro or cross-sectional micro approach has been followed, with elasticities estimated in macro models generally being lower than those from cross-sectional studies.[6] With regard to other variables, the macro-model studies indicate a relatively small effect from variables measuring quality of service or other non-price effects; a demographic variable that is positive with elasticity up to unity; and, particularly in more recent studies, an effect from e-substitution.

The recent decline in mail volumes has raised the issue of whether the relationships estimated in these studies still hold. With regard to price elasticities, there is some evidence, for example from France and the UK, that their (absolute) values have increased a little, but at the total traffic level perhaps by only 0.2 or 0.3. On economic activity, some have claimed that the relationship between the economy and mail volumes has been 'broken'. However, evidence from the UK (Jarosik et al., chapter 14 this volume) suggests that the economy–mail volume association remains with an elasticity close to unity for data to 2011, implying that mail volumes continue to be cyclical around a trend. What has changed there, and perhaps elsewhere, is that the trend is no longer close to the underlying expansion of the economy plus a measure of demographic growth. Rather, the growth rate has been displaced downwards and become negative, because to the positive impacts on volumes of economic activity and demography needs to be added the negative impact of e-substitution.

Understanding E-substitution

Nikali (1995) modeled the effect of a number of teleservices (for example, telefax) on letter mail, in two steps: first, a diffusion model (as a logistic curve), where the diffusion of a new technology is a function of time; and, second, the effect of that developing technology on the demand for a particular type of mail (for example, bills). Diffusion has followed an S-shaped curve in later forms such as broadband penetration. Electronic media compete not only with mail but also with other such media, and may replace those rather than letter mail, as shown by the experience of fax. The idea of successive or multiple technologies can be captured through a sequence of time-dependent diffusion curves forming a 'large corrugated S-curve' (Nikali, 2008). This suggests that e-substitution cannot be captured fully through a single variable, but is a more complex multi-dimensional process. While the form of this process is likely to be nonlinear and only partially observed, some of the econometric models also include trend breaks, which reflect, in a simple way, structural breaks in the demand for mail that are almost certainly due to the effects of e-substitution. Recent examples of this type for the UK include Cazals et al. (2011) and Jarosik et al. (chapter 14 this volume).

The replacement of mail requires both the sender and the recipient of targeted communication to have both the technology and the willingness to accept an electronic substitute. Elkelä (2011) considers this issue using survey information by examining the form of invoicing in 16 European countries in 2010. In the UK, for example, an above EU average percentage of enterprises sent (89 percent) or received (76 percent) electronic invoices, but a below EU average of consumers (34 percent) received them, and respondents stated that they did not expect to change their preferences appreciably in the following two to three years. This is an important result, because the business-to-consumer mail flow is the largest and the one where e-substitution has probably advanced least. A related aspect is differences in the use of mail by generation. Jimenez et al. (2006a, 2006b) report data from the US, which indicate that households with a head in an older age group receive significantly more mail than younger households. Using plausible assumptions on future mailing, the authors conclude that the decline in mail due to e-substitution might be no more than 3 percent per annum on average to 2025. These survey and demographic approaches add significant insights to the process and possible quantitative effects of e-substitution, complementing econometric analysis.

Forecasting and the Treatment of Uncertainty

Trinkner and Grossman (2006a, p. 279) comment that it is 'nearly impossible to make long term forecasts with the applied techniques, because there is no unique proxy for e-substitution'. Using Monte Carlo techniques, Cazals et al. (2008) show that the errors around a forecast increase with the period ahead of that forecast, and that a structural break (for example, caused by a step change in e-substitution) can be a second and potentially larger source of such errors. Nevertheless, there is a requirement for long-term forecasts. Fève et al. (2010, 2012) formulate an approach to forecasting that is Bayesian in character combining econometric estimates from analysis of historical data with informative priors using 'non-identified' models from other sources of information, such as surveys. They propose this as a way to address the increased level of uncertainty arising from e-substitution. This has become a dominant consideration in forecasting mail volumes over the longer term, particularly where projections support decisions that are irreversible. Both Fève et al. (2012) for the UK and Martin et al. (2012) for Australia provide examples of forecasts that move in the direction of this approach.

3 COSTS AND EFFICIENCY

The cost structure of posts has particular features that are important in understanding the operation of postal markets. A large amount of analysis on this area has been presented at the conferences.

Cost Structure of Postal Networks and Variability of Costs

Posts is a network industry where the value chain can be characterized as a sequence of activities from collection of mail, through outward processing/sorting and transportation (collectively upstream), to inward processing and delivery to the addressee (collectively downstream). Network industries typically have some element of natural monopoly. At the first conference, Panzar posed the fundamental question, 'Is postal service a natural monopoly?' (Panzar, 1991). Although he considered that there was a lack of conclusive empirical evidence, he answered the question in the affirmative because of the expectation that 'there were significant economies of scale in delivery'. However, competition may be possible for posts may be a monopoly network only in part, and sunk costs probably quite low due to its labor-intensive nature. Rogerson and Takis (1993) presented the first set of estimates to the conferences of cost elasticities for parts of the value chain in the US. Econometric evidence indicated a cost elasticity of about 0.35 for outdoor delivery, indicating very significant economies of scale (of about 3) consistent with the hypothesis that delivery is a natural monopoly. Transportation and mail processing cost elasticities were estimated closer to unity.

The basic proposition outlined in these two papers on the structure of postal networks (that is, that there are significant economies of scale in delivery but approximately constant returns to scale in much of the rest of the network) represents a cornerstone of postal economics, largely accepted throughout the conferences. Analytical models of the postal market have also tended to follow this structure, positing a fixed cost in the delivery network, to which there is also a marginal cost of delivery, while upstream costs are treated as variable.

With regard to delivery, a number of subsequent studies have been broadly consistent with the result reported in Rogerson and Takis. Roy (1999) uses an operational model to simulate how delivery costs vary by a number of factors including volume, delivery point density and grouping index (apartment blocks), finding cost elasticities that vary from 0.1 to closer to unity. Cazals et al. (2005) separate their econometric estimates of the effects of volumes on delivery costs in the UK (cost elasticity of 0.42) into those arising from volume per delivery point and number of delivery points. Delivery costs rise approximately in line with delivery points, so that the main effect in generating low cost elasticities comes from increases in volumes per delivery point. Cazals et al. also find, consistent with results from other countries, that cost elasticities for delivery in rural areas are lower than in urban areas. With mail volumes contracting in recent years, the issue arises not only of whether delivery costs would decline less rapidly than volume but also whether there is an asymmetry and delivery costs decline even less than in proportion to volumes when volumes decline. As Bradley et al. (2012) note, using data from the US between 2006 and 2010, this asymmetry might arise for a number of reasons: for example, the need to maintain universal service at fixed levels or union contracts. For 'street hours' (outdoor delivery), they indeed find that the short-run elasticity of hours with respect to volume for periods when delivered volume declines (0.07) is 'about a third less' than periods when it rises (0.11), while for 'office hours' (indoor delivery) there appears to be no corresponding asymmetry.

Costing Methodologies

USPs are large multi-product firms. A key feature of their cost structure is the widespread occurrence of common and joint costs. A number of papers have outlined approaches to costing for pricing-related issues, which grapple with this complexity to some extent. In the US, the prices of postal products are based on unit volume variable costs (a proxy for marginal costs) (Bradley et al., 1993), and there has been significant work there also on incremental costs relevant for testing cross-subsidy (Bradley et al., 1997, 1999). In Europe, there has been some focus on approaches to costing where prices reflect fully allocated costs. However, as in the US, there is a requirement to estimate incremental costs to ensure that prices set are not an abuse of dominant position. Mautino et al. (chapter 10 this volume) consider, from a UK perspective, the issues involved in estimating long-run incremental and stand-alone costs to satisfy these requirements.

Efficiency

A related area considered at the conferences has been efficiency. The primary approach followed has been stochastic frontier analysis (SFA). A boundary of efficient units within the relevant part of a USP is estimated econometrically, and the unexplained 'distances' of individual units from that frontier are allocated between statistical noise and the unit's level of inefficiency relative to that frontier. As part of the work for the Third Price Control Review in the UK, Horncastle et al. (2006b) and Moriarty et al. (2006b) report results from applying SFA to data on over 1,000 Royal Mail delivery offices for 2003–04, covering over a third of Royal Mail's costs.[7] Horncastle et al. (2006b) concluded that the average inefficiency of delivery offices was in the range of 7.5 to 12.5 percent compared with units on the efficient frontier that they had estimated, while Moriarty et al. (2006b) estimated a figure of about 11 percent. Postcomm used the latter estimate as one of its main inputs in determining that Royal Mail would be able to increase its efficiency by 3 percent per annum over the period 2006 to 2010. Further work has been undertaken on the use of SFA in measuring (in)efficiency. Cazals et al. (2012) show that results from panel SFA can be sensitive to the specification used and unknowable variables such as the assumed form of noise. Additionally, many factors may impact on delivery costs in practice, but it is difficult to capture this heterogeneity. Cazals et al. suggest that a full range of specifications should be tested and interpreted in reaching a decision regarding the degree of inefficiency, but that cross-section SFA has reasonably good properties for estimating its overall level.

4 UNIVERSAL SERVICE AND ITS FUNDING

In posts, a USO is the 'provision of a ubiquitous service at a uniform price and quality' (Crew and Kleindorfer, 2000, p. 5). In 1990, national postal operators in most countries were monopolies, with a reserved area to fund these obligations. However, in Europe the Single European Act began a process for opening markets to competition. An emerging issue in 1990 and a central one ever since has been to reconcile the provision of universal service with the opening of postal markets so that consumers benefit from both. This section considers the contribution of the conferences on universal service and its funding. The next section discusses competitive entry.

The USO: Content and Rationale

Although specifics vary across countries, typically the USO includes collection/clearance of mail five or six days a week; delivery to (virtually) every address to the same frequency; a uniformly priced stamp service; and other services (for example, international mail, parcels, registered mail).[8] Ambrosini et al. (2006a) surveyed 19 countries and described

USOs in three dimensions: the scope of products covered by the USO; non-price characteristics such as delivery frequency; and price constraints. Crew and Kleindorfer (2006b) criticize the concept of a social USO (SUSO) as one response to these constraints with postal market liberalization, which would limit the scope of products in the USO to uniformly priced social mail. Leskinen et al. (2009, p. 277) argue that a 'broad USO should no longer exist' in Finland and should be replaced by a USO that combines aspects of postal and e-communication. Nevertheless, there is agreement that some form of USO is needed. Crew and Kleindorfer (2000) develop an economic argument for the benefits of the uniform price component of the USO in terms of reducing transactions costs compared with varying prices by location. Cremer et al. (2008) set out other important economic considerations supporting it: first, the USO as a form of redistributive pricing and, second, its justification in efficiency terms because an extensive, high-quality network adds to the demand for mail that the market would undervalue. Surveys of consumers also suggest that they value positively the existence of the USO. In the UK, Sheldon and Lawrence (2011) report evidence from an extensive survey of consumers of a high level of satisfaction with the USO.

Costs and Funding of Universal Service

The costs of universal service and their funding became an area of interest at the conference with postal market liberalization. From a UK/EU perspective, a key policy issue in the late 1990s (in the context of the postal directives) was to ensure that the market could be opened while safeguarding the provision of the USO – that is, that the 'cost of the USO' could be funded. How should this question be posed and cost measured? In two important papers, Cremer et al. (2000) and Panzar (2001) showed that the cost of the USO in posts should be defined as a profitability cost: that is, as the difference between two estimates of profits rather than between two estimates of costs. As Cremer et al. (2000, p. 49) state: 'To assess the burden that universal service imposes on an operator, one has to compare its profits at the *market equilibria* that obtain under two competitive scenarios: one with USO and one without USO'.[9] Cremer et al. also identified a measure they termed the 'cost of liberalization', which they defined as the difference between the profit of the incumbent USP pre-liberalization and its profit under the competitive scenario without the USO. The measure used in the telecomms sector for measuring profitability costs – net avoided cost (NAC) – was not appropriate, not least because in the postal sector in the 1990s such a calculation would have been for a monopolist pre-liberalization. Another way of addressing the question of whether the postal market could be opened while meeting the USO was to consider directly the profitability cost of continuing to provide that USO post-liberalization. Here, the counterfactual was a liberalized market with that USO rather than a monopolist without the USO as under NAC. This is the entry pricing measure of the cost of the USO (Rodriguez et al., 1999) and a similar methodology was also developed by others (for example, Bradley and Colvin, 2000).[10] Unlike NAC, which took no account of liberalization, these measures are forward looking and require an explicit assessment of at least one competitive scenario (under entry pricing) and two under the Cremer et al./Panzar measure.

Crew and Kleindorfer (2000) set out three scenarios for the prospects of financing the USO in a liberalized environment. Much would depend on the extent of entry. Scenario 1 posited a 'graveyard spiral' (GYS), where USPs are extremely vulnerable to entry and lose the mailings of large customers to entrants. Here raising prices becomes self-defeating as more and more volume and profitable contribution are lost but the USP retains the fixed costs of operation, and financial deficits become unsustainable. Scenario 2 is a 'successful liberalization', where the USO is met and entry provides benefits to consumers. Scenario 3 is an 'intermediate case', which the authors consider to be the likeliest outcome. Some entry occurs and the USO might need to be reduced but the situation was uncertain. A number of papers followed that focused on whether full liberalization would result in a GYS but reached a wide range of conclusions on its likelihood. One of the reasons for this was not just the possible impact of market opening but also that of other factors, such as the decline of the mail market. The likelihood of a GYS would also depend on the competitive response of the USP, particularly its pricing. Postcomm had considered the potential financial impact on Royal Mail of market opening in reaching its decisions on postal market liberalization (Postcomm, 2002). The question of Royal Mail's financial viability under FMO continued to be one of major significance during the work for the price control that came into operation in 2006.[11] More recently, a number of USPs, including Royal Mail, have been under financial pressure as mail volumes have declined, whether due to a contraction in the mail market, competitive entry, or both.

With FMO, there has been a second round of interest in the cost of the USO at the conference. Directive 2008/06/EC implements the Cremer et al. (2000) profitability cost approach to the measurement of the net cost of universal service. The directive (at Annex 1) proposes that the cost be calculated as the sum of the individual components of the USO. However, as Jaag et al. (2009) show, this may not lead to the same result as considering a counterfactual of the withdrawal of the USO as a whole as set out in Cremer et al. (2000), and conclude that a global approach is required to calculation to avoid either under or double counting. Examples of calculations for the USO in total include cross-country comparisons made by Boldron et al. (2006b). There have also been assessments of the net costs of individual components of the USO, for example, in the UK, by Bradley et al. (2009) for the net cost of Saturday delivery. It is apparent from these studies that the demand side in the profitability cost calculation has proved challenging. Carslake et al. (2011), using UK data, model such effects by indirect methods for the case of reducing delivery by one day, concluding that the demand reduction would be under 1 percent, while De Donder et al. (2010) analyze the complex interaction between changes in quality and demand in a formal model.

Financing Mechanisms

Directive 2008/06/EC allows financing through either compensation from public funds or cost sharing between providers of services and/or users, although, as the mail market has contracted, it is perhaps uncertain whether cost sharing between the USP and entrants alone could be adequate to fund an extensive USO. Such arrangements can be established where there is shown to be, first, a positive net cost and, second, an unfair financial burden borne by the USP.[12] The interpretation of this second condition is not unambiguous. Both Boldron et al. (2009) and De Donder et al. (2010) consider aspects of this issue in the financing of the net cost. However, there have been few analyses of approaches to the specifics of cost-sharing mechanisms. An important consideration here is that the financing mechanism itself affects the behavior of both the USP and other providers and hence is an endogenous component that needs to be allowed for in the arrangements for cost sharing. De Donder et al. (2002a) and Borsenberger et al. (2010) have considered this issue through formal models and simulations on stylized data and, in particular, alternative forms of taxation that might be levied in the case of cost sharing.

5 COMPETITIVE ENTRY

Bypass and Downstream Access

Bypass and access are the two generic forms of competitive entry in the postal sector, and their impacts on the operation of the market differ markedly. As discussed by Panzar (1993), it is possible to introduce competition into the value chain of a vertically integrated postal operator by unbundling the constituent components of the mail process. Entry upstream had been developed in posts from the 1970s in the US through workshare discounts. In principle, he suggested, it would be possible to extend access downstream to the delivery function. The issue rose in importance with the adoption of Directive 2002/39/EC and the issuing of a license to Royal Mail, which in the former offered the possibility of, and in the latter required the mandating of, access. However, downstream access might be wasteful because of cream-skimming against the uniform tariff and its mandating in posts could be viewed as unnecessary because sunk costs are low in the sector (Panzar, 2002b). By contrast, based on evidence of limited entry into the German market, Schwarz-Schilling (2002b) considers that significant entry by a single operator does involve substantial sunk costs in the form of, for example, recruitment and training of a reliable workforce. The theme of the desirability of access has been revisited by Crew and Kleindorfer (2011). Access is complex to regulate, and regulatory intervention should be at a minimum. At the same time, they argue that it is in the interests of USPs to promote access, appropriately priced, as a way to maximize the use of delivery networks, so helping to retain contribution and underpin the funding of the USO. Their theorem on superiority of access (to bypass) reinforces the benefits of this strategic approach by USPs by highlighting the welfare economic advantages of access.

A number of papers have addressed the question of the optimal pricing of access, which is complicated both by the possibility of cream-skimming and, in Europe, bypass. These include Crew and Kleindorfer (2002b), Panzar (2002b), Billette de Villemeur et al. (2004) and De Donder et al. (2005). In De Donder et al., the optimal access price derived from a basic model includes the following terms:[13] the marginal cost of delivery; the opportunity cost of a displaced retail item multiplied by the displacement ratio; and a Ramsey-based markup to achieve financial break-even where bypass occurs. The first two terms correspond to the efficient component pricing rule (ECPR).[14] Welfare is maximized when access prices are differentiated at a zonal level to capture differences in delivery costs by area. While detailed formulae from formal models provide clear insights into the constituent parts of optimal pricing regimes, these may be difficult to apply in practice. A simplified scheme which captures some of the features of optimal prices is delivery area access pricing (DAP) proposed by Crew and Kleindorfer

(2002b). Here, the access price in a zone is the higher of the ECPR access price and the average incremental cost of delivery, capped at the relevant single-piece price.[15] Hill and Robinson (2006a) outline the approach to zonal access pricing initially followed in the UK, which calculated delivery costs by zones to which were added a national average markup.

The possibility of bypass in the UK/EU, however, means that the access customer will deliver its mail if it has the capability to do so and its delivery cost is below the USP's access price. While access prices may be optimal or some approximation to these, this does not preclude entry through bypass. In general, in these models the impact of bypass compared with access is to reduce economic welfare by reducing volume in the delivery network, thus raising average costs and prices. As a result, there is also the potential for a GYS. These welfare-maximizing models of access and bypass are set in a comparative static framework, but the dynamic benefits of bypass would need to be substantial to reverse these effects. Much then depends on the form and extent of entry.

Understanding Entry and Its Impacts

Several conference papers have developed approaches to understanding entry and its possible impacts, much of it based on modeling. Entrants are typically modeled as being profit maximizing and not subject to a USO, although approaches differ in the ways entrants seek to maximize profits. In contrast to those that emphasize entrants competing for routes or segments of traffic with the greatest profit, Crew and Kleindorfer (2001a) focus on entrants competing for mail from large mailers with low-cost delivery characteristics, passing higher-cost mail to the USP for delivery. Burns et al. (2002b) develop a model where a USP gains advantage in the market in the form of brand loyalty to its services, while Hill et al. (2005) outline a model which contains a switching function which takes account of price, non-price and inertia effects to assess the movement of customers to entrants. Cohen et al. (2005) take the perspective of a venture capitalist assessing whether to invest in a startup operation modeled on Citymail in Sweden. They conclude that returns on such a business would be inadequate to satisfy US investors.

In considering the UK market from the perspective of Postcomm, Moriarty and Smith (2005) note that, despite a partial opening of the market, very little entry had occurred, and highlight economies of scale as a major barrier to entry through bypass. This was particularly so for delivery six days a week or in rural areas, although less in urban areas or where delivery was less frequent. Entry through access was seen by Postcomm as a way to promote effective competition in the UK market. Other barriers to entry the authors identify included Royal Mail's VAT exemption. Through this the authors argued that Royal Mail gained a price advantage over entrants by not charging VAT. At the same time, it could not reclaim input tax associated with VAT. Entrants, however, have to charge VAT (but reclaim input tax, thus lowering their base price). This provides them with a price disadvantage with customers who are VAT exempt, such as banks, but a price advantage for their VAT-rated customers who also can reclaim input tax.

Empirical Evidence on Competitive Entry

Entry has varied significantly across countries. In the US, the United States Postal Service (USPS) retains a monopoly in delivery, but extensive private sector activity has developed upstream. Elcano et al. (2000, p. 337) describe this as 'the quiet liberalisation of the United States postal system', and estimated the extent of private sector activity to be about 20 percent of combined USPS revenue and workshare discounts. In Europe, there has been FMO. Jonsson and Selander (2006a) outline developments in the Swedish market. By the mid-2000s, Citymail had been able to gain about 25 percent of presorted bulk mail or about 8 percent of the total market. A number of local operators jointly held less than 1 percent, so that Sweden Post retained over 90 percent. In considering the early development of the German market, Schwarz-Schilling (2002b) notes that, while entry into the (partially liberalized) market was easy (over 1,000 licenses were issued by the German regulator within four years of this in 1998), so was exit. Less than 10 percent of the part of the market opened was being served by entrants after four years.

The development of competition in Germany, the Netherlands, Spain and the UK prior to FMO was examined by de Bas and van der Lijn (2008), who consider that regulation has affected the way competition has developed in these countries. Other than in the UK, entry has been mainly bypass. By the end of 2006, entrants had taken about 8 to 12 percent of the addressed market, although in these countries letter mail under 50g remained within the reserved area. By contrast, in the UK, entry had taken place to a similar extent but through downstream access, which the authors believe was due to 'regulatory uncertainty' deterring bypass before the first access agreement, and low access prices thereafter. Dudley et al. (2009) consider this issue further. By 2008, access had increased to over 20 percent of all addressed delivered volumes in the UK. They review the constraint introduced by Postcomm in 2006 to prevent price squeezes of entrants offering access and conclude that this was greater than required under competition law.

6 ECONOMIC REGULATION, COMPETITION POLICY AND PRICING ISSUES

The framework for the operation of postal markets is determined by statute. In the EU/UK there are the provisions of the directives and their translation into domestic legislation. The postal sector is also subject to the provisions of competition law. Directive 97/67/EC required the creation of independent national regulatory authorities. The dominant focus of regulation in many EU countries initially was sector specific, aiming both to constrain the market position and pricing of USPs, and to promote competition. The UK market was opened in full from January 2006, and most of the EU from January 2011. As a result, as Wojtek and Zauner (2012, p. 32) note, 'With full liberalization of the postal markets the focus of price regulation shifts from *ex ante* price setting to detecting and preventing abuses in the liberalized market'. Papers to the conferences have analyzed these developments.

Economic Regulation: Approaches and Models

The theory of incentive or price-cap regulation (PCR) had largely been developed by 1990 but a core component of the theory underpinning PCR is the existence of residual claimants. As Crew and Kleindorfer (2001b) showed, such incentives are likely to be weak in publicly owned corporations, so it was unlikely that the full benefits of efficiency gains would be achieved by publicly owned postal operators. Nevertheless, compared with possible alternatives for regulation, Crew and Kleindorfer (2008) considered that an amended version of PCR could have benefits, for example, in terms of allowing pricing flexibility to USPs. In practice, PCR has been introduced in many countries and the details of some of these country examples have been presented at the conferences. Correia da Silva et al. (2004) review the application of price controls in the postal sector, based on both theory and experience from other regulated sectors in the UK. Many of the elements they considered were contained in the price control set by Postcomm that ran from 2006, including mechanisms for managing external risks to the profitability of Royal Mail.

A number of other areas relating to PCR in the postal sector were addressed by other papers. First, in principle, a USP could allow quality of service (QoS) to deteriorate in meeting a price cap unless its regulator put in place a counterbalance. Postcomm introduced a formal control on QoS in 2003 that penalized Royal Mail if it failed to meet QoS targets. Balogh et al. (2006a) set out Postcomm's work in extending this mechanism for the control commencing in 2006. Second, a competitive environment has implications for PCR. Dudley et al. (2005) examine the issue of the coverage of the control, and consider tests for the removal of price caps as competition increases. The implications of competition on price controls are considered in a welfare economic framework by De Donder et al. (2006b). Confirming a result from the wider economics literature, economic welfare is maximized where the price control has a single basket with a global price cap. However, if additional constraints are placed on prices (for example, from a regulatory objective to minimize single-piece prices) then, in general, there is a decline in economic welfare.[16] Quantitatively, the negative effects on welfare from additional constraints may be modest, although this is not likely to be the case where competitive entry is through bypass, for this acts to reduce delivery volumes and raise average costs of the USP continuing to provide universal service. De Donder et al. (2006b) consider examples where not only does welfare decline due to bypass, but also deficits emerge, thus resulting in a GYS.[17]

Crew and Kleindorfer (2008) also develop a model of PCR and emphasize the potential negative effect on economic welfare of restricting price flexibility to USPs in response to competitive entry. In particular, as competitive entry develops, they propose a scheme where increased pricing flexibility is allowed; a price cap is applied only to some single-piece rates to protect small customers and also on some access prices; and greater use is made of the publishing of information. The significant changes made by Ofcom to the regulatory framework for the UK mail market from April 2012 reflect many of these elements.

Competition Policy and Constraints on Pricing

FMO in the UK/EU has led, then, to a powerful shift in the balance from sector-specific regulation to regulation through competition law. The main issues here arise from the potential of USPs to contravene Article 102 TFEU on the abuse of dominant position. The possibility of such abuses is assessed on a case-by-case basis. The first step is to establish market structure: is a USP dominant in a market, which itself requires a procedure for defining the relevant market? A second step, if dominance is established, is to assess behavior for evidence of abuses, many of which relate to pricing, so constraints on the ability to price remain at the heart of regulation.

Definition of relevant markets was first examined by Plum and Schwarz-Schilling (2000). They set out the approach to this question in some detail, beginning with the hypothetical monopolist (SSNIP) test and considering the examination of demand- and supply-side substitution in defining product and geographical markets. Gibson and Race (2012) report the results of a study on the definition of packets and parcels services markets in the UK undertaken by Postcomm and used for decisions on whether particular Royal Mail products were to continue to be price controlled. However, broadly the same approach would apply in identifying relevant markets for competition policy purposes. The European Commission has proposed that the approach to assessing possible abuses of dominance should change from being 'form based' to 'effects based', which would be more in line with modern economic theory (Geradin and Henry, 2010). They review the guidance paper published by the Commission on its proposed approach to enforcement against potential abuses (European Commission, 2009). The two key cost benchmarks against which to compare prices in applying tests to investigate these are average avoidable costs and long-run average incremental costs (LRAIC). In particular, the authors highlight that price above LRAIC appears to be a (strong) test to show absence of abuse of a dominant position. Davies (2011) reviews some of this material also in the context of investigations undertaken by Postcomm of alleged abuses of dominant position by Royal Mail, and a number of papers at recent conferences have reviewed case law on possible abuse of dominant position in the context of price discrimination.

An example where the relaxation of constraints on pricing may be welfare economic enhancing is considered in De Donder et al. (2011) who examine differentiation of prices between direct mail and other bulk mail. They show that reducing the price of direct mail relative to other bulk mail (because of its higher (absolute) price elasticity) can result in both higher total mail volumes and higher economic welfare when compared with a counterfactual of all bulk mail being priced at the same rate. Flórez Duncan et al. (2011) examine some of the issues involved in applying such approaches to pricing in practice. As competition grows, the operation of regulation through competition law seems set to increase, and so too its importance at future conferences.

7 CONCLUSION

This chapter has reviewed the contribution of the Rutgers CRRI conferences to the analysis of postal markets and policy since the first conference in 1990. The areas covered in the chapter have been among those of particular interest in, although not exclusively to, the UK, namely demand, cost, universal service and competition, and regulation and pricing. In all of these areas, the conference has been a key forum for the exchange and development of analysis on postal markets and policy. Looking ahead, the environment within which the postal sector operates is changing and the sector itself is evolving in response to these changes. Demand for mail is in decline while multi-modal competition is increasing, competitive entry is expanding and growth continues in express, parcel and logistics markets. Securing universal service remains a primary objective of governments but the form of that service may be modified as users' needs change, while the focus of regulation and the pricing structures of postal operators are also changing in response to the realities of today's postal markets. USPs are undergoing major changes in many countries and that process seems set to advance further. All these areas and more provide rich material for papers to future conferences.

NOTES

* The author is very grateful for comments received in the preparation of this chapter from Robert Bishopp, Catherine Cazals, Philippe De Donder, Paul Dudley, Frédérique Fève, Jean-Pierre Florens, Leonardo Mautino and Soterios Soteri. The views contained in the chapter are those of the author, as are any errors that remain. A longer version of this chapter is available at www.oxera.com.

1. Center for Research in Regulated Industries, Rutgers Business School, Rutgers University.
2. Additional information on the Post Office Group at that time is contained in Dobbs and Richards (1991).
3. See Post Office Group, *Annual Report and Accounts*.
4. As contained in the nearly 400 papers published in the conferences' 18 books.
5. For example, income elasticities for First Class (next day) traffic above those for Second Class in both France and the UK (see Boldron et al., 2010; Jarosik et al., chapter 14 this volume)
6. Cazals and Florens (2002b) assess whether there is systematic bias in these alternative approaches and conclude that both approaches are sensitive to estimation bias, which may be reduced by the use of panel datasets.
7. Horncastle et al. (2006b) also analyzed the dataset using data envelopment analysis and ordinary and corrected least squares regression, while Moriarty et al. (2006b) also applied OLS techniques.
8. For example, in the UK see the Postal Services (Universal Postal Service) Order 2012 (Ofcom, 2012).
9. Emphasis in original. This contrasted with the efficiency or welfare cost approach (Cremer et al., 1997).
10. In Cremer et al. (2000) the sum of the cost of the USO as defined in Cremer et al. and the cost of liberalization was shown to equal an entry-pricing type measure (see equation (2)).
11. The analysis undertaken by Postcomm and Royal Mail in those studies for market demand made use of the models reported in Fève et al. (2012). On the modeling of competitive entry, Postcomm's analysis was based on a development of the model reported in Burns et al. (2002b), while that of Royal Mail used the entry-pricing model reported in Hill et al. (2005).
12. Eccles (2011) reviews the cost-sharing arrangements set out in the directive from a legal perspective.
13. Both Crew and Kleindorfer (2002b) and Billette de Villemeur et al. (2004) contain a very similar result.
14. As defined by Armstrong (2002).
15. Panzar (2002b) proposes a very similar approach.
16. A similar result has been derived by Borsenberger et al. (2012).
17. In practice, e-substitution may have a similar effect on the sustainability of the USP under PCR.

REFERENCES

Papers from the Conferences

Papers from the conferences cited in the current chapter and referenced below have been published in 18 books edited by Michael A. Crew and Paul R. Kleindorfer. From 1991 to 2005 the books were published by Kluwer Academic (Boston, MA); 2006a by Springer (New York); and since 2006b by Edward Elgar (Cheltenham, UK, and Northampton, MA, USA):

(1991), *Competition and Innovation in Postal Services.*
(1993), *Regulation and the Nature of Postal and Delivery Services.*
(1995), *Commercialization of Postal and Delivery Services: National and International Perspectives.*
(1997), *Managing Change in the Postal and Delivery Industries.*
(1999), *Emerging Competition in Postal and Delivery Services.*
(2000), *Current Directions in Postal Reform.*
(2001), *Future Directions in Postal Reform.*
(2002a), *Postal and Delivery Services: Pricing, Productivity, Regulation and Strategy.*
(2002b), *Postal and Delivery Services: Delivering on Competition.*
(2004), *Competitive Transformation of the Postal and Delivery Sector.*
(2005), *Regulatory and Economic Challenges in the Postal and Delivery Sector*
(2006a), *Progress Toward Liberalization of the Postal and Delivery Sector.*
(2006b), *Liberalization of the Postal and Delivery Sector.*
(2008), *Competition and Regulation in the Postal and Delivery Sector.*
(2009), *Progress in the Competitive Agenda in the Postal and Delivery Sector.*
(2010), *Heightening Competition in the Postal and Delivery Sector.*
(2011), *Reinventing the Postal Sector in an Electronic Age.*
(2012), *Multi-modal Competition and the Future of Mail.*

Unless otherwise stated, the articles cited below are contained in these books identified by year.

Ambrosini, Xavier, François Boldron and Bernard Roy (2006a), 'Universal service obligations in the postal sector: economic learnings from cross-country comparisons'.

Balogh, Tom, Richard Moriarty, Paul Smith, Roisin Doherty and Ian Leigh (2006a), 'The economic implications of quality of service regulation in a liberalized postal market'.

Billette de Villemeur, Etienne, Helmuth Cremer, Bernard Roy and Joëlle Toledano (2004), 'Access and (non-) uniform pricing in the postal sector'.

Boldron, François, Claire Borsenberger, Denis Joram, Sébastien Lécou and Bernard Roy (2009), 'A dynamic and endogenous approach to financing the USO in a liberalized environment'.

Boldron, François, Catherine Cazals, Jean-Pierre Florens and Sébastien Lécou (2010), 'Some dynamic models for mail demand: the French case'.

Boldron, François, Denis Joram, Lise Martin and Bernard Roy (2006b), 'From the size of the box to the costs of universal service obligation: a cross-country comparison'.

Borsenberger, Claire, Sébastien Bréville, Helmuth Cremer, Philippe De Donder and Denis Joram (2012), 'Price-cap regulation in the postal sector: single versus multiple baskets'.

Borsenberger, Claire, Helmuth Cremer, Philippe De Donder, Denis Joram and Bernard Roy (2010), 'Funding the cost of universal service in a liberalized postal sector'.

Bradley, Michael D., Christopher S. Brehm, Jeff Colvin and William M. Takis (1999), 'Empirical estimation of incremental costs for the U.S. Postal Service'.

Bradley, Michael D. and Jeff Colvin (2000), 'Measuring the cost of universal service for posts'.

Bradley, Michael D., Jeff Colvin and John C. Panzar (1997), 'Issues in measuring incremental cost in a multi-function enterprise'.

Bradley, Michael D., Jeff Colvin and Mary K. Perkins (2012), 'Do volume increases and decreases have the same effect on labor hours?'.

Bradley, Michael D., Jeff Colvin and Marc A. Smith (1993), 'Measuring product costs for ratemaking: the United States Postal Service'.

Bradley, Richard, Phil Burns and George Houpis (2009), 'Costing elements of the universal service'.

Burns, Phil, Isabelle Carslake and George Houpis (2002b), 'Brand loyalty and limited entry to postal markets'.

Carslake, Isabelle, George Houpis and Christian Strobel (2011), 'Costing the universal service: evaluating the demand response'.

Cazals, Catherine, Paul Dudley, Jean-Pierre Florens and Mike Jones (2012), 'A panel data analysis of inefficiency and heterogeneity in the postal sector'.

Cazals, Catherine and Jean-Pierre Florens (2002b), 'Econometrics of mail demand: a comparison between cross-section and dynamic data'.
Cazals, Catherine, Jean-Pierre Florens, Frank Rodriguez and Soterios Soteri (2008), 'Forecast uncertainty in dynamic models: an application to the demand for mail'.
Cazals, Catherine, Jean-Pierre Florens and Soterios Soteri (2005), 'Delivery costs for postal services in the UK: some results on scale economies with panel data'.
Cazals, Catherine, Jean-Pierre Florens, Leticia Veruete-McKay, Frank Rodriguez and Soterios Soteri (2011), 'UK letter mail demand: a content-based time-series analysis using overlapping market survey statistical techniques'.
Cohen, Robert, Matthew Robinson, Renee Sheehy, John Waller and Spyros Xenakis (2005), 'Will entrants into a liberalized delivery market attract investors'.
Correia da Silva, Luis, Paul Dudley, Leonardo Mautino and Sophie Richard (2004), 'RPI-X price control regulation in the postal sector'.
Cremer, Helmuth, Philippe De Donder, François Boldron, Denis Joram and Bernard Roy (2008), 'Social costs and benefits of the universal service obligation in the postal market'.
Cremer, Helmuth, Marc De Rycke and Andre Grimaud (1997), 'Costs and benefits of universal service obligations in the postal sector'.
Cremer, Helmuth, Andre Grimaud and Jean-Jacques Laffont (2000), 'The cost of universal service in the postal sector'.
Crew, Michael A. and Paul R. Kleindorfer (2000), 'Liberalisation and the universal service obligation in postal service'.
Crew, Michael A. and Paul R. Kleindorfer (2001a), 'Whither the USO under competitive entry: a microstructure approach'.
Crew, Michael A. and Paul R. Kleindorfer (2001b), 'A critique of the theory of incentive regulation'.
Crew, Michael A. and Paul R. Kleindorfer (2002b), 'Balancing access and the universal service obligation'.
Crew, Michael A. and Paul R. Kleindorfer (2006b), 'Approaches to the USO under entry'.
Crew, Michael A. and Paul R. Kleindorfer (2008), 'Regulation and the USO under entry'.
Crew, Michael A. and Paul R. Kleindorfer (2011), 'Competitive strategies under FMO and intermodal competition'.
Davies, Mary (2011), 'Assessing anti-competitive behavior in a postal market'.
de Bas, Patrick and Nick van der Lijn (2008), 'Development of competition in EU postal markets: the influence of the regulatory framework on the pattern of competition'.
De Donder, Philippe, Helmuth Cremer, Paul Dudley and Frank Rodriguez (2006b), 'A welfare analysis of price controls with end-to-end mail and access services'.
De Donder, Philippe, Helmuth Cremer, Paul Dudley and Frank Rodriguez (2010), 'Welfare and profit implications for changes in service specification within the universal service'.
De Donder, Philippe, Helmuth Cremer, Paul Dudley and Frank Rodriguez (2011), 'Optimal pricing for mail and welfare implications in a communications market'.
De Donder, Philippe, Helmuth Cremer and Frank Rodriguez (2002a), 'Funding the universal service obligation under liberalization'.
De Donder, Philippe, Helmuth Cremer and Frank Rodriguez (2005), 'Access pricing in the postal sector: results from a model with bypass and customer direct access'.
Dobbs, Ian and Paul Richards (1991), 'Assessing the welfare effects of entry into letter delivery'.
Dudley, Paul, Stephen Agar, Leonardo Mautino and Felipe Flórez Duncan (2009), 'Competition through downstream access in the UK postal sector: the first four years'.
Dudley, Paul, Helen Jenkins, Leonardo Mautino and Sophie Richard (2005), 'Competition and the coverage of price controls in the postal sector'.
Eccles, Richard (2011), 'State funding and cost sharing of the USO under the 2008 EU Postal Services Directive'.
Elcano, Mary S., R. Andrew German and John T. Pickett (2000), 'Hiding in plain sight: the quiet liberalization of the United States postal system'.
Elkelä, Kari (2011), 'Invoicing in 16 European countries'.
Fève, Frédérique, Jean-Pierre Florens, Frank Rodriguez and Soterios Soteri (2010), 'Forecasting mail volumes in an evolving market environment'.

Fève, Frédérique, Jean-Pierre Florens, Leticia Veruete-McKay, Soterios Soteri and Frank Rodriguez (2012), 'Uncertainty and projections of the demand for mail'.
Flórez Duncan, Felipe, Dawn Longman, Leonardo Mautino and Paul Dudley (2011), 'Price discrimination and price differentiation within direct mail'.
Geradin, Damien and David Henry (2010), 'Abuse of dominance in the postal sector: the contribution of the Guidance Paper on Article 82 EC'.
Gibson, Stephen and Nancy Race (2012), 'A market study of packets and parcels services'.
Hill, Roger and Richard Robinson (2006a), 'Establishing non-uniform access prices in the UK'.
Hill, Roger, Richard Robinson and Frank Rodriguez (2005), 'The financial equilibrium of universal service providers in a liberalized postal market'.
Horncastle, Alan, David Jevons, Paul Dudley and Emmanuel Thanassoulis (2006b), 'Efficiency analysis of delivery offices in the postal sector using stochastic frontier and data envelopment analyses'.
Jaag, Christian, Martin Koller and Urs Trinkner (2009), 'Calculating the cost of the universal service obligation: the need for a global approach'.
Jimenez, Luis, Elena Diakova and Chrystal Szeto (2006a), 'Generational analysis of mail users'.
Jimenez, Luis, Anna Owsiany and Chrystal Szeto (2006b), 'Scenarios of mail receipt patterns across generations'.
Jonsson, Per and Sten Selander (2006a), 'The "real" graveyard spiral: experiences from the liberalized Swedish postal market'.
Leskinen, Pekka, Peter Karlsson, Heikki Nikali and Paivi Rokkanen (2009), 'How should regulation be adjusted when universal service substitution grows?'.
Martin, Vance L., Chris Paterson and Jessie Xiaokang Wang (2012), 'Forecasting letter volumes: augmenting econometric baseline projections'.
Moriarty, Richard and Paul Smith (2005), 'Barriers to entry in post and regulatory responses'.
Moriarty, Richard, Sophie Yorke, Greg Harman, John Cubbin, Meloria Meschi and Paul Smith (2006b), 'Economic analysis of the efficiency of Royal Mail units and the implications for regulatory policy'.
Nikali, Heikki (1995), 'Replacement of letter mail by electronic communications to the year 2010'.
Nikali, Heikki (2008), 'Substitution of letter mail for different sender-receiver segments'.
Panzar, John C. (1991), 'Is postal service a natural monopoly?'.
Panzar, John C. (1993), 'Competition, efficiency and the vertical structure of postal services'.
Panzar, John C. (2001), 'Funding universal service obligations: the costs of liberalization'.
Panzar, John C. (2002b), 'Reconciling competition, downstream access and universal service in postal markets'.
Plum, Monika and Cara Schwarz-Schilling (2000), 'Defining postal markets: an antitrust perspective'.
Rodriguez, Frank, Stephen Smith and David Storer (1999), 'Estimating the cost of the universal service obligation in postal service'.
Rogerson, Cathy M. and William M. Takis (1993), 'Economies of scale and scope and competition in postal services'.
Roy, Bernard (1999), 'Technico-economic analysis of the costs of outside work in postal delivery'.
Schwarz-Schilling, Cara (2002b), 'Market results of postal reform in Germany: current trends'.
Sheldon, Rob and Alison Lawrence (2011), 'The UK service obligation: what do the public think and how do they value it?'.
Trinkner, Urs and Martin Grossman (2006a), 'Forecasting Swiss mail demand'.
Wojtek, Ralf and Martin Zauner (2012), 'Postal price regulation in a competitive environment'.

Other References

Armstrong, Mark (2002), 'The theory of access pricing and interconnection', in M. Cave, S. Majumdar and I. Vogelsang (eds), *Handbook of Telecommunications Economics*, Amsterdam: North-Holland.

Directive 97/67/EC on common rules for the development of the internal market of EU postal services and the improvement of quality of service OJ (1998) L15/14.
Directive 2002/39/EC amending Directive 97/67/EC with regard to the further opening of the EU postal services to competition, OJ (2002) L176/21.
Directive 2008/06/EC amending Directive 97/67/EC with regard to the full accomplishment of the internal market of community postal service OJ (2008) L52/3.
European Commission (2009), Guidance on the Commission's enforcement priorities applying Article 82 EC Treaty to exclusionary conduct by dominant undertakings.
Hooper, Richard, Deidre Hutton and Ian R. Smith (2008), 'Modernise or Decline: Policies to Maintain the Universal Postal Service in the United Kingdom', Cm 7529.
Ofcom (2012), 'Securing the Universal Postal Service', March.
Postcomm (2002), 'Promoting Effective Competition in UK Postal Services'.
Post Office Group (n.d.), 'Annual Report and Accounts'.

27. Social media challenges the entire postal industry*

Kari Elkelä[†] and Heikki Nikali[‡]

1 INTRODUCTION

Internet penetration has rapidly increased across the developed world. Internet household penetration was 71 percent in the EU in 2011 (Eurostat, 2012). In Finland, 89 percent of all Finns and 99 percent of 16–50-year-olds use the Internet today, and in addition 60 percent of these use it several times a day (Statistics Finland, 2011). This means that the Internet has become an absolutely necessary channel in daily searches for information, news follow-up and communication. This has resulted in declining mail volumes in many countries and a trend towards letters and advertising becoming increasingly digitalized. In addition there is an increasing tendency for newspapers and magazines to be read in digital formats. Consequentially, at the same time, postal organizations providing traditional paper-based communication services will be faced with financial problems.

The most significant feature in today's media is increasing globalization. This kind of new media is rarely under the control of a single owner and when the media compete with one another, new dynamics and media convergences will develop. Tools such as Facebook and Twitter have brought people closer together and created new online communities. Within these social media communities, members create and share content that connects group members to one another. Social media users also filter information, whereby influential individuals can direct the attention of the members of the community to specific news, advertisements, goods and services.

This sort of social filtering of media is mainly put into practice among community members, but it threatens traditional professional journalism even today. First, it presents a challenge to the delivery and reading of printed newspapers and magazines. For example, in Finland the number of newspapers delivered has decreased 10 percent from 2008 to 2012. During the same period, the decrease in magazines was 20 percent. Here, one should note the special position held by newspapers and magazines with regard to postal delivery in the Nordic countries. For example, in 2011 newspapers and magazines accounted for one-third of all shipments delivered by Itella.

In Finland, 13 percent of consumers already prefer socially filtered media use, although 62 percent still prefer to receive their news directly through traditional professional journalistic sources (Elkelä, 2011). Individuals preferring social filtering are mainly

† Research Manager, Itella Corporation.
‡ Research Director, Itella Corporation.

in the younger age groups, but their share seems to be growing rapidly. In this research it was also found that socially filtered media use is accompanied by the substitution of paid newspapers with Internet and free papers. Many social media users are also cynical about the professional media. This change has not only affected the use of the printed media, but also influenced the willingness to send and receive letters, postcards and advertising leaflets. This is presenting a major challenge to the postal industry as a whole.

This chapter considers the substitution of traditional paper-based and other analog forms of communication and media with the new digital ways of media use and evaluates what this means for postal organizations as well as the whole of the postal industry. This study is of international significance, because social media use quickly diffuses in line with Internet penetration growth and will increasingly influence media consumption and communication behavior globally.

Section 2 examines how digitalization has led to media convergence and enabled the triumph of social media. Furthermore, it specifies the concept and diversity of social media and describes how social media will alter our behavior. Section 3 presents our empirical study from Finland investigating the effects of social media. The results of the analyses included user segmentation and an explanatory model for social media use, suggesting a trend towards increasing use of social media services. In Section 4 a future vision for media delivery and social interaction is presented, outlining a rationale for the possibilities of all media and communication to become digitalized leaving only the transport of goods for delivery companies. Section 5 presents the conclusions and implications.

2 DIGITALIZATION HAS LED TO MEDIA CONVERGENCE AND SOCIAL MEDIA

The adoption of digital technology has, and will continue to cause, significant changes in both mass communication and interaction between people. In particular, it is challenging analog and paper-based forms of communication. Technologically speaking, digitalization implies the following new opportunities: First, *numerical expression* makes it possible to present information using a systematic and programmable method. Second, *modularity* enables the linking of individual objects to one another, which makes it easy to combine text, pictures, videos, and other content produced by different parties into a message entity. Third, *automation* will make the transmission and targeting of messages more efficient. Rich site summary (RSS) feeds are a good example of this. Furthermore, automation enables real-time news monitoring, which conventional newspapers cannot offer. Fourth, *variability* enables the provision of customized content, so that, for example, users registered at Amazon are each offered different recommendations, or each consumer can subscribe to a digital newspaper which is customized based on his or her areas of interest. *Transcoding* enables the reshaping of message content so that it can be interpreted and read using new or different communication devices that are taken into use (Meikle and Young, 2012, pp. 15–16).

The progressive nature of digital technology has enabled diverse media convergence. With regard to *technology*, messages can be transmitted over diverse systems and the same message can be converted so that it is compatible with multiple systems. With regard to *content*, digitalization has resulted in an enormous increase in the easy availability of a wide range of materials and information. Indeed, opportunities for combining available content and producing new content utilizing them have reached a new level. With regard to *organizations*, new versatile players have rapidly emerged in the communications industry while traditional industry players have reorganized. At the same time, the business of communications organizations has become increasingly global.

Consumers encounter media convergence especially when using *social media*, where they can interact with friends or businesses. They may also receive and comment on news, entertainment and anything else that they find interesting. This community phenomenon could have already been predicted as a future Internet trend in the late 1990s, but as a concept and mode of operation, social media use is just a couple of years old. What is unique is the growth rate of social media services and use, and their global impact on communication behavior. Underlying the transformation is, naturally, the fact that the Internet is used by almost all consumers. In addition to this, increasingly high-speed connections and extensive mobile broadband services are becoming ubiquitously available.

The transition to the new phase substantially began in 2004 when talk of Web 2.0 started, describing new kinds of community software platform where content and applications are produced so that they can be edited by all users, all the time. Kaplan and Haenlein (2010, p. 61) coined a clear definition on this basis: 'Social media is a group of Internet-based applications that build on the ideological and technological foundations of Web 2.0, and that allow the creation and exchange of user generated content'. An obvious difference to previous forms of communication is that users are now, at least in part, also content producers.

With social media, the previously passive audience has become a new kind of a creative audience to which the Internet offers *access* to an enormous amount of material. They can *organize* this material into desired entities or *remix* their own versions from the huge volume of material. Social media also offer an easy and encouraging channel for *writing* one's own experiences and opinions for public view. On the web, consumers can also *collaborate* to produce materials; for example, write articles for the Wikipedia Internet encyclopedia. It is also essential in social media that the material thereby produced can be *shared* with one's communities and the whole world (Meikle and Young, 2012, pp. 103–26).

'Social media' is a broad concept, and its services are being developed continuously. Table 27.1 describes the diversity of social media, with the richness of media and social presence in the columns, and the user's self-presentation or self-disclosure along the rows. One can see in the table that self-expression is emphasized in blogs, networking sites and virtual social worlds. One's identity need not be revealed, on the other hand, in collaborative projects, content communities, or virtual game worlds.

A key feature of social media is, in fact, that the user can choose the roles that he or she assumes in the increasingly community-oriented media. It is also easy to jump from one role to another, as there are infinite opportunities. There are also an infinite number of communities to which one can belong; each user can create the community that he/she wants. However, it should be emphasized that a social world is not making people community oriented. Rather, it is offering new, easier and more diverse opportunities to realize people's inherent sense of community. This is enabled by ubiquitously accessible

Table 27.1 Classification of social media

		Richness of social presence and media		
		Low	Medium	High
Self-presentation and self-disclosure	High	Blogs	Social network sites (e.g., Facebook)	Virtual social worlds (e.g., Second Life)
	Low	Collaborative projects (e.g., Wikipedia)	Content communities (e.g., YouTube)	Virtual game worlds (e.g., World of Warcraft)

Source: Adapted from Kaplan and Haenlein (2010).

and scalable digital communication techniques, and the result is that social media have already substantially changed the way organizations, communities, and individuals communicate.

Social media influence the everyday lives of users in various ways. Upon joining a community, there is social pressure to maintain an ongoing role within the environment. The more active the role one has taken, the more difficult the decision to leave becomes. Even though a sense of a virtual communality is based on consumers' normal social needs, the special significance is that it considerably improves opportunities to fulfill those needs. Social media combine personal one-to-one communication and few-to-many mass communication; the result is a form of any-to-any communication.

Social media are also transforming the way news is transmitted and received. Traditionally, news has been offered in the same ready-made package for everyone in the form of a newspaper or television news broadcast, for example. Digital news, on the other hand, is a database based on one's own choices. Traditionally, news has been transmitted to the recipient via a distribution channel, such as in the form of a newspaper distributed by delivery organizations or a television broadcast. Digital news is often shared by the community in social media. Traditional news is a monologue from the journalists. As for digital news, authors and readers engage in conversations within the same channel where the news is published (Meikle and Young, 2012, pp. 51–8).

The further that media convergence proceeds, the more analog and paper-based communication will be replaced by digital communication that enables effective networking. The impact of social media also extends to shopping behavior, as companies' products and services are an important topic of discussion, besides their own advertising. Even companies without an active presence in social media cannot avoid its effects; customers comment on the products, services and activities of such companies in social media.

Social media are currently being developed as a marketing channel in particular, which can be seen in the abundant literature in the field. Some authors, however, address the topic in more depth than marketing tricks. Qualman (2011) tries to explain in his book *Socialnomics* how value is created and shared via social media. He also says that in social media, 'word of mouth' becomes 'world of mouth'. In his optimistic vision, this means that in the future we will no longer search for products and services, but rather they will find us through social media. Qualman understands that the use of social media is like living in a glasshouse. He concludes – again optimistically – that for this reason we shall adopt *preventive* behavior, doing less stupid things, and also adopt *braggadocian* behavior, becoming braver to do things that we can be proud of.

Jensen (2010) reduces the changes in communications into three development phases: interpersonal communication, mass communication, and network communication. From the point of view of our review, the most interesting is the comparison between mass and network communication. Mass communication emerged and developed through the utilization of the opportunities provided by analog technology, while the adoption of digital technology provided the resources for network communication. Printed magazines and postal delivery, as well as broadcasting of radio and television programs, are typical of mass communication. Networking with computers, the Internet and smartphones is typical of digital communication. Mass communication is made by few for many, whereas anyone can communicate to anyone on the network. The area of effect for interpersonal communication is typically local, while in mass communication it is national or covering a group of states. Network communication, on the other hand, is typically global.

3 EMPIRICAL RESULTS ILLUSTRATE THE IMPACT

In order to assess the current status of the use and effects of social media, empirical data comprising 1,000 respondents, a representative sample of Finns aged 15–64, was collected in M3 Research's Internet panel in April 2012. All analysis in this section is based on these data. According to the survey, social media are used by approximately 70 percent of Finns, and in the youngest age group, those aged 15–24, users number more than 90 percent. The users spend an hour a day using social media on average, and users aged 15–24 as much as an hour and a half. Of all Finns, 22 percent report using social media for more than an hour a day. Social media is the third most used media channel; only television and radio are used to a greater extent. Searching for information on the Internet approaches almost the same level as social media, but the fifth most important channel, speaking on the telephone, is already clearly behind these.

Kaplan and Haenlein (2010) presented the extensive nature of social media well by classifying the various forms in terms of media richness and the users' self-expression opportunities (Table 27.1, above). This classification was used as the basis when inquiring into the typical uses of social media. Discussion forums have been added to the categorization, and the use and production of content have been separated in the modes of use.

Table 27.2 presents the social media appreciation segments, based on a k-means cluster analysis of the significance of modes of use. The significance of the different modes of use was measured with a five-step scale, with 'not at all important' and 'very important' as the extremes. When taking a look at social media users overall, one can see that the use of content produced by others is considered clearly more important than producing one's own content. This is particularly emphasized in terms of collaboratively produced content and content community materials. On social networking sites, such as Facebook, however, the situation is almost in balance.

The cluster analysis produced four segments describing the appreciation of social media. *Tech lovers* or technology enthusiasts clearly appreciate social media the most. They appreciate all its forms and will also participate in their production. They also are the first to have utilized the versatile possibilities of social media. *Networkers* appreciate

Table 27.2 Modes of use and appreciation segments of social media

	Importance of use in appreciation groups			
	Tech lovers	Networkers	Content utilizers	Suspicious bystanders
Main modes of use for social media				
Collaborative content, e.g., Wikipedia	Utilizing + participating	Utilizing	Utilizing	Occasional utilizing
Social networking sites, e.g., Facebook	Reading + publishing	Reading + publishing		
Content communities, e.g., YouTube	Utilizing + publishing	Utilizing	Occasional utilizing	
Discussion forums	Reading + writing	Occasional reading	Occasional reading	
Blogs	Reading + writing	Occasional reading	Occasional reading	
Consumer share, %	21	26	21	32
Typical group features				
Gender	Male	Female	Male	
Age, years	15–24	15–34		35–64
Income group of 5	2 lowest	Lowest		3 highest
Work or study	Studies	Studies		Works
Mobile phone	Smartphone			Regular
Daily use of SoMe	63 minutes	75 minutes	24 minutes	17 minutes
Daily net music/videos	35 minutes	24 minutes	15 minutes	8 minutes

social media as channels of interaction, since they consider it important to keep in touch with other people by following their activity and comments, for example, on Facebook, and by sharing their own observations, experiences and opinions on social networking sites. This group also considers it important to follow content produced by others. They are not, however, particularly interested in discussion forums, but they may follow blogs to some extent. *Content utilizers* particularly appreciate socially produced materials and might read Wikipedia articles. They may also occasionally read discussion forums and use materials on content community sites, such as videos on YouTube. The most skeptical attitudes towards social media are held by *suspicious bystanders*, who do not much appreciate any use of social media. However, even they can sometimes utilize collaborative content.

Tech lovers appreciate all social media services and thus have a basically positive attitude towards them. Persons under 25, students, and low incomes individuals are emphasized among this group. This segment has the highest number of smartphones, tablets, gaming consoles, and TV dongles in their computers. This group clearly spends the most time compared to other groups using the newest technology. In addition to interacting via social media, they listen to music, watch videos and TV programs on the Internet, and play online games. On the other hand, this segment spends the least time in face-to-face interaction.

Networkers appreciate social media particularly as channels of interaction. Women, those aged under 35 and students and people with low incomes are emphasized among this group. In terms of devices owned, networkers conformed to the average. However, they spend the most time of all segments using social media, particularly on Facebook and other networking sites.

Social media *content utilizers* are mainly users of materials produced and shared in online communities and do not actually want to be personally involved in creating social media content. Men and people living in sparsely populated areas are emphasized among content utilizers. Managers and salaried employees are the most prominent occupational groups. Similarly to content utilizers, the devices owned conformed to the average. However, they tend to possess slightly more smartphones than the average. This segment has the most face-to-face interaction, which is why their use of social media is below average.

Suspicious bystanders of social media are typically aged over 35, white-collar workers and pensioners, working full-time and have average incomes. This group uses the latest technology, such as smartphones, tablets, TV dongles or paid entertainment service packages, the least. However, they use pay TV more frequently than the other segments. This segment spends the most time among conventional media, such as television, radio and printed newspapers and the least time with new digital media.

In summary, the effect of age is such that those aged 15–34 tend to be tech lovers and networkers, and those over 35 are more often suspicious bystanders. Different age groups are fairly evenly represented in content utilizers, only the 25-year-olds are slightly underrepresented. Thus, young people use social media more and more diversely, while older age groups mainly use it as a reception channel similarly to conventional media consumption. Networkers spend the most time on social media among almost all age groups. Use by tech lovers is also above average among all other age groups except the oldest age group, those aged 55–64, whose positive attitude seems to be about utilizing social media in principle rather than in practice. Suspicious bystanders and content utilizers use social media less than the average, but the youngest age group, 15–24, spends quite a lot of time using social media even among these groups.

The transformation brought about by social media proceeds by generation. Tapscott (2010) has divided Americans into four generations, based on the year of birth: baby boomers (1946–64), Generation X (1965–76), Generation Y (1977–97) and Generation Z (1997–2012). A corresponding division is largely applicable in Finland and other developed countries as well (Säntti and Säntti, 2011). Generation Z consists of social media natives, so it is a natural thing for them. Generation Y comprises digital media natives who have also mastered social media. Generation X consists of digital immigrants who are actively learning to use social media. Older generations are also rapidly moving towards using social media – as communication partners for their children and grandchildren – even though, in this group, use is often focused on receiving messages, meaning that social media are used in the same, familiar way as conventional media.

Attitudes towards social media and digitalization were measured through 71 statements in the survey, with the extremes of the five-step scale being 'fully agree' and 'fully disagree' bracketed at one and five, respectively. Principal components analysis indicated eight perceived practical benefits of using social media. Age has a clear effect on how users perceive these benefits. We found that those aged 15–24 appreciate the practical benefits of social media as being implemented the best by far. Among this group, social media function particularly as a fast and reliable news sharer, support work and studies, and help in purchasing decisions. Those aged 25–34 also see social media as more useful than consumers on average. Those aged over 35 have a clearly more suspicious attitude towards the benefits of social media than younger consumers.

The image of the meaning of social media was complemented through a linear regression model. The model had the perceived overall importance of social media as a channel of reception and publishing as well as interaction and receiving information, which is the average of the four variables describing the different ways of using social media, as the dependent variable. The principal components analysis combined these factors into significance dimensions of social media.

The explanatory linear regression model estimated from the data is presented with statistical indicators in Table 27.3. The model clarifies the meaning of social media rather well, as the explanatory degree, with five explanatory variables that are acceptable according to statistical criteria, is 55 percent According to the model, the meaning of social media is best described by *increased interaction possibilities*. Social media, can keep users in touch with friends, and find new friends, or even a new partner. Social media are also deemed to help in understanding other people, their lives, and their problems. In addition, congratulations and greetings sent via social media are replacing conventional postcards.

A second strong explanatory factor is that social media are considered *good channels of self-expression*. Users can describe their successes and achievements and generally present their own thoughts freely. Via social media, anyone can boast of their achievements. When one submits his or her opinions and materials for others to freely use, one also learns, based on shared comments and discussion, to understand oneself better.

Third, social media offer users practical benefits by *helping to make purchasing decisions*. When other users evaluate products and services in social media, these reviews are

Table 27.3 Explanatory linear regression model for importance of social media

Perceived benefits of social media	Unstandardized coefficients		Standardized Beta	*t*	Sig.
	B	Std error			
(Constant)	−0.08	0.091			
Increases interaction possibilities	0.36	0.045	0.30	8.03	0.00
Good channel for self-expression	0.29	0.040	0.25	7.07	0.00
Supports in purchasing decisions	0.18	0.042	0.13	4.16	0.00
Fast and reliable news sharing	0.13	0.037	0.11	3.62	0.00
Supports work and studies	0.07	0.036	0.06	2.02	0.04
Dependent variable: importance of social media for consumers					
Adjusted R-square:					0.554

trusted more than companies' advertisements. Online shopping, on the other hand, is made easier by following the links in social media. Social media also have a strong impact on how corporate images are shaped, as consumers readily describe their experiences of good and, in particular, bad services. There is not much enthusiasm over actual advertising on social media sites, but it is accepted as an inevitable evil. Furthermore, discussions of products and services and shared tips and links are a significant challenge for conventional push marketing.

Fourth, social media are deemed *a quick and reliable means of sharing news*, through which active users most often get information on the most recent news. News and other information shared by one's friends are considered reliable in the same way as their estimates of marketed products and services. Social media have thus become not only new interaction channels, but also news channels that combine personal and public information. It is precisely here where it can be seen that social media have become new social filters that, in part, question choices made by professional journalists regarding which news items are important to publish (Elkelä, 2011; Keränen et al., 2011).

Fifth, social media are considered to *support work and studies*. It is possible to network with people important to one's work and career on LinkedIn, for example. Social media also help users to keep up to date, and through which it is easy to get help from friends with problems encountered in work and studies. Companies, on the other hand, already utilize social media quite extensively in searching for and evaluating new employees.

As a whole, the model indicates that the benefits that explain the significance of social media diversely cover the needs of people's daily lives. Social media function as interaction and news channels, and also support key daily activities, work, studies, and purchases. It could also be said that social media provide channels for entertainment and leisure, even though these factors were not included in the model due to them being difficult to measure.

Social media services are already available almost everywhere, and in the future their use will be promoted by the decreasing prices of mobile terminal devices and their development towards user friendliness. The evolution of cloud services, on the other hand, will make media content even more extensively available to everyone, resulting in its use being linked increasingly closely with social interaction. Social media have become a factor that accelerates and boosts the impact of digital technology through the convergence of the already many available services and the services that will be further developed.

4 FUTURE VISION FOR MEDIA DELIVERY AND SOCIAL INTERACTION

Based on the theoretical perspectives and empirical results presented above, it is possible to specify a future vision of media delivery and social interaction. We begin the examination with a simplified description of the delivery history. Messaging and media delivery started with the *physical delivery* services offered by the post organizations and other transport companies. At this first stage, all letters, newspapers, magazines, advertisements and packages were artifacts, things in molecular form. At the second stage, electronic devices and services with *analog technology*, such as telephone, radio and television, came to supplement these.

The third stage of the development was *digital* information networks, and the most familiar of these are the Internet, email and text messages. The digitalizing of communication has proved to be a significant change factor. In quite a short time, a large part of analog electronic communication has been replaced by digital communication in which all content can be presented in easily convertible and editable bit format. Mobile phone services and television especially have been digitalized. Digital technology has also started to replace traditional paper communication. Nowadays email messages are often sent instead of letters and, as a substitute for paper newspapers and magazines, many consumers read news and receive entertainment through the Internet. Altogether, content distributed via different channels can be classified into communication, such as information, entertainment and interpersonal interaction, and goods. One could also say that it is a business where either bits or molecules are delivered. Because everything else but physical goods can already today be delivered in bits and the delivery of bits is both quicker and cheaper, their share has increased rapidly. Even the technology of three-dimensional printing of objects has been introduced. These three stages in the development of communication are presented on the left-hand side of Figure 27.1.

Digital technology has also provided the necessary conditions for the fourth stage of communication development, *social media*, which are best known for networking sites such as Facebook. Social media not only facilitate the mutual interaction of friends, but have also become a filter for all media consumption because the hints and links to interesting news, videos, music and TV programs are shared there. As services and terminal devices evolve, this digital interaction and use of media will become increasingly intertwined. Currently, particular efforts are being made to harness social media as marketing channels, and therefore applications where the Internet and television can be combined into a form of 'social television' are also being developed. In the next few years, entertainment and interaction will increasingly be offered to consumers as 'cloud services', which are available at all times, and in any place. The use of these services is facilitated by mobile terminal devices such as tablets and smartphones, which are rapidly becoming more commonplace.

Increasing use of social media is transforming people's lives and the economy, so it could be said that we are moving into a social–economic culture, which Qualman

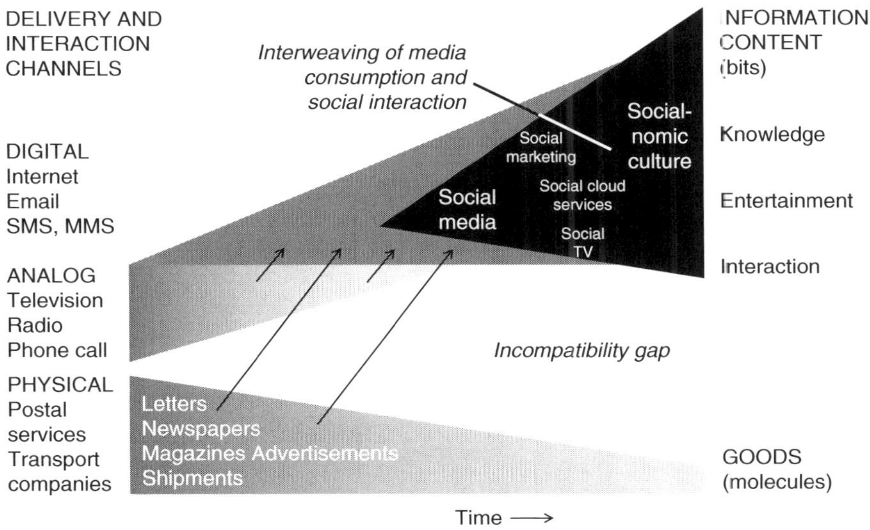

Figure 27.1 A future vision for media delivery and social interaction

(2011) has named 'socialnomic'. The use of social media also transforms one's brain and mindset, so we are also adopting a new way of thinking at the same time, which Amerland (2012) in turn calls the 'social media mindset'. So the change accomplished by social media will be really significant, even though at this stage only the first signs of it are distinctly visible.

The empirical results from Finland presented above suggest that the youngest age groups have already adopted the new mindsets and ways of acting, but older age groups are suspicious of them. This is first indicated by the fact that those aged 15–24 consider social media to be more important interaction channels than letters or email. Second, they deem news shared via social media to be more important than newspapers. Third, they deem music listened to and videos watched on the Internet more important than radio or television broadcasting. The special significance of social media could also be seen in being an interaction and news channel at the same time, while also helping in key daily activities such as work, studies, and making purchasing decisions.

This transformation means the interweaving of the consumption of information and entertainment and interpersonal interaction, because digital technology facilitates their linkage. Thus, the ownership and use of information and entertainment is no longer desired in inconvenient location-dependent forms, such as books, newspapers or disks, but is available in digital format everywhere. The digital interweaving of information, entertainment and interaction is becoming a social norm, which results in a clear distinction from, for example, conventional paper-based communication. In this way, social media will accelerate the adoption of digital communication.

An incompatibility gap will emerge between old and new forms of communication, meaning that there will be no demand for a physical format for content that can be offered in digital format. The reasons for abandoning physical forms of communication include the use of conventional services being deemed inconvenient, or out of concern for the environment. This will lead to a situation where only goods that must exist by their very nature in a physical format are transported by postal services and other transport companies. The new social–economic culture will also shape the human mind, and may result in an alliance between social interaction and the commercial marketing of products and services, where social is commercial and commercial is social. Consumers were referred to as producers of information in the early years of social media; now they are increasingly becoming marketers, and they also seem to be silently accepting it. On the other hand, there will be a permanent problem of who owns the content and who has the right to share it with others, that is, the borders between piracy and legitimate use.

This transition will take some time, but it will be easy to accept, at least for digital natives. There will naturally be a delay in change, even if it is considered good. In addition, nostalgia for old forms of communication will occur, just as some people nowadays are returning to LP albums. However, the trend towards a more social digital media and social–economic culture emerging as a result seems to be unavoidable, and it can be assumed to be the prevailing situation within a few decades.

The trend forecast here is somewhat analogous to communities having already been seen as the future of the Internet early in the 1990s, but the truly significant social media solutions were invented and adopted only after the turn of the millennium. Social media can, for the time being, be considered a fashion phenomenon, but this means ignoring its probable development into becoming a new highway for digital–social media that combines the Internet and all other media consumption and interaction. Even though solutions are still fragmented and terminal devices have their limitations, the new integrated future can easily be imagined, and what can be imagined, can also be realized.

5 CONCLUSIONS AND IMPLICATIONS

The results show that the introduction of social media is clearly accelerating the move towards digital communication. Social media use is becoming a new significant phase in digital communication because for consumers social media combine person-to-person interaction and all kinds of media consumption. When consumers have a single, easy-to-use channel which caters to different communication needs, they tend to stop using traditional letters, newspapers, magazines and other printed communication. This will then generate a new kind of consumption culture which will also have a considerable impact on the demand for physical delivery services. Therefore, it is important that postal services and other distribution organizations closely monitor the development of social media and evaluate its impact in order to be able to adjust to the rapidly changing business environment.

At the moment, about 90 percent of consumers in Finland use the Internet. Some 73 percent of Finns are also users of social media which are seen as particularly good interaction channels that also enable self-expression. Especially the young (under 35) appreciate these social media characteristics. At the same time, they do not want to send letters and postcards because they send messages via their online communities. Such communication enables immediate interaction and the links forwarded provide a fast access to news, entertainment and other online content. As a result, consumers who have stopped sending letters want to receive digital messages. In Finland, this is shown by the fact that the share of digital consumer bills in 2007–12 has increased from almost zero to a third, while the letter volume has decreased by 15 percent. Previously, the letter volume had remained rather stable (Nikali and Rantaseppä, 2012). In some other countries, especially in Nordic countries, letter volumes have decreased to a clearly greater extent. In such a transition, postal organizations also have to re-think their services and marketing. This means easy service access over the Internet and also the provision of partially and fully digital delivery services. In addition, service providers must actively monitor the online discussion concerning their services and quickly comment on the discussion in the social media.

Consumers find that social media provide good support for their purchasing decisions. An online culture of recommendations has been adopted, where product and shopping location information is linked to discussions. Moreover, consumers trust such recommendations more than advertisements. This particularly promotes online commerce and also gives new opportunities to goods transport organizations. To achieve success, online stores need a product range which matches the customer needs, and a quick and reliable supply chain. Therefore, transport operators and online stores should engage in close cooperation in service development and marketing. The consumer benefits of this cooperation should be notified via social media, which means that in the best-case scenario, consumers become marketers who share this information with their friends.

Social media have also become important channels for sharing news. In 2008–12, the demand for magazines in Finland decreased by almost a fifth. Consumers give three reasons for this: it is faster to find the corresponding information online even from the magazine websites. Content shared via an online community replaces magazine reading and social media take up so much time that there is less time to read magazines than before. Over the last 20 years, newspaper demand has decreased by about 2 percent per year. Currently, users find social media to be one of the quickest ways to share news, which means that printed newspaper news is considered as outdated. In this way, social media are undermining the status of printed communication, which will further decrease the demand for newspapers and magazines. The transition means that media distribution is a rapidly declining business which is why distribution organizations must evaluate whether it is possible for them to contribute to content production or expand their role in the media value chain in other ways.

The decrease in the volumes and the increase in the competition require postal organizations to operate more openly and effectively than before. The adjustment inevitably requires a re-evaluation of the service level of the delivery of traditional paper-based messages and therefore increase cost efficiency. Possible ways to implement this include decreasing the weekly delivery frequency and limiting the highest service quality to the most densely populated areas. Since postal delivery is regulated by the Universal Service Obligation, it is important to prepare for probable future scenarios well in advance, so that the service-level requirements related to delivery and possible compensation can also be determined before the situation escalates. Media convergence will also inevitably result in the need to regulate paper and digital communication with common principles, taking into account the services offered to customers by the overall market.

NOTE

* The views expressed in this chapter are those of the authors and do not necessarily reflect the views of Itella Corporation.

REFERENCES

Amerland, David (2012), *The Social Media Mind: How the Social Media Is Changing Business, Politics and Science and Helps Create a New World Order*, New Line Publishing.

Elkelä, Kari (2011), 'Lehtibarometri 11/2011', Helsinki: Itella BI, Research Series 44/2011.

Eurostat (2012), Database.

Jensen, Klaus Bruhr (2010), *Media Convergence: The Three Degrees of Network, Mass and Interpersonal Communication*, London: Routledge.

Kaplan, Andreas M. and Michael Haenlein (2010), 'Users of the world, unite: the challenges and opportunities of social media', *Business Horizons*, **53**, 59–68.

Keränen, Markus, Riikka Lätti, Kari Elkelä and Heikki Nikali (2011), 'Media-alan mahdollisuuksien kentät, Neljä suuntaa tulevaisuuteen', Helsinki: Itella BI, Research Series 10/2011, June.

Meikle, Graham and Sherman Young (2012), *Media Convergence: Networked Digital Media in Everyday Life*, Basingstoke: Palgrave Macmillan.

Nikali, Heikki and Minna Rantaseppä (2012), 'Content survey of letter mail', Helsinki: Itella BI, Research Series 7/2012.

Qualman, Eric (2011), *Socialnomics: How Social Media Transforms the Way We Live and Do Business*, Hoboken, NJ: Wiley.

Säntti, Risto and Petra Säntti (2011), 'Organisaatio ja sosiaalisen median ajattelutapa', in T. Aaltonen-Ogbeide, P. Saastamoinen, H. Rainio and T. Vartiainen (eds), *Silmät auki sosiaaliseen mediaan*, Helsinki: Eduskunnan tulevaisuusvaliokunnan julkaisu.

Statistics Finland (2011), 'Tieto- ja viestintätekniikan käyttö 2011', Helsinki.

Tapscott, Don (2010), *Syntynyt Digiaikaan*, Jyväskylä: Docendo.